MW01073648

Mental Health of Refugee and Conflict-Affected Populations

Nexhmedin Morina • Angela Nickerson
Editors

Mental Health of Refugee and Conflict-Affected Populations

Theory, Research and Clinical Practice

Editors
Nexhmedin Morina
Department of Clinical Psychology
and Psychotherapy
University of Münster
Münster, Germany

Angela Nickerson
School of Psychology
University of New South Wales
Sydney, NSW, Australia

ISBN 978-3-319-97045-5 ISBN 978-3-319-97046-2 (eBook)
https://doi.org/10.1007/978-3-319-97046-2

Library of Congress Control Number: 2018957833

Cover Illustration: WANGECHI MUTU, Video Still of The End of carrying All, 2015. 3 Screen Animated Video (color, sound). 9 minutes 27 seconds loop. Edition of 3. Courtesy of the Artist, Gladstone Gallery, Susanne Vielmetter Los Angeles Projects, and Victoria Miro Gallery.

This Springer imprint is published by the registered company Springer Nature Switzerland AG
The registered company address is: Gewerbestrasse 11, 6330 Cham, Switzerland

Dedicated to individuals and families affected by violence, persecution, and displacement worldwide

Foreword

This timely volume brings together the accumulated experience of clinical scientists who are determined to improve our approach to improving the mental health of refugees and individuals in conflict-affected settings. The challenge is enormous given the millions of refugees and internally displaced people, half of whom are children, as well as the multitude of regions in the world in a state of war. Their needs are complex and ever changing.

Traditionally, refugees and conflict-affected groups were offered help by NGOs. Some excellent work was developed, often incorporating a human rights perspective within a humanitarian framework. However, as is discussed, the various projects were rarely scientifically evaluated. In contrast, mental health responders seized on the then recently described posttraumatic stress disorder and introduced training which was evaluated. A major problem was that often other mental health needs – notably depression, anxiety and bereavement reactions – were ignored. Over the past 20 years or so, there have been strenuous efforts to blend these two contrasting approaches. Contributors discuss how this can be developed.

As reflected in the chapters, there have been many examples of interventions being adapted and applied to groups of refugees and conflict-affected populations. The trouble is that all too often studies are of small number of participants and rarely have follow-ups of more than 2–3 months. In addition, more thought needs to be given as to what measures are developed and applied in order to judge the effects. Understandably, when responding to a crisis, well-meaning people want to get going quickly and so use whatever materials they are familiar with. A strong message from this text is that we should think through beforehand what may be needed, how it should be implemented and how it will be evaluated. The intervention literature is full of examples that "show promise", but that rarely deters their authors from then implementing their approach without further development.

Many NGOs still eschew the use of concepts of trauma, depression and so on, believing that this medicalises normal human reactions and that such labelling can be harmful. They talk of using "psychosocial" approaches to avoid such terminology. But this does not absolve them from properly evaluating what they do. For example, providing child friendly spaces is welcomed, but unless active interventions are included, there is little evidence that they have a beneficial effect on children's adjustment. Similarly, ensuring access to education is a matter of right and of urgency, but unless some attention is paid to children's stress reactions, opportunities will be wasted.

Overall, the book moves on from seeing mental health needs solely in terms of individual treatment for specific diagnostic entities to how best to support people at many points throughout their lengthy journeys. Indeed, one radical suggestion is that it may be better to concentrate on providing skills so as to sustain everyday living. Social context is important and can bolster resilience. One recent technological development has been the wide-scale use of smartphones and Wi-Fi-enabled devices. Refugees are no longer totally separated from their families of origin and keep in contact, at times checking back home that advice being given is acceptable.

People can and will join online support groups just as they will access the internet. Not all will be moderated by mental health professionals. Whilst partially empowering individuals affected by war and persecution, it means professionals will have to learn new ways of interacting with them.

Lest it be thought that the book is debunking all that is currently undertaken in the name of improving the mental health of refugees, far from it. The argument is that much broader issues have to be tackled simultaneously and across time. CBT-based interventions remain the most powerful currently in use. However, there is a strong move towards more transdiagnostic approaches looking at underlying psychological processes such as emotional regulation and memory. A far better understanding of the effects of stress on recall is needed to avoid some of the injustices encountered in the judicial processes when apparent contradictions in providing testimony are taken as evidence of lying.

The need to provide some help to as many people as possible has led to the call for low-intensity interventions. Certainly it would be good to see more of these developed and evaluated. But it should not be forgotten that group interventions, often of only a few sessions, can encourage relevant skills that in turn ensure access to community resources. For some, there will still be a need for very long-term support. The question is: who should be responsible for providing all these desirable activities. Different countries have different ways of funding mental health treatment. Whatever protection is theoretically available under international human rights legislation, services can still be overwhelmed unless properly planned and funded. This book is full of up-to-date information that will make for huge improvements in the way societies respond to the needs of refugees and conflict-affected groups.

London, UK
February 2018

William Yule

Preface

Millions of individuals around the globe carry physical and psychological scars following exposure to mass violence. Mass violence violates the basic psychological needs of humans, damaging both the physical and mental integrity of the individual. Survivors of war and other forms of systematic oppression often endure multiple and varying traumatic experiences, such as assaults, injuries, torture, rape, and lack of food and water. In addition, many have witnessed violence toward, and even the murder of, family members, friends, or strangers. These experiences typically occur in the context of the destruction of property and infrastructure and may erode the basic values that underpin societal cohesion. Even after enduring such experiences, survivors of war and persecution may be forced to leave their homes and face the perils of flight into the unknown, as well as the prospect of starting a new life far from home.

Such experiences are likely to significantly affect the well-being of survivors of mass violence. On the individual level, the individual must come to terms with his or her own physical and mental injuries, potential loss of family members and friends, or loss of faith in societal norms and solidarity. Additionally, he or she is likely to live in an environment characterized by daily hardship, either in a postwar society or as a refugee in a host country. Many survivors of organized violence suffer from psychological problems that arise from their experiences of systematic violence, as well as the daily hardships they endure. On the societal level, organized violence may have diminished trust in others and led to the dismantling of infrastructure necessary for successful societal functioning. Evidently, wars and other forms of mass violence represent a major global challenge to well-being. The magnitude of the problems resulting from mass violence becomes clear when one considers the fact that, since the end of the Cold War in 1989, more than half of the countries in the world have been affected by armed conflicts (Marshall & Cole, 2014), with about 68 million people currently forcibly displaced worldwide (UNHCR, 2017). Hence, mass violence has led to enormous suffering among millions of individuals and has caused destruction of social, educational, economic, and health-related structures among many societies.

During the last two decades, increasing efforts have been made to bring mental health to the forefront of the global health agenda. A growing body of research has investigated the factors underlying mental health in refugee and other conflict-affected populations and evaluated treatments to reduce psychological distress in these groups. At the same time, several initiatives by different organizations or groups of individuals have promoted greater collaboration in humanitarian mental health. Global efforts in this regard are urgently needed since most countries with a recent history of mass conflict lack effective mental health services as a consequence of the destruction of infrastructure during conflict.

In developing this book, we aimed to create a comprehensive and up-to-date resource on the mental health of refugee and other conflict-affected populations. The overarching goal of this book was to offer a review of theoretical, empirical, and clinical conceptualizations on mental health following exposure to mass violence. The first part of the book includes a review of current research on the mental health of refugee and conflict-affected populations. Here, prevalences of mental disorders, stressors experienced during and after mass conflict, and psychological interventions implemented with war-affected populations are reviewed (chapters "Mental Health Among Adult Survivors of War in Low- and Middle-Income Countries: Epidemiology and Treatment Outcome", "Mental Health, Pre-migratory Trauma and Post-migratory Stressors Among Adult Refugees", and "Child Mental Health in the Context of War: An Overview of Risk Factors and Interventions for Refugee and War-Affected Youth"). The second part of the book provides a historical analysis of military violence that offers an important context in which the mental health of survivors of organized violence can be understood (chapter "Variations of Military Violence: Structures, Interests, and Experiences of War from the Nineteenth to the Twenty-First Century"). This part further offers psychological, neurobiological, and psychosocial frameworks that can guide the investigation and treatment of psychological symptoms and disorders in refugee and post-conflict populations (chapters "Pathways to Recovery: Psychological Mechanisms Underlying Refugee Mental Health", "Drive to Thrive: A Theory of Resilience Following Loss", "A Neurobiological Perspective of Mental Health Following Torture Trauma", and "Interventions for Mental Health and Psychosocial Support in Complex Humanitarian Emergencies: Moving Towards Consensus in Policy and Action?"). The third part of the book outlines prominent psychological and psychosocial interventions for refugees and other conflict-affected groups (chapters "Narrative Exposure Therapy (NET) as a Treatment for Traumatized Refugees and Post-conflict Populations", "Culturally Sensitive CBT for Refugees: Key Dimensions", "Alcohol and Drug Misuse Interventions in Conflict-Affected Populations", "Trauma Systems Therapy for Refugee Children and Families", and "Supporting Children Affected by War: Towards an Evidence Based Care System"). In addition, this part presents relevant clinical, ethical, and legal considerations for practitioners working with refugees and other conflict-affected groups (chapters "Clinical Considerations in the Psychological Treatment of Refugees", and "Legal and Ethical Considerations Related to the Asylum Process"). The final part details important considerations in conducting research with refugees and war-affected populations in terms of measurement of mental health status (chapter "Conceptualization and Measurement of Traumatic Events among Refugees and Other War-Affected Populations"), evaluation of psychosocial interventions (chapter "Development and Evaluation of Mental Health Interventions for Common Mental Disorders in Post-conflict Settings"), enhancement of feasibility and dissemination of interventions via low-intensity treatments (chapter "Low Intensity Interventions for Psychological Symptoms Following Mass Trauma"), and application of technology to assist psychosocial interventions (chapter "Development and Evaluation of Mental Health Interventions for Common Mental Disorders in Post-conflict Settings").

We were fortunate to have internationally renowned clinicians and researchers contribute to this text and share their research and clinical insights derived from years of experience working with refugee and conflict-affected populations. We hope that this book will be informative to academics, researchers, clinicians, students, community workers, human rights advocates, journalists, public policymakers, and others throughout the globe who work to support individuals exposed to systematic violence.

Münster, Germany — Nexhmedin Morina
Sydney, NSW, Australia — Angela Nickerson

References

Marshall, M. G., & Cole, B. R. (2014). *Global report 2014: Conflict, governance, and state fragility.* Vienna, VA: Center for Systemic Peace.

UNHCR. (2017). *Global trends: Forced displacement in 2017.* Geneva: UNHCR.

Contents

Contributors

Saida M. Abdi Boston Children's Hospital, Boston, MA, USA

Molly A. Benson Department of Psychiatry, Boston Children's Hospital/Harvard Medical School, Boston, MA, USA

Paul Bolton Department of International Health and Department of Mental Health, Johns Hopkins University Bloomberg School of Public Health, Baltimore, MD, USA

Felicity Brown Research and Development, War Child, Amsterdam, North Holland, The Netherlands

Richard A. Bryant School of Psychology, University of New South Wales, Sydney, NSW, Australia

Jessica Carlsson Competence Centre for Transcultural Psychiatry, Mental Health Centre Ballerup, Mental Health Services of the Capital Region of Denmark, Copenhagen, NA, Denmark

M. Claire Greene Mental Health, Johns Hopkins Bloomberg School of Public Health, Baltimore, MD, USA

April Coetzee Research and Development, War Child, Amsterdam, North Holland, The Netherlands

Katie S. Dawson Psychology, University of New South Wales, Sydney, NSW, Australia

Jörg Echternkamp Center for Military History and Social Sciences (ZMSBw), Potsdam, Germany

Martin Luther University Halle-Wittenberg, Halle, Germany

Thomas Elbert Clinical Psychology and Neuropsychology, University of Konstanz, Konstanz, NA, Germany

Rinske Ellermeijer Research and Development, War Child, Amsterdam, North Holland, The Netherlands

Mina Fazel Department of Psychiatry, Oxford University, Oxford, UK

Brian J. Hall Department of Psychology, University of Macau, Macau SAR, China

Kim Hartog Research and Development, War Child, Amsterdam, North Holland, The Netherlands

B. Heidi Ellis Department of Psychiatry, Boston Children's Hospital/Harvard Medical School, Boston, MA, USA

Jane Herlihy Centre for the Study of Emotion and Law, London, UK

Devon E. Hinton Psychiatry, Harvard University, Boston, MA, USA

Stevan E. Hobfoll Department of Behavioral Sciences, Rush University Medical Center, Chicago, IL, USA

Wai Kai Hou Department of Psychology, The Education University of Hong Kong, Hong Kong, SAR, China

Mark J. D. Jordans Faculty of Social and Behavioral Sciences, University of Amsterdam, Amsterdam, The Netherlands

Research and Development, War Child, Amsterdam, North Holland, The Netherlands

Jeremy C. Kane Mental Health, Johns Hopkins Bloomberg School of Public Health, Baltimore, MD, USA

Shraddha Kashyap School of Psychology, University of New South Wales, Sydney, NSW, Australia

Kaveh Khoshnood Yale School of Public Health, Epidemiology of Microbial Diseases, New Haven, CT, USA

Christine Knaevelsrud Division of Clinical Psychological Intervention, Freie Universität Berlin, Berlin, Germany

Noa Krawczyk Mental Health, Johns Hopkins Bloomberg School of Public Health, Baltimore, MD, USA

Belinda J. Liddell School of Psychology, University of New South Wales, Sydney, NSW, Australia

Thomas Maier Psychiatric Services of St. Gallen North, Wil, St. Gallen, Switzerland

Alisa B. Miller Department of Psychiatry, Boston Children's Hospital/Harvard Medical School, Boston, MA, USA

Kenneth E. Miller Research and Development, War Child, Amsterdam, North Holland, The Netherlands

Naser Morina Department of Consultation-Liaison-Psychiatry and Psychosomatic Medicine, University Hospital Zurich, Zurich, Switzerland

Nexhmedin Morina Department of Clinical Psychology and Psychotherapy, University of Münster, Münster, Germany

Laura Murray Mental Health, Johns Hopkins Bloomberg School of Public Health, Baltimore, MD, USA

Frank Neuner Clinical Psychology, Bielefeld University, Bielefeld, NA, Germany

Elizabeth A. Newnham School of Psychology, Curtin University, Perth, WA, Australia

Angela Nickerson School of Psychology, University of New South Wales, Sydney, NSW, Australia

Anushka Patel Department of Psychology, University of Tulsa, Tulsa, OK, USA

Atif Rahman Institute of Psychology, Health and Society, University of Liverpool, Liverpool, Merseyside, UK

Andrew Rasmussen Department of Psychology, Fordham University, Bronx, NY, USA

Maggie Schauer Centre of Excellence for Psychotraumatology, University of Konstanz, Konstanz, NA, Germany

Matthis Schick Department of Consultation-Liaison-Psychiatry and Psychosomatic Medicine, University Hospital Zurich, Zurich, Switzerland

Ulrich Schnyder University of Zurich, Zurich, Switzerland

Charlotte Sonne Competence Centre for Transcultural Psychiatry, Mental Health Centre Ballerup, Mental Health Services of the Capital Region of Denmark, Copenhagen, NA, Denmark

Frederik Steen Research and Development, War Child, Amsterdam, North Holland, The Netherlands

Jana Stein Division of Clinical Psychological Intervention, Freie Universität Berlin, Berlin, Germany

Jessica Tearne State Major Trauma Unit, Royal Perth Hospital, Health Department of Western Australia, Perth, WA, Australia

Wietse A. Tol Mental Health, Johns Hopkins Bloomberg School of Public Health, Baltimore, MD, USA

Stuart Turner Trauma Clinic, London, UK

Myrthe van den Broek Research and Development, War Child, Amsterdam, North Holland, The Netherlands

Peter Ventevogel Public Health Section, Division of Programme Management and Support, United Nations High Commissioner for Refugees, Geneva, Switzerland

Jay Verkuilen Educational Psychology, City University of New York, New York, NY, USA

Part I
Mental Health in Refugee and Conflict-Affected Populations

Mental Health Among Adult Survivors of War in Low- and Middle-Income Countries: Epidemiology and Treatment Outcome

Nexhmedin Morina

Abstract Millions of survivors of war live in low- and middle-income countries (LMICs). This chapter critically reviews literature on prevalences of mental disorders, in particular depression and posttraumatic stress disorder (PTSD), among adult survivors of war in LMICs. In addition, current publications on the efficacy of psychological interventions for depression and PTSD applied within this population are discussed. The findings suggest that more than a fourth of a population with a recent history of mass violence suffer from depression and/or PTSD at any given time. There is lack of research on mental disorders other than PTSD and depression among war survivors in LMICs. Furthermore, current evidence suggests that psychological interventions have the potential to successfully reduce symptoms of depression and PTSD in LMICs. Yet, given the lack of mental health services in many LMICs, a major challenge for global mental health remains developing more low-intensity interventions that can provide cost-effective solutions to large numbers of war survivors in need of mental health services.

Keywords War · Mental health · Depression · PTSD · Psychological interventions · Meta-analysis

Millions of individuals have been exposed to recent and ongoing armed conflicts (Pettersson & Wallensteen, 2015). The overwhelming majority of survivors of war are civilians who live in areas of (former) conflict in low-and middle-income countries (LMICs). There is much evidence of the psychological costs for individuals exposed to trauma in LMICs, resulting in this issue being at the forefront of many global health initiatives. Most epidemiological research in this population has focused on posttraumatic stress disorder (PTSD) and to a lesser extent on depression. Both conditions are known to contribute significantly to the global burden of

N. Morina (✉)
Department of Clinical Psychology and Psychotherapy, University of Münster, Münster, Germany
e-mail: morina@uni-muenster.de

N. Morina, A. Nickerson (eds.), *Mental Health of Refugee and Conflict-Affected Populations*, https://doi.org/10.1007/978-3-319-97046-2_1

disease (Kessler, 2012; Nemeroff et al., 2006; Sabes-Figuera et al., 2012). Yet, despite the evidence of the mental health burden of war and conflict, there is a disturbing gap between the evidence base for treating mental health problems such as PTSD and depression in LMICs and the expansive evidence that exists in developed nations, which has evolved as a result of many controlled trials of various psychological interventions (Bisson, Roberts, Andrew, Cooper, & Lewis, 2013; Morina, Koerssen, & Pollet, 2016). This chapter first reviews the literature on prevalences of depression, PTSD, and other mental disorders among adult survivors of war in LMICs. Then, the chapter discusses results of clinical trials assessing the efficacy of psychological interventions for PTSD and depression in patients who have been exposed to war-related events and live in LMICs.

Prevalences of Mental Disorders Among Survivors of War in LMICs

Dozens of survey reports provide information about prevalences of PTSD and depression among survivors of organized violence. Steel et al. (2009) report in their meta-analysis of 161 published surveys conducted before May 2009 on the prevalences of PTSD and depression among populations exposed to mass conflict and displacement. Whereas about two thirds of the included studies had been conducted with refugee samples in both high and low income countries, the remaining surveys had been carried out in conflict-affected populations in LMICs. The reported prevalences for PTSD and depression in the included publications varied from 0% to 99% for PTSD and 3% to 86% for depression. The authors reported weighted prevalences of 31% for PTSD and depression, respectively. Yet, Steel and colleagues did not separately report prevalences for depression and PTSD from studies conducted with war survivors in the areas of former conflict.

To review the current literature on PTSD and depression among adult survivors of war in areas of former conflict, we conducted a systematic review and a meta-analysis. To this end, surveys conducted less than 26 years after the end of the war were included. In contrast to the meta-analysis conducted by to Steel et al., we included only surveys undertaken in areas of (former) conflict as defined by the Uppsala Conflict Data Program (Pettersson & Wallensteen, 2015). This database defines wars as conflicts that generate 1000 or more battle-related deaths in one calendar year. Journal articles published on this topic before December 31, 2015 were located using the databases PsycINFO, MEDLINE and PILOTS (the latter is managed by the United States National Center for PTSD). We used the following search terms in titles, abstracts and key concepts related to (1) Depression (major depression/OR depress*); (2) PTSD (posttraumatic stress disorder OR posttraumatic stress OR posttraumatic stress OR posttraumatic syndrome OR post traumatic syndrome OR PTSD); (3) General mental health ("mental disorders OR mental health), and (4) War victims (genocide OR holocaust OR war OR warfare OR prisoners of war OR mass conflict OR post-conflict OR political conflict OR armed conflict OR terrorism OR torture OR persecution OR civilian OR ethnic cleansing). The inclusion criteria for the meta-analysis were: (1) a sample size of 50 or more participants with exposure to war-related events who were living in the area of former conflict at the time the survey was conducted; (2) participants had experienced war-related events within 25 years prior to conducting the survey; (3) at least 80% of the participants were older than 18 years. Exclusion criteria were: (1) study participants had received mental health interventions; (2) the sample consisted of combatants in armed forces (given the focus of the review on civilian war survivors); and (3) refugees (given the focus on war survivors living in the area of conflict). Similarly to Steel et al. (2009), studies conducted with Israeli participants were excluded since they mostly involve a small group of the population who were exposed to specific terrorist attacks and are therefore not representative of the general population. If a publication reported on more than one sample because the study was conducted in more than one country or because the study was conducted with different groups of war survivors (such as bereaved and non-bereaved survivors of war), the samples in question were treated as distinct samples. To analyze the weighted prevalence for PTSD and depression, the software program MetaXL was used (Barendregt, Doi, Lee, Norman, & Vos, 2013) and the random effects model was applied.

A total of 95 surveys fulfilled our criteria and provided the needed data to be included into the meta-analysis. Of these publications, 86 surveys (with a total of 68,076 participants) reported on prevalence of PTSD and 59 surveys (with a total of 56,961 participants) reported on prevalence of depression. The mean overall age of participants was 38.2 years (SD = 10.8) and 59.4% of participants were female. The assessment took place after a mean of 6 years following conflict. The majority of surveys were conducted in Africa (42.1%), followed by Asia (29.5%), Europe (23.2%), and South America (5.3%). The three most frequently used instruments to measure PTSD were the Harvard Trauma Questionnaire (n = 32), the Composite International Diagnostic Interview (n = 11), and the Mini International Neuropsychiatric Interview (n = 10). Depression was mostly measured with the Hopkins Symptom Checklist (n = 21), followed by the Mini International Neuropsychiatric Interview (n = 9) and the Composite International Diagnostic Interview (n = 8).

The weighted prevalence of PTSD was 29.5% (CI: 25.3–33.9, I^2 = 99.9%). The high I^2 indicates that there was large heterogeneity in the prevalences across the studies. For example, Siriwardhana et al. (2013) reported a PTSD prevalence of 2.4% among a randomly selected sample of 450 individuals in Sri Lanka who had been displaced due to conflict. On the other hand, Igreja et al. (2009) reported that 95% of their sample of 240 individuals in postwar Mozambique were PTSD cases. With regards to depression, the 59 surveys led to a weighted prevalence of 31% (95% CI = 0.25–0.36, I^2 = 99.0%). Here, too, large heterogeneity was observed. For example, Ayazi, Lien, Eide, Ruom, and Hauff (2012) found a prevalence of 6.4% among a community sample of 1200 war survivors in South Sudan. Yet, Mutabaruka, Sejourne, Bui, Birmes, and Chabrol (2012) reported a depression prevalence of 94.1% among 102 survivors of the Genocide in Rwanda.

Only a minority of the included studies in this systematic review reported on prevalences of other mental disorders, with anxiety disorders being the most frequently-reported. Accordingly, no weighted prevalences of other mental disorders were estimated. Similar to the prevalences of PTSD and depression, prevalences of other mental disorders varied greatly across surveys. The large heterogeneity remained even when only surveys applying a structured psychiatric interview were reviewed. For example, whereas some publications reported prevalences of suicide risk to be lower than 8% (Morina, von Lersner, & Prigerson, 2011; Mugisha, Muyinda, Wandiembe, & Kinyanda, 2015), others reported that more than one third of war survivors suffered from suicide risk (Morina & Emmelkamp, 2012; Schaal, Dusingizemungu, Jacob, & Elbert, 2011). A limited number of studies reported on prevalences of several mental disorders. For example, Priebe et al. (2010) conducted a survey with more than 3300 survivors of war in five countries of former Yugoslavia and applied a random walk technique to randomly select participants for face-to-face interviews with a structured psychiatric interview. In this study, the prevalences for mood disorders and anxiety disorders (including PTSD) varied enormously across the five countries (12–47% and 16–42%, respectively). The prevalences with the largest range across the five countries were major depression episode which ranged from 4% to 37%, manic episode which ranged from 0% to 4%, PTSD which ranged from 11% to 35%, generalized anxiety disorder which ranged from 4% to 24%, panic disorder which ranged from 3% to 10%, social anxiety disorder which ranged from 1% to 6%, substance use disorder which ranged from 1% to 9%, psychotic disorder which ranged from 0.3% to 4.5%, and somatization disorder which ranged from 0% to 1.3%.

Many studies have indicated that exposure to torture is associated with higher levels of psychopathology than exposure to other forms of mass violence (Gola et al., 2012; Steel et al., 2009). Similarly, higher prevalence rates have been reported for survivors of war who have lost a first degree relative due to war violence. Morina and Emmelkamp (2012) reported that as many as 96% of widowed lone mothers who had survived the war in Kosovo in the late 1990s and lost their husband during the war met criteria for major depressive disorder, PTSD, an anxiety disorder, or a substance use disorder, compared to 54.9% of non-bereaved mothers who had also experienced the war in Kosovo. In particular, widowed lone mothers reported significantly higher prevalences of PTSD (82%), major depressive disorder (71%), generalized anxiety disorder (48%), and suicide risk (45%) than non-bereaved mothers (18.3%, 29.6%, 9.9%, and 16.9%, respectively). Morina et al. (2011) also reported that exposure to war experiences involved the loss of first-degree relatives may lead to higher levels of psychopathology than exposure to war without loss of relatives. In this study, young war survivors who had lost their father during the war before the age of 18 reported significantly higher prevalences of generalized anxiety disorder (11% vs 7%), panic disorder (6% vs 2%), obsessive-compulsive disorder (3% vs 1%), and suicide risk (12% vs 6%) than matched non-bereaved young survivors of war. Related to this, several publications included in the meta-analysis reported on the prevalence of prolonged grief disorder (PGD). Schaal, Jacob, Dusingizemungu, and Elbert (2010) reported a prevalence of PGD of 8% in 400 survivors of the Rwandan genocide who had lost their parents and/or their husbands before, during, or after the genocide in 1994. Morina and colleagues reported PGD prevalences between 34.6% and 69% in three samples of war survivors who had lost first-degree relatives during the Kosovo war of 1998/1999 (Morina & Emmelkamp, 2012; Morina, Reschke, & Hofmann, 2011; Morina, Rudari, Bleichhardt, & Prigerson, 2010). Finally, Stammel et al. (2013) reported a PGD prevalence of 14.3% among 775 survivors of the Khmer Rouge regime in Cambodia.

In summary, research indicates that more than a fourth of war survivors suffer from either PTSD or depression. Prevalences of several other disorders seem also to be elevated, yet, there is less research on other mental disorders than PTSD and depression. Furthermore, we know little about the impact of nature and amount of different traumatic experiences during war on current mental health. More importantly, there is lack of research on potential psychosocial and environmental factors that moderate the long-term impact of exposure to war-related events on mental health among war survivors living in the areas of former conflict.

Psychological Interventions for PTSD and Depression

Several randomized controlled trials (RCTs) of psychological interventions for PTSD and associated symptoms (mostly depression) have been conducted in LMICs. Recent systematic reviews and meta-analyses have reported on such interventions. Tol et al. (2011) provided an overview and a meta-analysis of psychosocial support for survivors of natural disasters, technological disasters, or armed conflicts in LMICs. The authors included seven RCTs with adult participants in their meta-analysis that produced an aggregated effect size of 0.38 when psychological interventions were compared to control conditions (wait lists or usual care). However, several factors limit the generalizability of these findings to war survivors in LMIC. Two of the included clinical trials were conducted with earthquake survivors rather than survivors of mass violence. In addition, one of the trials with war survivors (Dybdahl, 2001) had examined the efficacy of a psychosocial intervention program for patients in an ongoing medical care program, which prohibits conclusions about the sole efficacy of the psychosocial intervention. Weiss et al. (2016) published a review of the current literature on psychological interventions for survivors of torture and other systematic violence. The authors included trials from across the globe and concluded that cognitive behavior interventions produce the best treatment effects among survivors of mass violence with PTSD and/or depression. Furthermore, the authors stated that the quality of reporting of RCTs was generally good, whereas publications on other forms of clinical trials showed poor quality of documentation.

More recently, Morina, Malek, Nickerson, and Bryant (2017b) published a meta-analysis on the efficacy of RCTs for adult survivors of mass violence with PTSD and/or depression living in LMICs. The authors included a total of 18 RCTs that were published in peer-reviewed journals before the end of November 2016. Of these, 17 assessed PTSD and 13 assessed depression. This included a total of 2124 treated participants and 934 participants in the wait-list condition. With regards to PTSD, Morina et al. reported large pre-post and pre-follow-up effect sizes across active treatments (g = 1.29 and 1.75, respectively). When active treatments were compared to control conditions at post-treatment or at follow-up, the effect sizes were medium to large (g = 0.39 and 0.93, respectively). Psychotherapy seemed to be effective also for depressive symptomatology. Both pre-post as well as pro-follow-up effect sizes were large (g = 1.28 and 1.56, respectively). When active treatments were compared to control conditions at post-treatment or at follow-up, effect sizes were large in both cases (g = 0.86 and 0.90, respectively). The authors further reported that six trials also assessed the effect of treatment on functional impairment. In these trials, large pre-post and pre-follow-up effect sizes were found (g = 0.73 and 0.91, respectively). Finally, four trials compared active treatments to control conditions at post-treatment and produced a medium effect (g = 0.59) with regards to functional impairment. It should be noted, however, that the authors also reported that the risk of bias was rated as high in half of the cases, which might indicate that some of the current results might underestimate or overestimate the intervention effect. Furthermore, the rather limited number of existing RCTs in this population indicates that the results of the current literature should be interpreted with caution.

Discussion

Current literature suggests that more than one fourth of survivors of war suffer from depression and/or PTSD. These prevalences are much higher in war-affected populations than in individuals without a recent exposure to mass violence. For example, prevalences of less than 7% for major depression and less than 4% for PTSD have been reported in the European Union and the USA (Kessler, Chiu, Demler, & Walters, 2005; Wittchen et al., 2011). Furthermore, the findings demonstrate that depression is at least as prevalent among war survivors as PTSD. Additionally, comorbidity of mental disorders is prevalent among survivors of war, with about one fourth of war survivors suffering from at least two mental disorders (Priebe et al., 2010). Research indicates that comorbidity between depression and PTSD is characterized by significantly higher levels of psychopathological distress, including suicide risk, than either condition alone (Morina et al., 2013).

The finding that depression is at least as prevalent as PTSD among survivors of war is another relevant result that should guide future research and health care policy. This is somewhat in contract to the rather stronger research focus on PTSD than on depression in this population. In fact, PTSD has been overrepresented in both epidemiological as well as psychotherapy research among war survivors. Relevant avenues to investigate in the future are related to psychological, socio-economical and physical factors associated with depression and other mental health complaints beyond PTSD. In addition, future research should more carefully investigate the impact of both war-related as well as post-war related factors on psychopathological complaints in war survivors.

Although limited, the literature on other mental disorders than depression and PTSD indicates that some of these disorders might also be very prevalent in war survivors. This finding is worrisome when one considers the fact that most affected survivors of war live in LMICs, which are not adequately resourced by mental health services (Saxena, Thornicroft, Knapp, & Whiteford, 2007). Consequently, many millions of survivors of war with mental disorders lack access to mental health services. Accumulating empirical findings suggest that children and adolescents with a history of exposure to war events are also more likely to suffer from poor mental health then children without such a history (Attanayake et al., 2009; Reed, Fazel, Jones, Panter-Brick, & Stein, 2012; Slone & Mann, 2016). This situation represents a global challenge and urgently requires a process of rethinking in finding new ways to more effectively address mental health needs of those suffering because of exposure to war.

The large heterogeneity across the studies measuring prevalences of PTSD, depression, and other mental disorders might be explained by different factors. Study characteristics, such as recruitment procedures and psychometric characteristics of the applied instruments may account for some of the variance. Yet, studies that have applied a similar recruitment strategy and methodology to assess prevalences of mental disorders in two or more samples also produced heterogeneous prevalences. Perhaps the best example in this area is the study by Priebe et al. (2010) conducted in five countries of former Yugoslavia. As reported above, prevalences for mood disorders and anxiety disorders varied substantially across the samples. Given that the authors of this study applied an identical methodology and recruitment strategy in all countries, we can assume that differences across and within samples may play a significant role in explaining the heterogeneity across studies. Hence, the nature and amount of traumatic experiences during war as well as post-conflict psychosocial and environmental factors are likely to be significantly associated with current prevalences of mental disorders. The survey by Morina and Emmelkamp (2012) might provide an illustrative example for this notion. In this survey, almost all widowed lone mothers who had survived the war in Kosovo and lost their husband during the war met criteria for a mental disorder. This population must cope with the psychological difficulties associated with their own war-related memories, need to overcome the loss of their husband, manage without a husband and co-parent for practical and emotional support, and perceive major difficulties in their role as a sole caretaker for their children. Furthermore, social norms might negatively affect mental health in this population. For example, it was customary in the post-war Kosovar society that a widowed mother not remarry, which in many cases may have resulted in forced lone motherhood and may have negatively affected coping with traumatic memories and post-war stressors (Morina & Emmelkamp, 2012). Finally, ongoing societal and political instability and poor mental health and social care services are likely to further contribute to psychopathology.

Mitigating the effects of trauma and adversity has increasingly become a global public health objective (Belfer, Remschmidt, Nurcombe, Okasha, & Sartorius, 2007; Collins et al., 2011; World Health Organization, 2003). Yet, significant challenges hinder implementing evidence-based interventions in LMICs. These include insufficient mental health services, barriers in adapting established interventions to the needs of LMIC contexts, and the lack of adequately qualified practitioners to deliver interventions (Dawson et al., 2015). Current research indicates that psychological interventions have the potential to effectively reduce symptoms of PTSD and depression in war survivors in LMICs. Evidence-based psychological treatments that have been shown to work effectively in developed countries also demonstrate efficacy when applied to treating the mental health needs of both children and adolescents, as well as adults in LMICs (Morina, Malek, Nickerson, & Bryant, 2017a; Morina et al., 2017b). It is often proposed that the treatment of choice in developed countries for individuals affected by traumatic experiences is trauma-focused psychotherapy, which typically involves strategies that address intrusive memories of the traumatic experience (Ehlers et al., 2010). However, the extent to which psychological treatment should focus on past traumatic experiences or rather address more immediate problems of current adversity, which are commonly experienced in LMICs, is frequently debated (Hubbard & Pearson, 2004). It is proposed that mass violence does not simply result in psychopathology emanating from the stress of war-related experiences. Mental health among war survivors is also strongly affected by the subsequent social upheaval, poverty, marginalization, lack of infrastructure, and overcrowding (Miller & Rasmussen, 2010). Supporting this view is much evidence that ongoing stressors have a significant impact on the mental health of survivors of war and conflict (de Jong et al., 2001; Lev-Wiesel, Al-Krenawi, & Sehwail, 2007; Miller, Omidian, Rasmussen, Yaqubi, & Daudzai, 2008; Rasmussen et al., 2010). Currently, there is indication that addressing both the psychological effects of trauma and the daily stressors encountered by war-affected populations in LMICs may effectively reduce psychopathology. Yet, there is a need for caution about the capacity of these interventions to be implemented in LMICs at population levels. Given the large number of war survivors in need of mental health support, interventions for war survivors in LMICs need to be both efficacious as well as capable of being scaled up to the point that they can be readily implemented in countries with limited access to mental health services. Accordingly, low intensity interventions that can achieve reasonable treatment effects but simultaneously provide cost-effective solutions are needed to develop the long-term and sustainable capacity to disseminate these interventions to large numbers of those in need in LMICs (Patel et al., 2010; Rahman et al., 2016; Singla et al., 2017; Tol et al., 2011).

In conclusion, current research findings indicate that millions of war survivors who live in war-afflicted regions suffer from depression, PTSD, and other mental disorders that may directly or indirectly be associated with war experiences as well as post-war psychosocial and environmental factors. Additionally, preliminary evidence suggests that existing psychological interventions may successfully reduce mental health complaints. Yet, a major challenge for global mental health is to develop more low-intensity interventions for large numbers of war survivors in need psychological assistance.

References

Attanayake, V., McKay, R., Joffres, M., Singh, S., Burkle, F., Jr., & Mills, E. (2009). Prevalence of mental disorders among children exposed to war: A systematic review of 7,920 children. *Medicine, Conflict, and Survival, 25*(1), 4–19.

Ayazi, T., Lien, L., Eide, A. H., Ruom, M. M., & Hauff, E. (2012). What are the risk factors for the comorbidity of posttraumatic stress disorder and depression in a war-affected population? A cross-sectional community study in South Sudan. *BMC Psychiatry, 12*, 175. https://doi.org/10.1186/1471-244X-12-175

Barendregt, J. J., Doi, S. A., Lee, Y. Y., Norman, R. E., & Vos, T. (2013). Meta-analysis of prevalence. *Journal of Epidemiology and Community Health, 67*(11), 974–978. https://doi.org/10.1136/jech-2013-203104

Belfer, M. L., Remschmidt, H., Nurcombe, B., Okasha, A., & Sartorius, N. (Eds.). (2007). *A global programme for child and adolescent mental health: A challenge in the new millennium.* West Sussex, UK: Wiley.

Bisson, J. I., Roberts, N. P., Andrew, M., Cooper, R., & Lewis, C. (2013). Psychological therapies for chronic post- traumatic stress disorder (PTSD) in adults. *Cochrane Database of Systematic Reviews, 12*, CD003388–CD003388. https://doi.org/10.1002/14651858.CD003388.pub4

Collins, P. Y., Patel, V., Joestl, S. S., March, D., Insel, T. R., Daar, A. S., ... Executive Comm Grand Challenges Gl. (2011). Grand challenges in global mental health. *Nature, 475*(7354), 27–30.

Dawson, K. S., Bryant, R. A., Harper, M., Tay, A. K., Rahman, A., Schafer, A., & van Ommeren, M. (2015). Problem management plus (PM plus): A WHO transdiagnostic psychological intervention for common mental health problems. *World Psychiatry, 14*(3), 354–357. https://doi.org/10.1002/wps.20255

de Jong, J. T., Komproe, I. H., Van Ommeren, M., El Masri, M., Araya, M., Khaled, N., ... Somasundaram, D. (2001). Lifetime events and posttraumatic stress disorder in 4 postconflict settings. *JAMA, 286*, 555–562.

Dybdahl, R. (2001). Children and mothers in war: An outcome study of a psychosocial intervention program. *Child Development, 72*, 1214–1230. Retrieved from https://doi.org/10.1111/1467-8624.00343

Ehlers, A., Bisson, J., Clark, D. M., Creamer, M., Pilling, S., Richards, D., ... Yule, W. (2010). Do all psychological treatments really work the same in posttraumatic stress disorder? *Clinical Psychology Review, 30*, 269–276. Retrieved from https://doi.org/10.1016/j.cpr.2009.12.001

Gola, H., Engler, H., Schauer, M., Adenauer, H., Riether, C., Kolassa, S., ... Kolassa, I. (2012). Victims of rape show increased cortisol responses to trauma reminders: A study in individuals with war- and torture-related PTSD. *Psychoneuroendocrinology, 37*(2), 213–220. https://doi.org/10.1016/j.psyneuen.2011.06.005

Hubbard, J., & Pearson, N. (2004). Sierra leonean refugees in Guinea: Addressing the mental health effects of massive community violence. In K. E. Miller & L. M. Rasco (Eds.), *The mental health of refugees: Ecological approaches to healing and adaptation* (pp. 95–132). Mahwah, NJ: Lawrence Erlbaum Associates, Inc.

Igreja, V., Kleijn, W., Dias-Lambranca, B., Hershey, D. A., Calero, C., & Richters, A. (2009). Agricultural cycle and the prevalence of posttraumatic stress disorder: A longitudinal community study in postwar Mozambique. *Journal of Traumatic Stress, 22*(3), 172–179. https://doi.org/10.1002/jts.20412

Kessler, R. C. (2012). The costs of depression. *Psychiatric Clinics of North America, 35*, 1–14. Retrieved from https://doi.org/10.1016/j.psc.2011.11.005

Kessler, R. C., Chiu, W. T., Demler, O., & Walters, E. E. (2005). Prevalence, severity, and comorbidity of 12-month DSM-IV disorders in the national comorbidity survey replication. *Archives of General Psychiatry, 62*(6), 617–627.

Lev-Wiesel, R., Al-Krenawi, A., & Sehwail, M. A. (2007). Psychological symptomatology among palestinian male and female adolescents living under political violence 2004–2005. *Community Mental Health Journal, 43*, 49–56.

Miller, K. E., Omidian, P., Rasmussen, A., Yaqubi, A., & Daudzai, H. (2008). Daily stressors, war experiences, and mental health in Afghanistan. *Transcultural Psychiatry, 45*, 611–638. Retrieved from https://doi.org/10.1177/1363461508100785

Miller, K. E., & Rasmussen, A. (2010). War exposure, daily stressors, and mental health in conflict and post-conflict settings: Bridging the divide between trauma-focused and psychosocial frameworks. *Social Science & Medicine, 70*, 7–16. Retrieved from https://doi.org/10.1016/j.socscimed.2009.09.029

Morina, N., Ajdukovic, D., Bogic, M., Franciskovic, T., Kucukalic, A., Lecic-Tosevski, D., … Priebe, S. (2013). Co-occurrence of major depressive episode and posttraumatic stress disorder among survivors of war. *The Journal of Clinical Psychiatry, 74*, e212–e218. Retrieved from https://doi.org/10.4088/jcp.12m07844

Morina, N., & Emmelkamp, P. M. G. (2012). Mental health outcomes of widowed and married mothers after war. *British Journal of Psychiatry, 200*(2), 158–159. https://doi.org/10.1192/bjp.bp.111.093609

Morina, N., Koerssen, R., & Pollet, T. V. (2016). Interventions for children and adolescents with posttraumatic stress disorder: A meta-analysis of comparative outcome studies. *Clinical Psychology Review, 47*, 41–54. https://doi.org/10.1016/j.cpr.2016.05.006

Morina, N., Malek, M., Nickerson, A., & Bryant, R. A. (2017a). Psychological interventions for post-traumatic stress disorder and depression in young survivors of mass violence in low- and middle-income countries: Meta-analysis. *The British Journal of Psychiatry, 210*, 247–254. https://doi.org/10.1192/bjp.bp.115.180265

Morina, N., Malek, M., Nickerson, A., & Bryant, R. A. (2017b). Meta-analysis of interventions for posttraumatic stress disorder and depression in adult survivors of mass violence in low- and middle-income countries. *Depression and Anxiety, 34*(8), 679–691. https://doi.org/10.1002/da.22618

Morina, N., Reschke, K., & Hofmann, S. G. (2011). Long-term outcomes of war-related death of family members in Kosovar civilian war survivors. *Death Studies, 35*(4), 365–372. https://doi.org/10.1080/07481187.2011.553340 Pii 935975006.

Morina, N., Rudari, V., Bleichhardt, G., & Prigerson, H. G. (2010). Prolonged grief disorder, depression, and posttraumatic stress disorder among bereaved Kosovar civilian war survivors. A preliminary investigation. *International Journal of Social Psychiatry, 56*(3), 288–297. https://doi.org/10.1177/0020764008101638

Morina, N., von Lersner, U., & Prigerson, H. G. (2011). War and bereavement: Consequences for mental and physical distress. *PLoS One, 6*(7), e22140. https://doi.org/10.1371/journal.pone.0022140

Mugisha, J., Muyinda, H., Wandiembe, P., & Kinyanda, E. (2015). Prevalence and factors associated with posttraumatic stress disorder seven years after the conflict in three districts in Northern Uganda (the wayo-nero study). *BMC Psychiatry, 15*, 170. https://doi.org/10.1186/s12888-015-0551-5

Mutabaruka, J., Sejourne, N., Bui, E., Birmes, P., & Chabrol, H. (2012). Traumatic grief and traumatic stress in survivors 12? Years after the genocide in Rwanda. *Stress and Health, 28*(4), 289–296. https://doi.org/10.1002/smi.1429

Nemeroff, C. B., Bremner, J. D., Foa, E. B., Mayberg, H. S., North, C. S., & Stein, M. B. (2006). Posttraumatic stress disorder: A state-of-the-science review. *Journal of Psychiatric Research, 40*(1), 1–21. https://doi.org/10.1016/j.jpsychires.2005.07.005

Patel, V., Weiss, H. A., Chowdhary, N., Naik, S., Pednekar, S., Chatterjee, S., … Simon, G. (2010). Effectiveness of an intervention led by lay health counsellors for depressive and anxiety disorders in primary care in Goa, India (MANAS): A cluster randomised controlled trial. *The Lancet, 376*(9758), 2086–2095. https://doi.org/10.1016/S0140-6736(10)61508-5

Pettersson, T., & Wallensteen, P. (2015). Armed conflicts, 1946–2014. *Journal of Peace Research, 52*, 536–550. Retrieved from https://doi.org/10.1177/0022343315595927

Priebe, S., Bogic, M., Ajdukovic, D., Franciskovic, T., Galeazzi, G. M., Kucukalic, A., ... Schutzwohl, M. (2010). Mental disorders following war in the balkans: A study in 5 countries. *Archives of General Psychiatry, 67*(5), 518–528. https://doi.org/10.1001/archgenpsychiatry.2010.37

Rahman, A., Hamdani, S. U., Awan, N. R., Bryant, R. A., Dawson, K. S., Khan, M. F., ... van Ommeren, M. (2016). Effect of a multicomponent behavioral intervention in adults impaired by psychological distress in a conflict-affected area of Pakistan: A randomized clinical trial. *JAMA, 316*(24), 2609–2617. https://doi.org/10.1001/jama.2016.17165

Rasmussen, A., Nguyen, L., Wilkinson, J., Vundla, S., Raghavan, S., Miller, K. E., & Keller, A. S. (2010). Rates and impact of trauma and current stressors among Darfuri refugees in Eastern Chad. *American Journal of Orthopsychiatry, 80*, 227–236. Retrieved from https://doi.org/10.1111/j.1939-0025.2010.01026.x

Reed, R. V., Fazel, M., Jones, L., Panter-Brick, C., & Stein, A. (2012). Mental health of displaced and refugee children resettled in low-income and middle-income countries: Risk and protective factors. *Lancet, 379*(9812), 250–265. https://doi.org/10.1016/S0140-6736(11)60050-0

Sabes-Figuera, R., McCrone, P., Bogic, M., Ajdukovic, D., Franciskovic, T., Colombini, N., ... Priebe, S. (2012). Long-term impact of war on healthcare costs: An eight-country study. *PloS one, 7*, e29603. Retrieved from https://doi.org/10.1371/journal.pone.0029603

Saxena, S., Thornicroft, G., Knapp, M., & Whiteford, H. (2007). Resources for mental health: Scarcity, inequity, and inefficiency. *The Lancet, 370*(9590), 878–889. https://doi.org/10.1016/S0140-6736(07)61239-2

Schaal, S., Dusingizemungu, J., Jacob, N., & Elbert, T. (2011). Rates of trauma spectrum disorders and risks of posttraumatic stress disorder in a sample of orphaned and widowed genocide survivors. *European Journal of Psychotraumatology, 2*, 6343. https://doi.org/10.3402/ejpt.v2i0.6343

Schaal, S., Jacob, N., Dusingizemungu, J. P., & Elbert, T. (2010). Rates and risks for prolonged grief disorder in a sample of orphaned and widowed genocide survivors. *BMC Psychiatry, 10*, 55. https://doi.org/10.1186/1471-244X-10-55

Singla, D. R., Kohrt, B., Murray, L. K., Anand, A., Chorpita, B. F., & Patel, V. (2017). Psychological treatments for the world: Lessons from low-and middle-income countries. *Annual Review of Clinical Psychology, 13*(1), 149–181. https://doi.org/10.1146/annurev-clinpsy-032816-045217

Siriwardhana, C., Adikari, A., Pannala, G., Siribaddana, S., Abas, M., Sumathipala, A., & Stewart, R. (2013). Prolonged internal displacement and common mental disorders in Sri Lanka: The COMRAID study. *PLoS One, 8*(5), e64742. https://doi.org/10.1371/journal.pone.0064742

Slone, M., & Mann, S. (2016). Effects of war, terrorism and armed conflict on young children: A systematic review. *Child Psychiatry & Human Development, 47*(6), 950–965. https://doi.org/10.1007/s10578-016-0626-7

Stammel, N., Heeke, C., Bockers, E., Chhim, S., Taing, S., Wagner, B., & Knaevelsrud, C. (2013). *Prolonged grief disorder three decades post loss in survivors of the Khmer Rouge regime in Cambodia* (Vol. 144, pp. 87–93). https://doi.org/10.1016/j.jad.2012.05.063

Steel, Z., Chey, T., Silove, D., Marnane, C., Bryant, R. A., & van Ommeren, M. (2009). Association of torture and other potentially traumatic events with mental health outcomes among populations exposed to mass conflict and displacement. *JAMA, 302*, 537. Retrieved from https://doi.org/10.1001/jama.2009.1132

Tol, W. A., Barbui, C., Galappatti, A., Silove, D., Betancourt, T. S., Souza, R., ... van Ommeren, M. (2011). Mental health and psychosocial support in humanitarian settings: Linking practice and research. *The Lancet, 378*, 1581–1591. Retrieved from https://doi.org/10.1016/s0140-6736(11)61094-5

Weiss, W. M., Ugueto, A. M., Mahmooth, Z., Murray, L. K., Hall, B. J., Nadison, M., … Bass, J. (2016). Mental health interventions and priorities for research for adult survivors of torture and systematic violence: A review of the literature. *Torture, 26*, 17–44.

Wittchen, H. U., Jacobi, F., Rehm, J., Gustavsson, A., Svensson, M., Jonsson, B., … Steinhausen, H. C. (2011). The size and burden of mental disorders and other disorders of the brain in europe 2010. *European Neuropsychopharmacology, 21*(9), 655–679. https://doi.org/10.1016/j.euroneuro.2011.07.018

World Health Organization. (2003). *Caring for children and adolescents with mental disorders: Setting WHO directions*. Geneva, Switzerland: World Health Organization.

Nexhmedin Morina, Ph.D., is professor of Clinical Psychology and Psychotherapy at the University of Münster, Germany, and director of the Centre for the Treatment of Traumatic Stress Disorders. His research interests include investigating mental health in survivors of mass conflict as well as the evaluation of mental health services.

Mental Health, Pre-migratory Trauma and Post-migratory Stressors Among Adult Refugees

Jessica Carlsson and Charlotte Sonne

Abstract The refugee experience is characterised by exposure to multiple traumatic events both in one's country of origin and during displacement. Researchers have found that severity of traumatic events and cumulative trauma are associated with an increased prevalence of mental health problems. Refugees typically also experience numerous post-migratory stressors following arrival in the resettlement country. Accordingly, several studies have found an association between pre-migratory traumatic events, post-migratory stressors and mental health outcomes in refugees. In this chapter, common trauma-related mental health problems among refugees will be presented. The influence of traumatic events and post-migratory stressors on refugee mental health will be discussed. The information provided in the chapter is based on available research as well as the authors' clinical experience at the Competence Centre for Transcultural Psychiatry (CTP) in Denmark.

Keywords Trauma · Post-migratory stressors · Refugee · Mental health · PTSD

Introduction

Existing evidence suggests that mental disorders are highly prevalent in refugees and asylum-seekers (Fazel, Wheeler, & Danesh, 2005; Marshall, Schell, Elliott, Berthold, & Chun, 2005; Steel et al., 2009). Studies have demonstrated that the severity of traumatic events, and repeated exposure to persecution and war-related trauma, as well as early childhood trauma, influence the prevalence and the complexity of symptoms in trauma-related mental health disorders such as Post Traumatic Stress Disorder (PTSD) (Bhui et al., 2003; Carlsson, Mortensen, & Kastrup, 2006; Jaranson et al., 2004; Lie, Lavik, & Laake, 2001; Palić & Elklit, 2014). When fleeing the home country, extensive losses are experienced by refugees who are often obliged to leave behind almost everything that defines their identity.

J. Carlsson (✉) · C. Sonne
Competence Centre for Transcultural Psychiatry, Mental Health Centre Ballerup, Mental Health Services of the Capital Region of Denmark, Copenhagen, NA, Denmark
e-mail: jessica.carlsson.lohmann@regionh.dk; charlotte.sonne@regionh.dk

N. Morina, A. Nickerson (eds.), *Mental Health of Refugee and Conflict-Affected Populations*, https://doi.org/10.1007/978-3-319-97046-2_2

Furthermore, the often difficult and dangerous journey to the country of resettlement is typically followed by a period of insecurity as the individual waits for asylum claims to be processed (Laban, Komproe, Gernaat, & de Jong, 2008; Silove, Steel, & Watters, 2000). Subsequently, even if offered secure residency, refugees typically face a high number of resettlement stressors, as well as fear related to ongoing conflict in the home country impacting on family left behind (Laban, Gernaat, Komproe, van der Tweel, & de Jong, 2005). The available literature provides evidence that, even several years after resettlement, a high level of exposure to both war-related traumatic events and post-migration stressors is associated with increased rates of mental health disorders (Bogic et al., 2012; Carlsson, Olsen, Mortensen, & Kastrup, 2006; Marshall et al., 2005; Steel, Silove, Phan, & Bauman, 2002).

Mental Health Problems Among Trauma-Affected Refugees

The reported prevalence of PTSD and other trauma-related mental health disorders in non-clinical samples of refugees and asylum-seekers differs widely across studies due to differences in study populations and methodology. A review by Fazel and colleagues of the prevalence of PTSD, depression, generalized anxiety and psychotic disorders included 20 studies with a total of 6743 adult refugees and asylum-seekers resettled in Western countries. Seventeen of the included studies reported point prevalence, whereas three studies reported 1-year prevalence. In contrast to several other reviews, Fazel et al. excluded studies where findings were based on self-report questionnaires only. This resulted in a relatively low PTSD prevalence of 9% (Fazel et al., 2005). The estimated prevalence for major depression was 5%. The review included only a handful of studies on generalized anxiety (five studies) and psychotic illness (two studies) with the estimated prevalence being 4% and 2%, respectively. A large-scale meta-analysis by Steel and colleagues on refugees and post-conflict populations worldwide found the prevalence of PTSD and depression to be substantially higher with an unadjusted weighted prevalence of 31% for both PTSD and depression (Steel et al., 2009). This meta-analysis included 161 papers with a total of 81,866 participants. The studies included in the analysis used both point prevalence and period prevalence (6–12 months or lifetime) and both self-report and interview-based measures. Bogic and colleagues conducted a review of depression and anxiety disorders among refugees who had been in the country of resettlement for 5 years or longer and found considerable variation in reported prevalences of mental health disorders, although most studies reported rates of both PTSD and depression that were above 20% (Bogic, Njoku, & Priebe, 2015). In this review, 29 studies were included, comprising a total of 16,010 participants. The included studies reported point prevalence or 1-year prevalence. Furthermore, Lindert and colleagues undertook a systematic review and meta-analysis of prevalence rates of depression and anxiety among refugees and labour migrants. They found that refugees reported rates of depression that were double those observed in labour migrants (44% versus 20%) (Lindert, von Ehrenstein, Priebe, Mielck, & Brähler, 2009).

While PTSD and depression are the most commonly-researched trauma-related mental health disorders among refugees and asylum-seekers, a range of other psychological and physical symptoms have been found in such groups including prolonged or complicated grief (Craig, Sossou, Schnak, & Essex, 2008), explosive anger (Hecker, Fetz, Ainamani, & Elbert, 2015; Silove et al., 2009; Spiller et al., 2016), dissociation (Palić, Carlsson, Armour, & Elklit, 2015), anxiety (Hinton, Nickerson, & Bryant, 2011) and medically unexplained somatic symptoms (Rohlof, Knipscheer, & Kleber, 2014). In studies conducted with refugees, it has been demonstrated that having other psychiatric disorders comorbid with PTSD, is often associated with greater functional impairment (Momartin, Silove, Manicavasagar, & Steel, 2004; Palić, Kappel, Nielsen, Carlsson, & Bech, 2014).

Moreover, large epidemiological studies have shown an excess burden of psychosis among migrants and findings from several high quality studies have suggested that migration itself may represent a risk factor for developing a psychotic disorder (Bourque, van der Ven, & Malla, 2011; Cantor-Graae, Pedersen, Mcneil, & Mortensen, 2003). A large Swedish study demonstrated that this risk is even higher among refugees (Hollander et al., 2016). In this registry-based study, carried out in a high-income setting, the incidence rate of a non-affective psychotic disorder was 66% higher in refugees compared to non-refugee migrants from similar regions of origin, and nearly three times higher than in the native-born Swedish population. The authors noted that their findings support the theory that exposure to psychosocial adversity may increase the risk of psychosis. In another study, comprising a clinical sample of 181 trauma-affected refugees with PTSD, psychotic symptoms were identified in 41% of participants. The majority of symptoms identified were auditory hallucinations and persecutory delusions. Among those with PTSD and psychotic symptoms there were significantly more patients exposed to torture and imprisonment (Nygaard, Sonne, & Carlsson, 2017). These findings emphasise the need to consider signs of psychosis in refugee populations with respect to both clinical assessment and treatment.

In addition to the mental health problems discussed above, the experience of multiple traumas and forced migration may also alter a refugee's view of themselves, their identity and social relations (Silove, 2013). Separation from family members and social networks necessarily disrupts existing relationships, and experiences of interpersonal violence often cause distrust that may serve as a hindrance to the formation of new social relations in the resettlement country (Morina, Schnyder, Schick, Nickerson, & Bryant, 2016). Furthermore, human rights violations committed by state officials often lead to a lack of trust in authorities, which might act as a barrier to help-seeking behaviour and consequently prevent refugees from receiving appropriate and timely treatment of trauma-related mental health difficulties.

For at least 20 years, there have been attempts to identify a separate diagnosis to encompass the complex pattern of distress and very high levels of comorbidity described above in populations exposed to repeated and protracted traumatic experiences, such as trauma-affected refugees (Davidson et al., 1996). The concept of disorders of extreme stress not otherwise specified (DESNOS) was put forward as a potential diagnosis covering a broader spectrum of symptoms. DESNOS has been researched and identified in only a small number of studies with trauma-affected refugees and post-conflict populations (Morina & Ford, 2008; Palić & Elklit, 2014; Teodorescu, Heir, Hauff, Wentzel-Larsen, & Lien, 2012; Weine et al., 1998). When studied, DESNOS was found to be a rather diffuse syndrome with varying psychopathological patterns, and thus has not been included in the present diagnostic manuals. Currently, the stress-related diagnosis "enduring personality change after catastrophic experience" (EPCACE) exists in the ICD-10 and the DSM-5 has broadened the PTSD diagnosis to include some of the former DESNOS symptoms such as impulsivity and negative self-evaluation. In the upcoming ICD-11, the acknowledgement of potential differential symptom profiles in persons exposed to protracted and inter-personal trauma has led to a division of the PTSD diagnosis into PTSD and complex PTSD (CPTSD) (Palić et al., 2016). As the DMS-5 PTSD diagnosis is rather new and the ICD-11 CPTSD has not yet officially been implemented, only limited research has been carried out, including on refugees (Nickerson et al., 2016; Tay, Rees, Chen, Kareth, & Silove, 2015). Research on EPCACE has been rather scarce generally and in refugees almost non-existent (Nygaard et al., 2017). It remains debatable whether these diagnoses fully capture the complex pattern of mental health and psychosocial problems that are frequently found among trauma-affected refugees.

Pre-migratory Traumatic Events Among Refugees

The pre-migratory traumatic events experienced by refugees may start in early life and can include traumatic events directly related to armed conflicts (such as being an active combatant or, as a civilian, witnessing killings) or persecution, or indirectly by the consequences of conflict and upheaval on the societal structure, family patterns and living conditions. Studies assessing past traumatic experiences use a range of measurement tools. Self-reports or semi-structured interviews may be the instrument of choice in research studies and clinical practice depending on the purpose of the assessment as well as the practical circumstances in the specific setting.

Early Childhood Trauma

Due to the circumstances in their country of origin, with conflicts lasting for years or even decades, refugees have often experienced war-related trauma early in their lives. Accordingly, a recent study on trauma-affected refugees carried out at the Competence Centre for Transcultural Psychiatry (CTP) in Denmark found a high prevalence of childhood traumatic events, such as physical and sexual abuse (Riber,

2015a, 2015b). In this sample, different types of childhood maltreatment were endorsed at rates as high as 63% by both men and women from Iraqi and Palestinian-Lebanese backgrounds. Participants in the study reported that experienced child abuse had a personal impact on emotional, behavioural and relational domains, which lead to a lack of autonomy, insecurity, low self-esteem and feeling unappreciated. The findings indicated that childhood maltreatment, in combination with war-related traumatic events, affected attachment patterns (Riber, 2015b). In another study conducted with treatment-seeking Bosnian refugees resettled in Denmark, 29% of participants reported having experienced at least one adverse childhood event (Palić & Elklit, 2014). The childhood events assessed included emotional, physical and sexual maltreatment as well as physical neglect and witnessing violence between parents before the age of 18 years. In this study, refugees with experiences of childhood trauma reported higher levels of psychopathology than refugees without childhood trauma.

Trauma Related to Armed Conflicts, Persecution, Imprisonment and Torture

Many refugees and asylum-seekers have lived in war zones and either participated in armed conflicts or have been civilians in the midst of war. Additionally, many have been persecuted due to (for example) political, religious or ethnic reasons, and some have been imprisoned or held in custody and tortured.

Traumatic events experienced in the context of armed conflict or individual persecution are often marked by interpersonal traumas, inflicted on purpose by one or more human beings on another, such as torture. The UN Convention against Torture defines torture as an act by which severe pain or suffering, whether physical or mental, is intentionally inflicted on a person for such purposes as obtaining information or a confession. The UN Convention against Torture, Article 14, also describes the right to rehabilitation for torture survivors, which provides survivors of torture with a special legal status (United Nations, 2003). In their meta-analysis, Steel and colleagues found that, after adjusting for methodological factors, torture was most strongly associated with PTSD, followed by cumulative traumatic events. Furthermore Steel et al. found the prevalence of reported torture to be 21% (95% CI, 17–26%) and this estimate remained unchanged after excluding seven surveys specifically targeting torture survivors (Steel et al., 2009).

Among refugees who have been actively involved in war or conflict, some may have had the role of a violent offender. Research has shown that having inflicted interpersonal trauma on others is a negative predictor of treatment outcome (Stenmark, Guzey, Elbert, & Holen, 2014). These events are often associated with feelings of shame and guilt, and accordingly may be difficult to assess in the clinical context due to patients being unwilling to disclose these experiences.

The Flight

The flight itself, both internally in the home country, during displacement to neighbouring countries or refugee camps, and during the journey to the host country, often involves difficult experiences. The organisation of the flight often involves many risks and a substantial financial burden, for example, paying smugglers. Furthermore, family and friends, as well as personal goods, are often left behind. Many refugees leave their home country without knowing where and when the journey will end or whether they will manage to escape to safety. A number of hardships can affect displaced people. Lack of resources in refugee camps is a current challenge as well as a lack of rights when displaced to neighbouring countries including having no legal rights as well as no access to schooling or education (Regional Refugee & Resilience Plan, 2015; United Nations High Commissioner for Refugees, 2017). Additionally, exposure to conflict may continue in some of the neighbouring countries. People smuggling by sea, for example, across the Mediterranean Sea, has increased drastically in recent years. In April 2015 as many as 1308 refugees and migrants travelling by boat drowned or went missing (United Nations High Commissioner for Refugees, 2015).

Case A – Part 1

A was born in a country in the Middle East and arrived in Denmark when he was 20 years old. His mother left the family when he was only 3 years old and he has not seen her since. When his mother left, he was told to take care of his 3-month-old baby brother together with his older sister (aged five). The baby brother died 4 weeks later. A and his sister were blamed for the baby brother's death by their father. A went to school and continued with a military education. He then obtained a rather high position in the army and participated in war as a young adult. After 6 months of warfare he was suspected of being a traitor and he was imprisoned and severely tortured for 2 years. A was released and fled the country with assistance from his family. After escaping the country, A was informed that his father had been imprisoned. A considered returning to help his father, but his older sister begged him not to return. A used all his savings to pay people to help him to safety in Europe. The flight to Denmark lasted one and a half years and the journey took A through several countries. A's physical sequelae after torture started during imprisonment and subsequently got worse, including severe pain in his shoulders and neck after hanging with his shoulders behind his body. His mental health problems, however, only commenced after his arrival in Denmark.

Gender Differences and Trauma

For refugees, the prevalence of specific traumatic events often differs according to gender, as a consequence of, for example, the typically different roles played by men and women during armed conflicts as well the vulnerable position of unaccompanied women during flight and in refugee camps (Freedman, 2016).

In a sample of 91 refugees and asylum-seekers in Australia, men reported exposure to more types of traumatic events than women and in the same sample men had been exposed to more interpersonal traumatic events compared to women (Haldane & Nickerson, 2016). In accordance with these results, in the population offered treatment at CTP, men are overrepresented when it comes to imprisonment and torture. In the population at CTP, women often report having lived alone during wartime, often with the added responsibility of taking care of and trying to keep the children safe. Sometimes the women had been forced to leave the country of origin with the children, with little or no news regarding the whereabouts of other family members. During the flight, women were at elevated risk of both sexual harassment and rape (Keygnaert et al., 2014). Furthermore, women reported a larger proportion of early life trauma, including sexual abuse, although it is well known that sexual abuse is often underreported. Consistent with this finding, studies in other populations have observed substantially greater exposure to sexual abuse among girls compared to boys (Helweg-Larsen & Bøving Larsen, 2006). Although gender differences in childhood trauma have not been studied systematically among trauma-affected refugees, the gender difference found in other trauma-affected populations regarding sexual abuse might also apply to refugees. It is important to keep potential gender differences in mind not only in relation to clinical work but also in relation to research when developing instruments for screening of traumatic events to make sure that all relevant traumatic events are covered.

Case B – Part 1

B was born in a traditional family in the countryside. She had seven siblings and was the second oldest among the children. In her family, only boys were sent to school and B never learned to read and write in her home country. She was married to a man from the same village at the age of 15. The young couple had a daughter and after a few years they moved to a neighbouring country together with other members of the husband's family. In the new country it was not possible for the husband to support his family and after 3 years in the new country B's husband decided to continue the journey to Europe. After the husband had left, their daughter was hit by a car bomb on her way to school and was instantly killed. B could not get in touch with her husband at this time and could not give him the news until after a few months. B was reunited with her husband in Denmark 12 months later.

Post-migratory Stressors Among Trauma-Affected Refugees

It has been shown that, in addition to pre-migration trauma, adversities experienced following displacement impact the psychopathology of refugees. It is well documented that refugees experience a wide range of ongoing stressors following arrival in a host country, including social problems and acculturation difficulties. Indeed, there is evidence to suggest that the impact of post-migratory living difficulties on refugee mental health is stronger than the impact of trauma experienced in the country of origin (Gorst-Unsworth & Goldenberg, 1998; Laban, Gernaat, Komproe, Schreuders, & de Jong, 2004; Li, Liddell, & Nickerson, 2016). Post-migratory stressors can be related to the asylum process, such as detention of asylum-seekers or fear of being sent back to the country the asylum-seeker has fled, or they can be related to life after obtaining a visa, such as discrimination, unemployment or poverty. Some factors might be experienced both during the flight and after arrival in the host country, such as worry about family members left behind.

Post-migratory stressors can be studied in several ways. While some studies have investigated the overall impact of resettlement stress on mental health, others have assessed the prevalence of specific stressors in different populations and/or their correlation with psychopathology. A frequently used measure when studying post-migratory stressors is the Post-Migration Living Difficulties (PMLD) Questionnaire (Silove, Sinnerbrink, Field, Manicavasagar, & Steel, 1997). The questionnaire includes 23 items that may be modified or re-grouped into fewer or more categories (Carswell, Blackburn, & Barker, 2011). In this chapter, we have divided post-migratory stressors into the following broad categories: stressors related to the asylum process and visa status, healthcare, family-related stressors, socio-economic difficulties, loss of culture and social support, poor language skills and discrimination.

Stressors Related to Asylum Process and Visa Status

Stressors throughout the asylum process have been less thoroughly investigated compared to living difficulties experienced after a residence permit has been obtained (Filges, Montgomery, & Kastrup, 2016). This likely has more to do with accessibility than relevance, since asylum process stressors, such as lengthy detention and problems with immigration officials, are significantly related to PTSD symptomatology (Robjant, Hassan, & Katona, 2009; Silove, Austin, & Steel, 2007). For example, Laban et al. found that stress related to the asylum procedure and lengthier processing of asylum claims increase the risk of psychopathology (Laban et al., 2004, 2005). Furthermore, the asylum process per se often involves repeated questioning about past trauma and the flight. This might be experienced as stressful for refugees, particularly if it reminds them of previously experienced interrogation by authorities in their home country. Accordingly, repeated questioning during the asylum process has been demonstrated to lead to worsening of trauma symptoms (Schock, Rosner, & Knaevelsrud, 2015). Additionally, difficulties with this process may negatively influence the outcome of asylum claims due to the impact of memory disturbances on the refugee's narrative (Herlihy & Turner, 2007; Steel, Frommer, & Silove, 2004).

Living conditions and access to healthcare during the asylum process vary a great deal depending on the asylum system of the host country. In a number of low- and middle-income countries, asylum seekers often have very limited or no access to health care. While high-income countries usually acknowledge the individuals' rights to receive emergency healthcare, asylum-seekers seldom have the same rights to receive care for chronic conditions and prenatal visits, which might cause stress as well as lead to a worsening of physical and mental health problems for those with unmet treatment needs. In many countries, asylum-seekers may additionally have no or very limited employment rights, which can result in further deterioration of their mental health (Hocking, Kennedy, & Sundram, 2015a, 2015b).

Once a visa is granted it might only be for a certain period, such as a temporary protection visa, or it might be conditional, such as a family reunification visa, which can be revoked in the case of divorce. The insecurity of residence status might therefore last substantially longer than the asylum process. Several studies have shown that this uncertainty negatively affects mental health (Bogic et al., 2012; Nickerson, Steel, Bryant, Brooks, & Silove, 2011). For example, in a study by Carswell et al., almost half of the participants reported fear of being sent home to be a serious or very serious problem, however a significant correlation between this item and PTSD symptoms was not observed (Carswell et al., 2011). Although sparsely investigated, the fear of being sent home might indirectly lead to other stressful events, such as women staying in a violent marriage out of fear of losing either their residence permit or the right to be with their children (Raj & Silverman, 2002).

Case A – Part 2

Upon arrival in Denmark, A lived in an asylum centre for 3 years. During this time, one of his roommates took his own life. After obtaining asylum, A went to language school for 2 years after which he applied for technical university admission and completed a 3-year engineering degree. Through his studies, he met a woman that he started dating and later married. He also got a job, but found it difficult to perform as well as his colleagues at work due to concentration and memory problems in addition to poor sleep. He had many short-term positions, but rarely managed to hold on to a job for more than a year. Additionally, his marriage was strained by both A's mental and physical health problems as well as his wife having several spontaneous miscarriages. One of these miscarriages coincided with A losing his job. This worsened A's mental health symptoms considerably, and as a result of this his wife moved out of their house. When A was referred to treatment he had severe PTSD symptoms as well as depressive symptoms with suicidal ideation.

Stressors After Obtaining Residence Permit

Resettlement stressors are the obstacles and difficulties experienced by refugees while building a new life in a society which is often fundamentally different from their home country both culturally and linguistically. While most refugees will experience challenges during the process of cultural transition, these may turn into overwhelming problems for those whose coping capacity may already be compromised by severely traumatising experiences. For example, a study by Wright and colleagues investigated the relationship between pre-migratory traumatic events, post-migratory stressors and unemployment in the host country. While neither pre-migratory traumatic events nor post-migratory stressors were found to be independently related to employment rates, the interaction between the two significantly predicted a high level of unemployment 2 years after arrival to the host country (Wright et al., 2016).

Healthcare

In countries with a primarily privately funded healthcare system, the lack of healthcare coverage is inevitably a stressor for those in need of healthcare services but without sufficient funds to access such services. Accordingly, a study of Bosnian refugees in Chicago found a statistically significant association between the severity of PTSD symptoms and poor access to healthcare (Delic-Ovcina, 2010). Although refugees who have obtained visas in Western countries that provide free access to public healthcare might officially have equal access to healthcare compared to the native population of the country, a number of barriers remain for refugees in need of healthcare assistance. Language problems as well as a lack of understanding of how the healthcare system is organized influence help-seeking behavior and can lead to conflicts with healthcare professionals (Slewa-Younan et al., 2015). Although many struggle with the physical and/or psychological consequences of trauma, the individual's perception of psychological distress often differs from that of healthcare professionals in the host country. This might, in combination with stigma surrounding mental health problems, discourage help-seeking behavior (May, Rapee, Coello, Momartin, & Aroche, 2014; Savic, Chur-Hansen, Mahmood, & Moore, 2016). Not only can these barriers lead to worse health outcomes for refugees, but they can also add to the stress of being ill in a country where the refugee has only limited or no social network.

Family-Related Stressors

Fears for Family in the Home Country

Refugees often have relatives in their home countries with ongoing conflicts, or who experience continued persecution. Consequently, fears for threatened family remaining in the country of origin is one of the most frequent self-reported stressors in refugees and asylum-seekers (Laban et al., 2008; Schweitzer, Melville, Steel, & Lacherez, 2006; Silove et al., 1997). In some cases, family members left behind might even have been attacked or punished by government officials as a direct consequence of the refugee's escape. In a study by Carswell and colleagues with refugees and asylum–seekers, separation from close family members was reported to be a serious problem by 77% of participants and worries for family in the home country by 57% of participants (Carswell et al., 2011). Nonetheless, family-related problems were not found to correlate significantly with PTSD symptomatology in this study, whereas other studies have found that threat to immediate family is correlated with mental health outcomes (Laban et al., 2005). For example, in a study with refugees from Iraq, Nickerson et al. found that intrusive fear for family in the home country predicted PTSD and depression symptoms independent of pre-migration trauma exposure and post-migration stress (Nickerson, Bryant, Steel, Silove, & Brooks, 2010).

Change of Family Structure

Integration into a new and often fundamentally different cultural context might challenge traditional family structures as well as parental authority. Although the mental health consequences of these challenges for refugee parents are yet to be thoroughly researched, parenthood in cultural transition has been acknowledged as a resettlement stressor (Osman, Klingberg-Allvin, Flacking, & Schön, 2016). Some refugees will additionally suffer from severe psychological consequences of past trauma, which might affect their ability to work and to financially support their families. The combination of trauma symptoms, such as explosive anger and the challenges of altered family structures, can potentially lead to further trauma such as domestic violence (Rees & Pease, 2007).

Socio-economic Difficulties

Socio-economic difficulties have been shown to be a substantial post-migratory stressor in many refugee studies (Blair, 2000; Bogic et al., 2012; Laban et al., 2005). It is well-known that refugees often have higher unemployment rates than the native population in the host country, especially during the first years after resettlement (Bevelander, 2016). A large number of highly educated refugees end up in unskilled jobs in the host country. This might be due to a range of factors such as poor language skills, differences in the educational system in the home and host countries resulting in qualifications not being recognised, as well as disabling psychical and mental sequelae of experienced trauma. Unemployment, as well as the potential associated decrease in social status, might not only lead to poverty and problems in supporting one's family but also to loss of identity, boredom and social isolation. These factors, in turn, may contribute to the worsening of mental health in refugee populations. It is therefore not surprising that socio-economic problems such as unemployment and financial hardship have been found to correlate significantly with psychopathology in a number of studies (Beiser & Hou, 2001; Carlsson, Olsen, Mortensen, & Kastrup, 2006; Carswell et al., 2011; Teodorescu et al., 2012). It should be noted, however, that most studies have used a cross-sectional design and therefore it remains unclear how psychopathology and socio-economic difficulties affect each other over time. Severe psychopathology is also likely to impact a person's ability to adapt to a new environment as well as the ability to obtain and maintain a job. Hence, these factors may potentially form a vicious cycle whereby trauma-related psychopathology leads to decreased job opportunities and unemployment, resulting in loss of identity and social isolation and further deterioration of mental health. Relatedly, uncertainty concerning employment status and finances have been demonstrated to correlate negatively with treatment outcome (Sonne et al., 2016).

Loss of Culture and Social Support

Loss of culture and social support, including social isolation, has also been identified as a significant post-migratory stressor in refugee populations (Birman & Tran, 2008; Carlsson, 2005; Carswell et al., 2011). Several studies have found that refugees living alone are more vulnerable to mental health problems than those living with their families (Miller et al., 2002; Steel et al., 2002). Similarly, lack of support from family and friends has been found to correlate with mental health difficulties. The presence of a well-established local ethnic community and opportunities to live in accordance with religious and cultural customs can ease the cultural transition for newcomers and prevent social isolation and distress (Birman & Tran, 2008; Schweitzer et al., 2006).

Poor Language Skills

Many refugees are challenged by learning the language of the host country, especially if they suffer from concentration and memory problems as a result of trauma-related mental disorders. Several studies have found that poor language skills are correlated with mental health complaints, such as PTSD, depression and anxiety symptoms in refugees (Bogic et al., 2012; Chung & Kagawa-Singer, 1993). Additionally, poor language skills can interact with several of those stressors discussed above, such as access to employment and healthcare, and contribute to cultural adaptation difficulties, financial problems and social isolation. Beiser and colleagues conducted a study with 608 Southeast Asian refugees resettled in Canada. They found that, at the end of the first decade following resettlement in Canada as a refugee, English language fluency was a significant predictor of depression and unemployment, particularly among refugee women and those who did not become engaged in the labour market during the earliest years of resettlement (Beiser & Hou, 2001).

Case B – Part 2

After her arrival in Denmark, B started language school, but she found it difficult to pay attention in class. She experienced low self-esteem as her classmates learned the language a lot faster than she did. Nevertheless, she slowly learnt to speak Danish, but still had poor writing and reading skills. She had nightmares about her daughter's death and she greatly missed her mother and sisters back home. However, after giving birth to twin sons she started feeling better; she felt that she now had a purpose in life. She had some good years enjoying life with her sons and husband, but when the boys were 4 years old, her husband had a serious accident at work, after which he was unable to return to work due to his injuries. This turned B's life upside down. The family had financial problems and B managed to get a cleaning job in order to provide for the family. Although it was hard work for B to manage the job as well as the family (and her husband was of little help), she enjoyed the job and made friends with the other women who had the same cultural and linguistic background as her own. She stayed at the same job for 2 years until her shoulder started hurting very badly and she could no longer lift her arm. Her doctor found that she had developed neuritis in the shoulder and told her that recovery could take a long time. He advised her to find a job with less strain on the arms. She therefore applied for a course to become an interpreter, but was turned down due to her poor writing skills. She started feeling very sad and low in energy, and she started having flashbacks and nightmares about her daughter's death again. Her doctor referred her to treatment in a transcultural mental health facility.

Discrimination

Discrimination can act as a stressor directly or indirectly through its effect on, for example, job opportunities. In situations where a large number of refugees arrive concurrently, which has occurred in many European countries since the outbreak of the civil war in Syria in 2011, the negative rhetoric towards refugees often intensifies, which can lead to the experience of greater discrimination among refugees. Several studies have found that perceived lack of acceptance by the resettlement country impacts the mental health of refugees (Beiser & Hou, 2016; Bogic et al., 2012). Accordingly, researchers have proposed that discrimination and racism should not only be considered as societal problems, but also be acknowledged as a health risk (Kim, 2016; Mölsä, Kuittinen, Tiilikainen, Honkasalo, & Punamäki, 2016).

Other Post-migratory Stressors and Stressful Life Events

The post-migratory stressors discussed above exemplify only some of many potential problems refugees may face while struggling to build a new life in a country where the culture may often fundamentally differ from their own. As illustrated by the case reports in this chapter, refugees may also face living difficulties in the resettlement country that they may have already experienced in their country of origin, such as physical illness, unemployment, family conflict, and discrimination. However, because they are out of the cultural and social context of the home country and psychologically vulnerable due to trauma and acculturation stress, these problems may have a stronger impact on their mental health than they would in other circumstances.

Furthermore, refugees arriving in a new country may have imagined life there to be unrealistically easy and without complications. Discovering that their dreams are far from reality, as life in exile often begins with a number of obstacles and complications as described above, can lead to disappointment, a feeling of hopelessness or exacerbation of trauma-related mental health symptoms, which might, for some refugees, evolve into delayed onset PTSD or depression (Uribe Guajardo, Slewa-Younan, Smith, Eagar, & Stone, 2016).

The Interaction Between Trauma and Post-migratory Stressors: Implications for Clinical Work and for Future Research

As described above, it is well documented that both trauma and post-migratory stressors can affect the mental health and quality of life in refugees. Models acknowledging the complexity of the interaction between pre-migration trauma, post-migratory stressors and the stressors of everyday life experienced in foreign or insecure contexts have replaced a previously more narrow focus on pre-migration trauma only (Aroche & Coello, 1994; Miller & Rasmussen, 2010). While many years after the original trauma, post-migratory living difficulties might show the strongest association with present mental health and quality of life. (Beiser & Hou, 2001; Carlsson, Olsen, Mortensen, & Kastrup, 2006). A narrow focus on post-migratory stressors might on the other hand lead to underestimation of the effects of pre-migration trauma on the mental health and psychosocial function of refugees (Kartal & Kiropoulos, 2016). It is important to acknowledge that over time, the effects of the trauma can increasingly become mediated by post-migratory factors and that post-migratory stressors can accentuate the effect of the pre-migratory stressors, as demonstrated by Wright and colleagues among others (Wright et al., 2016). This also emphasises the importance of interventions that do not solely focus on either trauma or current psychosocial stressors but deal with both in order to maximize the possibilities of a successful outcome.

The interplay between severely traumatising experiences and post-migratory stressors can not only help explain the high rates of mental health problems among refugees but presumably also the difficulties experienced when offering treatment for this target group. It is possible that this combination of factors explains the rather poor treatment effects found in some studies with severely trauma-affected refugees (Buhmann, Nordentoft, Ekstroem, Carlsson, & Mortensen, 2015). Although scarcely studied, perpetrator status as well as post-migratory socio-economic problems have been demonstrated to correlate with poor treatment outcome, whereas no such relation has been demonstrated for torture or other war-related pre-migratory traumatic experiences (Sonne, 2016; Stenmark et al., 2014). As post-migratory stressors are often malleable, these stressors are of particular interest in relation to improving treatment outcome. The effect of post-migratory stressors on treatment outcome should therefore be further investigated.

Post-migratory stressors are also of interest with regard to the increased focus on understanding late onset PTSD. A study in a mixed trauma-affected population found that severity of trauma, pain and social support can be of importance for the trajectory of developing mental health problems after trauma (Forbes et al., 2016). Although the direct link between specific post-migratory events and the onset of PTSD remains to be studied, it is our clinical impression that social stressors, such as dismissal from a job followed by severe financial strain, as well as physical illness, can be factors related to deterioration of mental health among refugees who have presented with few or only subclinical mental health complaints during early years of resettlement. This theory is supported by studies which have demonstrated late onset PTSD to be a significant contributor to the persistence of a high prevalence of PTSD among both adults and unaccompanied refugee minors several years after resettlement (Lamkaddem et al., 2014; Smid, Lensvelt-Mulders, Knipscheer, Gersons, & Kleber, 2011).

Considering the burden of pre-migratory trauma followed by the post-migratory stressors that some refugees face, it can be hard to imagine how refugees and asylum-seekers can ever overcome their experiences. However, it is important to bear in mind that although most refugees have a history of severely traumatising experiences, not all develop a trauma-related mental health disorder (Steel et al., 2009). As such, a greater understanding is needed about the trajectories of emotional distress and resilience in trauma-affected refugees. In particular, research should examine whether the provision of early psychosocial or mental health interventions can help prevent mental health problems from escalating into a mental health disorder and significant functional impairment.

In conclusion, pre- and peri-migration trauma, post-migratory stressors and "normal" life cycle events in a foreign context all contribute to the complex pattern of mental health, physical health and psychosocial complaints found among severely trauma-affected refugees. This interaction, together with the influence of personal resources and social support of the individual, must be considered in all aspects of assessment and clinical work with trauma-affected refugees.

References

Aroche, J., & Coello, M. (1994). *Towards a systematic approach for the treatment and rehabilitation of torture and trauma survivors: The experience of STARTTS in Australia*. Retrieved from http://www.startts.org.au/media/Research-Doc-Towards-a-systematic-approach.pdf

Beiser, M., & Hou, F. (2001). Language acquisition, unemployment and depressive disorder among Southeast Asian refugees: A 10-year study. *Social Science & Medicine, 53*(10), 1321–1334.

Beiser, M., & Hou, F. (2016). Mental health effects of premigration trauma and postmigration discrimination on refugee youth in Canada. *The Journal of Nervous and Mental Disease, 204*(6), 464–470. https://doi.org/10.1097/NMD.0000000000000516

Bevelander, P. (2016). Integrating refugees into labor markets. *IZA World of Labor, 269*. https://doi.org/10.15185/izawol.269

Bhui, K., Abdi, A., Abdi, M., Pereira, S., Dualeh, M., Robertson, D., … Ismail, H. (2003). Traumatic events, migration characteristics and psychiatric symptoms among Somali refugees – Preliminary communication. *Social Psychiatry and Psychiatric Epidemiology, 38*(1), 35–43.

Birman, D., & Tran, N. (2008). Psychological distress and adjustment of Vietnamese refugees in the United States: Association with pre- and postmigration factors. *The American Journal of Orthopsychiatry, 78*(1), 109–120. https://doi.org/10.1037/0002-9432.78.1.109

Blair, R. G. (2000). Risk factors associated with PTSD and major depression among Cambodian refugees in Utah. *Health and Social Work, 25*(1), 23–30.

Bogic, M., Ajdukovic, D., Bremner, S., Franciskovic, T., Galeazzi, G. M., Kucukalic, A., … Priebe, S. (2012). Factors associated with mental disorders in long-settled war refugees: Refugees from the former Yugoslavia in Germany, Italy and the UK. *British Journal of Psychiatry, 200*(3), 216–223. https://doi.org/10.1192/bjp.bp.110.084764

Bogic, M., Njoku, A., & Priebe, S. (2015). Long-term mental health of war-refugees: A systematic literature review. *BMC International Health and Human Rights, 15*(1), 29. https://doi.org/10.1186/s12914-015-0064-9

Bourque, F., van der Ven, E., & Malla, A. (2011). A meta-analysis of the risk for psychotic disorders among first- and second-generation immigrants. *Psychological Medicine, 41*(5), 897–910. https://doi.org/10.1017/S0033291710001406

Buhmann, C. B., Nordentoft, M., Ekstroem, M., Carlsson, J., & Mortensen, E. L. (2015). The effect of flexible cognitive-behavioural therapy and medical treatment, including antidepressants on post-traumatic stress disorder and depression in traumatised refugees: Pragmatic randomised controlled clinical trial. *The British Journal of Psychiatry, 208*(3), 252–259. https://doi.org/10.1192/bjp.bp.114.150961

Cantor-Graae, E., Pedersen, C. B., Mcneil, T. F., & Mortensen, P. (2003). Migration as a risk factor for schizophrenia: A Danish population-based cohort study. *The British Journal of Psychiatry, 182*(2), 117–122. https://doi.org/10.1192/bjp.02.299

Carlsson, J. M. (2005). *Mental health and health-related quality of life in tortured refugees*. Copenhagen, Denmark: Rehabilitation and Research Centre for Torture Victims.

Carlsson, J. M., Mortensen, E. L., & Kastrup, M. (2006). Predictors of mental health and quality of life in male tortured refugees. *Nordic Journal of Psychiatry, 60*(1), 51–57.

Carlsson, J. M., Olsen, D. R., Mortensen, E. L., & Kastrup, M. (2006). Mental health and health-related quality of life: A 10-year follow-up of tortured refugees. *The Journal of Nervous and Mental Disease, 194*(10), 725–731. https://doi.org/10.1097/01.nmd.0000243079.52138.b7

Carswell, K., Blackburn, P., & Barker, C. (2011). The relationship between trauma, post-migration problems and the psychological well-being of refugees and asylum seekers. *The International Journal of Social Psychiatry, 57*(2), 107–119. https://doi.org/10.1177/0020764008105699

Chung, R. C., & Kagawa-Singer, M. (1993). Predictors of psychological distress among Southeast Asian refugees. *Social Science & Medicine, 36*(5), 631–639. https://doi.org/10.1016/0277-9536(93)90060-H

Craig, C. D., Sossou, M.-A., Schnak, M., & Essex, H. (2008). Complicated grief and its relationship to mental health and well-being among Bosnian refugees after resettlement in the United States: Implications for practice, policy, and research. *Traumatology, 14*(4), 103–115. https://doi.org/10.1177/1534765608322129

Davidson, J., Foa, E. B., Blank, A. B., Brett, E. A., Fairbank, J., Green, B. L., et al. (1996). Posttraumatic stress disorder. In T. A. Widiger, A. J. Frances, H. A. Pincus, R. Ross, M. B. First, & W. W. Davis (Eds.), *DSM-IV sourcebook* (pp. 577–606). Washington, DC: American Psychiatric Association.

Delic-Ovcina, L. (2010). *The case of adult Bosnian Muslim male refugees in Chicago: Current health behavior outcomes and PTSD symptomatology.* Doctoral dissertation. Retrieved from https://www.ideals.illinois.edu/handle/2142/15543

Fazel, M., Wheeler, J., & Danesh, J. (2005). Prevalence of serious mental disorder in 7000 refugees resettled in western countries: A systematic review. *Lancet, 365*(9467), 1309–1314.

Filges, T., Montgomery, E., & Kastrup, M. (2016). The impact of detention on the health of asylum seekers: A systematic review. *Research on Social Work Practice*, 1–16. https://doi.org/10.1177/1049731516630384

Forbes, D., Alkemade, N., Nickerson, A., Bryant, R. A., Creamer, M., Silove, D., … O, Donnell, M. (2016). Prediction of late-onset psychiatric disorder in survivors of severe injury: Findings of a latent transition analysis. *The Journal of Clinical Psychiatry, 77*(6), 807–812.

Freedman, J. (2016). Sexual and gender-based violence against refugee women: A hidden aspect of the refugee "crisis". *Reproductive Health Matters, 24*(47), 18–26. https://doi.org/10.1016/j.rhm.2016.05.003

Gorst-Unsworth, C., & Goldenberg, E. (1998). Psychological sequelae of torture and organised violence suffered by refugees from Iraq. Trauma-related factors compared with social factors in exile. *The British Journal of Psychiatry, 172*(1), 90–94.

Haldane, J., & Nickerson, A. (2016). The impact of interpersonal and noninterpersonal trauma on psychological symptoms in refugees: The moderating role of gender and trauma type. *Journal of Traumatic Stress, 29*(5), 457–465. https://doi.org/10.1002/jts.22132

Hecker, T., Fetz, S., Ainamani, H., & Elbert, T. (2015). The cycle of violence: Associations between exposure to violence, trauma-related symptoms and aggression—Findings from Congolese refugees in Uganda. *Journal of Traumatic Stress, 28*(5), 448–455. https://doi.org/10.1002/jts.22046

Helweg-Larsen, K., & Bøving Larsen, H. (2006). The prevalence of unwanted and unlawful sexual experiences reported by Danish adolescents: Results from a national youth survey in 2002. *Acta Paediatrica, 95*(10), 1270–1276. https://doi.org/10.1080/08035250600589033

Herlihy, J., & Turner, S. W. (2007). Asylum claims and memory of trauma: Sharing our knowledge. *The British Journal of Psychiatry, 191*(1), 3–4.

Hinton, D. E., Nickerson, A., & Bryant, R. A. (2011). Worry, worry attacks, and PTSD among Cambodian refugees: A path analysis investigation. *Social Science & Medicine, 72*(11), 1817–1825. https://doi.org/10.1016/j.socscimed.2011.03.045

Hocking, D. C., Kennedy, G. A., & Sundram, S. (2015a). Mental disorders in asylum seekers: The role of the refugee determination process and employment. *The Journal of Nervous and Mental Disease, 203*(1), 28–32. https://doi.org/10.1097/NMD.0000000000000230

Hocking, D. C., Kennedy, G. A., & Sundram, S. (2015b). Social factors ameliorate psychiatric disorders in community-based asylum seekers independent of visa status. *Psychiatry Research, 230*(2), 628–636. https://doi.org/10.1016/j.psychres.2015.10.018

Hollander, A.-C., Dal, H., Lewis, G., Magnusson, C., Kirkbride, J. B., & Dalman, C. (2016). Refugee migration and risk of schizophrenia and other non-affective psychoses: Cohort study of 1.3 million people in Sweden. *BMJ, 353*, i2865. https://doi.org/10.1136/bmj.i1030

Jaranson, J. M., Butcher, J., Halcon, L., Johnson, D. R., Robertson, C., Savik, K., … Westermeyer, J. (2004). Somali and Oromo refugees: Correlates of torture and trauma history. *American Journal of Public Health, 94*(4), 591–598.

Kartal, D., & Kiropoulos, L. (2016). Effects of acculturative stress on PTSD, depressive, and anxiety symptoms among refugees resettled in Australia and Austria. *European Journal of Psychotraumatology, 7*(1), 28711. https://doi.org/10.3402/ejpt.v7.28711

Keygnaert, I., Dialmy, A., Manço, A., Keygnaert, J., Vettenburg, N., Roelens, K., & Temmerman, M. (2014). Sexual violence and sub-Saharan migrants in Morocco: A community-based participatory assessment using respondent driven sampling. *Globalization and Health, 10*(1), 32. https://doi.org/10.1186/1744-8603-10-32

Kim, I. (2016). Beyond trauma: Post-resettlement factors and mental health outcomes among Latino and Asian refugees in the United States. *Journal of Immigrant and Minority Health, 18*(4), 740–748. https://doi.org/10.1007/s10903-015-0251-8

Laban, C. J., Gernaat, H. B. P. E., Komproe, I. H., Schreuders, B. A., & de Jong, J. T. V. M. (2004). Impact of a long asylum procedure on the prevalence of psychiatric disorders in Iraqi asylum seekers in the Netherlands. *The Journal of Nervous and Mental Disease, 192*(12), 843–851. Retrieved from http://www.ncbi.nlm.nih.gov/pubmed/15583506

Laban, C. J., Gernaat, H. B. P. E., Komproe, I. H., van der Tweel, I., & de Jong, J. T. V. M. (2005). Postmigration living problems and common psychiatric disorders in Iraqi asylum seekers in the Netherlands. *The Journal of Nervous and Mental Disease, 193*(12), 825–832. Retrieved from http://www.ncbi.nlm.nih.gov/pubmed/16319706

Laban, C. J., Komproe, I. H., Gernaat, H. B. P. E., & de Jong, J. T. V. M. (2008). The impact of a long asylum procedure on quality of life, disability and physical health in Iraqi asylum seekers in the Netherlands. *Social Psychiatry and Psychiatric Epidemiology, 43*(7), 507–515. https://doi.org/10.1007/s00127-008-0333-1

Lamkaddem, M., Stronks, K., Devillé, W. D., Olff, M., Gerritsen, A. A., & Essink-Bot, M.-L. (2014). Course of post-traumatic stress disorder and health care utilisation among resettled refugees in the Netherlands. *BMC Psychiatry, 14*(1), 90. https://doi.org/10.1186/1471-244X-14-90

Li, S. S. Y., Liddell, B. J., & Nickerson, A. (2016). The relationship between post-migration stress and psychological disorders in refugees and asylum seekers. *Current Psychiatry Reports, 18*(9), 82. https://doi.org/10.1007/s11920-016-0723-0

Lie, B., Lavik, N. J., & Laake, P. (2001). Traumatic events and psychological symptoms in a non-clinical refugee population in Norway. *Journal of Refugee Studies, 14*(3), 276–294.

Lindert, J., von Ehrenstein, O. S., Priebe, S., Mielck, A., & Brähler, E. (2009). Depression and anxiety in labor migrants and refugees – A systematic review and meta-analysis. *Social Science & Medicine, 69*(2), 246–257. https://doi.org/10.1016/j.socscimed.2009.04.032

Marshall, G. N., Schell, T. L., Elliott, M. N., Berthold, S. M., & Chun, C. A. (2005). Mental health of Cambodian refugees 2 decades after resettlement in the United States. *JAMA, 294*(5), 571–579.

May, S., Rapee, R. M., Coello, M., Momartin, S., & Aroche, J. (2014). Mental health literacy among refugee communities: Differences between the Australian lay public and the Iraqi and Sudanese refugee communities. *Social Psychiatry and Psychiatric Epidemiology, 49*(5), 757–769. https://doi.org/10.1007/s00127-013-0793-9

Miller, K. E., & Rasmussen, A. (2010). War exposure, daily stressors, and mental health in conflict and post-conflict settings: Bridging the divide between trauma-focused and psychosocial frameworks. *Social Science & Medicine, 70*(1), 7–16. https://doi.org/10.1016/j.socscimed.2009.09.029

Miller, K. E., Weine, S. M., Ramic, A., Brkic, N., Bjedic, Z. D., Smajkic, A., … Worthington, G. (2002). The relative contribution of war experiences and exile-related stressors to levels of psychological distress among Bosnian refugees. *Journal of Traumatic Stress, 15*(5), 377–387. https://doi.org/10.1023/A:1020181124118

Mölsä, M., Kuittinen, S., Tiilikainen, M., Honkasalo, M.-L., & Punamäki, R.-L. (2016). Mental health among older refugees: The role of trauma, discrimination, and religiousness. *Aging & Mental Health, 21*(8), 829–837. https://doi.org/10.1080/13607863.2016.1165183

Momartin, S., Silove, D., Manicavasagar, V., & Steel, Z. (2004). Comorbidity of PTSD and depression: Associations with trauma exposure, symptom severity and functional impairment in

Bosnian refugees resettled in Australia. *Journal of Affective Disorders, 80*(2), 231–238. https://doi.org/10.1016/S0165-0327(03)00131-9

Morina, N., & Ford, J. D. (2008). Complex sequelae of psychological trauma among kosovar civilian war victims. *International Journal of Social Psychiatry, 54*(5), 425–436. https://doi.org/10.1177/0020764008090505

Morina, N., Schnyder, U., Schick, M., Nickerson, A., & Bryant, R. A. (2016). Attachment style and interpersonal trauma in refugees. *The Australian and New Zealand Journal of Psychiatry, 50*(12), 1161–1168. https://doi.org/10.1177/0004867416631432

Nickerson, A., Bryant, R. A., Steel, Z., Silove, D., & Brooks, R. (2010). The impact of fear for family on mental health in a resettled Iraqi refugee community. *Journal of Psychiatric Research, 44*(4), 229–235. https://doi.org/10.1016/j.jpsychires.2009.08.006

Nickerson, A., Cloitre, M., Bryant, R. A., Schnyder, U., Morina, N., & Schick, M. (2016). The factor structure of complex posttraumatic stress disorder in traumatized refugees. *European Journal of Psychotraumatology, 7*(1), 33253. https://doi.org/10.3402/ejpt.v7.33253

Nickerson, A., Steel, Z., Bryant, R., Brooks, R., & Silove, D. (2011). Change in visa status amongst Mandaean refugees: Relationship to psychological symptoms and living difficulties. *Psychiatry Research, 187*(1), 267–274. https://doi.org/10.1016/j.psychres.2010.12.015

Nygaard, M., Sonne, C., & Carlsson, J. (2017). Secondary psychotic features in refugees diagnosed with post-traumatic stress disorder: A retrospective cohort study. *BMC Psychiatry, 17*(1), 5. https://doi.org/10.1186/s12888-016-1166-1

Osman, F., Klingberg-Allvin, M., Flacking, R., & Schön, U.-K. (2016). Parenthood in transition – Somali-born parents' experiences of and needs for parenting support programmes. *BMC International Health and Human Rights, 16*(1), 7. https://doi.org/10.1186/s12914-016-0082-2

Palić, S., Carlsson, J., Armour, C., & Elklit, A. (2015). Assessment of dissociation in Bosnian treatment-seeking refugees in Denmark. *Nordic Journal of Psychiatry, 69*(4), 307–314. https://doi.org/10.3109/08039488.2014.977344

Palić, S., & Elklit, A. (2014). Personality dysfunction and complex posttraumatic stress disorder among chronically traumatized Bosnian refugees. *The Journal of Nervous and Mental Disease, 202*(2), 111–118. https://doi.org/10.1097/NMD.0000000000000079

Palić, S., Kappel, M. L., Nielsen, M. S., Carlsson, J., & Bech, P. (2014). Comparison of psychiatric disability on the health of nation outcome scales (HoNOS) in resettled traumatized refugee outpatients and Danish inpatients. *BMC Psychiatry, 14*(1), 330. https://doi.org/10.1186/s12888-014-0330-8

Palić, S., Zerach, G., Shevlin, M., Zeligman, Z., Elklit, A., & Solomon, Z. (2016). Evidence of complex posttraumatic stress disorder (CPTSD) across populations with prolonged trauma of varying interpersonal intensity and ages of exposure. *Psychiatry Research, 246*, 692–699. https://doi.org/10.1016/j.psychres.2016.10.062

Raj, A., & Silverman, J. (2002). Violence against immigrant women. *Violence Against Women, 8*(3), 367–398.

Rees, S., & Pease, B. (2007). Domestic violence in refugee families in Australia. *Journal of Immigrant & Refugee Studies, 5*(2), 1–19. https://doi.org/10.1300/J500v05n02_01

Regional Refugee & Resilience Plan. (2015). *3RP regional progress report*. Retrieved from http://www.unhcr.org/558aa6566.html

Riber, K. (2015a). *Attachment, complex trauma, and psychotherapy – A clinical study of the significance of attachment in adult Arabic-speaking refugees with PTSD*. Unpublished doctoral dissertation. University of Copenhagen.

Riber, K. (2015b). Attachment organization in Arabic-speaking refugees with post traumatic stress disorder. *Attachment & Human Development, 18*(2), 154–175. https://doi.org/10.1080/14616734.2015.1124442

Robjant, K., Hassan, R., & Katona, C. (2009). Mental health implications of detaining asylum seekers: Systematic review. *British Journal of Psychiatry, 194*(4), 306–312. https://doi.org/10.1192/bjp.bp.108.053223

Rohlof, H. G., Knipscheer, J. W., & Kleber, R. J. (2014). Somatization in refugees: A review. *Social Psychiatry and Psychiatric Epidemiology, 49*(11), 1793–1804. https://doi.org/10.1007/s00127-014-0877-1

Savic, M., Chur-Hansen, A., Mahmood, M. A., & Moore, V. M. (2016). 'We don't have to go and see a special person to solve this problem': Trauma, mental health beliefs and processes for addressing 'mental health issues' among Sudanese refugees in Australia. *The International Journal of Social Psychiatry, 62*(1), 76–83. https://doi.org/10.1177/0020764015595664

Schock, K., Rosner, R., & Knaevelsrud, C. (2015). Impact of asylum interviews on the mental health of traumatized asylum seekers. *European Journal of Psychotraumatology, 6*(1), 26286. https://doi.org/10.3402/ejpt.v6.26286

Schweitzer, R., Melville, F., Steel, Z., & Lacherez, P. (2006). Trauma, post-migration living difficulties, and social support as predictors of psychological adjustment in resettled Sudanese refugees. *The Australian and New Zealand Journal of Psychiatry, 40*(2), 179–187. https://doi.org/10.1111/j.1440-1614.2006.01766.x

Silove, D. (2013). The ADAPT model: A conceptual framework for mental health and psychosocial programming in post conflict settings. *Intervention, 11*(3), 237–248. https://doi.org/10.1097/WTF.0000000000000005

Silove, D., Austin, P., & Steel, Z. (2007). No refuge from terror: The impact of detention on the mental health of trauma-affected refugees seeking asylum in Australia. *Transcultural Psychiatry, 44*(3), 359–393. https://doi.org/10.1177/1363461507081637

Silove, D., Brooks, R., Steel, C. R., Steel, Z., Hewage, K., Rodger, J., & Soosay, I. (2009). Explosive anger as a response to human rights violations in post-conflict Timor-Leste. *Social Science & Medicine, 69*(5), 670–677. https://doi.org/10.1016/j.socscimed.2009.06.030

Silove, D., Sinnerbrink, I., Field, A., Manicavasagar, V., & Steel, Z. (1997). Anxiety, depression and PTSD in asylum-seekers: Assocations with pre-migration trauma and post-migration stressors. *The British Journal of Psychiatry, 170*(4), 351–357. Retrieved from http://www.ncbi.nlm.nih.gov/pubmed/9246254

Silove, D., Steel, Z., & Watters, C. (2000). Policies of deterrence and the mental health of asylum seekers. *JAMA, 284*(5), 604–611. Retrieved from http://www.ncbi.nlm.nih.gov/pubmed/10918707

Slewa-Younan, S., Mond, J. M., Bussion, E., Melkonian, M., Mohammad, Y., Dover, H., … Jorm, A. F. (2015). Psychological trauma and help seeking behaviour amongst resettled Iraqi refugees in attending English tuition classes in Australia. *International Journal of Mental Health Systems, 9*(1), 5. https://doi.org/10.1186/1752-4458-9-5

Smid, G. E., Lensvelt-Mulders, G. J. L. M., Knipscheer, J. W., Gersons, B. P. R., & Kleber, R. J. (2011). Late-onset PTSD in unaccompanied refugee minors: Exploring the predictive utility of depression and anxiety symptoms. *Journal of Clinical Child and Adolescent Psychology, 40*(5), 742–755. https://doi.org/10.1080/15374416.2011.597083

Sonne, C. (2016). *Trauma-affected refugees: Pharmacological treatment and predictors of treatment outcome*. Odense, Denmark: University of Southern Denmark.

Sonne, C., Carlsson, J., Bech, P., Vindbjerg, E., Mortensen, E. L., & Elklit, A. (2016). Psychosocial predictors of treatment outcome for trauma-affected refugees. *European Journal of Psychotraumatology, 7*(1), 30907. https://doi.org/10.3402/ejpt.v7.30907

Spiller, T. R., Schick, M., Schnyder, U., Bryant, R. A., Nickerson, A., & Morina, N. (2016). Somatisation and anger are associated with symptom severity of posttraumatic stress disorder in severely traumatised refugees and asylum seekers. *Swiss Medical Weekly, 146*, w14311. https://doi.org/10.4414/smw.2016.14311

Steel, Z., Chey, T., Silove, D., Marnane, C., Bryant, R. A., & Van, O. M. (2009). Association of torture and other potentially traumatic events with mental health outcomes among populations exposed to mass conflict and displacement: A systematic review and meta-analysis. *JAMA, 302*(5), 537–549.

Steel, Z., Frommer, N., & Silove, D. (2004). Part I—The mental health impacts of migration: The law and its effects: Failing to understand: Refugee determination and the traumatized applicant. *International Journal of Law and Psychiatry, 27*(6), 511–528. https://doi.org/10.1016/j.ijlp.2004.08.006

Steel, Z., Silove, D., Phan, T., & Bauman, A. (2002). Long-term effect of psychological trauma on the mental health of Vietnamese refugees resettled in Australia: A population-based study. *Lancet, 360*(9339), 1056–1062.

Stenmark, H., Guzey, I. C., Elbert, T., & Holen, A. (2014). Gender and offender status predicting treatment success in refugees and asylum seekers with PTSD. *European Journal of Psychotraumatology, 5*(1), 20803. https://doi.org/10.3402/ejpt.v5.20803

Tay, A. K., Rees, S., Chen, J., Kareth, M., & Silove, D. (2015). The structure of post-traumatic stress disorder and complex post-traumatic stress disorder amongst West Papuan refugees. *BMC Psychiatry, 15*(1), 111. https://doi.org/10.1186/s12888-015-0480-3

Teodorescu, D.-S., Heir, T., Hauff, E., Wentzel-Larsen, T., & Lien, L. (2012). Mental health problems and post-migration stress among multi-traumatized refugees attending outpatient clinics upon resettlement to Norway. *Scandinavian Journal of Psychology, 53*(4), 316–332. https://doi.org/10.1111/j.1467-9450.2012.00954.x

United Nations. (2003). *The Convention against torture and other inhuman or degrading treatment or punishment*. New York, NY: Author.

United Nations High Commissioner for Refugees. (2015). *The sea route to Europe: The Mediterranean passage in the age of refugees*. Retrieved from http://www.unhcr.org/5592bd059.html.

United Nations High Commissioner for Refugees. (2017). *Left behind – Refugee education in crisis*. Retrieved from http://www.unhcr.org/59b696f44.pdf

Uribe Guajardo, M. G., Slewa-Younan, S., Smith, M., Eagar, S., & Stone, G. (2016). Psychological distress is influenced by length of stay in resettled Iraqi refugees in Australia. *International Journal of Mental Health Systems, 10*(1), 4. https://doi.org/10.1186/s13033-016-0036-z

Weine, S. M., Becker, D. F., Vojvoda, D., Hodzic, E., Sawyer, M., Hyman, L., … McGlashan, T. H. (1998). Individual change after genocide in Bosnian survivors of "ethnic cleansing": Assessing personality dysfunction. *Journal of Traumatic Stress, 11*(1), 147–153. https://doi.org/10.1023/A:1024469418811

Wright, A. M., Dhalimi, A., Lumley, M. A., Jamil, H., Pole, N., Arnetz, J. E., & Arnetz, B. B. (2016). Unemployment in Iraqi refugees: The interaction of pre and post-displacement trauma. *Scandinavian Journal of Psychology, 57*(6), 564–570. https://doi.org/10.1111/sjop.12320

Jessica Carlsson, MD, Ph.D. is Associated Professor at the University of Copenhagen and head of Research at the Competence Centre for Transcultural Psychiatry (CTP), Mental Health Services of the Capital Region of Denmark. She is a clinical psychiatrist and researcher. Her primary research areas are clinical research in trauma-affected refugees and transcultural psychiatry.

Charlotte Sonne, MD, Ph.D. is a postdoctoral research fellow at the Competence Centre for Transcultural Psychiatry (CTP), Mental Health Services of the Capital Region of Denmark. Her primary research area is trauma-affected refugees with special interests in integrating research into real-life clinical settings.

Child Mental Health in the Context of War: An Overview of Risk Factors and Interventions for Refugee and War-Affected Youth

Elizabeth A. Newnham, Shraddha Kashyap, Jessica Tearne, and Mina Fazel

Abstract An unprecedented number of children and adolescents are migrating to escape war and persecution, often unaccompanied by family (UNHCR: Global trends forced displacement in 2015. The UN Refugee Agency, Geneva, 2016). These children face security and health risks in their country of origin, on the journey to safety, and sometimes in their place of resettlement. The trauma and hardships that accompany these experiences have potential to create significant mental health difficulties. This chapter aims to review the risk factors associated with mental health disorders among refugee children and adolescents exposed to war, violence and displacement, and to critically review the effectiveness of psychological interventions recently used with this population. Precipitating and maintaining factors that influence the expression of mental health difficulties and resilience among children and adolescents affected by war are discussed according to a social ecological framework. While the effectiveness of individual, group- and school-based interventions is compelling, more evidence is needed to determine optimal models of intervention delivery for this population.

Keywords Child · Adolescent · Refugee · Post-conflict · Interventions · Resettlement

E. A. Newnham (✉)
School of Psychology, Curtin University, Perth, WA, Australia
e-mail: elizabeth.newnham@curtin.edu.au

S. Kashyap
School of Psychology, University of New South Wales, Sydney, NSW, Australia
e-mail: Shradhha.kashyap@unsw.edu.au

J. Tearne
State Major Trauma Unit, Royal Perth Hospital, Health Department of Western Australia, Perth, WA, Australia
e-mail: jessica.tearne@health.wa.gov.au

M. Fazel
Department of Psychiatry, Oxford University, Oxford, UK
e-mail: mina.fazel@psych.ox.ac.uk

N. Morina, A. Nickerson (eds.), *Mental Health of Refugee and Conflict-Affected Populations*, https://doi.org/10.1007/978-3-319-97046-2_3

Safety and security are considered foundational elements for healthy child development. Yet for many children and adolescents affected by war, development occurs within a dangerous and uncertain environment. This can have variable effects; many children demonstrate considerable resourcefulness, capacity and self-efficacy in the face of adversity (Saigh, Mroueh, Zimmerman, & Fairbank, 1995), utilising a range of supports and opportunities that may be available. There is, however, a significant proportion of children affected by violence who develop mental health difficulties that negatively impact their wellbeing, physical health, access to education, family and peer relationships, and often, sense of identity (Ellis et al., 2010; Hassan, Ventevogel, Jefee-Bahloul, Barkil-Oteo, & Kirmayer, 2016; Newnham, Pearson, Stein, & Betancourt, 2015). In 2015, the number of people escaping violence and persecution grew to the highest rate seen since World War II, numbering more than 65 million (UNHCR, 2016). Half of those seeking refuge are children. As the global humanitarian crisis escalates, the need for interventions to address posttraumatic stress disorder, depression, anxiety, grief and behavioural difficulties in this population becomes increasingly evident.

This chapter presents a critical examination of the factors that moderate and mediate the relationship between exposure to trauma and mental health outcomes for war-affected and refugee children and adolescents. The review will build on a socio-ecological framework to examine the interaction between individual experiences and the social environment in determining psychological health (Betancourt & Khan, 2008). To address these factors, a number of psychological treatments have demonstrated effectiveness when delivered in high, middle and low-income nations. Recent evaluations of individual, group, family and community interventions are illustrated, with attention to feasibility and effectiveness data.

Chapter Outline

A review of the literature was conducted with a focus on the epidemiology of psychological disorders, and evidence-supported interventions for refugee and war-affected youth. Relevant studies published between January 2005 and December 2016 were identified through scientific databases including PsycINFO, Medline and Proquest Psychology Journals and a review of reference sections of key articles. Studies published after January 2005 were included to build on the findings of earlier reviews conducted by Fazel and colleagues (Fazel, Wheeler, & Danesh, 2005; Tyrer & Fazel, 2014). Search terms included "child and adolescent refugee" together with, "risk factors", "mental health problems", "exposure to conflict", "posttraumatic stress disorder", "anxiety", "depression", "grief", "traumatic loss", "psychological interventions" and "mental health interventions". The application of interventions across low, middle and high-income countries will be described.

Prevalence

Rates of mental health disorders reported in studies of war-affected and refugee youth vary considerably. A recent systematic review reported wide-ranging prevalence rates, including incidence of posttraumatic stress disorder (PTSD) spanning 0–87%, and rates of anxiety and depression ranging from 9.5 to 95.5% among youth living in refugee camps (Vossoughi, Jackson, Gusler, & Stone, 2016). Common barriers to conducting research among war exposed and refugee youth may account for the broad-ranging differences across studies (Hebebrand et al., 2016; Reed, Fazel, Jones, Panter-Brick, & Stein, 2012). Challenges include addressing the large heterogeneity within this population, particularly with regard to country of origin, cultural background, and the types of trauma experienced; differences between the types of measures used to assess mental health disorders; different methods of translation; type of reporting (e.g., self-report versus other-report); difficulty accessing individuals in dangerous conflict zones; reliance on small sample sizes; and a paucity of studies using diagnostic clinical interviews (Graham, Minhas, & Paxton, 2016; Hebebrand et al., 2016; Reed et al., 2012; Vossoughi et al., 2016). Nevertheless, despite the variability in prevalence estimates, records suggest that there is an elevated rate of psychological disorders and maladjustment among war-affected and refugee children and adolescents (Attanayake et al., 2009; Fazel & Stein, 2002; Ramel, Taljemark, Lindgren, & Johansson, 2015; Vossoughi et al., 2016).

High Income Countries

In high-income nations, clinical reports have highlighted the prevalence of mental health difficulties for resettled war-affected youth. High rates of generalized anxiety (26.8%), probable PTSD (30.4%), behavioral difficulties (44.6%), somatization (26.8%), and traumatic grief (21.4%) were identified through clinical interviews with 60 refugee children and adolescents seeking treatment for trauma in the United States (US) (Betancourt et al., 2012). Comorbidity was common. Of note, high-risk behaviours and alcohol and drug use were less often reported in this group, in comparison with a matched sample of youth originating from the U.S. (Betancourt et al., 2017). In Norway, clinical interviews with unaccompanied asylum seeking adolescents suggested that 41.9% of individuals met diagnostic criteria for a current psychiatric disorder (Jakobsen, Demott, & Heir, 2014). The most common disorders were PTSD (30.6%), depression (9.4%), agoraphobia (4.4%) and generalized anxiety (3.8%) (Jakobsen et al., 2014). Similarly, unaccompanied refugee minors were found to be overrepresented in inpatient psychiatric care following presentations to the emergency department at a hospital in Sweden, where self-injurious behaviors were more common among refugee minors than non-refugee minors (Ramel et al., 2015).

Beyond clinical reports, population and community based studies report increased but variable levels of psychological distress among refugee and war-affected youth. For example, assessments conducted with a non-clinical sample of 530 refugees aged 4–17 years resettled in Australia revealed elevated rates of emotional and behavioral difficulties among 11% of the sample (Ziaian, de Anstiss, Antoniou, Baghurst, & Sawyer, 2013). Recent findings from Denmark showed a 26% rate of self-reported mental health difficulties in asylum-seeking children as measured by the *Strengths and Difficulties Questionnaire* (Nielsen et al., 2008; Tousignant et al., 1999). Beyond general mental health difficulties, a Cochrane review reported levels of PTSD (19–54%) and depression (3–30%) that varied among refugee youth resettled in Western countries (Bronstein & Montgomery, 2011). Unaccompanied refugee minors (URM) appear to be at highest risk for the development of psychopathology relative to refugee adolescents living with family, with studies showing that URM resettled in The Netherlands consistently reported higher rates of psychiatric symptoms and disorders, internalizing behaviours, stressful life events, and traumatic stress reactions (Bean, Derluyn, Eurelings-Bontekoe, Broekaert, & Spinhoven, 2007; Wiese & Burhorst, 2007). Furthermore, a recent study in the United Kingdom (UK) suggests that despite URM being at high risk of developing mental health disorders, mental health services are under-utilized by this population (Sanchez-Cao, Kramer, & Hodes, 2013).

Low and Middle Income Countries (LMIC)

Mirroring the findings for youth resettled in high-income countries, war-affected youth in LMIC have an increased risk of developing posttraumatic stress symptoms, anxiety and depression. Child mental health assessments conducted via caregiver reports in a Syrian-Turkish refugee camp indicated that rates of anxiety among 4–10 year olds were as high as 49%, and more than one third met a clinical threshold for behavioural issues (Cartwright, El-Khani, Subryan, & Calam, 2015). Among 38 Yazidi youth (aged 2–18 years old) assessed in a Turkish refugee camp, all participants were found to have at least one psychiatric disorder, while 50% reported comorbidity (Ceri et al., 2016). The most prevalent issues were depression (36.8%), conversion disorders (28.9%), adjustment disorders (21.8%), acute stress (18.4%) and PTSD (10.5%) (Ceri et al., 2016).

The psychological impacts of war can be lasting. Four years after the cessation of conflict in Northern Uganda, 205 adolescents aged 12–19, recruited from primary schools in the area were assessed for psychological distress (McMullen, O'Callaghan, Richards, Eakin, & Rafferty, 2012. More than half (57%) of participants were found to have clinically significant posttraumatic stress, and these symptoms were highly correlated with anxiety and depression-like symptoms (McMullen et al., 2012). Higher rates of mental health difficulties among war-affected and refugee youth signal a need for tailored clinical interventions, specialist training in trauma for psychologists working with cross-cultural clients, and investigative research into the risk and protective pathways for trauma-affected children.

Individual Level Factors

Exposure to Conflict

War exposures are complex and severe in nature. In contrast to single-incident traumas, war-affected youth can experience chronic exposure to potentially traumatic events for weeks, months or even years (Betancourt, Newnham, McBain, & Brennan, 2013). Among the range of traumatic incidents common in war, children may witness violence, be separated from or experience the death of family members and friends, experience physical, sexual and psychological harm, be deprived of food, water or shelter, or forced to inflict harm on others. These exposures have varying impacts for each child, but some experiences have been found to be particularly harmful (Betancourt, McBain, Newnham, & Brennan, 2013).

Among war-affected youth in Sierra Leone, experiencing rape predicted higher anxiety and hostility two years post-war (Betancourt et al., 2010). Similarly, forced engagement in violence predicted increased hostility in the post-conflict period (Betancourt, Borisova, et al., 2010). Increased exposure to war-related stressors was associated with higher risk of PTSD among war-affected youth from Afghanistan (Bronstein, Montgomery, & Dobrowolski, 2012), and Palestine (Kolltveit et al., 2012). In contrast, the effects of war exposure on depression symptoms are mixed. Exposure to war was not associated with depression among adolescents from Sierra Leone (Betancourt, Borisova, et al., 2010) and Palestine (Kolltveit et al., 2012), but positively associated with slower improvements in depression and anxiety among adolescents in Northern Uganda (Haroz, Murray, Bolton, Betancourt, & Bass, 2013).

Migration is a particularly vulnerable time for displaced children. Security risks include trafficking, bonded labour and sexual exploitation, with severe psychological impacts (Hebebrand et al., 2016; Kiss, Yun, Pocock, & Zimmerman, 2015). For example, adolescent Syrian boys exploited into child labour reported experiencing humiliation, anxiety and hopelessness (Mercy Corps, 2014) and sexually-exploited trafficked girls in the Mekong Delta reported high rates of posttraumatic stress, depression, hostility and suicidal ideation related to their experience of abuse (Kiss et al., 2015). Refugee children in Greece have experienced high rates of physical and sexual abuse during the journey to safety and in migrant camps, with substantial implications for their psychological health (Digidiki & Bhabha, 2017).

Upon resettlement, exposure to conflict-related stressors continues to be a factor associated with an increased risk of psychological problems (Bronstein et al., 2012). For example, the risk of experiencing PTSD was found to be increased amongst URM resettled in Belgium, Norway, and The Netherlands (Jensen, Fjermestad, Granly, & Wilhelmsen, 2015; Smid, Lensvelt-Mulders, Knipscheer, Gersons, &

Kleber, 2011; Vervliet et al., 2014; Vervliet, Lammertyn, Broekaert, & Derluyn, 2014). War exposure was positively associated with depression among URM on arrival in Belgium (Vervliet, Meyer Demott, et al., 2014) and 6 months post-arrival in Norway (Jensen et al., 2015). Similarly, psychological problems were significantly higher among refugee groups than non-refugee youth re-settled in Italy (Thommessen, Laghi, Cerrone, Baiocco, & Todd, 2013). Among a treatment-seeking sample of refugee youth from various backgrounds in the US, high rates of emotional and behavioural problems were associated with exposure to war, violence or displacement (Betancourt et al., 2017).

Daily Hardships

It is not only war exposures that play a critical role in long-term mental health outcomes. Daily hardships, the living conditions caused or worsened by war and poverty, encompass experiences of domestic violence, housing insecurity, food and water shortages, family disintegration, and lack of access to core services (Miller & Rasmussen, 2010). These stressors have consistently been found to contribute to worsening PTSD and depression symptoms among war-affected youth in post-conflict settings (Newnham, Pearson, et al., 2015), and young people resettled in both low and high-income countries (Ellis et al., 2010; Fazel, Reed, Panter-Brick, & Stein, 2012; Reed et al., 2012). For Sri Lankan, Sierra Leonean, and Bosnian war-affected youth, the association between war trauma and later psychological distress was largely mediated by daily hardships, highlighting the significant influence of the post-conflict environment in recovery (Fernando, Miller, & Berger, 2010; Layne et al., 2010; Newnham, Pearson, et al., 2015). Similarly, despite efforts to seek safety and stability, refugee youth resettled in new countries face a range of daily hardships including economic insecurity, exposure to community violence, prejudice and acculturation stressors (Fazel et al., 2012; Miller & Rasmussen, 2017; Vervliet, Lammertyn, et al., 2014).

Gender and Age

Associations between demographic variables such as age and gender and rates of psychopathology in youth have been mixed. For example, older age was associated with higher rates of PTSD among Palestinian youth (Kolltveit et al., 2012) and URM arriving in the Netherlands (Smid et al., 2011), but not among URM arriving in Norway (Jensen et al., 2015) or Belgium (Vervliet, Meyer Demott, et al., 2014). Female gender was associated with psychological difficulties among war-affected Palestinian (Kolltveit et al., 2012), and Chechen youth (Betancourt et al., 2012) and among URM seeking asylum in Austria and Belgium (Huemer et al., 2011; Vervliet, Lammertyn, et al., 2014; Vervliet, Meyer Demott, et al., 2014). However, gender was not associated with psychopathology among URM in Norway (Jensen et al., 2015). More males were found to report resilient outcomes among Palestinian youth (Punamäki, Qouta, Miller, & El-Sarraj, 2011), and more females had higher resilience scores among refugees settled in Australia (Ziaian, de Anstiss, Antoniou, Baghurst, & Sawyer, 2012). Methodological differences such as sampling methods, differences in measures of resilience, and previous trauma exposures between these studies could account for conflicting findings.

Cognitive and Behavioural Factors

Cognitive manifestations of loss and displacement may include a sense of guilt, shame, loss of control, helplessness, boredom and rumination (Hassan et al., 2016). In some cases, coherence of identity may be disturbed by the experience of trauma, but can also be a function of migration, resettlement, and cultural adaptation (Fazel et al., 2012). Reports of behavioural changes among displaced Syrian refugees suggest that social withdrawal, aggression and interpersonal difficulties are common, but are not necessarily indicative of psychological disorders (Cartwright et al., 2015; Hassan et al., 2016; James, Sovcik, Garoff, & Abbasi, 2014). While violent and war-related role playing is sometimes displayed by children who have experienced prolonged exposure to trauma, as documented among child refugees from Syria (James et al., 2014), this form of play has been found to be common, particularly among boys, in peaceful societies (Malloy, McMurray-Schwarz, Reifel, & Brown, 2004) and likely meets a developmental need for mastery and control.

Psychological Resilience

The rate and pattern of the development of psychopathology differs across individuals. Even when exposed to severe trauma, many children and youth recover quickly from acute reactions or do not exhibit psychological distress. For example, in a study of war-affected Palestinian youth who were exposed to high levels of trauma, one in five individuals showed low levels of psychological difficulties (Punamäki et al., 2011). Ugandan former child soldiers who did not have PTSD reported fewer guilt cognitions, less motivation for revenge and more perceived spiritual support (Klasen et al., 2010). More pro-social behaviours were associated with better well-being among refugee youth in Australia (Ziaian et al., 2012) and among war-affected adolescents in Northern Uganda (Haroz et al., 2013); while social competence among refugees settled in Canada was protective against emotional problems (Beiser, Puente-Duran, & Hou, 2015). Among Palestinian youth, better physical health, cognitive functioning and emotion regulation were associated with fewer psychological problems (Punamäki et al., 2011). A recent study in Australia indicated that higher levels of school connectedness, acculturation, and permanent visa status were associated with increased wellbeing and lower levels of psychological distress (Tozer, Khawaja, & Schweitzer, 2017).

Family Level Factors

Caregiver Mental Health

Parental mental health plays an important role in psychological outcomes for children affected by trauma. Caregiver psychological distress was associated with higher levels of psychopathology among war-affected youth from Ethiopia (Betancourt, Yudron, Wheaton, & Smith-Fawzi, 2012), Afghanistan (Panter-Brick, Grimon, & Eggerman, 2014), Sierra Leone (Betancourt, McBain, Newnham, & Brennan, 2015), Palestine (Khamis, 2016), and among young refugees from various backgrounds settled in Canada (Beiser et al., 2015). Indeed, among 364 Afghani child-caregiver dyads, caregiver distress predicted child depression and posttraumatic stress over and above exposure to war stressors (Panter-Brick et al., 2014). It has been theorised that emotional distress may impact upon a caregiver's parenting efficacy, with one study indicating that mothers displaying depressed mood post-war exposure were less likely to nurture their young children (Lai, Hadi, & Llabre, 2014; Morris et al., 2012). There may also be reciprocal causality, in which low mood and problem behaviours in each party influence the emotional state of the other (Betancourt et al., 2015). A recent assessment of coping among displaced Syrian refugee parents revealed the difficulties inherent in parenting as children develop increasingly problematic behaviours and trauma reactions (El-Khani, Ulph, Peters, & Calam, 2017). To address these challenges, parents reported coping in three ways: embodying acceptance and gratitude, using faith to maintain strength and motivate good parenting, and seeking help from others.

Family Environment

Warm and supportive parenting was protective against emotional problems among war-affected youth in Palestine (Punamäki et al., 2011) and among young refugees living in Canada (Beiser et al., 2015). Family unity was associated with more pro-social behaviour and fewer impacts of exposure to war-related stressors among Afghani youth (Panter-Brick et al., 2014). Similarly, stronger family connectedness predicted fewer internalizing problems among war-affected Chechen youth (Betancourt, Salhi, Buka, et al., 2012), although the protective effect of family connectedness was found only for males. Family acceptance of returning child soldiers in Sierra Leone was also associated with lower depression, anxiety, hostility and more pro-social behaviours and confidence (Betancourt, Brennan, Rubin-Smith, Fitzmaurice, & Gilman, 2010).

In contrast, negative family environments involving domestic violence (Panter-Brick et al., 2014), neglect, abuse (Betancourt, McBain, et al., 2013), and discord (Dura-Vila, Klasen, Makatini, Rahimi, & Hodes, 2013) were associated with increased psychopathology among war-affected and refugee youth. Among conflict-affected youth in Northern Uganda (Haroz et al., 2013) and Sierra Leone (Betancourt, McBain, et al., 2013), caregiver death was associated with a worsening of depression (Haroz et al., 2013) and deteriorating internalizing symptoms (Betancourt, McBain, et al., 2013) over time. Living alone versus with a foster family was associated with higher PTSD among male Afghani refugees (Bronstein et al., 2012).

Family Socio–economic Status and Access to Income

Belonging to a family with higher socio-economic status (SES) was associated with lower rates of PTSD among former child soldiers in Northern Uganda (Klasen et al., 2010) and lower internalizing problems among Ethiopian youths living in refugee camps (Betancourt, Yudron, Wheaton, & Smith-Fawzi, 2012). Having an unemployed father was associated with more psychological problems among young Palestinians (Kolltveit et al., 2012), yet other assessments have suggested that SES was not associated with resilience among war-affected Palestinian youth (Punamäki et al., 2011). Qualitative interviews from Guinea in communities affected by violent conflict forward the notion of a negative cycle in which loss of livelihoods and experience of trauma contribute to the genesis of psychological ill health, and that psychological symptoms in turn affect efforts to regain wealth in the long-term (Abramowitz, 2005). It is plausible that this cycle may contribute to mental ill-health in families affected by conflict.

School and Community Level Factors

Stigma and Acceptance

Stigma and discrimination are frequently reported risks for young people who remain in the post-conflict setting, as well as those who resettle in new countries. Despite the increased safety of resettlement, many young people experience stigma related to race, economic position, language, disability, religion and gender (Fazel et al., 2012). Refugee children resettled in the US and Canada reported discrimination and stigma that had significant impacts on mental health outcomes (Beiser et al., 2015; Ellis et al., 2010). In post-conflict settings, stigma plays a damaging role. Children who have previously been associated with armed groups, or were the victim of rape or physical assault, face particularly severe stigma, later associated with psychological difficulties (Betancourt, McBain, et al., 2013).

The loss of social connections that occurs with displacement has potential to create feelings of estrangement, disorientation, loss of identity and social capital, and yearning for familiarity (Hassan et al., 2016). As recently resettled groups begin the search for housing, services and community, the burden of adaptation to new systems and culture can weigh heavily. Women and children can be particularly isolated in new settings, with the impacts of stigma and discrimination leading to physical as well as emotional seclusion (Hassan et al., 2016).

In contrast, community inclusion can have very positive effects on mental health. Perceived community acceptance predicted lower rates of depression, better pro-social attitudes and behaviours, more confidence and improvements in internalizing symptoms over 6 years among former child soldiers in Sierra Leone (Betancourt, Borisova, et al., 2010; Betancourt, McBain, et al., 2013). In addition, staying in school predicted more pro-social attitudes in this population (Betancourt, Borisova, et al., 2010). Acculturation style (the manner in which refugees associate with both their original culture and the culture of their destination location) was associated with psychological wellbeing among Somali refugees in the US (Ellis et al., 2010) and young refugees living in Canada (Beiser et al., 2015).

Detention

There is an emerging body of evidence to indicate that migration detention is associated with poor mental health outcomes in children and adolescents. One systematic review of the impact of prolonged detention suggested evidence of a causal relationship between detention and conditions injurious to mental health in children and adolescents (Robjant, Hassan, & Katona, 2009). Several studies from the UK and Australia show that the majority (if not all) children surveyed in detention centres meet criteria for at least one psychiatric illness (Lorek et al., 2009; Steel et al., 2004), and comparative analyses have shown a tenfold increase in psychiatric symptomatology following detention (Steel et al., 2004). These studies revealed high incidence of PTSD, anxiety including separation anxiety, major depression, oppositional defiant disorder, and somatic complaints, as well as sleep difficulties, deliberate self-harm and suicidal ideation (Dudley, Steel, Mares, & Newman, 2012). Factors such as ongoing uncertainty and stress, disrupted peer and family relationships, exposure to further traumatic events and attempts at self-harm, parental psychological distress, and potential exposure to human rights abuses have been forwarded as potential mediators of this relationship (Coffey, Kaplan, Sampson, & Tucci, 2010; Fazel, Karunakara, & Newnham, 2014). Despite difficulties in carrying out research on detention and the limitations of several studies (e.g., small sample size, difficulty accessing persons in detention), it appears clear that detention is associated with deleterious mental health impacts for children and adolescents, and that alternatives to detention are urgently required.

Visa Status

There is a paucity of literature regarding the impact of visa status on youth mental health. Tozer et al. (2017) found that visa certainty was significantly associated with increased report of subjective wellbeing in refugee youth resettled in Australia. Refugee youth attending school in the UK reported that worry about uncertainty in the asylum process had negative effects on social functioning and concentration at school (Fazel, Garcia, & Stein, 2016). Previous studies in adults have indicated that temporary protection visa status strongly predicted increased incidence of depression, anxiety including PTSD symptoms, and mental health related disability relative to those who held permanent residence (Momartin et al., 2006; Steel et al., 2006), and that change to a more stable visa status was associated with significant improvements in mental health symptoms (Nickerson, Steel, Bryant, Brooks, & Silove, 2011). There are myriad factors that may underlie this relationship, including prolonged uncertainty regarding residency and one's future, limited access to services, separation from family, living difficulties, and prolonged provocation of past-trauma (Nickerson et al., 2011). It stands to reason that these findings in adult populations may extend to youth affected by uncertainty associated with visa status. Further, given the known relationship between caregiver psychopathology and youth psychiatric symptomatology (Beiser et al., 2015; Huemer et al., 2011; Panter-Brick et al., 2014), it is possible that the distress associated with uncertain visa status in caregivers may be passed on to the child.

Interventions for Children and Adolescents Affected by War

The interplay of risk factors that manifest during and following war creates significant potential for psychological harm. Mechanisms to address the effects of this complex system of vulnerability, and to determine optimal modes of intervention, are needed. The next section of this chapter will outline existing evidence for interventions trialled across low, middle and high-income nations.

Individual Interventions

Narrative Exposure Therapy (NET) for youth (KID-NET) is an evidence-based treatment for survivors of multiple severe traumatic events (Catani et al., 2009; Robjant & Fazel, 2010; Ruf et al., 2010). It builds on the principles of cognitive behavioural therapy, with the inclusion of a historical narrative within which the experience of trauma is processed. KID-NET involves the therapist working with the child or adolescent to record a chronological narrative of their whole life, focussing on the full range of positive and traumatic events they have experienced (Ruf et al., 2010). The objective is to help the child or adolescent better understand the details of each traumatic event, making them less distressing and debilitating by facilitating their encoding within the autobiographical details of that person's life (Ruf et al., 2010). NET is an effective, brief intervention that has demonstrated cultural universality and feasibility in low resource settings. KID-NET has been assessed in a series of trials (both controlled and uncontrolled), and has demonstrated effectiveness for treating PTSD among children in Northern Sri Lanka (Catani et al., 2009), Northern Uganda (Ertl, Pfeiffer, Schauer, Elbert, & Neuner, 2011; Onyut et al., 2005), and at an outpatient refugee clinic in Germany (Ruf et al., 2010). Ruf et al. (2010) reported post-treatment symptom reductions of 60% (Cohen's $d = 1.9$), with sustained improvement over 12 months ($d = 1.8$). Similar to this study, in which a 6-month PTSD remission rate of 83% was reported, Catani et al. (2009) reported an 81% PTSD recovery rate at 6 months post-treatment, with similar effect sizes (post-treatment $d = 1.76$, 6 month follow up $d = 1.96$). Applications of KID-NET suggest that it has the potential to be used effectively in both high and low income countries, and in settings in which instability and volatility continue (Robjant & Fazel, 2010).

Group-Based Interventions

Group based interventions for improving mental health outcomes among war-affected and refugee youth have had promising results. Group-based Interpersonal Therapy (IPT) has been evaluated for adolescent survivors of war living in camps for internally displaced persons (IDP) in Northern Uganda (Bolton et al., 2007). Adolescents were randomly allocated to the IPT group, an activity-based group or a wait-list control group (Bolton et al., 2007). IPT resulted in a statistically significant decline in depression for all females and male former child soldiers, but not for males who did not have a history of abduction (Betancourt et al., 2012). The significant improvement in this population suggests that group IPT can be feasibly delivered within an IDP camp.

Conflict-affected youth in the Democratic Republic of the Congo (DRC) were randomly allocated to a community participative psychosocial intervention ($n = 79$), which provided psychoeducation, problem-solving skills, relaxation techniques and healthy interpersonal communication training for families; or a waitlist control group ($n = 80$) (O'Callaghan et al., 2014). The treatment group reported significantly lower posttraumatic stress and higher prosocial behaviours, with these gains sustained at 3-month follow-up (O'Callaghan et al., 2014). Another study in the DRC evaluated the effectiveness of Trauma-Focused CBT among 50 boys aged 13–17, of whom 39 were former child soldiers (McMullen, O'Callaghan, Shannon, Black, & Eakin, 2013). Boys in the treatment group showed significantly improved posttraumatic stress, depression/anxiety-like symptoms, prosocial behaviours and conduct problems compared to waitlist controls, which were sustained at 3-month follow-up (McMullen et al., 2013). Group based therapies have therefore been effectively delivered in areas affected by past and ongoing insecurity with demonstrated improvements in psychological and behavioural outcomes.

Another group based intervention evaluated in an area of ongoing insecurity assessed Mind-Body Skills (relaxation, guided imagery and movement skills) training to treat PTSD and depression among 129 Palestinian youth aged 8–18 in Gaza (Staples, Abdel Atti, & Gordon, 2011). Results suggested that PTSD and depression scores post-intervention, and at 3-month follow-up had significantly improved, and this improvement was greater for older children (Staples et al., 2011). The lack of a control group, however, limits conclusions that can be drawn about the efficacy of the intervention. Similarly, an art therapy group intervention was provided for 63 Syrian refugee children living in Turkey (Ugurlu, Akca, & Acarturk, 2016). Scores from 30 youth measured post-intervention suggest that trauma symptoms and depression had significantly reduced. However, the effectiveness of this intervention cannot be determined due to the absence of a control group and high rate of drop-out: Less than half the sample were assessed post-intervention.

It is not only the traumas of conflict that cause psychological distress. In the aftermath of war, youth are forced to navigate the challenges of a post-conflict environment that is often devoid of health services, food and clean water, security, and supportive community structures (Newnham, Pearson, et al., 2015). The stress inherent in post-conflict recovery was the focus of the Youth Readiness Intervention (Betancourt et al., 2014; Newnham et al., 2015), an evidence-based treatment for war-affected youth. Building on the foundations of cognitive behavioural therapy and interpersonal therapy, the intervention was designed to address the comorbid psychological issues that are common among war-affected youth, delivered in a low-resource setting (Newnham, McBain, et al., 2015). In a randomized controlled trial in Sierra Leone, the Youth Readiness Intervention was effective in improving emotion regulation, prosocial behaviours, social support and functioning (Betancourt et al., 2014). Further to this, young people who received the intervention demonstrated significant improvements in school enrolment, attendance and classroom behaviour (Betancourt et al., 2014). The Youth Readiness Intervention provides indication not only that psychological treatment is effective in improving psychological and social outcomes, but that psychological improvements have a positive impact on engagement in education.

Family Interventions

To date there is little research on family-based therapy for young refugees. To the authors' knowledge, only three studies have been conducted between 2005 and 2016. First, among 10 war-affected families from Bosnia-Herzegovina living in Sweden (Bjorn, Boden, Sydsjo, & Gustafsson, 2013), results showed that three sessions of family therapy reduced the rate of pathological versus normal sandbox play in refugee children aged 5–12, as measured by the "Erica play-diagnostic" method (Bjorn et al., 2013). However, the efficacy of this treatment is yet to be established and cannot be determined based on the small sample size, the lack of a control group and the absence of a strong empirical evidence base for the intervention. Second, brief psychoeducation for parents of war-affected youth (10–14 years old) in Burundi was associated with significant reductions in child-reported aggression in the intervention group ($n = 58$), compared to 62 waitlist control children (Jordans, Tol, Ndayisaba, & Komproe, 2013). However, reductions in aggression were only found among boys, and no differences in depression or perceived family support were found between intervention and control groups (Jordans et al., 2013). Further, measures of depression, aggression and family support did not include both child and parent reports, which limits the validity of these results.

A parenting skills intervention entitled *The Happy Families Program* was evaluated using a randomized control trial, with 479 Burmese migrant and displaced youth, aged 7–15, living in Thailand (Annan, Sim, Puffer, Salhi, & Betancourt, 2016). One month post-intervention, both children and caregivers in the intervention group ($n = 240$) reported significant reductions in externalizing problems compared to waitlist controls ($n = 239$) (Annan et al., 2016). However, only caregivers reported a reduction in children's attention problems, and only children reported an improvement in psychosocial protective factors compared to controls. Therefore, while more research is needed to confirm the efficacy of these interventions among refugee and war-affected youth, emerging evidence points to the potential capacity of parenting skills interventions to improve aggression and other externalizing problems.

School-Based Interventions

Low and Middle Income Countries

School-based interventions have been implemented across a range of peri and post-conflict settings. For example, five studies assessed school-based interventions among Palestinian youth. Three of these evaluated the effectiveness of Teaching Recovery Techniques (TRT), a skills-based Cognitive Behavioural Therapy program, in improving posttraumatic stress, depressive symptoms (Qouta, Palosaari, Diab, & Punamaki, 2012), traumatic grief, negative school impact (Barron, Abdallah, & Smith, 2013), psychological wellbeing and pro-social behaviors, compared to wait-list control groups (Diab, Peltonen, Qouta, Palosaari, & Punamaki, 2015). TRT teaches coping strategies, problem solving and emotion regulation skills, and also aims to mobilise family and community resources (Diab et al., 2015). The techniques taught to manage psychological distress include play, psycho-education about normal trauma responses, relaxation to manage hyper-arousal, graded exposure to manage avoidance, and mental imagery exercises to manage intrusive symptoms. The first study in Gaza found that posttraumatic symptoms were reduced only in boys in the TRT group and in girls with low peri-traumatic dissociation, with no overall differences between TRT and wait-list controls (Qouta et al., 2012). A second study in Gaza found no improvement in pro-social behavior or psychological wellbeing in the TRT group post-intervention (Diab et al., 2015). The lack of significant improvements may be due to the continued insecurity in Gaza, and a more targeted intervention based on specific trauma processing may be more effective (Diab et al., 2015; Qouta et al., 2012). Nevertheless, significant reductions in PTSD, depression, traumatic grief and negative school impact were reported in the TRT treatment group (n = 90), compared to the waitlist controls (n = 50), among youth aged 11–14 attending school in the West Bank (Barron et al., 2013). It is not known if gains were sustained beyond post-intervention testing, as follow-up scores were not measured. Additionally, two studies implemented a school mediation program that aimed to provide psychosocial support to improve conflict resolution and decrease disruptive school behavior in Gaza (Peltonen, Qouta, El Sarraj, & Punamäki, 2012; Thabet, Tawahina, & Vostanis, 2009). Teachers, parents and peers were provided with psychoeducation around interpersonal relationships, trained in socio-emotional skills, and trained to mediate conflict. Compared to pre-intervention measures, children aged 12+ reported significant reductions in obsessive and over-anxious symptoms, and parents of children aged 6–12 reported reductions in hyperactivity (Thabet et al., 2009). Yet, this study was limited by the absence of a control group, the use of different reporters for children of different ages, a lack of follow-up measures and the fact that it was not clear if analyses controlled for potentially confounding factors such as gender, as 87.17% of the sample was male. Indeed, results of a second study evaluating school mediation in Gaza; which did account for gender and trauma exposure in treatment and control groups; suggest that there was no improvement in PTSD, depression or prosocial behaviors in the treatment group compared to wait-list controls (Peltonen et al., 2012).

Evidence for the effectiveness of other psychosocial support programs implemented in low and middle income countries is also limited. One program entitled "Prijateljice", adapted for 336 children aged 12–15 in post-war Bosnia Herzegovina, involved dealing with issues such as prejudice, and aimed to link students, parents and teachers to form support networks and school clubs (Hasanović et al., 2009). Youth who engaged in the program reported significant reductions in PTSD post intervention, compared to 72 age-matched controls who reported no change (Hasanović et al., 2009). Yet post-intervention differences could have been due to significantly higher pre-intervention traumatic exposure and PTSD scores in the treatment group. In addition, psychosocial support programs in South Sudan and India aimed to teach healthy coping, critical thinking and problem solving skills. These programs were I DEAL, a life skills training program delivered to 122 war-affected youth in South Sudan aged 8–16 (Eiling, Van Diggele-Holtland, Van Yperen, & Boer, 2014), and Life Skills Training, implemented among 150 Tibetan refugee adolescents aged 13–19 living in India (Yankey & Biswas, 2012). While the contribution of the intervention itself cannot be evaluated due to the absence of a control group, qualitative interviews suggest that I DEAL was associated with improved social and emotional coping skills (Eiling et al., 2014). The Life Skills Training program appeared to be associated with lower school, leisure and self-stress in the treatment versus control group. However, not all forms of stress were different between groups (Yankey & Biswas, 2012).

Psychosocial activities, including art therapy, group play and music are also often delivered in refugee camp settings. A 12-month Psychosocial Structured Activities intervention was delivered in post-conflict Northern Uganda with 203 school children, aged 7–12 years (Ager et al., 2011). Activities including drama and art, together with components addressing parental and community support resulted in significant improvements in wellbeing among these children compared to a waitlist control, however, since psychological symptoms were not measured, it is not known if the intervention resulted in any reductions in symptoms (Ager et al., 2011). A lack of follow-up data, and inter-teacher reporting variability further limits interpretation of the findings (Ager et al., 2011).

A Classroom Based Intervention (CBI) that combined cognitive behavioral strategies (psychoeducation, coping skills training) with creative expression elements (music, drama, dance) was evaluated in cluster randomized controlled trials among war-affected school children in Indonesia (Tol et al., 2008), Nepal (Jordans et al., 2010) and Burundi (Tol et al., 2014). After 15 sessions of CBI among children aged 7–15 in Indonesia, the treatment group (n = 182) reported significant reductions in PTSD and improved hope compared to waitlist controls (n = 221) (Tol et al., 2008). These gains were maintained at 6 months post-intervention (Tol et al., 2008). However, only females in the treatment group reported reductions in functional impairment following the intervention, while neither females nor males reported improvements in depression, anxiety or stress-related physical symptoms (Tol et al., 2008). Furthermore, after accounting for variance associated with measures conducted at different schools in Nepal, no overall differences in psychological symptoms between treatment (n = 164) and waitlist controls (n = 161) were found post-intervention (Jordans et al., 2010). Still, gender and age-specific differences were found, where females showed more pro-social behaviors, males reported less aggression and psychological difficulties, while older children reported higher levels of hope (Jordans et al., 2010). Finally, in Burundi, results suggested that there were no significant differences in psychological wellbeing between treatment and control groups among war affected children aged 8–17 (Tol et al., 2014). While some differences were found, such as younger children reporting higher levels of hope, conflicting findings suggest that while CBI may be beneficial, gains were gender, age and context specific (Tol et al., 2014).

In Sierra Leone, 315 children aged 8–17 years enrolled in schools within IDP camps were administered an education intervention (Rapid-ED) which combined literacy and numeracy skills with a trauma healing program (Gupta & Zimmer, 2008). This intervention aimed to provide a safe environment for locally-trained teachers to encourage children to share experiences, normalize traumatic reactions through drawing, writing and role-playing, and to provide accurate information about the war to counteract magical thinking (Gupta & Zimmer, 2008). A significant decrease in arousal and intrusive symptoms of posttraumatic stress was reported at post-intervention (Gupta & Zimmer, 2008). However, the lack of a control group limits inferences that can be made about the effectiveness of the intervention (Gupta & Zimmer, 2008).

The Writing for Recovery intervention comprising reflective writing about participants' experience of trauma and current daily stressors, was delivered in Iran for 61 adolescent Afghani refugees (Kalantari, Yule, Dyregrov, Neshatdoost, & Ahmadi, 2012). The treatment group showed significantly lower traumatic grief symptoms post-intervention compared to wait-list controls (Kalantari et al., 2012). In contrast, a cognitive behavior therapy based intervention containing expressive elements such as guided exposure through drawing, music, movement, and games, conducted in Sri Lanka with war-affected children, was not found to impact directly upon longitudinal mental health outcomes such as anxiety, depression, and PTSD (Tol et al., 2012). The intervention was, however, found to affect the incidence of conduct problems, and a significant interaction with age was evident, such that younger children exposed to the intervention showed the largest improvements in conduct problems. Despite the barriers inherent in evaluating treatments conducted in post-conflict and refugee settings, there is promising evidence for school and community-based interventions in low income countries (Tyrer & Fazel, 2014).

High Income Countries

School and community interventions have gained increasing attention for refugees resettled in high-income countries. For example, three studies evaluated the efficacy of school-based, creative expression programs. In Canada, teachers reported significant reductions in internalizing behaviors for participants in a treatment group ($n = 73$) compared to waitlist controls ($n = 65$), following 12 weeks of Art Therapy among immigrant and refugee youth aged 7–13 (Rousseau, Drapeau, Lacroix, Bagilishya, & Heusch, 2005). Further, treatment recipients reported higher self-esteem post-intervention compared to controls in this study, where this effect was stronger among males. However, assignment to treatment or control groups was not random, but based on which school the student attended (Rousseau et al., 2005). This, together with a lack of long term follow-up measures beyond the 2-week post-intervention test, and that 32% of participants were born in Canada and therefore not directly affected by war, suggests that more research is needed before generalizations about the efficacy of this intervention among war-affected youth can be made. In another study, a group-based music therapy program was delivered to 31 refugee adolescents of various backgrounds settled in Australia (Baker & Jones, 2006). Measurements were taken at five time points over 20 weeks, and results suggested that only teacher-reported classroom externalizing behaviors reduced significantly over the entire course of therapy, while no differences were reported for adaptive behavior skills, internalizing behaviors, or school problems (Baker & Jones, 2006). Moreover, the small sample sizes for both studies ($n = 30$ and $n = 31$, respectively), together with the lack of a control group, follow-up measures, and having only teacher or youth reports on symptoms, limits the conclusions that can be drawn about the validity and efficacy of these interventions among refugee youth.

School-based group Cognitive Behaviour Therapy (CBT) has been implemented with varying success. CBT incorporates psychoeducation related to posttraumatic stress reactions, relaxation, behavioral activation, problem solving and cognitive restructuring. In the UK, a small controlled trial testing the effectiveness of the CBT group-based Teaching Recovery Techniques (TRT) (Diab et al., 2015; Qouta et al., 2012) demonstrated significant improvements in PTSD symptoms for the treatment group at post-intervention assessment (Ehntholt, 2005). However, limited follow up data 2 months later suggested that gains were not sustained (Ehntholt, 2005). Indeed, another randomised controlled trial evaluating TRT was conducted in Australia with 82 refugee youth aged 10–17, of various backgrounds (Ooi et al., 2016). Significant post-test improvements in depression were found in the treatment group ($n = 45$) compared to waitlist controls, and these gains were maintained at 3-months follow-up. However, no differences in PTSD, externalizing or internalizing problems, and psychosocial outcomes were reported for the treatment group. A study in the U.S. compared two specific psychological interventions; Trauma Focused CBT (TF-CBT, $n = 17$), and Child Centred Play Therapy (CCPT, $n = 14$) among refugee school children (ages 6–13 years, 54.8% male) who met criteria for at least partial PTSD (Schottelkorb, Doumas, & Garcia, 2012). Only children who met full criteria for PTSD ($n = 15$) in both groups showed significant reductions in symptoms post-intervention, and there were no differences between groups (Schottelkorb et al., 2012).

Project SHIFA in the US is a multi-tiered service that combines school and community mental health resources to improve mental health outcomes for Somali refugee school children (Ellis et al., 2013). Utilizing a stepped-care approach, the first two tiers provide community and school-based skills training, while the second two tiers provide Trauma Systems Therapy (TST) for children who required more intensive clinical intervention (Ellis et al., 2013). TST combines techniques from empirically validated treatments to enhance emotion regulation skills and address environmental stressors (Ellis et al., 2013). Across the four tiers, all participants ($n = 30$) reported lower depression scores and participants in tiers 2, 3 and 4 showed a reduction in PTSD symptoms. There were no significant differences in outcomes between participants in tiers 2 compared to the higher intensity tiers 3 and 4 which may be a function of the small sample size (Ellis et al., 2013). Although the lack of a control group makes it difficult to draw conclusions, the study explored the effectiveness of a school/community based model of intervention, where existing resources were used to facilitate the work of mental health professionals.

A similar model has been delivered in the UK, where school and mental healthcare resources were combined to support refugee and asylum-seeker students with emotional and behavioral problems (Fazel, Doll, & Stein, 2009). Teachers identified at-risk children and referred them to treatment, which was delivered within the school setting. Compared to a control group of ethnic minority students and white UK-origin students, refugee students who were chosen to receive clinical intervention showed a significant improvement in hyperactivity and peer relationships (Fazel et al., 2009). The close collaboration of teachers, parents and mental health professionals highlights opportunities to engage children and adolescents in a supportive environment.

Recent findings indicate that refugee children and adolescents largely prefer to access mental health interventions at school (Fazel et al., 2016). Schools present a safe and convenient location for young people to engage with health services and establish trusting relationships with mental health professionals. Despite emerging evidence supporting the use of psychological intervention in schools, small sample sizes, the absence of significant differences between conditions and an absence of longitudinal data suggest that more research is needed to determine best practices for young refugees (Sullivan & Simonson, 2016). It is important that future evaluations include randomized allocation to conditions, control groups, and post-intervention follow-up assessments so that an evidence base on treatment effectiveness can be built. Future intervention research must take into account the large numbers of unaccompanied and homeless youth in urban settings, and determine optimal models and settings for treatment delivery, as well as the important role of parents and teachers in mediating relationships with health services.

Conclusion

Despite the difficulties inherent in conducting research with children affected by violence, existing evidence underscores the significant and long-lasting psychological impacts of exposure to war and displacement in children. It is vital that clinicians attend to a range of moderating and mediating variables such as post-conflict or resettlement stressors (Newnham, Pearson, et al., 2015), cognitive self-regulatory processes (Punamäki et al., 2011; Ziaian et al., 2012), and family environment (Betancourt et al., 2015; Panter-Brick et al., 2014), in addition to the severity and chronicity of experienced war exposures. Yet, despite the toxic trauma that characterizes violence exposure, child and adolescent survivors of war are often tremendously resilient. The experience of trauma and ongoing hardships do not result in psychological difficulties for all children (Betancourt, Newnham, et al., 2013). Many cope well with adversity, and others experience posttraumatic growth that contributes to resilient health outcomes (Kimhi, Eshel, Zysberg, & Hantman, 2010).

Preliminary evidence across a number of settings indicates promising outcomes for interventions, with the strongest evidence base supporting ‘verbal exposure’ therapies, consistent with findings from the adult literature (Tyrer & Fazel, 2014). Innovative mechanisms to overcome ethical and methodological constraints to conducting intervention research in these settings will be crucial to further iterations of feasible and efficacious interventions. In addition to interventions and longitudinal follow-up, macro level changes such as alternatives to immigration detention and the provision of temporary protection visas will help to mitigate the psychological impacts of war and displacement for children.

References

Abramowitz, S. A. (2005). The poor have become rich, and the rich have become poor: Collective trauma in the Guinean Languette. *Social Science & Medicine, 61*(10), 2106–2118. https://doi.org/10.1016/j.socscimed.2005.03.023

Ager, A., Akesson, B., Stark, L., Flouri, E., Okot, B., McCollister, F., & Boothby, N. (2011). The impact of the school-based psychosocial structured activities (PSSA) program on conflict-affected children in Northern Uganda. *Journal of Child Psychology and Psychiatry, 52*(11), 1124–1133. https://doi.org/10.1111/j.1469-7610.2011.02407.x

Annan, J., Sim, A., Puffer, E. S., Salhi, C., & Betancourt, T. S. (2016). Improving mental health outcomes of Burmese migrant and displaced children in Thailand: A community-based randomized controlled trial of a parenting and family skills intervention. *Prevention Science, 18*(7), 793–803. https://doi.org/10.1007/s11121-016-0728-2

Attanayake, V., McKay, R., Joffres, M., Singh, S., Burkle, F., Jr., & Mills, E. (2009). Prevalence of mental disorders among children exposed to war: A systematic review of 7,920 children. *Medicine Conflict and Survival, 25*(1), 4–19. https://doi.org/10.1080/13623690802568913

Baker, F., & Jones, C. (2006). The effect of music therapy services on classroom behaviours of newly arrived refugee students in Australia—A pilot study. *Emotional and Behavioural Difficulties, 11*(4), 249–260. https://doi.org/10.1080/13632750601022170

Barron, I. G., Abdallah, G., & Smith, P. (2013). Randomized control trial of a CBT trauma recovery program in Palestinian schools. *Journal of Loss and Trauma, 18*(4), 306–321. https://doi.org/10.1080/15325024.2012.688712

Bean, T., Derluyn, I., Eurelings-Bontekoe, E., Broekaert, E., & Spinhoven, P. (2007). Comparing psychological distress, traumatic stress reactions, and experiences of unaccompanied refugee minors with experiences of adolescents accompanied by parents. *The Journal of Nervous and Mental Disease, 195*(4), 288–297. https://doi.org/10.1097/01.nmd.0000243751.49499.93

Beiser, M., Puente-Duran, S., & Hou, F. (2015). Cultural distance and emotional problems among immigrant and refugee youth in Canada: Findings from the New Canadian Child and Youth Study (NCCYS). *International Journal of Intercultural Relations, 49*, 33–45. https://doi.org/10.1016/j.ijintrel.2015.06.005

Betancourt, T. S., Borisova, I. I., Williams, T. P., Brennan, R. T., Whitfield, T. H., de la Soudiere, M., … Gilman, S. E. (2010). Sierra Leone's former child soldiers: A follow-up study of psychosocial adjustment and community reintegration. *Child Development, 81*(4), 1077–1095. https://doi.org/10.1111/j.1467-8624.2010.01455.x

Betancourt, T. S., Brennan, R. T., Rubin-Smith, J., Fitzmaurice, G. M., & Gilman, S. E. (2010). Sierra Leone's former child soldiers: A longitudinal study of risk, protective factors, and mental health. *Journal of the American Academy of Child & Adolescent Psychiatry, 49*(6), 606–615. https://doi.org/10.1016/j.jaac.2010.03.008

Betancourt, T. S., & Khan, K. T. (2008). The mental health of children affected by armed conflict: Protective processes and pathways to resilience. *International Review of Psychiatry, 20*(3), 317–328. https://doi.org/10.1080/09540260802090363

Betancourt, T. S., McBain, R., Newnham, E. A., Akinsulure-Smith, A. M., Brennan, R. T., Weisz, J. R., & Hansen, N. B. (2014). A behavioral intervention for war-affected youth in Sierra Leone: A randomized controlled trial. *Journal of the American Academy of Child & Adolescent Psychiatry, 53*(12), 1288–1297. https://doi.org/10.1016/j.jaac.2014.09.011

Betancourt, T. S., McBain, R., Newnham, E. A., & Brennan, R. T. (2013). Trajectories of internalizing problems in war-affected Sierra Leonean youth: Examining conflict and postconflict factors. *Child Development, 84*(2), 455–470. https://doi.org/10.1111/j.1467-8624.2012.01861.x

Betancourt, T. S., McBain, R. K., Newnham, E. A., & Brennan, R. T. (2015). The intergenerational impact of war: Longitudinal relationships between caregiver and child mental health in post-conflict Sierra Leone. *Journal of Child Psychology and Psychiatry, 56*(10), 1101–1107. https://doi.org/10.1111/jcpp.12389

Betancourt, T. S., Newnham, E. A., Birman, D., Lee, R., Ellis, B. H., & Layne, C. M. (2017). Comparing trauma exposure, mental health needs, and service utilization across clinical samples of refugee, immigrant, and U.S.-origin children. *Journal of Traumatic Stress, 30*(3), 209–218. https://doi.org/10.1002/jts.22186

Betancourt, T. S., Newnham, E. A., Brennan, R. T., Verdeli, H., Borisova, I., Neugebauer, R., … Bolton, P. (2012). Moderators of treatment effectiveness for war-affected youth with depression in northern Uganda. *Journal of Adolescent Health, 51*(6), 544–550. https://doi.org/10.1016/j.jadohealth.2012.02.010

Betancourt, T. S., Newnham, E. A., Layne, C. M., Kim, S., Steinberg, A., Ellis, B. H., & Birman, D. (2012). Trauma history and psychopathology in war-affected refugee children referred for trauma-related mental health services in the United States. *Journal of Traumatic Stress, 25*(6), 682–690. https://doi.org/10.1002/jts.21749

Betancourt, T. S., Newnham, E. A., McBain, R., & Brennan, R. T. (2013). Post-traumatic stress symptoms among former child soldiers in Sierra Leone: Follow-up study. *The British Journal of Psychiatry, 203*(3), 196–202. https://doi.org/10.1192/bjp.bp.112.113514

Betancourt, T. S., Salhi, C., Buka, S., Leaning, J., Dunn, G., & Earls, F. (2012). Connectedness, social support and internalising emotional and behavioural problems in adolescents displaced by the Chechen conflict. *Disasters, 36*(4), 635–655. https://doi.org/10.1111/j.1467-7717.2012.01280.x

Betancourt, T. S., Yudron, M., Wheaton, W., & Smith-Fawzi, M. C. (2012). Caregiver and adolescent mental health in Ethiopian Kunama refugees participating in an emergency education program. *Journal of Adolescent Health, 51*(4), 357–365. https://doi.org/10.1016/j.jadohealth.2012.01.001

Bjorn, G. J., Boden, C., Sydsjo, G., & Gustafsson, P. A. (2013). Brief family therapy for refugee children. *The Family Journal, 21*(3), 272–278. https://doi.org/10.1177/1066480713476830

Bolton, P., Bass, J., Betancourt, T., Speelman, L., Onyango, G., Clougherty, K., … Verdeli, H. (2007). Interventions for depression symptoms among adolescent survivors of war and displacement in Northern Uganda: A randomised controlled trial. *JAMA, 298*(5), 519–527.

Bronstein, I., & Montgomery, P. (2011). Psychological distress in refugee children: A systematic review. *Clinical Child and Family Psychology Review, 14*(1), 44–56. https://doi.org/10.1007/s10567-010-0081-0

Bronstein, I., Montgomery, P., & Dobrowolski, S. (2012). PTSD in asylum-seeking male adolescents from Afghanistan. *Journal of Traumatic Stress, 25*(5), 551–557. https://doi.org/10.1002/jts.21740

Cartwright, K., El-Khani, A., Subryan, A., & Calam, R. (2015). Establishing the feasibility of assessing the mental health of children displaced by the Syrian conflict. *Global Mental Health, 2*, e8. https://doi.org/10.1017/gmh.2015.3

Catani, C., Kohiladevy, M., Ruf, M., Schauer, E., Elbert, T., & Neuner, F. (2009). Treating children traumatized by war and Tsunami: A comparison between exposure therapy and meditation-relaxation in North-East Sri Lanka. *BMC Psychiatry, 9*, 22. https://doi.org/10.1186/1471-244X-9-22

Ceri, V., Özlü-Erkilic, Z., Özer, Ü., Yalcin, M., Popow, C., & Akkaya-Kalayci, T. (2016). Psychiatric symptoms and disorders among Yazidi children and adolescents immediately after forced migration following ISIS attacks. *Neuropsychiatrie, 30*(3), 145–150. https://doi.org/10.1007/s40211-016-0195-9

Coffey, G. J., Kaplan, I., Sampson, R. C., & Tucci, M. M. (2010). The meaning and mental health consequences of long-term immigration detention for people seeking asylum. *Social Science & Medicine, 70*(12), 2070–2079. https://doi.org/10.1016/j.socscimed.2010.02.042

Diab, M., Peltonen, K., Qouta, S. R., Palosaari, E., & Punamaki, R. L. (2015). Effectiveness of psychosocial intervention enhancing resilience among war-affected children and the moderating role of family factors. *Child Abuse and Neglect, 40*, 24–35. https://doi.org/10.1016/j.chiabu.2014.12.002

Digidiki, V., & Bhabha, J. (2017). *Emergency within an emergency: The growing epidemic of sexual exploitation and abuse of migrant children in Greece*. Boston, MA: FXB Center for Health and Human Rights, Harvard University.

Dudley, M., Steel, Z., Mares, S., & Newman, L. (2012). Children and young people in immigration detention. *Current Opinion in Psychiatry, 25*(4), 285–292. https://doi.org/10.1097/yco.0b013e3283548676

Dura-Vila, G., Klasen, H., Makatini, Z., Rahimi, Z., & Hodes, M. (2013). Mental health problems of young refugees: Duration of settlement, risk factors and community-based interventions. *Clinical Child Psychology and Psychiatry, 18*(4), 604–623. https://doi.org/10.1177/1359104512462549

Ehntholt, K. A. (2005). School-based cognitive-behavioural therapy group intervention for refugee children who have experienced qar-related trauma. *Clinical Child Psychology and Psychiatry, 10*(2), 235–250. https://doi.org/10.1177/1359104505051214

Eiling, E., Van Diggele-Holtland, M., Van Yperen, T., & Boer, F. (2014). Psychosocial support for children in the Republic of South Sudan: An evaluation outcome. *Intervention, 12*(1), 61–75. https://doi.org/10.1097/wtf.0000000000000023

El-Khani, A., Ulph, F., Peters, S., & Calam, R. (2017). Syria: Coping mechanisms utilised by displaced refugee parents caring for their children in pre-resettlement contexts. *Intervention, 15*(1), 34–50. https://doi.org/10.1097/wtf.0000000000000136

Ellis, B. H., Lincoln, A. K., Charney, M. E., Ford-Paz, R., Benson, M., & Strunin, L. (2010). Mental health service utilization of Somali adolescents: Religion, community, and school as gateways to healing. *Transcultural Psychiatry, 47*(5), 789–811. https://doi.org/10.1177/1363461510379933

Ellis, B. H., Miller, A. B., Abdi, S., Barrett, C., Blood, E. A., & Betancourt, T. S. (2013). Multi-tier mental health program for refugee youth. *Journal of Consulting and Clinical Psychology, 81*(1), 129–140. https://doi.org/10.1037/a0029844

Ertl, V., Pfeiffer, A., Schauer, E., Elbert, T., & Neuner, F. (2011). Community implemented trauma therapy for former child soldiers in Northern Uganda: A randomised controlled trial. *JAMA, 306*(5), 503–512. https://doi.org/10.1001/jama.2011.1060

Fazel, M., Doll, H., & Stein, A. (2009). A school-based mental health intervention for refugee children: An exploratory study. *Clinical Child Psychology and Psychiatry, 14*(2), 297–309. https://doi.org/10.1177/1359104508100128

Fazel, M., Garcia, J., & Stein, A. (2016). The right location? Experiences of refugee adolescents seen by school-based mental health services. *Clinical Child Psychology and Psychiatry, 21*(3), 368–380. https://doi.org/10.1177/1359104516631606

Fazel, M., Karunakara, U., & Newnham, E. A. (2014). Detention, denial, and death: Migration hazards for refugee children. *The Lancet Global Health, 2*(6), e313–e314. https://doi.org/10.1016/s2214-109x(14)70225-6

Fazel, M., Reed, R. V., Panter-Brick, C., & Stein, A. (2012). Mental health of displaced and refugee children resettled in high-income countries: Risk and protective factors. *The Lancet, 379*(9812), 266–282. https://doi.org/10.1016/s0140-6736(11)60051-2

Fazel, M., & Stein, A. (2002). The mental health of refugee children. *Archives of Disease in Childhood, 87*(5), 366–370. https://doi.org/10.1136/adc.87.5.366

Fazel, M., Wheeler, J., & Danesh, J. (2005). Prevalence of serious mental disorder in 7000 refugees resettled in western countries: A systematic review. *The Lancet, 365*(9467), 1309–1314. https://doi.org/10.1016/s0140-6736(05)61027-6

Fernando, G. A., Miller, K. E., & Berger, D. E. (2010). Growing pains: The impact of disaster-related and daily stressors on the psychological and psychosocial functioning of youth in Sri Lanka. *Child Development, 81*(4), 1192–1210. https://doi.org/10.1111/j.1467-8624.2010.01462.x

Graham, H. R., Minhas, R. S., & Paxton, G. (2016). Learning problems in children of refugee background: A systematic review. *Pediatrics, 137*(6), e20153994. https://doi.org/10.1542/peds.2015-3994

Gupta, L., & Zimmer, C. (2008). Psychosocial intervention for war-affected children in Sierra Leone. *British Journal of Psychiatry, 192*(3), 212–216. https://doi.org/10.1192/bjp.bp.107.038182

Haroz, E. E., Murray, L. K., Bolton, P., Betancourt, T., & Bass, J. K. (2013). Adolescent resilience in Northern Uganda: The role of social support and prosocial behavior in reducing mental health problems. *Journal of Research on Adolescence, 23*(1), 138–148. https://doi.org/10.1111/j.1532-7795.2012.00802.x

Hasanović, M., Srabović, S., Rašidović, M., Šehović, M., Hasanbašić, E., Husanović, J., & Hodžić, R. (2009). Psychosocial assistance to students with posttraumatic stress disorder in primary and secondary schools in post-war Bosnia Herzegovina. *Psychiatria Danubina, 21*(4), 463–473.

Hassan, G., Ventevogel, P., Jefee-Bahloul, H., Barkil-Oteo, A., & Kirmayer, L. (2016). Mental health and psychosocial wellbeing of Syrians affected by armed conflict. *Epidemiology and Psychiatric Sciences, 25*(02), 129–141. https://doi.org/10.1017/s2045796016000044

Hebebrand, J., Anagnostopoulos, D., Eliez, S., Linse, H., Pejovic-Milovancevic, M., & Klasen, H. (2016). A first assessment of the needs of young refugees arriving in Europe: What mental health professionals need to know. *European Child & Adolescent Psychiatry, 25*(1), 1–6. https://doi.org/10.1007/s00787-015-0807-0

Huemer, J., Karnik, N., Voelkl-Kernstock, S., Granditsch, E., Plattner, B., Friedrich, M., & Steiner, H. (2011). Psychopathology in African unaccompanied refugee minors in Austria. *Child Psychiatry & Human Development, 42*(3), 307–319. https://doi.org/10.1007/s10578-011-0219-4

Jakobsen, M., Demott, M. A., & Heir, T. (2014). Prevalence of psychiatric disorders among unaccompanied asylum-seeking adolescents in Norway. *Clinical Practice & Epidemiology in Mental Health, 10*(1), 53–58. https://doi.org/10.2174/1745017901410010053

James, L., Sovcik, A., Garoff, F., & Abbasi, R. (2014). The mental health of Syrian refugee children and adolescents. *Forced Migration Review, 47*, 42.

Jensen, T. K., Fjermestad, K. W., Granly, L., & Wilhelmsen, N. H. (2015). Stressful life experiences and mental health problems among unaccompanied asylum-seeking children. *Clinical Child Psychology and Psychiatry, 20*(1), 106–116. https://doi.org/10.1177/1359104513499356

Jordans, M. J., Komproe, I. H., Tol, W. A., Kohrt, B. A., Luitel, N. P., Macy, R. D., & De Jong, J. T. (2010). Evaluation of a classroom-based psychosocial intervention in conflict-affected Nepal: A cluster randomized controlled trial. *Journal of Child Psychology and Psychiatry, 51*(7), 818–826. https://doi.org/10.1111/j.1469-7610.2010.02209.x

Jordans, M. J., Tol, W. A., Ndayisaba, A., & Komproe, I. (2013). A controlled evaluation of a brief parenting psychoeducation intervention in Burundi. *Social Psychiatry and Psychiatric Epidemiology, 48*(11), 1851–1859. https://doi.org/10.1007/s00127-012-0630-6

Kalantari, M., Yule, W., Dyregrov, A., Neshatdoost, H., & Ahmadi, S. J. (2012). Efficacy of writing for recovery on traumatic grief symptoms of Afghani refugee bereaved adolescents: A randomized control trial. *OMEGA – Journal of Death and Dying, 65*(2), 139–150. https://doi.org/10.2190/OM.65.2.d

Khamis, V. (2016). Does parent's psychological distress mediate the relationship between war trauma and psychosocial adjustment in children? *Journal of Health Psychology, 21*(7), 1361–1370. https://doi.org/10.1177/1359105314553962

Kimhi, S., Eshel, Y., Zysberg, L., & Hantman, S. (2010). Postwar winners and losers in the long run: Determinants of war related stress symptoms and posttraumatic growth. *Community Mental Health Journal, 46*(1), 10–19. https://doi.org/10.1007/s10597-009-9183-x

Kiss, L., Yun, K., Pocock, N., & Zimmerman, C. (2015). Exploitation, violence, and suicide risk among child and adolescent survivors of human trafficking in the Greater Mekong Subregion. *JAMA Pediatrics, 169*(9), e152278. https://doi.org/10.1001/jamapediatrics.2015.2278

Klasen, F., Daniels, J., Oettingen, G., Post, M., Hoyer, C., & Adam, H. (2010). Posttraumatic resilience in former Ugandan child soldiers. *Child Development, 81*(4), 1096–1113. https://doi.org/10.1111/j.1467-8624.2010.01456.x

Kolltveit, S., Lange, N., II, Thabet, A. A., Dyregrov, A., Pallesen, S., Johnsen, T. B., & Laberg, J. C. (2012). Risk factors for PTSD, anxiety, and depression among adolescents in Gaza. *Journal of Traumatic Stress, 25*(2), 164–170. https://doi.org/10.1002/jts.21680

Lai, B. S., Hadi, F., & Llabre, M. M. (2014). Parent and child distress after war exposure. *British Journal of Clinical Psychology, 53*(3), 333–347. https://doi.org/10.1111/bjc.12049

Layne, C. M., Olsen, J. A., Baker, A., Legerski, J. p., Isakson, B., Pašalić, A., … Arslanagić, B. (2010). Unpacking trauma exposure risk factors and differential pathways of influence: Predicting postwar mental distress in Bosnian adolescents. *Child Development, 81*(4), 1053–1076. https://doi.org/10.1111/j.1467-8624.2010.01454.x

Lorek, A., Ehntholt, K., Nesbitt, A., Wey, E., Githinji, C., Rossor, E., & Wickramasinghe, R. (2009). The mental and physical health difficulties of children held within a British immigration detention center: A pilot study. *Child Abuse & Neglect, 33*(9), 573–585. https://doi.org/10.1016/j.chiabu.2008.10.005

Malloy, H. L., McMurray-Schwarz, P., Reifel, S., & Brown, M. (2004). War play, aggression, and peer culture: A review of the research examining the relationship between war play and aggression. *Advances in Early Education and Day Care, 13*, 235–265. https://doi.org/10.1016/s0270-4021(04)13009-7

McMullen, J. D., O'Callaghan, P. S., Richards, J. A., Eakin, J. G., & Rafferty, H. (2012). Screening for traumatic exposure and psychological distress among war-affected adolescents in post-conflict northern Uganda. *Social Psychiatry and Psychiatric Epidemiology, 47*(9), 1489–1498. https://doi.org/10.1007/s00127-011-0454-9

McMullen, J. D., O'Callaghan, P. S., Shannon, C., Black, A., & Eakin, J. G. (2013). Group trauma-focused cognitive-behavioural therapy with former child soldiers and other war-affected boys in the DR Congo: A randomised controlled trial. *Journal of Child Psychology and Psychiatry, 54*(11), 1231–1241. https://doi.org/10.1111/jcpp.12094

Mercy Corps. (2014). Advancing adolescence: Getting Syrian refugee and host-community adolescents back on track. Retrieved from *https://data.unhcr.org/syrianrefugees/download.php*.

Miller, K. E., & Rasmussen, A. (2010). War exposure, daily stressors, and mental health in conflict and post-conflict settings: Bridging the divide between trauma-focused and psychosocial frameworks. *Social Science & Medicine, 70*(1), 7–16. https://doi.org/10.1016/j.socscimed.2009.09.029

Miller, K. E., & Rasmussen, A. (2017). The mental health of civilians displaced by armed conflict: An ecological model of refugee distress. *Epidemiology and Psychiatric Sciences, 26*(2), 129–138. https://doi.org/10.1017/s2045796016000172

Momartin, S., Steel, Z., Coello, M., Aroche, J., Silove, D. M., & Brooks, R. (2006). A comparison of the mental health of refugees with temporary versus permanent protection visas. *Medical Journal of Australia, 185*(7), 357.

Morris, J., Jones, L., Berrino, A., Jordans, M. J. D., Okema, L., & Crow, C. (2012). Does combining infant stimulation with emergency feeding improve psychosocial outcomes for displaced mothers and babies? A controlled evaluation from northern Uganda. *American Journal of Orthopsychiatry, 82*(3), 349–357. https://doi.org/10.1111/j.1939-0025.2012.01168.x

Newnham, E. A., McBain, R. K., Hann, K., Akinsulure-Smith, A. M., Weisz, J., Lilienthal, G. M., … Betancourt, T. S. (2015). The Youth Readiness Intervention for war-affected youth. *Journal of Adolescent Health, 56*(6), 606–611. https://doi.org/10.1016/j.jadohealth.2015.01.020

Newnham, E. A., Pearson, R. M., Stein, A., & Betancourt, T. S. (2015). Youth mental health after civil war: The importance of daily stressors. *The British Journal of Psychiatry, 206*(2), 116–121. https://doi.org/10.1192/bjp.bp.114.146324

Nickerson, A., Steel, Z., Bryant, R., Brooks, R., & Silove, D. (2011). Change in visa status amongst Mandaean refugees: Relationship to psychological symptoms and living difficulties. *Psychiatry Research, 187*(1), 267–274. https://doi.org/10.1016/j.psychres.2010.12.015

Nielsen, S. S., Norredam, M., Christiansen, K. L., Obel, C., Hilden, J., & Krasnik, A. (2008). Mental health among children seeking asylum in Denmark–the effect of length of stay and number of relocations: A cross-sectional study. *BMC Public Health, 8*(1), 293. https://doi.org/10.1186/1471-2458-8-293

O'Callaghan, P. S., Branham, L., Shannon, C., Betancourt, T. S., Dempster, M., & McMullen, J. D. (2014). A pilot study of a family focused, psychosocial intervention with war-exposed youth at risk of attack and abduction in north-eastern Democratic Republic of Congo. *Child Abuse & Neglect, 38*(7), 1197–1207. https://doi.org/10.1016/j.chiabu.2014.02.004

Onyut, L. P., Neuner, F., Schauer, E., Ertl, V., Odenwald, M., Schauer, M., & Elbert, T. (2005). Narrative Exposure Therapy as a treatment for child war survivors with posttraumatic stress disorder: Two case reports and a pilot study in an African refugee settlement. *BMC Psychiatry, 5*(1), 7. https://doi.org/10.1186/1471-244X-5-7

Ooi, C. S., Rooney, R. M., Roberts, C., Kane, R. T., Wright, B., & Chatzisarantis, N. (2016). The efficacy of a group cognitive behavioral therapy for war-affected young migrants living in Australia: A cluster randomized controlled trial. *Frontiers in Psychology*, 7. https://doi.org/10.3389/fpsyg.2016.01641

Panter-Brick, C., Grimon, M. P., & Eggerman, M. (2014). Caregiver-child mental health: A prospective study in conflict and refugee settings. *Journal of Child Psychology and Psychiatry, 55*(4), 313–327. https://doi.org/10.1111/jcpp.12167

Peltonen, K., Qouta, S., El Sarraj, E., & Punamäki, R.-L. (2012). Effectiveness of school-based intervention in enhancing mental health and social functioning among war-affected children. *Traumatology, 18*(4), 37–46. https://doi.org/10.1177/1534765612437380

Punamäki, R.-L., Qouta, S., Miller, T., & El-Sarraj, E. (2011). Who are the resilient children in conditions of military violence? Family- and child-related factors in a Palestinian community sample. *Peace and Conflict: Journal of Peace Psychology, 17*(4), 389–416. https://doi.org/10.1080/10781919.2011.610722

Qouta, S. R., Palosaari, E., Diab, M., & Punamaki, R. L. (2012). Intervention effectiveness among war-affected children: A cluster randomized controlled trial on improving mental health. *Journal of Traumatic Stress, 25*(3), 288–298. https://doi.org/10.1002/jts.21707

Ramel, B., Taljemark, J., Lindgren, A., & Johansson, B. A. (2015). Overrepresentation of unaccompanied refugee minors in inpatient psychiatric care. *Springerplus, 4*(1), 131. https://doi.org/10.1186/s40064-015-0902-1

Reed, R. V., Fazel, M., Jones, L., Panter-Brick, C., & Stein, A. (2012). Mental health of displaced and refugee children resettled in low-income and middle-income countries: Risk and protective factors. *The Lancet, 379*(9812), 250–265. https://doi.org/10.1016/s0140-6736(11)60050-0

Robjant, K., & Fazel, M. (2010). The emerging evidence for narrative exposure therapy: A review. *Clinical Psychology Review, 30*(8), 1030–1039. https://doi.org/10.1016/j.cpr.2010.07.004

Robjant, K., Hassan, R., & Katona, C. (2009). Mental health implications of detaining asylum seekers: Systematic review. *The British Journal of Psychiatry, 194*(4), 306–312. https://doi.org/10.1192/bjp.bp.108.053223

Rousseau, C., Drapeau, A., Lacroix, L., Bagilishya, D., & Heusch, N. (2005). Evaluation of a classroom program of creative expression workshops for refugee and immigrant children. *Journal of child psychology and psychiatry, 46*(2), 180–185. https://doi.org/10.1111/j.1469-7610.2004.00344.x

Ruf, M., Schauer, M., Neuner, F., Catani, C., Schauer, E., & Elbert, T. (2010). Narrative exposure therapy for 7-to 16-year-olds: A randomized controlled trial with traumatized refugee children. *Journal of Traumatic Stress, 23*(4), 437–445. https://doi.org/10.1002/jts.20548

Saigh, P. A., Mroueh, M., Zimmerman, B. J., & Fairbank, J. A. (1995). Self-efficacy expectations among traumatized adolescents. *Behaviour Research and Therapy, 33*(6), 701–704. https://doi.org/10.1016/0005-7967(94)00092-x

Sanchez-Cao, E., Kramer, T., & Hodes, M. (2013). Psychological distress and mental health service contact of unaccompanied asylum-seeking children. *Child: Care, Health and Development, 39*(5), 651–659. https://doi.org/10.1111/j.1365-2214.2012.01406.x

Schottelkorb, A. A., Doumas, D. M., & Garcia, R. (2012). Treatment for childhood refugee trauma: A randomized, controlled trial. *International Journal of Play Therapy, 21*(2), 57–73. https://doi.org/10.1037/a0027430

Smid, G. E., Lensvelt-Mulders, G. J., Knipscheer, J. W., Gersons, B. P., & Kleber, R. J. (2011). Late-onset PTSD in unaccompanied refugee minors: Exploring the predictive utility of depression and anxiety symptoms. *Journal of Clinical Child & Adolescent Psychology, 40*(5), 742–755. https://doi.org/10.1080/15374416.2011.597083

Staples, J. K., Abdel Atti, J. A., & Gordon, J. S. (2011). Mind-body skills groups for posttraumatic stress disorder and depression symptoms in Palestinian children and adolescents in Gaza. *International Journal of Stress Management, 18*(3), 246–262. https://doi.org/10.1037/a0024015

Steel, Z., Momartin, S., Bateman, C., Hafshejani, A., Silove, D. M., Everson, N., … Blick, B. (2004). Psychiatric status of asylum seeker families held for a protracted period in a remote detention Centre in Australia. *Australian and New Zealand Journal of Public Health, 28*(6), 527–536. https://doi.org/10.1111/j.1467-842x.2004.tb00042.x

Steel, Z., Silove, D., Brooks, R., Momartin, S., Alzuhairi, B., & Susljik, I. N. A. (2006). Impact of immigration detention and temporary protection on the mental health of refugees. *The British Journal of Psychiatry, 188*(1), 58–64. https://doi.org/10.1192/bjp.bp.104.007864

Sullivan, A. L., & Simonson, G. R. (2016). A systematic review of school-based social-emotional interventions for refugee and war-traumatized youth. *Review of Educational Research, 86*(2), 503–530. https://doi.org/10.3102/0034654315609419

Thabet, A., Tawahina, B., & Vostanis, P. (2009). Effectiveness of student mediation program to decrease behavioural and emotional problems in Palestinian children affected by war and trauma in the Gaza strip. *Arabpsynet E Journal, 24*(1), 50–55.

Thommessen, S., Laghi, F., Cerrone, C., Baiocco, R., & Todd, B. K. (2013). Internalizing and externalizing symptoms among unaccompanied refugee and Italian adolescents. *Children and Youth Services Review, 35*(1), 7–10. https://doi.org/10.1016/j.childyouth.2012.10.007

Tol, W. A., Komproe, I. H., Jordans, M. J., Ndayisaba, A., Ntamutumba, P., Sipsma, H., … de Jong, J. T. (2014). School-based mental health intervention for children in war-affected Burundi: A cluster randomized trial. *BMC Medicine, 12*(1), 56. https://doi.org/10.1186/1741-7015-12-56

Tol, W. A., Komproe, I. H., Jordans, M. J., Vallipuram, A., Sipsma, H., Sivayokan, S., … Jong, J. T. (2012). Outcomes and moderators of a preventive school-based mental health intervention for children affected by war in Sri Lanka: A cluster randomized trial. *World Psychiatry, 11*(2), 114–122. https://doi.org/10.1016/j.wpsyc.2012.05.008

Tol, W. A., Komproe, I. H., Susanty, D., Jordans, M. J., Macy, R. D., & De Jong, J. T. (2008). School-based mental health intervention for children affected by political violence in Indonesia: A cluster randomized trial. *JAMA, 300*(6), 655–662. https://doi.org/10.1001/jama.300.6.655

Tousignant, M., Habimana, E., Biron, C., Malo, C., Sidoli-Lebianc, E., & Bendris, N. (1999). The Quebec adolescent refugee project: Psychopathology and family variables in a sample from 35 nations. *Journal of the American Academy of Child & Adolescent Psychiatry, 38*(11), 1426–1432. https://doi.org/10.1097/00004583-199911000-00018

Tozer, M., Khawaja, N. G., & Schweitzer, R. (2017). Protective factors contributing to wellbeing among refugee youth in Australia. *Journal of Psychologists and Counsellors in Schools*, 1–18. https://doi.org/10.1017/jgc.2016.31

Tyrer, R. A., & Fazel, M. (2014). School and community-based interventions for refugee and asylum seeking children: A systematic review. *PLoS One, 9*(2), e89359. https://doi.org/10.1371/journal.pone.0089359

Ugurlu, N., Akca, L., & Acarturk, C. (2016). An art therapy intervention for symptoms of post-traumatic stress, depression and anxiety among Syrian refugee children. *Vulnerable Children and Youth Studies, 11*(2), 89–102. https://doi.org/10.1080/17450128.2016.1181288

UNHCR. (2016). *Global trends forced displacement in 2015.* Geneva, Switzerland: The UN Refugee Agency.

Vervliet, M., Lammertyn, J., Broekaert, E., & Derluyn, I. (2014). Longitudinal follow-up of the mental health of unaccompanied refugee minors. *European Child & Adolescent Psychiatry, 23*(5), 337–346. https://doi.org/10.1007/s00787-013-0463-1

Vervliet, M., Meyer Demott, M. A., Jakobsen, M., Broekaert, E., Heir, T., & Derluyn, I. (2014). The mental health of unaccompanied refugee minors on arrival in the host country. *Scandinavian Journal of Psychology, 55*(1), 33–37. https://doi.org/10.1111/sjop.12094

Vossoughi, N., Jackson, Y., Gusler, S., & Stone, K. (2016). Mental health outcomes for youth living in refugee camps: A review. *Trauma, Violence, & Abuse, 1524838016673602*. https://doi.org/10.1177/1524838016673602

Wiese, E. B. P., & Burhorst, I. (2007). The mental health of asylum-seeking and refugee children and adolescents attending a clinic in the Netherlands. *Transcultural Psychiatry, 44*(4), 596–613. https://doi.org/10.1177/1363461507083900

Yankey, T., & Biswas, U. N. (2012). Life skills training as an effective intervention strategy to reduce stress among Tibetan refugee adolescents. *Journal of Refugee Studies, 25*(4), 514–535. https://doi.org/10.1093/jrs/fer056

Ziaian, T., de Anstiss, H., Antoniou, G., Baghurst, P., & Sawyer, M. (2012). Resilience and its association with depression, emotional and behavioural problems, and mental health service utilisation among refugee adolescents living in South Australia. *International Journal of Population Research, 2012*, 1–9. https://doi.org/10.1155/2012/485956

Ziaian, T., de Anstiss, H., Antoniou, G., Baghurst, P., & Sawyer, M. (2013). Emotional and behavioural problems among refugee children and adolescents living in South Australia. *Australian Psychologist, 48*(2), 139–148. https://doi.org/10.1111/j.1742-9544.2011.00050.x

Elizabeth A. Newnham, Ph.D., is a Research Fellow in the School of Psychology at Curtin University, and at the FXB Center for Health and Human Rights at Harvard University. Her central research focus is child and adolescent mental health in settings affected by conflict, disaster or adversity, and she has led studies in China, Nepal, Hong Kong, Sierra Leone and Australia.

Shraddha Kashyap, Ph.D. is a Postdoctoral Research Fellow at the Refugee Trauma and Recovery Program at the School of Psychology, University of New South Wales (UNSW), Sydney, Australia. Her research interests include the psychological and social mechanisms underlying the mental health of refugees and asylum-seekers.

Jessica Tearne, Ph.D., is a Clinical Psychologist and researcher with a strong interest in the impact of traumatic life events on mental health. She is particularly interested in predictors of risk and resilience for developing acute and posttraumatic stress disorders and in unique risks for women and girls post trauma. Jessica holds concurrent positions with the Health Department of Western Australia and the Telethon Kids Institute, and previously worked in the Global Resilience Lab in the School of Psychology at Curtin University.

Mina Fazel is an Associate Professor in the Oxford University Department of Psychiatry and a consultant child psychiatrist in the Oxford Children's Hospital. The focus of her work has been on improving access to mental health services for vulnerable children. She has expertise in refugee mental health; working for over a decade developing mental health services for refugee children and other children who might not easily access services.

Part II
Historical Perspectives and Theoretical Frameworks in Refugee and Conflict-Affected Mental Health

Variations of Military Violence: Structures, Interests, and Experiences of War from the Nineteenth to the Twenty-First Century

Jörg Echternkamp

Abstract Wars matter also in peace time. To better understand the characteristics of war and its impact, it is most revealing to analyse the historicity of modern warfare rather than assuming a war culture as an anthropological constant. If one looks back on the past two centuries – that were also marked by longer periods of peace – a structural change in war can be identified in several problem areas: the tendency towards "total war", the idea of humanitarian interventions, technological and cultural changes, the nationalisation of war, the invention of conscription, as well as the role of civilians. Modern military history with its interest also in political, social, and cultural aspects of the past, has shed new light on war and post-war from the late eighteenth century to the present.

Keywords Military history · World War I · World War II · Violence · War · Peace · Humanitarian interventions · Nationalism · Technology · Post war · Trauma

Military history as a specialist discipline, which has been completely overhauled beginning in the late 1990s and now involves aspects of social and cultural history, has fostered the scientific debate on the history of past wars (Echternkamp, Schmidt, & Vogel, 2010; Wolfrum, 2003). This has resulted in a broadening of research horizons beyond combatants to include affected civilian populations, the interest in the "experience" of violence used (actively) or violence suffered (passively) (Echternkamp, 2012; Echternkamp & Martens, 2013), the consideration of medium- and long-term psychological problems as well as the historicisation of the medical discourse which confirmed the existence of such problems. Eventually, the collective representations of war were reflected upon, for example, with the commemoration of fallen soldiers: The many-layered focusses of interest make it worthwhile examining the historical variations of military violence across the past two centuries, which will allow for a better understanding of the mental consequences of war.

J. Echternkamp (✉)
Center for Military History and Social Sciences (ZMSBw), Potsdam, Germany

Martin Luther University Halle-Wittenberg, Halle, Germany
e-mail: joerg.echternkamp@geschichte.uni-halle.de

N. Morina, A. Nickerson (eds.), *Mental Health of Refugee and Conflict-Affected Populations*, https://doi.org/10.1007/978-3-319-97046-2_4

New types of military conflict which have emerged since the late 1990s have at times created the impression that war as such has changed and that nowadays we have to deal with "new- type" wars. One could think that military conflict no longer erupts between the major industrialised countries of the Western world, but between the less developed countries or countries where there are asymmetrical balances of power; this, again, impacts on the conduct of war. The new complexity of the battlespace is reflected by what is vaguely called "hybrid warfare": a military strategy that combines conventional and subversive, irregular warfare. The impression that, in this field of international history, we are dealing with novel warfare is nourished by the technological leap reflected in high-tech weapons systems. No question, the face of war has changed. Whether this means that war has got a *new* face is debatable (Beyrau, Hochgeschwender, & Langewiesche, 2007; Strachan & Scheipers 2011a, 2011b).

In order to understand the variations of military violence, the most important area of enquiry is therefore not human "war culture" as an anthropological constant, that is, something inherent to life (van Creveld, 2008) or the – according to the Prussian military theorist Carl von Clausewitz (1984) – unchangeable nature of war. Rather, the historicity of war in the sense of orienting historical knowledge from an interdisciplinary angle is more informative: the variations in each distinctive character of various wars. If one looks back on the past two centuries, a structural change in war can be identified in several problem areas. More meaningful than a chronological perusal of the history of events of wars is therefore to select central aspects of war and access them systematically, to take a closer look at them with the help of longitudinal historical analysis and expand international perspectives at the same time.

In an initial perusal one should ask about warfare in the wider sense: How has the use of military violence been justified? What influence has the technological development had on the conduct of war? What role does the triad of state, nation and war play? In a second step, the focus should be on the actors: How has the soldier's role changed? What share has the civilian population had in war? How "transnational" has the aftermath of war been? One may then come to a conclusion regarding the changing nature of warfare and provide an overview of structural problems in terms of security since the end of the Cold War.

War and Peace

What actually is war? To the extent that the familiar image of war between states fades, the conceptual dividing lines appear also to become indistinct; hence, it is worthwhile to give a definition first. A group of Oxford researchers has recently formulated five criteria to determine whether a particular conflict constitutes a "war". Firstly, war involves the violent use of force – though there are phases of war without active use of violence – and, as one might argue, even the threat of violence as happened during the Cold War (Gaddis, 2005). Secondly, war rests upon reciprocity: The attack launched by one side must be countered with violence by the other side, even if the force ratio is "asymmetrical". Thirdly, war requires a minimum in intensity and duration of combat, distinguishing war from a flaring border conflict. Fourthly, the actors involved in war do not function as private individuals. And fifthly, with war the warring parties pursue a goal which goes beyond warfare in itself (Strachan & Scheipers, 2011a). In modern times, there has been no shortage of wars so defined.

Still, there would be a distorted picture if, in the early twenty-first century and in the long shadow of both World Wars, one were to see the nineteenth and twentieth centuries as a heyday of continued military violence. Rather, the opposite is true. Before there is talk about war, the long periods of peace should be remembered. After Napoleon Bonaparte's last battle near Waterloo on 18 June 1815, there followed a peaceful phase of 39 years in which none of the great powers instigated war. The Crimean War (1853–1856) and the War of Italian Unification (1859) were wars limited in space; the Franco-Austrian War (1859) and the German Wars of Unification (1864, 1866, 1870–1871) did not last long. A peaceful period of 43 years, from 1871 to 1914, followed among the great powers – a then new record in European history. Even during the Age of Imperialism there was no major general war, albeit the great powers were sometimes on the verge of starting one (Dülffer, 2003; Dülffer, Kröger, & Wippich, 1997). The World Wars of 1914–1918 and 1939–1945, separated by an inter-war period of 21 years, were followed by another record: peace between the great powers lasting more than 70 years to date, which ultimately can be attributed to the existence of nuclear weapons. The tendency towards extended periods of peace became apparent as early as during the nineteenth and twentieth centuries. The three longest peaceful phases amongst the great powers happened in the years after 1815 (Gat, 2011; Pinker, 2011). By contrast, it is an illusion to believe that the number of wars has decreased considerably since 1945. Indeed, this is only true when one – under the impression of the nuclear scenario during the Cold War – considers only a major general war. Minor wars between states have happened quite as frequently, except for the short span from 1990 to 1992.

The decreased tendency for engagement in major warfare is often explained in terms of international economic development: The Industrial Revolution reduced the probability of war; prosperity was no longer a question of distribution in which, like in a number game, growth on one side happens at the cost of the other side; internationalisation of markets and their mutual dependency made national prosperity dependent on the prosperity of foreign countries; finally, the prospect of land gain – a central reason for war in pre-industrial times – lost its worth as economic openness made it possible to benefit from another territory without dominating it politically. In the light of economic competition war consequently became less attractive. Yet, the limitation of this idea lies in its premise of rationality as the importance of nationalist ideology for the conflicts of the 1990s has shown recently.

"Total War"

The total war of Germany's national socialist government has quite plainly shown that ideologies care very little about facts, be they economic or otherwise, when war must be justified. Theatres of war in World War II spanned almost all continents. Never before had so many persons – over 70 million – been mobilised for military service in armed forces whose warfare became ever more radicalised, supported by economic systems in which men and women, among them prisoners of war and forced labourers in their millions, generated a gross national product of which more than half was pumped into warfare. The brutality of warfare, in particular on the German, Soviet and Japanese sides, was also unprecedented; likewise was the radical nature of the war aims and the inhumane enemy stereotype with which they were underpinned. The fact that the idea of a "total war" was widely accepted in 1945 laid the mental ground for its final escalation: the dropping of the nuclear bomb.

Hence, the model of "total war" served historians as a heuristic tool for analysing the development of war in the past two centuries. One can study the historical dynamics of a specific military conflict from a synchronic perspective, taking into account the respective constellation of international relations and intra-societal conditions of the same time period to trace the causes, characteristic features and consequences of that conflict. However, one can also undertake a systematic comparison of modern military conflicts by way of a diachronic approach to the phenomenon of war with the wider aim of making out one, if not *the* line of historical development of war. The following features ideally indicate the totality of war: mobilisation of men and the economy for the purpose of war, the control of war-making societies, the methods of warfare and the aims of war. The model dynamics are based on the hypothesis that the wars under consideration evolved into "total war" in the course of a "radicalisation" process, that is, in the course of an ever more total manifestation of its single features; the war that most closely conforms to this ideal type is World War II (Boemeke, 1999; Chickering & Förster, 2000; Förster & Chickering, 2003; Förster & Nagler, 1997).

Such a model, however, carries the risk of a teleological reduction of 150 years of war history to the five and a half years from 1939 to 1945. Therefore, one should be reminded of the implication of the definition of World War II as a total war on the narrative logic of its historiography. While the benchmark for previous wars is their nearness to World War II, a master narrative too soon underlies modern military history and makes 1939–1945 the vanishing point, if not the crown of an evolvement which began in the late eighteenth century with the people's wars during the revolution age. There is the danger that historical contingency is disregarded and temporary peculiarities and developments which do not fit into the current interpretive pattern are too easily ignored.

Objection is raised also to the premature assumption of totality itself in respect to the war from 1939 to 1945. This is because recent research qualifies the statement that World War II was a "total" war (Chickering, Förster, & Greiner, 2010). When one looks at the elements of totality stated, it becomes apparent that their degree of totality varies. The war was geographically focused in Asia, Central and Eastern Europe. The degree of economic mobilisation and social control varied. This held true for the USA whose war was global but not total, but also for the totalitarian National Socialist regime, although the exploitation of forced labourers was undoubtedly a pinnacle of the "total" warfare. For Great Britain, a combination of state control and market mechanisms can be observed. There are even numerous examples that World War II was in some respects less total than its predecessor. For example, traditional gender roles limited the military employment of women in Germany and Great Britain. Further, those persons who became prisoners of war in Western Europe or Northern Africa had good prospects of surviving under comparatively humane conditions. The objectives of World War II were also not entirely compatible with those that define a "total war". For example, while the National Socialists' aim of a new order for Europe was based on racist criteria, the Allies of World War II in their attempts to stop German, Italian and Japanese aggression had no intention at all to fundamentally destroy the societies of their opponents – despite the repetitively cited formula of "unconditional surrender". Thus, in regards to the period 1939–1945, it appears useful to understand the intermixture of warfare instead of implying totality.

Humanitarian Interventions

In both World Wars, representing the tradition of the "just" war, the aim was that soldiers killed the enemy in the name of a common identity (the community of the national socialist people, staying with the present example). By contrast, killing in humanitarian interventions was justified in the name of a higher moral. In such cases, a military operation or the threat thereof was intended to punish crimes against humanity. One speaks of a military intervention for humanitarian reasons when three criteria are fulfilled: The intervention takes place in a foreign country; it is coupled with bringing pressure to bear or threatening the use of force, both of which are directed against the government of that country; and the intervention is, at least pro forma, aimed at preventing the death or suffering brought by the state upon large sections of its population, or at stopping or averting a repetition of such actions. The use of military violence distinguishes humanitarian intervention from other, civilian forms of humanitarian aid. Unlike state wars conducted in the national interest, wars as an expression of humanitarian intervention are a more recent phenomenon. The relative novelty of humanitarian interventions is highlighted by politicians and the military when they emphasise that their responsibility for the victims of atrocities committed in other states is a lesson learned from the genocide during World War II. But again, the impression of humanitarian intervention as a novel phenomenon is wrong as historical farsightedness shows. Military intervention in the name of humanity occurred before the end of the Cold War. Moreover, since the sixteenth century, at the latest since the Early Modern Age, there has been military intervention from outside in favour of a third party suffering under "tyranny", not continually but repeatedly (Simms & Trim, 2011; Trim, 2011, pp. 151–53). Even the term goes back to the second half of the nineteenth century when interventions were a particularly common occurrence. One should recall the numerous interventions by the great powers in the Ottoman Empire intended to establish law and order and protect Christians and Jews against violence; the *Royal Navy* operations off the coast of West Africa in the 1820s and 1830s aimed at stopping the slave trade by way of a blockade; and the US-American invasion of Cuba in 1898–1999 legitimised by the civilizational objective of freeing the Cubans from Spanish rule. A "humanitarian-minded public" evolved and was evidently pervasive in the nineteenth century; the repression of any (preferably Christian) minority was considered sufficient reason for war, and public opinion was therefore influenced accordingly. It is therefore no wonder that experts of the recent academic discipline of international law have found a new concept for this international dimension of war: "humanitarian intervention".

With the ratification of the Charter of the United Nations (UN) in 1945, the potential for humanitarian intervention seemed to have come to an end. Article 2, sub-section 4 demanded that member states "shall refrain in their international relations from the threat or use of force against the territorial integrity or political independence of any state". Article 2, sub-section 7 made it clear that the Charter did not permit any authorisation by the United Nations – let alone by single member states – "to intervene in matters which are essentially within the domestic jurisdiction of any state" (Charter, 1945). While this principle of non-intervention was widely accepted, military operations on foreign land were conducted repeatedly over the following 45 years; they were legitimised as humanitarian intervention or considered necessary to ensure compliance with the principle of non-intervention after an intervention by the other side, for example, the US invasion of Grenada in autumn 1983. After the conflict of systems ended, it appeared for a while that the concept of humanitarian intervention would be anointed by the UN Security Council. To a certain extent, humanitarian reasons served as an external justification, i.e., in press releases, for the use of military violence, for example, by the USA and other Western states in Iraq in 1991, by the USA and the UN in Somalia in 1992–1993 or by NATO in Kosovo in 1999. By contrast, the demolition of weapons of mass destruction was presented to the public as the main reason for the US and British attack on Iraq in 2003 – wrongly, as the stunned global public were to learn later. Yet, it is important to note that, since the 1990s, humanitarian aspects have been and still are widely accepted as a legitimate reason for war in practice, although they have to date not been enshrined in the theory of international law. Progress in armament technology and the illusion that it is possible to conduct clean wars with minimal loss of life have contributed to this.

Warfare: Technological Advances and Cultural Particularities

Technological quantum leaps can be observed in both conventional and nuclear warfare. Military theorists and military historians like to speak of a "revolution in military affairs" (RMA). In general, the catalysts of change are considered to be economic, technological or political change within a state or the international system. Military transformation is, according to the premises of organisational theory, the answer to these challenges and is fuelled by the purposeful adaptation of strategic and operational objectives and military training. The familiar, but by no means specific RMA formula is primarily aimed at the strategic implications of "revolutionary" developments in the field of conventional weapons technology.

Indeed, the pace of advance in military technology in the nineteenth and twentieth centuries did invariably depend on technological advancement in general. There are three distinguishable phases of accelerated change. Initially, the use of railway steam engines in the course of the first Industrial Revolution transformed army mobility and logistics. In shipping, it influenced warfare and the design of warships. At the same time, the telegraph drastically shortened ways of transmission. Secondly, since the 1880s, chemical inventions such as dynamite and combat agents, but equally electrics and above all the combustion engine had their impact on warfare. Motor vehicles, tractors and, eventually, tanks improved military mobility in World War I beyond inflexible track networks. Radio broadcasting allowed information to be transmitted without delay and independent of telegraph posts. Without the combustion engine there would not have been aircrafts, and without the electric motor no submarines. This so-called second Industrial Revolution transformed the face of warfare. When in 1914, men went to war on horseback, armed with bayonets, in colourful uniforms and with a song on their lips, the scene was reminiscent of the nineteenth century. Less than 4 years later, the first tanks and aircrafts were deployed (Leonhard, 2014).

Further, the "information revolution" changed warfare in its entirety: Radar in the late 1930s, then electro-optics, television and laser-guided rocket systems since the 1970s revolutionised the acquisition and destruction of targets as distance had almost become irrelevant. Electronic weapon systems used in both Gulf Wars – 1990–1991 and 2003 – made warfare reach its temporary pinnacle. Television broadcasting familiarised a global audience with this change. Who cannot even today remember CNN's images of zooming target-homing cameras? The contrast between state-of-the-art weapons technology on the US side and vulnerable conventional weapons on the Iraqi side could not have been more striking. Technologized determinism, that is, the belief in the crucial technological superiority of one's own weapons, was associated both with Operation *Desert Storm* in 1991 and the air war in Kosovo in 1999. Unmanned aerial vehicles and drones remote-controlled via satellite, such as the "Predator", served reconnaissance and surveillance purposes, and, when fitted with weapons they could also be employed in combat. Robots did not render human warriors obsolete, but they tempted the public in Western countries to jump to the false conclusion that warfare in the early twenty-first century had become an (almost) risk-free business (Singer, 2011). Yet, global proliferation of state-of-the-art technology, such as the Global Positioning System (GPS), the availability of global computer networks and the omnipresence of mobile telephones enabled lesser developed states to use high-tech products in conventional military conflict.

In non-conventional conflict, nuclear, biological and chemical weapons of mass destruction have massively changed warfare in the twentieth century. The proliferation of these products has turned the scales even more so than the technological development evidenced throughout the past century. Terrorism as we understand it nowadays only became possible in the late nineteenth century when explosives and automatic weapons, motor vehicles and telecommunication means enabled individuals to exercise power, to cause great damage in relation to their small number and to evoke a disproportionately large-scale response via the mass media. Nuclear weapons still played a special role as there was no defence against them – other than reciprocal deterrence. Yet, what might have worked between the superpowers during the Cold War was no longer effective where small, volatile terrorist groups were concerned. On the one hand, they were not suitable targets for retaliatory strikes. On the other hand, the logic of deterrence failed as a result of the willingness of the opponents to risk their lives on religious grounds. In contrast to the deterrent effect of strategic thinking as the operating principle in the nuclear age, i.e. *mutual assured destruction,* it is considered possible that terrorists might use nuclear weapons. Terrorism exercised by a few individuals has become a threat worldwide.

Technological innovation had functional equivalents in the past. With the invention of aviation, the battlefield did indeed obtain a "third dimension" without which there would have been no strategic bomb war. But as a strategic asset intended to demoralise the enemy's civilian population, this new tool came to play an important role in the tradition of sea blockade and siege. Time and again, strategists would integrate pioneering inventions into well-known concepts. In the 1920s and 1930s, German military integrated mechanised warfare into familiar concepts of operations, and as a result, operation planning for World War II was equivalent to a "Schlieffen plan on wheels" (Vardi, 2011). The simultaneity of old and new characterised also the individual soldier. The clash of conventional military virtues and traditions on the one hand, and the use of modern technology on the other hand revealed the ambivalence of "modern warriors" as becomes apparent in the example of air force pilots (Kehrt, 2010). While the military was at first skeptical about the military use of airplanes, it was not before long that the new technique was ideologically exploited as a symbol of national power and progress. Controlling the technique, pilots were considered the 'new heroes'combining older virtues such as courage and officiousness with the handling of modern technical problems. At the same time they served as a contrast to the anonymous death on the battlefield.

The respective military culture did not only set the course for change, but promoted the belief in continuity with the intention to gloss over disruptions and imponderabilities. According to this interpretation, strategic procedures are not so much a function of technological progress or of security developments, but rather a function of the deep-rooted cultural patterns of military command and control (the military culture) or of security politics (the strategic culture) (Hull, 2005; Kier, 1997). The undeniable influence technological progress has on the changing character of warfare should therefore not be overestimated. What should not be underestimated, however, is another influential factor: the redefining of the link between warfare and state in the early nineteenth century.

Nationalisation of War

The history of war has always been the history of states at the same time. The changing character of war since around 1800 should therefore be understood also as a change in its relationship with the state. Taking a closer look, it becomes clear that there is a connection with the changing character of the concept of state itself. As the state was progressively defined as a *nation* state, the image of war took a new shape. The concept of nation and nation state had an impact on the interdependence of domestic and foreign politics, as well as on the military aspects of state and foreign policy. Modern nationalism, with its ideological idealisation of military violence, made the nation a community of fighters and war its instrument of action (Echternkamp, 1998; Langewiesche, 2010). The nationalisation of the military – and the militarisation of the nation – was the reason why violent conflicts of the nineteenth and twentieth centuries changed completely in character. For minorities, however, war was often the litmus test for their national affiliation; in particular in those cases when they were suspected of fighting for the opposing side in the name of a superior religion or ideology, with the opposing side being the representation of that very religion or ideology. Many German Jews, for example, sought to become equal citizens through participation in the Franco-Prussian War of 1870–1871; at the same time, they saw themselves exposed to accusations of sympathising with France which had been regarded as the pioneer of Jewish emancipation since the French Revolution (Krüger, 2006).

Initially, civil wars were also characterised by an often Marxist-charged nationalism. The aim of mass mobilisation was to impose state structures in those regions which were controlled by insurgents. The latter either turned against the national idealisation of war or used it themselves; this happened frequently in the wars of decolonisation after 1945. With the end of the Cold War, the link between nation and civil war dissipated. Since then, the ideology of rebels has been drawing from the sources of local or transnational identities. Where the ideology pursues terrorist aims, it has no longer anything in common with the insurgency oriented towards *state-building* based on the Marxist-nationalistic pattern (Kalyvas, 2011). Unlike warlords of the early modern period, present-day warlords are not concerned about playing a role on the central political stage; hence why they prefer to operate on the periphery of a state (Marten, 2011).

Recently, colonial wars have increasingly become the focus of researchers as a violent form of transcultural conflict, which carries military violence not only beyond state frontiers but also beyond cultural frontiers. In the era of imperialism and colonial expansion, the violent clash of opponents who had until then not known of each other, could also lead to a better mutual understanding. For instance, both sides learned about each others armament and doctrine – a learning process under the conditions of hostility. This is true for the assaults of German colonial troops in East Africa against the ethnic group of the Hehe in 1891; and is relevant even more so for terrorist groups such as Al Qaida whose anti-Western ideology is not opposed to using Western strategies and weapons (Bührer, Stachelbeck, & Walter, 2011; Walter & Kundrus, 2012).

The impression that asymmetric warfare is a novelty is based on the unspoken assumption that the war of states is typologically the normal case. But the direct link between state and war was an historical exception limited to the relatively short period of 200 years from 1750 to 1950. If one focusses on the delineated nationalisation of state and war in the wake of the French Revolution, the duration of irregularity is reduced again by almost 50 years. The triad of war, state and nation continues to be helpful as an analytical category for a military history beyond the concept of nation, albeit it has lost its real meaning in historical terms since the 1990s at the latest.

The downside of the nationalisation of war is the internationalisation of attempts to contain war. Multinational organisations such as the League of Nations, founded after World War I and based in Geneva (1920–1946), and the succeeding United Nations (UNO) were and still are intended to ensure permanent peace worldwide through mediation in conflicts and monitoring of peace treaties. After the seminal catastrophe of World War I – "the war that will end war", as British writer H. G. Wells had hoped – peace was defined as a normal condition between states. The fact that these multilateral security systems depend on those very systems to avert military violence has from the beginning been a paradox – and a reason for their repeated failure. The nationalisation of war not only had an impact on the relationship between belligerent powers. When a "nation" went to war, the role of the respective national players also changed; and that again impacted indirectly back on the interstate conflict. In this context, a distinction should be made between the military and the civilian population.

The Military and Conscription

Hand in hand with the technological progress and the national idealisation of war, the soldier's professional profile had been undergoing change since the turn of the nineteenth century – an inner-state change which was closely linked with the shaping of state structures. The political and societal upheavals of the French Revolution also led to radical structural change in Europe's military organisations (Planert, 2009). In particular, two de facto intertwined developments should be distinguished for a better understanding.

On the one hand, the introduction of general conscription henceforth allowed mass armies to be raised. Those who believe that wars fought between 1782 and 1815 marked dramatic change in warfare in-between the Early Modern Age and the nineteenth century are influenced by contemporary propaganda. A closer look shows that these wars were not the first "total wars" (Bell, 2007) but rather the last grand wars in which the tactics and technology of the early modern age were still used. Soldiers would march or ride on horseback to the battlefield, fight mostly with muskets and swords and act on order only. Natural circumstances, such as terrain, weather and seasons, had considerable influence. The revolutionary and Napoleonic wars therefore do not mark the beginning of a new era, but rather the end of an epoch (Chickering & Förster, 2010). What was new was how the state, its gendarmerie and its administration "managed" war, taking into account the Enlightenment concept of modern bureaucracy, in particular by using the much hated conscription to mobilise the rural population (Forrest, 1989). The sheer number of soldiers deployed in conventional war around 1814 was a ground-breaking change.

On the other hand, the self-image and external perception of soldiers underwent change. Far from hiring themselves out as mercenaries, men would go into battle for their "nation"; to protect one's own "people" and to defend the independence of one's "country", as was the motto of the patriots in uniform. A new enemy perception also emerged. According to the ideological idealisation, soldiers in the opposing ranks were no longer comrades of the same trade, but "enemies". The army in which they served was regarded as the military instrument of a hostile people.

In intra-societal terms, conscription can be seen as an initiation rite for entering the world of adult citizens. Not so much aristocratic descent, but personal bravery and know-how were the decisive criteria for the selection of officers; the social opening of the officer corps to the educated classes was the consequence. Conscription, which was maintained in most territories after the end of the anti-Napoleonic period, strengthened the three-level hierarchy of officers, non-commissioned officers and the rank and file. Unlike up to and including the eighteenth century, soldiers henceforth lived in barracks. Life in military installations, which was both isolated and controlled, made the army a "school of the nation". The revolution of 1848–1849 which started out from France showed that the army was resistant to liberal or even democratic ideas as the military obediently moved in on the civil militias (Müller, 1999). The more the nineteenth century society can pointedly be described as a "nation in barracks" due to conscription (Frevert, 1997, 2004), the greater the influence that the military and war had as a power on shaping the gender order can be ascribed. Certain images of men and women were associated with their mobilisation for war and, in turn, found their way into the national identity. War had a male connotation: Soldierly virtues were considered male virtues, heroes were men (Hagemann, 2002; Schilling, 2002).

National conscription also politicised the soldiers' role. In contrast to the more artisanal self-perception of the mercenaries who, in the pre-modern age, had made commercial military service an international business, soldiers of the modern age were supposed to identify with the political system of the state whom they served so that they were no longer suited as manpower on the international market. In other words, military professionalism alone was insufficient to qualify soldiers for modern warfare. In the case of the twentieth century, this is clearly apparent in relation to Germany. Be it the national socialist warrior in the "Third Reich", the "citizen in uniform" in West Germany or the "socialist soldier personality" in East Germany: Despite all normative differences the functional equivalence of these models cannot be overlooked. In this context, national and international conditions were also intertwined.

Internally, such a model limited the recruitment of qualified men (and women); externally, it defined and stabilised the delimitation among "comrades". There was one thing all military still had in common – to be distinct from "civilians".

Civilian Populations in War: Victims or Combatants?

At first glance, civilians have nothing to do with war, as they are defined as not being members of the regular armed forces of a particular country, nor are they members of the armed troops of non-governmental parties in a civil war. In theory, military violence in an ideal war is always a matter for combatants. However, wars were and are not conducted in unpopulated areas. In practice, non-combatants are involved in combat in many ways. In World War II, they fell victim to acts of war primarily because of the aerial war. The civilian experience of war was to a large extent shaped by life in an air-raid shelter. Elderly men, women, and children spent night after night in the bunkers. While at times they waited for the sirens, at other times they went there right after work or school to feel safe. They ate in the shelter and slept there, next to family, friends, or strangers. Evacuation to the countryside was another way to save one's life. Civilians also became directly involved in warfare when their encircled city was supposed to be defended at all costs. For example, when, by the end of World War II, Hitler declared the city of Breslau to be a "fortress" with the regional party leader as "battle commander". Thousands of civilians died or were wounded during the siege or after they were forced to leave their homes in the middle of the winter of 1944/1945.

Vice versa, the military could make deliberate use of civilians as a means of warfare. Letting civilians suffer or even starve to death to achieve military and/or political goals is one such example. Napoleon Bonaparte's large-scale embargo of British trade, the Continental blockade starting in 1809, is a case in point. Aiming to defeat Britain by destroying its trade, he brought about suffering amongst the British people when the import of food and raw materials dropped while the price of staple food increased. In the twentieth century the siege of Leningrad by the German Army Group North is an even harsher example of how civilians were used as a means of warfare. The military blockade started on 8 September 1941 and was lifted only on 27 January 1944. Regardless of a small land corridor, those 872 days are considered not only the longest, but also the most destructive siege in history with the largest loss of life in a modern city. The blockade caused extreme famine and led to the deaths of up to 1.5 million civilians and soldiers as well as the evacuation of 1.4 million people, mostly women and children, many of who died on the run (Ganzenmüller, 2005). Placing non-combatants deliberately in combat targets has become yet another way to drag civilians into warfare, despite the fact that this practice is illegal according to the 1949 Geneva Conventions. For example, following the Iraqi invasion of Kuwait in 1990, Iraq's dictator Saddam Hussein used hundreds of civilian citizens of Western countries as human shields in order to prevent those countries from taking part in military operations against Iraq.

Mass rapes occurred throughout World War II, mostly, but not only, committed by Red Army soldiers entering German territory during their last battles against the German troops. Raping German women can be understood as one way to humiliate and demoralize the enemy by 'stealing' the women from their husbands and harming their dignity. Rape as an instrument of warfare was also utilized by Serb troops in the war between Serbia and Kosovo 1998/1999. At least 20,000 women were raped prior to NATO intervention. The number of victims was most likely much higher, as many women might not have come forward due to feelings of shame surrounding the sexual assaults by foreign soldiers.

Population transfer has been a war-related means to make newly won territories ethnically homogeneous. This so-called ethnic cleansing was at the core of Nazi ideology and led to the deportation and killing of millions of people, especially in Eastern Europe. Ethnic cleansing has been closely linked to mass atrocities and genocide. In addition to the Nazi context, the term was also used by journalists to describe forced migration during the Yugoslav Wars of the 1990s.

Children are particularly prone to be used for warfare. In Asia and Africa, thousands of children have served as child soldiers. They were recruited by force or joined armed groups out of desperation. Boys served as messengers, fought on the front line or took part in suicide missions while girls were forced into sexual slavery. In South Sudan, for instance, hundreds of teenagers aged 14–17 were abducted in 2013 and forcibly recruited into the ranks of both government and rebel forces. Among refugees, unaccompanied children have become a particularly vulnerable group. During the first half of 2016, Greek authorities registered more than 3300 asylum-seeking and migrant children who escaped armed conflicts in Syria, Afghanistan, and Iraq without their parents. The kidnapping of schoolgirls by the terrorist organization Boko Haram in Nigeria on the night of 14–15 April 2014 is another case in point.

However, it would be short-sighted in this context to think of civilians only as victims of war. More long-sighted would be a concept which assumes the ambivalence of the civilian situation, which would do greater justice to the diverse roles of civilians in war. Indeed, civilians have played a range of roles in warfare: civilians observed war, supported war, participated in war or fell victim to war. Historians have previously highlighted mainly the passive role of civilians as suffering objects of warfare: as targets in strategic bomb wars or as hostages in the opponent's hands, either in occupied territories or in internment camps. Civilians as acting subjects of war is an emerging area in historical research. This may be related to the legal situation in which the "civilian" did not appear for a long time. Only the Fourth Geneva Convention in 1949 explicitly mentioned and put under protection the civilian population – here: in the hands of the opponent. In 1977, this Convention was extended with the first Additional Protocol and other agreements. The term "civilian" now defined *ex negativo* any person who could not be a prisoner of war. In general, the following rule has since then been applied: A distinction must always be made between civilian population and combatants, and acts of war may be directed against military targets only, indiscriminate attacks are forbidden (Art. 48, 51). Since World War II, the protection of civilians has repeatedly been the reason for respective legislation. International courts of justice count "crimes against the civilian population" as war crimes; the criminal offence "crimes against humanity" applies exclusively to civilian populations; the Ottawa Treaty of 1997 forbids anti-personnel mines, which in particular affect civilian populations long after the end of combat action. However, the discriminatory power of the concept "civilian" still reached its limits where individuals, who were not members of armed forces or part of a *levée en masse*, were involved in combat action: as partisans, as "human shields" or as civilian sub-contractors for formerly military tasks. A problem is also the fusion of identities when civilian staff of non-governmental organisations (NGOs) work side by side with military personnel within the framework of peace-building measures.

It has consequently become unclear what exactly non-combatants are. Their status eroded in the "total war" with its national community of fighters. Was the civilian worker in an armament factory not a legitimate target? Was the suicide attacker, possibly a child, a combatant or not? What about farmers who supply war-essential foodstuffs? After the Nazi regime's war based on race ideology, the dropping of nuclear bombs on Hiroshima and Nagasaki marked the historic moment at which the national security of the one side was supposed to legitimise the massive killing of innocent civilians on the other side. In this final act, not in its contentious deterrence function during the Cold War, lies the actual importance of the bomb (the USA and the USSR would most likely not have launched a war against each other, even without the existence of the bomb, such is the counterfactual argument) (DeGroot, 2011; Heuser, 1999; Mueller, 2010, pp. 29–54).

Three further developments had long before 1945 contributed to this tendential rapprochement, even exchangeability of military personnel and civilians, which Raymond Aron observed in 1951. Firstly, war became a media event. Media brought war dauntingly close. In the almost 40 years before World War I was triggered, reporting about the wars in the Balkans gave many newspaper readers in Europe a premonition that any future war would affect also the civilian populations to a much greater extent than previously (Daniel, 2006; Keisinger, 2008). The British Empire's Boer Wars, to give another example, featured constantly in the Austrian and German press. In their reports from the theatres of war, newspapers and magazines formed a hostile picture of Britain for German readers; they were sympathetic with the Boers as they were allegedly ethnically close (Bender, 2009). At the same time, the popular war paintings in monarchic national style also shaped the image of war (Arbeitskreis Historische Bildforschung, 2003; Parth, 2010). With their battlefield pictures, their presentation of war episodes, military parades and topoi such as death and wounding, the painters of war created a specific image of war for the public at large.

Secondly, women and children were involved in combat action. On the one hand, the mobilisation and self-mobilisation of women for regular and irregular combat – a neglected field of research – made women become a part of the fighting forces: Polish and Ukrainian female legionnaires in World War I, female Red Army soldiers in the Soviet armed forces and "gunwomen" in the German Wehrmacht are some examples (Latzel, Maubach, & Satjukow, 2011). On the other hand, women played their part in resistance movements against occupation regimes: In World War II, for example, as partisans in Yugoslavia or as members of the Résistance in France (von List, 2010). Even children did not only feature as passive victims of war fighting, but were misused as child soldiers to commit acts of violence as is well known from African theatres of war (Dahlmann, 2000).

Thirdly, the raping of women in war zones or in occupied territories mentioned above also underscores the rapprochement of military personnel and civilians. The connection between sexual and war-related violence for instance becomes apparent in the different way of punishing sexual offences committed by German military personnel in Western and Eastern Europe where rape was downplayed or, partly, tolerated in the context of the "war of annihilation" (Beck, 2004). In early 1945, it was mainly the Red Army soldiers who spread fear and terror among women of all age groups as they committed rape on a massive scale during their advance on Berlin. This experience of violence created a vast gulf between personal experience and official liberation rhetoric in the Soviet occupation zone, later East Germany, and was a burden for the relationship between the Germans and their Soviet "liberators".

Without mental acrobatics, the theoretical distinction between (military) combatants and (civilian) non-combatants cannot, for sure, be maintained in the practice of military violence. To dissolve the distinction of "civilian" and "military" is considered a new development. What calls in question this pattern of interpretation is the fact that civilians are assumedly put on the same level as non-combatants, and also the fact that the number of civilian deaths in previous wars, not least the colonisation and decolonisation wars, cannot be exactly determined because statistics are imprecise and civilian war casualties were not counted; all in all, the definition thereof was vague. But even though more civilians might have lost their lives in military conflict in the late twentieth century than in the first half of that century, the total number of dead would be lower because of the decreased number of conflicts.

The "wartime experience" of both groups, soldiers and civilians, impacted back on the inter-state relationship. Individual interpretations of events and the quest for their meaning to help the process of "coping" are an indication of collective patterns of assigning meaning; these became also relevant for political and military leaders (Buschmann & Carl, 2001; Schild, 2010; Schild & Schindling, 2009). Whether enthusiasm for war or war fatigue, whether confidence of victory or fear of defeat: the morale of society in war gained increasing importance in the twentieth century. It had a say in a military conflict, its continuation or discontinuation.

Refugees

War is the main reason for forced migration. The notion of refugee refers to escaping violence mostly motivated by political, nationalistic, racist, or religious ideas. In this regard the twentieth century can be considered the century of refugees. The two world wars, the Cold War, and the wars of de-colonialisation closely linked to the conflict between East and West prompted millions of people to flee from the violence of war and civil war. World War II alone forced approximately 60 million refugees, displaced persons, and deportees to leave their home; equivalent to approximately 10% of the population. This was not only true for Europe, but also for the theater of war in Asia. When the conflict between Japan, Manchuria and northern China smoldering since 1931 escalated in 1937, around 30 million people retreated from the frontline and occupation towards central and southern China. During the war between China and Japan (1937–1945) the number of refugees amounted to 100 million – clearly more than in Europe (Amrith, 2011). These numbers are much higher in comparison to the nineteenth century due to the change of warfare. Technological progress had led to a new dynamic during the "total wars" of the twentieth century. Now, within weeks or even days, the war zone could stretch out enormously and trigger waves of refugees in a flash. Internally, this holds particularly true for the new aerial warfare. The bombardments of towns blurred the lines of the war zone and mobilized millions of people who had to be evacuated before the attack or find a new place to stay after the destruction of their homes. Externally, the occupation of foreign territories made people get away from hostile troops. For instance, in the first three months after the German attack in 1914, 1.4 million Belgians – one fifth of the overall population – fled to the Netherlands, France, and Great Britain (Oltmer, 2016, p. 21). The end of war mobilized even more groups. On the one hand, prisoners of war, refugees and deportees tried to return to their hometown (if it was still there). On the other hand, the fact that in the winners' states minorities stood in the way of an ethnically homogeneous territory also caused people to escape from persecution.

In the second half of the twentieth century, during the Cold War, Asia and Africa became the continents of military conflicts. Here, so-called proxy wars caused mass escapes. In the early 1950s, the Korean War compelled millions of people to leave their homes. During the Vietnam War the United States used deportation as a means of warfare; when the war was over in 1975, again hundreds of thousands of Vietnamese left their country now under communist rule, especially between 1979 and 1982. Those 1.6 million Vietnamese men, women, and children who tried to reach secure foreign countries crossing the South China Sea by boat were described as "Boatpeople". The erosion of Dutch, French, and Portuguese imperial rule starting in the late 1940s led to new waves of migrants. Ironically, settlers and local elites who had cooperated with the colonial power came to Europe for the first time (Smith, 2002). Wars and civil wars have had a global impact because they made people flee to countries very far away. During the Russian Civil War, for example, Russians settled in towns as far away as Shanghai. In the first half of the twentieth century, the United States became the most important destination for refugees from Europe. In the 1980s it was the Soviet-Afghan conflict that prompted another mass escape. In order to get away from Soviet occupation, up to six million Afghans, about one third of the population, went mostly to Pakistan (more than three million by 1988) and, to a minor degree, to Iran (2.2 million). The war between Iraq and Iran (1980–1988) increased the number of refugees significantly. Since the 1980s, Afghanistan, Pakistan, as well as the regions in the Far and Middle East have turned into the most crucial areas of war until today. Primarily due to the change of warfare, civilians have become victims of war in many ways. Their experiences of military violence have changed their lives, just like how refugees have left their mark on conflict and post-conflict societies.

Post-war Situation

The cessation of warfare is not the end of the war. In any case, the end of war can no longer be fixed on a particular date such as the armistice or the signing of a peace treaty. Since the late twentieth century, security and strategic planning is based on the assumption that war and peace are the outer points that determine the parameters of a complex transformation process; particularly, as the modern concept of peace goes far beyond the mere absence of war, and is generally understood to include justice, political stability and "security" on a comprehensive scale. Wars have shaped the history of the international system, of the relations between states and societies and their networks far beyond the cessation of military operations. Not only the material and human losses and millions of war invalids – 2.7 million in Germany alone after the World War (Kienitz, 2008) – at the national level should be considered in this context, but also the transnational spaces which, in the long run, shaped the mutual perception of the parties involved as a consequence of the war and left their mark on international relations. Recent research focusses on three consequences of war which are of international importance: war captivity, occupation and *Transitional Justice*.

Firstly, soldiers were taken prisoner while World War I was still ongoing. Between 1914 and 1918, approximately eight to nine million soldiers were taken prisoner by the enemy (Oltmer, 2005; Overmans, 2008, 2014). After World War I, the last German, Austrian and Russian soldiers returned home in 1922. After World War II, the unresolved issue of the late returnees was one of the domestic and foreign-political problems the young state of West Germany was facing up until the mid-1950s (Echternkamp, 2014). For the Soviet leadership, the German prisoners of war in the Gulag served as a bargaining chip in their foreign-political power game. International complications were caused also by deserters who on foreign territory had defected to the enemy and were playing a role in the enemy's policy of occupation, as for example, former members of the "National Committee of a Free Germany" (*NKFD*) did (Koch, 2008). War captivity on a massive scale was not simply the sum of individual fates, but also a national and international problem with domestic and foreign-political ramifications. For an international organisation such as the Red Cross, this was a field in which they became actively involved.

Secondly, foreign troops often stayed as occupying powers in the enemy's territory beyond the end of war – for over 40 years, US and Soviet forces were stationed in West and East Germany, respectively (Müller, 2011) –, and were part of the international web of relations as much as they were part of the populations' everyday life. During this period of temporary foreign military rule, occupiers and occupied influenced each other. As international comparisons have shown, occupation can be interpreted as a forced encounter with the "others" which will always impact on the political, societal and cultural situation and gender relations. This, for example, held generally true for the southern states occupied by the US Army during the *Reconstruction* phase in the nineteenth century, as well as for Norway occupied by the German *Wehrmacht* in the twentieth century (Kronenbitter, Pöhlmann, & Walter, 2006). Sexual contacts between soldiers of the occupying forces and women of the occupied society were a taboo until far into the 1990s. Only very recently did historians find out how different societies stigmatised these women and the "war children" after the end of the war.

Thirdly, attention is given to the political and legal "cleansing" where the end of war coincides with regime change from a dictatorship to a democratic system. In the national and international context, the focus of attention is on addressing and reappraising the crimes committed and on stabilising a post-war order through a civil society; the overall aim is to achieve reconciliation within the society and internationally. The term *Transitional Justice* brings together various approaches which include legal proceedings, historical clarification and compensation, as well as the removal from office of personnel handicapped by their political past. The International Military Court of Justice at Nuremberg in 1945–1946 is the best-known example for the attempt at addressing war crimes of a former enemy by using legal means (von Lingen, 2009).

Conclusions

War changed in the nineteenth and twentieth centuries – how could it have been otherwise? But as historians' research on war has shown, this change did not always take a linear course, because development was happening in oscillations or at different rates. Change in military history does not always signify progress. Moreover, change as regards war is sluggish. While the end of the Cold War had drastic and long-term implications for the international system of states, it did not bring about a paradigm shift in the practice of war (Strachan & Scheipers, 2011b). A retrospective review of the changing character of war since the nineteenth century therefore allows for the methodological insight that a distinct presentation of its history in terms of dichotomous indicators is not feasible. Familiar dichotomies, such as (military) combatants / (civilian) non-combatants, former/recent wars or war/peace have dissolved in historical practice in favour of hybrid forms. This is also the conclusion reached by Strachan and Scheipers (2011a).

The end of the Cold War produced a contradiction. While the majority of people in the Western world reject military force in general, are concerned about "collateral damage" among innocent civilians and no longer understand the erstwhile war pathos, European governments show a growing willingness to use military means in the context of voluntary intervention on behalf of the European Union, the United Nations Organisation and NATO, as it did and still does happen in former Yugoslavia, in Afghanistan and off the coast of Africa (Deighton, 2011). Military operations, they now say, are a legitimate instrument to uphold internationally valid standards of behaviour for the purpose of a peaceful, just and functioning system of states. What astonishes at first glance is that the post-heroic attitude of large sections of the Western population and the wide-spread feeling, fostered by live reporting, of something needing to be done in view of striking injustice and hardship are two sides of one coin. This contradiction adds an underlying tension to the new security policy. Following a schematic shift, "security" has become a household term. What is meant in this context is a combination of military operation, civilian *peacekeeping* and social and economic reform. NATO, having lost its defensive *raison d'être* at the end of the conflict of systems, uses the offensive out-of-area operations to seek a new justification for its existence in the name of security.

This brief review of the history of war and warfare has shown that non-combatants are involved in combat in many ways: While civilians also play active roles in the war effort, the majority suffer as passive victims of blockades and bombardments, of ethnic cleansing, and/or of mass rape. Sometimes, civilians were deliberately used for warfare as child soldiers or human shields. Millions of them were separated for a long time from their homes and families as victims of deportation and forced labour, because they had to be evacuated or were retained in internment camps.

War-related violence is inextricably linked to the increasing number of refugees worldwide and the associated problems faced by refugees, whether it be scaping from the war zone, returning to one's home or moving on to find a new peaceful place to live. Forced migration has undoubtedly had a crucial impact on conflict and post-conflict societies. Indeed, the twentieth century can be characterised as the century of refugees. The origin of war-related escapes has shifted from Europe in the first half of the twentieth century to Asia and Africa in the second half. The increase of refugees as compared to the nineteenth century is mostly due to the advance of military technology that has led to the "total wars" of the twentieth century. While governments try to mobilize as many people as possible for the war effort, new means of warfare, especially the aerial warfare, make non-combatants suffer from combat.

References[1]

Amrith, S. A. (2011). *Migration and diaspora in modern Asia*. Cambridge, UK: Cambridge University Press.

Arbeitskreis Historische Bildforschung (Ed.). (2003). *Der Krieg im Bild – Bilder vom Krieg*. Frankfurt a.M., Germany: Peter Lang.

Aron, R. (1951). *Les guerres en chaînes*. Paris, France: Gallimard.

Beck, B. (2004). *Wehrmacht und sexuelle Gewalt. Sexualverbrechen vor deutschen Militärgerichten 1939–1945*. Paderborn, Germany: Schöningh.

Bell, D. A. (2007). *The first total war. Napoleon's Europe and the birth of warfare as we know it*. Boston, MA: Houghton Mifflin.

Bender, S. (2009). *Der Burenkrieg und die deutschsprachige Presse. Wahrnehmung und Deutung zwischen Bureneuphorie und Anglophobie 1899–1902*. Paderborn, Germany: Schöningh.

Beyrau, D., Hochgeschwender, M., & Langewiesche, D. (Eds.). (2007). *Formen des Krieges. Von der Antike bis zur Gegenwart*. Paderborn, Germany: Schöningh.

Boemeke, M. F. (1999). *Anticipating total war. The German and American experiences, 1871–1914*. Cambridge, UK: Cambridge University Press.

Bührer, T., Stachelbeck, C., & Walter, D. (Eds.). (2011). *Imperialkriege von 1500 bis heute. Strukturen – Akteure – Lernprozesse*. Paderborn, Germany: Schöningh.

Buschmann, N., & Carl, H. (Eds.). (2001). *Die Erfahrung des Krieges. Erfahrungsgeschichtliche Perspektiven von der Französischen Revolution bis zum Zweiten Weltkrieg*. Paderborn, Germany: Schöningh.

Charter of the United Nations, San Francisco, 26. (1945, June). http://www.unric.org/de/charta. Accessed 15 May 2015.

Chickering, R., & Förster, S. (Eds.). (2000). *Great War, total war. Combat and mobilization on the Western front, 1914–1918*. Cambridge, UK: Cambridge University Press.

Chickering, R., & Förster, S. (Eds.). (2010). *War in an age of revolution, 1775–1815*. Cambridge, UK: Cambridge University Press.

Chickering, R., Förster, S., & Greiner, B. (Eds.). (2010). *A world at total war. Global conflict and the politics of destruction, 1937–1945*. Cambridge, UK: Cambridge University Press.

Dahlmann, D. (Ed.). (2000). *Kinder und Jugendliche in Krieg und Revolution. Vom Dreißigjährigen Krieg bis zu den Kindersoldaten Afrikas*. Paderborn, Germany: Schöningh.

Daniel, U. (Ed.). (2006). *Augenzeugen. Kriegsberichterstattung vom 18. zum 21. Jahrhundert*. Göttingen, Germany: Vandenhoeck & Ruprecht.

DeGroot, G. J. (2011). 'Killing is easy': The atomic bomb and the temptation of terror. In H. Strachan & S. Scheipers (Eds., 2011b), *The changing character of war* (pp. 91–108). Oxford, UK: Oxford University Press.

Deighton, A. (2011). The European Union, multilateralism, and the use of force. In H. Strachan & S. Scheipers (Eds., 2011b), *The changing character of war* (pp. 315–332). Oxford, UK: Oxford University Press.

Dülffer, J. (2003). *Im Zeichen der Gewalt. Frieden und Krieg im 19. und 20. Jahrhundert*. Wien, Austria: Böhlau.

Dülffer, J., Kröger, M., & Wippich, R.-H. (1997). *Vermiedene Kriege. Deeskalation von Konflikten der Großmächte zwischen Krimkrieg und Erstem Weltkrieg (1856–1917)*. Munich, Germany: Oldenbourg.

Echternkamp, J. (1998). *Der Aufstieg des deutschen Nationalismus 1770–1840*. Frankfurt a.M, Germany: Campus.

Echternkamp, J. (2012). Krieg. In J. Dülffer & W. Loth (Eds.), *Dimensionen internationaler Geschichte* (pp. 9–28). Munich, Germany: Oldenbourg.

[1] The reference list concentrates on international works; country-specific expert literature cannot be considered here.

Echternkamp, J. (2014). *Soldaten im Nachkrieg. Historische Deutungskonflikte und westdeutsche Demokratisierung 1945–1955*. Munich, Germany: Oldenbourg.

Echternkamp, J., & Martens, S. (Eds.). (2013). *Experience and memory: The second world war in Europe*. New York, NY: Berghahn Books.

Echternkamp, J., Schmidt, W., & Vogel, T. (Eds.). (2010). *Perspektiven der Militärgeschichte. Raum, Gewalt und Repräsentation in historischer Forschung und Bildung*. Munich, Germany: Oldenbourg.

Forrest, A. (1989). *Conscripts and deserters. The army and French society during the revolution and the empire*. Oxford, UK: Oxford University Press.

Förster, S., & Chickering, R. (Eds.). (2003). *The shadows of total war. Europe, East Asia, and the United States, 1919–1939*. Cambridge, UK: Cambridge University Press.

Förster, S., & Nagler, J. (Eds.). (1997). *On the road to total war. The American Civil War and the German Wars of Unification, 1861–1871*. Cambridge, UK: Cambridge University Press.

Frevert, U. (Ed.). (1997). *Militär und Gesellschaft im 19. und 20. Jahrhundert*. Stuttgart, Germany: Klett.

Frevert, U. (2004). *A nation in barracks*. In *Modern Germany, military conscription, and civil society*. London, UK: Berg.

Gaddis, J. L. (2005). *The cold war. A new history*. London, UK: Penguin Books.

Ganzenmüller, J. (2005). *Das belagerte Leningrad 1941–1944*. Paderborn, Germany: Schöningh.

Gat, A. (2011). *The changing character of war*. In H. Strachan & S. Scheipers (Eds., 2011b), *The changing character of war* (pp. 27–47). Oxford, UK: Oxford University Press.

Hagemann, K. (2002). *Mannlicher Muth und Teutsche Ehre. Nation, Militär und Geschlecht zur Zeit der Antinapoleonischen Kriege Preußens*. Paderborn, Germany: Schöningh.

Heuser, D. B. G. (1999). *The bomb*. In *Nuclear weapons in their historical, strategic and ethical context*. London, UK: Routledge.

Hull, I. V. (2005). *Absolute destruction. Military culture and the practices of war in imperial Germany*. Ithaca, NY: Cornell University Press.

Kalyvas, S. N. (2011). The changing character of civil wars, 1800–2009. In H. Strachan & S. Scheipers (Eds., 2011b), *The changing character of war* (pp. 202–219). Oxford, UK: Oxford University Press.

Kehrt, C. (2010). *Moderne Krieger. Die Technikerfahrung deutscher Luftwaffenpiloten 1910–1945*. Paderborn, Germany: Schöningh.

Keisinger, F. (2008). *Unzivilisierte Kriege im zivilisierten Europa? Die Balkankriege und die öffentliche Meinung in Deutschland, England und Irland 1876–1913*. Paderborn, Germany: Schöningh.

Kienitz, S. (2008). *Beschädigte Helden. Kriegsinvalidität und Körperbilder 1914–1923*. Paderborn, Germany: Schöningh.

Kier, E. (1997). *Imagining war. French and British military doctrine between the wars*. Princeton, NJ: Princeton University Press.

Koch, M. (2008). *Fahnenfluchten. Deserteure der Wehrmacht im Zweiten Weltkrieg. Lebenswege und Entscheidungen*. Paderborn, Germany: Schöningh.

Kronenbitter, G., Pöhlmann, M., & Walter, D. (Eds.). (2006). *Besatzung: Funktion und Gestalt militärischer Fremdherrschaft von der Antike bis zum 20. Jahrhundert*. Paderborn, Germany: Schöningh.

Krüger, C. G. (2006). *Sind wir denn nicht Brüder? Deutsche Juden im nationalen Krieg 1870/71*. Schöningh: Paderborn, Germany.

Langewiesche, D. (2010). Nationalismus – ein generalisierender Vergleich. In G. Budde, S. Conrad, & O. Janz (Eds.), *Transnationale Geschichte. Themen, Tendenzen und Theorien* (2nd ed., pp. 175–189). Göttingen, Germany: Vandenhoeck & Rupprecht.

Latzel, K., Maubach, F., & Satjukow, S. (Eds.). (2011). *Soldatinnen. Gewalt und Geschlecht im Krieg vom Mittelalter bis heute*. Paderborn, Germany: Schöningh.

Leonhard, J. (2014). *Die Büchse der Pandora. Geschichte des Ersten Weltkriegs*. Munich, Germany: C. H. Beck.

Marten, K. (2011). Warlords. In H. Strachan & S. Scheipers (Eds., 2011b), *The changing character of war* (pp. 220–301). Oxford, UK: Oxford University Press.
Mueller, J. E. (2010). *Atomic obsession. Nuclear alarmism from Hiroshima to Al-Qaeda*. New York, NY: Oxford University Press.
Müller, C. T. (2011). *US-Truppen und Sowjetarmee in Deutschland*. In *Erfahrungen, Beziehungen, Konflikte im Vergleich*. Paderborn, Germany: Schöningh.
Müller, S. (1999). *Soldaten in der deutschen Revolution von 1848/49*. Paderborn, Germany: Schöningh.
Oltmer, J. (Ed.). (2005). *Kriegsgefangene im Europa des Ersten Weltkriegs*. Paderborn, Germany: Schöningh.
Oltmer, J. (2016). Kleine Globalgeschichte der Flucht im 20. Jahrhundert. In *Bundeszentrale für politische Bildung* (Ed.), Aus Politik und Zeitgeschichte (66 ed., Vol. 26–27, pp. 18–25). Bonn, Germany: Editor.
Overmans, R. (2008). Das Schicksal der deutschen Kriegsgefangenen des Zweiten Weltkriegs. In R. D. Müller (Ed.), *Das Dseutsche Reich und der Zweite Weltkrieg: Der Zusammenbruch des Deutschen Reiches 1945* (Vol. 2, 10th ed., pp. 379–507). Munich, Germany: DVA.
Overmans, R. (2014). German policy on prisoners of war, 1939 to 1945. In J. Echternkamp (Ed.), *Germany and the second world war: German wartime society 1939–1945: Exploitation, interpretations, exclusion* (Vol. 2, 4th ed., pp. 733–879). Oxford, UK: Oxford University Press.
Parth, S. (2010). *Zwischen Bildbericht und Bildpropaganda. Kriegskonstruktionen in der deutschen Militärmalerei des 19. Jahrhunderts*. Paderborn, Germany: Schöningh.
Pinker, S. (2011). *The better angels of our nature: Why violence has declined*. New York, NY: Viking Adult.
Planert, U. (Ed.). (2009). *Krieg und Umbruch: Mitteleuropa um 1800. Erfahrungsgeschichte(n) auf dem Weg in eine neue Zeit*. Paderborn, Germany: Schöningh.
Schild, G. (Ed.). (2010). *The American experience of war*. Paderborn, Germany: Schöningh.
Schild, G., & Schindling, A. (Eds.). (2009). *Kriegserfahrungen. Krieg und Gesellschaft in der Neuzeit. Neue Horizonte der Forschung*. Paderborn, Germany: Schöningh.
Schilling, R. (2002). *Kriegshelden*. In *Deutungsmuster heroischer Männlichkeit in Deutschland 1813–1945*. Paderborn, Germany: Schöningh.
Simms, B., & Trim, D. J. B. (Eds.). (2011). *Humanitarian intervention. A history*. Cambridge, UK: Cambridge University Press.
Singer, P. W. (2011). Robots at war: The new battlefield. In H. Strachan & S. Scheipers (Eds., 2011b), *The changing character of war* (pp. 333–353). Oxford, UK: Oxford University Press.
Smith, A. L. (Ed.). (2002). *Europe's invisible migrants. Consequences oft he Colonists' Return*. Amsterdam, The Netherlands: Amsterdam University Press.
Strachan, H., & Scheipers, S. (2011a). Introduction: The changing character of war. In H. Strachan & S. Scheipers (Eds., 2011b), *The changing character of war* (pp. 1–24). Oxford, UK: Oxford University Press.
Strachan, H., & Scheipers, S. (Eds.). (2011b). *The changing character of war*. Oxford, UK: University Press.
Trim, D. J. B. (2011). Humanitarian intervention. In H. Strachan & S. Scheipers (Eds., 2011b), *The changing character of war* (pp. 151–166). Oxford, UK: Oxford University Press.
van Creveld, M. (2008). *The culture of war*. New York, NY: Presidio Press.
Vardi, G. (2011). The change from within. In H. Strachan & S. Scheipers (Eds., 2011b), *The changing character of war* (pp. 79–90). Oxford, UK: Oxford University Press.
von Clausewitz, C. (1984). *On war* (M. Howard & P. Paret, Eds. & Trans.). Princeton, NJ: Princeton University Press.
von Lingen, K. (Ed.). (2009). *Kriegserfahrung und nationale Identität in Europa nach 1945. Erinnerung, Säuberungsprozesse und nationales Gedächtnis*. Paderborn, Germany: Schöningh.
von List, C. (2010). *Frauen in der Résistance 1940–1944. Der Kampf gegen die 'Boches' hat begonnen!* Paderborn, Germany: Schöningh.

Walter, D., & Kundrus, B. (Eds.). (2012). *Waffen Wissen Wandel. Anpassung und Lernen in transkulturellen Erstkonfllikten*. Hamburg, Germany: Hamburger Edition.

Wolfrum, E. (2003). *Krieg und Frieden in der Neuzeit. Vom Westfälischen Frieden bis zum Zweiten Weltkrieg*. Darmstadt, Germany: Wissenschaftliche Buchgesellschaft.

Jörg Echternkamp, Dr. phil. habil., is Research Director at the Bundeswehr Center for Military History and Social Sciences, Potsdam, and Adjunct Professor of Modern and Contemporary History at Martin Luther University Halle-Wittenberg. Since 2000, he has been co-editor of the journal „Militärgeschichtliche Zeitschrift". His area of research includes European military history, history of National Socialism, research of memory cultures, as well as the history of political ideas.

Pathways to Recovery: Psychological Mechanisms Underlying Refugee Mental Health

Angela Nickerson

Abstract It has been well-established that refugees evidence increased rates of psychological disorders such as posttraumatic stress disorder (PTSD) and depression. While the contribution of pre- and post-migration experiences to refugee mental health has been extensively examined, relatively less research has focused on the mechanisms that may contribute to the development and maintenance of psychological disorders in refugees. This chapter discusses three potential mechanisms that may impact on refugee mental health, namely emotion regulation, cognitive appraisals and memory processes. Examples of research to date with refugee populations on each of these mechanisms are presented, and potential future research directions are outlined. Implications for the development of psychological interventions tailored to the refugee context are discussed.

Keywords Refugees · Posttraumatic stress disorder · Depression · Appraisals · Memory · Emotion regulation

The number of individuals forcibly displaced worldwide is unprecedented in recent history (United Nations High Commissioner for Refugees (UNHCR); UNHCR, 2017). Numerous research studies have documented the deleterious impact of persecution and displacement on refugee mental health, with refugees reporting high rates of psychiatric disorders such as posttraumatic stress disorder (PTSD) and depression (Fazel, Wheeler, & Danesh, 2005; Steel et al., 2009). The focus on prevalence rates of mental disorders amongst refugee groups, however, has obscured the consistent finding that, across communities and contexts, many refugees do not meet criteria for a psychiatric diagnosis. In addition to highlighting the resilience of refugees and asylum-seekers, this provides strong evidence that exposure to persecution and displacement does not unequivocally lead to psychopathology. In fact, most refugees do not report clinically-significant psychological symptoms following resettlement (Fazel et al., 2005; Nickerson et al., 2014; Sondergaard, Ekblad, &

A. Nickerson (✉)
School of Psychology, University of New South Wales, Sydney, NSW, Australia
e-mail: anickerson@psy.unsw.edu.au

N. Morina, A. Nickerson (eds.), *Mental Health of Refugee and Conflict-Affected Populations*, https://doi.org/10.1007/978-3-319-97046-2_5

Theorell, 2003; Steel et al., 2009; Tay, Rees, Chen, Kareth, & Silove, 2015). Despite this, relatively little is known about pathways to refugee mental health. Research to date investigating factors that contribute to psychopathology amongst refugees has tended to focus on refugee experiences, in particular exposure to pre-migration traumatic events and post-migration living difficulties. In contrast, very little is known about the psychological processes that may influence pathways to psychopathology and recovery in refugees. Understanding these basic mechanisms is of critical importance if we are to develop psychological interventions that both specifically target maintaining factors of psychopathology in refugees, and are tailored to the needs of these vulnerable populations. Although research into psychological mechanisms underpinning refugee mental health is in its infancy, we can draw from the broader literature derived from studies conducted with other trauma and adversity-exposed groups. These studies can be used to develop testable hypotheses that guide empirical research on key psychological factors that may contribute to the psychological recovery of traumatized refugees.

This chapter will describe examples of key candidate mechanisms that may underpin refugee mental health (c.f. Nickerson, Bryant, Silove, & Steel, 2011). For each of these psychological processes, the existing evidence available with refugee and asylum-seeking groups will be reviewed, potential future research directions will be outlined and implications for the development of evidence-based psychological interventions for refugees will be discussed.

Psychological Disorders in Refugees: Prevalence and Impact of Contextual Factors

A large body of research conducted over the past three decades has focused on determining the prevalence of psychiatric disorders amongst refugees. Meta-analyses estimate that between 9% and 31% of refugees qualify for a diagnosis of PTSD while between 5% and 31% of refugees qualify for major depression (Fazel et al., 2005; Steel et al., 2009). When considering these figures, it is immediately apparent that many refugees do not meet criteria for PTSD or depression. While it is likely to be the case that a substantial proportion of refugees suffer from other psychiatric disorders, or even sub-syndromal levels of PTSD or depression, there is emerging evidence that the modal response amongst refugees is resilience. For example, in a latent class analysis of symptom profiles amongst Iraqi refugees, 43% of participants had a low probability of reporting all measured PTSD and prolonged grief symptoms (Nickerson et al., 2014). Similarly, in a latent class analysis of intermittent explosive disorder, PTSD, and depression symptoms in West Papuan refugees displaced to Papua New Guinea, 49% of participants had a low probability of endorsing all assessed mental health symptoms (Tay et al., 2015). Further, in a study conducted with 75 newly-resettled refugees from Iraq, 38% of the sample met criteria for full PTSD, 29% met criteria for partial PTSD and 33% did not meet criteria for full or sub-syndromal PTSD (Sondergaard et al., 2003). Taken together, these findings suggest that, despite almost universal exposure to traumatic events and displacement, many refugees do not go on to develop significant psychopathology.

Research seeking to understand pathways to these differential mental health outcomes in refugee groups has largely focused on contextual factors. Seminal studies conducted by Mollica and colleagues demonstrated, for the first time, a dose-effect relationship such that exposure to a greater number of types of traumatic experiences was associated with more severe symptomatology amongst Vietnamese and Cambodian refugees (Mollica, McInnes, Pham, et al., 1998; Mollica, McInnes, Poole, & Tor, 1998). These results have been replicated numerous times with refugees from a variety of different backgrounds (Lie, 2002; Lindencrona, Ekblad, & Hauff, 2008; Nickerson, Bryant, Steel, Silove, & Brooks, 2010; Schweitzer, Melville, Steel, & Lacharez, 2006). More recently, researchers have sought to understand the impact of the post-migration environment on refugee mental health. This research has consistently shown that stressors encountered after displacement and/or resettlement are strong predictors of psychopathology in refugees (see Li, Liddell, & Nickerson, 2016 for a review; Porter & Haslam, 2005). Recent studies have suggested that post-displacement stressors may mediate the impact of trauma exposure on refugee mental health (Rasmussen et al., 2010; Sachs, Rosenfeld, Lhewa, Rasmussen, & Keller, 2008). Overall, research conducted to date suggests that pre- and post-displacement factors play a powerful role in influencing mental health outcomes in refugees.

Psychological Mechanisms Underlying Refugee Mental Health

Research over recent decades has substantially increased our knowledge regarding external factors that may lead to psychopathology in refugees. However, relatively less empirical attention has been paid to the internal or psychological factors that contribute to mental health outcomes in these groups. The elucidation of these factors represents an important avenue for future research as it would increase understanding of psychological factors that may moderate or mediate the impact of refugee experiences of trauma and displacement on mental health. Further, identification of psychological processes that are amenable to change would significantly inform treatment interventions that facilitate the psychological recovery of refugees following displacement.

We have previously proposed a model of psychological reactions to refugee trauma, which hypothesized psychological mechanisms that may influence the relationship between refugee experiences and mental health outcomes (Nickerson et al., 2011). This chapter expands on the role of psychological mechanisms outlined in this model as potential factors underpinning the association between refugee experiences and mental health outcomes (Fig. 1). Specifically, we propose that exposure to potentially traumatic events, ongoing threat and daily stressors in the context of war, persecution, displacement and seeking asylum impacts on core psychological

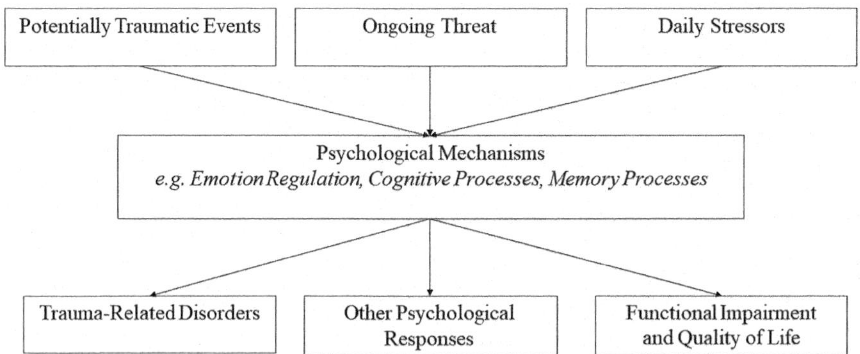

Fig. 1 Theoretical model of pathways from refugee experiences to psychological outcomes

processes. In turn, these psychological processes contribute to the development of trauma-related disorders (i.e., PTSD and depression), other psychological responses (e.g., other psychological disorders and responses such as grief, shame and guilt), and overall daily functioning and quality of life. While there is a myriad of potential processes that may be impacted by the refugee experience, this chapter will focus on three key potential mechanisms, namely emotion regulation, cognitive responses and memory processes. These psychological processes are the subject of a growing body of literature in the field of refugee mental health research, and are targeted by existing evidence-based interventions for posttraumatic stress reactions.

Emotion Regulation

Emotion regulation has been defined as the capacity to monitor, evaluate and modify emotional reactions in a way that facilitates adaptive functioning (Gratz & Roemer, 2004). Emotion dysregulation has been demonstrated to be a key factor implicated in a variety of psychological disorders including anxiety, mood, eating and substance use disorders (Aldao, Nolen-Hoeksema, & Schweizer, 2010). Studies conducted with trauma survivors have found that PTSD is associated with an impaired capacity to regulate emotional responses to stressors (Amstadter & Vernon, 2008; Kulkarni, Pole, & Timko, 2013; Sippel, Roy, Southwick, & Fichtenholtz, 2016; Tull, Barrett, McMillan, & Roemer, 2007), and that exposure to repeated interpersonal trauma confers additional risk for disrupted emotion regulation (Walsh, DiLillo, & Scalora, 2011). Further, there is a growing body of research examining the use and impact of specific emotion regulation strategies in trauma-affected groups. Studies suggest that emotional suppression is commonly used by individuals with PTSD and is associated with greater symptom severity (Amstadter & Vernon, 2006, 2008; Ehlers, Mayou, & Bryant, 1998; Roemer, Litz, Orsillo, & Wagner, 2001; Seligowski, Lee, Bardeen, & Orcutt, 2015; Shipherd & Beck, 1999).

While there is relatively less evidence regarding the use of "adaptive" emotion regulation strategies by trauma survivors, preliminary experimental evidence indicates that cognitive reappraisal (or thinking about the traumatic event in a more helpful way to reduce the intensity of an emotional response) may reduce intrusive memories in analogue samples (Woud, Holmes, Postma, Dalgleish, & Mackintosh, 2012; Woud, Postma, Holmes, & Mackintosh, 2013). Overall, the extant literature suggests that emotion regulation is strongly related to posttraumatic mental health.

Given the high rates of PTSD and exposure to repeated instances of interpersonal traumatization, it might be expected that emotion regulation difficulties are prominent in refugee groups. Research investigating emotion regulation in refugees has focused on understanding the association between specific types of emotion regulation difficulties and strategies, and mental health outcomes in refugees. For example, a study conducted with resettled refugees from a variety of backgrounds found that deficits in specific emotion regulation modalities mediated the association between refugee experiences and psychological outcomes (Nickerson, Bryant, et al., 2015). Specifically, trauma exposure was associated with difficulties engaging in goal-directed behavior and limited access to emotion regulation strategies, while exposure to post-migration living difficulties was associated with a variety of emotion regulation deficits. Lack of emotional clarity and difficulties engaging in goal-directed behavior were associated with PTSD symptom severity, impulse control difficulties were associated with anger responses and limited access to emotion regulation strategies was associated with depression symptoms. This study highlights the relationship between stressors encountered in the resettlement environment, emotion regulation difficulties and mental health outcomes in refugees.

Another stream of research has focused on the association between specific emotion regulation strategies and psychological outcomes in refugees. Two studies have investigated the association between alexithymia (difficulty identifying, describing and expressing emotional responses) and PTSD symptoms in refugees. In a study conducted with 199 North Korean refugees who had resettled in South Korea, Park et al. (2015) found that alexithymia was associated with greater PTSD symptoms. Specifically, the dose-response relationship between trauma exposure and PTSD symptoms was found to be especially strong for those with greater difficulties in identifying and expressing their emotions. A second study found that, amongst 86 resettled refugees, those with PTSD had greater difficulties identifying feelings than those without PTSD symptoms (Sondergaard & Theorell, 2004). Over a period of 9 months, increased difficulty naming emotions was associated with greater PTSD symptoms. Accordingly, alexithymia appears to be positively related to PTSD symptom severity in refugees.

Three studies have investigated the relationship between emotion-focused and problem-focused coping and mental health outcomes in refugees. A study conducted with Palestinian refugees who were former political prisoners found that emotion-focused coping (i.e., expressing emotional responses to others) was associated with lower psychological distress in the aftermath of exposure to a traumatic event, while problem-focused coping (i.e., attempting to change the situation) was related to reduced distress several months after the trauma. In a study conducted with 75 treatment-seeking refugees, emotion-focused disengagement coping (i.e., avoiding internal emotional experiences) was associated with greater PTSD symptoms, with this relationship being heightened amongst individuals who tend to see others as worse-off (Hooberman, Rosenfeld, Rasmussen, & Keller, 2010). Conversely, in a study conducted with 335 refugees resettled in the Netherlands, emotion-focused coping was related to greater quality of life – contrary to the authors' hypotheses (Huijts, Kleijn, van Emmerik, Noordhof, & Smith, 2012). Another study found that acceptance and "putting into perspective" partly mediated the association between trauma exposure and PTSD symptoms in 226 Tibetan refugees, with these strategies, surprisingly, being positively related to PTSD symptom severity (Hussain & Bhushan, 2011). An experimental study conducted with 82 refugees and asylum-seekers found that greater use of emotional suppression while viewing trauma-related images was associated with higher distress amongst torture survivors, with this pattern being especially strong for those with high levels of PTSD symptoms (Nickerson et al., 2016). In contrast, the opposite pattern was observed for refugees who had not been exposed to torture such that greater use of emotional suppression was associated with lower distress. Finally, findings from another experimental study conducted with the same sample indicated that implementing cognitive reappraisal instructions following the viewing of trauma-related images led to lower levels of intrusive memories in subsequent days for refugees high in PTSD, compared to using emotional suppression (Nickerson et al., 2017). In addition, trait suppression moderated the impact of cognitive reappraisal, with refugees with low trait suppression (and high PTSD symptoms) showing significantly lower levels of negative affect when implementing cognitive reappraisal compared to emotional suppression. This finding suggests that habitual emotion regulation may play an important role in influencing the effectiveness of implementing new emotion regulation strategies. Taken together, these studies highlight the complex association between specific emotion regulation strategies and psychological outcomes in refugees, suggesting that the efficacy of these strategies may differ across time-points, trauma exposure, refugee groups and contexts.

Despite the mixed findings to date, studies have consistently demonstrated that emotion regulation is implicated in psychopathology in refugees and other trauma survivors. These results point to emotion regulation as a potentially important target for interventions that aim to reduce posttraumatic symptomatology amongst refugees. Accordingly, in their investigation of mechanisms underlying the efficacy of cognitive behavioural interventions for PTSD in Cambodian refugees, Hinton and colleagues found that improvements in emotion regulation significantly mediated decreases in PTSD symptoms over the course of the intervention (Hinton, Hofmann, Pollack, & Otto, 2009). The impact of emotion regulation difficulties on treatment response is further exemplified by evidence that substantial emotion regulation difficulties (i.e., anger and aggression) interfere with the effectiveness of first-line trauma-focused therapy in non-refugee groups (Foa, Riggs, Massie, & Yarczower, 1995; Forbes et al., 2008). Taken together, these findings underscore the potential utility of phase-based interventions in which patients receive emotion regulation skills training prior to embarking on exposure-based interventions (Cloitre, Koenen,

Cohen, & Han, 2002; Cloitre et al., 2010). While these treatments have yet to be tested with refugees, they represent a promising direction for future enquiry.

The mixed findings from the studies reviewed above indicate that there is a need for further research to elucidate the mechanistic role of emotion regulation in refugee psychopathology, and to determine which strategies may be particularly useful, when and for whom. In terms of understanding the association between emotion regulation deficits and posttraumatic symptomatology, prospective and experimental research may be especially useful in disentangling the influence of important factors as these studies allow for inferences about causality. For example, tracking participants' emotion regulation capacity and symptom severity over time would allow us to determine whether emotion regulation difficulties indeed play a mechanistic role in the maintenance of posttraumatic stress reactions in refugees; and which deficits are most influential. To enhance knowledge regarding the strategies that may be most helpful for refugees experiencing posttraumatic stress reactions, experimental research in which individuals are randomly assigned to use specific emotion regulation strategies represents a promising direction of research that may directly inform the development of interventions tailored for refugee groups. Undertaking this research would also allow for the manipulation of context, which may shed light on how the efficacy of emotion regulation strategies vary according to circumstances. Investigating differences in emotional regulation capacity and strategies between refugees with significant psychopathology and those who do not experience psychological distress poses a unique opportunity to learn from those who are functioning well. Such an understanding could be used to inform interventions for PTSD and other disorders. In addition, there is a growing body of research indicating that emotion regulation flexibility may be more important in influencing psychological outcomes than the use of specific emotion regulation strategies (Aldao, Sheppes, & Gross, 2015), however this is yet to be examined empirically in refugees. It is important that research be conducted both with specific groups of refugees to understand the cultural influences on emotion regulation and psychopathology, and with refugees from varying backgrounds to facilitate identification of transcultural ways in which the refugee experience disrupts emotion regulation and impacts on psychological outcomes.

Cognitive Responses

There exists a vast body of theoretical and empirical literature detailing the importance of cognitive factors in predicting post-trauma psychological distress (Ehlers & Clark, 2000; Foa, Ehlers, Clark, Tolin, & Orsillo, 1999; Resick & Schnicke, 1992). The way in which traumatic events are interpreted critically contributes to psychological outcomes, with prospective research indicating that posttraumatic appraisals (e.g., about the traumatic event, the self, the future, symptoms etc.) predict subsequent PTSD severity in trauma survivors (Dunmore, Clark, & Ehlers, 2001; Halligan, Michael, Clark, & Ehlers, 2003; O'Donnell, Elliott, Wolfgang, &

Creamer, 2007). Research evidence regarding the contribution of cognitive appraisals to the disorder have also directly informed the development of efficacious interventions for PTSD (Ehlers, Clark, Hackmann, McManus, & Fennell, 2005; Ehlers et al., 2014; Resick et al., 2008; Resick, Nishith, Weaver, Astin, & Feuer, 2002; Resick & Schnicke, 1992). There is emerging evidence that interventions featuring cognitive strategies are effective in reducing symptoms of PTSD and associated impairment in both refugees (Hinton et al., 2005; Schulz, Resick, Huber, & Griffin, 2006) and post-conflict settings (Bass et al., 2013; Bolton et al., 2014).

While relatively less research has been undertaken examining the role of cognitive appraisals in contributing to posttraumatic stress reactions in refugees than in survivors of civilian trauma, those studies that have been conducted can be broadly divided into three categories. The first stream of research has focused on interpretation of posttraumatic psychological symptoms, the second has examined appraisals regarding the traumatic event itself, and the third has investigated broader appraisals regarding the nature of the world and other people.

A large body of work on the relationship between the interpretation of psychological symptoms and posttraumatic stress responses has been undertaken by Hinton and colleagues (e.g., Hinton, Chhean, Hofmann, Orr, & Pitman, 2008; Hinton et al., 2006; Hinton, Hinton, Pham, Chau, & Tran, 2003; Hinton, Hofmann, Pitman, Pollack, & Barlow, 2008; Hinton, Nickerson, & Bryant, 2011; Hinton & Otto, 2006; Hinton, Pich, Marques, Nickerson, & Pollack, 2010). Several of these studies detail how the catastrophic misinterpretation of somatic sensations (which may arise from and/or contribute to the experience of intrusive traumatic memories) exacerbate symptoms of posttraumatic stress and related disorders such as panic disorder (Hinton, Chhean, et al., 2008; Hinton et al., 2003; Hinton, Hofmann, et al., 2008; Hinton & Otto, 2006; Hinton et al., 2010). Hinton and colleagues have also demonstrated that negative cultural interpretations of nightmares (Hinton, Hinton, Pich, Loeum, & Pollack, 2009) and dreams of the dead (Hinton, Field, Nickerson, Bryant, & Simon, 2013) can lead to substantial psychological distress and the worsening of existing posttraumatic psychological symptoms in Cambodian refugees. Hinton and colleagues have published several articles and book chapters that draw on cultural conceptualizations of physical and psychological processes to inform clinicians' understanding of the mental and physical health impacts of trauma exposure (e.g., Hinton, 2012; Hinton et al., 2003; Hinton & Otto, 2006; Hinton et al., 2010). These theoretical models and empirical findings have led to the development of Culturally-Adapted Cognitive Behaviour Therapy, an intervention that combines cognitive techniques, which draw heavily on culturally-specific conceptions of physical and psychological processes, with exposure to emotional responses and emotion regulation training to reduce PTSD symptoms in refugees and patients from ethnic minority groups (Hinton, Hofmann, Rivera, Otto, & Pollack, 2011; Hinton et al., 2004; Hinton, Rivera, Hofmann, Barlow, & Otto, 2012; Otto & Hinton, 2006). This body of research definitively highlights the importance of interpretations of psychological symptoms in contributing to posttraumatic distress in refugees.

The second stream of research relating to cognitive appraisals has focused on how beliefs about the traumatic experience itself are associated with posttraumatic mental health outcomes. In a cross-sectional study conducted with torture survivors from the former Yugoslavia, Basoglu, Livanou, and Crnobaric (2007) found that perceived controllability over torture was linked to lower levels of psychological symptoms, while physical severity of torture was unrelated to PTSD or depression. In another study conducted with Palestinian former political prisoners, appraising the prison experience as being harmful and involving loss was associated with greater severity of PTSD symptoms (Kanninen, Punamaki, & Qouta, 2002). Collectively, these findings indicate that appraisals of the traumatic event(s) play an important role in refugee mental health.

A third area of research has implicated broader beliefs about the cause, society and the world in posttraumatic mental health in refugees. In a sample of resettled refugees in Switzerland, the perception that others had transgressed fundamental morals and values was found to be associated with more severe PTSD, depression and explosive anger, even after controlling for trauma exposure and post-migration stressors (Nickerson, Schnyder, et al., 2015). While this study was not conducted with refugees, a survey of 1358 survivors of the war in the former Yugoslavia revealed that fear and loss of control over life, loss of meaning in the war cause and lower levels of belief in benevolence and justice were associated with greater likelihood of having a diagnosis of PTSD (Basoglu et al., 2005). These factors, as well as greater desire for vengeance and loss of faith in God and religion were also associated with greater likelihood of having depression. While there is a need for further research conducted with refugees, these studies provide preliminary evidence that beliefs about society and the world at large may play a role in psychological outcomes in individuals exposed to human rights violations.

While there is emerging evidence highlighting the importance of cognitive appraisals in refugee mental health, this body of evidence is lagging behind compared to research available for non-refugee trauma survivors. In addition, the research conducted to date is not sufficient to provide a comprehensive understanding of how cognitive factors may mediate the association between refugee experiences and mental health outcomes. There is a need for the systematic identification of cognitive appraisals that arise from the traumatic events typically experienced by refugees (i.e., human rights violations), and the examination of how these interpretations contribute to the maintenance of posttraumatic psychological symptoms. The implementation of prospective designs would greatly strengthen the conclusions that could be drawn from such research, as it would allow for examination of how changes in beliefs over time might relate to changes in symptomatology.

Further, while there is a well-documented link between post-migration stressors and psychological outcomes in refugees, there has been scant research to date investigating how interpretation of post-migration experiences might underpin psychological symptoms in the resettlement environment. For example, it may be the case that a refugee who interprets his or her failure to find employment as reflecting his/her lack of value as a person, or an asylum-seeker who perceives the rejection of an application for permanent residency as being evidence of a breach of the broader social contract may experience higher levels of psychological symptoms in relation to such interpretations. Investigation of cognitive appraisals of refugee experiences (i.e., both pre- and post-migration), as well as psychological symptoms and broader beliefs about the world and other people is needed to better understand the cognitive impact of the refugee experience. In addition, increasing knowledge regarding how certain types of post-trauma appraisals might exacerbate (or ameliorate) psychological symptoms in refugees may facilitate the identification of treatment targets and further inform the development of targeted cognitive interventions to reduce psychological symptoms in refugees.

Memory Disturbances

PTSD has traditionally been conceptualized as a disorder rooted in memory disturbances, with hallmark symptoms relating to re-experiencing and avoiding memories of the traumatic event (American Psychiatric Association, 2013). Theoretical models posit that inadequate processing, integration or elaboration of the traumatic memory lead to intrusive memories and associated distress following the traumatic experience (Brewin, Dagleish, & Joseph, 1996; Ehlers & Clark, 2000; Foa, Steketee, & Rothbaum, 1989). Dominant treatment approaches, including Narrative Exposure Therapy—the psychological intervention for PTSD in refugees with the strongest evidence to date (Robjant & Fazel, 2010; Schauer, Neuner, & Elbert, 2005)—focus on correcting this deficit via techniques that promote reliving of the trauma memory (e.g., Foa, Dancu, et al., 1999; Foa & Kozak, 1986; Resick & Schnicke, 1992). Much research has focused on the development and phenomenology of intrusive memories in non-refugee trauma survivors (Catarino, Kupper, Werner-Seidler, Dalgleish, & Anderson, 2015; Ehlers, Hackmann, & Michael, 2004; Hackmann, Ehlers, Speckens, & Clark, 2004; Holmes & Bourne, 2008; Nicholson, Bryant, & Felmingham, 2014; Speckens, Ehlers, Hackmann, Ruths, & Clark, 2007), as well as examining how memory more broadly is affected by trauma exposure and PTSD (Brewin, 2011; Debiec, 2012; Glover, Jovanovic, & Norrholm, 2015; McNally, 2006; Ono, Devilly, & Shum, 2016).

In contrast, there has been relatively scant research investigating memory processes in refugee groups. Studies conducted with refugees to date have tended to focus either on how memory for traumatic experiences changes over time, or how refugee experiences may impact on other memory-related processes such as autobiographical memory and directed forgetting.

In relation to the first stream of research, Herlihy, Turner and colleagues have written extensively about the impact of memory disturbances following exposure to refugee trauma on the process of seeking asylum, noting that credibility in retelling traumatic events (i.e., providing a narrative that is coherent and consistent) is often a pre-condition for a positive asylum decision (Herlihy, Jobson, & Turner, 2012; Herlihy & Turner, S. 2007; Herlihy & Turner, S. W. 2007). In a study conducted with Kosovar and Bosnian refugees, Herlihy, Scragg and Turner (2002) found a high level of discrepancies in repeated accounts of traumatic and non-traumatic autobiographical memories, with the number of discrepancies increasing alongside time between interviews among refugees with PTSD. In a study examining consistency of trauma memories over a period of 3 years, Mollica and colleagues (Mollica, Caridad, & Massagli, 2007) found that Bosnian refugees demonstrated generally high consistency in recall. Where participants' reporting changed over this period, the trend was usually for decreased reporting of traumatic events. Where participants did evidence an increase in the reporting of traumatic events, this usually occurred in the context of a diagnosis of PTSD. These studies indicate that high levels of PTSD symptoms may be associated with poorer consistency in recalling details of traumatic experiences, which has important potential implications for the process of seeking asylum.

A handful of studies have examined specific processes such as autobiographical memory and directed forgetting amongst refugees. Graham et al. (2014) found evidence for an overgeneral memory bias, such that refugees and asylum-seekers with PTSD and depression were less able to recall specific memories than those without a psychiatric diagnosis. Moradi et al. (2008) observed greater overgeneral memory in refugees who more frequently experienced trauma-related flashbacks. This reduced specificity of memories was also associated with lower levels of effortful avoidance of traumatic memories in daily life. Baumann et al. (2013) found no difference between refugees with and without PTSD in their capacity to engage in directed forgetting, although refugees with PTSD were less able to discriminate previously presented items from novel items. While there is inadequate research evidence to date to draw firm conclusions, these studies provide preliminary evidence that there may be a link between memory processes and PTSD in refugees.

Given the primacy placed on the processing of trauma memories in psychological interventions for PTSD both in general and with refugees, further research should be undertaken that probes the specific phenomenology and mechanisms associated with memory disturbances following refugee trauma. In particular, it would be of great value to examine how the refugee experience uniquely impacts on memory processes in order to facilitate the adaptation of existing interventions specifically for refugees. For example, many refugees live in circumstances of ongoing threat either to themselves or to family members and close friends. A study conducted with Iraqi refugees found that participants experienced intrusive symptoms about potential traumatic events that might befall their family and friends who remained in the country of origin, and that these intrusions significantly contributed to psychological distress (Nickerson et al., 2010). While these were not memory disturbances per se, as they were about potential future events rather than past experiences, these findings highlight the fact that, for many refugees, traumatic experiences are not relegated to the past, but are instead very real threats in the present and future. This introduces important considerations for psychological interventions that focus on the processing of a *past* traumatic event from a *current* position of safety. For example, it is often argued that exposure-based interventions are contraindicated in the case of ongoing threat (e.g., domestic violence). Further research is required to understand how ongoing threat may impact on memory processes and psychopathology, and how individuals who experience continued threat may be best supported in therapy.

The implementation of experimental designs that include non-refugee trauma-exposed control groups also represents an important potential direction of research for determining how the refugee experience may uniquely impact on memory processes. This would facilitate the investigation of the specific phenomenology of intrusive symptoms following refugee trauma and how this differs from intrusions experienced by western survivors of civilian trauma. Refugee trauma is unique as it stems from persecution and is typically prolonged, repeated and human-instigated. To date, distinctive features of intrusive symptoms arising from these events are not well understood. Systematic study of the nature of these intrusive symptoms could directly inform the tailoring of existing treatment interventions to refugees. In addition, comparing refugees with and without significant psychological distress on memory processes would facilitate understanding of the mechanistic role of these processes in influencing psychopathology following refugee trauma.

Conclusions

Recent decades have seen an exponential increase in research investigating the psychological impact of the refugee experience. Many of these studies have focused on documenting rates of psychological disorders in refugee groups and/or considering the impact of pre- and post-migration experiences on refugee mental health. In contrast, there has been relatively little investigation of how psychological processes may contribute to mental health outcomes in refugees. This chapter has outlined research conducted to date on three psychological mechanisms that may underpin the mental health of refugees, namely emotion regulation, cognitive appraisals and memory processes. Further, this chapter has proposed potential future research directions that may facilitate the understanding of how these processes may impact on refugee mental health. Increasing knowledge regarding how psychological mechanisms that may be affected by pre-migration trauma and post-migration stressors influence mental health represents an important area of enquiry. This is especially the case given that the majority of refugees and asylum-seekers do not exhibit psychopathology despite having experienced persecution and displacement. Learning about how these processes differ in refugees with and without psychological symptoms, and how they vary from disruptions experienced by survivors of civilian trauma in high-income countries would provide us with a unique opportunity to understand the specific mechanisms by which refugee trauma impacts on mental health. Ultimately this would allow us to strengthen and tailor existing evidence-based interventions to facilitate recovery and adaptation in refugees.

References

Aldao, A., Nolen-Hoeksema, S., & Schweizer, S. (2010). Emotion-regulation strategies across psychopathology: A meta-analytic review. *Clinical Psychology Review, 30*(2), 217–237. https://doi.org/10.1016/j.cpr.2009.11.004

Aldao, A., Sheppes, G., & Gross, J. J. (2015). Emotion regulation flexibility. *Cognitive Therapy and Research, 39*(3), 263–278. https://doi.org/10.1007/s10608-014-9662-4

American Psychiatric Association. (2013). *Diagnostic and statistical manual of mental disorders* (5th ed.). Arlington, Virginia: American Psychiatric Publishing.

Amstadter, A. B., & Vernon, L. L. (2006). Suppression of neutral and trauma targets: Implications for posttraumatic stress disorder. *Journal of Traumatic Stress, 19*(4), 517–526. https://doi.org/10.1002/jts.20142

Amstadter, A. B., & Vernon, L. L. (2008). A preliminary examination of thought suppression, emotion regulation, and coping in a trauma-exposed sample. *Journal of Aggression, Maltreatment & Trauma, 17*(3), 279–295. https://doi.org/10.1080/10926770802403236

Basoglu, M., Livanou, M., & Crnobaric, C. (2007). Torture vs other cruel, inhuman, and degrading treatment: Is the distinction real or apparent? *Archives of General Psychiatry, 64*(3), 277–285. https://doi.org/10.1001/archpsyc.64.3.277

Basoglu, M., Livanou, M., Crnobaric, C., Franciskovic, T., Suljic, E., Duric, D., & Vranesic, M. (2005). Psychiatric and cognitive effects of war in former Yugoslavia: Association of lack of redress for trauma and posttraumatic stress reactions. *Journal of the American Medical Association, 294*(5), 580–590. https://doi.org/10.1001/jama.294.5.580

Bass, J. K., Annan, J., McIvor Murray, S., Kaysen, D., Griffiths, S., Cetinoglu, T., … Bolton, P. A. (2013). Controlled trial of psychotherapy for Congolese survivors of sexual violence. *New England Journal of Medicine, 368*(23), 2182–2191. https://doi.org/10.1056/NEJMoa1211853

Baumann, M., Zwissler, B., Schalinski, I., Ruf-Leuschner, M., Schauer, M., & Kissler, J. (2013). Directed forgetting in post-traumatic-stress-disorder: A study of refugee immigrants in Germany. *Frontiers in Behavioral Neuroscience, 7*, 94. https://doi.org/10.3389/fnbeh.2013.00094

Bolton, P., Bass, J. K., Zangana, G. A., Kamal, T., Murray, S. M., Kaysen, D., … Rosenblum, M. (2014). A randomized controlled trial of mental health interventions for survivors of systematic violence in Kurdistan, Northern Iraq. *BMC Psychiatry, 14*, 360. https://doi.org/10.1186/s12888-014-0360-2

Brewin, C. R. (2011). The nature and significance of memory disturbance in posttraumatic stress disorder. *Annual Review of Clinical Psychology, 7*(1), 203–227. https://doi.org/10.1146/annurev-clinpsy-032210-104544

Brewin, C. R., Dagleish, T., & Joseph, S. (1996). A dual representation theory of posttraumatic stress disorder. *Psychological Review, 103*(4), 670–686. https://doi.org/10.1037//0033-295x.103.4.670

Catarino, A., Kupper, C. S., Werner-Seidler, A., Dalgleish, T., & Anderson, M. C. (2015). Failing to forget: Inhibitory-control deficits compromise memory suppression in posttraumatic stress disorder. *Psychological Science, 26*(5), 604–616. https://doi.org/10.1177/0956797615569889

Cloitre, M., Koenen, K. C., Cohen, L. R., & Han, H. (2002). Skills training in affective and interpersonal regulation followed by exposure: A phase-based treatment for PTSD related to childhood abuse. *Journal of Consulting and Clinical Psychology, 70*(5), 1067–1074. https://doi.org/10.1037/0022-006X.70.5.1067

Cloitre, M., Stovall-McClough, K. C., Nooner, K., Zorbas, P., Cherry, S., Jackson, C. L., … Petkova, E. (2010). Treatment for PTSD related to childhood abuse: A randomized controlled trial. *American Journal of Psychiatry, 167*(8), 915–924. https://doi.org/10.1176/appi.ajp.2010.09081247

Debiec, J. (2012). Memory reconsolidation processes and posttraumatic stress disorder: Promises and challenges of translational research. *Biological Psychiatry, 71*(4), 284–285. https://doi.org/10.1016/j.biopsych.2011.12.009

Dunmore, E., Clark, D. M., & Ehlers, A. (2001). A prospective investigation of the role of cognitive factors in persistent posttraumatic stress disorder (PTSD) after physical or sexual assault. *Behaviour Research and Therapy, 39*(9), 1063–1084. https://doi.org/S0005-7967(00)00088-7 [pii]

Ehlers, A., & Clark, D. M. (2000). A cognitive model of posttraumatic stress disorder. *Behaviour Research and Therapy, 38*(4), 319–345. https://doi.org/S0005-7967(99)00123-0

Ehlers, A., Clark, D. M., Hackmann, A., McManus, F., & Fennell, M. (2005). Cognitive therapy for post-traumatic stress disorder: Development and evaluation. *Behaviour Research and Therapy, 43*(4), 413–431. https://doi.org/10.1016/j.brat.2004.03.006

Ehlers, A., Hackmann, A., Grey, N., Wild, J., Liness, S., Albert, I., … Clark, D. M. (2014). A randomized controlled trial of 7-day intensive and standard weekly cognitive therapy for PTSD and emotion-focused supportive therapy. *American Journal of Psychiatry, 171*(3), 294–304. https://doi.org/10.1176/appi.ajp.2013.13040552

Ehlers, A., Hackmann, A., & Michael, T. (2004). Intrusive re-experiencing in post-traumatic stress disorder: Phenomenology, theory, and therapy. *Memory, 12*(4), 403–415. https://doi.org/10.1080/09658210444000025

Ehlers, A., Mayou, R. A., & Bryant, B. (1998). Psychological predictors of chronic posttraumatic stress disorder after motor vehicle accidents. *Journal of Abnormal Psychology, 107*(3), 508–519. https://doi.org/10.1037//0021-843x.107.3.508

Fazel, M., Wheeler, J., & Danesh, J. (2005). Prevalence of serious mental disorder in 7000 refugees resettled in western countries: A systematic review. *The Lancet, 365*(9467), 1309–1314. https://doi.org/10.1016/S0140-6736(05)61027-6

Foa, E. B., Dancu, C. V., Hembree, E. A., Jaycox, L. H., Meadows, E. A., & Street, G. P. (1999). A comparison of exposure therapy, stress inoculation training, and their combination for reducing posttraumatic stress disorder in female assault victims. *Journal of Consulting and Clinical Psychology, 67*(2), 194–200. https://doi.org/10.1037//0022-006x.67.2.194

Foa, E. B., Ehlers, A., Clark, D. M., Tolin, D. F., & Orsillo, S. M. (1999). The posttraumatic cognitions inventory: Development and validation. *Psychological Assessment, 11*, 303–314. https://doi.org/10.1037//1040-3590.11.3.303

Foa, E. B., & Kozak, M. J. (1986). Emotional processing of fear: Exposure to corrective information. *Psychological Bulletin, 99*(1), 20–35. https://doi.org/10.1037/0033-2909.99.1.20

Foa, E. B., Riggs, D. S., Massie, E. D., & Yarczower, M. (1995). Impact of fear activation and anger on the efficacy of exposure treatment for posttraumatic stress disorder. *Behavior Therapy, 26*(3), 487–499. https://doi.org/10.1016/s0005-7894(05)80096-6

Foa, E. B., Steketee, G., & Rothbaum, B. O. (1989). Behavioral/cognitive conceptualizations of post-traumatic stress disorder. *Behavior Therapy, 20*(2), 155–176. https://doi.org/10.1016/s0005-7894(89)80067-x

Forbes, D., Parslow, R., Creamer, M., Allen, N., McHugh, T., & Hopwood, M. (2008). Mechanisms of anger and treatment outcome in combat veterans with posttraumatic stress disorder. *Journal of Traumatic Stress, 21*(2), 142–149. https://doi.org/10.1002/jts.20315

Glover, E. M., Jovanovic, T., & Norrholm, S. D. (2015). Estrogen and extinction of fear memories: Implications for posttraumatic stress disorder treatment. *Biological Psychiatry, 78*(3), 178–185. https://doi.org/10.1016/j.biopsych.2015.02.007

Graham, B., Herlihy, J., & Brewin, C. R. (2014). Overgeneral memory in asylum seekers and refugees. *Journal of Behavior Therapy and Experimental Psychiatry, 45*(3), 375–380. https://doi.org/10.1016/j.jbtep.2014.03.001

Gratz, K. L., & Roemer, L. (2004). Multidimensional assessment of emotion regulation and dysregulation: Development, factor structure, and initial validation of the difficulties in emotion regulation scale. *Journal of Psychopathology and Behavioral Assessment, 26*(1), 41–54. https://doi.org/10.1023/b:joba.0000007455.08539.94

Hackmann, A., Ehlers, A., Speckens, A., & Clark, D. M. (2004). Characteristics and content of intrusive memories in PTSD and their changes with treatment. *Journal of Traumatic Stress, 17*(3), 231–240. https://doi.org/10.1023/B:JOTS.0000029266.88369.fd

Halligan, S. L., Michael, T., Clark, D. M., & Ehlers, A. (2003). Posttraumatic stress disorder following assault: The role of cognitive processing, trauma memory, and appraisals. *Journal of Consulting and Clinical Psychology, 71*(3), 419–431. https://doi.org/10.1037/0022-006x.71.3.419

Herlihy, J., Jobson, L., & Turner, S. (2012). Just tell us what happened to you: Autobiographical memory and seeking asylum. *Applied Cognitive Psychology, 26*(5), 661–676. https://doi.org/10.1002/acp.2852

Herlihy, J., Scragg, P., & Turner, S. (2002). Discrepancies in autobiographical memories–implications for the assessment of asylum seekers: Repeated interviews study. *BMJ, 324*(7333), 324–327. https://doi.org/10.1136/bmj.324.7333.324

Herlihy, J., & Turner, S. (2007). Memory and seeking asylum. *European Journal of Psychotherapy and Counselling, 9*(3), 267–276. https://doi.org/10.1080/13642530701496872

Herlihy, J., & Turner, S. W. (2007). Asylum claims and memory of trauma: Sharing our knowledge. *The British Journal of Psychiatry, 191*(1), 3–4. https://doi.org/10.1192/bjp.bp.106.034439

Hinton, D. E. (2012). Multicultural challenges in the delivery of anxiety treatment. *Depression and Anxiety, 29*(1), 1–3. https://doi.org/10.1002/da.20889

Hinton, D. E., Chean, D., Pich, V., Safren, S., Hofmann, S., & Pollack, M. (2005). A randomized controlled trial of cognitive-behavior therapy for Cambodian refugees with treatment-resistant PTSD and panic attacks: A cross-over design. *Journal of Traumatic Stress, 18*(6), 617–629. https://doi.org/10.1002/jts.20070

Hinton, D. E., Chhean, D., Hofmann, S. G., Orr, S. P., & Pitman, R. K. (2008). Dizziness and palpitations-predominant orthostatic panic: Physiology, flashbacks and catastrophic cognitions. *Journal of Psychopathology and Behavioral Assessment, 30*(2), 100–110. https://doi.org/10.1007/s10862-007-9059-8

Hinton, D. E., Field, N. P., Nickerson, A., Bryant, R. A., & Simon, N. (2013). Dreams of the dead among Cambodian refugees: Frequency, phenomenology, and relationship to complicated grief and posttraumatic stress disorder. *Death Studies, 37*(8), 750–767. https://doi.org/10.1080/07481187.2012.692457

Hinton, D. E., Hinton, A. L., Pich, V., Loeum, J. R., & Pollack, M. H. (2009). Nightmares among Cambodian refugees: The breaching of concentric ontological security. *Culture, Medicine and Psychiatry, 33*(2), 219–265. https://doi.org/10.1007/s11013-009-9131-9

Hinton, D. E., Hinton, L., Tran, M., Nguyen, L., Hsia, C., & Pollack, M. H. (2006). Orthostatically induced panic attacks among Vietnamese refugees: Associated psychopathology, flashbacks, and catastrophic cognitions. *Depression and Anxiety, 23*(2), 113–115. https://doi.org/10.1002/da.20154

Hinton, D. E., Hinton, S., Pham, T., Chau, H., & Tran, M. (2003). 'Hit by the wind' and temperature-shift panic among Vietnamese refugees. *Transcultural Psychiatry, 40*(3), 342–376. https://doi.org/10.1177/13634615030403003

Hinton, D. E., Hofmann, S. G., Pitman, R. K., Pollack, M. H., & Barlow, D. H. (2008). The panic attack-posttraumatic stress disorder model: Applicability to orthostatic panic among Cambodian refugees. *Cognitive Behaviour Therapy, 37*(2), 101–116. https://doi.org/10.1080/16506070801969062

Hinton, D. E., Hofmann, S. G., Pollack, M. H., & Otto, M. W. (2009). Mechanisms of efficacy of CBT for Cambodian refugees with PTSD: Improvement in emotion regulation and orthostatic blood pressure response. *CNS Neuroscience & Therapeutics, 15*(3), 255–263. https://doi.org/10.1111/j.1755-5949.2009.00100.x

Hinton, D. E., Hofmann, S. G., Rivera, E., Otto, M. W., & Pollack, M. H. (2011). Culturally adapted CBT (CA-CBT) for Latino women with treatment-resistant PTSD: A pilot study comparing CA-CBT to applied muscle relaxation. *Behaviour Research and Therapy, 49*(4), 275–280. https://doi.org/10.1016/j.brat.2011.01.005

Hinton, D. E., Nickerson, A., & Bryant, R. A. (2011). Worry, worry attacks, and PTSD among Cambodian refugees: A path analysis investigation. *Social Science & Medicine, 72*(11), 1817–1825. https://doi.org/10.1016/j.socscimed.2011.03.045

Hinton, D. E., & Otto, M. (2006). Symptom presentation and symptom meaning among traumatized Cambodian refugees: Relevance to a somatically focused cognitive behavior therapy. *Cognitive and Behavioral Practice, 13*(4), 249–260. https://doi.org/10.1016/j.cbpra.2006.04.013

Hinton, D. E., Pham, T., Tran, M., Safren, S., Otto, M., & Pollack, M. (2004). CBT for Vietnamese refugees with treatment-resistant PTSD and panic attacks: A pilot study. *Journal of Traumatic Stress, 17*(5), 429–433. https://doi.org/10.1023/B:JOTS.0000048956.03529.fa

Hinton, D. E., Pich, V., Marques, L., Nickerson, A., & Pollack, M. H. (2010). Khyâl attacks: A key idiom of distress among traumatized Cambodia refugees. *Culture, Medicine and Psychiatry, 34*(2), 244–278. https://doi.org/10.1007/s11013-010-9174-y

Hinton, D. E., Rivera, E. I., Hofmann, S. G., Barlow, D. H., & Otto, M. W. (2012). Adapting CBT for traumatized refugees and ethnic minority patients: Examples from culturally adapted CBT (CA-CBT). *Transcultural Psychiatry, 49*(2), 340–365. https://doi.org/10.1177/1363461512441595

Holmes, E. A., & Bourne, C. (2008). Inducing and modulating intrusive emotional memories: A review of the trauma film paradigm. *Acta Psychologica, 127*(3), 553–566. https://doi.org/10.1016/j.actpsy.2007.11.002

Hooberman, J., Rosenfeld, B., Rasmussen, A., & Keller, A. (2010). Resilience in trauma-exposed refugees: The moderating effect of coping style on resilience variables. *American Journal of Orthopsychiatry, 80*(4), 557–563. https://doi.org/10.1111/j.1939-0025.2010.01060.x

Huijts, I., Kleijn, W. C., van Emmerik, A. A., Noordhof, A., & Smith, A. J. (2012). Dealing with man-made trauma: The relationship between coping style, posttraumatic stress, and quality of life in resettled, traumatized refugees in the Netherlands. *Journal of Traumatic Stress, 25*(1), 71–78. https://doi.org/10.1002/jts.21665

Hussain, D., & Bhushan, B. (2011). Posttraumatic stress and growth among Tibetan refugees: The mediating role of cognitive-emotional regulation strategies. *Journal of Clinical Psychology, 67*(7), 720–735. https://doi.org/10.1002/jclp.20801

Kanninen, K., Punamaki, R. L., & Qouta, S. (2002). The relation of appraisal, coping efforts, and acuteness of trauma to PTS symptoms among former political prisoners. *Journal of Traumatic Stress, 15*(3), 245–253. https://doi.org/10.1023/A:1015211529584

Kulkarni, M., Pole, N., & Timko, C. (2013). Childhood victimization, negative mood regulation, and adult PTSD severity. *Psychological Trauma: Theory, Research, Practice, and Policy, 5*(4), 359–365. https://doi.org/10.1037/a0027746

Li, S. S., Liddell, B. J., & Nickerson, A. (2016). The relationship between post-migration stress and psychological disorders in refugees and ssylum seekers. *Current Psychiatry Reports, 18*(9), 82. https://doi.org/10.1007/s11920-016-0723-0

Lie, B. (2002). A 3-year follow-up study of psychosocial functioning and general symptoms in settled refugees. *Acta Psychiatrica Scandinavica, 106*(6), 415–425. https://doi.org/10.1034/j.1600-0447.2002.01436.x

Lindencrona, F., Ekblad, S., & Hauff, E. (2008). Mental health of recently resettled refugees from the Middle East in Sweden: The impact of pre-resettlement trauma, resettlement stress and capacity to handle stress. *Social Psychiatry and Psychiatric Epidemiology, 43*(2), 121–131. https://doi.org/10.1007/s00127-007-0280-2

McNally, R. J. (2006). Cognitive abnormalities in post-traumatic stress disorder. *Trends in Cognitive Sciences, 10*(6), 271–277. https://doi.org/10.1016/j.tics.2006.04.007

Mollica, R. F., Caridad, K. R., & Massagli, M. P. (2007). Longitudinal study of posttraumatic stress disorder, depression, and changes in traumatic memories over time in Bosnian refugees. *Journal of Nervous and Mental Disease, 195*(7), 572–579. https://doi.org/10.1097/NMD.0b013e318093ed2c

Mollica, R. F., McInnes, K., Pham, T., Smith Fawzi, M. C., Murphy, E., & Lin, L. (1998). The dose-effect relationships between torture and psychiatric symptoms in Vietnamese ex-political detainees and a comparison group. *Journal of Nervous and Mental Disease, 186*(9), 543–553. https://doi.org/10.1097/00005053-199809000-00005

Mollica, R. F., McInnes, K., Poole, C., & Tor, S. (1998). Dose-effect relationships of trauma to symptoms of depression and post-traumatic stress disorder among Cambodian survivors of mass violence. *British Journal of Psychiatry, 173*(6), 482–488. https://doi.org/10.1192/bjp.173.6.482

Moradi, A. R., Herlihy, J., Yasseri, G., Shahraray, M., Turner, S., & Dalgleish, T. (2008). Specificity of episodic and semantic aspects of autobiographical memory in relation to symptoms of posttraumatic stress disorder (PTSD). *Acta Psychologica, 127*(3), 645–653. https://doi.org/10.1016/j.actpsy.2007.11.001

Nicholson, E. L., Bryant, R. A., & Felmingham, K. L. (2014). Interaction of noradrenaline and cortisol predicts negative intrusive memories in posttraumatic stress disorder. *Neurobiology of Learning and Memory, 112*, 204–211. https://doi.org/10.1016/j.nlm.2013.11.018

Nickerson, A., Bryant, R. A., Schnyder, U., Schick, M., Mueller, J., & Morina, N. (2015). Emotion dysregulation mediates the relationship between trauma exposure, post-migration living difficulties and psychological outcomes in traumatized refugees. *Journal of Affective Disorders, 173*, 185–192. https://doi.org/10.1016/j.jad.2014.10.043

Nickerson, A., Bryant, R. A., Silove, D., & Steel, Z. (2011). A critical review of psychological treatments of posttraumatic stress disorder in refugees. *Clinical Psychology Review, 31*(3), 399–417. https://doi.org/10.1016/j.cpr.2010.10.004

Nickerson, A., Bryant, R. A., Steel, Z., Silove, D., & Brooks, R. (2010). The impact of fear for family on mental health in a resettled Iraqi refugee community. *Journal of Psychiatric Research, 44*(4), 229–235. https://doi.org/10.1016/j.jpsychires.2009.08.006

Nickerson, A., Garber, B., Ahmed, O., Asnaani, A., Cheung, J., Hofmann, S. G., … Bryant, R. A. (2016). Emotional suppression in torture survivors: Relationship to posttraumatic stress symptoms and trauma-related negative affect. *Psychiatry Research, 242*, 233–239. https://doi.org/10.1016/j.psychres.2016.05.048

Nickerson, A., Garber, B., Liddell, B. J., Litz, B. T., Hofmann, S. G., Asnaani, A., … Bryant, R. A. (2017). Impact of cognitive reappraisal on negative affect, heart rate, and intrusive memories in traumatized refugees. *Clinical Psychological Science, 5*(3), 497–512. https://doi.org/10.1177/2167702617690857

Nickerson, A., Liddell, B. J., Maccallum, F., Steel, Z., Silove, D., & Bryant, R. A. (2014). Posttraumatic stress disorder and prolonged grief in refugees exposed to trauma and loss. *BMC Psychiatry, 14*(1), 106. https://doi.org/10.1186/1471-244X-14-106

Nickerson, A., Schnyder, U., Bryant, R. A., Schick, M., Mueller, J., & Morina, N. (2015). Moral injury in traumatized refugees. *Psychotherapy and Psychosomatics, 84*(2), 122–123. https://doi.org/10.1159/000369353

O'Donnell, M. L., Elliott, P., Wolfgang, B. J., & Creamer, M. (2007). Posttraumatic appraisals in the development and persistence of posttraumatic stress symptoms. *Journal of Traumatic Stress, 20*(2), 173–182. https://doi.org/10.1002/jts.20198

Ono, M., Devilly, G. J., & Shum, D. H. (2016). A meta-analytic review of overgeneral memory: The role of trauma history, mood, and the presence of posttraumatic stress disorder. *Psychological Trauma: Theory, Research, Practice, and Policy, 8*(2), 157–164. https://doi.org/10.1037/tra0000027

Otto, M., & Hinton, D. E. (2006). Modifying exposure-based CBT for Cambodian refugees with posttraumatic stress disorder. *Cognitive and Behavioral Practice, 13*(4), 261–270. https://doi.org/10.1016/j.cbpra.2006.04.007

Park, J., Jun, J. Y., Lee, Y. J., Kim, S., Lee, S. H., Yoo, S. Y., & Kim, S. J. (2015). The association between alexithymia and posttraumatic stress symptoms following multiple exposures to traumatic events in North Korean refugees. *Journal of Psychosomatic Research, 78*(1), 77–81. https://doi.org/10.1016/j.jpsychores.2014.09.007

Porter, M., & Haslam, N. (2005). Predisplacement and postdisplacement factors associated with mental health of refugees and internally displaced persons: A meta-analysis. *Journal of the American Medical Association, 294*(5), 602–612. https://doi.org/10.1001/jama.294.5.602

Rasmussen, A., Nguyen, L., Wilkinson, J., Vundla, S., Raghavan, S., Miller, K. E., & Keller, A. S. (2010). Rates and impact of trauma and current stressors among Darfuri refugees in Eastern Chad. *American Journal of Orthopsychiatry, 80*(2), 227–236. https://doi.org/10.1111/j.1939-0025.2010.01026.x

Resick, P. A., Galovski, T. E., O'Brien Uhlmansiek, M., Scher, C. D., Clum, G. A., & Young-Xu, Y. (2008). A randomized clinical trial to dismantle components of cognitive processing therapy for posttraumatic stress disorder in female victims of interpersonal violence. *Journal of Consulting and Clinical Psychology, 76*(2), 243–258. https://doi.org/10.1037/0022-006x.76.2.243

Resick, P. A., Nishith, P., Weaver, T. L., Astin, M. C., & Feuer, C. A. (2002). A comparison of cognitive-processing therapy with prolonged exposure and a waiting condition for the treatment of chronic posttraumatic stress disorder in female rape victims. *Journal of Consulting and Clinical Psychology, 70*(4), 867–879. https://doi.org/10.1037//0022-006x.70.4.867

Resick, P. A., & Schnicke, M. K. (1992). Cognitive processing therapy for sexual assault victims. *Journal of Consulting and Clinical Psychology, 60*(5), 748–756. https://doi.org/10.1037/0022-006X.60.5.748

Robjant, K., & Fazel, M. (2010). The emerging evidence for narrative exposure therapy: A review. *Clinical Psychology Review, 30*(8), 1030–1039. https://doi.org/10.1016/j.cpr.2010.07.004

Roemer, L., Litz, B. T., Orsillo, S. M., & Wagner, A. W. (2001). A preliminary investigation of the role of strategic withholding of emotions in PTSD. *Journal of Traumatic Stress, 14*(1), 149–156. https://doi.org/10.1023/a:1007895817502

Sachs, E., Rosenfeld, B., Lhewa, D., Rasmussen, A., & Keller, A. (2008). Entering exile: Trauma, mental health, and coping among Tibetan refugees arriving in Dharamsala, India. *Journal of Traumatic Stress, 21*(2), 199–208. https://doi.org/10.1002/jts.20324

Schauer, M., Neuner, F., & Elbert, T. (2005). *Narrative exposure therapy: A short-term intervention for traumatic stress disorders after war, terror or torture*. Cambridge, MA: Hogrefe & Huber.

Schulz, P. M., Resick, P. A., Huber, L. C., & Griffin, M. G. (2006). The effectiveness of cognitive processing therapy for PTSD with refugees in a community setting. *Cognitive and Behavioral Practice, 13*(4), 322–331. https://doi.org/10.1016/j.cbpra.2006.04.011

Schweitzer, R., Melville, F., Steel, Z., & Lacharez, P. (2006). Trauma, post-migration living difficulties and social support as predictors of psychosocial adjustment in resettled Sudanese refugees. *Australian and New Zealand Journal of Psychiatry, 40*, 179–187. https://doi.org/10.1111/j.1440-1614.2006.01766.x

Seligowski, A. V., Lee, D. J., Bardeen, J. R., & Orcutt, H. K. (2015). Emotion regulation and posttraumatic stress symptoms: A meta-analysis. *Cognitive Behaviour Therapy, 44*(2), 87–102. https://doi.org/10.1080/16506073.2014.980753

Shipherd, J. C., & Beck, J. G. (1999). The effects of suppressing trauma-related thoughts on women with rape-related posttraumatic stress disorder. *Behaviour Research and Therapy, 37*(2), 99–112. https://doi.org/10.1016/s0005-7967(98)00136-3

Sippel, L. M., Roy, A. M., Southwick, S. M., & Fichtenholtz, H. M. (2016). An examination of the roles of trauma exposure and posttraumatic stress disorder on emotion regulation strategies of operation Iraqi freedom, operation enduring freedom, and operation new Dawn veterans. *Cognitive Behaviour Therapy, 45*(5), 339–350. https://doi.org/10.1080/16506073.2016.1183037

Sondergaard, H. P., Ekblad, S., & Theorell, T. (2003). Screening for post-traumatic stress disorder among refugees in Stockholm. *Nordic Journal of Psychiatry, 57*(3), 185–189. https://doi.org/10.1080/08039480310001328

Sondergaard, H. P., & Theorell, T. (2004). Alexithymia, emotions and PTSD; findings from a longitudinal study of refugees. *Nordic Journal of Psychiatry, 58*(3), 185–191. https://doi.org/10.1080/08039480410006214

Speckens, A. E., Ehlers, A., Hackmann, A., Ruths, F. A., & Clark, D. M. (2007). Intrusive memories and rumination in patients with post-traumatic stress disorder: A phenomenological comparison. *Memory, 15*(3), 249–257. https://doi.org/10.1080/09658210701256449

Steel, Z., Chey, T., Silove, D., Marnane, C., Bryant, R. A., & van Ommeren, M. (2009). Association of torture and other potentially traumatic events with mental health outcomes among populations exposed to mass conflict and displacement: A systematic review and meta-analysis. *Journal of the American Medical Association, 302*(5), 537–549. https://doi.org/10.1001/jama.2009.1132

Tay, A. K., Rees, S., Chen, J., Kareth, M., & Silove, D. (2015). The coherence and correlates of intermittent explosive disorder amongst West Papuan refugees displaced to Papua New Guinea. *Journal of Affective Disorders, 177*, 86–94. https://doi.org/10.1016/j.jad.2015.02.009

Tull, M. T., Barrett, H. M., McMillan, E. S., & Roemer, L. (2007). A preliminary investigation of the relationship between emotion regulation difficulties and posttraumatic stress symptoms. *Behavior Therapy, 38*(3), 303–313. https://doi.org/10.1016/j.beth.2006.10.001

UNHCR. (2017). *Global trends in forced displacement in 2016*. Geneva, Switzerland: UNHCR.

Walsh, K., DiLillo, D., & Scalora, M. J. (2011). The cumulative impact of sexual revictimization on emotion regulation difficulties: An examination of female inmates. *Violence Against Women, 17*(8), 1103–1118. https://doi.org/10.1177/1077801211414165

Woud, M. L., Holmes, E. A., Postma, P., Dalgleish, T., & Mackintosh, B. (2012). Ameliorating intrusive memories of distressing experiences using computerized reappraisal training. *Emotion, 12*(4), 778–784. https://doi.org/10.1037/a0024992

Woud, M. L., Postma, P., Holmes, E. A., & Mackintosh, B. (2013). Reducing analogue trauma symptoms by computerized reappraisal training – Considering a cognitive prophylaxis? *Journal of Behavior Therapy & Experimental Psychiatry, 44*(3), 312–315. https://doi.org/10.1016/j.jbtep.2013.01.003

Angela Nickerson, Ph.D., is an Associate Professor and Director of the Refugee Trauma and Recovery Program at the University of New South Wales (UNSW), Sydney, Australia. She is a Clinical Psychologist and conducts research into psychological and social mechanisms underlying the mental health of refugees and asylum seekers, with the aim of informing policy and treatment development.

Drive to Thrive: A Theory of Resilience Following Loss

Wai Kai Hou, Brian J. Hall, and Stevan E. Hobfoll

Abstract Prior work has considered demand and distress, temporal dynamics, and differential outcomes in defining human stress resilience but not the processes and mechanisms of resilience across different life challenges. The purpose of this chapter is to outline the Drive to Thrive (DTT) theory in an attempt to advance existing understanding of stress adaptation and resilience among refugee and conflict-affected populations. The basic tenet of the DTT theory is that stress resilience is determined by sustaining the fabrics/routines (i.e., interwoven psychosocial and communal activities, procedures, and practices) and structure of everyday life. Primary and secondary fabrics/routines are distinguished to further current understanding on everyday life of stress adaptation based on theoretical and empirical evidence. Within the theory, the Sustaining Everyday Life Fabrics and Structure (SELFS) model outlines how consolidation, replacement, and addition of everyday life fabrics shape the association between trauma exposure and physical and mental health over time. The current literature on everyday adaptation among refugee and conflict-affected populations is critically reviewed. Applications of the theory to guide empirical investigation and intervention development among refugee populations and populations affected by war, are evaluated through the lens of principles derived from the theory.

Keywords Everyday life · Stress · Resilience · Refugees · Conflict-affected · Drive to thrive

W. K. Hou (✉)
Department of Psychology, The Education University of Hong Kong, Hong Kong, SAR, China
e-mail: wkhou@eduhk.hk

B. J. Hall
Department of Psychology, University of Macau, Macau SAR, China
e-mail: brianhall@umac.mo

S. E. Hobfoll
Department of Behavioral Sciences, Rush University Medical Center, Chicago, IL, USA
e-mail: shobfoll@hotmail.com

N. Morina, A. Nickerson (eds.), *Mental Health of Refugee and Conflict-Affected Populations*, https://doi.org/10.1007/978-3-319-97046-2_6

This chapter introduces a new theoretical framework called Drive to Thrive (DTT) theory with the aim of enhancing existing understanding of the fundamental everyday processes governing psychological resilience among refugee and conflict-affected populations. Major theoretical frameworks on psychological resilience are critically reviewed. The basic concepts, principles, and corollaries of the DTT theory are introduced. In the Sustaining Everyday Life Fabrics and Structure (SELFS) model, concrete pathways for sustaining daily routines and structure in the aid of resilience are outlined and explained in accordance with challenges faced by people in refugee and post-conflict settings. Testable hypotheses are suggested for investigating why and how everyday life processes contribute to both positive and negative health outcomes over and beyond traumatic exposure among refugee and post-conflict populations.

Human Stress Resilience

Existing conceptualizations of human stress resilience have a strong reference to adaptational outcomes following adversity. Early research looked to identify personality as an individual-level risk and protective factor (Anthony, 1974). Some children and adolescents were considered "invulnerable" despite experiencing multiple risks. As such, invulnerability or resilience referred to static durable individual differences without taking into account developmental progressions, ongoing challenges, and variations in functioning over time (Luthar, Cicchetti, & Becker, 2000). It was then suggested that individual, family, and larger sociocultural influences could be risk and protective processes that contribute to distress or resilience over time (Masten, Best, & Garmezy, 1990; Rutter, 1987). Extending the early concept of psychological resilience, Masten (2001, 2014) suggested "ordinary magic" among children and adolescents who demonstrated positive adaptation in the context of past and present adversity. "Ordinary magic" or resilience according to the concept are attributable to otherwise normative adaptation and coping resources in everyday life, which are composed of the biological and psychological characteristics of the children facing adversity, their close social partners, and their communities. This literature evolved from focusing on an individual, static quality to a more contextual understanding of resilience processes.

A recent definition receiving empirical support further argued that resilience is the absence of psychological distress in the face of highly disruptive or life-threatening events, not only at a single point in time, but also as a stable trajectory across time despite transient perturbations in functioning (Bonanno, 2004; Staudinger, Marsiske, & Baltes, 1995). Across traumatic and chronic life events, including bereavement (Bonanno et al., 2002), terrorist attack or mass violence (Bonanno, Galea, Bucciarelli, & Vlahov, 2007), natural disasters (Norris, Tracy, & Galea, 2009), and life-threatening medical conditions (Bonanno, Kennedy, Galatzer-Levy, Lude, & Elfström, 2012; Hou, Law, Yin, & Fu, 2010), a significant proportion of people (55–85%) followed a resilient trajectory, characterized by enduring normative psychological functioning (i.e., below a cutoff score of clinically significant distress). The focus of these investigations was on people without significant psychological distress and factors that contributed to the absence of distress. This perspective is a reversal of former theories and studies that focused instead on significant distress or psychopathology and their risk and protective factors. Nevertheless, a large body of literature has highlighted the pitfall of privileging psychological distress as the most important psychological outcome without also considering or incorporating subjective well-being, or quality of life, in stress adaptation (Lyubomirsky, King, & Diener, 2005; Seligman & Csikszentmihalyi, 2000).

A two-part theory suggested two fundamental aspects of human stress resilience, namely recovery and sustainability (Zautra, Hall, & Murray, 2010). Recovery refers to the capacity to recover from negative psychophysiological sequelae brought about by stressful events, whereas sustainability refers to the capacity to maintain or gain positive physical and psychological health throughout stressful encounters. The recovery and sustainability pathways interact with each other while developing independently in a stress process (Hou & Lam, 2014). The impact of recovery is more significant than sustainability at the acute, immediate phase of stressful events. Following the acute phase, sustainability emerges to have an increasingly important role especially in coping with on-going and sometimes chronic demands (Zautra et al., 2010). This perspective offers a more balanced view on how to conceptualize human stress resilience – a lack of distress is by no means sufficient for reflecting positive adaptation in terms of past or present adversity. What remains unclear is how people recover from distress and sustain positive functioning.

Another definition of resilience focused on the extent to which people remain involved and committed to their everyday life tasks despite significant challenges (Hobfoll, 2011a, 2011b; Hobfoll et al., 2012). Based on the concept of engagement (Schaufeli, Salanova, González-Romá, & Bakker, 2002), resilient people were suggested to demonstrate high levels of energy and mental effort when meeting life challenges (i.e., vigor), high levels of commitment to key everyday life tasks (i.e., dedication), and substantial involvement in life tasks (absorption). Engagement itself could be an outcome of resilience or a predictor of both absence of distress and presence of well-being following major life challenges. This perspective focuses on who continues to thrive and function as evidenced by their rich participation in the everyday life tasks amidst adversity. Engagement is akin to the sustainability pathway that is independent of the recovery pathway (Zautra et al., 2010). Previous studies have found that war zone residents who experienced posttraumatic stress and depressive symptoms were able to maintain their involvement in key life tasks (Hobfoll et al., 2012). Hobfoll's perspective on engagement in life tasks emphasized *how to build an everyday life context* that is conducive to resilience.

An ecological perspective added to the conceptualization of resilience by emphasizing contextual factors that confer positive outcomes following exposure to mass trauma (Bonanno, Romero, & Klein, 2015; Rosshandler, Hall, & Canetti, 2016; Tol, Song, & Jordans, 2013). People's positive and negative mental health outcomes are thought to be dependent on predictors at various socio-ecological levels including individual, family, peer, and community. Psychological resilience could be associated with family belief systems such as positive outlook and familial flexibility in mobilizing resources, social capital, collective efficacy, and community competence (Hall, Tol, Jordans, Bass, & de Jong, 2014; Kawachi, Kennedy, & Glass, 1999; Norris, Stevens, Pfefferbaum, Wyche, & Pfefferbaum, 2008; Walsh, 2016). Panter-Brick and colleagues describe resilience as a dynamic rather than static process of harnessing biological, psychosocial, structural, and cultural resources in order to sustain well-being (Panter-Brick & Eggerman, 2012). Resilience on the societal and structural levels was emphasized, with structural resilience referring to delivery of resources on socio-ecological levels to people for sustaining everyday life practices and preserving culture-specific dignity and meaningfulness of life (Panter-Brick & Eggerman, 2012). The primary aim for people in this framework is to *build a resourceful environment* instead of bolstering individual qualities for coping with adversity.

The Why and How of Psychological Resilience

A consensus among most, if not all, aforementioned major frameworks is that everyday life is the fundamental context for resilience during posttraumatic and chronic stress conditions. Resilience was considered as "ordinary magic" because resilience emerges in adaptation and coping resources in ordinary everyday life of children and adolescents facing adversity (Masten, 2001, 2014). Likewise, intertwined recovery and sustainability pathways were suggested to be the ongoing processes that characterize daily living of people adapting to different stressors (Zautra et al., 2010). The socio-ecological perspective argued that the key role of structural resilience is to sustain livelihood and preserve life and cultural meanings in everyday life (Eggerman & Panter-Brick, 2010; Panter-Brick, 2014; Panter-Brick & Eggerman, 2012). More importantly, in the face of immediate and unpredictable threats to life and societal stability, psychological resilience was realized in active behaviors for building or sustaining a more resourceful environment (Hobfoll, 2011a, 2011b; Hobfoll et al., 2012). What can be added to the existing understanding is a clear, explicit focus on everyday behavioral processes that characterize stress resilience.

Everyday Life Fabrics and Structure

This article introduces the term "fabric" to describe daily routines as interwoven, interdependent, and offering sustaining benefits for adaptation among refugee and conflict-affected populations. Hobfoll, Stevens, and Zalta (2015) adapted constructs from material science, from which the concept of stress in psychology was first borrowed, in a novel attempt to expand the current conceptualizations of human stress resilience. In material science, *tensile strength* is the amount of pressure that a material can withstand up to any changes in its form. It reflects the overall resistance of fabrics (Mott, 2007), and can be used to conceptualize how people's resources might allow them to withstand the pressures of stressful life circumstances. Fabrics are much stronger than individual threads if they are woven tightly together. This strength, called tensile strength, is maintained even under significant pressure. One of the measures of tensile strength is *yield strength*, which refers to the extent to which fabrics withstand tension and pressure by deformation and plastic changes. Fabrics demonstrate elasticity up to a yield point. Beyond this yield point, there is permanent, irreversible deformation in the fabric, reflecting a plastic range up to the tensile/break point. There might exist a rip in fabrics, and *tear strength* is the amount of force required to tear a fabric on an existing rip. It reflects how well a fabric could resist the growth of a tear under tension. But once a "fault" or rip develops in the fabrics, breakdown is rapid. This concept is important for human resilience and leads to our DTT theory, which posits that the personal, social, and material resources that people have are strongest when they are interdependent and sustained by life practices. For example, a fragmented social support system might be strong at first, but if refugees and people exposed to armed conflict are not in touch with their close social partners and sustained by geographical space, they might be quickly overwhelmed by an individual's or family's demands in crisis. We can see how social support or personal resources such as self-esteem and self-efficacy might work up to a point, and then be overwhelmed.

The DTT theory uses the term "fabrics" as a metaphor of biological, psychological, community, and sociocultural activities, procedures, and practices – these being everyday routines and rituals – that are interconnected and interwoven to make up the structure of everyday life. People sharing the same societal, community, or sociocultural backgrounds have more similar everyday life fabrics and structure, for the composition and quality of their everyday life fabrics and structure are partially dependent on community-level processes such as social networks, collective efficacy, and social capital. Fabrics/Daily routines encompass a broad range of everyday activities/procedures/practices, which could be primary or secondary (Baltes, Maas, Wilms, Borchelt, & Little, 1999).

Primary and Secondary Fabrics/Daily Routines

Primary fabrics / daily routines are essential for survival and satisfying biological needs. Eating and rest/sleep are basic human daily needs. Personal hygiene is one of the first steps of disease prevention and thus better physical health (Prüss, Kay, Fewtrell, & Bartram, 2002). Our home is both functional and meaningful to our lives (Oswald & Wahl, 2005). Secondary fabrics / daily routines refer to behaviors that are optional and selectively performed in accordance with preference, motivation, and appropriateness.

Exercise or leisure activities benefit physical and mental health (Chen & Pang, 2012) only if the circumstances are not restrictive like during social upheaval and heavy workload (Borodulin et al., 2016).

We tend to stay connected and interact with some social partners. Most people are involved in study or work to varying degrees; some people such as those who are self-employed, housewives, and retired might work within less socially organized structures.

The following sections will firstly outline the DTT theory and the Sustaining Everyday Life Fabrics and Structure (SELFS) model and previous supporting evidence, with examples of adaptation among the refugee and conflict-affected populations. Previous research on the associations between everyday life experiences and psychological adaptation of the populations will then be critically reviewed. Next, the added value and applicability of the DTT theory for empirical research and intervention for the populations will be discussed.

Drive to Thrive (DTT) Theory

The basic tenet of the DTT theory is that stress resilience is determined by sustaining the fabrics/routines and structure of everyday life. The main value of this theory is that prior work has considered demand and distress, temporal dynamics, and differential outcomes in defining human stress resilience but not fundamental developmental processes of stress resilience across different life challenges. If, according to Zautra's and Hobfoll's frameworks (Hobfoll et al., 2015; Zautra et al., 2010), positive functioning like engagement in important everyday life tasks is an essential pathway for resilience that parallels recovery from stress-related distress and dysfunctions, then the DTT theory could outline the courses of action for resilience and how people could act upon adaptive beliefs in their everyday life. Practical aspects of everyday life at various socio-ecological levels could be derived for courses of action for resilience. The DTT theory is particularly applicable to long-term adaptation following traumatic events and during chronic stressors, as the lasting consequences of trauma like armed conflict could alter routines and structure of everyday life. Intervention, following from the theory, could focus on maintaining daily routines under usually chronic refugee or post-war settings.

There is empirical evidence showing that stress alters daily routines and structure. Relative to home-living older adults, those living in long-term care facilities exhibited lower levels of active engagement in everyday life (Horgas, Wilms, & Baltes, 1998). Marked differences in everyday life events have been identified between disabled, bereaved, and otherwise healthy older women (Zautra, Reich, & Guarnaccia, 1990). Across the three distinctly different groups, levels of stability in everyday life events have the strongest predictive utility in psychological distress (i.e., anxiety and depressive symptoms) and well-being (i.e., positive emotions and self-esteem). Studies have also demonstrated that small everyday life events predict psychological distress and well-being among diverse populations. Negative everyday life events predicted bereaved and married women's generalized psychological distress over and above the effects of demographic variables, poor physical health, conjugal bereavement status, social support, and major life events (Murdock, Alcorn, Heesacker, & Stoltenberg, 1998). Those negative events were unexpected financial burdens, spousal discords, and arguments and dissatisfaction with friends. Recent reviews suggest that daily aversive events at work and at school contribute to more aversive marital or family interactions, which could have a cumulative, negative impact on psychological well-being over time (Neff & Karney, 2017; Repetti, Wang, & Saxbe, 2009).

The onset of traumatic stress is rapid and the impact of traumatic exposure could be long-lasting (de Jong et al., 2001). Everyday life after trauma exposure could be plagued with stressful conditions that undermine health more substantially than the trauma itself (Miller & Rasmussen, 2010, 2014; Morina, von Lersner, & Prigerson, 2011). Chronic stress could also be exacerbated by time-varying traumatic event exposures and precipitate development of posttraumatic stress symptoms (Cieslak et al., 2014; Kangas, Henry, & Bryant, 2002; Norris & Uhl, 1993). Preexisting risk factors of distress could be amplified and accelerate breakdown of daily routines. Examples of preexisting risk factors include age, sex, low socioeconomic status, minority status, prior trauma, and family history of psychopathology. If everyday life fabrics could withstand the immediate impact of traumatic stress without breaking down, then deformation and plastic changes will be an ongoing process.

Principles

The DTT theory suggests four principles that govern why and how daily routines and structure change and can be sustained in long-term adaptation following traumatic events and during chronic stress conditions.

Principle 1: Following traumatic stress or under chronic stress conditions, people are challenged to maintain their everyday personal, social, work, and leisure practices, while they increasingly focus their attention on the stressors or their own psychological distress.

Principle 2: As traumatic stress subsides and chronic stress continues, contexts restrict people from practicing tasks that continue to contribute to sustaining the routines and structure of their lives. For example, they quit jobs, limit social contact, and withdraw from leisure activities. Some of these routines might have been completely destroyed following extreme exposures to community-wide trauma like wars and disasters.

Principle 3: Because the routines and structure of everyday life are well-built, meaning they have sustaining power, breakdown of routines and structure may not appear at first, despite their initial weakening (i.e., damage). Then, when

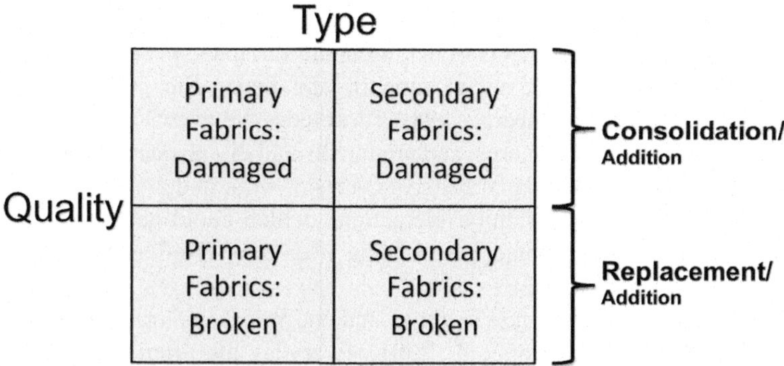

Fig. 1 Sustaining everyday life fabrics in terms of type and quality
Note. Type = primary or secondary fabrics; Quality = damaged or broken

some break point is reached, there appears to be a rapid acceleration of decline. For example, following personal or mass trauma, people might lose some friends but sustain a few good relationships, showing no negative impact on mental health. However, if further loss of these close ties occurs, we would see marked mental health impact when the threshold of some minimum number of sustaining interpersonal ties is reached. Hence, breakdown and loss accelerate after the break point is reached, but the actual decline of underlying resources often occurs earlier below the surface. Like fabric, strength is sustained despite some level of damage, and after some point the fabric no longer has strength to counteract further strain.

Principle 4: People engage in at least three processes for sustaining fabrics/routines and structure of everyday life, namely consolidation of damaged fabrics, replacement of broken fabrics, and addition of new fabrics (Fig. 1).

Corollaries

Based on the concepts and principles of the DTT theory, two corollaries are formulated to outline the association between quality of daily routines and structure and psychological resilience to posttraumatic and chronic stress conditions. Stress resilience is determined by the preexisting quality and ongoing sustainment of routines and structure, resulting in four hypothesized trajectories (Fig. 2):

1. Well-built preexisting daily routines and structure that are effectively sustained;
2. Less well-built but effectively sustained daily routines;
3. Well-built but not effectively sustained daily routines; and
4. Less well-built and not effectively sustained daily routines.

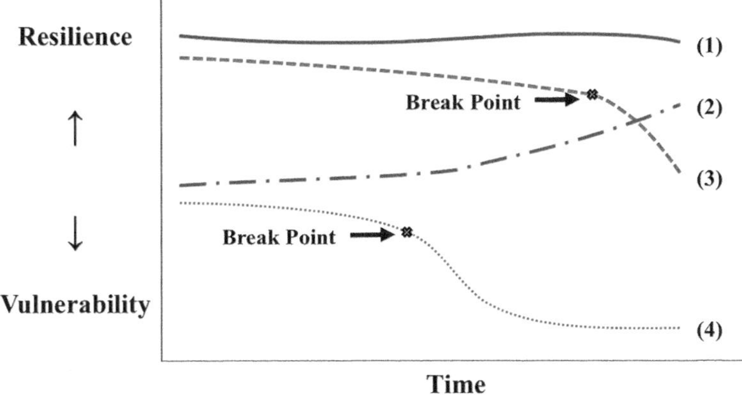

Fig. 2 Four trajectories of daily routines in stress resilience and vulnerability
Note. (1) Well-built preexisting daily routines and structure that are effectively sustained; (2) less well-built but effectively sustained daily routines; (3) well-built but not effectively sustained daily routines; (4) less well-built and not effectively sustained daily routines

Corollary 1: Those who have more "well-built" routines and structure of everyday life will be more resilient to posttraumatic and chronic stress. The "well-built" routines and structure could result from longstanding practices or sustaining routines and structure effectively.

Corollary 2: Those who lack "well-built" routines and structure of everyday life will be less resilient and will reach the break point at an earlier time or at lower levels of stress than those with "well-built" routines and structure. The velocity and timing of the break point depend on the extent to which people are able to sustain routines and structure.

Sustaining Everyday Life Fabrics and Structure (SELFS)

Three basic, sequential processes sustain everyday life fabrics/routines and structure. In presenting the SELFS model, we use "fabrics" instead of daily routines to highlight the dynamic changes. First, people *consolidate* the existing fabrics. While people consolidate the damaged life fabrics, they need to give up some other fabrics at the same time. Then, people attempt to *replace* the broken fabrics with alternative similar fabrics. Next, given the damaged and broken fabrics, people *add* new fabrics to complete the everyday life structure. Elastic range indicates the extent to which people consolidate existing fabrics, whereas plastic range indicates the extent to which people sustain fabrics and structure through replacement and addition. Consolidation and addition could be proactive or reactive and continuous procedures, throughout adaptation to stress and before and after breakdown of fabrics.

Replacement is reactive, occurring after fabrics break down and when consolidation does not work for certain fabrics. People work on either primary or secondary fabrics or both. Previous evidence has pointed out the importance of SELFS in prospective adaptation following different forms of trauma. A qualitative study has demonstrated that reconstructing everyday occupations and work participation endogenously emerged to be a key factor in adaptation to mild traumatic brain injury (Sveen, Søberg, & Østensjø, 2016). In a similar vein, the degree to which Japanese survivors of the 1995 Great Hanshin-Awaji earthquake consolidated motivation for civic participation was associated with lower physical and psychological distress (Tatsuki & Hayashi, 2000). After 11 years of civil war in Sierra Leone, remaking everyday life, which might include replacement of broken fabrics and addition of new fabrics, is suggested to parallel remaking society and is thus a crucial step for enhancing physical and mental health in the citizens' war-torn ecology (Ibrahim & Shepler, 2011).

SELFS: Engine

Resources are embedded in everyday life. The conservation of resources (COR) theory suggests that stress is experienced due to actual loss or threat of loss of resources and limited gain in resources (Hobfoll, 1998). Whether resource loss contributes to higher psychosocial distress is partially dependent upon the fabrics and structure of everyday life. In adjusting to posttraumatic or chronic stressors, resource loss is gradual, threat of loss is subtle, and sustaining everyday fabrics is continuing. This is a period when people invest resources to gain more resources, forming resource passageways for subsequent challenges. Resource passageways delay breakdown of fabrics by increasing elasticity and plasticity of fabrics. Resource changes also direct people to consolidate, replace, and add everyday life fabrics. According to COR theory, perceived stress indicates overall resource change, with higher perceived stress signifying higher overall resource loss (Hobfoll, 1998). There is evidence showing that perceived stress predicts consolidation of existing social ties but not addition of new communication ties (Kalish, Luria, Toker, & Westman, 2015). Resource change could be indicated for personal, social, and economic resources individually. It is important to look into loss and gain of resources in multiple dimensions and how these could drive sustainment of everyday life fabrics.

Loss of resources in a particular dimension could motivate people to consolidate fabrics in the same dimension. For example, people could change from being full-time workers to jobless refugees due to armed conflicts (i.e., loss of economic resources). With less income, they are motivated to be more careful in spending. Refugees could experience shrinkage of social networks due to separation from social partners in their home countries (i.e., loss of social resources). With limited facilities and time for leisure activities, they are motivated to spend quality time with family. Loss of resources in a particular dimension could also motivate people to replace broken fabrics with alternatives and add new fabrics from other dimensions. For example, migrants who have fled to other countries could experience decreased contact with friends. Such individuals, nevertheless, have more time to maintain existing hobbies or develop new hobbies. They could also spend time on developing friendships with local people around their neighborhood. Specific examples of consolidation, replacement, and addition among refugee and conflict-affected populations are given below.

Consolidation of Damaged Fabrics

Consolidation of primary and then secondary fabrics could result in a more well-built structure. For example, people following mass trauma or in refugee camps could make plans for preparing healthy food and maintain enough sleep, and then contact friends and relatives away from them and participate in hobbies regularly. They need to identify the most significant demands – whether it is the loss of a companion or family time, change in standard of living, or sleeping problems (Bonanno & Burton, 2013). If loss of a companion is the most significant, then consolidation of existing fabrics – maintaining relationships with other family members/relatives/friends/neighbors should be prioritized and given more attention. It is important to note that consolidation of fabrics is likely to be challenging in refugee and post-conflict settings – when survival is a struggle and luxuries like healthy food and engaging in hobbies may be difficult to access.

Replacement of Broken Fabrics with Alternatives

Replacement of fabrics occurs following loss of primary and/or secondary fabrics and when consolidation is unlikely. An example of this can be seen amongst African and Middle-Eastern refugees who built up encampments at the vicinity of Calais, France. They built not only homes (e.g., where mothers take care of the babies) but also a church and mosque for religious practices, schools and playgrounds for children, restaurants serving familiar cuisine, and theater and other recreation facilities. In the marketplace, shops and stalls sell food, drinks, snacks, and phone cards. They made an effort to replace their previous everyday life with similar alternatives (Davies & Isakjee, 2015). In particular, like other refugees who sought asylum in Europe, refugees in the Calais Jungle have been displaced from the social network that took years to establish in their home countries. It may also be difficult for people in conflict and post-conflict countries to regularly connect with their longtime friends. However, friendships could be maintained through other means, for example, through phone calls and social network sites. Maintaining social ties, nonetheless, is not necessarily exclusively beneficial. Contact with family and friends using social media might expose refugees to messages and images of the devastating consequences or continuation of persecution and violence that could inadvertently undermine mental health.

Addition of New Fabrics

This process could be understood as changes in the structure of everyday life fabrics. New fabrics refer to everyday activities and procedures that were not practiced pre-trauma and are added afterward. This is an essential step of thriving in the ongoing adaptation after trauma exposure and during chronic stress. For example, people who did not engage in health lifestyle practices before trauma exposure could develop new, regular eating and sleeping habits. They could explore new interests and develop new hobbies. They could make new friends and develop new social activities. Refugees who had a small social circle back in their home countries could obtain social resources over and above those in their life prior to trauma through participating in new activities such as local support groups. Instead of mere recovery to the original state and being non-distressed, addition of new fabrics is the precursor of thriving in refugee or post-conflict populations, which could represent gain in and pursuit of life opportunities for growth and development, both behaviorally and socially (Carver, 1998; Feeney & Collins, 2015).

SELFS: Resulting Structure

SELFS dictates whether the resulting structure is more well-built or fragile than the original structure. For example, people with more regular and stable lifestyles, family relationships, friendships, and management of work involvement would endorse a more well-built and well-sustaining everyday life structure. Those who merely consolidate and replace secondary fabrics and add new primary and secondary fabrics would have a more fragile everyday life structure, accelerating breakdown of fabrics and the damage brought about by the breakdown. At least three types of everyday life structures can result from SELFS: the original structure, a new structure, and a broad-base structure.

1. ***Restoring the Original Structure***

People can partially restore fabrics and structure following adversity. One core feature of all restored structures is traces of consolidation, replacement, and addition (i.e., deformation and plastic changes). People who are able to restore a structure so that it resembles the original one demonstrate resilience, which is reflected by lower distress and higher well-being. Restoration of the original structure benefits subsequent development of thriving. However, this in itself is not thriving, because thriving is not merely returning to the original state and being non-distressed.

2. ***Building a New Structure***

The quality of the new structure depends on the degree to which people take on a sequential process to build it. A more fragile structure results if people add new fabrics before existing fabrics are consolidated and broken fabrics are replaced by more adaptive ones. For example, people may try to add new hobbies despite the fact that they are incapable of balancing their work involvement. People may attempt to socialize with friends more by giving up time with their family. It is also possible for people to add new maladaptive fabrics like regular overuse of opioids or sleeping pills that do not benefit resilience. A new fragile structure contributes to an earlier break point and more rapid breakdown of fabrics, increasing the risk of psychological dysfunction.

3. ***Building a Broad-Base Structure***

A broad-base structure occurs after breakdown of the secondary fabrics. If people consolidate or replace solely the primary fabrics, their everyday life structure would take on a broad-base shape. The new structure is less likely to break but does not guarantee better functioning or resilience. A structure with only primary fabrics is likely to be basic, routine, low in vigor, commitment, and absorption, and comprise limited things to appreciate or savor, lacking psychological and behavioral processes that contribute to resilience (Hobfoll et al., 2012; Hou et al., 2016, 2017). With a solid structure, some people would be less likely to rebuild original secondary fabrics or add new adaptive secondary fabrics.

Drive to Thrive for the Global Migrant and Refugee Crisis

The previous sections outline principles and processes that could be applicable to refugee and conflict-affected populations, suggesting the importance of considering everyday experiences among these people. There is an increasing body of literature recognizing daily stressors as a missing yet essential component for investigating the link between direct exposure to trauma and health (Miller & Rasmussen, 2010, 2014). The Inter-Agency Standing Committee suggests a multi-layered system of Mental Health and Psychosocial Support (MHPSS) (Inter-Agency Standing Committee, 2007). MHPSS entails stepwise support in emergency settings: (re) establishing governance and services that address basic physical needs for the population as a whole, facilitating access to greater community and family supports for people to maintain their mental health and psychosocial well-being, providing focused individual, family, or group interventions to those in need, and providing specialized psychiatric services for the smaller percentage of the population whose severe mental disorders contribute to significant difficulties in everyday life (Hassan et al., 2015). The basic premise is that people face a wide range of recurrent stressors in everyday life in post-conflict settings, while existing evidence suggests that trauma exposure accounts for a limited amount of the variance in posttraumatic stress disorder (PTSD) symptoms or other psychological outcomes. Miller and Rasmussen (2010, 2014) suggest two kinds of daily stressors. One is low-intensity stressors such as poverty, social isolation, and poor or insecure neighborhoods, that could be experienced on a daily basis. The other is potentially traumatic stressors such as occasional armed conflicts, sexual violence, and death of loved ones; those that are highly distressing but do not occur on a daily basis.

A growing body of literature points out the possibility that the breakdown of daily routines mediates the impact of traumatic events on psychological outcomes following mass trauma, and that contrariwise support in sustaining daily routines may be restorative. The relevant studies are reviewed.

Daily Stressors

Supportive evidence is available to show that daily stressors are related to higher psychological distress over and above exposure to traumatic events in post-conflict settings. In a study in eastern Congo, a region disturbed by conflicts and conflict-related crimes including looting, massacres, torture, and sexual violence, more than one-third of 1305 adolescent girls (age = 11–23 years) reported having experienced rape or sexual violence during the conflict period (Verelst, De Schryver, Broekaert, & Derluyn, 2014). Relative to those without experience of sexual violence, these girls reported higher material and social daily stressors, such as insufficient food and clothing, skipping school due to work, a crowded home environment, and perceived stigmatization and social exclusion within community. For citizens in South Sudan (n = 1228), where poverty and armed conflicts have persisted for more than 20 years, insufficient clean drinking water, food, and medical care, together with previous serious injury, forced displacement, and more frequent experience of violent events were associated with poorer physical and psychological functioning (Roberts, Damundu, Lomoro, & Sondorp, 2010). In another study, a sample of 464 South Sudanese people have expressed unmet needs for drinking water and food, better hygiene, a sense of security (e.g., reduced alcohol or drug use in the community), education for the children, mutual and reciprocal support in the community, and material and health care support from authority as important everyday needs; they also considered having too much free time as a serious problem (Ayazi, Swartz, Eide, Lien, & Hauff, 2015). The association between exposure to traumatic events and psychological distress became non-significant after taking into account the effect of unmet everyday needs. In a longitudinal study of former child soldiers in Sierra Leone (n = 260), perceived everyday discrimination due to their status as a child soldier predicted higher post-war anxiety and depressive symptoms and hostility (Betancourt, Agnew-Blais, Gilman, Williams, & Ellis, 2010). The association between war exposures and psychological adjustment decreased after taking into account the effect of everyday discrimination.

Trauma Exposure, Daily Stressors, and Ill Health

The hypothesized mediating and moderating role of daily stressors in the association between trauma exposure and distress has also been formally tested. Unmet everyday needs mediated the association between trauma exposure (i.e., total number of traumatic events encountered) and psychological distress among Iraqi adults who were displaced in Jordan (n = 269) and Bhutanese adult refugees in Nepal (n = 269) (Jordans, Semrau, Thornicroft, & van Ommeren, 2012). The number of previous traumatic events was associated with higher psychological distress through its positive association with unmet everyday needs. Among Darfur refugees who were living in refugee camps in Chad (n = 848) and Afghans living under post-Taliban conflicts in Kabul (n = 320) (Miller, Omidian, Rasmussen, Yaqubi, & Daudzai, 2008; Rasmussen & Annan, 2009; Rasmussen et al., 2010), daily stressors including lack of money for living, unemployment, reduced sense of security, poor/crowded physical conditions, interpersonal conflicts, and others were stronger predictors of psychological distress than war exposure and increased the positive association between war exposure and psychological distress. War exposure resulted in psychological distress only if post-war/conflict daily stressors increased. At higher levels of daily stressors, psychological distress became unrelated to war exposure. Among Rohingya adults of Myanmar living in refugee camps in Bangladesh (n = 148), depressive symptoms were not positively associated with trauma exposure but daily stressors including shortage of food, restriction of moving freely, and lack of a sense of security, were, in aggregate, linked to depression symptoms (Riley, Varner, Ventevogel, Taimur Hasan, & Welton-Mitchell, 2017). The positive association between trauma exposure and PTSD symptoms was partially mediated by daily stressors, suggesting that trauma exposure increased PTSD symptoms partly because it increased daily stressors among refugees.

Similar findings have been identified among conflict-affected adolescents. While war exposure was only weakly associated with post-war symptoms of PTSD and depression in Sierra Leone Krio teenagers and younger adults (age = 13–24 years), daily stressors (i.e., housing, food, or economic insecurity, interpersonal conflicts, and neglect) were consistently moderately associated with the above symptoms ($r > 0.40$) (Newnham, Pearson, Stein, & Betancourt, 2015). The weak association between war exposure and depressive symptoms became non-significant after taking into account the mediating effect of daily stressors, suggesting that war exposure increases depressive symptoms, as a function of increasing challenges in sustaining daily living in post-war settings.

Sustaining Everyday Life Fabrics and Structure (SELFS) Among Refugee and Conflict-Affected Populations

Maintaining pre-displacement/pre-conflict daily life routines is recognized to be no easy task when post-displacement, refugee, and post-conflict settings may not offer the opportunity to engage in meaningful daily activities (Hassan et al., 2015). The daily stressor model opens up new agendas for investigating adaptation among refugee and conflict-affected populations. However, definition and measurement of the model could be further clarified. Although daily stressors were defined as stressful personal and social situations that are encountered by people in everyday life after trauma (Miller & Rasmussen, 2010, 2014), previous studies assessed a wide variety of experiences including lack of clean drinking water, poor or crowded living conditions, too much free time, unemployment, interpersonal conflicts, stigmatization, subjective feelings over the current conditions or the future, and even psychological distress. Although previous studies provided an important evidence base for investigating how everyday life impacts adaptation to refugee and post-conflict contexts, currently there is little investigation of how the everyday lives of refugee and conflict-affected populations change following trauma. Also, previous studies have aggregated all items together without looking at conceptually and realistically meaningful domains of everyday life.

Daily stressors could be either caused or worsened by war exposure or unrelated to the exposure (Miller & Rasmussen, 2010). Changes in daily routines and structure are nonetheless a definite condition following trauma exposure. Previous studies of conflict-affected people assessed and aggregated a wide variety of daily stressors including lack of clean drinking water, poor or crowded living conditions, too much free time, unemployment, and psychological distress. Some of these "*daily stressors*" are indeed ordinary everyday life fabrics/routines, damaged/broken fabrics/routines, or obstacles to sustaining these fabrics/routines. The DTT theory outlines principles and dynamic processes that could further the current understanding of adaptation in refugee and post-conflict settings. The theory differentiates between primary and secondary daily routines and provides a conceptual framework for explaining how health outcomes are attributable to everyday life in these populations. Refugees are challenged to sustain primary routines including hygiene, meal plans, shelter, housekeeping, and family relationships. Secondary routines could include free time and employment, religious practice, and friendship network. For instance, shortage of clean drinking water and food is obviously stressful, but how does this increase psychological distress? Possible mechanisms include the financial demands of water and food consumption and fear of malnutrition or dehydration for self and family (Hadley, Stevenson, Tadesse, & Belachew, 2012; Wutich & Ragsdale, 2008). How does living in crowded refugee camps contribute to poorer physical and mental health? Crowded living conditions could precipitate poorer interpersonal relationships and even interpersonal aggression (Evans, Lepore, Shejwal, & Palsane, 1998; Regoeczi, 2008). In conflict-affected regions, unemployed people, particularly those who feel that they have too much free time, could be more likely to have conflicts with family or neighbors. Concrete understanding of their everyday lives is crucial for us to fully understand and explain how daily hassles emerge to be salient concerns that impact health over and above trauma among refugee and conflict-affected populations.

Restoring the original everyday life structure may not be feasible following mass trauma given contextual limitations, such as disrupted social and economic systems, displacement from home, endless waiting in refugee camps, and alienation from social network in home countries. Neither is building a broad-base structure the most beneficial to the post-conflict populations. Although a broad-base structure is less likely to break down, it is made up of primary routines that are basic but lack psychological and behavioral processes of resilience such as fulfilling work involvement, friendship network, leisure activities, and community participation. Among consolidation, replacement, and addition for sustaining everyday life fabrics/routines, future studies could investigate which of these processes is/are more helpful. One possibility is that the three processes could be implemented sequentially for maximal benefit to post-conflict adaptation. Using interpersonal relationships in refugee camps as an example, maintaining family relationships could be prioritized at the outset (i.e., consolidation of primary fabrics). Being physically distant from the social network in their home countries, social media could be used (i.e., replacement of secondary fabrics). New interpersonal and communal connections could be established in the camps (i.e., addition of secondary fabrics). Those with less well-built daily routines and structure or those who are less capable of consolidating, replacing, or adding social relationships would be more likely to develop physical and psychological problems.

Conclusion

In the DTT theory, the term “fabrics” is a metaphor for psychological, community, and sociocultural activities, procedures, and practices that are interconnected and interwoven to make up the structure of everyday life. Fabrics encompass a broad range of everyday activities/procedures/practices (i.e., routines), which could be primary or secondary. Primary daily routines are essential for survival and satisfying biological needs, such as personal hygiene, eating healthy, sleep, and maintaining a home. Secondary daily routines refer to behaviors that are optional and selectively performed in accordance with preference, motivation, and appropriateness, such as exercising, social time, leisure activites, and work involvement.

The basic tenet of the DTT theory is that stress resilience is determined by sustaining the fabrics/routines and structure of everyday life, governed by four principles. First, while people increasingly become focused on post-trauma and chronic stressors, they are challenged to maintain everyday practices. Second, ongoing post-trauma and chronic stressful conditions restrict sustainment of routines and structure of everyday life (i.e., damage). Third, breakdown of daily routines and structure starts slow in the beginning but is accelerated once some break point is reached.

Fourth, everyday life fabrics/routines and structure are best sustained through sequential consolidation of existing fabrics, replacement of broken fabrics with alternatives, and addition of new fabrics. Whether daily routines and structure are "well-built" depends on longstanding practices and the extent to which people are able to sustain them in adaptation. More "well-built" routines and structure of everyday life confer resilience to traumatic and chronic stress (*Corollary 1*), whereas less "well-built" routines and structure result in earlier development and more rapid onset of significant distress (*Corollary 2*). The theory outlines concrete pathways through which people could act upon adaptive beliefs behaviorally in their everyday life. In the processes of sustaining daily routines, people either restore the original everyday life structure, build a new structure, or build a broad-base structure.

The DTT theory adds to existing theoretical and empirical literature by providing testable hypotheses for investigating which, when, and how everyday life processes contribute to both positive and negative health outcomes over and above traumatic exposure among refugee and conflict-affected populations. The daily stressor model asserts that daily stressors represent a missing yet essential component for investigating the link between direct exposure to trauma and health. There is a growing body of studies demonstrating the predictive utility of daily stressors in poorer mental health independent of exposure to traumatic events in different post-conflict populations. Previous studies have shown that traumatic exposure contribute to higher psychological distress only if the exposure increases daily stressors. Breakdown of daily routines could mediate or moderate the impact of traumatic events on psychological outcomes; alternatively support in sustaining daily routines may be restorative.

An evidence base is needed for testing the principles and processes that are proposed by the DTT theory. Recent years have witnessed a fast growing population of Smartphone users around the world. A free Wi-Fi and mobile phone charging service station was one of the most popular spots among African and Middle-East refugees in the Calais Jungle. One should not be surprised to see increasing use of internet services and social media among refugee and post-conflict populations due to their emotional, social, instrumental, informational, and even life-saving and health-promoting functions (Lau et al., 2016; United Nations High Commissioner for Refugees, 2016). Mobile apps could be programmed to help the people and health care professionals identify existing daily routines that are damaged or broken and additional routines that refugee and post-conflict populations might need. Using this data, apps could then be developed to administer evidence-based, theory-driven procedures for consolidating, replacing, and adding daily routines. The ultimate goal is to empower people to build new, adaptive daily routines and structure that enhance resilience.

Acknowledgements This chapter was prepared under the partial support of Early Career Scheme (Project No.: HKIED 859113) and the Fulbright-RGC Hong Kong Senior Research Scholar Award from the Research Grants Council of the Hong Kong Special Administrative Region, China (WK Hou). The Fulbright-RGC Hong Kong Award was in collaboration with the Consulate General of the United States in Hong Kong.

References

Anthony, E. J. (1974). The syndrome of the psychologically invulnerable child. In E. J. Anthony & C. Koupernik (Eds.), *The child in his family: Children at psychiatric risk* (pp. 529–545). New York, NY: Wiley.

Ayazi, T., Swartz, L., Eide, A. H., Lien, L., & Hauff, E. (2015). Perceived current needs, psychological distress and functional impairment in a war-affected setting: A cross-sectional study in South Sudan. *BMJ Open, 5*(8), e007534.

Baltes, M. M., Maas, I., Wilms, H.-U., Borchelt, M., & Little, T. D. (1999). Everyday competence in old and very old age: Theoretical considerations and empirical findings. In P. B. Baltes & K. U. Mayer (Eds.), The Berlin Aging Study: Aging from 70 to 100 (pp. 384–402). New York: Cambridge University Press.

Betancourt, T. S., Agnew-Blais, J., Gilman, S. E., Williams, D. R., & Ellis, B. H. (2010). Past horrors, present struggles: The role of stigma in the association between war experiences and psychosocial adjustment among former child soldiers in Sierra Leone. *Social Science & Medicine, 70*(1), 17–26.

Bonanno, G. A. (2004). Loss, trauma, and human resilience: Have we underestimated the human capacity to thrive after extremely aversive events? *American Psychologist, 59*(1), 20–28.

Bonanno, G. A., & Burton, C. L. (2013). Regulatory flexibility an individual differences perspective on coping and emotion regulation. *Perspectives on Psychological Science, 8*(6), 591–612.

Bonanno, G. A., Galea, S., Bucciarelli, A., & Vlahov, D. (2007). What predicts psychological resilience after disaster? The role of demographics, resources, and life stress. *Journal of Consulting and Clinical Psychology, 75*(5), 671–682.

Bonanno, G. A., Kennedy, P., Galatzer-Levy, I. R., Lude, P., & Elfström, M. L. (2012). Trajectories of resilience, depression, and anxiety following spinal cord injury. *Rehabilitation Psychology, 57*(3), 236–247.

Bonanno, G. A., Romero, S. A., & Klein, S. I. (2015). The temporal elements of psychological resilience: An integrative framework for the study of individuals, families, and communities. *Psychological Inquiry, 26*(2), 139–169.

Bonanno, G. A., Wortman, C. B., Lehman, D. R., Tweed, R. G., Haring, M., Sonnega, J., … Nesse, R. M. (2002). Resilience to loss and chronic grief: A prospective study from preloss to 18-months postloss. *Journal of Personality and Social Psychology, 83*(5), 1150–1164.

Baltes, M. M., Maas, I., Wilms, H.-U., Borchelt, M., & Little, T. D. (1999). Everyday competence in old and very old age: Theoretical considerations and empirical findings. In P. B. Baltes & K. U. Mayer (Eds.), *The berlin aging study: Aging from 70 to 100* (pp. 384–402). New York: Cambridge University Press.

Borodulin, K., Sipilä, N., Rahkonen, O., Leino-Arjas, P., Kestilä, L., Jousilahti, P., & Prättälä, R. (2016). Socio-demographic and behavioral variation in barriers to leisure-time physical activity. *Scandinavian Journal of Public Health, 44*, 62–69.

Carver, C. S. (1998). Resilience and thriving: Issues, models, and linkages. *Journal of Social Issues, 54*(2), 245–266.

Cieslak, R., Shoji, K., Douglas, A., Melville, E., Luszczynska, A., & Benight, C. C. (2014). A meta-analysis of the relationship between job burnout and secondary traumatic stress among workers with indirect exposure to trauma. *Psychological Services, 11*(1), 75–86.

Chen, M., & Pang, X. (2012). Leisure motivation: An integrative review. *Social Behavior and Personality: An International Journal, 40*, 1075–1081.

de Jong, J. T., Komproe, I. H., van Ommeren, M., El Masri, M., Araya, M., Khaled, N., … Somasundaram, D. (2001). Lifetime events and posttraumatic stress disorder in 4 post conflict settings. *Journal of the American Medical Association, 286*(5), 555–562.

Davies, T., & Isakjee, A. (2015). Geography, migration and abandonment in the Calais refugee camp. *Political Geography, 49*, 93–95.

Eggerman, M., & Panter-Brick, C. (2010). Suffering, hope, and entrapment: Resilience and cultural values in Afghanistan. *Social Science & Medicine, 71*(1), 71–83.

Evans, G. W., Lepore, S. J., Shejwal, B. R., & Palsane, M. N. (1998). Chronic residential crowding and children's well-being: An ecological perspective. *Child Development, 69*(6), 1514–1523.

Feeney, B. C., & Collins, N. L. (2015). A new look at social support: A theoretical perspective on thriving through relationships. *Personality and Social Psychology Review, 19*(2), 113–147.

Hadley, C., Stevenson, E. G. J., Tadesse, Y., & Belachew, T. (2012). Rapidly rising food prices and the experience of food insecurity in urban Ethiopia: Impacts on health and well-being. *Social Science & Medicine, 75*(12), 2412–2419.

Hall, B. J., Tol, W., Jordans, M., Bass, J., & de Jong, J. T. (2014). Understanding resilience in armed conflict: Social resources and mental health of children in Burundi. *Social Science and Medicine, 114*, 121–128.

Hassan, G., Kirmayer, L. J., Mekki-Berrada, A., Quosh, C., el Chammay, R., Deville-Stoetzel, J. B., … Ventevogel, P. (2015). *Culture, context and the mental health and psychosocial well-being of Syrians: A review for mental health and psychosocial support staff working with Syrians affected by armed conflict*. Geneva, Switzerland: United Nations High Commissioner for Refugees.

Hobfoll, S. E. (1998). *Stress, culture, and community: The psychology and philosophy of stress*. New York, NY: Plenum.

Hobfoll, S. E. (2011a). Conservation of resource caravans and engaged settings. *Journal of Occupational and Organizational Psychology, 84*(1), 116–122.

Hobfoll, S. E. (2011b). Conservation of resources theory: Its implication for success, health, and resilience. In S. Folkman (Ed.), *The Oxford handbook of stress, health, and coping* (pp. 127–147). New York, NY: Oxford University Press.

Hobfoll, S. E., Johnson, R. J., Canetti, D., Palmieri, P. A., Hall, B. J., Lavi, I., & Galea, S. (2012). Can people remain engaged and vigorous in the face of trauma? Palestinians in the West Bank and Gaza. *Psychiatry, 75*(1), 60–75.

Hobfoll, S. E., Stevens, N. R., & Zalta, A. K. (2015). Expanding the science of resilience: Conserving resources in the aid of adaptation. *Psychological Inquiry, 26*(2), 174–180.

Horgas, A. L., Wilms, H. U., & Baltes, M. M. (1998). Daily life in very old age: Everyday activities as expression of successful living. *The Gerontologist, 38*(5), 556–568.

Hou, W. K., & Lam, J. H. M. (2014). Resilience in the year after cancer diagnosis: A cross-lagged panel analysis of the reciprocity between psychological distress and well-being. *Journal of Behavioral Medicine, 37*(3), 391–401.

Hou, W. K., Lau, K. M., Ng, S. M., Cheng, S. T., Shum, T. C. Y., Cheng, A. C. K., & Cheung, H. Y. S. (2017). Savoring moderates the association between cancer-specific physical symptoms and depressive symptoms. *Psycho-Oncology, 26*(2), 231–238.

Hou, W. K., Lau, K. M., Ng, S. M., Lee, T. M. C., Cheung, H. Y. S., Shum, T. C. Y., & Cheng, A. C. K. (2016). Psychological detachment and savoring in adaptation to cancer caregiving. *Psycho-Oncology, 25*(7), 839–847.

Hou, W. K., Law, C. C., Yin, J., & Fu, Y. T. (2010). Resource loss, resource gain, and psychological resilience and dysfunction following cancer diagnosis: A growth mixture modeling approach. *Health Psychology, 29*(5), 484–495.

Ibrahim, A. F., & Shepler, S. (2011). Introduction: Everyday life in postwar Sierra Leone. *Africa Today, 58*(2), 5–12.

Inter-Agency Standing Committee. (2007). *IASC guidelines on mental health and psychosocial support in emergency settings*. Geneva, Switzerland: Author.

Jordans, M. J., Semrau, M., Thornicroft, G., & van Ommeren, M. (2012). Role of current perceived needs in explaining the association between past trauma exposure and distress in humanitarian settings in Jordan and Nepal. *British Journal of Psychiatry, 201*(4), 276–281.

Kalish, Y., Luria, G., Toker, S., & Westman, M. (2015). Till stress do us part: On the interplay between perceived stress and communication network dynamics. *Journal of Applied Psychology, 100*(6), 1737–1751.

Kangas, M., Henry, J. L., & Bryant, R. A. (2002). Posttraumatic stress disorder following cancer: A conceptual and empirical review. *Clinical Psychology Review, 22*(4), 499–524.

Kawachi, I., Kennedy, B. P., & Glass, R. (1999). Social capital and self-rated health: A contextual analysis. *American Journal of Public Health, 89*(8), 1187–1193.

Lau, K. M., Hou, W. K., Hall, B. J., Daphna, C., Ng, S. M., & Hobfoll, S. E. (2016). Social media and mental health in democracy movement in Hong Kong: A population-based study. *Computers in Human Behavior, 64*, 656–662.

Luthar, S. S., Cicchetti, D., & Becker, B. (2000). The construct of resilience: A critical evaluation and guidelines for future work. *Child Development, 71*(3), 543–562.

Lyubomirsky, S., King, L., & Diener, E. (2005). The benefits of frequent positive affect: Does happiness lead to success? *Psychological Bulletin, 131*(6), 803–855.

Masten, A. S. (2001). Ordinary magic: Resilience processes in development. *American Psychologist, 56*(3), 227–238.

Masten, A. S. (2014). Global perspectives on resilience in children and youth. *Child Development, 85*(1), 6–20.

Masten, A. S., Best, K. M., & Garmezy, N. (1990). Resilience and development: Contributions from the study of children who overcome adversity. *Development and Psychopathology, 2*(4), 425–444.

Miller, K. E., Omidian, P., Rasmussen, A., Yaqubi, A., & Daudzai, H. (2008). Daily stressors, war experiences, and mental health in Afghanistan. *Transcultural Psychiatry, 45*(4), 611–638.

Miller, K. E., & Rasmussen, A. (2010). War exposure, daily stressors, and mental health in conflict and post-conflict settings: Bridging the divide between trauma-focused and psychosocial frameworks. *Social Science & Medicine, 70*(1), 7–16.

Miller, K. E., & Rasmussen, A. (2014). War experiences, daily stressors and mental health five years on: Elaborations and future directions. *Intervention, 12*, 33–42.

Morina, N., von Lersner, U., & Prigerson, H. G. (2011). War and bereavement: Consequences for mental and physical distress. *PLoS One, 6*(7), e22140.

Mott, R. L. (2007). *Applied strength of materials* (5th ed.). Upper Saddle River, NJ: Pearson/Prentice Hall.

Murdock, N. L., Alcorn, J., Heesacker, M., & Stoltenberg, C. (1998). Model training program in counseling psychology. *The Counseling Psychologist, 26*(4), 658–672.

Neff, L. A., & Karney, B. R. (2017). Acknowledging the elephant in the room: How stressful environmental contexts shape relationship dynamics. *Current Opinion in Psychology, 13*, 107–110.

Newnham, E. A., Pearson, R. M., Stein, A., & Betancourt, T. S. (2015). Youth mental health after civil war: The importance of daily stressors. *British Journal of Psychiatry, 206*(2), 116–121.

Norris, F. H., Stevens, S. P., Pfefferbaum, B., Wyche, K. F., & Pfefferbaum, R. L. (2008). Community resilience as a metaphor, theory, set of capacities, and strategy for disaster readiness. *American Journal of Community Psychology, 41*(1–2), 127–150.

Norris, F. H., Tracy, M., & Galea, S. (2009). Looking for resilience: Understanding the longitudinal trajectories of responses to stress. *Social Science & Medicine, 68*(12), 2190–2198.

Norris, F. H., & Uhl, G. A. (1993). Chronic stress as a mediator of acute stress: The case of Hurricane Hugo. *Journal of Applied Social Psychology, 23*(16), 1263–1284.

Oswald, F., & Wahl, H.-W. (2005). Dimensions of the meaning of home. In G. D. Rowles & H. Chaudhury (Eds.), *Home and identity in late life: International perspectives* (pp. 21–45). New York: Springer.

Panter-Brick, C. (2014). Health, risk, and resilience: Interdisciplinary concepts and applications. *Annual Review of Anthropology, 43*, 431–448.

Panter-Brick, C., & Eggerman, M. (2012). Understanding culture, resilience, and mental health: The production of hope. In M. Ungar (Ed.), *The social ecology of resilience: A handbook of theory and practice* (pp. 369–386). New York, NY: Springer.

Prüss, A., Kay, D., Fewtrell, L., & Bartram, J. (2002). Estimating the burden of disease from water, sanitation, and hygiene at a global level. *Environmental Health Perspectives, 110*, 537–542.

Rasmussen, A., & Annan, J. (2009). Predicting stress related to basic needs and safety in Darfur refugee camps: A structural and social ecological analysis. *Journal of Refugee Studies, 23*(1), 23–40.

Rasmussen, A., Nguyen, L., Wilkinson, J., Vundla, S., Raghavan, S., Miller, K. E., & Keller, A. S. (2010). Rates and impact of trauma and current stressors among Darfuri refugees in Eastern Chad. *American Journal of Orthopsychiatry, 80*(2), 227–236.

Regoeczi, W. C. (2008). Crowding in context: An examination of the differential responses of men and women to high-density living environments. *Journal of Health and Social Behavior, 49*(3), 254–268.

Repetti, R., Wang, S. W., & Saxbe, D. (2009). Bringing it all back home how outside stressors shape families' everyday lives. *Current Directions in Psychological Science, 18*(2), 106–111.

Riley, A., Varner, A., Ventevogel, P., Taimur Hasan, M. M., & Welton-Mitchell, C. (2017). Daily stressors, trauma exposure, and mental health among stateless Rohingya refugees in Bangladesh. *Transcultural Psychiatry, 54*(3), 304–331.

Roberts, B., Damundu, E. Y., Lomoro, O., & Sondorp, E. (2010). The influence of demographic characteristics, living conditions, and trauma exposure on the overall health of a conflict-affected population in Southern Sudan. *BMC Public Health, 10*(1), 518.

Rosshandler, Y., Hall, B. J., & Canetti, D. (2016). An application of an ecological framework to understand risk factors of PTSD due to prolonged conflict exposure: Israeli and Palestinian adolescents in the line of fire. *Psychological Trauma: Theory, Research, Practice, and Policy, 8*(5), 641–648.

Rutter, M. (1987). Psychosocial resilience and protective mechanisms. *American Journal of Orthopsychiatry, 57*(3), 316–331.

Schaufeli, W. B., Salanova, M., González-Romá, V., & Bakker, A. B. (2002). The measurement of engagement and burnout: A two sample confirmatory factor analytic approach. *Journal of Happiness Studies, 3*(1), 71–92.

Seligman, M. E. P., & Csikszentmihalyi, M. (2000). Positive psychology: An introduction. *American Psychologist, 55*(1), 5–14.

Staudinger, U. M., Marsiske, M., & Baltes, P. B. (1995). Resilience and reserve capacity in later adulthood: Potentials and limits of development across the life span. In D. Cicchetti & D. Cohen (Eds.), *Developmental psychopathology* (Vol. 2, pp. 801–847). New York, NY: Wiley.

Sveen, U., Søberg, H. L., & Østensjø, S. (2016). Biographical disruption, adjustment and reconstruction of everyday occupations and work participation after mild traumatic brain injury. A focus group study. *Disability and Rehabilitation, 38*(23), 2296–2304.

Tatsuki, S., & Hayashi, H. (2000). Family system adjustment and adaptive reconstruction of social reality among the 1995 earthquake survivors. *International Journal of Japanese Sociology, 9*(1), 81–110.

Tol, W. A., Song, S., & Jordans, M. J. (2013). Annual research review: Resilience and mental health in children and adolescents living in areas of armed conflict – A systematic review of findings in low-and middle-income countries. *Journal of Child Psychology and Psychiatry, 54*(4), 445–460.

United Nations High Commissioner for Refugees. (2016). *Connecting refugees: How internet and mobile connectivity can improve refugee well-being and transform humanitarian action.* Retrieved from: http://www.unhcr.org/5770d43c4

Verelst, A., De Schryver, M., Broekaert, E., & Derluyn, I. (2014). Mental health of victims of sexual violence in eastern Congo: Associations with daily stressors, stigma, and labeling. *BMC Women's Health, 14*(1), 106.

Walsh, F. (2016). *Strengthening family resilience* (3rd ed.). New York, NY: Guilford.

Wutich, A., & Ragsdale, K. (2008). Water insecurity and emotional distress: Coping with supply, access, and seasonal variability of water in a Bolivian squatter settlement. *Social Science & Medicine, 67*(12), 2116–2125.

Zautra, A. J., Hall, J. S., & Murray, K. E. (2010). Resilience: A new definition of health for people and communities. In J. W. Reich, A. J. Zautra, & J. S. Hall (Eds.), *Handbook of adult resilience* (pp. 3–34). New York, NY: Guilford.

Zautra, A. J., Reich, J. W., & Guarnaccia, C. A. (1990). Some everyday life consequences of disability and bereavement for older adults. *Journal of Personality and Social Psychology, 59*(3), 550–561.

Wai Kai Hou, Ph.D., is Director of Centre for Psychosocial Health and Laboratory of Psychology and Ecology of Stress (LoPES) at The Education University of Hong Kong, Hong Kong SAR, China. Dr. Hou was Visiting Fulbright Scholar at Columbia University in New York. His research focuses on everyday processes and mechanisms of psychological resilience across posttraumatic and chronic stress conditions, with the ultimate goal of optimizing assessment and intervention for stress and health.

Brian J. Hall, Ph.D., is the Director of the Global and Community Mental Health Research Group at the University of Macau, in Macao (SAR), China. He is also an Associate in the Department of Health, Behavior, and Society, at the Johns Hopkins Bloomberg School of Public Health, and the first APA-IUPyS Global Mental Health Fellow of the World Health Organization. Dr. Hall's research group is focused on understanding the social determinants of population health, the consequences of adversity and traumatic stress, and developing and evaluating scalable interventions for marginalized populations.

Stevan E. Hobfoll, Ph.D., has authored and edited 12 books and authored over 250 journal articles, book chapters, and technical reports. He has been a consultant to several nations, military organizations, and major corporations on problems of stress and health. Dr. Hobfoll is currently the Judd and Marjorie Weinberg Presidential Professor and Chair of the Department of Behavioral Sciences at Rush Medical College in Chicago. His current research focuses on trauma in zones of conflict and on the connection between stress and biological-health outcomes in women's lives.

A Neurobiological Perspective of Mental Health Following Torture Trauma

Belinda J. Liddell and Richard A. Bryant

Abstract Torture can have significant long-term ramifications for the psychological and physical health of survivors. Here, we review the current neurobiological literature that suggests torture may have specific effects on the structure and functioning of the brain, perceptual and emotional functioning, and autonomic and neuroendocrinergic responses. We discuss these findings in the context of current neural models of PTSD, complex PTSD and the dissociative PTSD subtype. We also suggest that furthering the understanding of the neural impact of torture can only be achieved by conducting research that targets key disruptions characteristic to the interpersonal, prolonged and uncontrollable nature of torture trauma itself. Such research focusing on specific mechanisms underpinning the psychological effects of torture is critical to informing targeted treatments to alleviate suffering and promote recovery amongst survivors.

Keywords Torture · Refugee · Trauma · PTSD · Neuroimaging · Brain · Perception · Emotion · Social

Introduction

As a result of ongoing conflict around the world, there are more forcibly displaced individuals in 2017 than at any time since World War II. The rates of exposure to traumatic events, the threat of being returned to hostile environments, uncertainty regarding the future, and difficulties during the post-migration period can contribute to marked psychological difficulties in refugees. Despite the enormous public health challenges facing policy-makers regarding how to address the psychological burden suffered by millions of refugees, there is a remarkable paucity of empirical knowledge about the factors that underpin refugee mental health. This chapter focuses on the potential for recent advances in neuroscience research to partially address this gap. Although many advances have been made in understanding mental health

B. J. Liddell (✉) · R. A. Bryant
School of Psychology, University of New South Wales, Sydney, NSW, Australia
e-mail: b.liddell@unsw.edu.au; r.bryant@unsw.edu.au

N. Morina, A. Nickerson (eds.), *Mental Health of Refugee and Conflict-Affected Populations*, https://doi.org/10.1007/978-3-319-97046-2_7

conditions via neuroscientific research in mainstream populations, there has not been parallel research activity in refugee populations. This chapter outlines the need for such investigations, as well as the potential benefits of developing better knowledge of the neural effects of refugee experiences, including torture, which will advance opportunities for developing more suitable and/or targeted treatment strategies.

Psychological Responses to Refugee Trauma

There is overwhelming evidence that refugees experience elevated levels of mental health conditions, including posttraumatic stress disorder (PTSD), depression, suicide, and related comorbid conditions (Jankovic et al., 2013; Porter & Haslam, 2005; Song, Kaplan, Tol, Subica, & de Jong, 2015; Tay et al., 2015). Although the factors contributing to these conditions are complex and multifaceted (including the level of threat initially experienced, the duration of trauma exposure, exposure to threat during the emigration process, detention upon seeking asylum in a new country, or degree of post-migration stress), exposure to interpersonal violence represents one of the strongest risk factors for persistent psychiatric problems among refugees. For example, sexual violence has been shown to lead to elevated rates of PTSD (3.1–75.9%), anxiety (6.9–75%), and depression (8.8–76.5%) in refugees (Ba & Bhopal, 2016). Of the many forms of interpersonal trauma refugees are commonly exposed to, torture is experienced by over 20% of refugees, and has been shown to be the single biggest predictor of PTSD in conflict-affected individuals after controlling for other trauma exposure factors (OR, 2.01; 95% CI, 1.52–2.65) (Steel et al., 2009). Torture can lead to a range of other neuropsychiatric problems that impact functioning, including sleep disturbances, concentration and memory disruptions, headaches and muscle tension, and diverse somatic disturbances (Bradley & Tawfiq, 2006; Keatley, Ashman, Im, & Rasmussen, 2013; Spiller et al., 2016). This accords with accumulating evidence that PTSD reactions are associated with numerous memory, attentional, and concentration difficulties that are commonly reported following insults to the brain (Bryant et al., 2015; Meares et al., 2008; Meares et al., 2011).

Neural Models of PTSD

Current neural models of PTSD have been built on animal studies of fear conditioning and extinction, which have shown how persistent fear responses can be acquired following trauma and subsequently inhibited in recovery. Trauma adaption models posit that conditioned associations of fear with numerous trauma-related stimuli are stored in the basolateral nucleus of the amygdala, a pattern that has been observed in animals and humans (Maren & Quirk, 2004). When trauma reminders surface, fear responses are thus engaged via amygdala activity, while medial prefrontal regulation of fear via extinction learning and regulation systems are impaired in PTSD (Lanius, Bluhm, Lanius, & Pain, 2006; Milad, Rauch, Pitman, & Quirk, 2006; Rauch, 2003; Shin & Liberzon, 2010). The hippocampus is also a core brain region implicated in PTSD: It is critical to emotional memory, and particularly for the context of learnt fear associations. Meta-analytic studies have shown that people with PTSD have smaller hippocampi relative to healthy and trauma-exposed controls (Kitayama, Vaccarino, Kutner, Weiss, & Bremner, 2005), although one twin study suggests that smaller hippocampal volume may be a risk factor for PTSD rather than being a result of the disorder (Gilbertson et al., 2002). Although hundreds of studies have emerged in recent years investigating the neural bases of PTSD and trauma response, these have generally been conducted with survivors of single-incident traumas or veteran groups. As such, there is currently limited evidence regarding refugees, and particularly those exposed to torture. Specific features of the torture experience may have differential impacts on how PTSD manifests in the brain and these need to be considered in focused studies with torture survivors. The state of the current evidence-base on the neural effects of torture are reviewed in section "Evidence to Date of the Impact of Torture on Neurobiological Functioning" below.

Functional Deficits Associated with Torture

It is worth considering some of the major functional problems observed following torture because these are likely to contribute to the persistence of mental health problems. Apart from the evidence that refugees experience markedly high rates of PTSD and other disorders like depression (Steel et al., 2009), torture survivors appear less responsive to evidence-based treatments for PTSD that are effective in other trauma-exposed cohorts (Weiss et al., 2016). This highlights the need to understand the core processes affected by torture that may impede treatment response (Liddell, Nickerson & Bryant, 2018).

Arguably one of the fundamental challenges for torture survivors in the aftermath of their trauma is their diminished capacity to regulate the strong emotional reactions they can experience. Emotion regulation involves one's capacity to monitor and modify emotional responses in a manner that promotes adaptive functioning (Gratz & Roemer, 2004). There is convergent evidence that people with PTSD are impaired in this capacity (Amstadter & Vernon, 2008; Kulkarni, Pole, & Timko, 2013; Lilly & Hong Phylice Lim, 2013; Tull, Barrett, McMillan, & Roemer, 2007; Weiss et al., 2012). Of relevance to understanding the neural effect of torture is the observation that repeated interpersonal trauma is particularly associated with emotion regulation problems (Walsh, DiLillo, & Scalora, 2011). Initial evidence suggests that emotional dysregulation is an important mechanism that may underlie ongoing psychological distress in refugees. Adaptive emotion regulation strategies mediated the relationship between trauma and reduced PTSD in Tibetan refugees

(Hussain & Bhushan, 2011), enhanced emotion regulation capacity partly mediated PTSD symptom reduction following cognitive behaviour therapy in Cambodian refugees (Hinton, Hofmann, Pollack, & Otto, 2009), and difficulties in emotion regulation mediated the association between both trauma and post-migration living difficulties and psychological outcomes (Nickerson et al., 2015). Being exposed to torture can lead to impairments in the ability to manage one's emotional responses (Nickerson et al., 2015; Nickerson et al., 2016), and therefore may be one key factor in the persistent and treatment-resistant nature of refugees' mental health problems.

Another relevant process for torture survivors involves the loss of attachment systems. One model suggests that the prolonged interpersonal trauma and significant traumatic loss that defines the torture experience can substantially undermine or disrupt innate attachment systems (De Haene, Grietens, & Verschueren, 2010; Silove, 1999). There is evidence that interpersonal traumas increase risk for more severe adverse psychological outcomes to a greater extent than other traumatic events (Forbes et al., 2012; Forbes et al., 2014; Norris, Friedman, & Watson, 2002; Scott & Babcock, 2010). It is for this reason that it has been suggested that the interpersonal nature of torture may intensify a survivor's sense of vulnerability and contribute to posttraumatic stress reactions (Nickerson, Bryant, Rosebrock, & Litz, 2014). Attachment theories hold that people are programmed to seek the support of others at times of need (Bowlby, 1969), providing psychological benefit such as a more adaptive responses to stress (Mikulincer & Shaver, 2007), including for those with PTSD (Mikulincer, Shaver, & Horesh, 2006). If attachment availability is limited or fragmented at times of threat, such as in situations of interpersonal trauma, this could lead to exacerbated ongoing difficulties managing stress. Torture itself may erode an individual's natural coping systems, including interpersonal relationships and attachments (Quiroga & Jaranson, 2005). Experiencing torture may also reinforce beliefs that other people are dangerous and untrustworthy, thereby further interfering with a survivor's ability to engage in beneficial social support seeking during recovery.

Additionally, the potential benefits of attachments are limited if a person has an insecure attachment system because they cannot activate representations of attachment figures who can provide the comfort they may seek. For example, evidence points to people with avoidant attachment tendencies deactivating attachment seeking strategies when exposed to threat (Mikulincer, Shaver, Gillath, & Nitzberg, 2005), and if attachments are made available, they do not benefit from this proximity (Bryant & Foord, 2016). Similar deficits in benefiting from attachment availability have been found in prisoner-of-war survivors, who potentially have fragmented attachment systems (Mikulincer, Soloman, & Shaver, 2014). It is worth noting that one study of tortured refugees found that severity of interpersonal trauma predicted an avoidant attachment style (Morina, Schnyder, Schick, Nickerson, & Bryant, 2016). Accordingly, it is critical to understand how attachment systems are disrupted by torture, and how this impacts on mental health outcomes.

A third mechanism relevant to torture survivors involves loss of control. Indeed, loss of control is typical during trauma, and ongoing perceived loss of control following trauma exposure is associated with elevated anxiety and PTSD symptoms (Chorpita & Barlow, 1998; Grills-Taquechel, Littleton, & Axsom, 2011; Vujanovic,

Bonn-Miller, Potter, Marshall, & Zvolensky, 2011). However, the strong uncontrollable and prolonged nature of torture trauma may have specific and long-lasting effects (Le et al., 2018). Animal studies have demonstrated that cumulative exposure to uncontrollable stress modifies glutamatergic projections from the ventral medial prefrontal cortex (vmPFC), and causes persistent changes to GABAergic inhibition in the dorsal raphe nucleus (DRN) and subsequent serotonergic projections to the amygdala (Amat et al., 2005; Maier, 2015). Interestingly, some of these same processes have been observed in humans who perceive they lack control over a stressful event (Bryant, Felmingham, Das, & Malhi, 2013). It is possible that the neurobiological mechanisms disrupted by torture may reflect its uncontrollable characteristics, which exerts a significant impact on the mental health of survivors and their capacity to respond to stressful ongoing post-migration circumstances.

This review suggests that the mental health consequences of torture can be multifaceted and may be differentiated from the traditional conceptualisation of PTSD as a fear circuitry disorder (Liddell et al., 2018). The range of psychological effects of torture extends beyond the domain of fear and anxiety, with anger, shame, guilt, emotional lability, and interpersonal disturbances representing significant disruptions to emotional wellbeing (Nickerson et al., 2014; Stotz, Elbert, Muller, & Schauer, 2015). Indeed, the extension beyond fear-based responses accords with the DSM-5 definition of PTSD, which recognises the role of significant negative affect in non-fear domains and social alterations as being central to the manifestation of PTSD. The possibility that responses other than fear-based anxiety are present following torture suggests that neural investigations of the mental health outcomes of torture, and refugee experiences more widely, may need to consider broader models to fully accommodate the disruptions to emotional, social, and cognitive functioning noted in these populations. In this sense, prevailing neural models of PTSD may not suffice to adequately explain the psychological functioning of refugees. Evidence to date suggests that specialised attention to the neural underpinnings of torture trauma is critical in order to inform the development of effective treatments.

Evidence to Date of the Impact of Torture on Neurobiological Functioning

Structural Changes in the Brain

From the early 1980s, studies have been documenting the physical effect of torture on the body and the brain. Noting the common psychological and neurological symptoms reported by torture survivors and war detainees, Jensen and colleagues first observed significant cortical atrophy in five torture victims scanned 2–6 years post-torture exposure (Jensen et al., 1982). The authors suggest that evidence of cortical atrophy may reflect the long-term and possibly irreversible effects of these extreme experiences on the brain.

As neuroimaging methods have developed, research has provided a more accurate picture of the structural effects of torture. Torture related-PTSD has been associated with reductions in overall grey matter volume and ventricle size, as well as compromised diffusion weights in right frontal, left occipital and right cerebellar regions compared to healthy controls (Zandieh et al., 2016). Another study found that highly traumatized refugees with PTSD (including those exposed to torture), evidenced greater volumetric reductions in the bilateral inferior parietal lobe, dorsal anterior cingulate cortex, posterior cingulate cortex and orbitofrontal cortex, with the latter two regions associated with the degree of trauma exposure (Eckart et al., 2011). Changes have also been observed in sub-cortical structures, including decreases in the right amygdala volume predicted by greater trauma (Mollica et al., 2009) and in the hippocampus (Zandieh et al., 2016). Other studies did not report volumetric changes in the hippocampus or insula when comparing trauma-exposed refugees with and without PTSD, but rather neurometabolic reductions were observed in the left hippocampus – a finding that was correlated with adverse childhood experiences (Eckart et al., 2012). These mixed findings across studies suggest the influence of multiple factors, possibly including early life events, on the specific effect of severe adult experiences on the brain.

These findings accord with structural abnormalities observed in PTSD in general, so it remains unclear how specific these effects are to torture exposure. A recent meta-analysis of 20 voxel-based morphometry studies revealed robust reductions in the grey matter of the left anterior cingulate cortex (ACC), as well as smaller volumes of the left ACC, insula and parahippocampal gyrus in PTSD patients relative to trauma-exposed controls (TEC) without PTSD (Meng et al., 2014). Other meta-analyses suggest hippocampal volume reduction in PTSD (O'Doherty, Chitty, Saddiqui, Bennett, & Lagopoulous, 2015), which may be a pre-existing vulnerability factor for the development of the disorder (Pitman et al., 2012). This contrasts with no consistent differences in amygdala size being observed in PTSD patients relative to both trauma and non-trauma exposed control groups (Woon & Hedges, 2009). Interestingly, different traumatic events may impact on specific neural structures, with evidence that exposure to non-accidental traumas like mass violence are associated with particular decreases in medial prefrontal regions including the ACC (Meng et al., 2014).

One of the major challenges to understanding brain changes associated with torture is the fact that many torture survivors have also sustained traumatic brain injury (TBI) – either connected to their torture experience (e.g., blunt head trauma by beating) or from other displacement or conflict-related events. Research has documented rates of TBI amongst torture survivors to be as high as 69% (Bradley & Tawfiq, 2006; Keatley et al., 2013; Rasmussen, 1990), yet many of the brain structure studies reported here do not account for TBI in their sample, with the exception of Zandieh et al., (2016). In an MRI study of Vietnamese ex-political detainees, those with a history of TBI showed exaggerated cortical thinning in the left dorsolateral prefrontal cortex and bilateral superior temporal regions, relative to torture survivors without TBI (Mollica et al., 2009). Cortical thickness of these regions were negatively correlated with depression symptoms after controlling for trauma exposure and age but only in the TBI group. Such a finding suggests that it is critical to consider the possible contribution of TBI to torture sequaele as ongoing neurological symptoms can include severe headaches and migraines, loss of consciousness, and dizziness (Moreno & Grodin, 2002). When considering the neural impact of torture, it may be difficult to separate the long-term functional impact of the torture experience itself from the strong possibility that a TBI may have also been sustained.

The Impact of Torture on Basic Functional and Perceptual Processing

Changes in the neural processes underlying basic functioning and perceptual processing have also been observed amongst torture survivors. In a small study of 8 survivors of torture with PTSD, regional blood flow was observed to be more heterogeneous compared to healthy controls, particularly in the temporoparietal region (Mirzaei et al., 2001). Electrophysiological studies have focused on the EEG slow wave as a key marker of neuronal functional integrity. One study conducted with 97 survivors of war and torture with PTSD found enhanced slow wave activity over the left temporal cortex in the region of the insula, reduced slow wave activity over the parieto-occiptial cortex and differential slow wave patterns over the right frontal cortical region, relative to healthy controls (Kolassa et al., 2007). The insula is a region central to regulating autonomic arousal, interoceptive awareness and internal monitoring (Craig, 2009; Wager & Barrett, 2004). It is commonly reported as hyperactive in PTSD (Pitman et al., 2012), with insula activity being associated with greater PTSD symptom severity (Simmons et al., 2008), posttraumatic alexithymia (Frewen, Pain, Dozois, & Lanius, 2006), and dysregulated connectivity with the amygdala (Fonzo et al., 2010; Simmons et al., 2008); these changes in insula functioning have in turn been linked to hyperarousal symptoms (Turish et al., 2015). Many of these PTSD studies have been conducted with survivors of severe interpersonal violence and abuse – a trauma history that may have a similar effect as torture on the brain (McDonnell, Robjant & Katona, 2013). However it remains unclear from these studies as to whether these findings simply reflect general neural disruptions in PTSD or whether they are specific to torture.

Alterations to prefrontal regional functioning are also common markers of PTSD, but there may be specific effects following torture trauma. One study found dysregulated slow wave responses over the left ventrolateral frontal region in a torture-exposed sample, which was associated with severity of dissociative symptoms relative to culturally similar healthy controls, even after controlling for PTSD symptoms (Ray et al., 2006). The inverse relationship was observed in the right hemisphere and frontal regions, suggesting a decoupling between impaired verbal functioning in the left prefrontal cortex and affective regulation in the right prefrontal cortex that may be specific to dissociative symptoms amongst torture survivors

(Ray et al., 2006). Again, it is difficult to separate the effects of torture-exposure from the effects of PTSD in this study due to the lack of a non-tortured PTSD group.

Early perceptual alterations have also been observed in torture survivors. One study found evidence of diminished auditory P50 (relative to healthy controls) and visual N75 (relative to trauma-exposed and healthy controls) event-related potentials (ERPs) amongst a group of Iraqi refugee torture survivors with PTSD (Gjini et al., 2013). This reflects impaired bottom-up sensory encoding processes, with the P50 response being correlated with dissociation symptoms. Moreover, a measure of sensory gating was enhanced at P50 and N75 but not for later ERPs in the PTSD group, reflecting problems with suppressing unwanted sensory inputs. Intriguingly, stronger sensory gating was associated with better quality of life in this study. Other ERP studies conducted with past prisoners of war also showed evidence of altered automatic sensory and initial attentional components (Vrca, Bozikov, & Malinar, 1997).

The Impact of Torture on Emotion Processing and Regulation Systems

The aftermath of torture is also thought to be associated with disruptions to emotion processing and regulation systems (Nickerson et al., 2014; Nickerson et al., 2015). These disruptions appear to be reflected in alterations to emotion processing systems in the brain. Magnetoencephalography (MEG) studies have shown that survivors of war and torture engage differential neural responses during threat-related processing compared to healthy controls (Adenauer et al., 2010; Catani, Adenauer, Keil, Aichinger, & Neuner, 2009). War and torture survivors with and without PTSD demonstrated reduced visual evoked potentials over left occipital regions compared to healthy controls in response to aversive cues, but those with PTSD also showed increased responses over a left occipital region to positive cues. These findings are supportive of the notion that PTSD is associated with changes to sensory gating processes in response to affective stimuli, which have also been reported in civilian cohorts with PTSD (Felmingham, Bryant, & Gordon, 2003), suggesting inhibited responsivity to emotionally eliciting events that may be initially adaptive in stressful circumstances. Furthermore, the MEG studies found that only the PTSD group showed enhanced potentials over the superior parietal cortex to negative cues compared to trauma-exposed controls (Catani et al., 2009). Engagement of superior parietal regions coupled with reduced sensory activations has been interpreted to reflect reduced attentional deployment and enhanced disengagement to threat-related cues. The additional findings that superior parietal activity was correlated with degree of torture exposure and was specifically enhanced in those with dissociative symptoms (Catani et al., 2009) further supports this notion of elevated emotional withdrawal, demonstrated in terms of brain functioning, in the torture survivor group.

A second MEG study provided additional support for this finding of increased avoidance of aversive cues in a war and torture exposed group with PTSD via later stage activation in superior parietal regions. This pattern was preceded by initial (130–160 ms) increases over right ventrolateral prefrontal regions, supporting an initial hypervigilance-subsequent avoidance model of emotion dysregulation (Adenauer et al., 2010). Therapeutic gains following treatment with narrative exposure therapy have also been associated with changes in the superior parietal lobule in refugees with PTSD (Adenauer et al., 2011).

Studies of Survivors of Chronic Interpersonal Trauma Including Sexual Abuse and Domestic Violence

Commentators have suggested that the impact of torture in regards to complex PTSD representations may be likened to the effect of protracted physical abuse (McDonnell et al., 2013). Clinical studies conducted amongst survivors of prolonged sexual abuse in childhood and adulthood may offer further clues as to how the brain may be affected by torture. For example, research investigating the neural correlates of the dissociative subtype of PTSD in survivors of sexual abuse have found evidence of a neural profile characterized by over-modulation of emotion (Lanius et al., 2010). When exposed to trauma reminders, the medial prefrontal cortex over-regulates and dampens emotional reactivity regions including the amygdala and insula, resulting in emotional numbing and sympathetic nervous system withdrawal (Lanius, Bluhm, & Frewen, 2011; Lanius, Brand, Vermetten, Frewen, & Spiegel, 2012; Lanius et al., 2005; Lanius et al., 2002). Other studies with complex PTSD patients support this neural model. Thomaes et al. (2013) reported increased activity in the left ventral anterior cingulate, dorsomedial prefrontal cortex and hippocampus when encoding negative words in a group of complex PTSD patients vs controls. Furthermore, activation in the vACC was correlated with severity of child abuse in the patient group (as well as severity of comorbid depression). In one case study with a single torture survivor, exposure to trauma reminders was associated with increased cerebral blood flow in the precuneus and supplementary motor area in the prefrontal regions and reduced activity in the insula, prefrontal and inferior frontal areas, with SSRI treatment normalizing functioning in this cortico-limbic system (Fernandez et al., 2001). These findings suggest that the neural effect of torture may be one of emotional withdrawal and over-regulation during threat-related processing.

Conversely, other studies focusing on childhood abuse survivors indicate that automatic threat detection systems are hyperactivated, consistent with the classic neural model of PTSD. Steuwe et al., (2012) found that direct gaze perception (happy, sad, neutral faces) engaged automatic alarm networks (Liddell et al., 2005), including the locus coeruleus, superior colliculus and periaqueductal grey in patients with PTSD related to prolonged childhood abuse. Dannlowski et al., (2012) also reported amygdala hyper-activity in response to threatening faces associated with increased childhood maltreatment.

Relative to other PTSD investigations, there has been relatively little study of the neural correlates of emotion processing in complex PTSD. Differential findings may be related to a combination of clinical sampling and methodology, as we argue that it is likely that the nature, severity and length of trauma exposure, as well as potential characteristics of the recovery environment, play a significant role in how the emotional brain is altered in torture survivors with PTSD.

Neurobiological Effects of Torture and Other Common Refugee Experiences

The neurobiological effects of chronic and prolonged stress exposure are substantial, and manifest from the cellular level through to the functioning of entire neural circuits and regulation systems (McEwen, 2007; McEwen, Eiland, Hunter, & Miller, 2012). For example, the hypothalamic-pituatory-adrenal (HPA) axis, which regulates glucocorticoid functioning and stress hormone release (e.g., cortisol), is over-active following stress exposure. While increased cortisol secretion is linked to acute and chronic stress (McEwen, 2007), lowered cortisol plasma levels are commonly observed in PTSD (Daskalakis, Lehrner, & Yehuda, 2013), reflecting impairments in feedback mechanisms. While there has been little investigation of the specific neurobiological impact of torture, a number of studies have examined the neuroendogeneric, hormonal, autonomic and genetic effects of refugee and war-related trauma, with mixed findings. Seminal work conducted in a cohort of refugees from East Germany found evidence of disrupted HPA-axis activity including lowered cortisol responses as well as reduced thyroid functioning relative to healthy controls that was irrespective of psychiatric diagnosis (Bauer, Priebe, Graf, Kurten, & Baumgartner, 1994a; Bauer, Priebe, Kurten, Graf, & Baumgartner, 1994b). Other studies have reported elevated cortisol levels in displaced women (Sabioncello et al., 2000), perhaps reflecting acute stress. Elevated resting sympathetic autonomic nervous system functioning has also been observed amongst resettled highly traumatized Iraqi refugees compared to healthy controls (Slewa-Younan et al., 2012).

More recent studies have revealed that exposure to interpersonal violence may have a specific effect on stress systems. Refugees with trauma histories that included rape demonstrated increases in salivary (and not plasma) cortisol during a trauma interview compared to refugees with no rape exposure, despite having been exposed to a similar number of traumatic events overall and showing comparable levels of PTSD symptom severity (Gola et al., 2012). The authors suggest that proximity to the perpetrator during torture may alter arousal systems in specialized ways, as the combination of an uncontrollable stressor and physical contact triggers a shut-down response in the defense cascade at the time of exposure (Schauer & Elbert, 2010). Rather than being a fear-driven response, it may be the predominance of feelings of shame that engages enhanced HPA-axis activations during trauma recall (Miller, Chen, & Zhou, 2007), although shame was also reported by the non-rape exposed group in connection with their other traumatic experiences including torture (Gola et al., 2012). Understanding the interaction between specific traumatic experiences such as torture, post-recovery emotional states like fear and shame, and its neurobiological underpinnings will be an important research area in the future.

There is also a strong link between stress/trauma exposure and physical illness that is important to consider in the context of torture, with hyper-activation of the HPA-axis having detrimental effects on the body's immune and inflammatory systems. Amongst a cohort of war and torture survivors with chronic PTSD, the representation of peripheral T lymphocytes which regulate good physical health, was found to be significantly altered relative to matched trauma-exposed but otherwise healthy controls (Sommershof et al., 2009). Other studies have also found alterations in T cell distribution in displaced women (Sabioncello et al., 2000).

Genetic factors may also play a role in underlying an individual's vulnerability to the adverse effects of refugee and conflict-related trauma, although this research has not been extended specifically to torture. In a cohort of Rwandan genocide survivors, risk polymorphisms of two genes have been examined: those with the short-short allele in the promotor region of the SLC6A4 gene, which encodes serotonin (Kolassa, Ertl, et al., 2010a); and the Val158Met polymorphism of the catechol-O-methyltransferase (COMT) enzyme that regulates dopamine, epinephrine and norepinephrine activity (Kolassa, Kolassa, Ertl, Papassotiropoulos, & De Quervain, 2010b). Those who independently possessed these risk polymorphisms exhibited a 100% probability risk for PTSD regardless of the number of traumatic events experienced (Kolassa, Ertl, et al., 2010a; Kolassa, Kolassa, et al., 2010b). In both studies, those with the protective polymorphisms, exhibited the normal dose-response relationship between trauma exposure and increased risk for PTSD.

Conclusions and Next Steps

The current state of the literature suggests that the psychological impact of torture and war exposure may have specific neural underpinnings, including structural changes, early sensory processing alterations, disruptions to threat-related processes, and dysregulated autonomic and stress hormone release. However, it is not yet possible to draw clear inferences regarding the specific neural underpinnings of torture exposure, as differentiated from other war-experiences, the presence of PTSD symptoms, and the possibility of traumatic brain injury amongst many survivors. The evidence-base would be greatly strengthened by including appropriate control groups – such as torture survivors without PTSD – enabling the specific effects of torture to be elucidated. Comparisons with other groups with complex PTSD symptoms may also be warranted to discern potentially unique neural profiles of refugees relative to other groups with complex PTSD (e.g., survivors of childhood sexual abuse). Secondly, current research has focused on basic perceptual processes, with extension into threat-related perception. We argue that while these research targets are important, it is also critical that neurobiological studies are directed towards understanding the core elements related to torture experiences – such as the severance of emotional systems, violations of attachments and ongoing social stress, and long term effects of exposure to uncontrollable trauma. For example, given torture survivors are commonly exposed to severe violations of their attachment networks, coupled with ongoing family or community separation, attachment may be a major factor in their trauma recovery. There may be additional cultural factors to consider, given that the majority of refugees and torture survivors are from non-Western cultural groups that adhere to collectivistic cultural frameworks. There is evidence that there are cultural differences in the neural substrates of PTSD (Liddell & Jobson, 2016), which may have bearing on understanding the neural impact of torture in these cohorts. Building a solid neuroscientific evidence-base for mechanisms underlying the long-term psychological effects of torture is essential to advance knowledge regarding why torture survivors are less responsive to traditional PTSD treatments (Liddell et al., 2018). This knowledge could be harnessed to develop more effective and targeted treatments to facilitate the recovery and rehabilitation of torture survivors.

References

Adenauer, H., Catani, C., Gola, H., Keil, J., Ruf, M., Schauer, M., & Neuner, F. (2011). Narrative exposure therapy for PTSD increases top-down processing of aversive stimuli – evidence from a randomised controlled treatment trial. *BMC Neuroscience, 12*(1), 127. https://doi.org/10.1186/1471-2202-12-127

Adenauer, H., Pinösch, S., Catani, C., Gola, H., Keil, J., Kißler, J., & Neuner, F. (2010). Early processing of threat cues in posttraumatic stress disorder—evidence for a cortical vigilance-avoidance reaction. *Biological Psychiary, 68*(5), 451–458. https://doi.org/10.1016/j.biopsych.2010.05.015

Amat, J., Baratta, M. V., Paul, E., Bland, S. T., Watkins, L. R., & Maier, S. F. (2005). Medial prefrontal cortex determines how stressor controllability affects behavior and dorsal raphe nucleus. *Nature Neuroscience, 8*(3), 365–371. https://doi.org/10.1038/nn1399

Amstadter, A. B., & Vernon, L. L. (2008). A preliminary examination of thought suppression, emotion regulation, and coping in a trauma-exposed sample. *Journal of Aggression, Maltreatment & Trauma, 17*(3), 279–295. https://doi.org/10.1080/10926770802403236

Ba, I., & Bhopal, R. S. (2016). Physical, mental and social consequences in civilians who have experienced war-related sexual violence: a systematic review (1981–2014). *Public Health, 142*, 121–135. https://doi.org/10.1016/j.puhe.2016.07.019

Bauer, M., Priebe, S., Graf, K. J., Kurten, I., & Baumgartner, A. (1994a). Psychological and endocrine abnormalities in refugees from East Germany: Part II. Serum levels of cortisol, prolactin, luteinizing hormone, follicle stimulating hormone, and testosterone. *Psychiatry Research, 51*(1), 75–85. https://doi.org/10.1016/0165-1781(94)90048-5

Bauer, M., Priebe, S., Kurten, I., Graf, K. J., & Baumgartner, A. (1994b). Psychological and endocrine abnormalities in refugees from East Germany: Part I. Prolonged stress, psychopathology, and hypothalamic-pituitary-thyroid axis activity. *Psychiatry Research, 51*(1), 61–73. https://doi.org/10.1016/0165-1781(94)90047-7

Bowlby, J. (1969). *Attachment and loss, Volume 1. Attachment*. New York, NY: Basic Books.

Bradley, L., & Tawfiq, N. (2006). The physical and psychological effects of torture in Kurds seeking asylum in the United Kingdom. *Torture, 16*(1), 41–47. 2006-1.2005-9

Bryant, R. A., Baker, M. T., Mintz, J., Barth, J., Young-McCaughan, S., Creasy, B., … Peterson, A. L. (2015). The role of posttraumatic stress in acute postconcussive symptoms following blast injury in combat. *Psychotherapy and Psychosomatics, 84*(2), 120–121. https://doi.org/10.1159/000370049

Bryant, R. A., Felmingham, K. L., Das, P., & Malhi, G. (2013). The effect of perceiving control on glutamatergic function and tolerating stress. *Molecular Psychiatry, 19*(5), 533–534. https://doi.org/10.1038/mp.2013.60

Bryant, R. A., & Foord, R. (2016). Activating attachments reduces memories of traumatic images. *PLoS One, 11*(9), e0162550. https://doi.org/10.1371/journal.pone.0162550

Catani, C., Adenauer, H., Keil, J., Aichinger, H., & Neuner, F. (2009). Pattern of cortical activation during processing of aversive stimuli in traumatized survivors of war and torture. *European Archives of Psychiatry and Clinical Neuroscience, 259*, 340–351. https://doi.org/10.1007/s00406-009-0006-4

Chorpita, B. F., & Barlow, D. H. (1998). The development of anxiety: The role of control in the early environment. *Psychological Bulletin, 124*(1), 3–21. https://doi.org/10.1037//0033-2909.124.1.3

Craig, A. D. (2009). How do you feel now? The anterior insula and human awareness. *Nature Neuroscience, 10*(1), 59–70. https://doi.org/10.1038/nrn2555

Dannlowski, U., Stuhrmann, A., Beutelmann, V., Zwanzger, P., Lenzen, T., Grotegerd, D., … Kugel, H. (2012). Limbic scars: Long-term consequences of childhood maltreatment revealed by functional and structural magnetic resonance imaging. *Biological Psychiary, 71*(4), 286–293. https://doi.org/10.1016/j.biopsych.2011.10.021

Daskalakis, N. P., Lehrner, A., & Yehuda, R. (2013). Endocrine aspects of post-traumatic stress disorder and implications for diagnosis and treatment. *Endocrinology and Metabolism Clinics of North America, 42*(3), 503–513. https://doi.org/10.1016/j.ecl.2013.05.004

De Haene, L., Grietens, H., & Verschueren, K. (2010). Adult attachment in the context of refugee traumatisation: The impact of organized violence and forced separation on parental states of mind regarding attachment. *Attachment & Human Development, 12*(3), 249–264. https://doi.org/10.1080/14616731003759732

Eckart, C., Kaufmann, J., Kanowski, M., Tempelmann, C., Hinrichs, H., Elbert, T., … Kolassa, I. T. (2012). Magnetic resonance volumetry and spectroscopy of hippocampus and insula in relation to severe exposure of traumatic stress. *Psychophysiology, 49*(2), 261–270. https://doi.org/10.1111/j.1469-8986.2011.01303.x

Eckart, C., Stoppel, C., Kaufmann, J., Tempelmann, C., Hinrichs, H., Elbert, T., … Kolassa, I. T. (2011). Structural alterations in lateral prefrontal, parietal and posterior midline regions of men with chronic posttraumatic stress disorder. *Journal of Psychiatry & Neuroscience, 35*(6), 100010. https://doi.org/10.1503/jpn.100010

Felmingham, K. L., Bryant, R. A., & Gordon, E. (2003). Processing angry and neutral faces in post-traumatic stress disorder: An event-related potentials study. *Neuroreport, 14*(5), 777–780. https://doi.org/10.1097/01.wnr.0000065509.53896.e3

Fernandez, M., Pissota, A., Frans, O., von Knorring, L., Fischer, H., & Fredrikson, M. (2001). Brain function in a patient with torture related post-traumatic stress disorder before and after Fuoxetine treatment: A positron emission tomography provocation study. *Neuroscience Letters, 297*(2), 101–104. https://doi.org/10.1016/s0304-3940(00)01674-8

Fonzo, G. A., Simmons, A. N., Thorp, S. R., Norman, S. B., Paulus, M. P., & Stein, M. B. (2010). Exaggerated and disconnected insular-amygdalar blood oxygenation level-dependent response to threat-related emotional faces in women with intimate-partner violence posttraumatic stress disorder. *Biological Psychiatry, 68*(5), 433–441. https://doi.org/10.1016/j.biopsych.2010.04.028

Forbes, D., Fletcher, S., Parslow, R., Phelps, A., O'Donnell, M., Bryant, R. A., … Creamer, M. (2012). Trauma at the hands of another: Longitudinal study of differences in the posttraumatic stress disorder symptom profile following interpersonal compared with noninterpersonal trauma. *The Journal of Clinical Psychiatry, 73*(3), 372–376. https://doi.org/10.4088/JCP.10m06640

Forbes, D., Lockwood, E., Phelps, A., Wade, D., Creamer, M., Bryant, R. A., … O'Donnell, M. (2014). Trauma at the hands of another: Distinguishing PTSD patterns following intimate and nonintimate interpersonal and noninterpersonal trauma in a nationally representative sample. *The Journal of Clinical Psychiatry, 75*(2), 147–153. https://doi.org/10.4088/JCP.13m08374

Frewen, P. A., Pain, C., Dozois, D. J., & Lanius, R. A. (2006). Alexithymia in PTSD: Psychometric and FMRI studies. *Annals New York Academy of Sciences, 1071*(1), 397–400. https://doi.org/10.1196/annals.1364.029

Gilbertson, M. W., Shenton, M. E., Ciszewski, A., Kasai, K., Lasko, N. B., Orr, S. P., & Pitman, R. K. (2002). Smaller hippocampal volume predicts pathologic vulnerability to psychological trauma. *Nature Neuroscience, 5*(11), 1242–1247. https://doi.org/10.1038/nn958

Gjini, K., Boutros, N. N., Haddad, L., Aikins, D., Javanbakht, A., Amirsadri, A., & Tancer, M. E. (2013). Evoked potential correlates of post-traumatic stress disorder in refugees with history of exposure to torture. *Journal of Psychiatric Research, 47*(10), 1492–1498. https://doi.org/10.1016/j.jpsychires.2013.06.007

Gola, H., Engler, H., Schauer, M., Adenauer, H., Riether, C., Kolassa, S., … Kolassa, I. T. (2012). Victims of rape show increased cortisol responses to trauma reminders: A study in individuals with war- and torture-related PTSD. *Psychoneuroendocrinology, 37*(2), 213–220. https://doi.org/10.1016/j.psyneuen.2011.06.005

Gratz, K. L., & Roemer, L. (2004). Multidimensional assessment of emotion regulation and dysregulation: Development, factor structure, and initial validation of the difficulties in emotion regulation scale. *Journal of Psychopathology and Behavioral Assessment, 26*(1), 41–54. https://doi.org/10.1023/b:joba.0000007455.08539.94

Grills-Taquechel, A. E., Littleton, H. L., & Axsom, D. (2011). Social support, world assumptions, and exposure as predictors of anxiety and quality of life following a mass trauma. *Journal of Anxiety Disorders, 25*(4), 498–506. https://doi.org/10.1016/j.janxdis.2010.12.003

Hinton, D. E., Hofmann, S. G., Pollack, M. H., & Otto, M. W. (2009). Mechanisms of efficacy of CBT for Cambodian refugees with PTSD: Improvement in emotion regulation and orthostatic blood pressure response. *CNS Neuroscience and Therapeutics, 15*(3), 255–263. https://doi.org/10.1111/j.1755-5949.2009.00100.x

Hussain, D., & Bhushan, B. (2011). Posttraumatic stress and growth among Tibetan refugees: The mediating role of cognitive-emotional regulation strategies. *Journal of Clinical Psychology, 67*(7), 720–735. https://doi.org/10.1002/jclp.20801

Jankovic, J., Bremner, S., Bogic, M., Lecic-Tosevski, D., Adjukovic, D., Francisckovic, T., … Priebe, S. (2013). Trauma and suicidality in war affected communities. *European Psychiatry, 28*(8), 514–520. https://doi.org/10.1016/j.eurpsy.2012.06.001

Jensen, T. S., Genefke, I. K., Hyldebrandt, N., Pedersen, H., Petersen, H. D., & Weile, B. (1982). Cerebral atrophy in young torture victims. *New England Journal of Medicine, 307*(21), 1341. https://doi.org/10.1056/nejm198211183072112

Keatley, E., Ashman, T., Im, B., & Rasmussen, A. (2013). Self-reported head injury among refugee survivors of torture. *Journal of Head Trauma Rehabilitation, 28*(6), E8–E13. https://doi.org/10.1097/htr.0b013e3182776a70

Kitayama, N., Vaccarino, V., Kutner, M., Weiss, P., & Bremner, J. D. (2005). Magnetic resonance imaging (MRI) measurement of hippocampal volume in posttraumatic stress disorder: A meta-analysis. *Journal of Affective Disorders, 88*(1), 79–86. https://doi.org/10.1016/j.jad.2005.05.014

Kolassa, I. T., Ertl, V., Eckart, C., Glockner, F., Kolassa, S., Papassotiropoulos, A., … Elbert, T. (2010a). Association study of trauma load and SLC6A4 promoter polymorphism in posttraumatic stress disorder: Evidence from survivors of the Rwandan genocide. *Journal of Clinical Psychiatry, 71*(5), 543–547. https://doi.org/10.4088/JCP.08m04787blu

Kolassa, I. T., Kolassa, S., Ertl, V., Papassotiropoulos, A., & De Quervain, D. J. (2010b). The risk of posttraumatic stress disorder after trauma depends on traumatic load and the catechol-o-methyltransferase Val(158)Met polymorphism. *Biological Psychiatry, 67*(4), 304–308. https://doi.org/10.1016/j.biopsych.2009.10.009

Kolassa, I. T., Wienbruch, C., Neuner, F., Schauer, M., Ruf, M., Odenwald, M., & Elbert, T. (2007). Altered oscillatory brain dynamics after repeated traumatic stress. *BMC Psychiatry, 7*(1), 56. https://doi.org/10.1186/1471-244X-7-56

Kulkarni, M., Pole, N., & Timko, C. (2013). Childhood victimization, negative mood regulation, and adult PTSD severity. *Psychological Trauma: Theory, Research, Practice, and Policy, 5*(4), 359–365. https://doi.org/10.1037/a0027746

Lanius, R. A., Bluhm, R., Lanius, U., & Pain, C. (2006). A review of neuroimaging studies in PTSD: Heterogeneity of response to symptom provocation. *Journal of Psychiatric Research, 40*(8), 709–729. https://doi.org/10.1016/j.jpsychires.2005.07.007

Lanius, R. A., Bluhm, R. L., & Frewen, P. A. (2011). How understanding the neurobiology of complex post-traumatic stress disorder can inform clinical practice: a social cognitive and affective neuroscience approach. *Acta Psychiatrica Scandinavica, 124*(5), 331–348. https://doi.org/10.1111/j.1600-0447.2011.01755.x

Lanius, R. A., Brand, B., Vermetten, E., Frewen, P. A., & Spiegel, D. (2012). The dissociative subtype of posttraumatic stress disorder: Rationale, clinical and neurobiological evidence and implications. *Depression and Anxiety, 29*(8), 701–708. https://doi.org/10.1002/da.21889

Lanius, R. A., Vermetten, E., Loewenstein, R. J., Brand, B., Schmahl, C., Bremner, J. D., & Spiegel, D. (2010). Emotion modulation in PTSD: Clinical and neurobiological evidence for a dissociative subtype. *American Journal of Psychiatry, 167*(6), 640–647. https://doi.org/10.1176/appi.ajp.2009.09081168

Lanius, R. A., Williamson, P. C., Bluhm, R. L., Densmore, M., Boksman, K., Neufeld, R. W. J., … Menon, R. S. (2005). Functional connectivity of dissociative responses in posttraumatic stress disorder: A functional magnetic resonance imaging investigation. *Biological Psychiatry, 57*(8), 873–884. https://doi.org/10.1016/j.biopsych.2005.01.011

Lanius, R. A., Williamson, P. C., Boksman, K., Densmore, M., Gupta, M., Neufeld, R. W. J., … Menon, R. S. (2002). Brain Activation during script-driven imagery induced dissociative responses in PTSD: A functional magnetic resonance imaging investigation. *Biological Psychiatry, 52*(4), 305–311. https://doi.org/10.1016/s0006-3223(02)01367-7

Le, L., Morina, N., Schnyder, U., Schick, M., Bryant, R. A., & Nickerson, A. (2018). The effects of perceived torture controllability on symptom severity of posttraumatic stress, depression and anger in refugees and asylum seekers: A path analysis. *Psychiatry Research, 264*, 143–150.

Liddell, B. J., Brown, K. J., Kemp, A. H., Barton, M. J., Das, P., Peduto, A., … Williams, L. M. (2005). A direct brainstem-amygdala-cortical 'alarm' system for subliminal signals of fear. *Neuroimage, 24*(1), 235–243. https://doi.org/10.1016/j.neuroimage.2004.08.016

Liddell, B. J., & Jobson, L. (2016). The impact of cultural differences in self-representation on the neural substrates of posttraumatic stress disorder. *European Journal of Psychotraumatology, 7*(1), 30464. https://doi.org/10.3402/ejpt.v7.30464

Liddell, B. J., Nickerson, A., & Bryant, R. A. (2018). Clinical science and torture survivors' right to rehabilitation. *Lancet Psychiatry, 5*(2), 102–103.

Lilly, M. M., & Hong Phylice Lim, B. (2013). Shared pathogeneses of posttrauma pathologies: Attachment, emotion regulation, and cognitions. *Journal of Clinical Psychology, 69*(7), 737–748. https://doi.org/10.1002/jclp.21934

Maier, S. F. (2015). Behavioral control blunts reactions to contemporaneous and future adverse events: Medial prefrontal cortex plasticity and a corticostriatal network. *Neurobiology of Stress, 1*, 12–22. https://doi.org/10.1016/j.ynstr.2014.09.003

Maren, S., & Quirk, G. J. (2004). Neuronal signalling of fear memory. *Nature Reviews Neuroscience, 5*(11), 844–852. https://doi.org/10.1038/nrn1535

McDonnell, M., Robjant, K., & Katona, C. (2013). Complex posttraumatic stress disorder and survivors of human rights violations. *Current Opinion in Psychiatry, 26*(1), 1–6. https://doi.org/10.1097/YCO.0b013e32835aea9d

McEwen, B. S. (2007). Physiology and neurobiology of stress and adaptation: Central role of the brain. *Physiological Reviews, 87*(3), 873–904. https://doi.org/10.1152/physrev.00041.2006

McEwen, B. S., Eiland, L., Hunter, R. G., & Miller, M. M. (2012). Stress and anxiety: Structural plasticity and epigenetic regulation as a consequence of stress. *Neuropharmacology, 62*(1), 3–12. https://doi.org/10.1016/j.neuropharm.2011.07.014

Meares, S., Shores, E. A., Taylor, A. J., Batchelor, J., Bryant, R. A., Baguley, I. J., … Marosszeky, J. E. (2008). Mild traumatic brain injury does not predict acute postconcussion syndrome. *Journal of Neurology, Neurosurgery & Psychiatry, 79*(3), 300–306. https://doi.org/10.1136/jnnp.2007.126565

Meares, S., Shores, E. A., Taylor, A. J., Batchelor, J., Bryant, R. A., Baguley, I. J., … Marosszeky, J. E. (2011). The prospective course of postconcussion syndrome: The role of mild traumatic brain injury. *Neuropsychology, 25*(4), 454–465. https://doi.org/10.1037/a0022580

Meng, Y., Qui, C., Zhu, H., Lama, S., Lui, S., Gong, Q., & Zhang, W. (2014). Anatomical deficits in adult posttraumtic stress disorder: A meta-analysis of voxel-based morphometry studies. *Behavioural Brain Research, 270*, 307–315. https://doi.org/10.1016/j.bbr.2014.05.021

Mikulincer, M., & Shaver, P. R. (2007). Boosting attachment security to promote mental health, prosocial values, and inter-group tolerance. *Psychological Inquiry, 18*(3), 139–156. https://doi.org/10.1080/10478400701512646

Mikulincer, M., Shaver, P. R., Gillath, O., & Nitzberg, R. A. (2005). Attachment, caregiving, and altruism: Boosting attachment security increases compassion and helping. *Journal of Personality and Social Psychology, 89*(5), 817–839. https://doi.org/10.1037/0022-3514.89.5.817

Mikulincer, M., Shaver, P. R., & Horesh, N. (2006). Attachment bases of emotion regulation and posttraumatic adjustment. In D. K. Snyder, J. A. Simpson, & J. N. Hughes (Eds.), *Emotion regulation in families: Pathways to dysfunction and health* (pp. 77–99). Washington, DC: American Psychological Association.

Mikulincer, M., Soloman, Z., & Shaver, P. R. (2014). Attachment related consequences of war captivity and trajectories of posttraumatic stress disorder: A 17-year longitudinal study. *Journal of Social and Clinical Psychology, 33*(3), 207–228. https://doi.org/10.1521/jscp.2014.33.3.207

Milad, M. R., Rauch, S. L., Pitman, R. K., & Quirk, G. J. (2006). Fear extinction in rats: Implications for human brain imaging and anxiety disorders. *Biological Psychology, 73*(1), 61–71. https://doi.org/10.1016/j.biopsycho.2006.01.008

Miller, G. E., Chen, E., & Zhou, E. S. (2007). If it goes up, must it come down? Chronic stress and the hypothalamic-pituitary-adrenocortical axis in humans. *Psycholoigcal Bulletin, 133*(1), 25–45. https://doi.org/10.1037/0033-2909.133.1.25

Mirzaei, S., Knoll, P., Keck, A., Preitler, B., Gutierrez, E., Umek, H., … Pecherstorfer, M. (2001). Regional cerebral blood flow in patients suffering from post-traumatic stress disorder. *Neuropsychobiology, 43*(4), 260–264. https://doi.org/10.1159/000054900

Mollica, R. F., Lyoo, I. K., Chernoff, M. C., Bui, H. X., Lavelle, J., Yoon, S. J., … Renshaw, P. F. (2009). Brain structural abnormalities and mental health sequelae in South Vietnamese ex-political detainees who survived traumatic head injury and torture. *Archives of General Psychiatry, 66*(11), 1221–1232. https://doi.org/10.1001/archgenpsychiatry.2009.127

Moreno, A., & Grodin, M. A. (2002). Torture and its neurological sequelae. *Spinal Cord, 40*(5), 213–223. https://doi.org/10.1038/sj.sc.3101284

Morina, N., Schnyder, U., Schick, M., Nickerson, A., & Bryant, R. A. (2016). Attachment style and interpersonal trauma in refugees. *Australian & New Zealand Journal of Psychiatry, 50*(12), 1161–1168. https://doi.org/10.1177/0004867416631432

Nickerson, A., Bryant, R. A., Rosebrock, L., & Litz, B. T. (2014). The mechanisms of psychosocial injury following human rights violations, mass trauma, and torture. *Clinical Psychology Science and Practice, 21*(2), 172–191. https://doi.org/10.1111/cpsp.12064

Nickerson, A., Bryant, R. A., Schnyder, U., Schick, M., Mueller, J., & Morina, N. (2015). Emotion dysregulation mediates the relationship between trauma exposure, post-migration living difficulties and psychological outcomes in traumatized refugees. *Journal of Affective Disorders, 173*, 185–192. https://doi.org/10.1016/j.jad.2014.10.043

Nickerson, A., Garber, B., Ahmed, O., Asnaani, A., Cheung, J., Hofmann, S. G., … Bryant, R. A. (2016). Emotional suppression in torture survivors: Relationship to posttraumatic stress symptoms and trauma-related negative affect. *Psychiatry Research, 242*, 233–239. https://doi.org/10.1016/j.psychres.2016.05.048

Norris, F. H., Friedman, M. J., & Watson, P. J. (2002). 60,000 disaster victims speak: Part I. An emirical review of the empirical literature, 1981-2001. *Psychiatry: Interpersonal and Biological Processes, 65*(3), 207–239. https://doi.org/10.1521/psyc.65.3.207.20173

O'Doherty, D. C., Chitty, K. M., Saddiqui, S., Bennett, M. R., & Lagopoulous, J. (2015). A systematic review and meta-analysis of magnetic resonance imaging measurement of structural volumes in posttraumatic stress disorder. *Psychiatry Research, 232*(1), 1–33. https://doi.org/10.1016/j.pscychresns.2015.01.002

Pitman, R. K., Rasmussen, A., Koenen, K. C., Shin, L. M., Orr, S. P., Gilbertson, M. W., … Liberzon, I. (2012). Biological studies of post-traumatic stress disorder. *Nature Reviews Neuroscience, 13*(11), 769–787. https://doi.org/10.1038/nrn3339

Porter, M., & Haslam, N. (2005). Predisplacement and postdisplacement factors associated with mental health of refugees and internally displaced persons – A meta-analysis. *Journal of the American Medical Association, 294*(5), 602–612. https://doi.org/10.1001/jama.294.5.602

Quiroga, J., & Jaranson, J. M. (2005). Politically-motivated torture and its survivors: A desk study review of the literature. *Torture, 16*(203), 1–111.

Rasmussen, O. V. (1990). Medical aspects of torture. *Danish Medical Bulletin, 37*(Suppl 1), 1–88.

Rauch, S. L. (2003). Neuroimaging and neurocircuitry models pertaining to the neurosurgical treatment of psychiatric disorders. *Neurosurgery Clinics of North America, 14*(2), 213–223. https://doi.org/10.1016/s1042-3680(02)00114-6

Ray, W. J., Odenwald, M., Neuner, F., Schauer, M., Ruf, M., Wienbruch, C., … Elbert, T. (2006). Decoupling neural networks from reality: Dissociative experiences in torture victims are reflected in abnormal brain waves in left frontal cortex. *Psychological Science, 17*(10), 825–829. https://doi.org/10.1111/j.1467-9280.2006.01788.x

Sabioncello, A., Kocijan-Hercigonja, D., Rabatic, S., Tomasic, J., Jeren, T., Matijevic, L., … Dekaris, D. (2000). Immune, endocrine, and psychological responses in civilians displaced by war. *Psychosomatic Medicine, 62*(4), 502–508. https://doi.org/10.1097/00006842-200007000-00008

Schauer, M., & Elbert, T. (2010). Dissociation following traumatic stress: Etiology and treatment. *Zeitschrift fur Psychologie/Journal of Psychology, 218*(2), 109–127. https://doi.org/10.1027/0044-3409/a000018

Scott, S., & Babcock, J. C. (2010). Attachment as a moderator between intimate partner violence and PTSD symptoms. *Journal of Family Violence, 25*(1), 1–9. https://doi.org/10.1007/s10896-009-9264-1

Shin, L. M., & Liberzon, I. (2010). The neurocircuitry of fear, stress, and anxiety disorders. *Neuropsychopharmacology, 35*(1), 169–191. https://doi.org/10.1038/npp.2009.83

Silove, D. (1999). The psychosocial effects of torture, mass human rights violations, and refugee trauma: Toward an integrated conceptual framework. *Journal of Nervous and Mental Disease, 187*(4), 200–207. https://doi.org/10.1097/00005053-199904000-00002

Simmons, A. N., Paulus, M. P., Thorp, S. R., Matthews, S. C., Norman, S. B., & Stein, M. B. (2008). Functional activation and neural networks in women with posttraumatic stress disorder related to intimate partner violence. *Biological Psychiary, 64*(8), 681–690. https://doi.org/10.1016/j.biopsych.2008.05.027

Slewa-Younan, S., Chippendale, K., Heriseanu, A., Lujic, S., Atto, J., & Raphael, B. (2012). Measures of psychophysiological arousal among resettled traumatized Iraqi refugees seeking psychological treatment. *Journal of Traumatic Stress, 25*(3), 348–352. https://doi.org/10.1002/jts.21694

Sommershof, A., Aichinger, H., Engler, H., Adenauer, H., Catani, C., Boneberg, E.-M., … Kolassa, I. T. (2009). Substantial reduction of naïve and regulatory T cells following traumatic stress. *Brain, Behavior and Immunity, 23*(8), 1117–1124. https://doi.org/10.1016/j.bbi.2009.07.003

Song, S. J., Kaplan, C., Tol, W. A., Subica, A., & de Jong, J. (2015). Psychological distress in torture survivors: Pre- and post-migration risk factors in a US sample. *Social Psychiatry and Psychiatric Epidemiology, 50*(4), 549–560. https://doi.org/10.1007/s00127-014-0982-1

Spiller, T. R., Schick, M., Schnyder, U., Bryant, R. A., Nickerson, A., & Morina, N. (2016). Somatisation and anger are associated with symptom severity of posttraumatic stress disorder in severely traumatised refugees and asylum seekers. *Swiss Medical Weekly, 146*, w14311. https://doi.org/10.4414/smw.2016.14311

Steel, Z., Chey, T., Silove, D., Marnane, C., Bryant, R. A., & van Ommeren, M. (2009). Association of torture and other potentially traumatic events with mental health outcomes among populations exposed to mass conflict and displacement: A systematic review and meta-analysis. *Journal of the American Medical Association, 302*(5), 537–549. https://doi.org/10.1001/jama.2009.1132

Steuwe, C., Daniels, J., Frewin, P., Densmore, M., Pannasch, S., Beblo, T., … Lanius, R. (2012). Effect of direct eye contact in PTSD related to interpersonal trauma: An fMRI study of activation of an innate alarm system. *Social Cognitive and Affective Neuroscience, 9*(1), 88–97. https://doi.org/10.1093/scan/nss105

Stotz, S. J., Elbert, T., Muller, V., & Schauer, M. (2015). The relationship between trauma, shame, and guilt: Findings from a community-based study of refugee minors in Germany. *European Journal of Psychotraumatology, 6*(1), 25863. https://doi.org/10.3402/ejpt.v6.25863

Tay, A. K., Rees, S., Chen, J., Kareth, M., Lahe, S., Kitau, R., … Silove, D. (2015). Associations of conflict-related trauma and ongoing stressors with the mental health and functioning of West Papuan refugees in Port Moresby, Papua New Guinea (PNG). *PLoS One, 10*(4), e0125178. https://doi.org/10.1371/journal.pone.0125178

Thomaes, K., Dorrepaal, E., Draijer, N., de Ruiter, M. B., Elzinga, B. M., Sjoerds, Z., … Veltman, D. J. (2013). Increased anterior cingulate cortex and hippocampus activation in complex PTSD during encoding of negative words. *Scan, 8*(2), 190–200. https://doi.org/10.1093/scan/nsr084

Tull, M. T., Barrett, H. M., McMillan, E. S., & Roemer, L. (2007). A preliminary investigation of the relationship between emotion regulation difficulties and posttraumatic stress symptoms. *Behavior Therapy, 38*(3), 303–313. https://doi.org/10.1016/j.beth.2006.10.001

Turish, M., Ros, T., Frewen, P. A., Kluetsch, R. C., Calhoun, V. D., & Lanius, R. A. (2015). Distinct instrinsic network connectivity patterns of post-traumatic stress disorder symptom clusters. *Acta Psychiatrica Scandinavica, 132*(1), 29–38. https://doi.org/10.1111/acps.12387

Vrca, A., Bozikov, V., & Malinar, M. (1997). The use of visual evoked potentials to follow-up prisoners of war after release from detention camps. *Collegium antropologicum, 21*(1), 229–233.

Vujanovic, A. A., Bonn-Miller, M. O., Potter, C. M., Marshall, E. C., & Zvolensky, M. J. (2011). An evaluation of the relation between distress tolerance and posttraumatic stress within a trauma-exposed sample. *Journal of Psychopathology and Behavioral Assessment, 33*(1), 129–135. https://doi.org/10.1007/s10862-010-9209-2

Wager, T., & Barrett, L. F. (2004). From affect to control: Functional specialization of the insula in motivation and regulation. *Published Online at PsycExtra*. https://doi.org/10.1101/102368

Walsh, K., DiLillo, D., & Scalora, M. J. (2011). The cumulative impact of sexual revictimization on emotion regulation difficulties: An examination of female inmates. *Violence Against Women, 17*(8), 1103–1118. https://doi.org/10.1177/1077801211414165

Weiss, N. H., Tull, M. T., Davis, L. T., Dehon, E. E., Fulton, J. J., & Gratz, K. L. (2012). Examining the association between emotion regulation difficulties and probable posttraumatic stress disorder within a sample of African Americans. *Cognitive Behaviour Therapy, 41*(1), 5–14. https://doi.org/10.1080/16506073.2011.621970

Weiss, W. M., Ugueto, A. M., Mahmooth, Z., Murray, L. K., Hall, B. J., Nadison, M., … Bolton, P. (2016). Mental health interventions and priorities for research for adult survivors of torture and systematic violence: A review of the literature. *Torture, 26*(1), 17–44.

Woon, F. L., & Hedges, D. W. (2009). Amygdala volume in adults with posttraumatic stress disorder: A meta-analysis. *Journal of Neuropsychiatry & Clinical Neuroscience, 21*(1), 5–12. https://doi.org/10.1176/appi.neuropsych.21.1.5

Zandieh, S., Bernt, R., Knoll, P., Wenzel, T., Hittmair, K., Haller, J., ... Mirzaei, S. (2016). Analysis of the metabolic and structural brain changes in patients with torture-related post-traumatic stress disorder (TR-PTSD) using 18F-FDG PET and MRI. *Medicine, 95*(15), e3387. https://doi.org/10.1097/md.0000000000003387

Belinda J. Liddell is a Research Fellow and Deputy Director of the Refugee Trauma and Recovery Program, in the School of Psychology at the University of New South Wales (UNSW) Sydney Australia. Her research focuses on understanding the neurophysiological and psychological processes that are impacted by refugee trauma, and investigating how cultural factors shape the emotional and social brain.

Richard A. Bryant is a Scientia Professor and Director of the Traumatic Stress Clinic in the School of Psychology at the University of New South Wales (UNSW) Sydney Australia. His research focuses on identifying mechanisms underpinning adaptation to trauma, and development of more effective interventions for those affected by traumatic stress.

Interventions for Mental Health and Psychosocial Support in Complex Humanitarian Emergencies: Moving Towards Consensus in Policy and Action?

Peter Ventevogel

Abstract This chapter reviews international consensus guidance documents and tools for mental health and psychosocial support in 'complex humanitarian emergencies'. It pays specific attention to adaptions of such policies and tools for refugees residing in low and middle income countries. The chapter argues that there are three competing paradigms in humanitarian mental health: the 'trauma' paradigm, the 'psychosocial' paradigm, and the 'mental health in general health care' paradigm. While these three different ways of looking at mental health problems in humanitarian settings are not easily reconciled on a conceptual level, significant progress has been made to forge pragmatic consensus among providers of humanitarian assistance. Pivotal in this emerging consensus are two major documents that will be introduced and discussed in this chapter: The Sphere Handbook and the IASC Guidelines for Mental Health and Psychosocial Support in Emergencies. Both have deeply influenced the ways mental health and psychosocial support in refugees are being conceptualized and organized, as will be illustrated in the last parts of the chapter that details the content of the Operational Guidance for Mental Health and Psychosocial Support Programming in Refugee Operations of UNHCR, the UN Refugee Agency.

Keywords Mental health and psychosocial support (MHPSS) · Humanitarian emergencies · Guidelines · Refugees · Low and middle income countries

Mental Health and Psychosocial Support in Humanitarian Settings

Within the context of humanitarian assistance – a term to denote the whole of interventions to save lives and protect survival with dignity in situations such as armed conflict, natural disasters and complex political emergencies – the composite term

P. Ventevogel (✉)
Public Health Section, Division of Programme Management and Support, United Nations High Commissioner for Refugees, Geneva, Switzerland
e-mail: ventevog@unhcr.org

N. Morina, A. Nickerson (eds.), *Mental Health of Refugee and Conflict-Affected Populations*, https://doi.org/10.1007/978-3-319-97046-2_8

'Mental Health and Psychosocial Support' (MHPSS) is the consensus term to indicate 'any type of local or outside support that aims to protect or promote psychosocial well-being and/or prevent or treat mental disorder'(Inter-Agency Standing Committee, 2007). This may include support interventions in health, education, community-based protection and in other areas. The term 'MHPSS problems' is therefore wide ranging and may include social problems, emotional distress, common mental disorders (such as depression and posttraumatic stress disorder), severe mental disorders (such as psychosis and bipolar disorder), alcohol and substance use disorders, and intellectual or developmental disabilities. The use of the term MHPSS draws attention to the strong interaction of psychological and social factors in the development of 'mental problems', and conversely, underlines that interpersonal problems such as intimate partner violence (IPV), child abuse and neglect, and family conflicts are often intricately linked to the psychological state of the persons concerned. Although the term has been criticised for its lack of a valid operational definition which contributes to conceptual confusion (Tol, Purgato, Bass, Galappatti, & Eaton, 2015), it has proven to be an important construct in bringing together professionals who work from diverse and often competing paradigms. It is this heuristic value that has made the term MHPSS become 'a household name' in humanitarian emergencies (IASC Reference Group for Mental Health and Psychosocial Support, 2015). The term has contributed to a greater visibility of psychological problems of person in complex humanitarian situations and has enabled practitioners to reach minimum consensus about priority actions that need to be taken to address these issues (Ager, 2008).

Mental Health and Psychosocial Support in Complex Humanitarian Emergencies: A History of Clashing Paradigms and Competing Priorities

Within complex humanitarian emergencies increasing attention is being given to mental health and psychosocial wellbeing of affected populations (Ventevogel, 2016). In the 1970s and 1980s, attention to the psychological consequences of forced displacement and humanitarian emergencies was rather modest and mental health problems were easily overlooked amidst the plethora of needs. This has profoundly changed over the last decades. Several major humanitarian crises, particularly the wars in the Balkans in the 1990s in the wake of the break-up of Yugoslavia, and the 2004 South Asian Tsunami, forced the aid community and the general public to consider the mental health of affected populations in humanitarian settings. The Balkan wars and the Tsunami put mental health on the map as a priority issue in humanitarian emergencies and the birth of 'humanitarian psychiatry' can be traced to the 1990s (Fassin & Rechtman, 2009). However, these crises also demonstrated how divided the emerging field of 'humanitarian mental health' was, with different theoretical paradigms and sharp differences about what sort of interventions should be prioritized.

To generalize somewhat, there are three approaches to addressing the mental health issues of people in complex humanitarian emergencies. The first is the 'trauma approach', which regards 'psychological trauma' as the most important issue at stake, and, consequently, places trauma-focused interventions at the centre of the humanitarian mental health response. Within this approach, the mending of 'emotional scars' and the resolution of traumatic memories are key to humanitarian mental health care. The canonisation of posttraumatic stress disorder (PTSD) in the professional classification system of the American Psychiatric Association in 1980 and the subsequent great surge in research on psychological trauma, has given this approach a strong scientific backing. Over the years, various therapeutic approaches with a strong trauma focus have been developed and tested for use in humanitarian settings, such as Narrative Exposure Therapy (Schauer, Schauer, Neuner, & Elbert, 2011), trauma-focused cognitive behavioural therapy (Bass et al., 2013; O'Callaghan, McMullen, Shannon, Rafferty, & Black, 2013) and Eye Movement Desensitization and Reprocessing – EMDR (Shapiro, 2014). However, despite a relatively strong evidence base underpinning these approaches (Neuner, Schauer, & Elbert, 2014), many policy makers and practitioners within humanitarian organisations were and remain critical and at times even overtly hostile to trauma focused approaches (Ventevogel, 2014). The critiques can be summarized with the following overlapping arguments. Firstly, in humanitarian settings, PTSD is not the only mental health problem, nor necessarily clinically the most relevant one, and one-sided attention to it would divert attention away from other clinical issues such as acute and prolonged grief, depression and anxiety disorder (Jones, 2008; van Ommeren, Saxena, & Saraceno, 2005a). Secondly, in many cultural settings, people do not have words or concepts for 'trauma-related' mental disorders, or, if they have, these are remarkably different from the prevailing psychiatric definition of posttraumatic stress disorder (Kirmayer, Kienzler, Afana, & Pedersen, 2010; Patel, 1995; Rasmussen, Katoni, Keller, & Wilkinson, 2011; Ventevogel, Jordans, Reis, & de Jong, 2013). Thirdly, there has been sharp conceptual criticism of posttraumatic stress disorder as a 'psychological construct' that obscures the driving socio-political causes of emotional distress and transforms human suffering into a mental disorder in need of treatment (Summerfield, 1999; Zarowsky, 2004). Lastly, the emphasis on past traumatic events in the development of current emotional distress may ignore the pathogenic role of everyday stressors and the multiple hassles to survive in situations of hardship (Miller & Rasmussen, 2010; Riley, Varner, Ventevogel, Hassan, & Welton-Mitchell, 2017).

A second paradigm around mental health issues of refugees in humanitarian contexts is the 'psychosocial approach'. This approach has a very different lineage compared to the trauma approach. It has roots in community psychology, peace psychology and the human rights movement that blossomed in the 1970s and 1980s in Latin America and Southern Africa (Ager, 2002; Meyer, Bennouna, & Stark, 2016; Miller & Rasco, 2004; Wessells & Monteiro, 2001). This stream of humanitarian mental health work was partially a response to the profound discomfort many field workers felt with the emphasis on 'deficits' and highlighted the importance of repairing and strengthening a supportive social environment for overcoming psychological difficulties (Ager, 1997). Proponents of this approach emphasise the close relation between individual emotional wellbeing and the social context, that ranges from concrete relationships with others within family and community, to more abstract systems of traditions, shared history and cultural and spiritual values (Strang & Ager, 2003). Armed conflict and forced displacement deeply affect social and community cohesion and the capacity of individuals, families and communities to cope with adversity. The psychosocial approach is strongly influenced by the theoretical work around *social ecologies* locating social needs of individuals within the social context of a family or household which, in turn, is located within communities (Bronfenbrenner, 1986). Consequentially, the psychosocial approach emphasizes the importance of healing social ties *between* people. Key components of psychosocial reconstruction of conflict affected communities include healing of the 'collective wounds' of war, community mobilization for collective planning, use of local resources and capacities to support the (re)construction of social institutions that foster adaptation and survival (social fabric), fostering cooperation between displaced persons and host populations, and fostering truth and reconciliation and forgiveness (Boothby, Strang, & Wessells, 2008; Hamber, Gallagher, & Ventevogel, 2014; Wessells & Monteiro, 2001). An important characteristic of the psychosocial approach is the importance given to the active participation of local stakeholders in both the definition of what is 'at stake' as well how problems should be solved (Schinina & Tankink, 2018; Wessells, 2009a). Major criticisms of the psychosocial approach include the lack of robust documentation of outcomes and impact and the weak definitions of hypothesized causal pathways to wellbeing.

A third paradigm around mental health issues of refugees in humanitarian contexts is strongly related to the recent emergence of 'global mental health' as a branch of public health (Patel et al., 2011). The 'global mental health' approach emphasizes the importance of providing appropriate health interventions for a range of mental health issues including problems that can be found anywhere in the world and are not typical for humanitarian settings, such as psychotic disorders, bipolar disorders, alcohol and substance use problems, dementia and intellectual and developmental disabilities. Underpinning this approach is the notion that health care provision in any setting must include mental health components ('no health without mental health') and that this is perhaps especially true in humanitarian contexts. In refugee settings, health care providers are often overwhelmed by the massive health needs of the population and thus, within the plethora of health priorities, mental health may easily be under prioritized, while in fact a significant proportion of the visits to health facilities are related to mental health issues that remain undetected or are inappropriately managed. Consequently, the health system needs to be made more responsive to the needs of people with mental disorders, particularly the severe and disabling forms which undermine social functioning and pose major protection risks for the affected persons (Jones, Asare, Elmasri, & Mohanraj, 2007; Ostuzzi et al., Submitted; Silove, Ekblad, & Mollica, 2000). For decades, the World Health

Organization (WHO), and its allies have advocated for the integration of mental health into general health care (World Health Organization, 2001). The limitation of a pure 'global health approach' is that it does not distinguish the special experiences and reactions of refugees from those much larger populations where the major issues are related to deprivation in general and specifically to a lack of adequate mental health services. Refugee settings are unique, because of increased mental health needs including issues related to extreme stress and pervasive losses, but also due to decreased capacities of the health system to respond adequately to these mental health issues. Paradoxically however, humanitarian refugee settings can also provide new opportunities to tackle mental health needs within health care systems and to foster mental health care reforms (Epping-Jordan et al., 2015; Pérez-Sales, Férnandez-Liria, Baingana, & Ventevogel, 2011). For example, in Lebanon, the massive influx of refugees from Syria and the availability of NGOs and funding possibilities has prompted the Ministry of Health to set up a mental health unit in the ministry that actively promotes the integration of mental health into general health care and has led to the first mental health strategy in the country (El Chammay & Ammar, 2014). Similarly, in Jordan and Turkey, the refugee crisis fostered cooperation between WHO and the national ministries to decentralize mental health care and promote mental health training for general health workers (Weissbecker, Hanna, El Shazly, Gao, & Ventevogel, 2019).

Mental Health and Psychosocial Support in Practice: Competition and Conceptual Confusion

These major three paradigms, each with its own pedigree, led to diverse approaches of humanitarian agencies on the ground and to major disagreements between interventionists, to the detriment of collective and collaborative action (Silove, 2004; Ventevogel, 2008; Wickramage, 2006). Often, the situation was further complicated by a lack of adequate information from needs assessments in humanitarian settings, insufficient coordination between competing agencies and a tendency of organisations to highlight their success stories and downplay problems (Eloul et al., 2013; Zwi & Silove, 2002). A major problem in complex humanitarian emergencies is that, due to the absence of regulatory bodies, a magnitude of NGOs may emerge that provide often poorly coordinated services (Fritsche, 2001). NGOs, acting in parallel with what remains of the state systems and failing to support local capacity, increase the risk of little being left behind when humanitarian agencies withdraw (Farmer, 2011; Toole, Waldmann, & Zwi, 2006). Moreover, there is an inherent risk that such newly established services drain health workers from the existing health care system and undermine, rather than strengthen, the public sector and perpetuate the problem of weak governance (Ganesan, 2011; Wickramage, 2006). Moreover, a divide between NGOs (often working from an idealistic human rights or humanitarian perspective) and the government (with a bureaucratic 'civil service' way of working), may result in reticence to cooperate or to integrate NGO services into the local government systems (de Jong, 2014).

Various pioneers have developed integrated theoretic frameworks that attempt to capture a comprehensive account of the interplay between the refugee experience and mental health and psychosocial wellbeing (de Jong, 2002; Hobfoll et al., 2007; Miller & Rasmussen, 2014; Silove, 1999). These all have in common that they use a multisystem, ecosocial framework in which mental disorder is seen as the endpoint of an imbalance in (social) environmental factors rather than as merely an expression of innate or intrapsychic problems at an individual level (Silove, Ventevogel, & Rees, 2017). However, these models were not easily translated into programmatic action on the ground and were only slowly adopted (if at all) by a fragmented and polarized field and instead remained confined to academia or to single agency. For example, the work of the NGO HealthNet TPO was strongly influenced by the public mental health model for conflict settings of its founder de Jong. This model emphasizes the need for multileveled preventative and therapeutic interventions on individual, family, community and society level (Fairbank, Friedman, de Jong, Green, & Solomon, 2003). The model did not generalize or become widely accepted in other organisations. Currently, the field still lacks a unifying metatheory that captures individual psychological suffering as expressed in symptoms of psychological disorders such as PTSD, depression and prolonged grief disorder but also includes the effects of stress and social disruption on psychosis and disability.

Following these theoretical developments and the conceptual confusion, major donors, United Nations agencies and large international non-governmental organisations realized that coordinated action was needed to forge a pragmatic consensus among various actors that would improve mutual understanding and collaboration in the field of humanitarian mental health (Weiss, Saraceno, Saxena, & van Ommeren, 2003). The following section of this chapter will present two influential international guidance documents, discuss their content and consider how they have influenced and informed the emerging field of Mental Health and Psychosocial Support in humanitarian settings.

The *Sphere Handbook*

One of the most important collaborative initiatives in the field of humanitarian assistance is the Sphere Project, which is a joint initiative of large international non-governmental organisations to strengthen the quality of work of humanitarian agencies, and their accountability. It aimed to produce globally applicable minimum standards for humanitarian response services (Buchanan-Smith, 2003). This project was sparked by the deep discomfort many actors felt during the ill coordinated response to the Rwandan refugee crisis in 2004 where despite a massive aid operation an estimated 80,000 refugees in the refugee camps either died of preventable disorders or continued to live in appalling circumstances with ongoing human rights abuses. This crisis led to broad recognition that it was time to promote professionalism and the use of consensus based, evidence informed standards in humanitarian assistance (Walker & Purdin, 2004). The first two editions of the Sphere Handbook, in 1998 and 2000, did not contain guidance on mental health and psychosocial support because of a widely-shared view that there was not enough consensus among experts to formulate authoritative guidance (van Ommeren, Saxena, & Saraceno, 2005b). The 2004 edition of the handbook for the first-time contains a standard on 'mental and social aspects of health' that identifies eight 'social interventions' to describe activities that primarily aim to have social effects, and four 'psychological interventions' that are primarily meant to have psychological (or psychiatric) effects (Sphere Project, 2004). The handbook acknowledges the strong interactions between social and psychological domains (Batniji, van Ommeren, & Saraceno, 2006). The subsequent edition of 2011 has integrated most of the social considerations throughout the handbook and had one specific standard for mental health care in the health chapter. The latest revision of the handbook was published in 2018 and contain a separate mental health standard (see Box 1) and with psychosocial considerations interwoven throughout the handbook.

Box 1: Mental Health Standard and Related Key Actions in the Sphere Handbook 2018

Standard:

People have access to health services that reduce mental health problems and associated impaired functioning.

Key actions:

Coordinate mental health and psychosocial supports across sectors.

- Develop programmes on the basis of identified needs and resources.
- Work with community members, including marginalised people, to strengthen community self-help and social support.
- Orient staff and volunteers on how to offer psychological first aid.
- Make basic clinical mental health care available at every healthcare facility.
- Make psychological interventions available where possible for people impaired by prolonged distress.
- Protect rights of people with severe mental health conditions in the community, hospitals and institutions.
- Minimise harm related to alcohol and drugs.
- Take steps to develop a sustainable mental health system during early recovery planning and protracted crises.

The IASC Guidelines for Mental Health and Psychosocial Support on Emergency Settings

The experiences around mental health in the aftermath of the Asian Tsunami of 2004, that again showed paradigmatic fights and conceptual confusion among stakeholders willing to intervene in the field of mental health (Galappatti, 2005; Krishnakumar, Sivayokan, & Somasundaram, 2008; van der Veen & Somasundaram, 2006) prompted the main humanitarian players to embark on a major consensus building exercise. The Inter-Agency Standing Committee (IASC), which is the principal platform for global coordination of humanitarian assistance, initiated a Task Force to draft consensus guidelines that would facilitate effective coordination, identify useful practices and flag potentially harmful practices, and clarify how different approaches to mental health and psychosocial support complement one another (Inter-Agency Standing Committee, 2007). The extensive consultative process to come to the guidelines involved hundreds of different experts from nongovernmental organisations, United Nations agencies such as WHO, UNICEF and UNHCR, and academic institutions (Wessells & van Ommeren, 2008). The fact that it proved possible to forge a consensus among experts with widely diverging views was an important political achievement (Ager, 2008).

The IASC guidelines do not attempt to harmonize the various theoretical approaches and paradigms that were discussed in the first parts of this chapter, but they do provide a practical set of principles about which agreement could be reached. One of these was the shared realisation that mental health and psychosocial issues in humanitarian emergencies are highly interconnected. People in humanitarian crises experience a wide range of psychological and social problems at the individual, family, community and societal levels. Such problems can predate the emergency, for example pre-existing social problems (e.g. extreme poverty, belonging to discriminated or marginalized groups) or pre-existing mental disorders (such as chronic psychosis or substance use problems). They can also be directly related to the emergency experience e.g. social problems such as family separation; disruption of social networks and destruction of community structures) and psychological problems (acute stress, grief, depression and anxiety disorders, including PTSD). Moreover, the problems that people in emergencies experience can be caused or aggravated by the humanitarian response (e.g. anxiety due to a lack of information about food distribution, feelings of powerlessness and humiliation due to the way assistance is provided). Moreover, humanitarian emergencies may inadvertently erode existing protective supportive mechanisms and coping and undermine and overwhelm formal health care services and social services. This latter insight was fed by stinging critiques on the disempowering approaches of delivering humanitarian assistance leading to a state of dependency and demoralization (Harrell-Bond, 1986).

Six *guiding principles* should underpin programming to address mental health and psychosocial support in humanitarian settings:

- *Human rights and equity:* MHPSS should promote the rights of all affected people; promote equity among all affected groups; and avoid the discrimination that often harms affected people.
- *Participation:* Humanitarian action should stimulate the participation of affected people. This is a right of emergency affected people, but it is also a means of regaining a sense of control in the midst of overwhelming experiences.
- *Do No Harm:* An imperative for any humanitarian practitioner is to minimize the chances that interventions actually make things worse or cause additional harm (Wessells, 2009b). Humanitarian agencies and practitioners should participate in coordination groups, design programmes based on sufficient information, and be open to self-reflection and evaluation. An important point is to take into account power relations between outsiders and emergency-affected people.
- *Building on available resources and capacities:* Humanitarian agencies should not just come with pre-designed plans of action to be executed by themselves as expert but should attempt to build upon local resources and strengthen existing capacities.
- *Integrated support systems*: An important principle is to avoid stand-alone services such as those dealing only with survivors of Sexual and Gender Based Violence (SGBV), or dealing exclusively with people having a specific diagnosis such as PTSD because this could lead to a fragmented and non-sustainable care system that reaches few people and risks stigmatizing survivors. It is preferable to integrate activities into wider systems such as existing community support mechanisms, and (mental) health services, and social services.
- *Multi-layered supports:* In emergencies, people are affected in different ways and require different kinds of supports. Therefore, programmes for MHPSS should be conceptualized through a systems-based approach with multiple layers of complementary supports and functional referral systems between the different layers. It is important to develop a multi-layered system of MHPSS services, ranging from actions that benefit all persons of concern to targeted MHPSS interventions. This is illustrated in Fig. 1. (Wessells & van Ommeren, 2008)
- *Layer 1: Social considerations in basic services and security.*
  Ensure that the provision of basic needs and essential services (food, shelter, water, sanitation, basic health care, control of communicable diseases) and security is done in a way that facilitates the dignity of all people. This approach should be inclusive of those with special vulnerabilities but also avoid exclusively targeting a single group to prevent discrimination, stigma and potential further distress. This includes advocacy for good humanitarian practice that protects the dignity of persons of concern. Providing information on how, where and when humanitarian services can be accessed may be vital in reducing distress.
- *Layer 2: Strengthening community and family supports*
  Promote activities that foster social cohesion among refugee populations, including supporting the re-establishment or development of refugee community-based structures that are representative of the population in terms of age, gender and diversity. It also includes the promotion of community mechanisms which pro-

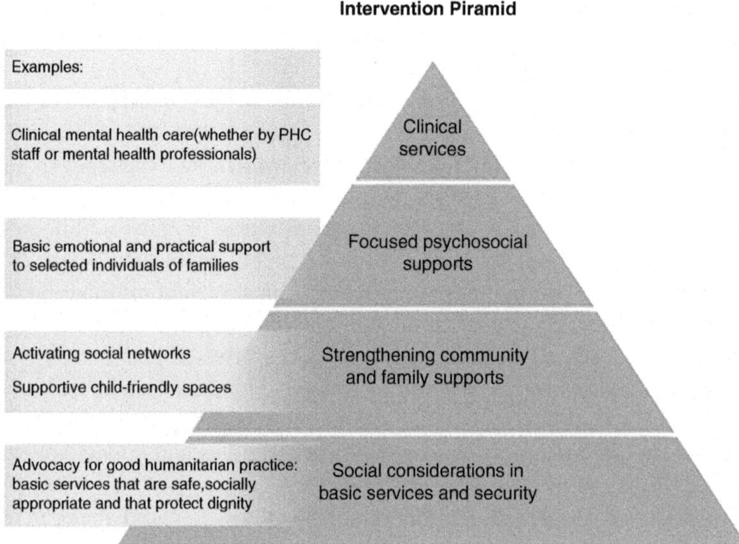

Fig. 1 The intervention pyramid for MHPSS in emergencies (Inter-Agency Standing Committee, 2007)

tect and support its members through participatory approaches. Ensuring play and recreation spaces and activities are an essential part of this layer, especially for children.

- *Layer 3: Focused psychosocial support*
  Provide emotional and practical support through individual, family or group interventions to those who are having difficulty coping using only their personal strengths and their existing support network. Usually non-specialised workers in health, education or social services deliver such interventions, after training and with ongoing supervision.
- *Layer 4: Clinical services*
  Deliver clinical mental health services to those with severe symptoms or an intolerable level of suffering, rendering them unable to carry out basic daily functions. This group consists of people with pre-existing mental health disorders and emergency-induced problems, including but not limited to: psychosis, drug abuse, severe depression, disabling anxiety symptoms, and those who are at risk to harm themselves or others. The interventions are usually led by mental health professionals.

Based on the six guiding principles, the main part of the IASC guidelines then consist of 11 chapters that describe the core actions for MHPSS to be taken in a humanitarian emergency. These chapters are divided in three sections: (a) Common functions (such coordination, assessment and human resources), (b) the core intervention sectors for MHPSS (health, education and community mobilisation and (c) MHPSS considerations in 'other' sectors such as nutrition, water, sanitation & hygiene (WASH), and shelter. See Box 2.

Box 2: Mental Health and Psychosocial Support: Suggested Minimum Responses in the Midst of Emergencies

A. Common functions

Coordination

- Establish coordination of intersectoral mental health and psychosocial support

Assessment, monitoring and evaluation

- Conduct assessments of mental health and psychosocial issues
- Initiate participatory systems for monitoring and evaluation

Protection and human rights standards

- Apply a human rights framework through mental health and psychosocial support
- Identify, monitor, prevent and respond to protection threats and failures through social protection
- Identify, monitor, prevent and respond to protection threats and abuses through legal protection

Human resources

- Identify and recruit staff and engage volunteers who understand local culture
- Enforce staff codes of conduct and ethical guidelines
- Organise orientation and training of aid workers in mental health and psychosocial support
- Prevent and manage problems in mental health and psychosocial well-being among staff and volunteers

B. Core mental health and psychosocial supports.

Community mobilisation and support

- Facilitate conditions for community mobilisation, ownership and control of emergency response in all sectors
- Facilitate community self-help and social support
- Facilitate conditions for appropriate communal cultural, spiritual and religious healing practices
- Facilitate support for young children (0–8 years) and their care-givers

Health services

- Include specific psychological and social considerations in provision of general health care
- Provide access to care for people with severe mental disorders

(continued)

Box 2 (continued)

- Protect and care for people with severe mental disorders and other mental and neurological disabilities living in institutions
- Learn about and, where appropriate, collaborate with local, indigenous and traditional health systems
- Minimise harm related to alcohol and other substance use

Education

- Strengthen access to safe and supportive education

Dissemination of information

- Provide information to the affected population on the emergency, relief efforts and their legal rights
- Provide access to information about positive coping methods

C. Social considerations in sectors

Food security and nutrition

- Include specific social and psychological considerations (safe aid for all in dignity, considering cultural practices and household roles) in the provision of food and nutritional support

Shelter and site planning

- Include specific social considerations (safe, dignified, culturally and socially appropriate assistance) in site planning and shelter provision, in a coordinated manner

Water and sanitation

- Include specific social considerations (safe and culturally appropriate access for all in dignity) in the provision of water and sanitation

The guidelines have generally been welcomed by a range of experts although some concerns were raised, particularly by those who would have preferred the guidelines to have been more strongly informed by insights from psychotraumatology and psychiatric epidemiology (Cardozo, 2008; Yule, 2008). Since 2007, the task group that developed the guidelines was transformed into the IASC Reference Group for Mental Health in Emergencies, which has released a series of supplementary implementation tools to accompany the full guidelines, including tools for coordinators in sectors such as health, camp management and protection. Separate documents were made, all through extensive consultation processes, on topics such as 'ethics of MHPSS research in emergencies' (Inter-Agency Standing Committee (IASC) Reference Group for Mental Health and Psychosocial Support in Emergency Settings, 2014), 'monitoring and evaluation' (Inter-Agency Standing Committee (IASC) Reference Group for Mental Health and Psychosocial Support in Emergency

Settings, 2016a) and 'interagency referral (Inter-Agency Standing Committee (IASC) Reference Group for Mental Health and Psychosocial Support in Emergency Settings, 2016b).

A review concluded that in the first seven years after their publication, the guidelines had important positive effects on the field, enabling various actors to communicate and coordinate across sectors, often bridging health and protection activities. The principle of multi layered services as shown in the intervention pyramid (see Fig. 1) was commonly described a useful tool for use in training and coordination (IASC Reference Group for Mental Health and Psychosocial Support, 2015).

Mental Health and Psychosocial Support Guidance for Refugee Settings

The materials that were described in the previous part of this chapter are not specific for refugee situations, but provide overall guidance for humanitarian emergencies. Refugee situations have additional layers of complexity that are related to the specific vulnerability of refugees and the legal context of protection their rights. The terms 'migrants' and 'refugees' are sometimes, erroneously, used as synonyms. There are crucial legal differences between the two. The 1951 Refugee Convention defines a refugee as 'someone who is unable or unwilling to return to their country of origin owing to a well-founded fear of being persecuted for reasons of race, religion, nationality, membership of a particular social group, or political opinion.'(United Nations General Assembly, 1951). Migrants can be defined as people moving from one country to another, unless they are specifically fleeing war or persecution, in which case they would be considered a refugee.

Being a refugee implies, per definition, that a person cannot count on the protection and assistance of the own government. Governmentals who signed the 1951 convention are legally obliged to assess claims for asylum and provide protection, and cannot deport refugees. Within the United Nations one specific agency is mandated to protect refugees: UNHCR. The UNHCR's major tasks are to offer refugees international protection, to seek durable solutions to their problems and provide them with assistance and services in the form of food, shelter, medical care, education and other social services. The provision of assistance and services for refugees is done in close cooperation with a range of actors including line ministries of the host governments, United Nations sister agencies such as WHO and UNICEF, and hundreds of nongovernmental organisations which may be funded directly by UNHCR and/or bring their own funds.

A 2013 review by UNHCR's Policy Development and Evaluation Service concluded that, although significant activities in the field of MHPSS are already employed across the organisation and its functional sectors, the organization as a whole has not yet adequately engaged with MHPSS concepts, definitions and approaches. This review advised that "UNHCR could more strongly and clearly articulate its role in the field of MHPSS by developing issuing guidance and by strengthening internal capacity to develop, implement and support MHPSS activities" (Meyer, 2013). Simultaneously, in 2013 UNHCR issued its first 'Operational Guidance for Mental Health and Psychosocial Support Programming in Refugee Operations' (United Nations High Commissioner for Refugees, 2013). It closely follows the 2007 IASC guidelines and does this with a specific focus on refugee settings in low and middle income countries.

MHPSS problems in refugee contexts can be addressed through activities such as supporting communities' resilience, promoting mechanisms for social support, and offering services to individuals with more complex mental health needs. Therefore, a central notion for UNHCR is that considerations around MHPSS are relevant for a wide range of actors within UNHCR operations. UNHCR distinguishes between an *MHPSS approach* and *MHPSS interventions*.

- Adopting an MHPSS approach means providing a humanitarian response in ways that are beneficial to the mental health and psychosocial wellbeing of the refugees. This is relevant for all actors involved in the assistance to refugees.
- MHPSS interventions consist of one or several activities with a primary goal to improve the mental health and psychosocial wellbeing of refugees. MHPSS interventions are usually implemented in the sectors for health, community protection and education.

Using an MHPSS Approach in Refugee Settings

An important way to improve the psychological state of refugees is by influencing humanitarian actors to deliver their assistance in ways that can support psychosocial wellbeing and mental health. Applying an 'MHPSS approach' to basic services and security requires working in close collaboration with refugees and providing them with adequate information. This can greatly reduce psychological distress in humanitarian settings and give refugees a sense of agency (United Nations High Commissioner for Refugees, 2017). Conversely, humanitarian assistance can undermine refugee psychosocial wellbeing if:

- Refugees are not being consulted/involved in decisions about humanitarian assistance that affect people's lives;
- Refugees are kept in a dependent and subordinate position, in receiving food rations or relief items;
- Refugees are being forced to use undignified or unsafe communal toilets and bathing facilities;
- Refugees have to live in shared shelters with no privacy;
- Refugees lack information about rights and what will happen next;
- Refugees perceive favouritism towards particular groups (United Nations High Commissioner for Refugees, 2017)

The best ways to prevent such negative effects of humanitarian assistance on wellbeing is to use participatory approaches that promote the dignitiy and agency of refugees, involve them in their own protection, and encourage them to actively shape a safe social environment. Within UNHCR, these are core elements of what is coined 'community-based protection' (United Nations High Commissioner for Refugees, 2014). Some organisations have developed sophisticated ways to use MHPSS approaches in their way of working. For example, the psychosocial specialists of the Act Alliance, a network of faith-based organisations, have developed an approach to mainstream community based psychosocial support within their programming in refugee settings in Ethiopia, Kenya and Uganda (Horn, Waade, & Kalisky, 2016). A multi-layered approach to mental health and psychosocial support (MHPSS) in emergencies involves the integration of psychosocial approaches into 'basic services and security' and 'community and family supports' services. Basic principles of MHPSS can assist organisations to integrate psychosocial approaches into their work and requires an awareness from staff working in these 'other sectors' that their activities have an effect in psychosocial wellbeing of staff.

MHPSS as Part of 'Protection' in Refugee Settings

An important source from which people can draw to maintain their mental health and psychosocial well-being is to seek support and assistance in their immediate trusted social environment: family members, friends, or neighbours. In many refugee settings, these community and family networks have been significantly affected: Family members are separated, neighbours do not know one another, trust among community members has been shattered, people who would normally support each other are not able to do so because they are in grief and pain themselves. It is, therefore, of paramount importance to help refugees to support each other and to foster social cohesion in refugee populations (see Box 2: strengthening community and family support). Key activities are thus to revitalize this mutual support among refugees, and between refugees and host communities.

Refugee outreach volunteers: In many refugee operations, refugees are engaged as volunteers in a wide range of programmes in health, education and social services. Particularly in urban settings, where refugees often find it challenging to navigate their way through services, networks of refugee outreach volunteers can be very relevant and constitute the missing link to assist refugees accessing services. Psychosocial elements can be integrated in the training and supervision of community outreach volunteers and enable them to be involved in information sharing, linking people to mental health services when needed, and setting up support groups amongst other functions (Hassan, 2013; Mirghani, 2013; Quosh, 2013).

Child friendly spaces: In acute refugee crises, when comprehensive services have not yet been established, the needs of children and adolescents can easily be overlooked. Wellbeing of children is often best fostered by the restoration of a sense of normalcy and safety in crises. For example, schools are often not yet established in the beginning of a refugee crisis and parents may be overwhelmed. A widely-used intervention for children in emergencies is the establishment of *child friendly spaces*: "specific, identifiable spaces that protect children and young people from physical harm and psychosocial distress whilst assisting them to play and develop through participation in organised and supervised activities during emergencies" (Davie, Stuart, Williams, & Erwin, 2014). These are often set up in a large tent or container, and are aimed to provide a supportive environment in which children can engage in a range of activities including song, drama, dance, drawing, play, storytelling/reading, sports, as well as learning basic literacy and numeracy. They are generally thought to have positive effects on emotional wellbeing of children but the evidence base for this is still scant (Ager, Metzler, Vojta, & Savage, 2013). Recent rigorous long term evaluation of child friendly spaces in various emergencies have shown positive effects, but not for all children in all settings. It is important to realize that child friendly spaces are temporary measures and when the education system is being set up Child Friendly Spaces may transform in child focused community centres (Bøgh, 2011).

Integrating MHPSS within schools: There are significant interactions between emotional wellbeing and capacities to learn and thrive in school. Children with good social and emotional skills do better in school, usually have better relationships with peers and adults and have a better mental health status. Therefore, organisations such as UNICEF and the Interagency Network for Education in Emergencies (INEE) promote the integration of social and emotional learning competencies within educational programmes for refugees (Interagency Network on Education in Emergencies, 2016).

MHPSS in Public Health Programmes for Refugees

UNHCR-supported health programmes for refugees in low and middle income countries strive to provide a basic level of services as defined by WHO standards, and to be equitable with health systems for non-refugees in the country (the host population). This may lead to tensions, in particular when the national health services in host countries are malfunctioning or when essential elements (such as mental health care) are neglected in national health services.

One of the key principles for mental health programming for refugees is integration within general health services. People with mental disorders frequently consult general health services, but their problems are frequently not properly identified and managed (Ventevogel, van Ommeren, Schilperoord, & Saxena, 2015). Therefore, general health care staff in refugee setting must have some basic knowledge that allows them to identify and manage people with MHPSS problems (which includes people with psychological distress, mental disorders, substance use problems, unexplained medical complaints and epilepsy). Key actions as defined in UNHCR's Operational Guidance (United Nations High Commissioner for Refugees, 2013) include:

- *Train and supervise primary health care providers*
  Train health staff (e.g. clinical officers, medical doctors, nurses) in identification and management of priority mental health problems, preferably using the mhGAP Humanitarian Intervention Guide (Cavallera, Jones, Weisbecker, & Ventevogel, 2019; World Health Organization & United Nations High Commissioner for Refugees, 2015) (See Box 3)
- *Regular support visits by psychiatrist for supervision and mentoring*
  Training must be followed by a supervision system. Some of the supervision activities can be done by general health workers with some advanced training, but it is preferable to have a service agreement with a mental health specialist to jointly see complicated cases and provide on the job training to the general health worker.
- *Ensure that people with severe mental disorders have access to care*
  Severe mental disorders (particularly psychosis and severe depression) lead to severe disability and make people highly vulnerable for human rights abuses. Access to minimum care for people with severe mental disorders must therefore be made available in all refugee operations. Hospitalizations need to be avoided because they sever ties of the patient with his social environment and they are generally not cost-effective, and dedicated hospitals are usually located in major urban centres, often far from the sites where refugees live. If hospitalization is required (for example if the person exhibits behaviour that is dangerous or harmful for the person or for others), they should be limited to short term admissions for emergencies. People with severe mental health problems should have access to a network of community-based social supports as well as clinical care through available health services (e.g., general hospitals, primary care clinics, etc.). Organizing basic clinical mental health care usually involves either organizing rapid training and supervision of general health staff or adding a mental health professional to the health facility. Mechanisms must be developed to identify

Box 3: Modules in the mhGAP Humanitarian Intervention Guide
(World Health Organization & United Nations High Commissioner for Refugees, 2015)

- Acute Stress
- Grief
- Moderate-severe Depressive Disorder
- Posttraumatic Stress Disorder (PTSD)
- Psychosis
- Epilepsy/Seizures
- Intellectual Disability
- Harmful Use of Alcohol and Drugs
- Suicide
- Other Significant Mental Health Complaints

people with severe mental disorders, particularly the most vulnerable among them, and link them to available services. This can be best done in consultation with key community informants, including religious leaders/healers and community workers, who often serve as a first contact. Some simple screening mechanisms have been developed for this aim (Jordans, Kohrt, Luitel, Komproe, & Lund, 2015; Llosa et al., 2017). It is critical that people who have been identified as having a severe mental disorder are regularly being followed-up by involving community workers and refugee outreach volunteers.

- *Provide essential drugs*
  Each health programme should make generic medication available for selected mental, neurological and substance use disorders, using the UNHCR essential medicine list (with 11 medications) or the more restricted Inter Agency Emergency Health Kit that has 5 medications (van Ommeren et al., 2011).
- *Ingrate mental health into the health information system*
  Since 2009 UNHCR routinely collects the number of consultations in the general health centres that are related to mental health (including epilepsy). This has shown major disparities between various settings (Kane et al., 2014).
- *Make sufficient human resources for MHPSS available*
  For camp based operations see Box 4. In non-camp based operations such as in urban settings different arrangements can be made based on available resources. Here too, the principle is to provide mental health services at logical and accessible locations, preferably integrated within general health care systems. If resources allow, consider assigning and training 'case managers'.

Box 4 Human Resources for MHPSS in the Health Sector in Camp-Based Operations

- A mental health professional (typically a psychiatric nurse, but in some contexts, this may be a psychiatrist) for assessment and management of people with severe or complex mental disorders and to provide guidance and support to primary health care staff.
- Availability of other mental health specialists (psychiatrists, clinical psychologists, psychiatric nurses) to support the primary health care staff and build their capacity through training, consultation, mentoring and supervision.
- Trained community based workers (refugee outreach volunteers or community health workers) to do home based follow up and support and link people with MHPSS problems (including epilepsy) to health and community services and to encourage /support self-help and mutual support for people with MHPSS problems.

- (United Nations High Commissioner for Refugees, 2013)

Additional elements that should be considered but are currently not yet routine part of refugee mental health programmes are:

- Evidence-based psychological treatments available for people with disabling forms of depression and other emotional disorders. There is, by now, clear evidence that brief structured psychological interventions based on the principles of cognitive behavioural therapy (Bolton et al., 2014; Rahman et al., 2016) and interpersonal therapy (Bolton et al., 2007; Verdeli et al., 2008) are effective. Simple manualized forms of such therapies have been developed by experts in cooperation with WHO (World Health Organization, 2016; World Health Organization & Columbia University, 2016). These should now be adapted, locally evaluated and scaled up in a wide range of refugee contexts (Sijbrandij et al., 2017).

Other neglected areas are the integration of integrated early child development (ECD) initiatives in the health sector (UNICEF & World Health Organization, 2012), the integration of MHPSS in programmes for nutrition (Dozio, Peyre, Morel, & Bizouerne, 2016), and the integrating of interventions for alcohol and drug use in refugee settings (Hanna, 2017; Greene, Kane, Krawczyk, Brown, Murray, Khoshnood, & Tol, 2018).

MHPSS Coordination in Refugee Settings

Refugee crises often pose major challenges to ensuring even a minimum level of services for mental health and psychosocial support. In their attempts to alleviate suffering as rapidly as possible, humanitarian programmes may inadvertently create problems in the long run such as creating parallel systems that are not sustainable and causing inequities between refugees and host populations, and are being driven by 'outsiders', ignoring what people already do themselves (Ventevogel, Pérez-Sales, Férnandez Liria, & Baingana, 2011). It is very important that the planning and exectution of services for refugees are well coordinated. In practice, services are coordinated through sectoral coordination groups of which those for health, protection and education are the most important for MHPSS. A continuing debate is where MHPSS should sit in the coordination mechanisms as it has links to particularly 'health' and 'protection'. The preferred option is to have an MHPSS working group that has functional links to both the health and protection coordination mechanisms (United Nations High Commissioner for Refugees, 2013). MHPSS working groups have been established in many refugee settings, bringing together organizations working in health as well as in 'protection'. In many of the more protracted and complex emergencies many dozens of organisations are active in the field of MHPSS posing significant coordination concerns (Baca, Fayyad, Marini, & Weissbecker, 2012; O'Connell et al., 2013).

Conclusions

This chapter focused on the slow but steady integration of mental health and psychosocial support into international policy documents and guidelines in humanitarian emergencies, particularly for refugees in low and middle income countries. Clearly, in the last decades, major steps have been taken, but there is still a long way to go to reach an acceptable level of services for mental health and psychosocial support for refugees in low and middle income settings. While the development of consensus guidelines has helped the field of MHPSS in humanitarian settings to become more coherent, more visible and probably more effective, various challenges impede the further development of the field.

Obviously, a major factor is the low level of funding for MHPSS in humanitarian settings. Increasingly, major funding agencies realize that addressing mental health and psychosocial wellbeing for refugees and others in humanitarian settings is not a luxury but essential. Unfortunately, until now this mounting insight has not been matched by equally mounting funding opportunities (Mackenzie & Kesner, 2016; Marquez, 2017).

Another factor impeding progress is the disconnect between the academic community of mental health researchers and those involved in the provision of humanitarian assistance. A growing group of global mental health researchers investigate practice-oriented questions, but still, unfortunately, much of mental health research is guided by academic concerns or debates that have limited relevance for humanitarian assistance (Tol, Barbui, et al., 2011; Tol, Patel, et al., 2011). Urgent issues that need to be addressed in future research on mental health and psychosocial support in refugee settings and other humanitarian emergencies in low and middle income countries include:

(1) How to foster community involvement in mental health interventions?
(2) How to make screening work: making sure that people get the care and support they need?
(3) How to scale up mental health interventions with proven efficacy in small scale research trials?
(4) How to best adapt interventions to context and culture? (Chowdhary et al., 2014),
(5) How to systematically translate findings of social ecological research around MHPSS in refugee settings into programmatic action? (Tol, 2015; Vindevogel, 2017).

Answers to such 'grand questions' cannot be found by consensus-making exercises as described in this chapter, but need to be addressed through a strong practice-focused research agenda to establish how MHPSS interventions for refugees can be made more effective and sustainable.

References

Ager, A. (1997). Tensions in the psychosocial discourse. *Development in Practice, 7*(4), 402–407.

Ager, A. (2002). Psychosocial needs in complex emergencies. *The Lancet, 360*(Suppl), 43–44.

Ager, A. (2008). Consensus and professional practice in psychosocial intervention: Political achievement, core knowledge-base and prompt for further enquiry. *Intervention, 6*(3), 261–264.

Ager, A., Metzler, J., Vojta, M., & Savage, K. (2013). Child friendly spaces: A systematic review of the current evidence base on outcomes and impact. *Intervention, 11*(2), 133–147.

Baca, M. J., Fayyad, K., Marini, A., & Weissbecker, I. (2012). The four W's (Who, Where, When, and What): The development of a comprehensive mapping service for mental health and psychosocial support in Jordan. *Intervention, 10*(2), 177–187.

Bass, J. K., Annan, J., McIvor Murray, S., Kaysen, D., Griffiths, S., Cetinoglu, T., … Bolton, P. A. (2013). Controlled trial of psychotherapy for Congolese survivors of sexual violence. *New England Journal of Medicine, 368*, 2182–2191.

Batniji, R., van Ommeren, M., & Saraceno, B. (2006). Mental and social health in disasters: relating qualitative social science research and the Sphere standard. *Social Science & Medicine, 62*(8), 1853–1864. https://doi.org/10.1016/j.socscimed.2005.08.050

Bøgh, C. (2011). *"The Desert Flower": From child friendly space to child education and welfare centre. Concept paper for Dadaab refugee camps Hagadera, Dagahaley, Ifo*. Retrieved from unpublished report.

Bolton, P., Bass, J., Betancourt, T., Speelman, L., Onyango, G., Clougherty, K. F., … Verdeli, H. (2007). Interventions for depression symptoms among adolescent survivors of war and displacement in northern Uganda: A randomized controlled trial. *JAMA, 298*(5), 519–527.

Bolton, P., Lee, C., Haroz, E. E., Murray, L., Dorsey, S., Robinson, C., … Bass, J. (2014). A transdiagnostic community-based mental health treatment for comorbid disorders: Development and outcomes of a randomized controlled trial among Burmese refugees in Thailand. *PLoS Med, 11*(11), e1001757.

Boothby, N., Strang, A., & Wessells, M. (Eds.). (2008). *A world turned upside down: Social ecological approaches to children in war zones*. Bloomfield: Kumarian Press.

Bronfenbrenner, U. (1986). Ecology of the family as a context for human development: Research perspectives. *Developmental Psychology, 22*(6), 723–742.

Buchanan-Smith, M. (2003). *How the Sphere Project came into being: A case study of policy-making in the humanitarian aid sector and the relative influence of research*. London, UK: Overseas Development Institute.

Cardozo, B. L. (2008). Guidelines need a more evidence based approach: A commentary on the IASC Guidelines on Mental Health and Psychosocial Support in Emergency Settings. *Intervention, 6*(3–4), 252–254.

Cavallera, V., Jones, L., Weissbecker, I., & Ventevogel, P. (2019). Mental health in complex emergencies. In A. Kravitz (Ed.), *Oxford handbook of humanitarian medicine* (pp. 117–153). Oxford, UK: Oxford University Press.

Chowdhary, N., Jotheeswaran, A. T., Nadkarni, A., Hollon, S. D., King, M., Jordans, M. J., … Patel, V. (2014). The methods and outcomes of cultural adaptations of psychological treatments for depressive disorders: A systematic review. *Psychological Medicine, 44*(6), 1131–1146. https://doi.org/10.1017/S0033291713001785

Davie, S., Stuart, M., Williams, F., & Erwin, E. (2014). Child friendly spaces: protecting and supporting children in emergency response and recovery. *Australian Journal of Emergency Management, 29*(1), 25–30.

de Jong, J. T. (2002). Public mental health, traumatic stress and human rights violations in low-income countries. In J. de Jong (Ed.), *Trauma, war, and violence: Public mental health in socio-cultural context* (pp. 1–91). New York, NY: Kluwer Academic/Plenum Publishers.

de Jong, J. T. (2014). Challenges of creating synergy between global mental health and cultural psychiatry. *Transcultural Psychiatry, 51*(6), 806–828.

Dozio, E., Peyre, L., Morel, S. O., & Bizouerne, C. (2016). Integrated psychosocial and food security approach in an emergency context: Central African Republic. *Intervention, 14*(3), 257–271.

El Chammay, R., & Ammar, W. (2014). Syrian crisis and mental health system reform in Lebanon. *The Lancet, 384*(9942), 494.

Eloul, L., Quosh, C., Ajlani, R., Avetisyan, N., Barakat, M., Barakat, L., … Diekkamp, V. (2013). Inter-agency coordination of mental health and psychosocial support for refugees and people displaced in Syria. *Intervention, 11*(3), 340–348.

Epping-Jordan, J. E., van Ommeren, M., Ashour, H. N., Maramis, A., Marini, A., Mohanraj, A., … Saxena, S. (2015). Beyond the crisis: building back better mental health care in 10 emergency-affected areas using a longer-term perspective. *International Journal of Mental Health Systems, 9*(1), 15. https://doi.org/10.1186/s13033-015-0007-9

Fairbank, J. A., Friedman, M. J., de Jong, J., Green, B. L., & Solomon, S. D. (2003). Intervention options for societies, communities, families, and individuals. In B. L. Green, M. J. Friedman, J. de Jong, S. D. Solomon, T. M. Keane, J. A. Fairbank, B. Donelan, & E. Frey-Wouters (Eds.), *Trauma interventions in war and peace* (pp. 57–72). New York, NY: Springer.

Farmer, P. (2011). *Haiti after the earthquake*. New York, NY: Public Affairs.

Fassin, D., & Rechtman, R. (2009). *The empire of trauma: An inquiry into the condition of victimhood*. Princeton, NJ: Princeton University Press.

Fritsche, G. (2001). Controlling humanitarian aid cowboys in Afghanistan. *The Lancet, 358*(9297), 2002. https://doi.org/10.1016/S0140-6736(01)06998-7

Galappatti, A. (2005). Psychosocial work in the aftermath of the Tsunami: Challenges for service provision in Batticaloa, eastern Sri Lanka. *Intervention, 3*(1), 65–69.

Ganesan, M. (2011). Building up mental health services from scratch: Experiences from eastern Sri Lanka. *Intervention, 9*(3), 359–363.

Greene, M. C., Kane, J. C., Krawczyk, N., Brown, F., Murray, L., Khoshnood, K., & Tol, W. A. (2018). Alcohol and drug misuse interventions in conflict-affected populations. In N. Morina & A. Nickerson (Eds.), *Mental health of refugee and conflict-affected populations* (pp. 221–241). Springer.

Hamber, B., Gallagher, E., & Ventevogel, P. (2014). Narrowing the gap between psychosocial practice, peacebuilding and wider social change. *Intervention, 12*(1), 7–15.

Hanna, F. B. (2017). Alcohol and substance use in humanitarian and post-conflict situations. *Eastern Mediterranean Health Journal, 23*(3), 231–235.

Harrell-Bond, B. E. (1986). *Imposing aid: Emergency assistance to refugees*. Oxford, UK: Oxford University Press.

Hassan, M. (2013). Personal reflections on a psychosocial community outreach programme and centre in Damascus, Syria. *Intervention, 11*(3), 330–335.

Hobfoll, S. E., Watson, P., Bell, C. C., Bryant, R. A., Brymer, M. J., Friedman, M. J., … Ursano, R. J. (2007). Five essential elements of immediate and mid-term mass trauma intervention: Empirical evidence. *Psychiatry: Interpersonal and Biological Processes, 70*(4), 283–315.

Horn, R., Waade, M., & Kalisky, M. (2016). Not doing more, but doing differently: Integrating a community based psychosocial approach into other sectors. *Intervention, 14*(3), 245–256.

Inter-Agency Standing Committee Reference Group on Mental Health and Psychosocial Support. (2015). *Review of the implementation of the IASC guidelines on mental health and psychosocial support in emergency settings*. Geneva, Switzerland: Inter-Agency Standing Committee.

Committee, I.-A. S. (2007). *IASC guidelines on mental health and psychosocial support in emergency settings*. Geneva, Switzerland: Author.

Inter-Agency Standing Committee (IASC) Reference Group for Mental Health and Psychosocial Support in Emergency Settings. (2014). *Recommendations for conducting ethical mental health and psychosocial research in emergency settings*. Geneva, Switzerland: Inter-Agency Standing Committee.

Inter-Agency Standing Committee (IASC) Reference Group for Mental Health and Psychosocial Support in Emergency Settings. (2016a). *A common monitoring and evaluation framework for mental health and psychosocial support in emergency settings*. Geneva, Switzerland: Inter-Agency Standing Committee.

Inter-Agency Standing Committee (IASC) Reference Group for Mental Health and Psychosocial Support in Emergency Settings. (2016b). *Inter-Agency referral form and guidance note*. Geneva, Switzerland: Inter-Agency Standing Committee.

Inter-Agency Network for Education in Emergencies. (2016). *Background paper on psychosocial support and social and emotional learning for children and youth in emergency settings*. New York, NY: Author.

Jones, L. (2008). Responding to the needs of children in crisis. *International Review of Psychiatry, 20*(3), 291–303.

Jones, L., Asare, J., Elmasri, M., & Mohanraj, A. (2007). Mental health in disaster settings. *British Medical Journal, 335*(7622), 679–680. https://doi.org/10.1136/bmj.39329.580891.BE

Jordans, M. J., Kohrt, B. A., Luitel, N. P., Komproe, I. H., & Lund, C. (2015). Accuracy of proactive case finding for mental disorders by community informants in Nepal. *British Journal of Psychiatry, 207*(6), 501–506. https://doi.org/10.1192/bjp.bp.113.141077

Kane, J. C., Ventevogel, P., Spiegel, P., Bass, J. K., van Ommeren, M., & Tol, W. A. (2014). Mental, neurological, and substance use problems among refugees in primary health care: analysis of the Health Information System in 90 refugee camps. *BMC Medicine, 12*(1), 228.

Kirmayer, L. J., Kienzler, H., Afana, A. H., & Pedersen, D. (2010). Trauma and disasters in social and cultural context. In C. Morgan & D. Bhugra (Eds.), *Principles of social psychiatry* (pp. 155–177). Chichester, UK: Wiley.

Krishnakumar, G., Sivayokan, S., & Somasundaram, D. (2008). Coordination of psychosocial activities at the Jaffna District level in Sri Lanka. *Intervention, 6*(3), 270–274.

Llosa, A. E., van Ommeren, M., Kolappa, K., Ghantous, Z., Souza, R., Bastin, B., ... Grais, R. F. (2017). A two-phase approach for the identification of refugees with priority need for mental health care in Lebanon: A validation study. *BMC Psychiatry, 17*(1), 28.

Mackenzie, J., & Kesner, C. (2016). *Mental health funding and the SDGs. What now and who pays?* London, UK: Overseas Development Institute.

Marquez, P. V. (2017). *Mental health among displaced people and refugees: making the case for action at the World Bank Group*. Washington, DC: World Bank Group.

Meyer, S. (2013). *UNHC's mental health and psychosocial support for persons of concern* (Global review 2013). Retrieved from UNHCR website: http://www.unhcr.org/research/evalreports/51bec3359/unhcrs-mental-health-psychosocial-support-persons-concern.html

Meyer, S., Bennouna, C., & Stark, L. (2016). Health and wellbeing in refugee camps. In F. Thomas (Ed.), *Handbook of migration and health* (pp. 379–401). Cheltenham, UK: Edward Elgar Publishing.

Miller, K. E., & Rasco, L. M. (2004). An ecological framework for addressing the mental health needs of refugee communities. In K. E. Miller & L. M. Rasco (Eds.), *The mental health of refugees. Ecological approaches to healing and adaptation* (pp. 1–64). Mahwah, NJ/London, UK: Erlbaum.

Miller, K. E., & Rasmussen, A. (2010). Mental health and armed conflict: The importance of distinguishing between war exposure and other sources of adversity: A response to Neuner. *Social Science & Medicine, 71*(8), 1385–1389.

Miller, K. E., & Rasmussen, A. (2014). War experiences, daily stressors, and mental health five years on: Elaborations and future directions. *Intervention, 12*, 33–42.

Mirghani, Z. (2013). Healing through sharing: An outreach project with Iraqi refugee volunteers in Syria. *Intervention, 11*(3), 321–329.

Neuner, F., Schauer, M., & Elbert, T. (2014). On the efficacy of Narrative Exposure Therapy: A reply to Mundt et al. *Intervention, 12*(2), 267–278.

O'Connell, R., Poudyal, B., Streel, E., Bahgat, F., Tol, W., & Ventevogel, P. (2013). Who is where, when, doing what: Mapping services for mental health and psychosocial support in emergencies. *Intervention, 10*(2), 171–176.

O'Callaghan, P., McMullen, J., Shannon, C., Rafferty, H., & Black, A. (2013). A randomized controlled trial of trauma-focused cognitive behavioral therapy for sexually exploited, war-affected

Congolese girls. *Journal of the American Academy of Child & Adolescent Psychiatry, 52*(4), 359–369.

Ostuzzi, G., Barbui, C., Hanlon, C., Chatterjee, S., Eaton, J., Jones, L., … Ventevogel, P. (Submitted). Mapping the evidence on pharmacological interventions for chronic non-affective psychosis in humanitarian non-specialized settings. *BMC Medicine, 15*, 197. https://doi.org/10.1186/s12916-017-0960-z. Manuscript submitted for publication.

Patel, V. (1995). Explanatory models of mental illness in sub-Saharan Africa. *Social Science & Medicine, 40*(9), 1291–1298. https://doi.org/10.1016/027795369400231H

Patel, V., Collins, P. Y., Copeland, J., Kakuma, R., Katontoka, S., Lamichhane, J., … Skeen, S. (2011). The movement for global mental health. *British Journal of Psychiatry, 198*(2), 88–90. https://doi.org/10.1192/bjp.bp.109.074518

Pérez-Sales, P., Férnandez-Liria, A., Baingana, F., & Ventevogel, P. (2011). Integrating mental health into existing systems of care during and after complex humanitarian emergencies: Rethinking the experience. *Intervention, 9*(3), 345–358.

Quosh, C. (2013). Mental health, forced displacement & recovery: Integrated mental health & psychosocial support programme for urban refugees in Syria. *Intervention, 11*(3), 295–320.

Rahman, A., Hamdani, S. U., Awan, N. R., Bryant, R. A., Dawson, K. S., Khan, M. F., … van Ommeren, M. (2016). Effect of a multicomponent behavioral intervention in adults impaired by psychological distress in a conflict-affected area of Pakistan: A randomized clinical trial. *JAMA, 316*(24), 2609–2617. https://doi.org/10.1001/jama.2016.17165

Rasmussen, A., Katoni, B., Keller, A. S., & Wilkinson, J. (2011). Posttraumatic idioms of distress among Darfur refugees: Hozun and Majnun. *Transcultural Psychiatry, 48*(4), 392–415. https://doi.org/10.1177/1363461511409283

Riley, A., Varner, A., Ventevogel, P., Hassan, M. M. T., & Welton-Mitchell, C. (2017). Daily stressors, trauma exposure and mental health among stateless Rohingya refugees in Bangladesh. *Transcultural Psychiatry, 54*(3), 304–331.

Schauer, M., Schauer, M., Neuner, F., & Elbert, T. (2011). *Narrative Exposure Therapy: A short-term treatment for traumatic stress disorders*. Göttingen, Germany: Hogrefe Publishing.

Schinina, G., & Tankink, M. (2018). Introduction to a special section on psychosocial support, conflict transformation and creative approaches in response to the needs of Syrian refugees in Turkey. *Intervention, 16*(2), 161–163.

Shapiro, F. (2014). EMDR therapy humanitarian assistance programs: Treating the psychological, physical, and societal effects of adverse experiences worldwide. *Journal of EMDR Practice and Research, 8*(4), 181–186.

Sijbrandij, M., Acarturk, C., Aktas, M., Bryant, R.A., Burchert, S., Carswell, K., … Cuijpers, P. (2017). *Strengthening mental health care systems for Syrian refugees in Europe and the Middle East: Integrating scalable psychological interventions in 8 countries*. Manuscript submitted for publication.

Silove, D. (1999). The psychosocial effects of torture, mass human rights violations, and refugee trauma: Toward an integrated conceptual framework. *Journal of Nervous and Mental Disease, 187*(4), 200–207.

Silove, D. (2004). The challenges facing mental health programs for post-conflict and refugee communities. *Prehospital and Disaster Medicine, 19*(1), 90–96.

Silove, D., Ekblad, S., & Mollica, R. (2000). The rights of the severely mentally ill in post-conflict societies. *The Lancet, 355*(9214), 1548–1549. https://doi.org/10.1016/S0140-6736(00)02177-2

Silove, D., Ventevogel, P., & Rees, S. (2017). The contemporary refugee crisis: An overview of mental health challenges. *World Psychiatry, 16*(2), 130–139.

Sphere Project. (2004). *Humanitarian charter and minimum standards in disaster response*. Geneva, Switzerland: Author.

Strang, A. B., & Ager, A. (2003). Psychosocial interventions: Some key issues facing practitioners. *Intervention, 1*(3), 2–12.

Summerfield, D. (1999). A critique of seven assumptions behind psychological trauma programmes in war-affected areas. *Social Science & Medicine, 48*(10), 1449–1462.

Tol, W. A. (2015). Stemming the tide: Promoting mental health and preventing mental disorders in low-and middle-income countries. *Global Mental Health, 2*, e11.

Tol, W. A., Barbui, C., Galappatti, A., Silove, D., Betancourt, T. S., Souza, R., … van Ommeren, M. (2011). Mental health and psychosocial support in humanitarian settings: Linking practice and research. *The Lancet, 378*(9802), 1581–1591. https://doi.org/10.1016/S0140-6736(11)61094-5

Tol, W. A., Patel, V., Tomlinson, M., Baingana, F., Galappatti, A., Panter-Brick, C., … van Ommeren, M. (2011). Research priorities for mental health and psychosocial support in humanitarian settings. *PLoS Medicine, 8*(9), e1001096. https://doi.org/10.1371/journal.pmed.1001096

Tol, W. A., Purgato, M., Bass, J. K., Galappatti, A., & Eaton, W. (2015). Mental health and psychosocial support in humanitarian settings: A public mental health perspective. *Epidemiology and Psychiatric Sciences, 24*(6), 484–494.

Toole, M. J., Waldmann, R. J., & Zwi, A. (2006). Complex emergencies. In M. H. Merson, M. H. Black, & A. J. Mills (Eds.), *International public health. Diseases, programs, systems, and policies* (pp. 445–511). Boston, MA: Jones and Bartlett.

United Nations High Commissioner for Refugees. (2014). *Understanding community-based protection. Protection Policy Paper*. Retrieved from http://www.refworld.org/pdfid/5209f0b64.pdf

UNICEF & World Health Organization. (2012). *Integrating early childhood development (ECD) into nutrition programmes in emergencies. Why, what and how.* Retrieved from https://www.unicef.org/earlychildhood/files/ecd_note_nutrition_whywhathow.pdf

United Nations General Assembly. (1951). *Convention relating to the status of refugees*. New York, NY: United Nations.

United Nations High Commissioner for Refugees. (2013). *Operational guidance for mental health and psychosocial support programming in refugee operations*. Geneva, Switzerland: Author.

United Nations High Commissioner for Refugees. (2017). *Community-based protection and mental health & psychosocial support*. Geneva, Switzerland: Author.

van der Veen, M., & Somasundaram, D. (2006). Responding to the psychosocial impact of the Tsunami in a war zone: Experiences from northern Sri Lanka. *Intervention, 4*(1), 53–57.

van Ommeren, M., Barbui, C., de Jong, K., Dua, T., Jones, L., Perez-Sales, P., … Saxena, S. (2011). If you could only choose five psychotropic medicines: Updating the interagency emergency health kit. *PLoS Medicine, 8*(5), e1001030. https://doi.org/10.1371/journal.pmed.1001030

van Ommeren, M., Saxena, S., & Saraceno, B. (2005a). Aid after disasters. *British Medical Journal, 330*(7501), 1160–1161.

van Ommeren, M., Saxena, S., & Saraceno, B. (2005b). Mental and social health during and after acute emergencies: Emerging consensus? *Bulletin of the World Health Organisation, 83*(1), 71–75. https://doi.org/10.1590/S0042-96862005000100017

Ventevogel, P. (2008). The IASC guidelines on mental health and psychosocial support in emergency settings, from discussion to implementation. *Intervention, 6*(3–4), 193–198.

Ventevogel, P. (2014). The role of brief trauma focused psychotherapies (such as Narrative Exposure Therapy) in areas affected by conflict. *Intervention, 12*(2), 244–249.

Ventevogel, P. (2016). *Borderlands of mental health: Explorations in medical anthropology, psychiatric epidemiology and health systems research in Afghanistan and Burundi.* (PhD), Universiteit van Amsterdam, Amsterdam.

Ventevogel, P., Jordans, M., Reis, R., & de Jong, J. (2013). Madness or sadness? Local concepts of mental illness in four conflict-affected African communities. *Conflict and Health, 7*(1), 3. https://doi.org/10.1186/1752-1505-7-3

Ventevogel, P., Pérez-Sales, P., Férnandez Liria, A., & Baingana, F. (2011). Integration of mental health into existing systems of care during and after complex humanitarian emergencies: An introduction to a special issue. *Intervention, 9*(3), 195–210.

Ventevogel, P., van Ommeren, M., Schilperoord, M., & Saxena, S. (2015). Improving mental health care in humanitarian emergencies. *Bulletin of the World Health Organization, 93*(10), 666–666A.

Verdeli, H., Clougherty, K., Onyango, G., Lewandowski, E., Speelman, L., Betancourt, T. S., … Bolton, P. (2008). Group interpersonal psychotherapy for depressed youth in IDP camps in Northern Uganda: Adaptation and training. *Child & Adolescent Psychiatric Clinics of North America, 17*(3), 605–624. https://doi.org/10.1016/j.chc.2008.03.002

Vindevogel, S. (2017). Resilience in the context of war: A critical analysis of contemporary conceptions and interventions to promote resilience among war-affected children and their surroundings. *Peace and Conflict, 23*, 76.
Walker, P., & Purdin, S. (2004). Birthing sphere. *Disasters, 28*(2), 100–111.
Weiss, M. G., Saraceno, B., Saxena, S., & van Ommeren, M. (2003). Mental health in the aftermath of disasters: Consensus and controversy. *Journal of Nervous and Mental Disease, 191*(9), 611–615. https://doi.org/10.1097/01.nmd.0000087188.96516.a3
Weissbecker, I., Hanna, F., El Shazly, M., Goa, J., & Ventevogel, P. (2019). Integrated mental health and psycosocial support interventions for refugees in humanitarian crisis settings. In T. Wenzel & B. Drozdek (Eds.), *Uncertain safety: Understanding and assisting the 21st century refugees* (pp. 117–153). Cham, Switzerland: Springer. https://doi.org/10.1007/978-3-319-72914-5_6
Wessells, M. (2009a). Community reconciliation and post-conflict reconstruction for peace. In J. de Rivera (Ed.), *Handbook on building cultures of peace* (pp. 349–361). New York, NY: Springer.
Wessells, M. (2009b). Do no harm: Toward contextually appropriate psychosocial support in international emergencies. *American Psychologist, 64*(8), 842.
Wessells, M., & Monteiro, C. (2001). Psychosocial interventions and post-war reconstruction in Angola: Interweaving Western and traditional approaches. In D. J. Christie, R. V. Wagner, & D. D. N. Winter (Eds.), *Peace, conflict, and violence: Peace psychology for the 21st century* (pp. 262–275). Upper Saddle River, NJ: Prentice Hall/Pearson Education.
Wessells, M., & van Ommeren, M. (2008). Developing inter-agency guidelines on mental health and psychosocial support in emergency settings. *Intervention, 6*(3–4), 199–218.
Wickramage, K. (2006). Sri Lanka's post-Tsunami psychosocial playground: Lessons for future psychosocial programming and interventions following disasters. *Intervention, 4*(2), 167–172.
World Health Organization. (2001). *The world health report 2001. Mental health: New understanding, new hope*. Geneva, Switzerland: Author.
World Health Organization. (2016). *Problem management plus (PM+): Psychological help by paraprofessionals for adults exposed to adversity*. Geneva, Switzerland: Author.
World Health Organization, & Columbia University. (2016). *Group Interpersonal Therapy (IPT) for depression*. Geneva, Switzerland: World Health Organization.
World Health Organization, & United Nations High Commissioner for Refugees. (2015). *mhGAP Humanitarian Intervention Guide (mhGAP-HIG): Clinical management of mental, neurological and substance use conditions in humanitarian emergencies*. Geneva, Switzerland: World Health Organization.
Yule, W. (2008). IASC guidelines – generally welcome, but…. *Intervention, 6*(3–4), 248–251.
Zarowsky, C. (2004). Writing trauma: Emotion, ethnography, and the politics of suffering among Somali returnees in Ethiopia. *Culture, Medicine, and Psychiatry, 28*(2), 189–209.
Zwi, A. B., & Silove, D. (2002). Hearing the voices: Mental health services in East Timor. *The Lancet, 360*(Suppl), 45–46.

Peter Ventevogel, M.D., Ph.D. is a psychiatrist and a medical anthropologist. He works as Senior Mental Health Officer in the head office of the United Nations High Commissioner for Refugees in Geneva. In 2016 he defended his doctoral dissertation 'Borderlands of mental health: explorations in medical anthropology, psychiatric epidemiology and health systems research in Afghanistan and Burundi.

Part III
Psychological Interventions and Relevant Clinical Considerations in Working with Refugee and Conflict-Affected Populations

Narrative Exposure Therapy (NET) as a Treatment for Traumatized Refugees and Post-conflict Populations

Frank Neuner, Thomas Elbert, and Maggie Schauer

Abstract Humans are experiencing wars that target primarily civilians and that are characterized by mass recruitment into armed forces and atrocities. An increasing number of victims is forced to flee from wars and persecution. Following the traumatic events experienced in the context of war and flight, a large proportion of post-conflict populations and refugees is traumatized. Refugees face additional stressors as host countries are not well prepared to meet the mental health needs of incoming refugees. Narrative Exposure Therapy (NET) is a short-term, robust, low-threshold, evidence-based and disseminable treatment module that aims to restore psychosocial functioning while counteracting human rights violations. This treatment has proven to reduce posttraumatic stress disorder even for war victims living in low resource settings and conditions of ongoing threat.

Keywords PTSD · Refugee · Treatment · Narration · Trauma-focus

The Principles of Narrative Exposure Therapy

Mental health provisioning for traumatized victims of war, persecution and torture is a global challenge. In war-affected populations, the amount of exposure to traumatic stressors is the most important predictor of trauma-related disorders (Neuner et al., 2004, Steel et al., 2009). The clinical presentations of survivors are typically complex and consist of symptoms related to posttraumatic stress disorder (PTSD),

---

F. Neuner (✉)
Clinical Psychology, Bielefeld University, Bielefeld, NA, Germany
e-mail: frank.neuner@uni-bielefeld.de

T. Elbert
Clinical Psychology and Neuropsychology, University of Konstanz, Konstanz, NA, Germany
e-mail: Thomas.Elbert@uni-konstanz.de

M. Schauer
Centre of Excellence for Psychotraumatology, University of Konstanz,
Konstanz, NA, Germany
e-mail: Maggie.Schauer@uni-konstanz.de

N. Morina, A. Nickerson (eds.), *Mental Health of Refugee and Conflict-Affected Populations*, https://doi.org/10.1007/978-3-319-97046-2_9

depression, somatization and substance abuse. In different countries, prevalence rates of PTSD and depression vary from 10% to more than 50% (Fazel, Reed, Panter-Brick, & Stein, 2012; Fazel, Wheeler, & Danesh, 2005; Karunakara et al., 2004; Miller, Elbert, & Rockstroh, 2005). Among populations affected by mass trauma, refugees are characterized by additional stressors as they are also faced with the need to adapt and integrate into the culture of the host communities. Refugees are typically confronted with a wide variety of stressful conditions and events, including an extended and sometimes unpredictable immigration procedure, restrictions of living opportunities and work, threats of detention, discrimination, and threats from the population of host countries etc. (Silove, Steel, & Watters, 2000).

Even well developed health care systems in industrialized countries have difficulties meeting the multiple mental health needs of traumatized refugees. The situation is even worse for the majority of victims of war and persecution who remain in war-affected regions or flee across the border to low-income countries where they are left without any opportunities for mental health assistance. In this context, Narrative Exposure Therapy (NET) has been developed as a short and pragmatic treatment approach (manualized in Schauer, Neuner, & Elbert, 2011). NET has proven to reduce traumatic stress symptoms to a clinically significant extent, even in refugees who live in unsafe and threatening environments. Within four to 14 individual sessions of 90 min, the client and therapist create a written autobiography containing the major emotional memories of the survivor from birth to the present. The focus of NET is on reconstructing the fragmented memories of traumatic experiences into coherent narrations that are connected to the temporal and spatial context of the life period. At the end of treatment, a copy of the final consistent life narration is handed over to the client, and the therapist keeps one copy that may, depending on the wishes of the client, be used for human rights purposes. NET has been developed based on the following principles:

Trauma-Focus In contrast to symptom-focused therapies or variants of problem-solving methods that teach individuals with PTSD to cope with symptoms and current stressors, the different variants of trauma-focused therapy aim to change trauma-related memories, cognitions and emotions. While there is some evidence for the efficacy of alternative approaches, trauma-focused therapies seem to be superior and are recommended as first-line therapies for individuals with PTSD (Bisson et al., 2007; Ehlers et al., 2010), including traumatized refugees (ter Heide, Mooren, & Kleber, 2016) and refugee children (Eberle-Sejari, Nocon, & Rosner, 2015). Trauma-focused therapy also differs from holistic psychosocial programs that often claim to simultaneously consider the various health, economic, educational and social needs of survivors of mass trauma. In contrast to this holistic approach, trauma-focused psychotherapy should be applied as one central component within a broad mental health structure that includes a clear clinical and organizational supervision structure as well as referral opportunities for other psychological and medical conditions (Schauer & Schauer, 2010).

Life-Span Approach Within the family of trauma-focused approaches, the unique feature of NET is the *life-span approach*. Most trauma-focused treatments require the client to identify the event that he/she experienced as most traumatic, often referred to as the index-trauma. However, victims of wars and persecution have typically experienced a series of traumatic events rather than a single traumatic stressor; thus whole periods of his/her life may have traumatized a survivor. A key assumption of NET is that it is the accumulation of aversive events and conditions over the life-span that brings about pathological memory representations and causes posttraumatic stress symptoms. In fact, the number of potentially traumatic event types experienced in life is the most important predictor of PTSD and depression in war-affected populations (Neuner et al., 2004; Steel et al., 2009). More recently, it was documented that, in addition to war events, traumatic events within families as well as adverse conditions in communities predict trauma-related symptoms and dysfunction (Catani, 2010; Nandi, Crombach, Bambonyé, Elbert, & Weierstall, 2015; Olema, Catani, Ertl, Saile, & Neuner, 2014; Saile, Ertl, Neuner, & Catani, 2016; Saile, Neuner, Ertl, & Catani, 2013). The life-span approach seeks to integrate the worst traumatic memories to enable the survivor to create a meaningful autobiographic memory representation, which is a key requisite of identity and self-acceptance.

Advocacy Due to fragmented autobiographic representations, avoidance behavior, and feelings of shame, as well as trauma-related feelings of helplessness and inferiority, victims of violence often have difficulties expressing themselves and talking about their experiences. This speechlessness of trauma is a double-sided phenomenon, as the society and public is also ignorant regarding the stories of trauma survivors. However, maintaining and improving human rights requires understanding and acknowledging the destructive power of human rights violations. From this perspective, NET can provide comprehensible documentations of individual life stories that facilitate feelings of empathy for the victims. Information resulting from individual trauma-focused narrations also facilitates the assembling of a template pattern of a region's dynamics of violence. Feeding back information about cruelties of war and torture to the public may be used to counter ongoing human rights violations. The social recognition of the suffering on both the victim's and perpetrator's side as well as the discussion of their needs may allow the community to develop their own healing process, increase stability, and make taboo torture practices and other human rights violations. For the victims, regaining access to their biography and communicating their history to others can empower them to stand up for their rights as victims of violence.

Task-Shifting NET has been developed for application in low-income countries affected by war and human rights violations. In such a context, any treatment approach has to be pragmatic, short, and teachable to talented local counselors with limited formal education. The World Health Organization recommends a task-shifting approach from academic professionals to trained lay health workers for countries with an insufficient health sector (Jordans & Tol, 2012). A series of randomized controlled trials has proven that NET can be successfully applied by trained lay therapists who do not have any medical or psychological background (for example, teachers and fellow refugees in a refugee camp) (Neuner et al., 2008; Robjant & Fazel, 2010). This allows for the scaling-up of NET within modern health care systems that provide referral structures, supervision and stepped care models including tasks delegated to lay counselors (Köbach, Schaal, Hecker, & Elbert, 2015).

Cross-Cultural Approach One of the basic assumptions of NET is that, with some cultural particularities in the expression of symptoms, trauma reactions are universal phenomena as they result from neurobiological processes involved in the processing of threat and stress. At the same time, sharing personal histories is a personal and cultural practice that helps the survivor to cope with life events and to foster interpersonal closeness. This may be the reason why the NET procedure has been successfully applied across cultures. While diagnostic instruments need to be carefully adapted for each language, only minor modifications in the NET procedure are required when this approach is implemented across cultures. Rather than focusing on the differences between cultures, the NET approach acknowledges that in each single culture survivors hold a wide variety of values and attitudes, and come from varying economic and educational backgrounds. Accordingly, any treatment approach has to be adjusted to the individual needs of each single client rather than according to clichés and stereotypes that are commonly ascribed to specific cultures (Schnyder et al. 2016).

The Theoretical Basis of NET: Trauma-Related Disorders Are Disorders of Memory

The rationale of NET is based on current psychological theories of PTSD that commonly identify dysfunctional memory processes as being at the core of the disorder (Brewin, 2013; Brewin, Dalgleish, & Joseph, 1996; Ehlers & Clark, 2000). In particular, these theories assume that associative and contextual memory structures code information about the traumatic experiences. The fundamental idea is that peritraumatic processes cause a dissociation of implicit and explicit memory structures that, in turn, cause PTSD symptoms and depression.

The Peritraumatic Reaction

Traumatic events present acute and imminent threats for the survival of the individual. Animals as well as humans are prepared to face such threats with a rapid and built-in defense reaction. During threat, a distinct neuronal circuitry that includes subcortical and cortical neuronal structures such as the amygdala and the ventral prefrontal cortex take over the command to coordinate automatic action patterns while the activity of brain regions that are associated with thoughtful planning, in particular frontal regions, is inhibited (Arnsten, 2009; Pessoa & Adolphs, 2010). This defense response involves rapid and marked alterations in a whole range of functions of the brain and the body, including sensory perception, cognitive processing and physiological reactions. Observations of animal and human reactions to threat have found that the defense reaction is not unidirectional but involves a consecutive sequence of reactions (Bracha, 2004). The human defense cascade includes phases of physiological and behavioral up- as well as down-regulations (Schauer & Elbert, 2010). The activating phase prepares the organism for a flight or fight reaction (Cannon, 1915), which consists of the activation of the sympathetic nervous system and the release of adrenaline, and results in heart rate acceleration, elevation of blood pressure, vasoconstriction and multiple other changes that prepare the organism for rapid action. However, in cases of perceived entrapment, for example if the predator has captured the prey, or in cases of physical restraint, this phase is followed by the *fright* response that consists of a sudden behavioral demobilization under high physiological arousal, also referred to as *tonic immobility* (Marx, Forsyth, Gallup, & Fusé, 2008). This stage of immobility has been explained as the last opportunity for survival for an animal that has already been defeated. Beyond the flight, fight and fright stages, Bracha (2004) as well as Schauer and Elbert (2010) have identified a further phase of the human fear cascade, that is characterized by a decrease of sympathetic arousal and a dominance of vagal activity that might progress to a fainting response. They refer to this response as *flag* reaction or *shut-down dissociation*. This phase has been exclusively observed in humans in situations of the highest proximity to danger, most commonly in victims of rape and sexual abuse, but also in grotesque situations that involve confrontation with blood and mutilations. This type of reaction is characterized by vasodilation, hypotension, bradycardia and loss of muscle tonus, and may proceed to a vasovagal syncope. While fear is the dominant emotion in the previous stages of the defense cascade, the flag reaction involves emotional numbing, an increasing sensory detachment, a higher pain threshold, derealization, depersonalization, and loss of responsiveness. Perception and learning, including conditioning, are inhibited in this phase, which may lead to a reduced memory of such experiences.

While the framework of psychological trauma considers threats to the physical integrity of a person as the key characteristics of traumatic events, it has to be emphasized that intense *threats to social integrity* trigger similarly phased defense cascades, including physiological and psychological up- as well as down-regulations. Threats to social integrity occur if one of the two most fundamental social motives, affiliation and social rank, is threatened. Separations from important relatives or friends involve an agitated protest phase as well as down-regulating phase of despair (Bowlby, 1982). While the protest reaction consists of the signaling of an emergency phase through lamenting, the despair phase is characterized by the inhibition of behavioral and physiological activity (Hofer, 2006; Mineka & Suomi, 1978). Recent research into social exclusion has shown that experiences of social exclusion can trigger intense agitating as well down-regulating reactions (Macdonald & Leary, 2005; Williams, 2007). A similar pattern of stress reactions follows the threat to the status of the individual. Based on evolutionarily mechanisms to defend one's place in the hierarchy of a herd, animals as well as humans respond with an intense behavioral as well as physiological reaction to threats to social status, such as degradations and humiliations (Chaouloff, 2013; Gilbert, 2006; Taylor, Gooding, Wood, & Tarrier, 2011). This response includes the sequence of resistance and fight that is followed by the so-called social defeat. Defeat is characterized by a submissive posture and a behavioral withdrawal, including a marked reduction of locomotion, a loss of social activity, and a decrease in heart rate and body temperature that, even after a single experience of defeat, may last for several days (Meerlo, Overkamp, Daan, van den Hoofdakker, & Koolhaas, 1996; Meerlo, Sgoifo, de Boer, & Koolhaas, 1999). While the defeat reaction itself may be adaptive by stopping the conflict and reducing the aggression of the rival, repeated experiences of defeat that are accompanied by ongoing aggression can trigger long-term consequences for the individual that consists of perseverating appraisals about his or her own inferiority and low adequacy. The endpoints of both social stress responses, despair as well as defeat, have been identified as the key experiences that cause depression (Bowlby, 1982; Price, Sloman, Gardner, Gilbert, & Rohde, 1994) and are featured in the most commonly used models of depression in animal research (Chaouloff, 2013).

The lives of war-affected populations as well as refugees are characterized by multiple threats to social integrity. Many war victims and refugees have lost family members in conflict or during flight. Some remain uncertain about the fate of relatives who could not leave the site of persecution. In addition, among refugees, most exile stressors, including the restrictions in the right to work, lack of recognition of education or professional qualifications, and being directly humiliated by representatives of the host country are essentially threats to social integrity. These may be responsible for the high rates of depressive disorders in refugees, an issue that needs to be especially addressed during treatment of refugees (Hensel-Dittmann et al., 2011). At the same time, counteracting fear with an appetite for aggression is a behavioral predisposition with immense social consequences, depending on the group and society.

The Threat Network

Threatening events, including traumatic experiences and interpersonal victimizations as well as calamities of nature and environment, are represented in two different memory systems; in associative memory (also referred to as situationally accessible memory, hot memory, fear structure, or s-rep) (Brewin, 2013; Brewin et al., 1996; Metcalfe & Jacobs, 1996) as well as in autobiographic memory (similar concepts have been referred to as verbally accessible memory, cold memory, or c-rep) (Brewin, 2013; Brewin et al., 1996; Metcalfe & Jacobs, 1996).

Threat networks refer to the associative representations of traumatic experiences that contain typical stimulus elements that provoke fear, shame or anger as well as the basic cognitive appraisals and the typical response elements of fear or counteracting fear, i.e., high physiological arousal and a tendency to avoid, flee, freeze, shut-down or act out, attack or dominate. The idea of threat networks is based on Lang, Davis, and Ohman's construct of *fear structures* (2000) as well as Foa and Kozak's (1986) model of *fear networks*, but acknowledges that the content of threat networks may include other emotional and behavioral response patterns than fear. Threat networks represent a network of the sensory, cognitive, emotional and physiological details of the traumatic situation. Threat networks differ from normal emotional memory representations in two ways. Firstly, they are unusually large and cover a wide variety of single elements, such as sight, sound, emotions, and physical sensations. This means that the items within these fear structures can be easily activated, as many stimuli in the environment have similarities to one or the other element and thus can act as cues. Secondly, the interconnections between single elements are unusually strong. Consequently, the activation of only a single stimulus that resembles an item of the network may be sufficient to activate the whole structure, causing all of the related memories to return. This explains why traumatized people can have sudden flashbacks when reminded of the traumatic event. According to this theory, an environmental stimulus or internal cue, like thinking about the event or an intense heartbeat that resembles one part of the stimulus configuration of the traumatic situation, can cause the full activation of the sensory information associated with the memory. In turn, the associated emotional, physiological, and motor responses stored in the fear structure will also be triggered. Depending on the peri-traumatic experience, threat networks may include the full cascade of defensive reactions, encompassing stages of tonic immobility, and shut-down reactions, such as a decrease of sympathetic arousal. From this perspective, dissociative reactions or aggressive dominance behaviors are conditioned in the same way as fear responses, and may be reactivated by reminders of the situation. This is why refugees often suffer from seemingly inadequate and dysfunctional reactions (such as hostile impulses or immobility) when exposed even to minor stressors years after the traumatic events.

Context Memory

Episodic learning is not restricted to the coding of stimulus-response associations, but involves embedding the associative responses into the context of the learning experience. Contextual learning has been identified as a key mechanism for the control of the activity of associative stimulus-response connections and provides a mechanism of basal learning principles such as extinction learning (Kindt, 2014). Context learning accounts for the fact that a stimulus can signal threat in a specific situation whereas it can be related to safety in other conditions. While in animal research the context is provided by the sensory and perceptual background of the learning experience, human context learning is much more complex and involves the embedding a learning experience into autobiographic memory. Autobiographic memory is a well-elaborated cognitive structure that provides a temporal and spatial framework of memories with chronological as well as thematic ordering principles.

The autobiographic context, also called the *conceptual frame* (Conway & Pleydell-Pearce, 2000) of the experience, refers to the interpretation of the perceptual episodic memory and provides a coherent connection of the episodic memory within a complex structure of autobiographic memory that involves knowledge about the sequence of *specific events*, *general events* as well as *lifetime periods* (Conway & Pleydell-Pearce, 2000) and includes information about the *meaning* of the event in the biographical perspective of a person.

Disconnection of Threat Structure from Context Memory

Associative learning as well as autobiographic learning are strongly influenced by stress hormones. While associative learning such as fear conditioning is augmented by high levels of adrenaline and nor-adrenaline, an excessive level of the glucocorticoid stress hormones at the hippocampus limits the functional plasticity of the hippocampus and impairs context learning (Cohen, Liberzon, & Richter-Levin, 2009). Without proper encoding of the context of a threat structure it is difficult to establish an inhibitory control over the stimulus-response structure (Kindt, 2014). This dissociation of associative and context learning is the basis of PTSD symptoms. Without the surrounding temporal and spatial context information (supported by the hippocampus, the retrosplenial cortex, the precuneus, and the ventromedial prefrontal cortex), intrusive recollections of trauma memories inevitably involve the "here and now" perception of the memory and the appraisal of current threat. Consistent with the weak autobiographic elaboration that typically characterize fear memories, several studies have shown that trauma narrations were more disorganized than the narrations of healthy control subjects (Jelinek, Randjbar, Seifert, Kellner, & Moritz, 2009), while other longitudinal studies have found that memory fragmentation predicted the maintenance of PTSD symptoms (Brewin, 2013; Ehring, Ehlers, & Glucksman, 2008; Halligan, Michael, Clark, & Ehlers, 2003).

The Rationale and Logic of NET

Current research indicates that the recreation of a context for dysfunctional associative stimulus-response connections is the key mechanism for the unlearning of fear (Craske et al., 2008; Craske, Treanor, Conway, Zbozinek, & Vervliet, 2014) and, in particular, for the treatment of PTSD (Ehlers & Clark, 2000; Neuner et al., 2008). Based on this principle, the aim of NET is to reestablish the autobiographical context of the traumatic events and to reconnect the context to the threat structure, or, in colloquial terms, to tie cold memories around hot memories, defined by their sensory representations. Therefore, the client, with the assistance of the therapist, constructs a chronological narrative of her/his life story with a focus on the traumatic experiences. Within a predefined time-frame, usually about four to twelve 90 min sessions, the fragmented reports of the traumatic experiences will be transformed into a coherent narrative that is documented in written form. For survivors of domestic or organized violence, the testimony can be recorded and used for human rights purposes.

The Procedure of NET for Traumatized Refugees

Diagnostics, Inclusion and Exclusion Criteria

The prerequisite of NET is a thorough review of the participant's life events and a diagnostic monitoring of current suffering. The assessment should include standardized instruments that assess the experience of traumatic events related to war and flight and the various forms of childhood adversities (event checklists). In addition, symptoms of PTSD and depression should be measured/indexed with the help of valid instruments. The current evidence supports the application of NET for subjects with a diagnosis of PTSD and comorbid disorders (see below). Exclusion criteria are typically associated with the treatment setting rather than the NET procedure itself. For example, some conditions, including severe suicidal ideation, self-harm or harm of others, may require hospitalization. If current substance abuse requires detoxification, this should be achieved first. At the same time, NET requires the ability to create elaborated narrations based on memories. Psychotic symptoms and mental retardation may limit this ability and NET should not be applied with children who do not yet possess the necessary skills.

Psychoeducation

A psychoeducational introduction is presented to the survivor, focusing on the explanation of his or her problems and symptoms according to the memory theory of trauma, and, if appropriate, a statement about the universality of human rights, followed by an outline of the treatment rationale. For participants with a low educational background, psychoeducation is often based on metaphors that allow the illustration of the memory theory including the emotional pain involved in exposure, such as the metaphor of trauma memory as a messy carpet that needs to be tidied up. More educated clients receive a more detailed explanation of the theory. In addition, survivors also receive an explanation about the motivation of the therapist and her/his ability to listen to the worst stories, that is founded on a professional basis to help the victim in the recovery process, but also emphasizes the readiness for empathic involvement in the treatment process. Psychoeducation closes with an invitation to engage in narrative exposure treatment.

Lifeline Exercise

The therapy continues with a biographical overview of the life span. Lifetime periods and important biographic events of the survivor are symbolized in a ritual called the lifeline. This exercise consists of placing positive and negative life events, symbolized by flowers and stones, along a rope in chronological order. The lifeline should reflect good and bad memories of moments with high physiological and emotional arousal in the biography of the individual. With the guidance of the therapist, the client places the symbols next to the line while classifying them briefly. The purpose of the lifeline is the re-construction of subjectively significant life events in chronological order. An initial, cursory overview of the times and locations in which events occurred within the overarching context of the individual's life serves as an introduction to the logic of the therapeutic process. The lifeline exercise should be conducted within one session.

The Narration

In the next session, the narration starts with essential background information and a summary of the first years of life the person cannot explicitly remember because of young age. A following pre-trauma period in childhood (if available) may be used as the time during which a foundation for the therapeutic core process is laid and a good rapport between therapist and client is established. In this phase, for example, the telling of emotional, warm, or exciting moments in the survivor's early life offer themselves as a training ground for emotional processing and communication between client and therapist.

During the narrative procedure, the survivor continues recounting his/her life-story in chronological order. Reestablishing a sequence is especially important for refugees and refugee children with broken lifelines. Wherever a 'stone' (traumatic incident) occurs, the event is relived in a slow-motion moment-by-moment reprocessing of the sensory, cognitive, emotional and bodily details of the traumatic scenes, ensuring the inter-weaving of hot and cold memory elements, meaning-making and integration. During the telling of the events, the therapist structures the topics and helps to clarify ambiguous descriptions. Inconsistencies in the survivor's report are gently pointed out and often resolved by raising in-depth awareness about recurring bodily sensations or thoughts. The client is encouraged to describe the traumatic events with sensory details and to reveal the perceptions, cognitions and emotions that were experienced at that time.

Empathic understanding, active listening, congruency and unconditional positive regard are key components of the therapist's behavior and attitude. For traumatic stress experiences, the therapist explores sensory information, resulting cognitions, and affective and physiological responding in detail and probes for respective observations. The survivor is encouraged to relive these experiences while narrating, without losing the connection to the present. Using permanent reminders that the feelings and physiological responses result from activation of hot memories, the therapist links these mnemonic representations to episodic facts, i.e., time, place, and chronology (cold memory). The imaginal exposure to the traumatic past is not terminated until the related affect, especially the fear presented by the patient, demonstrably decreases. In this way, the therapist is supportive yet directive in eliciting the narrative in order to recover the implicit information of the trauma in its entirety.

In the subsequent sessions, the autobiography is briefly repeated, now emphasizing the "where" and "when", i.e., the cold memories of the event. The client may add parts that he or she feels are important. Further emotionally arousing peaks (the next stones and flowers) are then processed, i.e., additional traumatic experiences are added to the narration. The procedure is repeated in subsequent sessions until a final version of the survivor's autobiography of arousing events across the life span has been completed.

The Closing Session

The lifeline – now available with greater precision – may be laid out once more and used as review of the patient's life. The final document may be read aloud to the patient. The refugee, the translator (if present) and the therapist sign the written narration. A copy of the signed document is handed to the survivor. With the agreement or upon request of the narrator, another copy may be passed on to lawyers or, in anonymized form, to human rights organizations as documentation of the atrocities that have happened. In addition, rituals can be used to ease the mourning and grief related to unresolved losses in the life history. In further sessions, beyond NET proper, the patient may be counseled on how to go on with life; for example, adjusting to a new role in the host society for a refugee or coping with further relationships for a battered woman.

NET as an Evidence-Based Treatment

Results from more than a dozen treatment trials in adults and children have demonstrated the power of using NET in reducing the suffering arising from interpersonal or organized violence, as well as other disasters. By the very nature of NET, it is constructed to counter the impact of multiple and complex traumatic stress experiences that have occurred across an entire lifetime. NET provides a well-supported treatment option to survivors of repeated torture as evidenced by large effect sizes (Hensel-Dittmann et al., 2011; Neuner et al., 2010). The most pronounced improvements are observed at follow up, suggesting a change in the dynamics of psychopathological symptoms, physical health, functioning and quality of life. NET has effectively been applied in situations that remain volatile and insecure, such as in continuous trauma settings. A number of reviews identified NET as an evidence-based treatment, especially for survivors of violence (Crumlish & O'Rourke, 2010; McPherson, 2011; Robjant & Fazel, 2010; ter Heide et al., 2016). A number of studies showing the effectiveness of NET have been independently conducted (e.g., Hijazi, 2012; Hijazi et al., 2014; Zang, Hunt, & Cox, 2013) in a variety of countries. Well established centers for torture victims and refugees, including Centrum 45 in the Netherlands and the Center for Victims of Torture in Minnesota, regularly use NET in their clinical practice. Manuals have appeared in print in Dutch, English, French, Italian, Slovakian, Korean, and Japanese and are also available from the authors in Spanish and Farsi.

Evidence for the effect of NET goes beyond subjective self-reports and clinical observations and includes biological markers. Successful psychotherapeutic interventions reorganize memory and modify the architecture of the brain. In a controlled trial, NET was compared to treatment as usual (Schauer et al., 2006). At the 6-month follow-up, oscillatory neural activity measured with magnetencephalography (MEG) was normalized in the NET group but not in the control group. Moreover, using magnetic source imaging, Adenauer et al. (2011) observed that NET caused an increase in activity associated with cortical top-down regulation of attention towards aversive pictures. The increase of attention allocation to potential threat cues seemingly allowed treated patients to re-appraise the actual danger of the current situation, thereby reducing PTSD symptoms. Morath, Gola et al. (2014) showed that symptom improvements caused by NET were mirrored in an increase in the originally reduced proportion of regulatory T cells in the NET group at a one-year follow-up. These cells are critical for maintaining balance in the immune system and regulating the immune response to infection without autoimmune problems. This finding fits with the observation that NET reduces the frequencies of cough, diarrhea, and fever for refugees living in a refugee settlement (Neuner et al., 2008). Moreover, NET is able to reverse the increased levels of damaged DNA in traumatized survivors back to a normal level (Morath, Moreno-Villanueva et al., 2014). These findings may have implications for physical health, in particular for carcinogenesis. The reversibility of pathophysiological processes in individuals with PTSD via psychotherapy indicates that there is a therapeutic window not only to revert the psychological burden associated with PTSD but also to reduce the long-term, and potentially lethal, somatic effects of this mental disorder. However, it should also be noted that not all immune parameters (like the proportion of naïve T lymphocytes) become normalized, and thus might render these patients more susceptible to infectious diseases across extended periods even after the completion of successful treatment.

Two decisive strengths of NET include its low dropout rate and its high potential for dissemination, including by lay counselors in low-income countries and war and crisis regions (Catani et al., 2009; Ertl, Pfeiffer, Schauer, Elbert, & Neuner, 2011; Jacob, Neuner, Maedl, Schaal, & Elbert, 2014; Köbach et al., 2015; Neuner et al., 2008). Stenmark et al. (2013) showed that, with NET, refugees as well as asylum seekers living in central Norway could be successfully treated for PTSD and depression in the general mental health care system. Recent randomized trials in Rwanda and the DR Congo demonstrated that local NET therapists successfully trained the next generation of therapists within a train-the trainer model (Jacob et al., 2014; Köbach et al., 2015), which is a further step towards making expatriate therapists dispensable in the process of providing trauma treatment in low income countries. As evidenced by the current refugee crisis in Europe, specific situations require a rethinking of health care even in countries with widespread mental health provision, like Germany. It will be difficult if not impossible to find any alternative to a task-shifting approach in order to provide the necessary care and support to the more than one million refugees – about one quarter of them with PTSD - arriving in 2015 alone.

References

Adenauer, H., Catani, C., Gola, H., Keil, J., Ruf, M., Schauer, M., & Neuner, F. (2011). Narrative exposure therapy for PTSD increases top-down processing of aversive stimuli – evidence from a randomized controlled treatment trial. *BMC Neuroscience, 12*(1), 127. https://doi.org/10.1186/1471-2202-12-127

Arnsten, A. F. T. (2009). Stress signalling pathways that impair prefrontal cortex structure and function. *Nature Reviews Neuroscience, 10*(6), 410–422. https://doi.org/10.1038/nrn2648

Bisson, J. I., Ehlers, A., Matthews, R., Pilling, S., Richards, D., & Turner, S. (2007). Psychological treatments for chronic post-traumatic stress disorder. Systematic review and meta-analysis. *The British Journal of Psychiatry, 190*(2), 97–104. https://doi.org/10.1192/bjp.bp.106.021402

Bowlby, J. (1982). *Attachment* (Vol. 2). New York, NY: Basic Books.

Bracha, H. S. (2004). Freeze, flight, fight, fright, faint: Adaptationist perspectives on the acute stress response spectrum. *CNS Spectrums, 9*(9), 679–685.

Brewin, C. R. (2013). Episodic memory, perceptual memory, and their interaction: Foundations for a theory of posttraumatic stress disorder. *Psychological Bulletin, 140*(1), 69–97. https://doi.org/10.1037/a0033722

Brewin, C. R., Dalgleish, T., & Joseph, S. (1996). A dual representation theory of posttraumatic stress disorder. *Psychological Review, 103*(4), 670–686.

Cannon, W. B. (1915). *Bodily changes in pain, hunger, fear, and rage: An account of recent researches into the function of emotional excitement*. New York, NY/London, UK: D. Appleton and Company.

Catani, C. (2010). War at home – a review of the relationship between war trauma and family violence. *Verhaltenstherapie, 20*(1), 19–27.

Catani, C., Kohiladevy, M., Ruf, M., Schauer, E., Elbert, T., & Neuner, F. (2009). Treating children traumatized by war and tsunami: A comparison between exposure therapy and meditation-relaxation in north-east Sri Lanka. *BMC Psychiatry, 9*(1), 22. https://doi.org/10.1186/1471-244X-9-22

Chaouloff, F. (2013). Social stress models in depression research: What do they tell us? *Cell and Tissue Research, 354*(1), 179–190. https://doi.org/10.1007/s00441-013-1606-x

Cohen, H., Liberzon, I., & Richter-Levin, G. (2009). Exposure to extreme stress impairs contextual odour discrimination in an animal model of PTSD. *The International Journal of Neuropsychopharmacology, 12*(3), 291–303. https://doi.org/10.1017/S146114570800919X

Conway, M. A., & Pleydell-Pearce, C. W. (2000). The construction of autobiographical memories in the self-memory system. *Psychological Review, 107*(2), 261–288.

Craske, M. G., Kircanski, K., Zelikowsky, M., Mystkowski, J., Chowdhury, N., & Baker, A. (2008). Optimizing inhibitory learning during exposure therapy. *Behaviour Research and Therapy, 46*(1), 5–27. https://doi.org/10.1016/j.brat.2007.10.003

Craske, M. G., Treanor, M., Conway, C. C., Zbozinek, T., & Vervliet, B. (2014). Maximizing exposure therapy: An inhibitory learning approach. *Behaviour Research and Therapy, 58*, 10–23. https://doi.org/10.1016/j.brat.2014.04.006

Crumlish, N., & O'Rourke, K. (2010). A systematic review of treatments for post-traumatic stress disorder among refugees and asylum-seekers. *The Journal of Nervous and Mental Disease, 198*(4), 237–251. https://doi.org/10.1097/NMD.0b013e3181d61258

Eberle-Sejari, R., Nocon, A., & Rosner, R. (2015). Zur Wirksamkeit von psychotherapeutischen Interventionen bei jungen Flüchtlingen und Binnenvertriebenen mit posttraumatischen Symptomen. *Kindheit und Entwicklung, 24*, 156–169.

Ehlers, A., & Clark, D. M. (2000). A cognitive model of posttraumatic stress disorder. *Behaviour Research and Therapy, 38*(4), 319–345.

Ehlers, A., Bisson, J., Clark, D. M., Creamer, M., Pilling, S., Richards, D., … Yule, W. (2010). Do all psychological treatments really work the same in posttraumatic stress disorder? *Clinical Psychology Review, 30*(2), 269–276. https://doi.org/10.1016/j.cpr.2009.12.001

Ehring, T., Ehlers, A., & Glucksman, E. (2008). Do cognitive models help in predicting the severity of posttraumatic stress disorder, phobia, and depression after motor vehicle accidents? A prospective longitudinal study. *Journal of Consulting and Clinical Psychology, 76*(2), 219–230. https://doi.org/10.1037/0022-006X.76.2.219

Ertl, V., Pfeiffer, A., Schauer, E., Elbert, T., & Neuner, F. (2011). Community-implemented trauma therapy for former child soldiers in northern Uganda: A randomized controlled trial. *JAMA, 306*(5), 503–512. https://doi.org/10.1001/jama.2011.1060

Fazel, M., Reed, R. V., Panter-Brick, C., & Stein, A. (2012). Mental health of displaced and refugee children resettled in high-income countries: Risk and protective factors. *The Lancet, 379*(9812), 266–282. https://doi.org/10.1016/S0140-6736(11)60051-2

Fazel, M., Wheeler, J., & Danesh, J. (2005). Prevalence of serious mental disorder in 7000 refugees resettled in western countries: A systematic review. *The Lancet, 365*(9467), 1309–1314. https://doi.org/10.1016/S0140-6736(05)61027-6

Foa, E. B., & Kozak, M. J. (1986). Emotional processing of fear: Exposure to corrective information. *Psychological Bulletin, 99*(1), 20–35.

Gilbert, P. (2006). Evolution and depression: Issues and implications. *Psychological Medicine, 36*(3), 287–297. https://doi.org/10.1017/S0033291705006112

Halligan, S. L., Michael, T., Clark, D. M., & Ehlers, A. (2003). Posttraumatic stress disorder following assault: The role of cognitive processing, trauma memory, and appraisals. *Journal of Consulting and Clinical Psychology, 71*(3), 419–431. https://doi.org/10.1037/0022-006x.71.3.419

Hensel-Dittmann, D., Schauer, M., Ruf, M., Catani, C., Odenwald, M., Elbert, T., & Neuner, F. (2011). Treatment of traumatized victims of war and torture: A randomized controlled comparison of narrative exposure therapy and stress inoculation training. *Psychotherapy and Psychosomatics, 80*(6), 345–352. https://doi.org/10.1159/000327253

Hijazi, A. M. (2012). *Narrative Exposure Therapy to treat traumatic stress in Middle Eastern refugees: A clinical trial* (Doctoral dissertation). Retrieved from ProQuest Dissertations and Theses database. (Order No. 3527991).

Hijazi, A. M., Lumley, M. A., Ziadni, M. S., Haddad, L., Rapport, L. J., & Arnetz, B. B. (2014). Brief narrative exposure therapy for posttraumatic stress in Iraqi refugees: A preliminary randomized clinical trial. *Journal of Traumatic Stress, 27*(3), 314–322. https://doi.org/10.1002/jts.21922

Hofer, M. A. (2006). Psychobiological roots of early attachment. *Current Directions in Psychological Science, 15*(2), 84–88. https://doi.org/10.1111/j.0963-7214.2006.00412.x

Jacob, N., Neuner, F., Maedl, A., Schaal, S., & Elbert, T. (2014). Dissemination of psychotherapy for trauma spectrum disorders in postconflict settings: A randomized controlled trial in Rwanda. *Psychotherapy and Psychosomatics, 83*(6), 354–363. https://doi.org/10.1159/000365114

Jelinek, L., Randjbar, S., Seifert, D., Kellner, M., & Moritz, S. (2009). The organization of autobiographical and nonautobiographical memory in posttraumatic stress disorder (PTSD). *Journal of Abnormal Psychology, 118*(2), 288–298. https://doi.org/10.1037/a0015633

Jordans, M. J., & Tol, W. A. (2012). Mental health in humanitarian settings: Shifting focus to care systems. *International Health, 5*(1), 9–10.

Karunakara, U. K., Neuner, F., Schauer, M., Singh, K., Hill, K., Elbert, T., & Burnha, G. (2004). Traumatic events and symptoms of post-traumatic stress disorder amongst Sudanese nationals, refugees and Ugandans in the west Nile. *African Health Sciences, 4*(2), 83–93.

Kindt, M. (2014). A behavioural neuroscience perspective on the aetiology and treatment of anxiety disorders. *Behaviour Research and Therapy, 62*, 24–36. https://doi.org/10.1016/j.brat.2014.08.012

Köbach, A., Schaal, S., Hecker, T., & Elbert, T. (2015). Psychotherapeutic intervention in the demobilization process: Addressing combat-related mental injuries with narrative exposure in a first and second dissemination stage. *Clinical Psychology and Psychotherapy, 24*, 807–825.

Lang, P. J., Davis, M., & Ohman, A. (2000). Fear and anxiety: Animal models and human cognitive psychophysiology. *Journal of Affective Disorders, 61*(3), 137–159.

Macdonald, G., & Leary, M. R. (2005). Why does social exclusion hurt? The relationship between social and physical pain. *Psychological Bulletin, 131*(2), 202–223. https://doi.org/10.1037/0033-2909.131.2.202

Marx, B. P., Forsyth, J. P., Gallup, G. G., & Fusé, T. (2008). Tonic immobility as an evolved predator defense: Implications for sexual assault survivors. *Clinical Psychology: Science and Practice, 15*(1), 74–90. https://doi.org/10.1111/j.1468-2850.2008.00112.x

McPherson, J. (2011). Does Narrative Exposure Therapy reduce PTSD in survivors of mass violence? *Research on Social Work Practice, 22*(1), 29–42. https://doi.org/10.1177/1049731511414147

Meerlo, P., Overkamp, G. J., Daan, S., van den Hoofdakker, R. H., & Koolhaas, J. M. (1996). Changes in behaviour and body weight following a single or double social defeat in rats. *Stress, 1*(1), 21–32.

Meerlo, P., Sgoifo, A., de Boer, S. F., & Koolhaas, J. M. (1999). Long-lasting consequences of a social conflict in rats: Behavior during the interaction predicts subsequent changes in daily rhythms of heart rate, temperature, and activity. *Behavioral Neuroscience, 113*(6), 1283–1290.

Metcalfe, J., & Jacobs, W. J. (1996). A "hot-system/cool-system" view of memory under stress. *PTSD Research Quarterly, 7*(2), 1–3.

Mineka, S., & Suomi, S. J. (1978). Social separation in monkeys. *Psychological Bulletin, 85*(6), 1376–1400. https://doi.org/10.1037/0033-2909.85.6.1376

Miller, G., Elbert, T., & Rockstroh, B. (2005). Judging psychiatric disorders in refugees. *The Lancet, 366*(9497), 1604–1605.

Morath, J., Gola, H., Sommershof, A., Hamuni, G., Kolassa, S., Catani, C., … Elbert, T. (2014). The effect of trauma-focused therapy on the altered T cell distribution in individuals with PTSD: Evidence from a randomized controlled trial. *Journal of Psychiatric Research, 54*, 1–10. https://doi.org/10.1016/j.jpsychires.2014.03.016

Morath, J., Moreno-Villanueva, M., Hamuni, G., Kolassa, S., Ruf-Leuschner, M., Schauer, M., … Kolassa, I. -T. (2014). Effects of psychotherapy on DNA strand break accumulation originating from traumatic stress. *Psychotherapy and Psychosomatics, 83*(5), 289–297.

Nandi, C., Crombach, A., Bambonyé, M., Elbert, T., & Weierstall, R. (2015). Predictors of posttraumatic stress and appetitive aggression in active soldiers and former combatants. *European Journal of Psychotraumatology, 6*(1), 26553. https://doi.org/10.3402/ejpt.v6.26553

Neuner, F., Kurreck, S., Ruf, M., Odenwald, M., Elbert, T., & Schauer, M. (2010). Can asylum-seekers with posttraumatic stress disorder be successfully treated? A randomized controlled pilot study. *Cognitive Behaviour Therapy, 39*(2), 81–91. https://doi.org/10.1080/16506070903121042

Neuner, F., Onyut, P. L., Ertl, V., Odenwald, M., Schauer, E., & Elbert, T. (2008). Treatment of posttraumatic stress disorder by trained lay counselors in an African refugee settlement: A randomized controlled trial. *Journal of Consulting and Clinical Psychology, 76*(4), 686–694. https://doi.org/10.1037/0022-006X.76.4.686

Neuner, F., Schauer, M., Karunakara, U., Klaschik, C., Robert, C., & Elbert, T. (2004). Psychological trauma and evidence for enhanced vulnerability for posttraumatic stress disorder through previous trauma among West Nile refugees. *BMC Psychiatry, 4*(1), 34. https://doi.org/10.1186/1471-244X-4-34

Olema, D. K., Catani, C., Ertl, V., Saile, R., & Neuner, F. (2014). The hidden effects of child maltreatment in a war region: Correlates of psychopathology in two generations living in Northern Uganda. *Journal of Traumatic Stress, 27*(1), 35–41. https://doi.org/10.1002/jts.21892

Pessoa, L., & Adolphs, R. (2010). Emotion processing and the amygdala: From a 'low road' to 'many roads' of evaluating biological significance. *Nature Reviews Neuroscience, 11*(11), 773–783. https://doi.org/10.1038/nrn2920

Price, J., Sloman, L., Gardner, R., Gilbert, P., & Rohde, P. (1994). The social competition hypothesis of depression. *The British Journal of Psychiatry, 164*(3), 309–315. https://doi.org/10.1192/bjp.164.3.309

Robjant, K., & Fazel, M. (2010). The emerging evidence for Narrative Exposure Therapy: A review. *Clinical Psychology Review, 30*(8), 1030–1039. https://doi.org/10.1016/j.cpr.2010.07.004

Saile, R., Ertl, V., Neuner, F., & Catani, C. (2016). Children of the postwar years: A two-generational multilevel risk assessment of child psychopathology in Northern Uganda. *Development and Psychopathology, 28*(2), 607–620. https://doi.org/10.1017/S0954579415001066

Saile, R., Neuner, F., Ertl, V., & Catani, C. (2013). Prevalence and predictors of partner violence against women in the aftermath of war: A survey among couples in Northern Uganda. *Social Science & Medicine, 86*, 17–25. https://doi.org/10.1016/j.socscimed.2013.02.046

Schauer, M., & Elbert, T. (2010). Dissociation following traumatic stress: Etiology and treatment. *Zeitschrift Für Psychologie/Journal of Psychology, 218*(2), 109–127. https://doi.org/10.1027/0044-3409/a000018

Schauer, M., Elbert, T., Gotthardt, S., Rockstroh, B., Odenwald, M., & Neuner, F. (2006). Wiedererfahrung durch Psychotherapie modifiziert Geist und Gehirn. *Verhaltenstherapie, 16*(2), 96–103. https://doi.org/10.1159/000093195

Schauer, M., Neuner, F., & Elbert, T. (2011). *Narrative Exposure Therapy: A short-term treatment for traumatic stress disorders* (2nd ed.). Cambridge, MA: Hogrefe Publishing.

Schauer, M., & Schauer, E. (2010). Trauma-focused public mental-health interventions: A paradigm shift in humanitarian assistance and aid work. In E. Martz (Ed.), *Trauma rehabilitation after war and conflict* (pp. 361–430). New York, NY: Springer Publishing.

Schnyder, U., Bryant, R. A., Ehlers, A., Foa, E. B., Hasam, A., Mwiti, G., … Yule, W. (2016). Culture-sensitive psychotraumatology. *European Journal of Psychotraumatology, 7*(1), 31179.

Silove, D., Steel, Z., & Watters, C. (2000). Policies of deterrence and the mental health of asylum seekers. *JAMA, 284*(5), 604–611.

Steel, Z., Chey, T., Silove, D., Marnane, C., Bryant, R. A., & van Ommeren, M. (2009). Association of torture and other potentially traumatic events with mental health outcomes among populations exposed to mass conflict and displacement: A systematic review and meta-analysis. *JAMA, 302*(5), 537–549. https://doi.org/10.1001/jama.2009.1132

Stenmark, H., Catani, C., Neuner, F., Elbert, T., & Holen, A. (2013). Treating PTSD in refugees and asylum seekers within the general health care system: A randomized controlled multicenter study. *Behaviour Research and Therapy, 51*(10), 641–647. https://doi.org/10.1016/j.brat.2013.07.002

Taylor, P. J., Gooding, P., Wood, A. M., & Tarrier, N. (2011). The role of defeat and entrapment in depression, anxiety, and suicide. *Psychological Bulletin, 137*(3), 391–420. https://doi.org/10.1037/a0022935

ter Heide, F. J. J., Mooren, T. M., & Kleber, R. J. (2016). Complex PTSD and phased treatment in refugees: A debate piece. *European Journal of Psychotraumatology, 7*(1), 28687. https://doi.org/10.3402/ejt.v7.28687

Williams, K. D. (2007). Ostracism. *Annual Review of Psychology, 58*, 425–452. https://doi.org/10.1146/annurev.psych.58.110405.085641

Zang, Y., Hunt, N., & Cox, T. (2013). A randomised controlled pilot study: The effectiveness of narrative exposure therapy with adult survivors of the Sichuan earthquake. *BMC Psychiatry, 13*(1), 41. https://doi.org/10.1186/1471-244X-13-41

Frank Neuner is head of Clinical Psychology at Bielefeld University including the university outpatient clinic. He has gained international reputation for the development of Narrative Exposure Therapy, a short-term mental health intervention for traumatic stress. He has published the first randomized treatment trial for posttraumatic stress disorder with refugees living in a war region that has been followed by more than ten highly cited RCTs of his working group. His expertise is epidemiology, etiology and treatment of severe trauma-associated psychological disorders following repeated intense adversities like war and child abuse. Currently he is funded from BMBF, DFG and Volkswagen Foundation for studies on the consequences of child maltreatment as well as relationship between trauma resulting from war and family violence.

Thomas Elbert, Ph.D., is Professor of Clinical Psychology and Behavioural Neuroscience at the University of Konstanz. Together with Dres. Frank Neuner and Maggie Schauer he developed the narrative exposure therapy (NET) in order to treat traumatic stress symptoms; NET has also been successfully tested in field studies in crisis regions in Africa and Asia. Professor Elbert is Hector fellow, member of the German National Academy of Sciences Leopoldina, the Berlin-Brandenburg Academy of Sciences and holds honorary professorships at the Université Lumiére in Burundi and the Mbarara University of Science and Technology in Uganda.

Maggie Schauer, Ph.D., is a clinical psychologist and director of the Centre of Excellence for Psychotraumatology at the University of Konstanz. Her research projects are focused on multiple and complex traumatization as well as the transgenerational consequences of violence and neglect. In collaboration with Professors Frank Neuner and Thomas Elbert, she developed Narrative Exposure Therapy (NET), an intervention for the treatment of trauma-related disorders after multiple and complex trauma. She is a founding member of vivo international (www.vivo.org), an NGO for the prevention and treatment of traumatic stress.

Culturally Sensitive CBT for Refugees: Key Dimensions

Devon E. Hinton and Anushka Patel

Abstract In increasingly multicultural societies, cognitive behavioral therapy (CBT) needs to be made appropriate for diverse groups. Refugees with mental health difficulties present particular therapeutic challenges that include complex trauma, different cultural traditions, and ongoing stress. The current chapter outlines how a contextually sensitive CBT can be developed for such refugee groups. It outlines key dimensions of culturally sensitive CBT, which can be therapeutically implemented among refugees in order to maximize efficacy and effectiveness. These guidelines can be followed to design culturally sensitive CBT studies among refugees, or what might be called "contextually sensitive CBT," and the guidelines can be used to evaluate such studies. Some examples of these key dimensions of care are the following: assessing and addressing key local complaints (e.g., somatic symptoms, spirit possession, and syndromes like "thinking a lot"); incorporating into treatment key local sources of recovery and resilience (e.g., CBT-compatible proverbs and techniques in that culture). Another example of a key dimension of care is making CBT techniques more tolerable and effective for the cultural group through various means: by using a phased approach, by utilizing culturally appropriate framing of CBT techniques (using local analogies), by making positive re-associations to problematic sensations during interoceptive exposure (e.g., to traditional games), and by using trauma-type exposure as an opportunity to practice emotion regulation. We describe such concepts as explanatory model bridging, cultural grounding, and contextual sensitivity.

Keywords Culture · CBT · Trauma · Refugees

D. E. Hinton (✉)
Harvard University, Boston, MA, USA
e-mail: devon_hinton@hms.harvard.edu

A. Patel
Department of Psychology, University of Tulsa, Tulsa, OK, USA
e-mail: anushka-patel@utulsa.edu

N. Morina, A. Nickerson (eds.), *Mental Health of Refugee and Conflict-Affected Populations*, https://doi.org/10.1007/978-3-319-97046-2_10

Psychological interventions that are effective across cultural groups are needed, with refugees being a case in point. There is a global refugee crisis with over 65.3 million people estimated to be forcibly displaced from their home countries (United Nations High Commissioner for Refugees, 2016). Refugees with mental health complaints are complex to treat for many reasons. As one challenge, ongoing stresses interact with complex trauma to make treatment more difficult. Refugees face several unique stressors in the course of the pre-displacement, displacement/resettlement, and post-migration context. For instance, refugees experience higher rates of trauma exposure compared to the general population (Porter & Haslam, 2005), as they are often subjected to and/or witness human rights violations during the conflicts from which they seek political asylum. The types of traumatic events experienced by refugees include starvation, loss of a loved one, physical violence, rape, torture, and brainwashing (Mollica et al., 1992). Refugees also experience loss on many levels; being exiled from their homelands, refugees lose material possessions of personal and cultural significance, in addition to social support networks, and connections with cultural traditions. These various risk factors predispose refugees to having post-traumatic stress disorder (PTSD) and other mental illnesses (Morina & Ford, 2008).

As another challenge in treating refugees, owing to having differing cultural traditions, there may be certain key presentations of distress, psychopathological processes, and local symptom meanings and healing traditions (Hinton & Good, 2009, 2016a; Kleinman & Good, 1985). For example, PTSD differs greatly across cultures with respect to the constellation of symptoms that emerge and their meaning (Hinton & Good, 2016b), as does panic disorder (Hinton & Good, 2009) and depression (Kleinman & Good, 1985).

Evidence demonstrates that cognitive-behavior therapy (CBT) is effective for a wide range of disorders including PTSD (Hofmann & Smits, 2008). However, most research on CBT has focused on Western populations, and research is just beginning to examine whether CBT is effective for ethnic minority and refugee groups and in global contexts and how it should be adapted (e.g., Bass et al., 2013; Drozdek, Kamperman, Tol, Knipscheer, & Kleber, 2014; Hinton, 2014; Hinton, Pich, Hofmann, & Otto, 2013; Murray et al., 2014; Naeem, Waheed, Gobbi, Ayub, & Kingdon, 2011; Nickerson, Bryant, Silove, & Steel, 2011). A systematic review of ten randomized controlled trials (RCTs) evaluating treatments for refugees with mental health problems found some promise in CBT, and argued that there is a need to adapt treatments to the local cultural context (Crumlish & O'Rourke, 2010).

How can CBT treatments be culturally adapted? Bernal and colleagues define cultural adaptation as the "systematic modification of an evidence-based treatment (EBT) to account for language, culture, and context in a way that is consistent with the client's cultural patterns, meanings and values" (Bernal, Jiménez-Chafey, & Domenech Rodríguez, 2009, p. 362). Griner and Smith (2006) reviewed 76 studies on culturally adapted mental health interventions for a wide range of disorders, and they found that interventions targeted to specific ethnic groups produced four times stronger effects than those provided to diverse ethnic groups. Benish, Quintana, and Wampold (2011) also found that culturally adapted treatment is more effective than un-adapted treatment ($d = .32$) in a direct-comparison meta-analysis. The only significant moderator accounting for this difference was modification of the explanatory model. This study highlights the importance of eliciting a group's explanatory model – that is, the way in which a group understands an illness experience, including ideas about causation, key symptoms, and cures – and adapting treatment in accordance with it. As this and many other studies show, understanding the client's interpretation of symptoms and providing treatment congruent with their explanatory model is a key ingredient in culturally adapted treatment (for further discussion of explanatory model, see Hinton, Lewis-Fernández, Kirmayer, & Weiss, 2016). Of note, this may entail changing the patient's explanatory model of the origins of the disorder: For a Western patient who has a purely biological model and expects only medication, creating illness models understandable to the patient as to why psychotherapy may work for panic disorder, or for a Cambodian patient who attributes panic symptoms to a *khyâl* attack, so too why psychotherapy may be effective. We refer to these various processes of working with the patient's explanatory model to further treatment as *explanatory model bridging*.

The present chapter aims to integrate knowledge of clinical science with cultural competence to present key considerations for adapting CBT across cultural settings. Specifically, this chapter provides recommendations on how to make the next wave of CBT treatments for refugees more culturally sensitive. We suggest parameters that can be used to develop culturally sensitive CBT interventions among refugees or other cultural groups in a given global location in what might be called "contextually sensitive CBT." Many of these parameters have guided our treatment development, and the global health research agenda more generally (Hinton et al., 2005; Hinton, Hofmann, Pollack, & Otto, 2009; Hinton, Hofmann, Rivera, Otto, & Pollack, 2011; Hinton et al., 2004; Hinton, Rivera, Hofmann, Barlow, & Otto, 2012; Patel, 2012; van Ginneken et al., 2013). Each dimension, and its constituent parts, is summarized in Table 1 and discussed below. These dimensions serve a twofold purpose: They can be addressed to attain contextual sensitivity in a treatment that is being developed, and also be used to evaluate the contextual sensitivity of extant treatments.

Key Dimensions of Culturally Sensitive CBT

Background Information

Identify the Cultural Group The exact cultural group needs to be specified, not just that the participants are from a certain broad group or a certain country. As an example, Latinos may be Caribbean Latino, Central American, South American, or Mexican, and each of these groups has a unique social and cultural history; or yet still, those treated may be members of a minority groups within the country, such as Quechua speakers in Peru.

Specify the Language of the Group and Language of Treatment The language the participants speak should be specified. It should be noted whether the treatment was conducted in the preferred or a secondary language, and whether an interpreter

Table 1 Dimensions of culturally sensitive CBT

Therapeutic dimensions	Subdimensions
Assess relevant background information	The exact cultural group
	The language of the group and language of treatment
	Key demographic variables
	Religious background of the group
Address key stressors and traumas	Key stressors
	Typical traumatic events in the group
Identify and address key local symptom and syndrome concerns	Complaints of most concern to those being treated: Somatic complaints and local illness categories and related catastrophic cognitions
	Complaints and behaviors of most concern to the community: Substance abuse, suicidality, violence
Address DSM disorders dimensions of psychopathology	Key DSM disorders
	Key psychopathological dimensions (e.g., worry, panic, and catastrophic cognitions)
Create universal and local models of how key complaints are generated	Universal model of how disorder is generated
	Local model of how disorder is generated
Utilize local sources of resilience and recovery	Proverbs, ethnopsychology, and religious practices (e.g., Dhikr or meditation) that promote resilience and recovery
Maximize credibility and positive expectancy	Take into consideration the local ethnopsychology, ethnophysiology, and ethnospirituality (e.g., address related catastrophic cognitions)
	Frame the treatment as addressing the problems of most concern
	Utilize local metaphors and proverbs and refer to local practices that teach CBT principles
	Testimonials by those who have recovered and by community leaders
Make CBT techniques more tolerable and effective for the cultural group	A phased approach when doing exposure
	Re-association to positive imagery during interoceptive exposure
	Exposure as an opportunity to teach emotion regulation techniques
	Culturally appropriate analogies and metaphors
Maximize access	Address stigma about the disorder and getting treatment for the disorder
	Address structural barriers to treatment
	Maximize adherence
	Specify scale-up and sustainability potential

was used. In many countries there are multiple languages spoken but a single national language, with variable fluency in the national language. For example, in Iraq, while Arabic is the national language, Arabic is not spoken in major parts of Northern Iraq, where Kurdish and Turkmen are the dominant languages.

Identify Key Demographic Variables The treatment population should be characterized in terms of key demographic variables such as gender, socio-economic status (SES), education, and literacy level. The level of education and literacy will determine whether written handouts can be used and may indicate whether use of technology (e.g., CDs containing therapeutic materials) can be a feasible treatment component or whether one must use easy-to-understand diagrams and figures. Furthermore, variables like SES may indicate current levels of stress, which may influence the ability to tolerate and benefit from therapy. For instance, exposure therapy may be contraindicated in groups experiencing a high degree of ongoing stress (Lester, Resick, Young-Xu, & Artz, 2010).

Detail the Religious Background of the Group and Its Impact on Treatment It should be determined whether the participants are members of a certain religion, such as Buddhism, Christianity, or Islam, and moreover, which denomination of that religion: Therevadan or Zen Buddhism, Pentecostal or Catholic Christianity, or Sunni or Shia Islam. The clinician should also determine the patient's attitude to that tradition: devout, agnostic, or hostile. Religious hybridity should also be taken into account; for example, Christianity among the Sepedi tribe of South Africa is an amalgamation of traditional Christianity and local beliefs in ancestral spirits, evil curses, and black magic. Religion may influence explanatory models of illness, and key aspects of the group's viewpoints of illness may be missed if religious identity has not been duly assessed. Ideally local religious leaders should first be consulted to determine their understanding of the types of distress in the population, what religious and other treatments they think should be implemented, and how they think Western-type interventions might be successfully conducted. Religious or spiritual traditions may provide sources of resilience or constitute obstacles to care. Incorporating sources of resilience from the religious traditions themselves and anticipating potential objections from the religious communities may improve the acceptability and efficacy of treatment in such settings: For example, in some Islamic cultures, it may be necessary to match therapist and client in respect to gender as a way of adapting treatment to religious beliefs (Murray et al., 2014).

Assess and Address Local Stressors and Traumas

Worry and current life concerns are a key generator of distress, particularly in traumatized populations (Hinton & Lewis-Fernández, 2011; Hinton, Nickerson, & Bryant, 2011). From a public health standpoint, when applying CBT in global contexts, it is important to be aware of local problems that may be addressed for the entire group: examples include security concerns, refugee status, and access to clean water (Bolton, Michalopoulos, Ahmed, Murray, & Bass, 2013; Hinton & Hinton, 2015). Ideally such concerns may be addressed at the community level as a public health intervention. Additionally, it should be specified whether the participant in CBT has an advocate, such as the equivalent of a social worker, who can help address key practical problems. As such, CBT may need to address practical problems as part of treatment, which also serves as a way to increase behavioral activation and improve participants' coping skills (Nezu, Nezu, & Lombardo, 2004).

In addition to ongoing stressors, past and current traumas common in the group should be clearly identified and the effects researched. The group in question may have endured mass violence of some kind. Prior to commencing CBT with a client, the client should be screened for current traumas (e.g., ongoing domestic violence), and if detected provided with resources that can facilitate coping. Ongoing trauma may include sexual and/or domestic violence, which is especially common in groups where gender disadvantage is culturally sanctioned (Patel, Kirkwood, Pednekar, Weiss, & Mabey, 2006).

Identify and Address Key Local Symptom and Cultural Syndrome Concerns

Identify and Address Distress Complaints of Most Concern to those Being Treated Failure to assess and treat key concerns such as somatic symptoms, possession, and cultural syndromes is to commit "category truncation," resulting in a lack of content validity (Hinton & Good, 2016b). In a particular cultural context, certain symptoms may be of great concern. For instance, among many Cambodian refugees, sleep paralysis, dizziness, poor sleep, and panic attacks warrant high levels of distress (Hinton, Kredlow, Pich, Bui, & Hofmann, 2013). The key local complaints may also manifest as cultural syndromes. For example, Cambodians frequently attribute anxiety symptoms to "heart weakness" and "wind attacks" (*khyâl* attacks), that is, a dangerous surge of *khyâl* and blood upward in the body (see below), and these attributions produce multiple catastrophic cognitions. Similarly, possession fears are prevalent in traumatized populations in certain African contexts, with PTSD and arousal symptoms sometimes being attributed to possession (de Jong & Reis, 2010, 2013). These complaints are experience-near categories; that is, they are the very terms that are used by members of the group to describe distress, and are therefore highly related to self-perceived well-being. The experience-near categories, according to which disorder is locally understood, are usually not Diagnostic and Statistical Manual of Mental Disorders (DSM) categories but other local categories such as *khyâl* attacks among Cambodian populations and "thinking a lot" among many cultural groups (Bolton, Surkan, Gray, & Desmousseaux, 2012; Kaiser et al., 2014; Patel, Simunyu, & Gwanzura, 1995; Yarris, 2014).

Ideally outcome studies in cross-cultural settings should include a list of locally salient complaints, particularly somatic complaints, and a list of cultural syndromes. These lists are referred to as a "Symptom and Syndrome Addendum", for example, a "Cambodian Symptom and Syndrome Addendum," or C-SSA (Hinton, Hinton, Eng, & Choung, 2012; Hinton, Kredlow, et al., 2013). Certain locally salient complaints may be particularly important to assess across treatment: For example, in the

Cambodian refugee groups, orthostatic dizziness (Hinton et al., 2009; Hinton, Hinton, et al., 2012; Hinton, Hofmann, et al., 2011; Hinton, Kredlow, et al., 2013), and in some Latino groups, *ataques de nervios* (Hinton, Hofmann, et al., 2011), which consists of the sense of a dangerous disorder of the "nerves" that may cause loss of control and various bodily disasters (e.g., uncontrollable shaking and asphyxia).

Framing treatment as addressing these key complaints greatly increases CBT acceptability and adherence, and helps to identify and address catastrophic cognitions. As a therapeutic intervention, the client can be told that the culturally salient items in the assessment battery should improve during treatment. This accomplishes many goals, such as addressing distress in terms of local explanatory models and symptoms of concern, alleviating catastrophic cognitions, and increasing positive expectancy (Benish et al., 2011; Hinton, Lewis-Fernández, et al., 2016).

Identify and Address Symptom and Syndrome Complaints of Most Concern to the Community One should ask local leaders, if present, about their key concerns relating to those in the community with psychological distress; for example, they may mention substance abuse or suicidality. Framing the treatment as addressing these issues may mobilize local leaders and the community to engage community members in treatment. Local leaders may include political, religious, and informal and formal health providers, as well as heads of local advocacy groups who have earned respect in the community. The aim of engaging such leaders is to have the community focus more on resolution rather than on blaming the victim or using other forms of non-productive labeling. It provides an alternative framing by contextualizing behaviors as resulting from social and psychological distress.

Address DSM Disorders and Dimensions of Psychopathology

Identify and Address Key DSM Disorders In some groups, such as traumatized refugees, certain disorders like PTSD and panic disorder may be particularly elevated owing to complex trauma, ongoing stressors, and catastrophic thought patterns about symptoms (Hinton & Lewis-Fernández, 2011). For example, Cambodian refugees not only experience PTSD but also have extremely high rates of panic attacks and panic disorder. If panic attacks are common in a locality, this will influence assessment and the recommended treatment modules. As such, each group may have a unique profile of DSM disorders. The profile of disorders will inform treatment and the design and implementation of modules.

Identify and Address Key Psychopathological Dimensions Other than DSM disorders, it is important to identify key psychopathological dimensions in a group, such as pathological worry, catastrophic cognitions, somatic symptoms, panic attacks, anger, substance abuse, or suicidality (Hinton, Nickerson, et al., 2011; Morris & Cuthbert, 2012); This analytic approach is consistent with the call to use dimensional analysis to identify treatment targets (Casey et al., 2013). Knowledge of these dimensions can inform treatment more specifically than simply focusing on DSM-5 symptoms, and can result in tailored culturally adapted care. Failing to address key distress dimensions among distressed traumatized populations in cross-cultural settings is an example of category truncation, which may lead to poor care (Hinton & Good, 2016a).

As an example of a key dimension to assess and track among traumatized refugee groups, it has been found that somatic symptoms form a prominent aspect of the illness experience in many non-Western populations (de Jong, Komproe, Spinazzola, van der Kolk, & van Ommeren, 2005; Hinton & Good, 2009; Hinton & Lewis-Fernández, 2011). Ideally one should identify key somatic concerns in a population so that these may be addressed in CBT; this can be considered as the assessment of a psychopathological dimension.

Another key psychopathology dimension relevant to the adaptation of CBT is catastrophic cognitions. A standard part of CBT is addressing catastrophic cognitions about symptoms, such as those concerning PTSD and somatic symptoms (Hinton, Rivera, et al., 2012). Learning the local ethnopsychology, ethnophysiology, and ethnospirituality as it applies to symptoms and processes like "worry" is a key way of identifying these catastrophic cognitions. In every culture, there will be local ideas about how symptoms of anxiety and depression are generated and treated. For example, many Cambodian refugees fear that neck soreness indicates the neck vessels will burst. Similarly, they hold that dizziness on standing indicates the onset of a dangerous *khyâl* attack, or "wind attack," in which a surge of *khyâl* and blood upward in the body is believed to cause various symptoms and disasters such as asphyxia by compressing the lungs, heart arrest by pressing on the heart, bursting of the neck vessels by dilating vessels, and fatal syncope by infiltrating the cranium (Hinton & Good, 2016a; Hinton, Pich, Marques, Nickerson, & Pollack, 2010). Cambodian refugees also tend to be concerned that worry will overheat the brain and cause permanent forgetfulness, and that palpitations will cause heart arrest. Among the Sepedi tribe of Northern Sotho, it has been found that PTSD symptoms and somatic symptoms give rise to fears of possession and attack by spirits (on possession fears elsewhere in Africa, see de Jong & Reis, 2010, 2013). The clinician can address catastrophic cognitions by giving an alternative framing in terms of the biology of anxiety, by teaching clients to control the symptom by relaxation methods (breath-focused techniques or applied stretching and muscle relaxation), and by interoceptive exposure[1] that teaches the innocuousness of these symptoms.[2]

[1] Interoceptive exposure is a cognitive behavioural therapy technique used in the treatment of panic disorder in which the individual is exposed to interoceptive sensations like dizziness to decrease fear of them.

[2] In many Buddhist countries symptoms may be attributed to bad spiritual status. If the client thinks the current state is due to "low merit" or past bad actions ("bad karma"), the client can be encouraged to use cultural means to elevate spiritual status. As such, meditating or projecting loving kindness are considered merit-making and by doing these activities, the client regains a sense of agency (there is a transformation of self-image). Thus, the client engages in a practice that is therapeutic by both local and "scientific" standards. Note that addressing concerns about a depleted or

Create Universal and Local Models of How Key Complaints Are Generated in the Population in Question in Order to Identify Treatment Targets and Modes of Intervention

How particular key complaints come to be generated should be identified in terms of two types of causal network models (McNally, 2012): universal and local models.

Construct Universal Models One should create universal models of how the complaint is generated. We have used multiplex models (Fig. 1) to show how key complaints are generated among Cambodian refugees with trauma-related symptoms. These causal models identify treatment targets, such as triggers of distress, and the nature of catastrophic cognitions, and provide a model of the generation of distress that can be shared with the client (Benish et al., 2011; Hinton & Lewis-Fernández, 2010). For example, we have used such models to explain why Cambodian refugees have high rates of somatic complaints and panic attacks and how they are generated. Among Cambodian refugees, we have determined that panic attacks often began with a somatic symptom that is caused by a trigger, such as worry or by standing up from a sitting or lying position. Next, the triggered somatic symptom may give rise to catastrophic cognitions, for example, worry-caused dizziness resulting in fears of the onset of a dangerous *khyâl* attack; and the triggered somatic symptom may evoke trauma associations, for example, worry-caused dizziness bringing about memories of doing slave labor while starving (Hinton et al., 2010; Hinton & Good, 2009; Hinton, Hofmann, Pitman, Pollack, & Barlow, 2008; Hinton, Nickerson, et al., 2011). The model takes into account local ideas about the workings of the body by emphasizing the assessment of catastrophic cognitions.

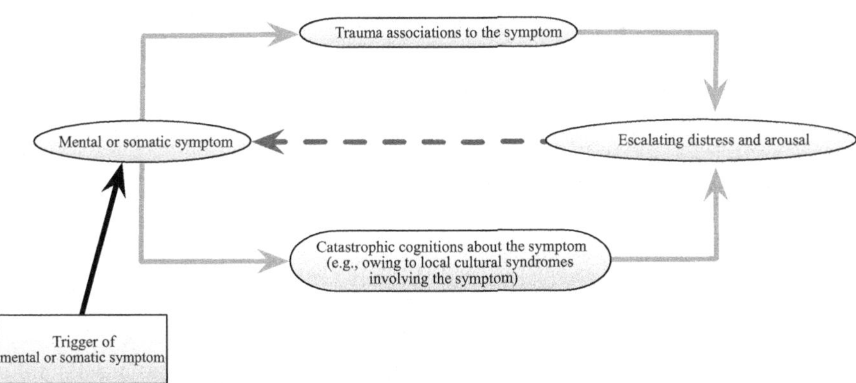

Fig. 1 A multiplex model of the generation of trauma-related distress

inauspicious spiritual status is often part of addressing catastrophic cognitions because the perception of low spiritual power and thus great vulnerability leads to multiple types of catastrophic cognitions: that spirit attack may lead to sleep paralysis and that somatic symptoms are due to invasion by a spirit.

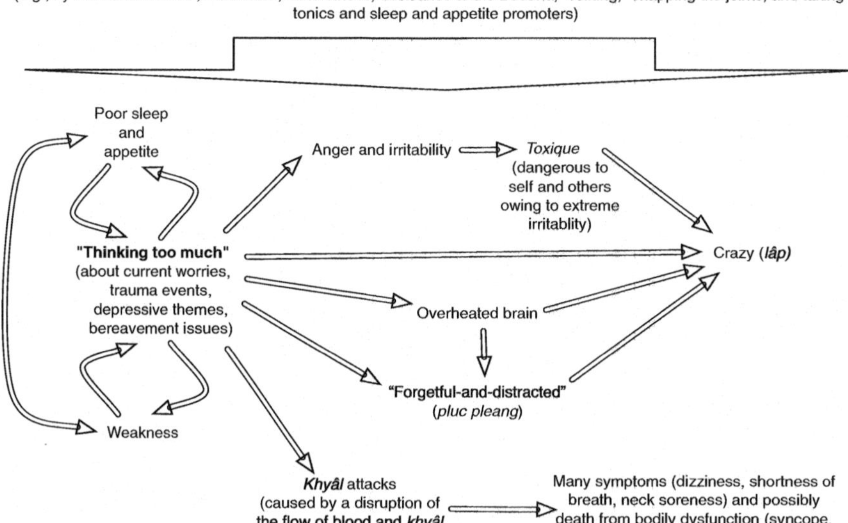

Fig. 2 The cambodian explanatory model of "thinking too much" and its treatment

Determine Local Models How key symptoms are generated according to the local ethnopsychology should also be determined, which often involves local cultural syndromes; this reveals the local explanatory models. These local models of mental distress highlight multiple possible treatment targets and support the discussion of symptoms and interventions in a way that will be locally understood. Determining local models allows the clinician/researcher to ground the treatment in the local context and to create a bridge from current psychological theory to local explanatory models. To give an example, one type of syndrome found in many cultures, "thinking a lot," can be investigated (Hinton et al., 2008; Hinton, Reis, & de Jong, 2015, 2016), providing an important entrée to local ethnopsychology and ethnophysiology. (On "thinking a lot," see also Bolton et al., 2012; Kaiser et al., 2014; Patel et al., 1995; Yarris, 2014.) Figure 2 shows how the syndrome of "thinking too much" is conceptualised among Cambodian refugees. According to the Cambodian conceptualization, there is the trigger of an episode, which is often worry, but also may be thoughts about past traumas, rumination over past failures, or pained recall of someone who has died or lives far away; then this "thinking too much" may cause poor sleep and weakness, which in turn causes more "thinking too much." Furthermore, according to the Cambodian conceptualization, "thinking too much" may cause anger and various serious disturbances of mind and body, such as permanent forgetfulness and "*khyâl* attacks". Figure 2 also shows how Cambodians traditionally treat "thinking a lot." Because of the commonality of "thinking a lot" across the globe, and its centrality in psychopathology, its evaluation is a key way of investigating local ideas about mental disorder. As such, we have proposed a questionnaire that can be used to conduct an assessment of "thinking a lot" in any cultural group (Hinton et al., 2015).

Utilize Local Sources of Resilience and Recovery

A key part of local resilience and recovery may be the local proverbs, ethnopsychology, and religious tradition. Incorporating such proverbs, teachings, and practices into CBT can increase cultural acceptability and positive expectancy related to the treatment. Useful proverbs may have religious origins. For instance, Rumi, a famous Persian poet, presented a proverb that helps to teach the virtue of gratitude: "Wear gratitude like a cloak and it will feed every corner of your life". In certain localities, there may be healing traditions such as Buddhist practices or Islamic spirituality (e.g., *Tazkiyah-tul-nafs*, or "purification of the soul") that are helpful to clients (Hinton & Kirmayer, 2013). These techniques can inform the application of CBT treatment itself, and participants may then be encouraged to use such methods. For Buddhists, incorporating meditation into the treatment may be useful. For some Islamic populations, incorporating a type of supplication known as *Dhikr* where God is repeatedly praised using various honorific names, may also be warranted. In our treatment for traumatized Southeast Asian refugees, we utilize multiple mindfulness techniques to improve the skills of clients in coping with anxiety (Hinton, Ojserkis, Jalal, Peou, & Hofmann, 2013; Hinton, Pich, et al., 2013).

In some cases, it is useful to end the CBT treatment with local rituals that indicate purification or healing in a general sense, which helps to change self-image and to create a sense of positive expectancy (Hinton, Rivera, et al., 2012). Such rituals help to improve one's self-imagery, which is a key issue in traumatized and other populations. These rituals create the sense of being transformed and thereby increase positive expectancy (Agger, Igreja, Kiehle, & Polatin, 2012; Hinton, Rivera, et al., 2012). For example, *Wudhu* and *Ghusl* (ritualistic washing of face, arms, and feet) for an Islamic population are types of spiritual purification techniques signifying a transition from spiritual impurity to purity (Amer & Jalal, 2011; Haque, 2004); among Southeast Asian populations, transition is often marked by various types of steaming rituals.

Maximize Credibility and Positive Expectancy

Increasing credibility and positive expectancy regarding treatment has various effects such as enhancing adherence and efficacy (Benish et al., 2011; Gone, 2013; Rutherford & Roose, 2013; Tsai, Ogrodniczuk, Sochting, & Mirmiran, 2014). Credibility and expectancy can be increased in the following ways.

Take into Consideration the Local Ethnopsychology, Ethnophysiology, and Ethnospirituality Credibility and positive expectancy will be increased by eliciting the client's explanatory model of disorder, explaining how that model relates to the

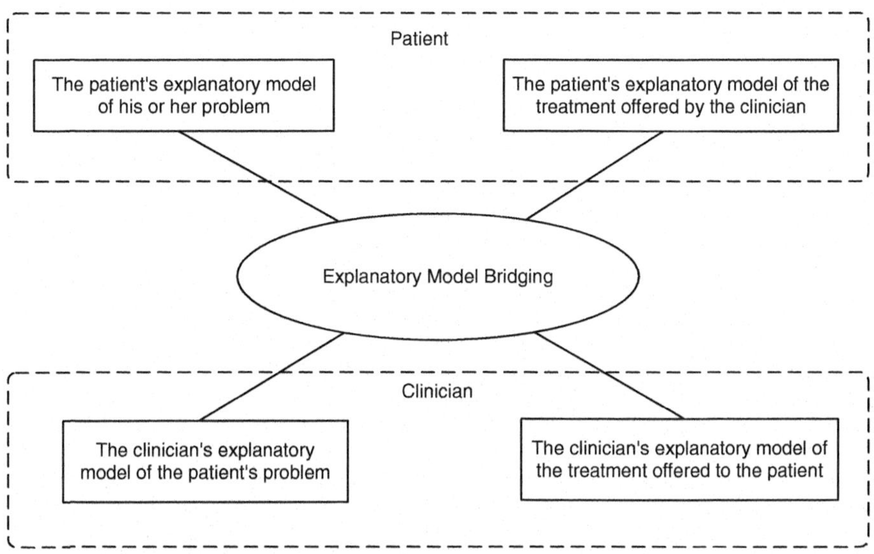

Fig. 3 The core clinical task of explanatory model bridging, with the clinical encounter configured as the negotiation of four types of explanatory models

proposed CBT treatment, and addressing concerns related to the client's explanatory model such as key complaints and catastrophic cognitions (Hinton, Lewis-Fernández, et al., 2016; Hinton, Rivera, et al., 2012; Ventevogel, Jordans, Reis, & de Jong, 2013). Giving explanations of the intervention that are culturally consonant might be called "explanatory model bridging" (Fig. 3).[3] Credibility and positive expectancy may be enhanced by referring to local therapeutic techniques in treatment, such as meditation in a Buddhist context, and, *Dhikr* or *Ruqyah* in Islamic contexts. Such techniques may also be used in the treatment when appropriate.

Frame the Treatment in Terms of the Problems of Most Concern It should be explained how the treatment will help with complaints of greatest concern, such as key symptoms like dizziness and sleep paralysis and key cultural syndromes like "weak heart" and "thinking a lot." For example, in our CBT treatments, we specifically mention that the treatment will relieve the complaints in the Symptom and Syndrome Addendum.

Use Local Metaphors and Proverbs and Refer to Local Practices Consonance between clinician and client explanatory models is a central mechanism of change

[3]The attempt at bridging, which requires eliciting the client's explanatory model, is seemingly efficacious for various reasons: increasing positive expectancy and credibility by increasing the client's feeling that the therapist's understands their concerns and by identifying catastrophic cognitions about symptoms (Hinton, Lewis-Fernández, et al., 2016). A recent review indicated that cultural adaptation of treatment increased effect size, and that the key aspect of cultural adaptation was eliciting the client's explanatory model of disorder (Benish et al., 2011).

in therapy. The use of local metaphors, proverbs, and practices is another example of explanatory model bridging; that is, creating a bridge between the clinician's and client's view of disorder. This is part of the cultural grounding of CBT, which increases credibility and positive expectancy, in addition to aiding a client in retaining information. For example, at the beginning of treatment we compare our CBT to the making of a special local dish that involves multiple culinary steps to promote positive expectancy and teach patience regarding timeframe of their improvement. When doing interoceptive exposure, we re-associate the induced sensations such as dizziness in head rolling to local games and practices that induce that same sensation. Similarly, we re-associate these types of sensations with more positive imagery germane to clients, for example, from the Islamic tradition, by introducing the holy image of whirling dervishes.

Metaphors, analogies, and proverbs may also be taken from the religious tradition to teach about emotion regulation such as anger control. In Cambodian Buddhism, for example, anger is compared to a dangerous fire; the proverb, "Controlling getting angry once results in a gain of a hundred days of happiness" (Nickerson & Hinton, 2011) may also be relevant to treatment. Likewise, anger is highly discouraged in the Islamic tradition. It is narrated that the Prophet of Islam, Muhammad, advised, "The strong man is not the one who can throw another down. The strong man is the one who can keep hold of himself when he is angry." Muhammad also stated that "Anger is from Satan, and Satan was created from fire. Fire is extinguished by water, so if one of you gets angry, he/she should perform *Wudhu*" (ritualistic washing of face, arms, and feet to cool down) (Amer & Jalal, 2011; Haque, 2004).

Utilize Testimonials by Community Leaders and Those Who Have Recovered Showing videos of local leaders who advocate treatment and attest to its efficacy may help improve credibility and positive expectancy, as may testimonial videos of those who have gotten better through the treatment (if permissions are obtained and it is culturally appropriate).

Make CBT Techniques Tolerable for the Cultural Group

To increase tolerability of interoceptive exposure, in our treatment we frame the techniques as a "game" and try to create positive associations to somatic sensations that are germane in that context. During head rolling exercises, the clinician can evoke the joy experienced by a child while rolling down a hill. It has been found that conducting exposure to trauma memories among ethnic populations presents challenges and may lead to drop out and worsening of symptoms (Hinton, 2012). With Western populations too, exposure conducted even by doctoral level therapists, has been problematic. However, narrative exposure therapy uses traditional exposure — with minimal preparation or modification — and has been shown to be effective in several countries (Morkved et al., 2014). Metaphors used to frame techniques may promote credibility and tolerability (Hinton, Rivera, et al., 2012; Hwang, 2006) and exposure may be facilitated by references to local practices. For example, one research group compared imaginal exposure to cleaning a wound (Murray et al., 2014). In another instance, the comparison equated the fear of exposure to the fear local women initially have of making bread on an open fire, as it is a fear that typically diminishes over time (Murray et al., 2014). In our treatment for Cambodian refugees, to increase tolerability and efficacy of exposure, we use the distress resulting from exposure as an opportunity to teach emotion regulation techniques (Hinton, Rivera, et al., 2012); for instance, by teaching loving kindness and mindfulness and providing self-metaphors of flexibility subsequent to exposure.

Maximize Access

Address Stigma About the Disorder and Getting Treatment for the Disorder One should determine how various psychological disorders and associated symptoms are locally viewed. The psychological disorders and associated symptoms should be normalized with the goal of reducing self-stigma and stigmatization by others. Family members may need to be educated about the illness. Videos of community leaders and possibly clients (if permissions are obtained and it is culturally appropriate) in which they talk about the disorder and the importance of treatment may be useful. Treatment can be framed as addressing locally salient concerns that are not stigmatizing, such as poor sleep, nightmares, or somatic complaints. If coming to the location of treatment remains stigmatizing, it may be necessary to provide treatment in a primary care or another non-stigmatizing locality.[4]

Address Structural Barriers to Treatment Structural barriers to treatment include transportation issues, difficulty paying for health care, and problems taking time off to go to the clinic. Transportation issues and time constraints may be alleviated by providing services in primary care. However, payment issues may well require governmental level shifts in policy.

Maximize Adherence Adherence includes attending sessions and trying to implement the treatment in daily life. Adherence will be increased by anything that decreases stigma, helps to increase credibility and positive expectancy, increases tolerability, or addresses structural barriers. So, for example, adherence will be increased by using metaphors that emphasize the need to complete all parts of the

[4] In respect to trauma, one may need to address social blaming and self-blaming: a rape victim may be blamed and stigmatized. In many Asian countries, the concept of karma (i.e., the idea that what happens to one is a result of past bad actions and so is deserved) can lead to a blaming of the victim. It should be noted that local models like that of karma may be used as a justificatory frame for perpetration of violence and need to be addressed at the community level. More generally, stigmatization of the survivor may need to be addressed at various levels such as through finding group consensus and utilizing local religious and transnational human-rights frames.

treatment, like the metaphor in which all elements of the treatment are analogized to the steps needed to prepare a dish that is highly prized in the culture.

Specify Scale-Up and Sustainability Potential Scale-up and sustainability will be greatly influenced by the level of education required of the service provider, how much time is needed to be trained in treatment provision, whether the treatment can be taught to multiple providers, how many sessions the treatment entails, whether the treatment is in a group or individual format, and the extent to which treatment can be delivered by non-specialists via task shifting (Chisholm et al., 2007; Patel, 2012). The scale-up and sustainability potential will be influenced by public health system variables as well. Examples of such factors include whether there is a place in the health care system to situate the treatment, whether the government is willing to incorporate the CBT into standard treatment, and whether funding is available for the program (Jordans & Tol, 2013). Therefore, keeping records of financial and labor costs can help to ascertain initial feasibility of such treatments.

Conclusion

In this chapter we have outlined some key ways of developing and implementing CBT in global contexts in a culturally sensitive way that maximizes efficacy and effectiveness. In studies involving CBT, the guidelines outlined (see Table 1) can be used as a checklist of cultural sensitivity, to support the development and implementation of contextually sensitive CBT. Ideally, preliminary research will be done to obtain the information shown in Table 1 prior to initiating CBT. The type of information specified in Table 1 can be gathered in various ways.

As an initial way to obtain the information in Table 1, there should be a review of the literature, discussion with community leaders, ethnographic surveys, and pilot treatment studies. As we have suggested, in designing a treatment, a good initial starting point is the determination of common presenting key complaints in a community. Then one can investigate the relationship of the complaint to DSM disorders and to dimensions of pathology, and one can evaluate local ideas about the complaint's cause, local ideas about the how the complaint arises from disturbance in the psychological, physiological, and spiritual state, and local ideas about how the complaint can be best treated. To facilitate evaluation of the complaint, the explanatory model from the cultural formulation can be used (Hinton, Lewis-Fernández, et al., 2016). In localities where "thinking a lot" is common, using the "thinking a lot" questionnaire (Hinton et al., 2015; Hinton, Reis, et al., 2016) is a good way to learn about the local ethnopsychology and ethnophysiology and about current stressors. The questionnaire can also be adapted to assess key complaints in context.

The CBT protocol itself may be structured in a way that takes into consideration the domains in Table 1, and the CBT protocol may ask participants about some of these domains. For example, in our CBT treatment (Hinton, Rivera, et al., 2012), we specifically ask participants whether they are using any other means to cope with distress, which often may be techniques from local religious traditions, and we use probes to elicit key somatic complaints and local catastrophic cognitions.

In summary, treatment developers can review the parameters presented in this chapter to further refine treatment at each stage of development of contextually sensitive CBT. The parameters can also be used to assess the cultural sensitivity of extant CBT treatments and treatment studies. However, the extent to which contextually sensitive CBT as operationalized in this chapter improves efficacy needs to be determined. One meta-analytic review (Benish et al., 2011) gave support for increased efficacy with cultural adaptation of treatment elements, in particular, eliciting the client's explanatory model of the disorder, but more studies need to be done to see how and why the various parameters of culturally sensitive treatments in general, and contextually sensitive CBT in particular, improve treatment outcomes.

References

Agger, I., Igreja, V., Kiehle, R., & Polatin, P. (2012). Testimony ceremonies in Asia: Integrating spirituality in testimonial therapy for torture survivors in India, Sri Lanka, Cambodia, and the Philippines. *Transcultural Psychiatry, 49*(3–4), 568–589.

Amer, M., & Jalal, B. (2011). Individual psychotherapy/counseling: Psychodynamic, cognitive behavioral and humanistic-experiential models. In S. Ahmed & M. Amer (Eds.), *Counseling Muslims: Handbook of mental health issues and interventions* (pp. 87–117). New York, NY: Routledge.

Bass, J. K., Annan, J., McIvor Murray, S., Kaysen, D., Griffiths, S., Cetinoglu, T., … Bolton, P. A. (2013). Controlled trial of psychotherapy for Congolese survivors of sexual violence. *New England Journal of Medicine, 368*(23), 2182–2191.

Benish, S. G., Quintana, S., & Wampold, B. E. (2011). Culturally adapted psychotherapy and the legitimacy of myth: A direct-comparison meta-analysis. *Journal of Counseling Psychology, 58*(3), 279–289.

Bernal, G., Jiménez-Chafey, M. I., & Domenech Rodríguez, M. D. (2009). Cultural adaptation of treatments: A resource for considering culture in evidence-based practice. *Professional Psychology: Research and Practice, 40*(4), 361–368.

Bolton, P., Michalopoulos, L., Ahmed, A. M., Murray, L. K., & Bass, J. (2013). The mental health and psychosocial problems of survivors of torture and genocide in Kurdistan, Northern Iraq: A brief qualitative study. *Torture, 23*(1), 1–14.

Bolton, P., Surkan, P. J., Gray, A. E., & Desmousseaux, M. (2012). The mental health and psychosocial effects of organized violence: A qualitative study in northern Haiti. *Transcultural Psychiatry, 49*(3–4), 590–612.

Casey, B. J., Craddock, N., Cuthbert, B. N., Hyman, S. E., Lee, F. S., & Ressler, K. J. (2013). DSM-5 and RDoC: Progress in psychiatry research? *Nature Reviews: Neuroscience, 14*(11), 810–814.

Chisholm, D., Flisher, A. J., Lund, C., Patel, V., Saxena, S., Thornicroft, G., & Tomlinson, M. (2007). Scale up services for mental disorders: A call for action. *The Lancet, 370*(9594), 1241–1252.

Crumlish, N., & O'Rourke, K. (2010). A systematic review of treatments for post-traumatic stress disorder among refugees and asylum-seekers. *Journal of Nervous and Mental Disease, 198*(4), 237–251.

de Jong, J. T., Komproe, I. H., Spinazzola, J., van der Kolk, B. S., & van Ommeren, M. H. (2005). DESNOS in three postconflict settings: Assessing cross-cultural construct equivalence. *Journal of Traumatic Stress, 18*(1), 13–21.

de Jong, J. T., & Reis, R. (2010). Kiyang-yang, a West-African postwar idiom of distress. *Culture, Medicine, and Psychiatry, 34*(2), 301–321.

de Jong, J. T., & Reis, R. (2013). Collective trauma resolution: Dissociation as a way of processing post-war traumatic stress in Guinea Bissau. *Transcultural Psychiatry, 50*(5), 644–661.

Drozdek, B., Kamperman, A. M., Tol, W. A., Knipscheer, J. W., & Kleber, R. J. (2014). Seven-year follow-up study of symptoms in asylum seekers and refugees with PTSD treated with trauma-focused groups. *Journal of Clinical Psychology, 70*(4), 376–387.

Gone, J. P. (2013). Redressing first Nations historical trauma: Theorizing mechanisms for indigenous culture as mental health treatment. *Transcultural Psychiatry, 50*(5), 683–706.

Griner, D., & Smith, T. B. (2006). Culturally adapted mental health intervention: A meta-analytic review. *Psychotherapy, 43*(4), 531–548.

Haque, A. (2004). Religion and mental health: The case of American Muslims. *Journal of Religion and Health, 43*(1), 45–58.

Hinton, D. E. (2012). Multicultural challenges in the delivery of anxiety treatment. *Depression and Anxiety, 29*(1), 1–3.

Hinton, D. E. (2014). Assessment and treatment in non-Western countries. In P. Emmelkamp & E. Ehring (Eds.), *The Wiley handbook of anxiety disorders* (pp. 1268–1278). Hoboken, NJ: Wiley.

Hinton, D. E., Chhean, D., Pich, V., Safren, S. A., Hofmann, S. G., & Pollack, M. H. (2005). A randomized controlled trial of cognitive-behavior therapy for Cambodian refugees with treatment-resistant PTSD and panic attacks: A cross-over design. *Journal of Traumatic Stress, 18*(6), 617–629.

Hinton, D. E., & Good, B. J. (Eds.). (2009). *Culture and panic disorder*. Palo Alto, CA: Stanford University Press.

Hinton, D. E., & Good, B. J. (2016a). The culturally sensitive assessment of trauma: Eleven analytic perspectives, a typology of errors, and the multiplex models of distress generation. In D. E. Hinton & B. J. Good (Eds.), *Culture and PTSD: Trauma in historical and global perspective* (pp. 50–113). Philadelphia, PA: University of Pennsylvenia Press.

Hinton, D. E., & Good, B. J. (Eds.). (2016b). *Culture and PTSD: Trauma in historical and global perspective*. Philadelphia, PA: University of Pennsylvenia Press.

Hinton, D. E., & Hinton, A. L. (2015). An anthropology of the effects of genocide and mass violence: Memory, symptom, and recovery. In D. E. Hinton & A. L. Hinton (Eds.), *Genocide and mass violence: Memory, symptom, and recovery* (pp. 1–45). Cambridge: Cambridge University Press.

Hinton, D. E., Hinton, A. L., Eng, K.-T., & Choung, S. (2012). PTSD and key somatic complaints and cultural syndromes among rural Cambodians: The results of a needs assessment survey. *Medical Anthropology Quarterly, 29*, 147–154.

Hinton, D. E., Hofmann, S. G., Pitman, R. K., Pollack, M. H., & Barlow, D. H. (2008). The panic attack–PTSD model: Applicability to orthostatic panic among Cambodian refugee. *Cognitive Behaviour Therapy, 37*(2), 101–116.

Hinton, D. E., Hofmann, S. G., Pollack, M. H., & Otto, M. W. (2009). Mechanisms of efficacy of CBT for Cambodian refugees with PTSD: Improvement in emotion regulation and orthostatic blood pressure response. *CNS Neuroscience and Therapeutics, 15*(3), 255–263.

Hinton, D. E., Hofmann, S. G., Rivera, E., Otto, M. W., & Pollack, M. H. (2011). Culturally adapted CBT for Latino women with treatment-resistant PTSD: A pilot study comparing CA-CBT to Applied Muscle Relaxation. *Behaviour Research and Therapy, 49*(4), 275–280.

Hinton, D. E., & Kirmayer, L. J. (2013). Local responses to trauma: Symptom, affect, and healing. *Transcultural Psychiatry, 50*(5), 607–621.

Hinton, D. E., Kredlow, M. A., Pich, V., Bui, E., & Hofmann, S. G. (2013). The relationship of PTSD to key somatic complaints and cultural syndromes among Cambodian refugees attending a psychiatric clinic: The Cambodian Somatic Symptom and Syndrome Inventory (SSI). *Transcultural Psychiatry, 50*(3), 347–370.

Hinton, D. E., & Lewis-Fernández, R. (2010). Idioms of distress among trauma survivors: Subtypes and clinical utility. *Culture, Medicine and Psychiatry, 34*(2), 209–218.

Hinton, D. E., & Lewis-Fernández, R. (2011). The cross-cultural validity of posttraumatic stress disorder: Implications for DSM-5. *Depression and Anxiety, 28*(9), 783–801.

Hinton, D. E., Lewis-Fernández, R., Kirmayer, L. J., & Weiss, M. G. (2016). Supplementary module 1: Explanatory module. In R. Lewis-Fernandez, N. Aggarwal, L. Hinton, D. Hinton, & L. J. Kirmayer (Eds.), *The DSM-5 handbook on the cultural formulation interview* (pp. 53–67). Washinton, DC: American Psychiatric Press.

Hinton, D. E., Nickerson, A., & Bryant, R. A. (2011). Worry, worry attacks, and PTSD among Cambodian refugees: A path analysis investigation. *Social Science and Medicine, 72*(11), 1817–1825.

Hinton, D. E., Ojserkis, R., Jalal, B., Peou, S., & Hofmann, S. G. (2013). Loving kindness to treat traumatized refugees and minority groups: A typology of mindfulness and the Nodal Network Model (NNM) of affect and affect regulation. *Journal of Clinical Psychology, 69*(8), 817–828.

Hinton, D. E., Pham, T., Tran, M., Safren, S. A., Otto, M. W., & Pollack, M. H. (2004). CBT for Vietnamese refugees with treatment-resistant PTSD and panic attacks: A pilot study. *Journal of Traumatic Stress, 17*(5), 429–433.

Hinton, D. E., Pich, V., Hofmann, S. G., & Otto, M. W. (2013). Mindfulness and acceptance techniques as applied to refugee and ethnic minority populations: Examples from culturally adapted CBT (CA-CBT). *Cognitive and Behavioral Practice, 20*(1), 33–46.

Hinton, D. E., Pich, V., Marques, L., Nickerson, A., & Pollack, M. H. (2010). Khyâl attacks: A key idiom of distress among traumatized Cambodian refugees. *Culture, Medicine and Psychiatry, 34*(2), 244–278.

Hinton, D. E., Reis, R., & de Jong, J. T. (2015). The "thinking a lot" idiom of distress and PTSD: An examination of their relationship among traumatized Cambodian refugees using the "Thinking a Lot" Questionnaire. *Medical Anthropology Quarterly, 29*(3), 357–380.

Hinton, D. E., Reis, R., & de Jong, J. T. (2016). A transcultural model of the centrality of "thinking a lot" in psychopathologies across the globe and the process of localization: A Cambodian refugee example. *Culture, Medicine, and Psychiatry, 40*(4), 570–619.

Hinton, D. E., Rivera, E., Hofmann, S. G., Barlow, D. H., & Otto, M. W. (2012). Adapting CBT for traumatized refugees and ethnic minority patients: Examples from culturally adapted CBT (CA-CBT). *Transcultural Psychiatry, 49*(2), 340–365.

Hofmann, S. G., & Smits, J. A. (2008). Cognitive-behavioral therapy for adult anxiety disorders: A meta-analysis of randomized placebo-controlled trials. *Journal of Clinical Psychiatry, 69*(4), 621–632.

Hwang, W. C. (2006). The psychotherapy adaptation and modification framework: Application to Asian Americans. *American Psychologist, 61*(7), 702–715.

Jordans, M. J., & Tol, W. A. (2013). Mental health in humanitarian settings: Shifting focus to care systems. *International Health, 5*(1), 9–10.

Kaiser, B., McLean, K., Kohrt, B. A., Hagaman, A., Wagenaar, B. H., Khoury, N. M., & Keys, H. M. (2014). *Reflechi twòp*–thinking too much: Description of a cultural syndrome in Haiti's Central Plateau. *Culture, Medicine, and Psychiatry, 38*(3), 448–472.

Kleinman, A., & Good, B. J. (Eds.). (1985). *Culture and depression: Studies in anthropology and cross-cultural psychiatry of affect and disorder*. Berkeley, CA: University of California Press.

Lester, K., Resick, P. A., Young-Xu, Y., & Artz, C. (2010). Impact of race on early treatment termination and outcomes in posttraumatic stress disorder treatment. *Journal of Consulting and Clinical Psychology, 78*(4), 480–489.

McNally, R. J. (2012). The ontology of posttraumatic stress disorder: Natural kind, social construction, or causal system? *Clinical Psychology Science and Practice, 19*(3), 220–228.

Mollica, R. F., Caspi-Yavin, Y., Bollini, P., Truong, T., Tor, S., & Lavelle, J. (1992). The Harvard trauma questionnaire. *Journal of Nervous and Mental Disease, 180*(2), 111–116.

Morina, N., & Ford, J. (2008). Complex sequelae of psychological trauma among Kosovar civilian war victims. *International Journal of Social Psychiatry, 54*(5), 425–436.

Morkved, N., Hartmann, K., Aarsheim, L. M., Holen, D., Milde, A. M., Bomyea, J., & Thorp, S. R. (2014). A comparison of narrative exposure therapy and prolonged exposure therapy for PTSD. *Clinical Psychology Review, 34*(6), 453–467.

Morris, S. E., & Cuthbert, B. N. (2012). Research domain criteria: Cognitive systems, neural circuits, and dimensions of behavior. *Dialogues in Clinical Neuroscience, 14*(1), 29–37.
Murray, L. K., Dorsey, S., Haroz, E., Lee, E., Alsiary, M. M., Haydary, A., … Bolton, P. (2014). A common elements approach for adult mental health problems in low- and middle-income countries. *Cogntive and Behavioral Practice, 21*(2), 111–123.
Naeem, F., Waheed, W., Gobbi, M., Ayub, M., & Kingdon, D. (2011). Preliminary evaluation of culturally sensitive CBT for depression in Pakistan: Findings from Developing Culturally-Sensitive CBT Project (DCCP). *Behavioural and Cognitive Psychotherapy, 39*(2), 165–173.
Nezu, A. M., Nezu, C. M., & Lombardo, E. (2004). *Cognitive-behavioral case formulation to treatment design a problem-solving approach*. New York, NY: Springer.
Nickerson, A., Bryant, R. A., Silove, D., & Steel, Z. (2011). A critical review of psychological treatments of posttraumatic stress disorder in refugees. *Clinical Psychology Review, 31*(3), 399–417.
Nickerson, A., & Hinton, D. E. (2011). Anger regulation in traumatized Cambodian refugees: The perspectives of Buddhist monks. *Culture, Medicine, and Psychiatry, 35*(3), 396–416.
Patel, V. (2012). Global mental health: From science to action. *Harvard Review of Psychiatry, 20*(1), 6–12.
Patel, V., Kirkwood, B. R., Pednekar, S., Weiss, H., & Mabey, D. (2006). Risk factors for common mental disorders in women. Population-based longitudinal study. *British Journal of Psychiatry, 189*(6), 547–555.
Patel, V., Simunyu, E., & Gwanzura, F. (1995). Kufungisisa (thinking too much): A Shona idiom for non-psychotic mental illness. *Central African Journal of Medicine, 41*(7), 209–215.
Porter, M., & Haslam, N. (2005). Predisplacement and postdisplacement factors associated with mental health of refugees and internally displaced persons: A meta-analysis. *JAMA, 294*(5), 602–612.
Rutherford, B. R., & Roose, S. P. (2013). A model of placebo response in antidepressant clinical trials. *American Journal of Psychiatry, 170*(7), 723–733.
Tsai, M., Ogrodniczuk, J. S., Sochting, I., & Mirmiran, J. (2014). Forecasting success: Patients' expectations for improvement and their relations to baseline, process and outcome variables in group cognitive-behavioural therapy for depression. *Clinical Psycholology and Psychotherapy, 21*(2), 97–107.
United Nations High Commissioner for Refugees. (2016). *Global trends: Forced displacement in 2015*. Geneva, Switzerland: Author.
van Ginneken, N., Tharyan, P., Lewin, S., Rao, G. N., Meera, S., Pian, J., et al. (2013). Non-specialist health worker interventions for the care of mental, neurological and substance-abuse disorders in low- and middle-income countries. *Cochrane Database Systemic Review, 11*, CD009149.
Ventevogel, P., Jordans, M., Reis, R., & de Jong, J. (2013). Madness or sadness? Local concepts of mental illness in four conflict-affected African communities. *Conflict and Health, 7*(1), 3.
Yarris, K. E. (2014). "Pensando mucho" ("thinking too much"): Embodied distress among grandmothers in Nicaraguan transnational families. *Culture, Medicine, and Psychiatry, 38*(3), 473–498.

Devon E. Hinton, MD, Ph.D., is an anthropologist and psychiatrist, and an Associate Professor of Psychiatry at Massachusetts General Hospital, Harvard Medical School, and the Department of Global Health and Social Medicine, Boston, Massachusetts. He has researched extensively culturally sensitive assessment and treatment of trauma.

Anushka Patel, M.A., is a doctoral student of clinical psychology at The University of Tulsa, OK. Her passions include examining trauma-related sequelae in low-income settings with cultural minorities, so as to inform cultural adaptation of treatment in these groups.

Alcohol and Drug Misuse Interventions in Conflict-Affected Populations

M. Claire Greene, Jeremy C. Kane, Noa Krawczyk, Felicity Brown, Laura Murray, Kaveh Khoshnood, and Wietse A. Tol

Abstract Despite the burden of substance misuse in conflict-affected populations, prevention and treatment services are often unavailable or neglected in policy and public health practice. This chapter reviews: (1) the epidemiology of substance misuse; (2) evidence for treatment and prevention services; and (3) implementation considerations for substance use services in conflict-affected populations. Overall, there is a significant lack of research evaluating implementation and impact of alcohol and drug misuse prevention and treatment services in conflict and post-conflict settings. Existing research indicates that substance misuse is common in conflict settings and displaced populations, and implementation of prevention and treatment programs is feasible, highlighting the importance of strengthening knowledge on how best to address this critical public health concern.

Keywords Substance misuse · Alcohol misuse · Drug misuse · Prevention · Treatment · Intervention · Conflict-affected · Post-conflict · Refugees

Introduction

Substance misuse, defined as use of alcohol or drugs for a purpose not consistent with legal or medical guidelines (World Health Organization, 2006), is often prevalent, but commonly neglected in settings affected by armed conflict. There are

M. C. Greene (✉) · J. C. Kane · N. Krawczyk · L. Murray · W. A. Tol
Mental Health, Johns Hopkins Bloomberg School of Public Health, Baltimore, MD, USA
e-mail: mgree116@jhu.edu; jkane29@jhu.edu; noa.krawczyk@jhu.edu; lmurra15@jhu.edu; wtol@jhu.edu

F. Brown
Research and Development, War Child, Amsterdam, North Holland, The Netherlands
e-mail: felicity.brown@warchild.nl

K. Khoshnood
Yale School of Public Health, Epidemiology of Microbial Diseases, New Haven, CT, USA
e-mail: kaveh.khoshnood@yale.edu

N. Morina, A. Nickerson (eds.), *Mental Health of Refugee and Conflict-Affected Populations*, https://doi.org/10.1007/978-3-319-97046-2_11

numerous pathways through which armed conflict can precipitate initiation and exacerbation of substance misuse, including self-medication for conflict-related distress, increased exposure to daily stressors, changes in availability and social norms, and the proliferation of risk factors in an environment that has been disrupted by conflict (Jack, Masterson, & Khoshnood, 2014). The individual-, family- and community-level consequences of substance misuse are substantial and can contribute to the challenge of recovering from armed conflict. In this chapter, we explore strategies for the prevention and treatment of substance misuse as well as the challenges and opportunities in addressing this burden in conflict-affected populations.

Methods

We conducted a broad review of the literature on substance misuse epidemiology, prevention and treatment strategies in conflict-affected populations by searching academic and grey literature databases (Pubmed, PILOTS, Embase, ALNAP, IRIN, mhpss.net, reliefweb, Anthrosource, PsycINFO, SCOPUS), agency websites (UNHCR, WHO, UNODC, UNICEF) and hand searching relevant journals (Intervention: Journal of Mental Health and Psychosocial Support in Conflict Affected Areas). Searches were conducted between April 8–26, 2016 using a systematic set of keywords combining terms for "drug", "alcohol", "substance", "war", "conflict", "displaced", "refugee", "prevention", "intervention", and "treatment" (available upon request). The searches yielded 14,252 results of which 3931 full text articles were screened. Articles were included if they were published in English, described a treatment or prevention strategy, guidelines for substance misuse interventions, epidemiology of substance misuse, or challenges to implementation of substance use programs in conflict-affected populations in any region of the world. Our review excluded publications that did not describe a substance misuse treatment or prevention intervention or epidemiological data, and those that were not implemented in a conflict-affected population. The search identified three prevention interventions implemented in post-conflict countries (Croatia) or with displaced populations (Burmese refugees, 2 interventions) and one qualitative evaluation of alcohol control policies in post-conflict settings globally. We identified four psychosocial/psychological treatment strategies implemented in conflict-affected populations in Thailand and Afghanistan, one systematic review of medication-assisted treatment in low- and middle-income countries (including conflict/post-conflict settings), and two harm reduction programs in Afghanistan.

Epidemiology of Substance Misuse in Conflict-Affected Populations

Searching the epidemiological literature yielded 1282 publications, 38 of which included information pertaining to measurement and prevalence of substance misuse, risk and protective factors, and consequences of substance misuse in conflict-affected populations, which are summarized below.

Measurement and Prevalence of Substance Misuse

Despite increased attention in recent years to mental health and other psychosocial problems associated with armed conflict, surprisingly few studies have focused on substance misuse in conflict-affected populations. A 2012 systematic review by Ezard identified 17 studies that measured substance misuse among populations displaced by conflict. Only half of these studies included prevalence estimates. Prevalence of alcohol misuse ranged from 14% reporting 'excessive use' in Colombia (Puertas, Rios, & Valle, 2006) to 30% reporting alcohol dependence in Croatia (Kozaric-Kovacic, Ljubin, & Grappe, 2000). Opium use ranged from 0.6% in Afghanistan (UNODC, 2005) to 5.5% in Laos (Westermeyer, 1982). The studies included in this review vary from large nationally representative household surveys of 799 conflict-affected persons in Afghanistan using validated measurement tools adapted to the local context through formative research to assess alcohol and drug misuse (Cardozo et al., 2004) to smaller convenience samples (n = 200) using non-standardized measurement tools to assess any use of opiates and/or alcohol (UNODC, 2003). The few epidemiologic studies that have been conducted in conflict-affected populations since the publication of the review by Ezard 2012 report comparable prevalence estimates for alcohol misuse (Massey et al., 2015; Roberts et al., 2014). These studies also vary in terms of sample size (range: 200–3600), timing (less than 1 year post-displacement to 13 years post-return to country/region of origin) and measurement method (self-administered questionnaires, semi-structured interviews). The majority of these studies did not use validated measures of alcohol misuse.

A clear limitation in the substance misuse literature is a lack of consistent measurement in the types of substances assessed; yet even when similar substances are assessed across studies, methodological differences preclude direct comparison. For example, across the five studies that included measures of alcohol use in the review by Ezard (2012), three included only measures of 'any use,' one measured 'alcohol dependence,' and one measured 'excessive use.' Additional methodological limitations include unrepresentative samples, the use of non-validated instruments, inappropriate statistical techniques, and a lack of differentiation between prevalence and incidence (Ezard, 2012; Roberts & Ezard, 2015; Weaver & Roberts, 2010). Difficulty in measurement of substance misuse in conflict settings is additionally compounded by the logistics of conducting surveys in potentially unsafe environments (Catani, Jacob, Schauer, Kohila, & Neuner, 2008; United Nations High Commissioner for Refugees and World Health Organization 2008) and a high risk for significant underreporting due to stigma or fear of losing protection by reporting use of illicit substances (e.g., legal refugee status in a resettled country or protection within a refugee camp) (Cardozo et al., 2004; Ezard, 2012).

Risk and Protective Factors

Substance misuse has been theorized to increase in conflict-affected settings because it is used as a coping mechanism for (1) distress that often occurs as a consequence of exposure to conflict, (2) adapting to new environments in difficult settings (e.g., refugee camps or low socioeconomic neighborhoods in countries of resettlement), (3) and loss of social and financial resources (Fig. 1) (Jack et al., 2014; United Nations High Commissioner for Refugees and World Health Organization 2008).

Patterns of misuse have varied across conflict settings and there is evidence of both an increase or exacerbation of use from pre-conflict to during and post-conflict periods (Ezard, 2012; Jack et al., 2014; Kozaric-Kovacic et al., 2000; Weaver & Roberts, 2010) and new cases of use among those with no previous history of substance misuse (UNODC, 2005). Moreover, increased uptake of one substance (e.g. alcohol) may be a risk factor for uptake of other substances (e.g. tobacco) (Luitel,

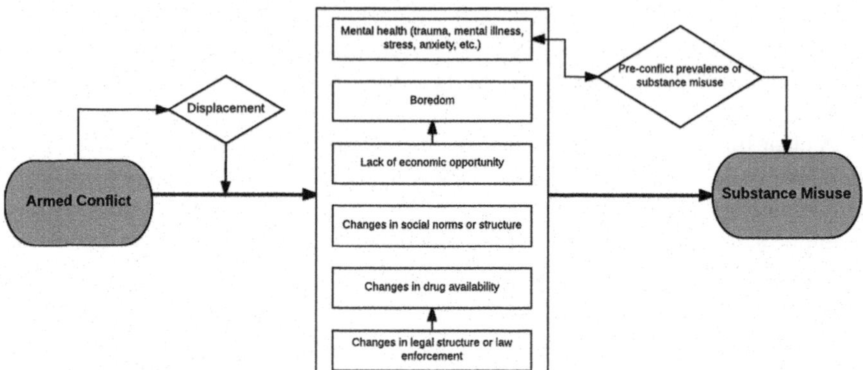

Fig. 1 Hypothesized mediators of the relationship between conflict and substance misuse. (Adapted from Jack et al., 2014)

Jordans, Murphy, Roberts, & McCambridge, 2013). Finally, access to substances may increase during conflict due to changes in the enforcement of drug policy, loss of security and increase in drug trafficking to conflict zones that are seen as emerging "open" drug markets, which may further increase prevalence (Strathdee et al., 2006). Due to the increased availability and potentially increased trafficking of substances, the types of substances used in conflict settings may differ from what is typically used in a particular country or community and also may differ from one conflict setting to the next. Examples of substance types have included both industrial, denatured alcohol not intended for consumption (Colombia), artisanal/homemade alcohol (Kenya refugee camps), opiates (Pakistan refugee camps), and benzodiazepines (Bosnia) (Ezard, 2012). Types of substances commonly used among conflict-affected populations are summarized in Table 1 (adapted from UNHCR & WHO, 2008).

Identified risk factors for substance use disorder (SUD), which is defined as substance misuse resulting in clinical and/or functional impairment (American Psychiatric Association, 2013), among conflict-affected populations have included individual characteristics (males, young adulthood, history of mental health or alcohol/substance misuse, extent of exposure to conflict stressors) and factors related to displacement (resettlement stressors) (UNODC, 2005; Weaver & Roberts, 2010). Low education, homelessness, and unemployment were also found to be associated with substance misuse among conflict-affected populations (Zafar, Brahmbhatt, Imam, ul Hassan, & Strathdee, 2003). Few studies have investigated

Table 1 Types of substances used in conflict-affected settings*

Substance type	Description
Alcohol	Sedative Most widely used substance in conflict settings Most commonly consumed as beer, wine, liquor, or home-brew Hazardous use results in impaired judgment, problems with coordination, drowsiness
Sedatives	Typically administered via pill Similar effects as alcohol Often used in conflict settings to cope with anxiety Most commonly used are benzodiazepines and barbiturates
Opioids	Sedative Associated with pain relief, euphoria High addictive potential Most commonly used are heroin, morphine, methadone, and codeine
Cannabis	Sedative and/or hallucinogenic effects Typically smoked, but sometimes ingested
Inhalants	Substances that are inhaled, typically aerosol sprays, paint thinners, and glues Sedative and/or hallucinogenic effects
Psychostimulants	Can be inhaled, injected, or ingested Common examples include cocaine, amphetamines, and khat Associated with hyperactivity, restlessness

*Table adapted from UNHCR & WHO, (2008)

protective factors for substance use, but Cardozo et al. (2004) found that increased religiosity might be associated with less misuse among conflict-affected populations in Afghanistan. Still, it is important to consider that the methodological limitations that exist for estimates of prevalence are similarly applicable to studies assessing risk and protective factors. According to Ezard (2012), the existing literature does not permit predictions with any reasonable accuracy of which conflict-affected groups may have an elevated risk for substance misuse.

Consequences of Substance Misuse in Conflict-Affected Populations

Substance misuse in any context is associated with adverse consequences, but the harm associated with misuse in conflict or post-conflict settings may be especially acute (United Nations High Commissioner for Refugees and World Health Organization 2008). Many of the world's conflicts occur in low and middle-income countries (LMIC), which are also disproportionately affected by the human immunodeficiency virus (HIV) epidemic. Since substance misuse is consistently linked to HIV incidence and disease course, it may exacerbate the burden of HIV in conflict-affected populations (Kalichman et al., 2008; Shuper et al., 2010; UNICEF, UNAIDS, & WHO, 2002; UNODC, 2012). Substance misuse in conflict settings is associated with other negative health outcomes such as injury and serious morbidity (including death) (United Nations High Commissioner for Refugees and World Health Organization 2008), co-occurring mental health problems and increased risk of suicide (Bosnar et al., 2005; Room, Babor, & Rehm, 2005; United Nations High Commissioner for Refugees and World Health Organization 2008), and social problems including domestic violence, child neglect, reduced food security and increased poverty resulting from financial resources being diverted to alcohol and other drugs (Ezard et al., 2011; United Nations High Commissioner for Refugees and World Health Organization 2008).

In short, few studies have focused on the epidemiology of substance misuse in conflict-affected populations, and these studies suffer from methodological limitations. Nevertheless, the limited available data indicates that substance misuse is likely a problem of critical public health importance. The following paragraphs discuss prevention and treatment interventions for substance misuse in conflict-affected populations.

Prevention Strategies

International guidelines recommend prevention programs as principal strategies for addressing the burden of substance-related harm in conflict-affected populations (Campello, Heikkila, & Maalouf, 2016; IASC, 2007); however, only 16 of 144 countries (9 LMIC) report provision of substance misuse prevention services for refugees and only 1/3 of conflict-affected countries allocate a portion of their budget to prevention efforts (UCDP, 2009; World Health Organization 2008, 2010).

Substance misuse prevention strategies can be categorized into interventions that aim to prevent or delay initiation of use and those that prevent development of SUD among persons currently using alcohol or drugs. Adolescence and emerging adulthood are known to be high risk developmental periods for initiation of substance misuse and onset of SUD, respectively (Schulte & Hser, 2014). Thus, it is recommended that interventions aiming to prevent or delay initiation of use be applied to youth in middle childhood or early adolescence. Similarly, it is recommended that interventions aiming to prevent transition from use to SUD target adolescents and emerging adults (Campello et al., 2016). In our searches, only 37 publications of prevention of substance misuse in conflict-affected populations were identified; furthermore, only four reported on specific prevention programs implemented in these settings. These four programs represent several different types of prevention strategies implemented in conflict-affected populations (Table 2).

Universal Prevention Strategies

Universal prevention strategies are interventions targeting an entire population regardless of risk or protective factors for individuals (Mrazek & Haggerty, 1994). In the context of substance misuse, universal interventions often aim to prevent initiation of substance use through increasing education on substance-related harms (e.g. through radio or television) or through implementation of policies intended to reduce supply or demand of alcohol and other drugs (e.g. raising the legal age for alcohol use). Substance misuse education programs can generally be described as knowledge-based (provide information about substance misuse), fear-based (use of scare tactics) or skills-based (teach self-management, social and cognitive skills) (Faggiano, Minozzi, Version, & Buscemi, 2014). Research in high-income countries (HICs) has found mixed evidence for the success of knowledge- and fear-based programs and more support for skills-based programs (Faggiano et al., 2014). In the same vein, an evaluation of a knowledge-based program conducted in post-conflict Croatia did not find positive intervention effects (Abatemarco et al., 2004).

Implementation of policies that aim to reduce availability, accessibility and affordability of alcohol and other drugs represent a universal prevention strategy that has shown promise and aligns with recommendations to minimize misuse of alcohol in refugee camps through sales restrictions (United Nations High Commissioner for Refugees 2013). However, evidence for these approaches comes primarily from HICs (Babor, 2010; Jernigan, Monteiro, Room, & Saxena, 2000; Toumbourou et al., 2007). A qualitative study exploring the perspectives of public health and policy experts revealed several challenges to implementation of

Table 2 Alcohol and substance misuse prevention interventions in conflict-affected populations

Study	Country	Sample Size	Objective	Type of Intervention	Intervention Description	Evidence
Abatemarco et al., (2004)	Croatia	1951	Delay initiation of alcohol use in 10–14 year old students	Universal prevention	Knowledge-based alcohol use education program	Cluster randomized trial displayed no intervention effects; increases in intentions to use in intervention and control group
Bolton et al., (2014)	Thailand	347	Prevent alcohol misuse in Burmese trauma survivors experiencing psychological distress	Indicated prevention	Transdiagnostic psychotherapy with brief motivational interviewing	In participants reporting harmful alcohol use at baseline, there was a decrease in alcohol use during follow-up; no difference between intervention and control group
Ezard et al., (2010)	Thailand	1256	Prevent progression from alcohol use to AUD among Burmese refugees	Indicated prevention	Screening, brief intervention and referral to treatment (SBIRT)	No outcome evaluation, but implementation was successful
Wallace & Roberts, (2014)	Post-conflict countries[a]	15	Prevention of alcohol use	Universal prevention	Alcohol control policy	Qualitative study describing challenges and opportunities for implementation; no outcome evaluation

[a]This qualitative study interviewed humanitarian actors with experience working in East Asia and Pacific, Europe and Central Asia, Latin America and the Caribbean, Middle East and North Africa, South Asia, and Sub-Saharan Africa

alcohol policy in post-conflict settings. First, policymakers and humanitarian actors often do not prioritize prevention of alcohol misuse. This may be explained by the prioritization of immediate, life-saving interventions as opposed to management of chronic diseases, such as SUD, as well as the limited available evidence on the effectiveness and implementation of SUD interventions in complex, humanitarian settings (Lai, 2014; Roberts & Ezard, 2015). Second, weak governments often lack resources and capacity to enforce alcohol control regulations. Lastly, the alcohol industry often capitalizes on the instability of post-conflict societies, identifying them as emerging markets and opportunistically colluding with policymakers to loosen regulations on marketing and distribution of alcohol (Bakke & Endal, 2010; Wallace & Roberts, 2014).

Selective Prevention Strategies

Selective interventions are prevention programs that target groups at increased risk of substance misuse (Mrazek & Haggerty, 1994). Individual risk may be based on biological, psychological or social factors. Peer-based interventions have been identified as an effective selective prevention strategy in LMICs not affected by armed conflict because of their ability to engage with high-risk individuals and transform peer influence, which is a commonly cited social risk factor for substance misuse, into a protective factor (Kasirye, 2015). This review of the literature did not identify any selective prevention strategies for substance misuse implemented or evaluated in conflict-affected populations.

Indicated Prevention Strategies

The objective of indicated prevention strategies in the context of substance misuse is not to prevent or delay initiation of use, but rather to prevent the progression to SUD in people currently using substances. Indicated interventions target individuals displaying early, but sub-threshold signs and symptoms of SUD (Mrazek & Haggerty, 1994). One example of an indicated prevention intervention is Screening, Brief Intervention and Referral to Treatment (SBIRT), which is intended to prevent SUD by exploring substance use patterns, consequences and motivations for behavior change to reduce risks (Babor et al., 2007; Ezard, Debakre, & Catillon, 2010). A pilot study assessing the feasibility of implementing SBIRT as a prevention strategy for Burmese refugees was conducted in Thailand and found that psychosocial workers were successfully trained and able to implement SBIRT into their existing services in this setting (see Case Example 1).

Case Example 1: SBIRT for Burmese Refugees in Thailand (Ezard et al., 2010)

Mae La refugee camp has been in operation along the Thai-Burma border since 1984. Alcohol is widely used by males in the camp. SBIRT was introduced to prevent alcohol use disorder (AUD) and related consequences in this high-risk group. The first element of SBIRT, screening, was accomplished using the 10-item Alcohol Use Disorders Identification Test (AUDIT), which was adapted and translated into Burmese and Sgaw Karen. Ten psychosocial workers from outpatient centers in the camp received a three-day training in brief intervention. Supervision and evaluation of trainees revealed increased competencies and confidence in providing brief intervention 1 month post-training.

In 4 months the psychosocial workers screened 1256 males between ages 15–49. One-third met criteria for high-risk use and 4% met criteria for an AUD. Among those that were high-risk, brief intervention was provided which consisted of information on alcohol-related consequences, advice on cutting down and referral to additional counseling as requested. Those meeting criteria for AUD were referred to specialized services; however very few referrals were completed. Although no outcome evaluation was conducted, investigators concluded that it was feasible to train workers in a refugee camp setting to successfully implement SBIRT for alcohol misuse. Further research is needed to identify the short- and long-term impact of SBIRT on alcohol misuse in this population.

Addressing broader mental health difficulties through integrated interventions that aim to prevent transition to SUD has also been recommended as an indicated prevention strategy (Meyer, 2013). This includes the use of non-medical strategies, such as psychological first aid, to deal with acute distress (IASC, 2007; World Health Organization and United Nations High Commissioner for Refugees 2015). Bolton et al. (2014) conducted a randomized controlled trial of transdiagnostic psychotherapy with Burmese trauma survivors in Thailand experiencing depression and/or posttraumatic stress. The intervention included brief, motivational interviewing if participants screened positive for alcohol misuse (not necessarily dependence). Participants screening positively for alcohol misuse at baseline showed decreases in alcohol misuse in both the treatment and control group, with no significant between-group differences (Bolton et al., 2014). Further studies with larger samples are needed to determine the potential for such transdiagnostic, integrated approaches to prevent SUD and related problems.

Treatment Strategies

A comprehensive search of the literature on treatment strategies for SUD amongst conflict-affected populations reveals a scarcity of published research such that only seven publications identified in the search process described treatment programs that met the eligibility criteria for this chapter. In addition, despite indications of higher rates of SUD in refugee populations and the priority placed on the problem amongst refugees themselves (Ezard, 2012; Ventevogel, 2015; Weaver & Roberts, 2010), there appears to be low service utilization rates for SUDs in primary care settings (Kane et al., 2014). Based on existing guidance, we discuss psychosocial treatments, medical management of withdrawal, and harm reduction strategies below (Meyer, 2013; IASC, 2007; United Nations High Commissioner for Refugees and World Health Organization 2008; United Nations High Commissioner for Refugees 2013; World Health Organization and United Nations High Commissioner for Refugees 2015;).

Psychosocial Treatments

Many treatment guidelines recommend delivery of psychosocial support for SUDs. Community based approaches are gaining momentum and primary care is increasingly recognized as an ideal place to identify individuals with SUD, provide brief intervention for mild to moderate cases, and refer to specialized services where indicated. An example is village-based treatment for opioid use disorders in Balkh Province, Afghanistan where a community-based psychosocial treatment delivered by trained outreach providers was implemented to overcome the problem of limited formal treatment services and resources available in the region (See Case Example 2) (How, Brian, Thirumagal, & Ayub, 2014).

Case Example 2: Opioid Treatment in Afghanistan (How et al., 2014)
A village-based treatment approach was implemented in rural Afghanistan by the Colombo Plan Drug Advisory Programme and International Narcotics and Law Enforcement Affairs, which consisted of 6 phases. The first two phases were village-based and included awareness (information sessions, community involvement) and motivation building (assessment/screening, motivational interviewing, counseling services, referrals). The next two phases were detoxification and primary treatment (psychoeducation, counseling,

(continued)

life-skills, recreational activities) at a 21-day residential treatment camp. Finally, two further village-based phases involved short- and longer-term aftercare (self-help groups, ongoing home-based counseling if needed, follow-up care and monitoring).

Over a pilot-implementation period of 12 months in 4 villages, 9000 villagers were reached through awareness sessions and 450 individuals (adults and children) with opioid dependence received motivational counseling. After-care consisted of recovery support groups, community volunteers, and local elder groups. While outcome data has not been presented, such community-based models have potential to deliver low-cost, accessible, and highly effective services in low resource settings.

In line with SBIRT described above (see Prevention Strategies), UNHCR recommends the Alcohol, Smoking and Substance Involvement Screening Test (ASSIST) – Linked Brief Intervention for Hazardous and Harmful Substance Use for those screening high on the ASSIST, an assessment tool recommended by WHO and UNHCR that screens for all substance types and assigns a risk score for each substance (Humeniuk et al., 2010; UNHCR, 2013). The ASSIST-Linked Brief Intervention is a single-session intervention of 3–15 minutes based on the FRAMES model (Feedback, Responsibility, Advice, Menu of options, Empathy and Self-efficacy) and motivational interviewing (Humeniuk et al., 2010). It involves personalized feedback, motivational techniques, providing advice, educational materials and is not designed to be a stand-alone intervention but rather an entry point to encourage engagement with more specialized services. The mhGAP humanitarian intervention guide for primary care similarly recommends brief motivational conversations, discussion of strategies to stop or reduce harmful use, psychosocial interventions (e.g. family counseling, problem-solving, cognitive behavioral therapy, motivational enhancement therapy, contingency management), and regular follow up. The DARE Network in Thailand is an example of a program offering a range of psychosocial outpatient services as well as referral to more specialized services (see Case Example 3) (DARE, 2014).

Brief Interventions have shown promise as both prevention and treatment strategies in a variety of primary care settings (Kaner et al., 2009) including those in low income countries (Pal, Yadav, Mehta, & Mohan, 2007; Simao et al., 2008; Tsai, Tsai, Lin, & Chen, 2009), and have been successfully implemented in post-conflict settings (Ezard et al., 2010). However, the efficacy of brief interventions as a treatment strategy specifically in conflict-affected populations is unknown.

Case Example 3: DARE Network Thailand (DARE, 2014)

The Drug and Alcohol Recovery and Education (DARE) Network in Thailand provides treatment (inpatient and outpatient), prevention and education programs in five of the nine refugee camps on the Thai-Burma border. The treatment programs consist of four phases: detoxification (acupuncture, massage, Burmese herbal medicine, and herbal saunas), recovery (self-care, coping, nutrition, sleep and exercise, and culturally appropriate counseling), education (addiction, HIV/AIDS and gender-based violence) and reintegration (preparing clients to return to families and the community). Relapse prevention includes follow-up workshops, individual meetings, and peer support groups with clients and families. Prevention and education initiatives include community events and campaigns, family home visits, a prevention program for teenagers, and women and men's groups (Fig. 2).

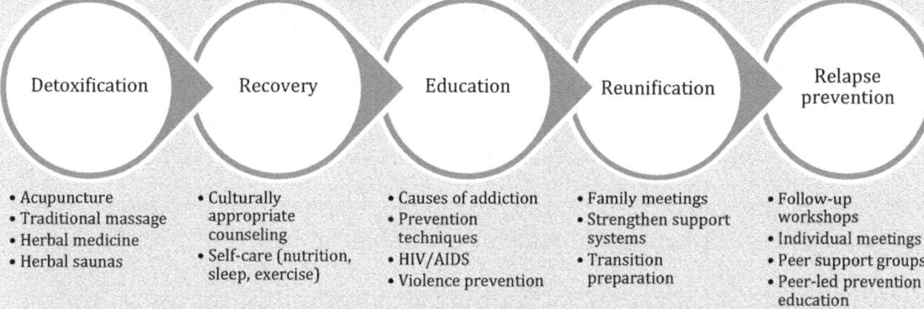

Fig. 2 Phases of DARE community based substance misuse treatment in Thailand

The Project Evaluation Report for 2014 indicates that 128 individuals participated in residential treatment, and 176 participated in non-residential treatment. Reported recovery rates at 12 months were 55% for inpatient and 69% for outpatient treatments.

Medical Management

The IASC guidelines for MHPSS in emergencies recommend that protocols are in place for medical management of withdrawal, intoxication and overdose (IASC, 2007), and WHO's and UNHCR's (2015) mhGAP provides guidance on this. It is recommended that service providers consider medication-assisted treatments (MATs) such as opioid substitution therapy (methadone, buprenorphine) or prescription of non-addictive medication alternatives (IASC, 2007).

Retention in MATs is important for longer-term improvements in substance use and other psychosocial outcomes (Ward, Hall, & Mattick, 1999). A recent systematic review investigated retention rates of participants in MATs in LMICs and found an average retention rate of 50% after 12 months (Feelmyer, Des Jarlais, Arasteh, Abdul-Quadar, & Hagan, 2014), which is similar to the benchmark for successful MATs delivered in HICs. However, evidence is needed for the effectiveness and acceptability of MATs in conflict-affected populations.

Harm Reduction

To reduce harm in the context of SUD (including increased HIV incidence, transmission of other infections, etc.), guidelines recommend community-level interventions such as provision of condoms, relocation of alcohol sale points, risk reduction information, access to safe injecting equipment, and harm-reduction awareness sessions among community leaders (IASC, 2007; United Nations High Commissioner for Refugees and World Health Organization 2008). A qualitative evaluation of a needle exchange program in Kabul indicated that beneficiaries were more likely to use clean needles for injection as compared to persons who inject drugs and do not utilize needle exchange programs (Todd et al., 2009). Respondents identified several benefits of the program including prevention of infection, provision of counseling, and motivation to seek treatment. Further qualitative and quantitative research is needed to determine the most effective ways to implement harm reduction strategies in conflict-affected populations.

Implementation Considerations

There are many challenges associated with implementing evidence-based substance misuse interventions in conflict-affected resource-limited settings, likely contributing to the overall lack of published intervention strategies. Even in settings without conflict, there are several barriers to establishing and sustaining substance misuse services, including inadequate treatment facilities, lack of trained personnel, stigma, limited transportation, and lack of political will to focus on prevention and treatment instead of persecution of illicit substance use (Odejide, 2006). In the time and aftermath of a conflict, these common barriers to the operation of substance misuse services become more pronounced as humanitarian agencies prioritize access to basic needs and emergency health care over substance misuse prevention and treatment and are operating with limited resources. Such circumstances, coupled with loss of income opportunities, displacement and additional stressors increase the risk for substance misuse and impair access to existent services (Streel & Schilperoord, 2010). For example, few refugees living in camps seek care for substance misuse in primary care despite the high prevalence of drug and alcohol-related problems (Kane et al., 2014). For highly stigmatized subgroups lack of treatment seeking may become more pronounced under conflict or high stress conditions (Mbwambo et al., 2012).

Adding to the challenge of substance misuse services are stringent laws that criminalize drug misuse, and may become more extreme following political unrest or government transitions. This can further isolate people using illicit substances and limit availability and accessibility of services (Flippovych, 2015; Todd et al., 2009). For example, following the annexation of the Crimea in 2014, the Russian government prohibited opioid substitution treatment centers from operating in these territories, which left many people in need of treatment without access to care (Flippovych, 2015). Even when substance misuse services are not forcibly shut down, their operations are often compromised during conflict (Mehic-Basara & Ceric, 2012). Furthermore, international actors and NGOs that operate in humanitarian settings have historically given low priority to provision of substance misuse services (Wallace & Roberts, 2014), which may in part be due to multilateral and humanitarian agencies' reluctance to address substance misuse because of concerns that such programs may attract negative publicity and add to stigma associated with refugees related to cultural prejudices, xenophobia and perceived threats to security and the economy.

Thus, interventions must be tailored to operate within available resources and infrastructure and to respond to unique needs of each population. In cases where services were existent before the conflict, prioritizing the restoration of such operations may be a first step in making substance misuse services available to the public (Mehic-Basara & Ceric, 2012). Where services are lacking and more expensive interventions or pharmacological treatments are not realistic, lower-resource strategies such as mutual-help groups, educational campaigns, and harm reduction interventions may be feasible alternatives (Brewer, 2010). A strategy that has been recommended for increasing access to substance misuse services among conflict-affected populations is to develop programs that concurrently address other immediate needs and are integrated within other health and community services (Todd et al., 2009; Streel & Schilperoord, 2010). However, in conflict and post-conflict settings this may be challenging given that humanitarian agencies have specific mandates for the types of services they provide, which often results in parallel systems that preclude service integration.

A promising area for integration is that of mental health and substance misuse services, both of which fall under the mandate of the health sector, but have had a tendency to be delivered in silos throughout the world. It is important that interventions address both substance misuse and the mental health problems that often co-occur with SUDs for several reasons (Ventevogel, 2015). First, integrating mental health problems into SUD services allows practitioners to address some of the known risk factors for substance misuse (e.g. psychological distress). Second, conflict-related experiences are common risk factors for both substance misuse and mental health problems. Thus, developing integrated psychosocial prevention and treatment programs for conditions that are likely to co-occur in conflict-affected populations, such as SUDs and mental health problems, may improve the efficiency and effectiveness of interventions.

Conclusions

Substance misuse is a prevalent public health problem in conflict-affected populations, yet the epidemiologic and intervention literature remains sparse. Research that is available suggests that implementation of substance misuse prevention and treatment programs are feasible, yet the effectiveness of these interventions remains unknown. Furthermore, barriers to successful implementation including inadequate human and material resources, ineffective alcohol and drug policies, and unstable health systems within which substance misuse services may be delivered remain a challenge. It is essential that public health leaders, researchers and policymakers prioritize efforts to overcome these barriers and address the potential rise in substance misuse in the aftermath of conflicts. Currently there is a dearth of high-quality epidemiological and intervention studies to guide programming and policy decisions. Furthermore, research into psychometric validation and adaptation of assessment tools is important for addressing the inconsistencies in measurement of substance misuse throughout the epidemiological and intervention literature. There is also a need to better characterize risk and protective factors for substance misuse in conflict-affected populations such that monitoring and intervention efforts may better target high-risk groups.

The existing research on prevention and treatment interventions for substance misuse rarely includes systematic, quantitative evaluations that employ rigorous methods necessary to make inferences about intervention effectiveness among conflict-affected populations. There is a need to evaluate implementation of brief interventions that are feasible in conflict-affected populations and can be integrated within existing systems of care. Additionally, evaluation of the effectiveness and implementation of interventions addressing both mental health and substance misuse is needed to determine whether an integrated intervention can improve efficiency and outcomes beyond parallel services, prevent the development of treatment 'silos' and increase cost-effectiveness of services in resource-limited settings.

Lastly, collaborative engagement in research, programming and policy development between international, national and local institutions is imperative to close these gaps in knowledge on substance misuse in conflict-affected populations (Flippovych, 2015; Todd et al., 2012; Wallace & Roberts, 2014). Only by prioritizing this issue can we make progress towards increasing accessibility to needed, evidence-based services and implement more effective alcohol and drug policies that minimize health and social harms among conflict-affected populations.

References

Abatemarco, D. J., West, B., Zec, V., Russo, A., Sosiak, P., & Mardesic, V. (2004). Project Northland in Croatia: A community-based adolescent alcohol prevention intervention. *Journal of Drug Education, 34*(2), 167–178.

American Psychiatric Association. (2013). *Diagnostic and statistical manual of mental disorders* (5th ed.). Arlington, VA: American Psychiatric Publishing.

Babor, T. F. (2010). *Alcohol: No ordinary commodity* (2nd ed.). New York, NY: Oxford University Press.

Babor, T. F., McRee, B. G., Kassebaum, P. A., Grimaldi, P. L., Ahmed, K., & Bray, J. (2007). Screening, Brief Intervention, and Referral to Treatment (SBIRT): Toward a public health approach to the management of substance abuse. *Substance Abuse, 28*(3), 7–30. https://doi.org/10.1300/J465v28n03_03

Bakke, O., & Endal, D. (2010). Vested interests in addiction research and policy alcohol policies out of context: Drinks industry supplanting government role in alcohol policies in sub-Saharan Africa. *Addiction, 105*(1), 22–28. https://doi.org/10.1111/j.1360-0443.2009.02695.x

Bolton, P., Lee, C., Haroz, E. E., Murray, L., Dorsey, S., Robinson, C., … Bass, J. (2014). A trans-diagnostic community-based mental health treatment for comorbid disorders: Development and outcomes of a randomized controlled trial among Burmese refugees in Thailand. *PLoS Medicine, 11*(11), e1001757. https://doi.org/10.1371/journal.pmed.1001757

Bosnar, A., Stemberga, V., Coldo, M., Koncar, G., Definis-Gojanovic, M., Sendula-Jengic, V., & Katic, P. (2005). Suicide and the war in Croatia. *Forensic Science International, 147*(Suppl), S13–S16.

Brewer, C. (2010). The hunting of the snark: Detecting and managing abusers of alcohol and other drugs in refugee camps – a commentary on Ezard et al., and Street & Schilperoord. *Intervention, 8*(3), 276–279.

Campello, G., Heikkila, H., & Maalouf, W. (2016). *International standards on drug use prevention*. Vienna, Austria: UNODC.

Cardozo, B. L., Bilukha, O. O., Crawford, C. A., Shaikh, I., Wolfe, M. I., Gerber, M. L., & Anderson, M. (2004). Mental health, social functioning, and disability in postwar Afghanistan. *JAMA, 292*(5), 575–584. https://doi.org/10.1001/jama.292.5.575

Catani, C., Jacob, N., Schauer, E., Kohila, M., & Neuner, F. (2008). Family violence, war, and natural disasters: A study of the effect of extreme stress on children's mental health in Sri Lanka. *BMC Psychiatry, 8*(1), 33. https://doi.org/10.1186/1471-244X-8-33

DARE. (2014). *Project Evaluation Report*, 2014. Retrieved from: http://www.darenetwork.com/images/documents/2014annualreport.pdf

Ezard, N. (2012). Substance use among populations displaced by conflict: A literature review. *Disasters, 36*(3), 533–557.

Ezard, N., Debakre, A., & Catillon, R. (2010). Screening and brief intervention for high-risk alcohol use in Mae La refugee camp, Thailand: A pilot project on the feasibility of training and implementation. *Intervention, 8*(3), 223.

Ezard, N., Oppenheimer, E., Burton, A., Schilperoord, M., MacDonald, D., Adelekan, M., … van Ommeren, M. (2011). Six rapid assessments of alcohol and other substance use in populations displaced by conflict. *Conflict and Health, 5*(1) 1–15.

Faggiano, F., Minozzi, S., Versino, E., & Buscemi, D. (2014). Universal school-based prevention for illicit drug use. *The Cochrane Database of Systematic Reviews, 12*, CD003020. https://doi.org/10.1002/14651858.CD003020.pub3

Feelmyer, J., Des Jarlais, D., Arasteh, K., Abdul-Quadar, A. S., & Hagan, H. (2014). Retention of participants in medication-assisted programs in low- and middle-income countries: An international systematic review. *Addiction, 109*(1), 20–32.

Flippovych, S. (2015). Impact of armed conflicts and warfare on opioid substitution treatment in Ukraine: Responding to emergency needs. *International Journal of Drug Policy, 26*(1), 3–5.

How, T. B., Brian, M., Thirumagal, V., & Ayub, M. (2014). Development of a village based treatment model for Afghanistan. *International Journal of Prevention and Treatment of Substance Use Disorders, 1*(2), 28–37.

Humeniuk, R. E., Henry-Edwards, S., Ali, R. L., Poznyak, V., & Monteiro, M. (2010). *The ASSIST-linked brief intervention for hazardous and harmful substance use: Manual for use in primary care*. Geneva, Switzerland: World Health Organization.

IASC. (2007). *IASC guidelines on mental health and psychosocial support in emergency settings*. Geneva, Switzerland: Inter-Agency Standing Committee.

Jack, H., Masterson, A. R., & Khoshnood, K. (2014). Violent conflict and opiate use in low and middle-income countries: A systematic review. *International Journal of Drug Policy, 25*(2), 196–203. https://doi.org/10.1016/j.drugpo.2013.11.003

Jernigan, D. H., Monteiro, M., Room, R., & Saxena, S. (2000). Towards a global alcohol policy: Alcohol, public health and the role of WHO. *Bulletin of the World Health Organization, 78*(4), 491–499.

Kalichman, S. C., Simbayi, L. C., Vermaak, R., Cain, D., Smith, G., Mthebu, J., & Jooste, S. (2008). Randomized trial of a community-based alcohol-related HIV risk-reduction intervention for men and women in Cape Town South Africa. *Annals of Behavioral Medicine, 36*(3), 270–279. https://doi.org/10.1007/s12160-008-9067-2

Kane, J. C., Ventevogel, P., Spiegel, P., Bass, J. K., van Ommeren, M., & Tol, W. A. (2014). Mental, neurological, and substance use problems among refugees in primary health care: Analysis of the Health Information System in 90 refugee camps. *BMC Medicine, 12*(228), 1–11.

Kaner, E., Bland, M., Cassidy, P., Coulton, S., Deluca, P., Drummond, C., … Newbury-Birch, D. (2009). Screening and brief interventions for hazardous and harmful alcohol use in primary care: A cluster randomised controlled trial protocol. *BMC Public Health, 9*(287). https://doi.org/10.1186/1471-2458-9-287

Kasirye, R. (2015). Efficacy of a peer interactive youth-led drug prevention programme: A UYDEL-UNODC project. *International Journal of Prevention and Treatment of Substance Use Disorders, 1*(3–4), 69–78.

Kozaric-Kovacic, D., Ljubin, T., & Grappe, M. (2000). Comorbidity of posttraumatic stress disorder and alcohol dependence in displaced persons. *Croatian Medical Journal, 41*(2), 173–178.

Lai, L. (2014). Treating substance abuse as a consequence of conflict and displacement: A call for a more inclusive global mental health. *Medicine, Conflict and Survival, 30*(3), 182–189. https://doi.org/10.1080/13623699.2014.917356

Luitel, N. P., Jordans, M., Murphy, A., Roberts, B., & McCambridge, J. (2013). Prevalence and patterns of hazardous and harmful alcohol consumption assessed using the AUDIT among Bhutanese refugees in Nepal. *Alcohol and Alcoholism, 48*(3), 349–355. https://doi.org/10.1093/alcalc/agt009

Massey, Z., Chartier, K. G., Stebbins, M. B., Canetti, D., Hobfoll, S. E., Hall, B. J., & Shuval, K. (2015). Explaining the frequency of alcohol consumption in a conflict zone: Jews and Palestinians in Israel. *Addictive Behaviors, 46*, 31–38. https://doi.org/10.1016/j.addbeh.2015.02.003

Mbwambo, J., McCurdy, S. A., Myers, B., Lambdin, B., Kilonzo, G. P., & Kaduri, P. (2012). Drug trafficking, use, and HIV risk: The need for comprehensive interventions. *SAHARA: Journal of Social Aspects of HIV/AIDS, 9*(3), 154–159.

Mehic-Basara, N., & Ceric, I. (2012). Treatment of addicts in Bosnia and Herzegovina – constraints and opportunities. *Psychiatria Danubina, 24*(Suppl 3), 392–397.

Meyer, S. (2013). *UNHCR's mental health and psychosocial support for persons of concern*. Geneva, Switzerland: UNHCR.

Mrazek, P., & Haggerty, R. (1994). *Reducing risks for mental disorders: Frontiers for preventive intervention research (Appendix A)*. Washington, DC: National Academy Press.

Odejide, A. O. (2006). Status of drug use/abuse in Africa: A review. *International Journal of Mental Health and Addiction, 4*(2), 87–102.

Pal, H. R., Yadav, D., Mehta, S., & Mohan, I. (2007). A comparison of brief intervention versus simple advice for alcohol use disorders in a North India community-based sample followed for 3 months. *Alcohol and Alcoholism, 42*(4), 328–332. https://doi.org/10.1093/alcalc/agm009

Puertas, G., Rios, C., & Valle, H. (2006). The prevalence of common mental disorders in urban slums with displaced persons in Colombia. *Revista Panamericana de Salud Publica/Pan American Journal of Public Health, 20*(5), 324–330.

Roberts, B., & Ezard, N. (2015). Why are we not doing more for alcohol use disorder among conflict-affected populations? *Addiction, 110*(6), 889–890.

Roberts, B., Murphy, A., Chikovani, I., Makhashvili, N., Patel, V., & McKee, M. (2014). Individual and community level risk-factors for alcohol use disorder among conflict-affected persons in Georgia. *PLoS One, 9*(5), e98299. https://doi.org/10.1371/journal.pone.0098299

Room, R., Babor, T., & Rehm, J. (2005). Alcohol and public health. *The Lancet, 365*(9458), 519–530. https://doi.org/10.1016/S0140-6736(05)17870-2

Schulte, M. T., & Hser, Y. I. (2014). Substance use and associated health conditions throughout the lifespan. *Public Health Reviews, 35*(2), 1–23.

Shuper, P. A., Neuman, M., Kanteres, F., Baliunas, D., Joharchi, N., & Rehm, J. (2010). Causal considerations on alcohol and HIV/AIDS – a systematic review. *Alcohol and Alcoholism, 45*(2), 159–166. https://doi.org/10.1093/alcalc/agp091

Simao, M. O., Kerr-Correa, F., Smaira, S. I., Trinca, L. A., Floripes, T. M., Dalben, I., ... Tucci, A. M. (2008). Prevention of "risky" drinking among students at a Brazilian university. *Alcohol and Alcoholism, 43*(4), 470–476. https://doi.org/10.1093/alcalc/agn019

Strathdee, S. A., Stachowiak, J. A., Todd, C. S., Al-Delaimy, W. K., Wiebel, W., Hankins, C., & Patterson, T. L. (2006). Complex emergencies, HIV, and substance use: No "big easy" solution. *Substance Use & Misuse, 41*(10–12), 1637–1651. https://doi.org/10.1080/10826080600848116

Streel, E., & Schilperoord, M. (2010). Perspectives on alcohol and substance abuse in refugee settings: Lessons from the field. *Intervention, 8*(3), 268–275.

Todd, C. S., MacDonald, D., Khoshnood, K., Mansoor, G. F., Eggerman, M., & Panter-Brick, C. (2012). Opiate use, treatment, and harm reduction in Afghanistan: Recent changes and future directions. *International Journal of Drug Policy, 23*(5), 341–345. https://doi.org/10.1016/j.drugpo.2012.05.004

Todd, C. S., Stibich, M. A., Stanekzai, M. R., Rasuli, M. Z., Bayan, S., Wardak, S. R., & Strathdee, S. A. (2009). A qualitative assessment of injection drug use and harm reduction programmes in Kabul, Afghanistan: 2006–2007. *International Journal of Drug Policy, 20*(2), 111–120.

Toumbourou, J. W., Stockwell, T., Neighbors, C., Marlatt, G. A., Sturge, J., & Rehm, J. (2007). Interventions to reduce harm associated with adolescent substance use. *Lancet, 369*(9570), 1391–1401. https://doi.org/10.1016/S0140-6736(07)60369-9

Tsai, Y. F., Tsai, M. C., Lin, Y. P., & Chen, C. Y. (2009). Brief intervention for problem drinkers in a Chinese population: A randomized controlled trial in a hospital setting. *Alcoholism: Clinical and Experimental Research, 33*(1), 95–101. https://doi.org/10.1111/j.1530-0277.2008.00815.x

UCDP. (2009). UCDP Database Categorical Variables 1989–2008. In U. University (Ed.). http://www.ucdp.uu.se: Uppsala Conflict Data Program.

UNICEF, UNAIDS, & WHO. (2002). *Young people and HIV/AIDS: Opportunity in crisis*. Retrieved from https://www.unicef.org/publications/files/pub_youngpeople_hivaids_en.pdf

United Nations High Commissioner for Refugees. (2013). *Operational guidance mental health and psychosocial support programming for refugee operations*. Retrieved from http://www.unhcr.org/525f94479.pdf

United Nations High Commissioner for Refugees, & World Health Organization (2008). *Rapid assessment of alcohol and other substance use in conflict-affected and displaced populations: A field guide*. Retrieved from http://www.who.int/mental_health/emergencies/unhcr_alc_rapid_assessment.pdf?ua=1

UNODC. (2003). *Afghanistan community drug profile #5: An assessment of problem drug use in Kabul City*. Retrieved from http://www.unodc.org/pdf/afg/report_2003-07-31_1.pdf

UNODC. (2005). *Afghanistan drug use survey* 2005. Retrieved from http://www.unodc.org/pdf/afg/2005AfghanistanDrugUseSurvey.pdf

UNODC. (2012). *World drug report 2012*. New York, NY: United Nations.

Ventevogel, P. (2015). The effects of war: Local views and priorities concerning psychosocial and mental health problems as a result of collective violence in Burundi. *Intervention, 13*(3), 216–234.

Wallace, K., & Roberts, B. (2014). An exploration of the alcohol policy environment in post-conflict countries. *Alcohol and Alcoholism, 49*(3), 356–362. https://doi.org/10.1093/alcalc/agt142

Ward, J., Hall, W., & Mattick, R. P. (1999). Role of maintenance treatment in opioid dependence. *Lancet, 353*(9148), 221–226. https://doi.org/10.1016/S0140-6736(98)05356-2

Weaver, H., & Roberts, B. (2010). Drinking and displacement: A systematic review of the influence of forced displacement on harmful alcohol use. *Substance Use & Misuse, 45*(13), 2340–2355.

Westermeyer, J. (1982). *Poppies, pipes and people: Opium and its use in Laos*. Berkeley, CA/Los Angeles, CA/London: University of California Press.

World Health Organization. (2006). *Lexicon of alcohol and drug terms*. Geneva, Switzerland: World Health Organization.

World Health Organization. (2008). Prevention programmes for special populations: Data by country. In World Health Organization (Ed.), Global Health Observatory data repository. Geneva, Switzerland: World Health Organization.

World Health Organization. (2010). *Atlas on substance use (2010): Resources for the prevention and treatment of substance use disorders*. Geneva, Switzerland: World Health Organization.

World Health Organization, & United Nations High Commissioner for Refugees. (2015). *mhGAP humanitarian intervention guide (mhGAP-HIG): Clinical management of mental, neurological and substance use conditions in humanitarian emergencies*. Geneva, Switzerland: World Health Organization.

Zafar, T., Brahmbhatt, H., Imam, G., ul Hassan, S., & Strathdee, S. A. (2003). HIV knowledge and risk behaviors among Pakistani and Afghani drug users in Quetta, Pakistan. *Journal of Acquired Immune Deficiency Syndromes, 32*(4), 394–398.

M. Claire Greene, MPH is a Ph.D. candidate in the Drug Dependence Epidemiology Training Program at Johns Hopkins Bloomberg School of Public Health. Her research focuses on the epidemiology, prevention and treatment of substance misuse and co-occurring violence and mental health problems, particularly in humanitarian settings and conflict-affected populations.

Jeremy C. Kane, Ph.D., MPH is Assistant Scientist in the Applied Mental Health Research Group, Department of Mental Health at Johns Hopkins Bloomberg School of Public Health. He is a psychiatric epidemiologist and his research investigates the impacts of culture and migration on substance and alcohol use patterns and how these relationships are related to experienced trauma and co-occurring mental health problems. His work concentrates on these issues both globally among HIV and trauma-affected populations in low- and middle-income countries as well as among refugee and immigrant populations living in the United States.

Noa Krawczyk, is a Ph.D. student in the Department of Mental Health and a trainee of the Drug Dependence Epidemiology Training Program at Johns Hopkins Bloomberg School of Public Health. Her research interests center on evaluating access to and quality of drug and alcohol treatment services and understanding barriers to evidence-based care.

Felicity Brown, Ph.D., is clinical psychologist and researcher at War Child in the Netherlands. Her research primarily focuses on the development and evaluation of evidence-based psychological interventions for individuals and families exposed to armed conflict and other adversity, with particular interests in the training of non-specialists to deliver interventions in low resource settings, cultural adaptations, and the role of the family environment in child outcomes.

Laura Murray, Ph.D, is a Licensed Clinical Psychologist and Associate Scientist in the Department of Mental Health at the Johns Hopkins Bloomberg School of Public Health. She conducts research on the effectiveness of mental and behavioral health treatments for children and adults in low and middle income countries, how to train lay providers, and how to implement and sustain evidence-based approaches in lower resource settings.

Kaveh Khoshnood is an Associate Professor at the Yale School of Public Health. He is trained as an infectious disease epidemiologist and has more than two decades of domestic and international experience in HIV prevention research among drug users and other at-risk populations, including its ethical aspects. Dr. Khoshnood is the principal investigator of a study of "Rapid Assessment and Response to Substance Use and Risk of HIV and other Blood-borne Infections among Lebanese nationals and Displaced Populations in Lebanon".

Wietse A. Tol, Ph.D. is Associate Professor at the Department of Mental Health, Johns Hopkins Bloomberg School of Public Health and Program Director of the Peter C. Alderman Foundation. His research and practice focus on integrated interventions that promote mental health and prevent mental ill health in populations living in situations of severe adversity, and the interplay between research, policy, and practice in this field.

Trauma Systems Therapy for Refugee Children and Families

Molly A. Benson, Saida M. Abdi, Alisa B. Miller, and B. Heidi Ellis

Abstract Trauma Systems Therapy for Refugees (TST-R) is an innovative, trauma-informed multi-tiered approach to mental health prevention and intervention with refugee children and their families. TST-R was developed as an adaptation of Trauma Systems Therapy (TST), which is an organizational and clinical model that focuses on both a child's dysregulation and the social environmental context that may be contributing to ongoing symptoms in the aftermath of trauma. TST-R adaptations address multiple barriers to care for refugees and their families through innovative mental health service delivery including multi-tiered approaches to community engagement and stigma reduction, embedding of services in the school setting, partnership building, and the integration of cultural brokering throughout all tiers of intervention to provide cultural knowledge, engagement, and attention to the primacy of resettlement stressors. TST-R has been shown to be effective in engaging refugee youth in services and reducing symptoms of PTSD and depression.

Keywords Refugee · Children and adolescents · Trauma · Cultural brokering · Trauma systems therapy

Background

In recent years the world has witnessed a growing refugee epidemic, with approximately 65 million people forcibly displaced from their homes by the end of 2015 (United States High Commissioner for Refugees (UNHCR), 2016). In 2016, the United States resettled 84,995 refugees while other nations received millions of

M. A. Benson (✉) · A. B. Miller · B. Heidi Ellis
Department of Psychiatry, Boston Children's Hospital/Harvard Medical School, Boston, MA, USA
e-mail: molly.benson@childrens.harvard.edu; Alisa.Miller@childrens.harvard.edu; Heidi.Ellis@childrens.harvard.edu

S. M. Abdi
Boston Children's Hospital, Boston, MA, USA
e-mail: Saida.Abdi@childrens.harvard.edu

N. Morina, A. Nickerson (eds.), *Mental Health of Refugee and Conflict-Affected Populations*, https://doi.org/10.1007/978-3-319-97046-2_12

refugees and displaced persons fleeing across their borders or seeking refuge upon their soil (Bureau of Population, Refugees, & Migration, 2017; UNHCR, 2016). Refugees and displaced persons are seeking refuge from multiple conflicts worldwide and related exposure to violence, terrorism, torture, and loss of resources. Of those displaced, approximately 21.3 million are considered refugees and over half of these refugees are under the age of 18 years old (UNHCR, 2016). The number of new asylum applications submitted by unaccompanied or separated children worldwide also increased significantly from 34,300 in 2014 to 98,400 in 2015 (UNHCR, 2016). The mounting impact of conflict and displacement on young people and their caregivers calls for increased innovation and responsiveness to meet this population's health and mental health needs.

Trauma Exposure and Mental Health Needs Among Refugees

Throughout their journeys, refugee children and their families are often exposed to traumatic events such as direct and indirect acts of violence, physical and sexual abuse, torture, physical injury, loss and family separation, exposure to extreme living conditions, malnutrition, and lack of access to basic resources (Fazel & Stein, 2002; Reed, Fazel, Jones, Panter-Brick, & Stein, 2012). Refugees also demonstrate exceptional resilience, as evidenced by their survival of extreme circumstances and efforts to seek relative safety in a new country (Betancourt & Khan, 2008). Refugee children are at risk, however, for short and long-term health and mental health difficulties including posttraumatic stress disorder (PTSD), depression, anxiety, attention, and behavioral problems (Bogic, Njoku, & Priebe, 2015; Fazel & Stein, 2002; Reed et al., 2012). Further, while heightened exposure to violence and trauma can increase the risk of these symptoms, studies suggest that other factors in their social environment may exacerbate or ameliorate these symptoms over time (Reed et al., 2012; Sundquist, Bayard-Burfield, Johansson, & Johansson, 2000). The refugee experience is defined by disruptions in the social-ecological environment of children during the course of their development and throughout their pre-migration, flight, and resettlement journey. Research suggests that the long-term impact of trauma exposure can be related to multiple factors including parental adjustment, child temperament, and other social environmental factors such as financial strain, lack of social support, discrimination, family conflict, and reminders of trauma (Brewin, Andrews, & Valentine, 2000; Catani, Jacob, Schauer, Kohila, & Neuner, 2008; Khawaja, White, Schweitzer, & Greenslade, 2008; Sundquist et al., 2000). Upon resettlement, social environmental stressors associated with resettlement, acculturation, and social isolation may also be important factors to consider in the adjustment of youth. Therefore, even once families are resettled in new communities, they remain at risk not only of exposure to new trauma such as community or domestic violence, but also to the ongoing stressors associated with the refugee and resettlement experience.

Innovations in Addressing Barriers to Care with Refugee Families and Children

Despite the potentially high need for psychosocial support among some refugee children and their families, refugee and immigrant youth are grossly underserved by mental health services (Ellis et al., 2010; Huang, Yu, & Ledsky, 2006; Munroe-Blum, Boyle, Offord, & Kates, 1989). Multiple barriers have been identified for refugee families and children in seeking assistance/care including difficulty in accessing services (e.g., transportation, health insurance), a paucity of available linguistically and culturally sensitive care, distrust of authorities and/or systems, stigma, differing cultural models of "mental health" and help seeking, and other priority needs (e.g., financial assistance, food insecurity) (Ellis, Miller, Baldwin, & Abdi, 2011; Kirmayer et al., 2011; Watters, 2001; Wong et al., 2006). Effective engagement of refugee children and families in mental health services thus requires innovations in where and in what manner mental health services are delivered. Innovations in mental health care of refugee children and their families include embedding comprehensive services into community and school settings, integrating cultural values and understandings into appropriate evidence-based practices, and building cultural knowledge and capacity within the larger workforce by both training providers in the needs of refugees as well as building capacity among refugees themselves to participate in providing mental health care (American Psychological Association (APA), 2010; Ellis et al., 2011; Lustig et al., 2004).

Trauma Systems Therapy for Refugees (TST-R) is a model of care that explicitly integrates these innovations, and has demonstrated success in engaging and treating young refugees. Ellis et al. (2011) initially developed the approach to specifically address a key problem they identified through their clinical experience and research with Somali refugee youth: Although a majority of these youth were exposed to high levels of trauma and many reported significant mental health symptoms, very few were receiving mental health care (Ellis, MacDonald, Lincoln, & Cabral, 2008). Parents and children both described a heavy stigma associated with "mental health" and traditional therapy services. Rather than seeking Western mental health treatment, most families sought help through traditional community supports such as family members and religious leaders (Ellis et al., 2010). In addition, both parents and adolescents identified schools as a trusted service system that could be turned to in times of need.

In this chapter, we describe the model and the ways in which it addresses critical barriers to engagement, and integrates evidenced-based trauma-informed care with an understanding of the specific socio-contextual needs and experiences of refugee youth and families.

Trauma Systems Therapy for Refugees

TST-R is an adaptation of Trauma Systems Therapy (TST) (Saxe, Ellis, & Kaplow, 2006; Saxe, Ellis, & Brown, 2015). TST is both an organizational model that guides the collaboration of care providers within service delivery systems to provide integrated treatment to traumatized children, as well as a clinical model that explicitly focuses on trauma-related emotional dysregulation. TST addresses a child's "trauma system" based on the theory that children are impacted by both the emotional and neurobiological sequelae of trauma, as well as the stressors or reminders in their environment that can contribute to the exacerbation or maintenance of symptoms in the aftermath of traumatic events. TST emphasizes the importance of targeting both aspects of the trauma system through phased-based clinical intervention. In earlier phases of treatment where the child may demonstrate higher levels of dysregulation and where the social environment is less stable, more intensive, community-based care that focuses on safety and stabilization of a child's environment is indicated. As a child progresses through the phases of treatment and their regulation and environment are correspondingly more stable, skill-building and trauma processing may be indicated.

TST as an organizational model seeks to provide integrated care. Organizational planning is a critical component of TST. At the inception of a TST/TST-R program, an organizational plan is developed that involves building partnerships across multiple disciplines and cultural backgrounds in order to provide the various levels and types of care needed across the different phases of treatment. This planning phase also includes a mapping of available resources, potential partners and strategies to identify potential funding/reimbursement mechanisms. It is a fundamental tenet of TST that a "formalized and well implemented" organizational plan that is endorsed by agency leaders is necessary to sufficiently support TST programs and team members (Saxe et al., 2015).

Initial trials of TST suggest that it is well tolerated and provide evidence that it significantly reduced PTSD symptoms, hospitalization rates, utilization of physical restraints, and significantly improved children's capacity to regulate their emotions and behaviors (Brown, McCauley, Navalta, & Saxe, 2013; Saxe, Ellis, Fogler, Hansen, & Sorkin, 2005). Saxe et al. (2005) reported small to medium effect sizes (Cohen's d = .18–.37) related to changes in PTSD symptoms, emotional and behavioral regulation, and the stability of the social environment. Since its development, TST has been disseminated and adapted for a variety of settings including outpatient mental health services, psychiatric residential settings, child welfare settings, and in dual treatment settings for trauma and substance abuse (Brown et al., 2013; Hidalgo, Maravić, Milet, & Beck, 2016). TST has demonstrated clinical and cost effectiveness (Ellis et al., 2011) as well as high levels of treatment retention (Saxe, Ellis, Fogler, & Navalta, 2012). In addition, implementing TST with fidelity in a Child Welfare system was associated with improvements in child well-being (functioning, emotional regulation, and behavioral regulation) and greater placement stability as indicated by the number of care placements a child received while in foster care (Moore et al., 2016).

Although the theoretical framework of TST is well-suited to address the mental health needs of refugee children, adaptation of this model was necessary to address specific barriers to care in this population. Community engagement and stigma reduction were identified as essential components of developing a sustainable and acceptable intervention for resettled refugee community members. In addition, services were located within the schools to reduce barriers to accessing care and provide a more culturally acceptable context for help seeking. Within the schools, preventative groups offered to resettled refugee youth were an additional adaptation that provided an opportunity to further reduce stigma, engage youth and their families in services, and support the unique needs of refugee youth in the school setting. Lastly, the integration of cultural brokering was identified as an important adaptation to providing culturally sensitive services and building capacity among community members. The resulting model is a multi-tiered school-based intervention that integrates a public health approach to community engagement and stigma reduction with increasing levels of support at the higher tiers, with the highest being home-based TST safety-focused services (see Fig. 1; Model of Trauma Systems Therapy for Refugees). Across the four tiers of services, cultural brokers partner with mental health providers to deliver the intervention.

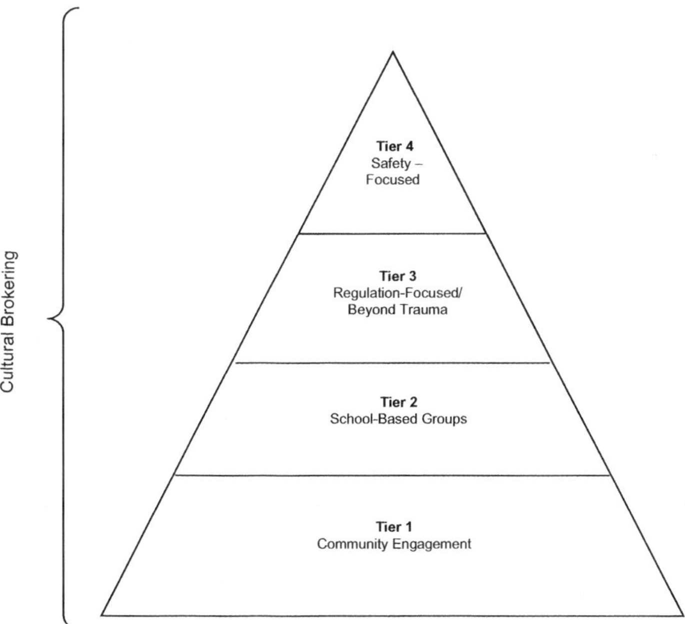

Fig. 1 Trauma Systems Therapy for Refugees (TST-R) Multi-tiered Prevention and Intervention Model

Cultural Brokering

According to Kaczorowski et al. (2011), delivering clinical services to refugees necessitates that clinicians develop cultural awareness and knowledge, as well as unique therapeutic skills. Moreover, research has shown that lack of cultural competence in the care system can be an important barrier to treatment engagement and adherence leading to negative outcomes (Barr, 2014; Carpenter-Song, Whitley, Lawson, Quimby, & Drake, 2011; Dixon et al., 2011). Traditionally, interpreters have been used to address cultural and linguistic barriers in health care, but creating culturally accessible care requires moving beyond linguistic interpretation. Culturally sensitive care must address the community/client's distrust of mental health systems of care, stigma around mental illness, and providers' lack of cultural knowledge so that they can tailor treatment approaches to a patient's cultural understanding of the illness and treatment. To deliver mental health care that is culturally sensitive, providers must not only learn about the culture of patient populations and their health seeking practices, but providers and institutions must also conduct a self-examination to investigate how their assumptions and beliefs affect their interactions with and service provision to clients from different backgrounds.

One key innovation of TST-R is the integration of the role of a cultural broker into community engagement and clinical service delivery activities. Cultural brokering is defined as "the act of bridging, linking, or mediating between groups or persons of differing cultural backgrounds" (Goode, Sockalingam, & Snyder, 2004; Jezewski, 1990). This model provides an innovative approach to mental health care provision because cultural brokers work closely with both the provider/care system and the client with the purpose of facilitating communication, enhancing provider knowledge of patient's culture and understanding of the illness, and improving the patient's understanding of the health care system and the proposed treatment. Cultural brokers, therefore, are not a conduit of information between the provider and the patient but connectors whose role is to create a trusting relationship and a common purpose. Cultural brokering in TST-R incorporates both cultural competency, which focuses on increasing provider cultural awareness and knowledge (Kohn-Wood & Hooper, 2014), and cultural humility, a practice that encourages providers to practice critical self-awareness, self-evaluation, mutual respect, and to "say that they do not know when they do not know" in cross-cultural interactions (Tervalon & Murray-Garcia, 1998, p. 119). Ultimately, adding cultural brokering to mental health services creates a more culturally responsive service system, a more critically self-aware mental health workforce, and engaged, educated and empowered clients.

TST-R cultural brokers help to address key identified barriers such as stigma and resettlement stressors while also providing cultural and linguistic support to both clients and providers. Cultural brokers are integrated into all phases of the intervention and are considered integral members of the clinical team. The cultural broker holds cultural and system of care knowledge and plays a key role in the engagement of both community and individual clients, as well as the implementation of the intervention and building of cultural competency of providers. Cultural brokers are typically identified through working with community leaders and are often members of the community who already formally or informally act as helpers and liaisons within their culture.

Description of TST-R Model/Services

Tier 1: Community Engagement

The first tier of intervention in TST-R is community engagement. Community engagement focuses on reducing stigma and increasing education related to mental health needs and services. The development of TST-R was driven by principles of Community-Based Participatory Research (CBPR), which emphasizes the importance of developing equal partnerships between academics and community members; the resulting research or, in this case, intervention is expected to be more culturally-informed and responsive to community-identified needs, and to build knowledge and capacity among both providers and community partners. An active community advisory board guided the initial implementation and subsequent adaptations of TST-R. The work with the advisory board established the importance of building strong community partnerships within each new community participating in subsequent implementations of the TST-R model. These community partnerships play a key role in community engagement and stigma reduction. Cultural brokers also play a central role in community engagement and education.

Tier 1 activities focus on creating an open and active dialogue with refugee community members. Community partners, cultural brokers, and/or staff members involved in TST-R services typically seek opportunities to participate in existing community activities (e.g., cultural fairs or education sessions), offer small groups for discussion in informal or formal settings, and engage parents through school-based activities (e.g., parent nights). Within these settings, discussions focus on understanding the concerns that refugee parents and community members have about their children's development in their resettlement communities, stressors facing families, issues related to navigating the school systems and other services, and goals that community members have for their young people. Cultural brokers and clinical staff engage community members in this dialogue, offer resources or education as appropriate, and integrate into the discussion topics related to wellness, mental health, and the potential benefits of a program like TST-R. These discussions serve as a platform for the community to learn about the intervention and for the clinical team to learn about the community, address concerns, and integrate community input in the implementation. Throughout Tier 1 activities, care is taken to use language that is in line with the community's cultural understanding of the issues. For example, given the stigma and different cultural concepts surrounding mental health, descriptive terms that are consistent with community members' concerns and goals for their children (e.g., reducing stress, improving behavior, improving academic success, supporting families) are typically integrated into the discussion in lieu of western terms such as "mental health", "depression", or "PTSD."

Community engagement also involves building partnerships and training service providers who work with refugees, particularly those in school and health/mental health systems.

Awareness of key refugee serving agencies, local culturally specific organizations, mental health and health providers, and school administration is an important aspect of organizational planning when developing a TST-R program. Identifying cultural brokers and other staff willing to engage flexibly with refugee communities is also essential. These partnerships are key to successful implementation of TST-R because refugees have a myriad of needs and face multiple barriers which one single agency cannot address. A more integrated service system and a workforce that is knowledgeable about the unique experiences and needs of refugees can mitigate key barriers such as lack of linguistic and cultural support and refugees' lack of familiarity with Western service systems.

Tier 2: School-Based Groups

Based on feedback from community partners that acculturative stress was a significant concern, and that relationships between providers and families were best built in the context of non-stigmatized supportive services, a second tier of group-based services was included in TST-R. The groups offer a non-stigmatizing way to provide support to a broader range of refugee youth entering school systems. The goals of the groups are to support the acculturation of refugee children, while simultaneously providing them with social and emotion regulation skill building. The groups function as both a preventative intervention and an opportunity for screening those with mental health needs. TST-R cultural brokers act as co-leaders for the students in groups, but also as a connection to parents. Cultural brokers can play an important role in answering parents' questions about the groups, maintaining ongoing contact, and building connections and trust with families.

The group curriculum is a 12-session manualized protocol that was originally developed for Somali middle school age students and co-led by a Somali cultural broker and school-based clinician (Abdi & Nisewaner, 2009; Nisewaner & Abdi, 2010). The curriculum is designed to be fun, interactive and activity-based. Given that boys and girls may have different experiences of the acculturation process and varying levels of comfort discussing their experience with children of the opposite gender due to their developmental stage or cultural expectations, groups are typically gender specific. When possible, they are offered to an entire class of incoming refugee students (e.g., 7th grade boys). In each session, students engage in a warm-up activity, group activity focused on a specific topic, discussion about this topic and how it relates to culture and the youth's experiences, and a cool-down activity. The topics are not trauma specific, but instead focus on group cohesion and skill building. The topics include, but are not limited to verbal and nonverbal communication, similarities and differences, positive peer interactions, emotional identification and regulation skills, and conflict resolution. Special attention is paid to issues that immigrant and refugee youth struggle with, such as the process of navigating two or more cultures, dealing with peer conflict, effective communication skills and understanding emotions, and developing coping skills to manage daily stressors across different social environments. To date, the group curriculum has been implemented in multiple sites within the United States (U.S.) with Somali youth, and adapted and piloted with Bhutanese students and multi-cultural groups. Subsequent adaptations of the group manual have also included options for extending activities for younger and older age ranges.

Groups also serve as a means to connect youth who might need a higher level of care to clinical services in a culturally and linguistically appropriate manner. As children participate in the groups, group leaders develop relationships and build trust with parents and teachers by participating in school meetings with parents, connecting the family to additional services such as housing agencies or after school programs, facilitating parent/teacher communication and helping parents better understand how the American school system works. TST-R staff members, especially the cultural broker, thus become a bridge between school and refugee families whose children participate in the program. As a result, when children are identified as needing therapeutic mental health services, parents are already familiar with and may trust the program; this existing relationship often facilitates engaging parents in discussion around referral to TST-R individual therapy services.

Tiers 3 and 4: TST Clinical Services

While for many refugee students group work provides sufficient support, students with more specific trauma-related mental health problems may require more focused treatment. Within a TST-R program, these students may be identified through the groups or other sources of referral (e.g., teachers, parents); they are then referred to Tiers 3 and/or 4 of the program and receive TST therapeutic clinical services. TST clinical services can include: (1) skill-based therapy, (2) home-based care, (3) psychopharmacology, and (4) advocacy (Saxe et al., 2015). Students who present with dangerous emotions or behaviors (e.g., suicidality, physical aggression, poor judgment resulting in dangerous activities) and/or who live in social environments that are threatening (e.g., gang violence in neighborhood, domestic violence in the home) receive "safety-focused treatment", or Tier 4. These services are typically home-based and include a partnership between a clinician and a cultural broker. Those students with sufficient stability to be assessed as safe, but who struggle with trauma-related dysregulation and/or significant stress in their social environments, receive “regulation focused” or “beyond trauma” phases of care (Tier 3), which are typically school-based.

In safety-focused treatment the goals of TST-R intervention are “to establish and maintain the safety and stability of the child’s social environment and to minimize the risk to the child and others based on the child’s difficulty regulating emotional and behavioral states” (Saxe et al., 2015, p.26). In TST-R, a cultural broker is paired with a clinician who is providing home-based services (Saxe et al., 2015). The cultural broker plays an important role in enhancing communication among family members and the clinician, attending to nonverbal and cultural cues, engaging the family, and facilitating clinical interventions. Even prior to beginning services, cultural brokers can help build the trust needed for refugee clients to invite strangers to their homes. Once a family accepts in-home services, the cultural broker can help clinicians by teaching them about the culture and what to expect during home visits. Additionally, cultural brokers work closely with outside providers (these often include child protection teams, school-based clinicians and community agencies) to ensure that there is service coordination and provide cultural lenses through which the family’s issues can be considered. Once services begin, cultural brokers work in partnership with clinicians to develop a language that would make sense to the client based on their cultural background. During visits, cultural brokers provide interpretation and cultural connection, helping the clinician and the family communicate in a meaningful way, while also using his/her cultural connection to the family to bridge the relationship. After encounters, cultural brokers and clinicians process what happened through an integrated clinical/cultural lens, therefore working to provide more integrated care and reduce misunderstandings.

Within safety-focused treatment, the cultural broker and clinician are working with families to identify collaborative goals focused on safety and stabilization. Systems advocacy plays an integral role in safety-focused treatment as it offers a mechanism and concrete tools for working on larger systemic problems that are fundamental contributors to a child’s dysregulation (Saxe et al., 2015). When working with refugee families, the importance of addressing concrete needs that may be contributing to threats or distress in the social environment, and therefore impacting the child, are central. Acculturation differences within families, which can lead to conflict and therefore stress in the social environment, are often a treatment focus that can be addressed through the collaborative work of clinicians and cultural brokers. Depending on how the roles of team members are established within service delivery systems, the cultural broker can also act as a case manager who attends to the identified stressors in the child and/or family’s environment such as housing or financial concerns. Attending to the primacy of these resettlement stressors is an important aspect of engaging refugee families, but also a means to identifying and reducing the stressors that may be most distressing to refugee families and children. In-home services are provided in lieu of, or in coordination with, a child’s individual therapy services. In both cases, the clinical team is focused on addressing priority problems in the child’s social environment that are impacting on their emotional and/or behavioral dysregulation. The child may still be receiving individual therapeutic support with some regulation-focused coping skills development.

However within TST and TST-R safety-focused treatment, the importance of addressing external reminders or stressors/triggers that provoke a trauma response is recognized. For example, for a child living in an area with active community violence in which they feel threatened, TST focuses on establishing a safer environment for that child as the first priority.

When it is determined that a child is no longer experiencing dangerous survival states and that his or her environment is safe enough, the child is ready for Tier 3, or the regulation-focused or beyond trauma phases of treatment. In TST-R these phases are typically provided as school-based individual therapy focused on the development of coping skills to help the child learn new ways of self-regulating. Regulation focused treatment is provided by a clinician who may or may not involve a cultural broker in session, depending on the child's and therapist's language proficiencies. The primary goals of regulation-focused treatment are to help children develop emotion regulation capacities, identify ways caregivers can support this regulation, and to share this information with caregivers so that they can develop their own capacities to help and protect their children, therefore reducing or preventing their child's switch to survival states (Saxe et al., 2015). Clinical strategies used in sessions focus on the concept of a trauma response, including identifying patterns of dysregulation in response to trauma triggers, reducing triggers when possible, and learning self-regulation skills to implement when reacting to trauma triggers. The understanding of these triggers and related intervention skills is constantly informed by cultural knowledge and/or cultural humility. The clinician is encouraged to be open to cultural aspects of emotion identification and coping skills and to integrate flexible ways of engaging refugee children (e.g., drawing or using pictures instead of relying on verbal communication). For example, some cultures/languages may have a limited range of vocabulary for describing emotions or ways of describing or expressing emotion that differ from the English language or the culture of the mental health provider. Role-playing and the discussion of somatic aspects of symptom expression are examples of tools that can further facilitate cross-cultural dialogue for the clinician and client. These skills are practiced with the therapist and shared with the child's caregivers and clinical team.

The beyond trauma phase of treatment is an extension of this work, for children whose emotion regulation and social environment are more stabilized, that incorporates cognitive processing and restructuring skills and encourages the child to develop a trauma narrative. The primary goal of this phase of treatment is "to work with the child and family to gain sufficient perspective on the trauma experience so that the trauma no longer defines the child's view of the self, world, and future," (Saxe et al., 2015, p.26). In this phase of treatment, children work with their individual therapist to further develop coping skills, primarily related to building cognitive awareness and learning cognitive restructuring. For those with persistent trauma-related symptoms, developing a trauma narrative in a format that is appropriate to the child's developmental and/or language capacity (e.g., writing a book, poetry, drawings, pretend play) and engagement in cognitive processing related to this narrative may be indicated. Given the history of multiple traumatic events in the lives of many refugee children, language/cultural differences, and the intergenerational trauma aspect of the refugee experience, trauma narratives may be flexible, creative, and reflect more of a timeline or narrative of the family migration experience as opposed to a focus on single traumatic incidents. The final stages of beyond trauma treatment aim to help children and families orient towards the future, set life goals, and nurture close relationships.

In the regulation-focused and beyond trauma phases of treatment (Tier 3) the cultural broker may participate in individual sessions when needed for language and cultural support. In this context s/he would serve as more than an interpreter of language, but also a source of cultural knowledge for both the clinician and the client, providing deeper context and cultural knowledge that enhances the understanding of the issues by all involved. Beyond involvement in individual treatment, cultural brokers can also facilitate parents' interactions with school personnel and clinical staff, providing linguistic and cultural support as needed. Cultural brokers may also provide ongoing case management or facilitate contact with partner community services that can continue to attend to social environmental stressors for the child and family during these phases of treatment. The TST-R clinical team format provides an opportunity for cultural brokers to share their cultural and community knowledge with clinicians even when they are not providing direct services within individual therapy sessions.

Tiers 1–4 Organizational/Team Meetings

A weekly multidisciplinary team meeting inclusive of those partnerships identified during the organizational planning of the program is a critical aspect that ensures the smooth integration of systems and services across all tiers of care. As such, for all TST-R program staff, a weekly team meeting is held during which new and existing client cases are reviewed. Case discussions during the team meeting include a review of the background of the case, an assessment of the child's current emotional or behavioral regulation status and social-environment, a determination of the phase of treatment based on this assessment, priority problems, targeted intervention approaches to address priority problems, and a discussion of cultural considerations. During the team meeting, the cultural broker(s) play an integral role in contributing information about engagement, cultural perceptions of the problems, related cultural or historical context, community knowledge, and strategies to enhance communication between families and providers.

Outcomes and Future Directions

TST-R was initially developed and implemented with Somali middle school youth (Ellis et al., 2013; Ellis et al., 2011). CBPR approaches to research within the Somali community guided community engagement activities and the adaptation of the TST model. The model was developed in partnership with school administrators, local community-based organizations, and mental health providers. The program was successful in engaging 100% (N = 30) of families who were referred for services (Ellis et al., 2013; Ellis et al., 2011). Preliminary findings from the first trial of this intervention demonstrated improvements in symptoms of PTSD and depression for children at all tiers of intervention and evidence that those with higher symptoms were appropriately matched with higher levels of care within this multi-tier model (Ellis et al., 2013). The outcomes also suggested an important role for the stabilization of social environmental stressors (resource hardships) in the reduction of mental health symptoms over time (Ellis et al., 2013).

Since this initial trial of the intervention, TST-R has been disseminated and piloted with Somali and Somali Bantu children and families in Maine, Kentucky, and Minnesota. The group intervention curriculum and TST-R intervention services were also adapted for, and implemented with, Bhutanese children and families in western Massachusetts. In each community, partnership development and community engagement has been an important element in determining the initial success and long term sustainability of the intervention. Initial evaluation findings from these dissemination projects suggest that the intervention is feasible, accepted, and viewed positively by students participating in services.

Strengths, Challenges, and Future Directions

TST-R is a unique prevention and intervention program that focuses on decreasing barriers to mental health care for refugee children and their families by providing integrated, multi-tiered approaches to intervention embedded within trusted service systems (i.e., schools). The strengths of this program include the flexibility in approaches to service delivery and an emphasis on community engagement and partnerships. Most importantly, services recognize the refugee experience and the importance of directly intervening in a child's social environment to affect change. Further, the cultural broker role is an innovation that increases the capacity for programs to provide culturally and linguistically sensitive care, helps to build trust and engagement, and also increases the ability of services to directly intervene in a child's family and community system. TST-R programs also have the potential to increase collaboration and efficiency across care delivery systems.

A recent sustainability study of TST-R dissemination sites identified several key elements that are important factors in developing this comprehensive program, including investment of key leadership within schools and community mental health organizations, a history of successful collaboration between key agencies, organizations, and/or refugee communities, a history of providing mental health providers services within schools, the size and organization of the refugee communities being served, and champions at the community and organizational level (Behrens, 2015). Given the complexity of the organizational readiness, partnership building, and community engagement that are essential to the success of this program, one of the greatest challenges of implementation can be identifying the funding to support the initial stages of program development.

Dissemination efforts have focused on identifying options for mapping services onto existing billing and mental health service structures within the U.S. mental health system. Funding and reimbursement for mental health services is variable by state within the U.S., and in some cases TST-R programs have advocated for state healthcare systems to fund certain aspects of the program. For example, in the state of Maine, home-based teams advocated to lift restrictions on the level of education required to fill a behavioral support position so that qualified refugee community members could serve as cultural brokers within this role designation for home-based TST-R teams. Although there is a growing recognition of the importance of comprehensive and preventative behavioral health interventions, there are aspects of the program that remain challenging to fund without the support of grants or philanthropy, particularly the cultural broker role and school-based groups. In some service systems this has been addressed by identifying ways to creatively bring together resources and existing roles (e.g., case management, school-based positions).

The initial stages of TST-R evaluation and implementation show promising efficacy in engaging refugee children and families with mental health services and reducing symptoms of distress in this traditionally underserved population. These promising outcomes suggest that this trauma-focused model is efficacious in meeting the needs of refugee children and families through innovative practice, including the integration of community engagement, cultural competency/cultural humility, cultural brokering, and tiered levels of school-based care. By incorporating these elements of service delivery, TST-R successfully addresses recommendations to tailor programs to the cultural needs of target populations and focus on more integrated, holistic models of care (APA, 2010; Kaczorowski et al., 2011). The knowledge gained from TST-R prevention and intervention efforts contributes to raising the standard of care for refugee children and families and informing responses to the ever-changing critical needs of new cultural populations seeking refuge and asylum.

References

Abdi, S. & Nisewaner, A. (2009). *Group work with Somali youth manual.* Unpublished manual.

American Psychological Association. (2010). *Resilience & recovery after war: Refugee children and families in the United States*. Retrieved from http://www.apa.org/pi/families/refugees.aspx

Barr, D. A. (2014). *Health disparities in the United States: Social class, race, ethnicity, and health.* Baltimore, MD: Johns Hopkins University Press.

Behrens, D. (2015). *Financing Strategies for TST-R Project.* Unpublished internal document, George Washington University.

Betancourt, T. S., & Khan, K. T. (2008). The mental health of children affected by armed conflict: Protective processes and pathways to resilience. *International Review of Psychiatry, 20*(3), 317–328. https://doi.org/10.1080/09540260802090363

Bogic, M., Njoku, A., & Priebe, S. (2015). Long-term mental health of war-refugees: A systematic literature review. *BMC International Health and Human Rights, 15*(1), 29. https://doi.org/10.1186/s12914-015-0064-9

Brewin, C. R., Andrews, B., & Valentine, J. D. (2000). Meta-analysis of risk factors for posttraumatic stress disorder in trauma-exposed adults. *Journal of Consulting and Clinical Psychology, 68*(5), 748–766. https://doi.org/10.1037//0022-006x.68.5.748

Brown, A., McCauley, D., Navalta, K., & Saxe, C. (2013). Trauma systems therapy in residential settings: Improving emotion regulation and the social environment of traumatized children and youth in congregate care. *Journal of Family Violence, 28*(7), 693–703. https://doi.org/10.1007/s10896-013-9542-9

Bureau of Population, Refugees, and Migration. (2017). *Fact sheet: Fiscal year 2016 refugee admissions*. Retrieved from: https://www.state.gov/j/prm/releases/factsheets/2017/266365.htm

Carpenter-Song, E., Whitley, R., Lawson, W., Quimby, E., & Drake, R. E. (2011). Reducing disparities in mental health care: Suggestions from the Dartmouth–Howard collaboration. *Community Mental Health Journal, 47*(1), 1–13. https://doi.org/10.1007/s10597-009-9233-4

Catani, C., Jacob, N., Schauer, E., Kohila, M., & Neuner, F. (2008). Family violence, war, and natural disasters: A study of the effect of extreme stress on children's mental health in Sri Lanka. *BMC Psychiatry, 8*(1), 33. https://doi.org/10.1186/1471-244x-8-33

Dixon, L., Lewis-Fernandez, R., Goldman, H., Interian, A., Michaels, A., & Kiley, M. C. (2011). Adherence disparities in mental health: Opportunities and challenges. *The Journal of Nervous and Mental Disease, 199*(10), 815–820. https://doi.org/10.1097/nmd.0b013e31822fed17

Ellis, B. H., Lincoln, A. K., Charney, M. E., Ford-Paz, R., Benson, M., & Strunin, L. (2010). Mental health service utilization of Somali adolescents: Religion, community, and school as gateways to healing. *Transcultural Psychiatry, 47*(5), 789–811. https://doi.org/10.1177/1363461510379933

Ellis, B. H., MacDonald, H. Z., Lincoln, A. K., & Cabral, H. J. (2008). Mental health of Somali adolescent refugees: The role of trauma, stress, and perceived discrimination. *Journal of Consulting and Clinical Psychology, 76*(2), 184–193. https://doi.org/10.1037/0022-006x.76.2.184

Ellis, B. H., Miller, A. B., Abdi, S., Barrett, C., Blood, E. A., & Betancourt, T. S. (2013). Multi-tier mental health program for refugee youth. *Journal of Consulting and Clinical Psychology, 81*(1), 129–140. https://doi.org/10.1037/a0029844

Ellis, B. H., Miller, A. B., Baldwin, H., & Abdi, S. (2011). New directions in refugee youth mental health services: Overcoming barriers to engagement. *Journal of Child & Adolescent Trauma, 4*(1), 69–85. https://doi.org/10.1080/19361521.2011.545047

Fazel, M., & Stein, A. (2002). The mental health of refugee children. *Archives of Disease in Childhood, 87*(5), 366–370. https://doi.org/10.1136/adc.87.5.366

Goode, T. D., Sockalingam, S., & Snyder, L. L. (2004). *Bridging the cultural divide in health care settings: The essential role of cultural broker programs*. Washington, DC: National Center for Cultural Competence.

Hidalgo, J., Maravić, M., Milet, C., & Beck, R. (2016). Promoting collaborative relationships in residential care of vulnerable and traumatized youth: A playfulness approach integrated with trauma systems therapy. *Journal of Child & Adolescent Trauma, 9*(1), 17–28. https://doi.org/10.1007/s40653-015-0076-6

Huang, Z., Yu, S., & Ledsky, R. (2006). Health status and health service access and use among children in U.S. immigrant families. *American Journal of Public Health, 96*(4), 634–640. https://doi.org/10.2105/ajph.2004.049791

Jezewski, M. A. (1990). Culture brokering in migrant farm worker health care. *Western Journal of Nursing Research, 12*(4), 497–513. https://doi.org/10.1177/019394599001200406

Kaczorowski, J. A., Williams, A. S., Smith, T. F., Fallah, N., Mendez, J. L., & Nelson–Gray, R. (2011). Adapting clinical services to accommodate needs of refugee populations. *Professional Psychology: Research and Practice, 42*(5), 361–367. https://doi.org/10.1037/a0025022

Khawaja, N. G., White, K. M., Schweitzer, R., & Greenslade, J. (2008). Difficulties and coping strategies of Sudanese refugees: A qualitative approach. *Transcultural Psychiatry, 45*(3), 489–512. https://doi.org/10.1177/1363461508094678

Kirmayer, L. J., Narasiah, L., Munoz, M., Rashid, M., Ryder, A. G., Guzder, J., et al. (2011). Common mental health problems in immigrants and refugees: General approach in primary care. *Canadian Medical Association Journal, 183*(12), E959–E967. https://doi.org/10.1503/cmaj.090292

Kohn-Wood, L. P., & Hooper, L. M. (2014). Cultural competency, culturally tailored care, and the primary care setting: Possible solutions to reduce racial/ethnic disparities in mental health care. *Journal of Mental Health Counseling, 36*(2), 173–188. https://doi.org/10.17744/mehc.36.2.d73h217l81tg6uv3

Lustig, S. L., Kia-Keating, M., Knight, W. G., Geltman, P., Ellis, H., Kinzie, J. D., … Saxe, G. N. (2004). Review of child and adolescent refugee mental health. *Journal of the American Academy of Child & Adolescent Psychiatry, 43*(1), 24–36. https://doi.org/10.1037/e318832004-001

Moore, K. A., Redd, Z., Beltz, M., Malm, K., Murphy, K., Schusterman, G., & Sticklor, L. (2016). *KVC's bridging the way home: An innovative approach to the application of trauma system therapy in shild welfare.*. Lexington, KY: KVC Health Systems.

Munroe-Blum, H., Boyle, M., Offord, D., & Kates, N. (1989). Immigrant children: Psychiatric disorder, school performance, and service utilization. *American Journal of Orthopsychiatry, 59*(4), 510–519. https://doi.org/10.1111/j.1939-0025.1989.tb02740.x

Nisewaner, A., & Abdi, S. M. (2010, June). Challenges, strategies and rewards of an adaptation of trauma systems therapy for newly arriving refugee youth: School-based group work with Somali adolescent boys. In V. Roy, G. Berteau, & S. Genest-Dufault (Eds.), *Strengthening Social Solidarity through Group Work: Research and Creative Practice.* Paper presented at the Proceeding of the XXXII International Symposium on Social Work with Groups, Montreal, June 3–6, (pp.129–147). London, UK: Whiting & Birch.

Office of Refugee Resettlement. (2016). *Unaccompanied children released to sponsors by state.* Retrieved from: http://www.acf.hhs.gov/programs/orr/programs/ucs/state-by-state-uc-placed-sponsors

Reed, R. V., Fazel, M., Jones, L., Panter-Brick, C., & Stein, A. (2012). Mental health of displaced and refugee children resettled in low-income and middle-income countries: Risk and protective factors. *The Lancet, 379*(9812), 250–265. https://doi.org/10.1016/s0140-6736(11)60050-0

Saxe, G. N., Ellis, B. H., & Brown, A. D. (2015). *Trauma systems therapy for children and teens* (2nd ed.). New York, NY: Guilford.

Saxe, G. N., Ellis, B. H., Fogler, J., Hansen, S., & Sorkin, B. (2005). Comprehensive care for traumatized children: An open trial examines treatment—Using trauma systems therapy. *Psychiatric Annals, 35*(5), 443–448. https://doi.org/10.3928/00485713-20050501-10

Saxe, G. N., Ellis, B. H., & Kaplow, J. (2006). *Collaborative care for traumatized teens and children: A trauma systems therapy approach.* New York, NY: Guilford.

Saxe, G. N., Ellis, H. B., Fogler, J., & Navalta, C. P. (2012). Innovations in practice: Preliminary evidence for effective family engagement in treatment for child traumatic stress–trauma systems therapy approach to preventing dropout. *Child and Adolescent Mental Health, 17*(1), 58–61. https://doi.org/10.1111/j.1475-3588.2011.00626.x

Sundquist, J., Bayard-Burfield, L., Johansson, L. M., & Johansson, S. E. (2000). Impact of ethnicity, violence and acculturation on displaced migrants: Psychological distress and psychosomatic complaints among refugees in Sweden. *The Journal of Nervous and Mental Disease, 188*(6), 357–365. https://doi.org/10.1097/00005053-200006000-00006

Tervalon, M., & Murray-Garcia, J. (1998). Cultural humility versus cultural competence: A critical distinction in defining physician training outcomes in multicultural education. *Journal of Health Care for the Poor and Underserved, 9*(2), 117–125. https://doi.org/10.1353/hpu.2010.0233

United Nations High Commissioner for Refugees. (2015). *UNHCR global trends 2015: Forced displacement in 2015.* Retrieved from: https://s3.amazonaws.com/unhcrsharedmedia/2016/2016-06-20-global-trends/2016-06-14-Global-Trends-2015.pdf

United Nations High Commissioner for Refugees. (2016). *Facts and figures about refugees.* Retrieved from: http://www.unhcr.ie/about-unhcr/facts-and-figures-about-refugees

Watters, C. (2001). Emerging paradigms in the mental health care of refugees. *Social Science & Medicine, 52*(11), 1709–1718. https://doi.org/10.1016/s0277-9536(00)00284-7

Wong, E. C., Marshall, G. N., Schell, T. L., Elliott, M. N., Hambarsoomians, K., Chun, C. A., & Berthold, S. M. (2006). Barriers to mental health care utilization for US Cambodian refugees. *Journal of Consulting and Clinical Psychology, 74*(6), 1116–1120. https://doi.org/10.1037/0022-006x.74.6.1116

Molly A. Benson, Ph.D. is an Attending Psychologist at Boston Children's Hospital and Assistant Professor of Psychology, Part-Time, in the Department of Psychiatry at Harvard Medical School. She is the former Associate Director for Treatment and Services at the Refugee Trauma and Resilience Center at Boston Children's Hospital. Her research and clinical interests include a focus on training providers in adapting and delivering evidence-based practices for diverse populations in real-world settings, with a specific emphasis on child and adolescent refugee mental health.

Saida M. Abdi, LICSW, MSW, M.A. is a Licensed Clinical Social Worker, the Associate Director for Community Relations at the Refugee Trauma and Resilience Center at Boston Children's Hospital, and a Ph.D. Candidate at Boston University. She has extensive experience in providing trauma informed care to refugees and immigrants, with particular expertise in community engagement, cultural humility, and the use of interpreters and cultural brokers to reduce health disparities. Her research interests focus on risk and resilience factors in the experience of Somali refugee youth in North America.

Alisa B. Miller, Ph.D., is Research Associate at the Refugee Trauma and Resilience Center and Assistant in Psychology in the Department of Psychiatry at Boston Children's Hospital and an Instructor in Psychology at Harvard Medical School. Her research interests include improving mental health equity among refugee and immigrant groups and the overall health and well-being of youth in our society.

B. Heidi Ellis, Ph.D., is an Associate Professor in Psychology and Psychiatry at Harvard Medical School and Boston Children's Hospital Boston, and a licensed clinical psychologist. She is also the Director of the Refugee Trauma and Resilience Center at Boston Children's Hospital, a partner in the National Child Traumatic Stress Network. Dr. Ellis' primary focus is on understanding and promoting refugee youth mental health and adjustment, with a particular emphasis on understanding how trauma exposure, violence, and social context impact developmental trajectories. She is also co-developer of the nationally recognized trauma treatment model, Trauma Systems Therapy.

Supporting Children Affected by War: Towards an Evidence Based Care System

Mark J. D. Jordans, Myrthe van den Broek, Felicity Brown, April Coetzee, Rinske Ellermeijer, Kim Hartog, Frederik Steen, and Kenneth E. Miller

Abstract One in ten children globally lives in an area affected by armed conflict. Armed conflict has both direct and indirect effects on children's social, emotional, and educational outcomes, and impacts can occur at multiple levels of the child's ecosystem- the individual, family, community, and society. This chapter will provide an overview of the impacts of war on children, outline existing intervention research and sector standards, and provide recommendations and future directions for research and implementation. The chapter will then detail War Child Holland's research and development agenda which aims to develop a multi-sectoral, multi-level system of care for children affected by war that addresses children's needs across different ecological levels. This system of care is complemented by mechanisms to ensure access and quality of care. The chapter describes how evidence-based principles can be developed and implemented in such a way that they are scalable and can achieve actual real-world impact, despite the complexities and challenges of working in low-resource humanitarian settings.

Keywords Armed conflict · Psychosocial · Mental health · Child protection · Education · Integrated care

M. J. D. Jordans (✉)
Faculty of Social and Behavioral Sciences, University of Amsterdam, Amsterdam, The Netherlands

Research and Development, War Child, Amsterdam, North Holland, The Netherlands
e-mail: mark.jordans@warchild.nl

M. van den Broek · F. Brown · A. Coetzee · R. Ellermeijer · K. Hartog · F. Steen · K. E. Miller
Research and Development, War Child, Amsterdam, North Holland, The Netherlands
e-mail: Myrthe.vandenBroek@warchild.nl; felicity.brown@warchild.nl; April.Coetzee@warchild.nl; Rinske.Ellermeijer@warchild.nl; Kim.Hartog@warchild.nl; Frederik.Steen@warchild.nl; Kenneth.Miller@warchild.nl

N. Morina, A. Nickerson (eds.), *Mental Health of Refugee and Conflict-Affected Populations*, https://doi.org/10.1007/978-3-319-97046-2_13

Introduction

Worldwide, nearly 250 million children – one in every ten of the world's children- live in countries and areas affected by armed conflict (UNICEF, 2016). The world is witnessing unprecedented numbers of displaced people and the highest numbers of war-related fatalities since 1989 (UNHCR, 2015). It is estimated that more than 2 million children have lost their lives in the past decade due to conflict (HIIK, 2016) and beyond that, 9.9 million children are refugees and a further 19 million children are internally displaced (ECHO, 2016). The 2016 annual report of the Secretary-General on Children and Armed Conflict reported ongoing serious concerns regarding both the protection of children affected by armed conflict, and the increased intensity of grave violations against children in many conflict-affected settings (including killing and maiming, child recruitment and use, sexual violence, abductions, attacks on schools and hospitals, and denial of humanitarian access) (UN, 2016).

The nature of modern conflict has seen an increasing shift towards wars of destabilization; that is, conflicts are increasingly fought within states, and are commonly not confined to distinct battlefields but rather specifically target civilian populations, along with essential infrastructure. Social networks, community structures and processes, service systems, and religious institutions can be disrupted or purposefully destroyed, and deep ethnic or political divides in society can be created or exacerbated (Barber, 2013; Betancourt & Khan, 2008). Thus, beyond the direct threat to life and individual impact of exposure to conflict-related violence and destruction, armed-conflicts affect the entire social ecology of children.

In this chapter, we will discuss how War Child Holland, an international non-governmental organisation (NGO) that aims to improve the wellbeing, and strengthen the resilience, of children affected by armed conflict, is working towards a comprehensive evidence-based system of care that can be implemented at scale. To put that work in context, we first discuss the impact that war and community violence might have on children and provide an overview of current research into the effectiveness of interventions for conflict-affected children. Based on this discussion, we formulate a number of recommendations that should be taken into account when developing a system of care.

Impact of War on Children

At the individual level the impact of armed conflict on the physical, mental and psychosocial wellbeing of children and youth has been well established (Barber, 1999; Barenbaum, Ruchkin, & Schwab-Stone, 2004; Panter-Brick, Goodman, Tol, & Eggerman, 2011). High rates of posttraumatic stress disorder (PTSD) symptoms, behavioral and emotional symptoms and disorders, sleep problems, disturbed play, and psychosomatic symptoms are found among conflict-affected children and youth (Attanayake et al., 2009; Betancourt et al., 2014; Fazel, Reed, Panter-Brick, & Stein, 2012; Miller & Jordans, 2016; Slone & Mann, 2016; Stichick, 2001).

It is widely recognised that a positive and nurturing family environment is essential for child development and wellbeing. Indeed, secure and consistent caregiving relationships can play a critical role in helping children to cope effectively with exposure to conflict and the many other ongoing stressors in these environments (Betancourt, Meyers-Ohki, Charrow, & Tol, 2013; Miller & Jordans, 2016; Tol, Song, & Jordans, 2013). Yet, in conflict-affected settings, caregivers exposed to conflict-related and other common daily stressors can have high rates of psychopathology and may have difficulty in providing responsive and effective parenting (Slone & Mann, 2016). There is evidence that conflict-affected parents often have difficulties interacting with children, become less sensitive and responsive to children's needs, and may be less effective at maintaining rules and setting boundaries (Barenbaum et al., 2004; Khamis, 2014; Miller & Jordans, 2016). Furthermore, there is growing evidence across multiple settings that family violence increases significantly in settings of armed conflict (Catani, Schauer, & Neuner, 2008; Panter-Brick et al., 2011). Taken together, these findings suggest that the family environment, and parental wellbeing and parenting behaviour in particular, represent key mediators on the relationship between armed conflict and children's mental health and psychosocial wellbeing (Miller & Jordans, 2016).

Community-level conditions, such as the prevalence of child labour and poverty, negatively impact upon children and increase a child's risk of experiencing harm (McLeod & Shanahan, 1993; Srivastava, 2011). In times of crisis, child protection risks such as violence and exploitation increase and become exacerbated (Bartels & Hamill, 2014). Ongoing conflict may lead families and communities to resort to harmful coping mechanisms, such as early marriage—a strategy sometimes used to protect adolescent girls from sexual violence (Bartels & Hamill, 2014). In addition, ongoing conflict results in damage to the community fabric, including the generation of distrust among members of different religious or ethnic groups, and damage to structures and available services such as education and health facilities (CPWG, 2015).

Interventions to Address the Impact of War on Children

Historically many explanatory and intervention models have focused on the direct impact of exposure to war-related violence on children's mental health. However, increasing attention is now being paid to both the direct and indirect impact of armed conflict on children as well as understanding the multiple pathways by which armed conflict affects children's ongoing development and psychosocial wellbeing more broadly (Miller & Jordans, 2016; Tol, Jordans, Kohrt, Betancourt, & Komproe, 2013; Tol, Song, et al., 2013). This more comprehensive model considers the "daily stressors" caused or exacerbated by exposure to armed conflict and draws attention to multiple risk factors at all levels of the social ecology i.e., the family, peers, school and wider-community. Protective factors have also been identified that may positively mediate the impact of exposure to violence on mental health and wellbeing and function as a buffer (Betancourt et al., 2013; Tol, Song, et al., 2013).

Therefore, in attempting to understand and respond to the effects of war on children, it is important to consider each of these multiple pathways of impact.

Several recent literature reviews (including systematic reviews and meta-analyses) have synthesised mental health interventions and their evidence, and have specifically focused on interventions aimed at children and adolescents affected by armed conflict (Barry, Clarke, Jenkins, & Patel, 2013; Betancourt et al., 2013; Jordans, Pigott, & Tol, 2016; Jordans, Tol, Komproe, & de Jong, 2009; O'Sullivan, Bosqui, & Shannon, 2016; Tol, Barbui, et al., 2011). Altogether, these reviews have included 150 unique publications. In recent years, there has been a promising increase in the number and quality of research evaluations of the effectiveness of interventions targeting the mental health and psychosocial wellbeing of children in adversity in low and middle income countries (LMIC).

There is empirical support for the use of individual as well as group-based psychosocial interventions for children to improve mental health and promote psychosocial wellbeing, particularly among children experiencing clinical levels of distress (Jordans et al., 2016; Jordans et al., 2009; O'Sullivan et al., 2016; Tol, Barbui, et al., 2011). Evidence tends to be limited to sub-groups of children (e.g., only boys or girls, only older or younger children) and centred around a few treatment types (i.e., Trauma Focused-Cognitive Behavioural Therapy, Narrative Exposure Therapy), with evidence for CBT-based interventions generally showing larger effects than interventions based on other theoretical frameworks (O'Sullivan et al., 2016). The generalizability of these findings is limited, however, by an over-reliance on highly resourced efficacy studies, as the relevance of such studies for everyday practice remains largely unknown. The higher quality evidence available to date has also tended to focus mostly on trauma-focused interventions that are infrequently implemented outside research settings (Tol et al., 2012). Interventions that are more commonly implemented in the field, such as structured social activities and developing or strengthening community-based social supports, are rarely subjected to rigorous evaluation (Tol, Barbui, et al., 2011). The same conclusion can be drawn for interventions in child protection (Wessells, 2009). In order to bridge this divide between research and practice, there is a need for further robust evaluations using pragmatic designs that more closely approximate the real world of everyday practice in which NGOs and local institutions operate. There is also a compelling need to transcend the dominant focus on providing direct services to children, by including interventions that address other socio-ecological levels, such as families, schools, and other community organizations and structures (Jordans & Tol, 2015).

To date, only a handful of controlled evaluations have been published with parents and/or families in conflict-affected settings, with varying outcomes. A two-session parent group psychoeducation intervention delivered in rural Burundi led to reductions in aggressive behaviours in boys compared to a waitlist group; however, no treatment effect was seen for depression symptoms or family social support (Jordans, Tol, Ndayisaba, & Komproe, 2013). A study comparing a multi-component psychosocial intervention plus medical care to medical care only for parents in Bosnia found mixed results. The psychosocial intervention led to greater improvements in some measures of child psychosocial functioning and mental health as well as mother's wellbeing, but no significant improvements on other measures of these outcomes (Dybdahl, 2001). Similarly, a family-focused group psychosocial intervention delivered in the Democratic Republic of Congo (DRC) for war-exposed youth at risk of attack or abduction, found significant intervention effects compared to a waitlist control group on PTSD symptoms, but no effect on depression and anxiety symptoms, conduct problems, or prosocial behaviour (O'Callaghan, McMullen, Shannon, Rafferty, & Black, 2013). A structured activities program combined with parent psychoeducation led to significant treatment effects (compared to a no-treatment comparison group) on behavioural and emotional difficulties for certain subgroups of children (Loughry et al., 2006). Finally, Puffer, Annan, Sim, Salhi, and Betancourt (2017), in their waitlist RCT of a 12 week family support and parenting intervention with Burmese refugees in Thailand, found improvements in family cohesion and parent-child relationships, and a parent-reported decrease in harsh parenting behavior (children did not report a decrease in harsh parenting). However, no effect was found for positive parenting and measures of child wellbeing were not included in the study.

Increasing attention is also being paid to interventions that strengthen social networks and reinforce traditional support mechanisms to help promote children's wellbeing. However, there is a scarcity of well-designed studies focusing on community support (Betancourt et al., 2013; Jordans et al., 2016; Wessells, 2009). A number of studies suggest that community support may play a protective role for children affected by armed conflict (Betancourt et al., 2013). Community level support is likely to reach large groups of children, tends to be low cost and therefore more sustainable, and community-level actors are often well-positioned to support families and children when problems come to light. When working towards the improved wellbeing of children, community-level action to prevent harm is required (Wessells, 2009). Moreover, there is agreement within the humanitarian sector that education, crucial as in intervention in itself, is significant for psychosocial wellbeing as it restores a sense of normalcy, dignity and hope (INEE, 2012).

Recommendations and Future Directions

The following section discusses a number of recommendations that we believe should be taken into account when developing services for children affected by armed conflict.

More Attention for Multi-level Interventions

Multi-level interventions focusing on the mental health and psychosocial wellbeing of children in adversity, including complex emergencies, are commonly advocated. The Inter-Agency Standing Committee (IASC) Guidelines for Mental Health and Psychosocial Support (MHPSS) in Emergency Settings specifically promote this approach via a four-tiered model; Level 1: *basic security and service* to enhance wellbeing of the general population; Level 2: responses to a smaller group that is able to maintain their wellbeing through the *support of family and community networks*; Level 3: *focused, non-specialised supports* for the still smaller number of people requiring more focused individual, family or group interventions to recover from their distress; and Level 4: *specialised services* delivered by qualified professionals to severely distressed and/or impaired individuals (IASC, 2007). Multi-level interventions have demonstrated feasibility and promising preliminary findings. However, they are rarely reported and evaluated (Betancourt et al., 2013; Jordans et al., 2016). A systematic review in 2016 found that 52% of the publications reviewed recommended that interventions should apply multi-level approaches (Jordans et al., 2016). Text Box 1 provides a promising example of a multi-level intervention.

Box 1: Multi-levelled Child Mental Health Program
A multi-levelled care system, where different levels of support interventions are available to address the psychosocial needs, for children in five conflict affected countries (Indonesia, Sri Lanka, Nepal, South Sudan and Burundi) was positively evaluated, with high levels of satisfaction and considerable levels of perceived post-treatment outcomes among children and parents (Jordans, Tol, et al., 2010). The program included organizing recreational activities, a 15-session group intervention that incorporated various components, such as structured expressive behavioral activities for children with elevated distress, non-specialized individual (or group) counselling for children with more severe problems in combination with family support, as well as specific referrals to specialized support (Jordans, Tol, et al., 2010), corresponding to levels 2 and 3 as described above.

Boosting Multi-sectoral Interventions

In the IASC MHPSS guidelines the importance of working inter-sectorally is articulated, reflecting growing consensus that the various sectors impact on psychosocial wellbeing (IASC, 2007). Protection and education guidelines and standards further emphasise the effect of both sectors on psychosocial wellbeing (CPWG, 2012; INEE, 2012). An inter-agency review of child protection interventions cited multiple studies related to the mental health and psychosocial wellbeing of children but also noted a lack of rigorous study designs, which limits any conclusions about the effectiveness of interventions. Moreover, these evaluations focused heavily on process and output indicators, while paying insufficient attention to psychosocial and mental health *outcomes* for children and their families. A recent review on health interventions argues for the need for more evidence of inter-sectoral approaches (nutrition, education, protection) in relation to mental health and psychosocial support (Blanchet et al., 2015). Text Box 2 provides an example of an education programme with psychosocial benefits.

Box 2: Healing Classrooms
The International Rescue Committee conducted a program that emphasizes education's role towards enhanced mental health and psychosocial wellbeing. Classrooms were converted into places of not only academic learning but also of healing. The program aimed to improve teachers' wellbeing, with a subsequent effect on students' wellbeing and academic performance. The research indicated significant psychological benefit for the children as they could picture themselves being able to provide support to their families in the future (Winthrop & Kirk, 2005). The importance of each teacher's identity and competences was identified, and further research into teacher professional development was recommended.

Interventions from a Socio-ecological Perspective

As we discussed earlier, it is imperative that interventions go beyond focusing solely on direct work with children, and focus on the critical factors in the environment that impact on children's wellbeing: family, school, peers, community, and a larger macro or societal context. The various ecological levels include protective factors that influence the psychosocial wellbeing and resilience of an individual child. Research suggests that interventions targeting risk and protective factors beyond an individual child are essential for helping children deal effectively with adversities (Betancourt & Khan, 2008). Indeed, interventions targeting the family and linking child protection and mental health have shown promise in improving child psychosocial outcomes (Sim, Annan, Puffer, Salhi, & Betancourt, 2014). Text Box 3 describes an intervention that simultaneously focuses directly on children as well as their families.

Box 3: Building Happy Families
Sim et al. (2014) conducted an RCT on parenting and family skills in a low-resourced displacement setting to evaluate feasibility and effectiveness in reducing behavioral problems, as well as promoting psychosocial wellbeing and resilience. Caregivers and children attended sessions separately, which were succeeded by joint family activities afterwards. Both caregivers and children expressed high interest and satisfaction. The intervention led to improvement on many family factors such as positive parenting and improved caregiver-child interaction. Though no impact was reported on children's emotional problems, improvement in resilience and reduction in negative behavioral issues were demonstrated. This intervention unintendedly also showed potential in improving caregiver mental health.

Need for Increased Scientific Rigour

The evidence-base for interventions for children in areas of armed conflict is mixed, and significant gaps in knowledge persist as outlined above (Betancourt et al., 2013; Brown, Graaff, Annan, & Betancourt, 2017; Jordans et al., 2016; O'Sullivan et al., 2016). Furthermore, there are a number of lessons that can be drawn from recent literature reviews regarding the future development and improvement of services. Although the intervention research base has increased significantly in recent years, many evaluations continue to lack rigor (e.g., frequent use of un-controlled studies, use of waitlist control designs rather than active comparison groups) (Jordans et al., 2016). O'Sullivan et al. (2016) stress that future research needs to consider more appropriate (culturally adapted) outcomes. There is a call for diversification as intervention studies seem to be skewed both geographically (some conflict-affected settings are over-represented) and by type of intervention (a disproportionate number of trauma-focused interventions). Programs are commonly implemented as one-off initiatives and with little conclusive longitudinal data available or ongoing implementation of services within the setting (O'Sullivan et al., 2016). Unfortunately, research results are often not used nor translated for the improvement of programs in humanitarian settings (Tol et al., 2012). Further, there is a lack of empirical knowledge in this field about active therapeutic ingredients and clinical processes driving change in effective interventions (i.e., through dismantling studies and mediational analyses) (Brown et al., 2017). In order to adequately inform the development and implementation of optimally effective, targeted, efficient, and sustainable interventions, it is vital that future work consider these issues.

Importance of Attending to Stigmatisation and Discrimination

Worldwide, people are excluded from participation in their society, including making optimum use of services, because of aspects of their identity such as gender, race, health status, sexual orientation, age and ability (Thornicroft, 2008). Although research specifically concerning mental health-related (experienced) stigma has increased over the last decades, intervention studies have only recently been conducted, mostly in high-income countries (HICs) and mostly focused on adult populations. Recent research indicates that globally over 70% of young people and adults with mental illnesses receive no treatment, with a higher percentage in LMICs where potential barriers to accessing treatment include prejudice against people with a mental illness as well as expectations of discrimination (Thornicroft, 2008). Social contact-based interventions with people with mental illness seem promising for short-term attitudinal changes but caution is warranted in generalizing these findings to other stigmatized groups and populations (Thornicroft et al., 2015).

Beyond stigma and discrimination, issues of inclusion can extend to other groups – for example, out-of-school children who are unable to participate in school-based interventions (Fazel & Tol, 2014).

Cultural Adaptation of Interventions

Cultural adaptation of existing evidence-based interventions when delivering them in different linguistic and cultural contexts is important not only to 'do no harm' and build upon local strengths and contexts, but also to increase the potential of positive outcomes and promote sustainability (Bernal & Sáez-Santiago, 2006; Castro, Barrera Jr, & Holleran Steiker, 2010). For an example of a cultural adapted intervention, see Box 4. Studies of culturally adapted psychotherapeutic interventions have demonstrated increased effect sizes compared to studies of non-adapted interventions (Benish, Quintana, & Wampold, 2011; Griner & Smith, 2006), with a recent review indicating that effectiveness increases the greater the number of adaptations made (Harper, Heim, Chowdhary, Maercker, & Albanese, 2016). Although many reports of program implementations in different settings report some kind of cultural adaptation, often no (detailed) account of adaptation is given.

Less than half of the studies in a recent systematic review mentioned the development of locally adapted versions of outcome measures (Jordans et al., 2016). Such adaptations are necessary in order to ensure the cross-cultural validity of the measures, as expression of symptoms can vary between different cultural contexts, which can lead to inaccurate findings during intervention evaluation (O'Sullivan et al., 2016). It is imperative that further research considers the value and process of cultural adaptations of both intervention methods and assessment tools (Jordans et al., 2016; O'Sullivan et al., 2016; Tol et al., 2012).

Box 4: School-Based Psychosocial Structured Activities

The impact of a school-based Psychosocial Structured Activities (PSSA) program in Northern Uganda has been positively evaluated (Ager et al., 2011). It serves as an example of a culturally adapted intervention, based on a Classroom Based intervention that has previously been used amongst others in Palestine. The program adopted an approach that went beyond children's individual symptomatology and incorporated different ecological levels, by asking parents and teachers to report on the child's wellbeing, in addition to the child's self-report. Significant improvements in wellbeing were observed for the children in the intervention group in comparison to those in the control group, indicating that girls make greater progress than boys.

Replication and Sustainability

Replicability of interventions is determined by various factors. The quality of research is crucial to assessing the validity of its outcomes. In their review of mental health promotion interventions in LMIC, Barry et al. (2013) noted that cost-effectiveness is imperative in order to establish whether the intervention is feasible in non-research settings, and whether the cost of the intervention is justified by the level of desired change achieved. However, very few studies integrate a cost-benefit element into their research design, creating challenges for replication as well as sustainability. Group-based interventions demonstrate higher cost-effectiveness, and are commonly implemented, with most indicating moderate to strong treatment effects on children's socio-emotional wellbeing (Barry et al., 2013). Schools are an optimal delivery platform for these kind of interventions because of the structure they provide (Barry et al., 2013; Betancourt et al., 2013). Internet-based mental health interventions, which have seldom been studied in LMICs but have shown value in HICs as a relatively low-cost intervention modality, may prove to have considerable potential (Arjadi, Nauta, Chowdhary, & Bockting, 2015). Although none of the studies mentioned by Arjadi et al. (2015) refer to children, a scoping review conducted in 2014 highlighted the potential of using technology, for example, videoconferencing, mobile phone applications and internet-based applications, for mental health interventions for children in HICs (Boydell et al., 2014).

Ethical Issues

Ethical issues in intervention research with conflict-affected children and families have received comparatively limited attention in the literature. Yet there are numerous ethical points that merit consideration. Examples include; (1) the use of untested interventions, or interventions tested in other contexts, without careful monitoring for untoward effects; (2) research interventions not relevant to the actual local needs and main problems that need addressing (O'Mathúna & Siriwardhana, 2017; Tol et al., 2012); (3) a focus on getting approval for studies from Ethics Review Boards, instead of actually focusing on the goal of research ethics, which is, amongst others, the protection of participants (O'Mathúna & Siriwardhana, 2017); (4) the use of passive versus active consent procedures by caregivers, and the use or non-use of children's own assent to participate in intervention studies; (5) weighing the benefits of longitudinal research that allow for patterns of recovery, resilience and persistent distress to be examined, versus the imperative to provide treatments when these are available; and (6) providing treatment to children without adequately assessing ongoing stressors such as child abuse that may be contributing to their distress. If these and related considerations are taken into account when planning and conducting research, investigators can improve their ethical practice in humanitarian research, thereby ensuring the actual protection of participants (O'Mathúna & Siriwardhana, 2017) – something that is crucially needed in humanitarian contexts given the especially vulnerable position of participants.

Developing a Multi-sectoral System of Care: War Child Holland's Response

Commonly in humanitarian response programs, interventions are defined in specific sectors that focus on a particular thematic area (e.g., psychosocial, child protection, education), creating silos without a focus on a shared goal or outcome. For many children and communities this approach is not adequate nor responsive enough to meet the complex and varied mental health and psychosocial needs found within post-conflict contexts. Rather, a system of complementary support mechanisms is required, targeting mental health problems or stress directly, as well as indirectly, through addressing the major social determinants of mental health and psychosocial wellbeing (de Jong, 2002; Jordans, Komproe, et al., 2010; Saltzman, Layne, Steinberg, Arslanagic, & Pynoos, 2003; Stichick, 2001; Tol, Jordans, Reis, & de Jong, 2009; Wessells & Monteiro, 2006; Williamson & Robinson, 2006).

War Child Holland is one among few international organisations that primarily focus on the mental health and wellbeing of children and communities affected by conflict. Drawing on the aforementioned recommendations, it combines a focus on psychosocial support, child protection and education through the development of an integrated, multi-level system of care. This care system entails *an integrated approach* in which interventions are interconnected and mutually strengthening, with a range of intervention methods available to respond to the varying needs of children and their caregivers. The care system is *multi-level*, in that interventions range from low-intensity and least restrictive access interventions that aim to promote wellbeing and prevent problems from arising, to higher-intensity and more targeted interventions designed specifically for children experiencing significant and enduring distress. Finally, the care system is *socio-ecological* in its approach, with services targeted at different ecological levels (individual and peers, families, schools, communities, civil society and state authorities). This approach reflects the reality that children's development is inextricably linked to the families, communities, economic situation, social values and cultural influences in which their lives are embedded and which provide for their basic needs and protection.

At the core of the War Child Holland care system (see Fig. 1) is a set of complementary interventions, outlined in Table 1. Together they target community systems (both formal and non-formal), the school as a place to enable children to reach their full potential, all children in communities affected by armed violence to promote their wellbeing, children for whom more focused support is needed (either with regard to significant psychosocial distress or severe protection issues), and families who may have been adversely affected by conflict. We believe that this care system will therefore address both mental health consequences and related social determinants, by responding to the needs of individual children whilst also strengthening child protection and education services, building the mechanisms and confidence necessary within communities to facilitate the care and protection of children under their care. Two interventions directly target children's common mental health problems, either through an intervention that combines specific therapeutic components or through a family systems treatment. Other interventions prevent these problems

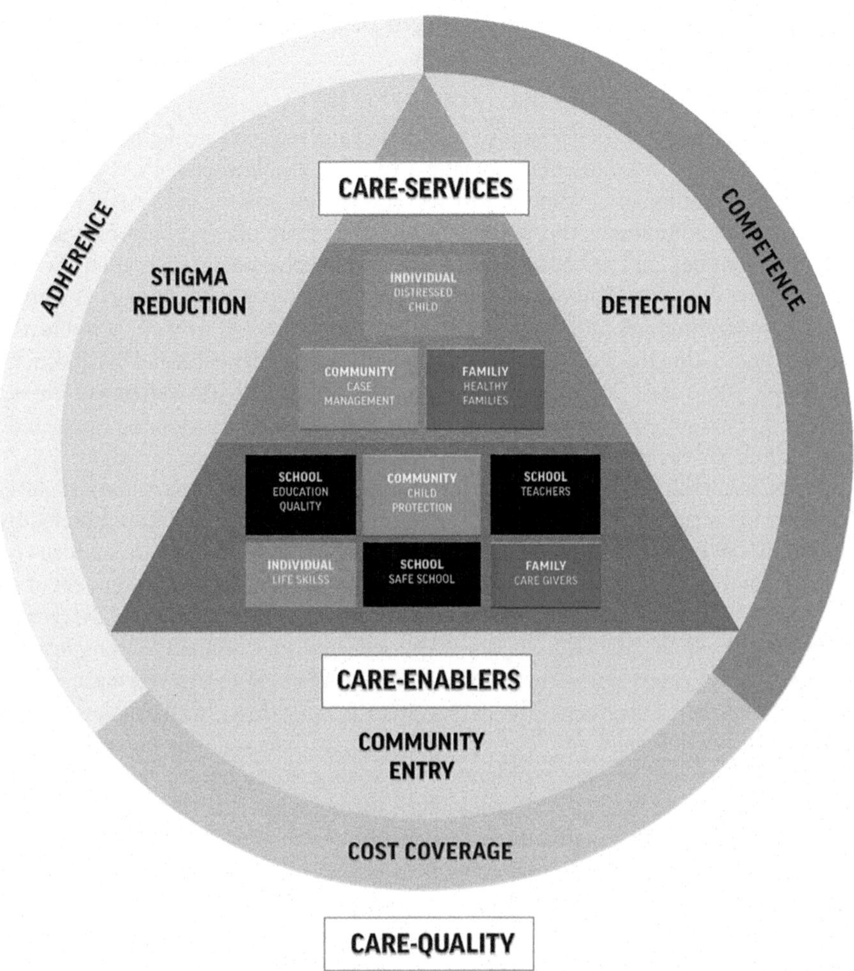

Fig. 1 Care system

from developing through either life skills interventions, which aim to strengthen children's resources to cope with the adversity they experience, or interventions focused on improving parental wellbeing and strengthening parenting under conditions of adversity. Reinstating structural education supports normalization, stability and continuity and also promotes continuation of the social role of a student, all of which are particularly important in conflict or post-conflict settings. Furthermore, a protective education environment is important to reduce the risk of children becoming involved in the worst forms of child labour, including being associated with armed groups and armed forces. Similarly, child protection services aim to deal with root causes of children's psychosocial and mental health problems, for example, by establishing community structures to prevent, or respond to, child abuse. While

Table 1 Overview of interventions

Interventions[a]	Description*
Caregiver support intervention	Group intervention for parents and caregivers to promote their wellbeing and support their parenting (with a trickle down effect to their children) (*)
Focused psychosocial support	Group intervention targeting children and adolescents that experience emotional problems (i.e., distress, anxiety, depression)
I-DEAL	Group-based life-skills intervention to promote children and young people's resources to cope with adversity (*)
Case management	Targeted social work type support for individual children and their families (CPWG, 2014)
Community based child protection	Strengthening community owned and led prevention and response to abuse, neglect, violence and exploitation of children (*)
Teacher professional development	Building the competencies of teachers to provide social, emotional and academic learning environments (*)
Safe schools [b]	School-level intervention that promotes schools as protective spaces for learning and healing, where children can reach their full potential (*)
Can't wait to learn	Game-based e-learning intervention to provide education, as well as stress reduction, primarily for out-of-school children (*)
Family network intervention [b]	Family-level intervention focusing on, and supporting, multiple-problem families

[a]This is not the full spectrum of services that War Child offers, but those that are included in the program described in this chapter

[b]Development yet to start

*Interventions indicated with an 'asterisk' are universal/preventive interventions, the others are targeted or indicated interventions

each intervention has specific goals and expected outcomes, overall the care system aims to contribute to (1) building increased resilience at different socio-ecological levels and; (2) improving psychosocial wellbeing in children. In short, this is done by targeting groups of children (with universal and targeted interventions), parents, families and key structures and processes within communities as a whole.

We recognise the need for the care system to be implemented within the real-world contexts of humanitarian work, which are often complex, variable and unpredictable. A number of enabling components will support the development and implementation of the interventions and promote access to care.

First, we are developing a structured tool to proactively identify children and families who may benefit from more targeted interventions, and to increase awareness, access and the uptake of these services. Using this tool will enable us to more effectively allocate interventions to higher risk children and families, based on identified needs. Particularly, because the (multi-level) care system includes interventions aimed at small groups of children with more severe problems, such a detection tool will become an integral component of this approach. Previous studies have found that a similar detection methodology with adults, using pictorial vignettes, led to acceptable accuracy in detection (Jordans, Kohrt, Luitel, Komproe, & Lund, 2015) and subsequent help seeking (Jordans, Kohrt, Luitel, Lund, & Komproe, 2017).

Second, we are aiming to ensure equitable inclusion of children. It is crucial to view this integrated programming framework from an inclusive perspective as, due to a variety of barriers and factors, some children are excluded from participating in their societies. These barriers need to be recognised and overcome to ensure that the care system is inclusive and responsive to all. This may include interventions that directly address stigmatization and discrimination to ensure that services can be accessed by all children and families who might benefit from them.

Lastly, we are developing a thorough and sensitive process of 'community entry', which will ensure that the services being offered are in line with the needs and expectations of relevant community stakeholders, and build on existing resources and structures.

Research and Development

The War Child Holland care system is complemented by a comprehensive research agenda to support the development process and evaluate its core interventions and their inter-related functioning. The research program works towards combining evidence-based care services with quality implementation standards. This entails going beyond demonstrating evidence for interventions, and towards creating an improved understanding of how interventions are implemented adequately and with sufficient quality in real-world low-resource settings. This combination will allow us to make real progress towards replication and scale-up efforts and closing the evidence-practice gap in humanitarian settings (Proctor et al., 2009; Shidhaye, 2015; Tol, Patel, et al., 2011).

A systematic approach of development and evaluation designed especially for complex interventions will be followed (Craig et al., 2008). This iterative process focuses on: (a) formative research towards the development and modelling of interventions, which can be achieved through systematic reviews of existing intervention evidence and related constructs, preliminary qualitative work and development of a Theory of Change (Anderson, 2004); (b) pilot studies to test procedures and assess relevance of interventions within the target settings and populations, via small-scale qualitative and quantitative studies, typically resulting in adaptions to interventions and evaluation protocols; (c) evaluation to assess effectiveness of the interventions, ideally with the use of randomized controlled trials, and; (d) an implementation phase focusing on surveillance of implementation outside a controlled study setting, which centrally includes assessment of quality of care.

To achieve these ends, we will develop and pilot-test standards for *quality of implementation* for each of these interventions. Following Miller's (1990) clinical skills hierarchy, we operationalize these standards as the extent to which a service provider has the knowledge and skill required to deliver a treatment to the standard needed for it to achieve its expected effects (competence) and the extent to which a psychological treatment was delivered well enough for it to achieve its expected effects (adherence) (Fairburn & Cooper, 2011). Similar work has already been conducted with adults (Kohrt et al., 2015), which will need to be replicated both for children and for interventions covering multiple sectors (child protection, education and psychosocial support). Furthermore, additional implementation research will need to address remaining gaps in understanding; for example, the optimal model and dose of training and supervision, the most adequate delivery agent, strategies for integration into existing care systems, recruitment and retention strategies for competent lay workers, and the extent of equity in proposed service delivery models.

In addition to intervention-level research, there is a vast need for system-level thinking in the design and evaluation of care. We have argued that a broader systems approach is more capable of addressing the variety of needs of children affected by armed conflict. A systems-of-care approach raises obvious questions with regard to feasibility and sustainability (Jordans & Tol, 2013, 2015). Especially in settings where existing support systems are weakened by conflict, the development and continuation of a system of care will be challenging. Consequently, we will review whether and how a care system is feasible and applicable in terms of service uptake (*coverage*) and *cost* – again developing standards to assess these in practice. At the same time, it will allow for an assessment of the added value of an integrated or multi-sectoral approach towards improving wellbeing over single intervention or 'silo-ed' sector-specific approaches.

In summary, we are advocating, and making progress towards, a care system that can be implemented in humanitarian settings, and is evidence-based, scalable and equitable. This requires a trajectory that moves from a research space through an implementation space to achieve actual impact (see Fig. 2). The research space involves intervention-level work that transfers current practice to meaningful evidence-based practice by establishing *efficacy/effectiveness* on the one hand and *relevance* on the other. Subsequently, the implementation space involves system-level work that transfers meaningful evidence-based interventions to large-scale

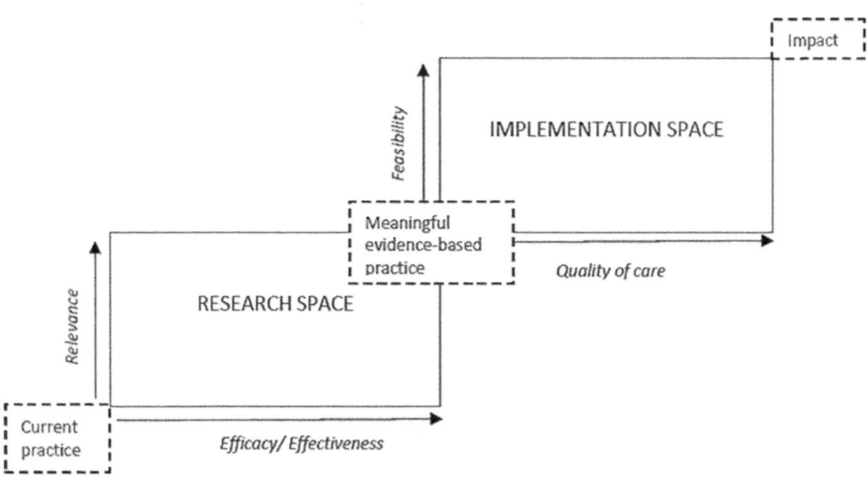

Fig. 2 Overview research and development trajectory

impact through assessing maintenance of quality of care via a set of competence and adherence standards, as well as assessing feasibility of the multi-sectoral service delivery framework through cost and coverage standards. The thinking behind this model is that once evidence for interventions has been established, implementation of services at scale can be assessed through a limited and defined set of standards for service providers and planners, with the assumption that if these standards are met impact is achieved.

Conclusions

To address the myriad psychosocial and mental health issues of children in areas of armed conflict, there is a need for comprehensive care systems that bring together prevention and treatment approaches. This can only truly be achieved if the social determinants of children's mental health are adequately addressed. We therefore propose a care system that integrates targeted psychosocial support and mental health care with child protection services that address and prevent issues of child abuse and neglect as well as interventions that aim to promote the school environment – jointly geared towards improving children's wellbeing and promoting resilience. The care system combines a set of interventions at different levels of the child's ecology and of differing intensity. It addresses common barriers to care, notably stigmatization and under-detection of children in need of care. An enormous 'service gap' exists whereby the support needs in low resource settings vastly outweigh the capacity of available services, and thus for any care package to have impact it must be capable of being provided at scale. Consequently, this requires the research agenda to gradually shift from demonstrating effectiveness of such interventions in LMIC to demonstrating how they can work optimally outside the boundaries of a study context. A set of standards to monitor quality and feasibility of service provision when implemented at scale will be vital to contribute towards impacting large groups of children affected by armed conflict that are currently not receiving the care they might need.

References

Ager, A., Akesson, B., Stark, L., Flouri, E., Okot, B., McCollister, F., & Boothby, N. (2011). The impact of the school-based psychosocial structured activities (PSSA) program on conflict-affected children in northern Uganda. *Journal of Child Psychology and Psychiatry, 52*(11), 1124–1133. https://doi.org/10.1111/j.1469-7610.2011.02407.x

Anderson, A. A. (2004). *The community builder's approach to theory of change: A practical guide to theory development.* Retrieved from http://www.dochas.ie/Shared/Files/4/TOC_fac_guide.pdf

Arjadi, R., Nauta, M. H., Chowdhary, N., & Bockting, C. L. H. (2015). A systematic review of online interventions for mental health in low and middle income countries: A neglected field. *Global Mental Health, 2*, e12.

Attanayake, V., McKay, R., Joffres, M., Singh, S., Burkle, F., & Mills, E. (2009). Prevalence of mental disorders among children exposed to war: A systematic review of 7,920 children. *Medicine, Conflict and Survival, 25*, 3–17.

Barber, B. K. (1999). Political violence, family relations, and palestinian youth functioning. *Journal of Adolescent Research, 14*(2), 206–230.

Barber, B. K. (2013). Annual research review: The experience of youth with political conflict–challenging notions of resilience and encouraging research refinement. *Journal of Child Psychology and Psychiatry, 54*(4), 461–473.

Barenbaum, J., Ruchkin, V., & Schwab-Stone, M. (2004). The psychosocial aspects of children exposed to war: Practice and policy initiatives. *Journal of Child Psychology and Psychiatry, 45*(1), 41–62.

Barry, M. M., Clarke, A. M., Jenkins, R., & Patel, V. (2013). A systematic review of the effectiveness of mental health promotion interventions for young people in low and middle income countries. *BMC Public Health, 13*(1), 835.

Bartels, S., & Hamill, K. (2014). *Running out of time: Survival of Syrian refugee children in Lebanon*. Boston, MA: FXB Center for Health and Human Rights at Harvard University.

Benish, S. G., Quintana, S., & Wampold, B. E. (2011). Culturally adapted psychotherapy and the legitimacy of myth: A direct-comparison meta-analysis. *Journal of Counseling Psychology, 58*(3), 279–289.

Bernal, G., & Sáez-Santiago, E. (2006). Culturally centered psychosocial interventions. *Journal of Community Psychology, 34*(2), 121–132.

Betancourt, T. S., & Khan, K. T. (2008). The mental health of children affected by armed conflict: Protective processes and pathways to resilience. *International Review of Psychiatry, 20*(3), 317–328.

Betancourt, T. S., McBain, R., Newnham, E. A., Akinsulure-Smith, A. M., Brennan, R. T., Weisz, J. R., & Hansen, N. B. (2014). A behavioral intervention for war-affected youth in Sierra Leone: A randomized controlled trial. *Journal of the American Academy of Child & Adolescent Psychiatry, 53*(12), 1288–1297.

Betancourt, T. S., Meyers-Ohki, S., Charrow, A., & Tol, W. A. (2013). Interventions for children affected by war: An ecological perspective on psychosocial support and mental health care. *Harvard Review of Psychiatry, 21*(2), 70–91.

Blanchet, R., Sistenich, V., Ramesh, A., Frison, S., Warren, E., Smith, J., … Roberts, B. (2015). *An evidence review of research on health interventions in humanitarian crises*. Retrieved from http://www.elrha.org/wp-content/uploads/2015/01/Evidence-Review-22.10.15.pdf

Boydell, K. M., Hodgins, M., Pignatiello, A., Teshima, J., Edwards, H., & Willis, D. (2014). Using technology to deliver mental health services to children and youth: A scoping review. *Journal of the Canadian Academy of Child and Adolescent Psychiatry, 23*(2), 87–99.

Brown, F. L., Graaff, A. M., Annan, J., & Betancourt, T. S. (2017). Annual research review: Breaking cycles of violence – A systematic review and common practice elements analysis of psychosocial interventions for children and youth affected by armed conflict. *Journal of Child Psychology and Psychiatry, 58*(4), 507–524.

Castro, F. G., Barrera, M., Jr., & Holleran Steiker, L. K. (2010). Issues and challenges in the design of culturally adapted evidence-based interventions. *Annual Review of Clinical Psychology, 6*, 213–239.

Catani, C., Schauer, E., & Neuner, F. (2008). Beyond individual war trauma domestic violence against children in Afghanistan and Sri Lanka. *Journal of Marital and Family Therapy, 34*(2), 165–176.

CPWG. (2012). *Minimum standards for child protection in humanitarian action*. Geneva, Switzerland: Child Protection Working Group.

CPWG. (2014). *Inter agency guidelines for case management & child protection. The role of case management in the protection of children: A guide for policy & programme managers and caseworkers*. Retrieved from http://cpwg.net/wp-content/uploads/sites/2/2014/09/Interagency-Guidelines-for-Case-Management-and-Child-Protection.pdf

CPWG. (2015). *A matter of life and death: Child protection programming's essential role in ensuring child wellbeing and survival during and after emergencies*. Retrieved from http://cpwg.net/?get=010222|2015/10/A_Matter_of_life_and_death_LowRes.pdf

Craig, P., Dieppe, P., Macintyre, S., Michie, S., Nazareth, I., & Petticrew, M. (2008). Developing and evaluating complex interventions: The new Medical Research Council guidance. *British Medical Journal, 337*, a1655. https://doi.org/10.1136/bmj.a1655

de Jong, J. T. V. M. (Ed.). (2002). *Trauma, war, and violence: Public mental health in socio-cultural context*. New York, NY: Kluwer Academic/Plenum Publishers.

Dybdahl, R. (2001). Children and mothers in war: An outcome study of a psychosocial intervention program. *Child Development, 72*(4), 1214–1230.

ECHO. (2016). *ECHO factsheet – Education in emergencies*. Retrieved from: http://ec.europa.eu/echo/files/aid/countries/factsheets/thematic/education_in_emergencies_en.pdf

Fairburn, C. G., & Cooper, Z. (2011). Therapist competence, therapy quality, and therapist training. *Behaviour Research and Therapy, 49*(6), 373–378.

Fazel, M., Reed, R. V., Panter-Brick, C., & Stein, A. (2012). Mental health of displaced and refugee children resettled in high-income countries: Risk and protective factors. *The Lancet, 379*(9812), 266–282.

Fazel, M., & Tol, W. A. (2014). Mental health interventions in schools in low-income and middle-income countries. *The Lancet Psychiatry, 1*(5), 388–398.

Griner, D., & Smith, T. B. (2006). Culturally adapted mental health interventions: A meta-analalytic review. *Psychotherapy: Theory, Research, Practice, Training, 43*(4), 531–548.

Harper, M. S., Heim, E., Chowdhary, N., Maercker, A., & Albanese, E. (2016). Cultural adaptation of minimally guided interventions for common mental disorders: A systematic review and meta-analysis. *Journal of Medical Internet Research Mental Health, 3*, 1–27.

HIIK. (2016). *Conflict barometer 2015*. Retrieved from http://www.hiik.de/en/konfliktbarometer/pdf/ConflictBarometer_2015.pdf

IASC. (2007). *IASC guidelines on mental health and psychosocial support in emergency settings*. Geneva, Switzerland: Inter-Agency Standing Committee.

INEE. (2012). *Minimum standards for education: Preparedness, response, recovery*. New York, NY: Inter-Agency Network for Education in Emergencies.

Jordans, M. J. D., Kohrt, B. A., Luitel, N. P., Komproe, I. H., & Lund, C. (2015). Accuracy of proactive case finding for mental disorders by community informants in Nepal. *The British Journal of Psychiatry, 207*(6), 501–506.

Jordans, M. J. D., Kohrt, B. A., Luitel, N. P., Lund, C., & Komproe, I. H. (2017). Proactive community case-finding to facilitate treatment seeking for mental disorders, Nepal. *Bulletin of the World Health Organization, 95*(7), 531–536.

Jordans, M. J. D., Komproe, I. H., Tol, W. A., Susanty, D., Vallipuram, A., Ntamatumba, P., … de Jong, J. T. V. M. (2010). Practice-driven evaluation of a multi-layered psychosocial care package for children in areas of armed conflict. *Community Mental Health Journal, 47*(3), 267–277. https://doi.org/10.1007/s10597-010-9301-9

Jordans, M. J. D., Pigott, H., & Tol, W. A. (2016). Interventions for children affected by armed conflict: A systematic review of mental health and psychosocial support in low- and middle-income countries. *Current Psychiatry Reports, 18*(9), 1–15.

Jordans, M. J. D., & Tol, W. A. (2013). Mental health in humanitarian settings: Shifting focus to care systems. *International Health, 5*(1), 9–10.

Jordans, M. J. D., & Tol, W. A. (2015). Mental health and psychosocial support for children in areas of armed conflict: Call for a systems approach. *British Journal of Psychiatry International, 12*(3), 72–75.

Jordans, M. J. D., Tol, W. A., Komproe, I. H., & de Jong, J. T. V. M. (2009). Systematic review of evidence and treatment approaches: Psychosocial and mental health care for children in war. *Child and Adolescent Mental Health, 14*(1), 2–14.

Jordans, M. J. D., Tol, W. A., Komproe, I. H., Susanty, D., Vallipuram, A., Ntamatumba, P., & de Jong, J. T. V. M. (2010). Development of a multi-layered psychosocial care system for children in areas of political violence. *International Journal of Mental Health Systems, 4*(15), 1–12.

Jordans, M. J. D., Tol, W. A., Ndayisaba, A., & Komproe, I. H. (2013). A controlled evaluation of a brief parenting psychoeducation intervention in Burundi. *Social Psychiatry and Psychiatric Epidemiology, 48*(11), 1851–1859.

Khamis, V. (2014). Does parent's psychological distress mediate the relationship between war trauma and psychosocial adjustment in children? *Journal of Health Psychology, 21*(7), 1361–1370.

Kohrt, B. A., Jordans, M. J. D., Rai, S., Shrestha, P., Luitel, N. P., Ramaiya, M. K., … Patel, V. (2015). Therapist competence in global mental health: Development of the ENhancing assessment of common therapeutic factors (ENACT) rating scale. *Behaviour Research and Therapy, 69*, 11–21.

Loughry, M., Ager, A., Flouri, E., Khamis, V., Afana, A. H., & Qouta, S. (2006). The impact of structured activities among Palestinian children in a time of conflict. *Journal of Child Psychology and Psychiatry, 47*(12), 1211–1218.

McLeod, J. D., & Shanahan, M. J. (1993). Poverty, parenting, and children's mental health. *American Sociological Review, 58*(3), 351–366.

Miller, G. E. (1990). The assessment of clinical skills/competence/performance. *Academic Medicine, 65*(9), S63–S67.

Miller, K. E., & Jordans, M. J. D. (2016). Determinants of children's mental health in war-torn settings: Translating research into action. *Current Psychiatry Reports, 18*(6), 58.

O'Callaghan, P., McMullen, J., Shannon, C., Rafferty, H., & Black, A. (2013). A randomized controlled trial of trauma-focused cognitive behavioral therapy for sexually exploited, war-affected Congolese girls. *Journal of the American Academy of Child & Adolescent Psychiatry, 52*(4), 359–369.

O'Mathúna, D. P., & Siriwardhana, C. (2017). Research ethics and evidence for humanitarian health. *The Lancet, 390*, 2228–2229. https://doi.org/10.1016/S0140-6736(17)31276-X

O'Sullivan, C., Bosqui, T., & Shannon, C. (2016). Psychological interventions for children and young people affected by armed conflict or political violence: A systematic literature review. *Intervention Journal, 14*(2), 142–164.

Panter-Brick, C., Goodman, A., Tol, W. A., & Eggerman, M. (2011). Mental health and childhood adversities: A longitudinal study in Kabul, Afghanistan. *Journal of the American Academy of Child & Adolescent Psychiatry, 50*(4), 349–363. https://doi.org/10.1016/j.jaac.2010.12.001

Proctor, E. K., Landsverk, J., Aarons, G., Chambers, D., Glisson, C., & Mittman, B. (2009). Implementation research in mental health services: An emerging science with conceptual, methodological, and training challenges. *Administration and Policy in Mental Health and Mental Health Services Research, 36*(1), 24–34.

Puffer, E. S., Annan, J., Sim, A. L., Salhi, C., & Betancourt, T. S. (2017). The impact of a family skills training intervention among Burmese migrant families in Thailand: A randomized controlled trial. *PLoS One, 12*(3), e0172611.

Saltzman, W. R., Layne, C. M., Steinberg, A. M., Arslanagic, B., & Pynoos, R. S. (2003). Developing a culturally and ecologically sound intervention for youth exposed to war and terrorism. *Child and Adolescent Psychiatric Clinics of North America, 12*(2), 319–342.

Shidhaye, R. (2015). Implementation science for closing the treatment gap for mental disorders by translating evidence base into practice: Experiences from the PRIME project. *Australasian Psychiatry, 23*(6 suppl), 35–37.

Sim, A., Annan, J., Puffer, E., Salhi, C., & Betancourt, T. S. (2014). *Building happy families: Impact evaluation of a parenting and family skills intervention for migrant and displaced Burmese families in Thailand.* New York, NY: International Rescue Committee.

Slone, M., & Mann, S. (2016). Effects of war, terrorism and armed conflict on young children: A systematic review. *Child Psychiatry and Human Development, 47*(6), 950–965.

Srivastava, K. (2011). Child labour issues and challenges. *Industrial Psychiatry Journal, 20*, 1–3.

Stichick, T. (2001). The psychosocial impact of armed conflict on children. Rethinking traditional paradigms in research and intervention. *Child Adolescent Psychiatric Clinics of North America, 10*(4), 797–814.

Thornicroft, G. (2008). Stigma and discrimination limit access to mental health care. *Epidemiology and Psychiatric Sciences, 17*(1), 14–19.

Thornicroft, G., Mehta, N., Clement, S., Evans-Lacko, S., Doherty, M., Rose, D., … Henderson, C. (2015). Evidence for effective interventions to reduce mental-health-related stigma and discrimination. *The Lancet, 387*(10023), 1123–1132.

Tol, W. A., Barbui, C., Galappattti, A., Silove, D., Betancourt, T. S., Souza, R., … Van Ommeren, M. (2011). Mental health and psychosocial support in humanitarian settings: Linking practice and research. *The Lancet, 378*(9802), 1–11.

Tol, W. A., Jordans, M. J. D., Kohrt, B. A., Betancourt, T. S., & Komproe, I. H. (2013). Promoting mental health and psychosocial Well-being in children affected by political violence: Part I – Current evidence for an ecological resilience approach. In C. Fernando & M. Ferrari (Eds.), *Handbook of resilience in children of war* (pp. 11–27). New York, NY: Springer.

Tol, W. A., Jordans, M. J. D., Reis, R., & de Jong, J. T. V. M. (2009). Ecological resilience: Working with child-related psychosocial resources in war-affected communities. In D. Brom, R. Pat-Horenczyk, & J. Ford (Eds.), *Treating traumatized children: Risk, resilience, and recovery*. London, UK: Routledge.

Tol, W. A., Patel, V., Tomlinson, M., Baingana, F., Galappatti, A., Panter-Brick, C., … van Ommeren, M. (2011). Research priorities for mental health and psychosocial support in humanitarian settings. *PLoS Medicine, 8*, 1–6.

Tol, W. A., Patel, V., Tomlinson, M., Baingana, F., Galappatti, A., Silove, D., … Panter-Brick, C. (2012). Relevance or excellence? Setting research priorities for mental health and psychosocial support in humanitarian settings. *Harvard Review of Psychiatry, 20*(1), 25–36. https://doi.org/10.3109/10673229.2012.649113

Tol, W. A., Song, S., & Jordans, M. J. D. (2013). Annual research review: Resilience and mental health in children and adolescents living in areas of armed conflict – A systematic review of findings in low-and middle-income countries. *Journal of Child Psychology and Psychiatry, 54*(4), 445–460.

UN. (2016). *Children and armed conflict: Report of the Secretary-General.* Retrieved from http://www.un.org/ga/search/view_doc.asp?symbol=S/2016/360

UNHCR. (2015). *World at war: UNHCR global trends: Forced displacement in 2014.* Retrieved from http://www.unhcr.org/556725e69.pdf

UNICEF. (2016). *The state of the world's children*. Retrieved from https://www.unicef.org/publications/files/UNICEF_SOWC_2016.pdf

Wessells, M. G. (2009). *What are we learning about protecting children in the community? An inter-agency review of the evidence on community-based child protection mechanisms in humanitarian and development settings.* Retrieved from http://educationcluster.net/wp-content/uploads/sites/2/2011/10/What-We-Are-Learning-About-Protecting-Children-in-the-Community_Full-Report.pdf

Wessells, M. G., & Monteiro, C. (2006). Psychosocial assistance for youth: Towards reconstruction for peace in Angola. *Journal of Social Issues, 62*(1), 121–139.

Williamson, J., & Robinson, M. (2006). Psychosocial interventions, or integrated programming for well-being. *Interventions, 4*(1), 4–25.

Winthrop, R., & Kirk, J. (2005). Teacher development and student well-being. *Forced Migration Review, 22*, 18–21.

Mark J. D. Jordans, PhD, child psychologist is Professor of Child and Adolescent Global Mental Health at the University of Amsterdam and works as Director of Research & Development for War Child in the Netherlands. Prof. Jordans is a Reader in Child and Adolescent Mental Health in Humanitarian Settings at the Center for Global Mental Health, King's College London. His work focuses on the development, implementation and evaluation of psychosocial and mental health care systems in low and middle income countries, especially for children in adversities and in fragile states. Mark Jordans is the founder and Senior Technical Advisor of TPO Nepal, a leading mental health NGO in Nepal.

Myrthe van den Broek, MSc, anthropologist and researcher at the Research & Development department of War Child Holland. She is involved in the development of a tool for proactive identification of children and families indicated for more targeted interventions to increase access to and uptake of services.

Felicity Brown, Ph.D., is clinical psychologist and researcher at War Child in the Netherlands. Her research primarily focuses on the development and evaluation of evidence-based psychological interventions for individuals and families exposed to armed conflict and other adversity, with particular interests in the training of non-specialists to deliver interventions in low resource settings, cultural adaptations, and the role of the family environment in child outcomes.

April Coetzee, MA, is the Senior Education Advisor in the Research & Development department of War Child in the Netherlands. She is leading the research on improving teachers' competencies through professional development and the addressing violence in schools. She has a particular interest in research that looks at the relationship between academic and social and emotional learning outcomes in education.

Rinske Ellermeijer, MSc, is the Senior Child Protection Advisor at the Research and Development department of War Child Holland in Amsterdam. She is a social- and cultural anthropologist with research interests in indigenous community structures and traditions involved in the protection of children from maltreatment.

Kim Hartog, MSc, human geographer, researcher at the Research & Development department of War Child in the Netherlands. Her research interests focus on stigma reduction and strengthening meaningful participation with a specific focus on children in conflict-affected communities.

Frederik Steen, MSc, researcher at the Research & Development department of War Child Holland. He is involved in research regarding an instrument to measure competencies for service providers working directly with children and a study to evaluate a psychological intervention for children with severe emotional distress.

Kenneth E. Miller, Ph.D., is a psychologist and researcher at War Child Holland, where he develops and evaluates mental health and psychosocial interventions for war-affected children and families. His research has also focused on identifying the diverse pathways by which armed conflict and forced migration impact the mental health of civilians.

Clinical Considerations in the Psychological Treatment of Refugees

Matthis Schick, Naser Morina, Ulrich Schnyder, and Thomas Maier

> *The passport is the most noble part of the human being. It also does not come into existence in such a simple fashion as a human being does. A human being can come into the world anywhere, in the most careless way and for no good reason, but a passport never can. When it is good, the passport is also recognized for this quality, whereas a human being, no matter how good, can go unrecognized.*
>
> *Bertolt Brecht, Refugee Conversations, 1961*

Abstract The refugee experience is a complex phenomenon and subject to a multitude of influencing factors including reminiscences of the traumatic past, and distress related to post-migration and ecological factors. While posttraumatic stress disorder (PTSD) is highly prevalent among refugees, psychiatric comorbidity is rather the rule than the exception. Though the literature provides evidence for the effectiveness of trauma-focused treatment in reducing symptoms of PTSD among refugees, PTSD may neither be the only nor the most important aspect, and the

M. Schick (✉)
Department of Consultation-Liaison-Psychiatry and Psychosomatic Medicine, University Hospital Zurich, Zurich, Switzerland
e-mail: matthis.schick@usz.ch

N. Morina
Department of Consultation-Liaison-Psychiatry and Psychosomatic Medicine, University Hospital Zurich, Zurich, Switzerland
e-mail: naser.morina@usz.ch

U. Schnyder
University of Zurich, Zurich, Switzerland
e-mail: ulrich.schnyder@access.uzh.ch

T. Maier
Psychiatric Services of St. Gallen North, Wil, St. Gallen, Switzerland
e-mail: thomas.maier@psgn.ch

N. Morina, A. Nickerson (eds.), *Mental Health of Refugee and Conflict-Affected Populations*, https://doi.org/10.1007/978-3-319-97046-2_14

exclusive therapeutic focus on PTSD often does not result in satisfactory treatment responses. This chapter seeks to put the refugee experience into a broader context integrating clinically relevant aspects of pre- and post-migration. Practical recommendations are given in order to overcome obstacles and pitfalls and to achieve more favorable outcomes in the treatment of this vulnerable population. Clinical considerations are illustrated by two case reports.

Keywords Refugee mental health · Asylum seekers · Posttraumatic stress disorder · PTSD · Transcultural psychiatry

Introduction

The refugee experience is a highly complex phenomenon. It comprises two diametrical, but equally fundamental dimensions: the view back on the past, often including violence, threat, separation, loss, and helplessness; and the view ahead, containing incertitude, isolation, and often, again, helplessness. Experiences in the past influence the perception and assumptions regarding the present and future, and the experiences in exile affect the appraisal of the past. Human rights violations in the country of origin may be compounded by the experience of injustice, hardship and discrimination in the hosting society and challenge beliefs about trust, justice, and mastery. The refugee experience affects not only the individual with his or her personality, biography, strengths and shortcomings, but also the family, clan, ethnicity, or nation, including the antecedent as well as the subsequent generation. It is, at the same time, individual and collective, and comprises i.e. political, cultural, religious, moral, and most often legal and bureaucratic aspects. It is, about life and death, good and evil, it involves hope and despair, courage and fear, grief and solace, perspectives, embitterment and resignation. War, persecution and displacement are the ultimate existential experiences. And as complex as the refugee experience is, so is refugee mental health. The psychological perspective is only one among many, subjectively often not the most significant one, and the distinction between pathological and normal reactions to trauma and blows of fate is not always obvious.

Research on refugee mental health has for a long time primarily focused on the effects of direct exposure to organized violence. The introduction of posttraumatic stress disorder (PTSD) as a clinically compelling and well operationalized diagnosis, followed by the consistent evidence of a dose-response relationship between direct trauma exposure and PTSD symptom levels (Mollica et al., 1998; Smith, Perrin, Yule, Hacam, & Stuvland, 2002) has fueled fruitful clinical and research activity. The past four decades generated an abundance of insights and evidence regarding trauma and its psychological impact and led to the development of effective treatment interventions for PTSD.

In addition to PTSD as a consequence of direct trauma exposure, there is a growing body of evidence indicating that refugee mental health is not only defined by traumatic events but also by post-migration or exile-related stressors. Post-migration stressors have consistently emerged as stronger predictors than war exposure of depression, functional impairment, and general distress, while war exposure seems more strongly related than post-migration stressors to PTSD (Ellis, MacDonald, Lincoln, & Cabral, 2008; Gorst-Unsworth & Goldenberg, 1998; Miller et al., 2002; Steel, Silove, Bird, McGorry, & Mohan, 1999). Nonetheless, post-migration stressors have also consistently been related to PTSD symptom levels among refugees, though the mechanism by which they may affect PTSD symptomatology remains unclear at present (for overview see Miller & Rasmussen, 2010b). Therefore, trauma-related and exile-related stressors may best be viewed as interdependent factors influencing refugees' health.

Diverging emphasis on traumatic or post-migration stressors respectively has led to a contentious and unfruitful divide between two opposing treatment approaches. Where trauma-focused advocates primarily see evidence of enduring war related trauma requiring specialized clinical treatment (Neuner, Schauer, Klaschik, Karunakara, & Elbert, 2004), psychosocial advocates see distress rooted largely in the stressful conditions and adversities of everyday life in conflict or post-conflict settings. From a psychosocial viewpoint, altering those stressful conditions is likely to improve people's mental health, while also fostering their inherent capacity to recover – with adequate social support and the passing of time – from the lingering effects of exposure to war-related violence and loss (Betancourt & Williams, 2008). Conversely, trauma-focused advocates believe that ameliorating symptoms of war-related trauma will not only improve mental health, but will also enable people to cope more effectively with ongoing environmental stressors (Neuner et al., 2004).

While the literature provides evidence for the effectiveness of trauma-focused treatment in reducing symptoms of PTSD among refugees, this does not (yet) hold for approaches exclusively focusing on counseling or multimodal interventions (for review see Nickerson, Bryant, Silove, & Steel, 2011). From a clinical perspective, however, the conflict between advocates of trauma-focused versus psychosocial approaches seems rather academic and might be influenced by the institutional affiliation of their promoters: Unlike in specialized trauma units which are by nature highly or exclusively focused on PTSD, clinicians operating in general (mental) health care institutions are confronted with a broad range of conditions including physical, psychosomatic, psychological and social problems. Comorbid depression, for instance, was found in over 70% of refugees with PTSD (Marshall, Schell, Elliott, Berthold, & Chun, 2005), and physical complaints were reported by more than 80% of refugees with PTSD (Teodorescu et al., 2015) and torture survivors (Van Ommeren et al., 2002). In a clinical sample of severely traumatized refugees, an average of 10 post-migration living difficulties were rated as a moderately serious, serious or very serious problem during the last 12 months (Schick et al., 2016). Not all refugees with mental health problems suffer from PTSD, and those who do may not necessarily rate PTSD as their top priority problem. Many refugees would identify current threats and problems rather than past trauma as their most stressful challenge (for overview see Miller & Rasmussen, 2010b) (cf. case report 2).

Despite the meritorious improvements in the treatment of PTSD that the diagnosis of PTSD and specific PTSD treatment interventions have enabled, trauma-focused psychotherapy is obviously not a one-fits-all solution for any refugee mental health problem, and a broader perspective is needed. Many clinically relevant questions remain to be answered, some of which will be discussed below.

Clinical Challenges

Potential Limitations of and Contra-Indications to Trauma-Focused Psychotherapy

Trauma-focused psychotherapy has proven effective in reducing PTSD symptoms in traumatized populations in general, in both adults as well as children and adolescents (Bisson, Roberts, Andrew, Cooper, & Lewis, 2013; Bradley, Greene, Russ, Dutra, & Westen, 2005; Gutermann et al., 2016; Morina, Koerssen, & Pollet, 2016; Schnyder & Cloitre, 2015; Watts et al., 2013), and in refugees in particular (Maier, 2015; Neuner, Onyut, et al., 2008; Neuner, Schauer, et al., 2004). However, in some patients trauma-focused therapy may not be applicable, or sufficiently effective, for manifold reasons.

Patients may be ambivalent or reluctant, or may even refuse trauma-focused psychotherapy straightforwardly (cf. case report 2). This is very common in severely traumatized individuals in general, especially in the beginning of treatment. In many cases, a patient's reluctance to undergo exposure-based psychotherapy can be understood as part of their avoidance behavior in the context of PTSD. On top of this, in multiply traumatized refugees, issues such as trust, shame, disgust, social stigma and social sanctioning (e.g., expulsion of female rape survivors from their families) frequently arise, thus creating impediments to trauma-focused treatment approaches that may at times seem insurmountable. In addition, depending on their individual cultural backgrounds, patients may have developed models of illness, and beliefs regarding appropriate treatment approaches that differ from their therapists' theories and attitudes. For all these reasons, it sometimes takes more time than usual to start trauma-focused psychotherapy. A number of preparatory sessions may be needed so that the therapist can better understand the cultural components of a patient's illness and help-seeking behaviors, as well as their treatment expectations. Based on such deeper understanding, mutual trust may develop, and eventually the patient will be ready to engage in trauma-focused work (cf. case report 1). Moreover, empirically supported treatments may need to be modified depending on the patient's cultural background (Schnyder et al., 2016). For instance, patients who are reluctant to talk may be willing to use other ways of accessing the traumatic memories such as writing, painting, dancing, or singing. Clearly, patients should be informed about effective treatments for trauma related disorders, and encouraged to consider these options. However, given the multitude of stressors traumatized refugees usually are exposed to, including the post-migration living difficulties they have to deal with, they should never be coerced into, for example, undergoing exposure sessions or cognitive restructuring. Rather, therapists should respect their patients' concerns, show an interest in their reasoning, and always try to "keep the door open": If a patient does not want to start trauma-focused psychotherapy today, it may well be that next week, or next month, or next year, they will be ready to muster the courage to confront their traumatic memories.

Furthermore, psychiatric comorbidity may limit the effectiveness of trauma-focused psychotherapy. Severe depression impacts on the patient's cognitive functions. Psychotic symptoms will likely impair a patient's trust in their therapist. Suicidal ideation and impulses may temporarily require psychiatric hospitalization. Substance use disorders decrease the patient's emotional responsiveness and hamper their ability to attend treatment sessions regularly. Moreover, especially in tortured refugees, somatic symptom disorders, in many cases with predominant chronic pain, are very common. While we know from the literature that trauma-focused psychotherapy can be safely and effectively used in the presence of psychiatric comorbidity (van Minnen, Harned, Zoellner, & Mills, 2012), such situations may make it necessary to provide integrated or concurrent treatment to monitor and address the comorbid problems.

In some patients, long-term, sequential exposure to trauma and its psychosocial consequences are so severe that it may take the patient a very long time to start engaging in trauma-focused psychotherapy in its proper sense. Even after undergoing successful trauma-focused psychotherapy, many of these patients will still fulfill diagnostic criteria for PTSD and suffer from substantial functional impairment and/or other psychiatric conditions (Bradley et al., 2005). These patients will remain in need of support and have to be offered alternative treatment options (cf. case report 2).

Other patients, particularly those with more acute symptom profiles, initially suffer from low distress tolerance. They may present with suicidal, self-harming and/or aggressive behavior, or show highly dissociative reactions especially when confronted with their traumatic memories. These patients may benefit from phase-based treatment approaches such as Skills Training in Affective and Interpersonal Regulation (STAIR) Narrative Therapy (Cloitre, Cohen, & Koenen, 2006; Cloitre & Schmidt, 2015) in which emotion regulation and other coping skills are trained prior to engaging in trauma-focused work. It has to be emphasized, however, that STAIR Narrative Therapy has not yet been evaluated with traumatized refugees.

Lack of safety due to insecure visa status, pending or negative asylum decisions, or social threats from within the patient's social network may present another obstacle, forcing both the therapist and their patient to defer trauma-focused treatment (cf. case report 1). Ongoing trauma such as repetitive domestic violence usually precludes trauma-focused psychotherapy until at least some degree of safety is established. Even if formal safety is achieved, many refugees remain deeply emotionally connected with their country of origin and their people. They rigorously follow the news via satellite TV and are updated on every incident by their relatives who have been left behind in situations of ongoing threat and conflict. Due to their high identification with their collective, witnessing their people being exposed to ongoing trauma is frequently perceived as a re-traumatization, which may reinforce negative beliefs and feelings of helplessness (Schock, Böttche, Rosner, Wenk-Ansohn, & Knaevelsrud, 2016). All of this can render trauma-focused therapy with refugees more challenging than with other populations.

Mental Health Problems Other than PTSD

Though PTSD is extremely prevalent among refugee populations, not all refugees with mental health problems suffer from PTSD: Many present with affective or anxiety disorders or chronic pain, which may be, but do not necessarily have to, be related to traumatic experiences. Some refugees suffer from pre-existing, non-trauma related disorders such as schizophrenia or bipolar disorder which might or might not be aggravated by traumatic or post-migration stress. All these conditions can also co-occur with PTSD, and it is not always obvious which disorder should primarily be addressed, and which is comorbid and would possibly resolve after successful PTSD treatment. In addition, the diagnostic attribution of symptoms can be challenging. Hearing voices and feeling persecuted, for instance, are quite common in PTSD resulting from organized violence (Nygaard, Sonne, & Carlsson, 2017). They can, however, also represent paranoid-hallucinatory symptoms of a psychotic disorder or a culture-specific expression of depression in the context of loss or interpersonal conflicts, each of which would require a different treatment approach. Finally, among the most commonly presented symptoms are physical complaints (Rohlof, Knipscheer, & Kleber, 2014). Again, the distinction between eligible causes such as genuine physical disability, somatic intrusions, dissociation, somatoform symptoms or non-specific expressions of distress is sometimes difficult. Eventually, the diagnostic procedure is complicated by typical refugee issues such as mistrust of others, language barriers, or culturally differing concepts and symptom presentations.

Before starting an intervention, the mechanisms behind the presented symptoms and their diagnostic affiliation should be properly understood. Sometimes, however, the initial evaluation is not conclusive, and treatment decisions have to be based on preliminary hypotheses under ongoing revision. Given the common co-occurrence and mutual dependence of psychological, biological and social factors in the emergence of refugee mental health problems, a close, interdisciplinary collaboration between psychologists, psychiatrists and somatic medicine is advisable. The diagnostic procedure should ideally distinguish between complaints in need of somatic or psychiatric treatment, and symptoms that can be treated with psychological intervention. In addition, assessment should include clarification regarding which symptoms are subjectively causing the most distress and functional impairment, and which issues the patient is ready to address. This assessment should intermittently be repeated as priorities usually change along the treatment trajectory. With the patient's approval, family members can be an important source of information not only with regard to symptom presentation and (familial) level of functioning, but also in terms of the evolution, context and the intracultural conceptualization of the condition.

Dual Focus of Distress: Trauma and Post-migration Living Difficulties

Learning a new language, finding appropriate and affordable accommodation or securing employment represent a challenge for most people. Achieving all this in a foreign country, unfamiliar in language, culture, custom, and procedures, is even more challenging. When additional burdens emerge from worries about family back home, precarious living conditions, or traumatic memories and functional impairment due to PTSD, a pathogenic stress level is easily surpassed. In consequence, refugee mental health is – beyond the adverse effects of traumatic experiences – also affected by difficulties arising *after* successful entry in a formally safe host country. Research suggests that length of asylum procedure, insecure visa status, detention in refugee camps or being prohibited to work account for a substantial proportion of psychological impairment (Brabant & Raynault, 2012; Laban, Gernaat, Komproe, Schreuders, & De Jong, 2004; Nickerson, Steel, Bryant, Brooks, & Silove, 2011; Ryan, Benson, & Dooley, 2008; Silove, Sinnerbrink, Field, Manicavasagar, & Steel, 1997). Even after potentially obtaining a secure visa status, refugees are often confronted with continuing challenges. Communication problems, financial austerity, poor quality accommodation, inability to find work, separation from family members and discrimination experiences have been shown to contribute to psychological distress and to the incidence of mental disorders (Laban, Gernaat, Komproe, van der Tweel, & De Jong, 2005; Nickerson, Bryant, Brooks, et al., 2011; Nickerson, Bryant, Steel, Silove, & Brooks, 2010; Porter & Haslam, 2005). While founding a new existence would require self-efficacy, courage and confidence, living in ongoing insecurity and being at the mercy of authorities in the host society may exacerbate the feelings of mental defeat and helplessness arising from precedent persecution and traumatic experiences. The "system" and the underlying political reluctance to welcome and support refugees may be perceived as hostile, and the initial relief about the successful escape is often replaced by new feelings of threat and embitterment. Psychological distress resulting from post-migration experiences is often felt as even more proximate and tormenting than past traumatic experiences, and its long-lasting continuance may gradually exhaust psychological resources.

This day-to-day clinical experience leads many agencies engaged in refugee support to offer multimodal approaches including social and legal counseling. Though counseling has not proven effective in reducing PTSD symptoms, successful coaching and social interventions may substantially reduce subjective distress (Miller & Rasmussen, 2010a, 2010b), allow corrective emotional experiences and a sense of achievement, improve trust, therapeutic alliance and compliance, and therefore potentially increase the likelihood of successful trauma-focused psychotherapy (cf. case report 2). On the other hand, many aspects of the post-migration environment are political in nature and are beyond therapeutic influence. Under such conditions, the vain therapeutic efforts to induce a feeling of safety, control and confidence in traumatized refugees can therefore become a source of continuous frustration and helplessness in patients as well as therapists – a fact that has to be carefully taken into account with regard to its impact on motivation, working atmosphere, and coherence of treatment teams.

Communication

The language barrier is often a particularly complex issue in the treatment of refugees. As language is one of the most important tools in psychotherapy, a treatment is not possible if there is no common language between therapist and patient. People can mostly express their feelings and emotions best in their mother tongue. The ability to describe one's own suffering in one's native language may promote the feeling of being taken seriously and may thus improve compliance with treatment and improve quality of care and satisfaction (Karliner, Jacobs, Chen, & Mutha, 2007). Medical organizations often use lay people (e.g., health service staff or family members) to help patients communicate with them. The use of these untrained ad-hoc interpreters, especially of family members or lay hospital interpreters, however, has been shown to have negative clinical consequences, because this could lead, for example, to misevaluation of a patient's mental status or sensitive psychological problems that cannot be discussed in front of a family member (Ebden, Carey, Bhatt, & Harrison, 1988; Jacobs et al., 2001; Marcos, 1979; Westermeyer, 1990). To enable communication between therapists and patients not speaking a common language, therefore, the use of qualified interpreters is inevitable. Beyond interpreting what is said, interpreters are also useful regarding the interpretation of verbal symbolism and cultural behaviors that feed into the therapy. Studies have shown that interpreter-assisted trauma-focused therapy can be effective (d'Ardenne, Ruaro, Cestari, Fakhoury, & Priebe, 2007; Schulz, Resick, Huber, & Griffin, 2006).

However, the presence of a third person – the interpreter – alters the traditional therapeutic relationship from a dyad to a triad, which introduces both challenges and opportunities. It can have an impact on the establishment of trust and confidentiality, particularly when it comes to the recounting of traumatic experiences (cf. case report 1). In addition, the presence of the interpreter can have a significant impact on the therapy process. Even though they are expected to be invisible in a therapy session, it is evident that patients regard interpreters as anything but invisible. Traumatized patients often have strong emotional reactions to interpreters. Interpreters can be a member of the patient's local community and therefore hinder disclosure of sensitive information. Age/gender discordance or differences in cultural, religious, and political affiliation may also hinder the development of a trusting therapeutic alliance. Ethnic characteristics can be particularly sensitive as some people who have experienced torture and war may not want a member of their own community interpreting for reasons of perceived confidentiality and shame. For instance, if someone has been forced to humiliate another person under the threat of torture the patients often do not want to talk about this in front of an own community member. On the other hand, in some cases, it may also be problematic if an interpreter is from a different group, i.e., because the group may have been involved in persecution, or there may be cultural misunderstandings. Further distortions could be interpreter-client or interpreter-therapist over-identification. In summary, the use of qualified and trained interpreters is highly recommended in order to establish a professional relationship and to achieve good treatment adherence (Crosby, 2013; Karliner et al., 2007).

In order to ensure good therapy in a triad therapist-patient-interpreter relationship the following issues might be important (Miletic et al., 2006): A session with an interpreter is best structured into a before – during – after the meeting, with different foci, respectively. It should be ensured at the beginning of a therapy session so that the patient can clarify any possible questions, and to ensure that he/she is satisfied with the interpretation/the interpreter. To avoid the above-mentioned difficulties and to facilitate the therapeutic process, interpreters should be familiarized with the principles of psychotherapeutic methods, and they should understand the rationale of a trauma-focused treatment. They should not omit, add or shorten what has been said, but translate exactly and accurately (sometimes simultaneously) so that meaning is not lost. If cultural consultation or clarification is needed, this could be done after the session in order to not interrupt the process of a therapy. Further, the responsibilities and roles of both interpreters and therapists should be clearly defined. The therapist should ensure that the seating is arranged to facilitate communication. Recommended seating is in a triangle formation, where all three parties are at an equal distance apart. Finally, supportive debriefing with the interpreter at the end of a session is important in helping interpreters manage distressing clinical material (Miller, Martell, Pazdirek, Caruth, & Lopez, 2005).

Loss of Trust and Faith

The severity of traumatic events experienced by refugees often surpasses the levels of trauma that clinicians are used to treating in civilian resident patients. The duration of traumatizing conditions, the number of traumatic events, the cruelty of the experienced trauma, the unsettling character of interpersonal violence, and the magnitude of loss are often extraordinary. In consequence, these patients not only suffer from 'regular, classical' posttraumatic stress symptoms but also from a deep and fundamental blow to what could be called self-sameness or identity as a person (Bettelheim, 1943; Mollica et al., 2001; Wilson, 2004). Severe depression, identity confusion, loss of meaning, and deep feelings of shame are challenges for clinicians working with traumatized refugees. Many severely traumatized refugees remain deeply depressed about their losses and cannot find a way to cope with helpless anger or recover from paralyzing shame. These patients have experienced a fundamental shattering of their assumptions about the trustworthiness of the world (Janoff-Bulman, 1992). Ordinary human life in the community with other people has lost meaning, and basic social values such as trust, respect, and compassion are mere words to these patients. They have experienced an amount of ruthlessness and malice that they may never again have faith in anybody. This damage to the basic sense of trust makes it highly demanding for therapists to establish a therapeutic relationship with such patients. Many of these patients have abandoned their faith in fairness and ethical values, and in consequence, may be fundamentally distrustful and dismissive. Often therapists are challenged by their patients' mistrustful attitude over a longer period of time until finally some degree of trust is built up by patients. Patience, reliability, authentic empathy, and constancy are therefore crucial qualities for therapists who intend to help traumatized refugees.

The Cultural and Social Dimensions of Suffering

Refugees who suffer from posttraumatic stress symptoms are often culturally and socially uprooted. Many lack social support and are distant from their families, their cultural background, and their traditional means of coping. This isolation is particularly distressing for traumatized individuals because the process of coping with extremely stressful experiences is often embedded in a cultural perspective (Aroche & Coello, 2004; Charuvastra & Cloitre, 2008). Ethnocultural beliefs, religious practices, and social behaviors are intimately linked to the process of how individuals integrate traumatic experiences into their lives and how they recover to a higher level of functioning. When treating victims of war and torture, clinicians must try to enter into the cultural and historical reality of their patients and evaluate the collectivistic dimension of individual traumata (Eisenbruch, de Jong, & van de Put, 2004). In recent research, the social ecology of posttraumatic symptoms has increasingly been highlighted. Not only do PTSD symptoms lead to relational difficulties in the family and society, but the reverse is also true: Lack of social support leads to more severe PTSD symptoms (Ozbay et al., 2007). Factors like family acceptance, stigma, education, economic circumstances, prosecution of perpetrators, and political development are intimately related to the course of posttraumatic stress symptoms. Concealment and denial of human rights violations, corrupted post-war societies and ongoing political and economic insecurity strongly affect mental health of traumatized individuals. Despite the importance of societal and collective factors, however, most evidence-based treatment modalities for trauma victims focus on the individual. Kohrt (2013) rightly argues:

> From a cross-cultural perspective, the social and relational aspects of trauma also can be more distressing than individual symptoms of PTSD. There is often a connection between social distress and post-traumatic psychosomatic complaints that resolve through community processes rather than solely through individual treatment (Kohrt, 2013).

Therapists treating traumatized refugees should carefully explore the patient's social environment. Also, some knowledge about the patient's cultural background is very helpful for evaluating the context of the therapy (Schnyder et al., 2016). Even if a patient is reluctant to involve family members or friends in treatment, the significance of others for the patient's recovery has to be clarified before initiating therapy. If a patient feels like an outcast from his community or disregarded by the family patriarch because of his posttraumatic stress symptoms, the patient may be reluctant to enter into therapy. In some cases, the involvement of cultural brokers (i.e., reputable members of the migrant's own community) facilitating the dialogue between patient and health professionals can be useful.

In addition, an individual-centred treatment approach may sometimes be inappropriate or insufficient: Structural violence and systematic human rights violations often do not target individuals but, rather, collectives with the aim of disrupting families and communities and destroying their bonds, their sense of belonging and togetherness. In such situations, therapy should not exclusively focus on individuals but should also address community needs in terms of coping with hatred and rifts, and the reconsolidation of victims and perpetrators within the same collective. As there is hardly any evidence available to guide such interventions, future research addressing these issues is urgently needed. Given this insight, the impact of religious and political leaders, mass media coverage of human rights violations, international persecution of perpetrators, and post-war reconciliation processes on the recovery of individuals becomes obvious. Therapists of traumatized refugees always act in a cultural, societal, yet political context and have to integrate various perspectives in their work.

Survivor's Guilt and Moral Injury

Traumatized refugees have to cope not only with feelings of fear, helplessness, and horror but also with shame, guilt, hatred, and anger. This mixture of different emotions is sometimes hard to disentangle and may be unsettling to patients and therapists. Survivors of war and torture often believe they survived only because others were less fortunate. To survive is indeed sometimes the result of mere chance and sometimes the result of the survivor's own acts. To survive in situations where reliable rules and moral values are annulled inevitably carries ethical dilemmas. The individual is challenged with how to remain fair and honest in situations where the will to survive becomes a mere biological drive. Especially in contexts of war and torture some experiences inevitably transgress deeply held moral beliefs. The psychological consequences of transgressions that lead to serious inner conflict because the experience is at odds with core ethical and moral beliefs is called *moral injury* (Litz et al., 2009; Nickerson, Bryant, Rosebrock, & Litz, 2014; Nickerson et al., 2015). From the comfortable armchair of the doctor's office, it is easy to moralize and to argue about right or wrong. Nevertheless, survivors of war and torture often rigorously apply moral reasoning to their acts and omissions, aggrieving themselves with reproaches and accusations. Feelings of guilt, persistence in self-reproach or even self-harm are, of course, symptoms of major depression; however, they also can be understood as the re-enactment of traumatizing experiences. In fact, torturers purposefully entangle their victims in moral dilemmas and inflict on them feelings of guilt (Modvig & Jaranson, 2004). Torturers aim to cause long-term damage to individuals as well as to societies by eroding their moral fundaments and by destroying their human values.

For therapists, the treatment of victims of war and torture holds the potential for confusion, anguish, and pain as, in countertransference, the patient's horrors are re-experienced. In fact, patients' experiences can also involve acts of cruelty or even crime. Some severely traumatized patients desperately seeking help are, in fact, perpetrators at the same time. It is rare, however, that patients expose themselves as perpetrators and want to focus their therapies on committed acts of violence. The example of child soldiers or war veterans shows, though, that even committed violence is potentially traumatizing and has detrimental effects on perpetrators (Klasen, Reissmann, Voss, & Okello, 2015; Schaal, Weierstall, Dusingizemungu, & Elbert, 2012). The crucial problem in these therapies is often the handling of actual guilt and moral injury, which is obviously not a psychotherapeutic issue. The therapist must wrestle with how to advise a patient who believes he is guilty, potentially not only morally but also legally. From a therapeutic perspective, the involvement of societal, religious, or legal authorities can pave the way to eventual recovery. When working in this field, clinicians must be prepared to enter into the most complex realities of patients, where truth, certainty, and clarity are not easy to recognize. They must find a way to address issues of morality, guilt, responsibility, and compensation without falling into a moralizing or condemning attitude.

Summary and Recommendations

Refugee mental health is a complex phenomenon and subject to a multitude of influencing factors including reminiscences of the traumatic past, distress related to current traumatic and life events (e.g., family back home, ongoing war, domestic violence), and distress related to post-migration and ecological factors (e.g., language, work, housing, visa status, integration). In consequence, psychiatric comorbidity is rather the rule than the exception, and the exclusive therapeutic focus on PTSD is often insufficient, even if an extended conceptualization including grief, embitterment, guilt and shame is taken into account. In view of the abundance of different (and therefore mostly unfamiliar) cultural, biographical, or sociopolitical backgrounds and mechanisms, it is prudent not to rely too uncritically on western concepts, nor on cultural stereotypes or putative transcultural expertise, but to seek a specific approach of understanding for each individual patient (Schnyder et al., 2016). It is important to keep in mind that assumptions that seem to be logical or obvious to us may not necessarily make sense in the eyes of our patients, and vice versa. A treatment approach exclusively based on an extra-cultural interpretation of symptom presentation can be misleading and provoke wrong treatment decisions. Therapy is often not only about relieving symptoms, but about initiating, facilitating and empowering long-term processes regarding self-competence, resilience, and, progressively, social integration.

From a practical point of view, it is advisable to primarily focus on (1) the disorder that is in the subjective focus of distress, (2) the disorder that is causing the most impairment, (3) the disorder that is accessible for treatment under given circumstances, or, ideally, a combination of these conditions. In view of the challenging surrounding conditions, a close interdisciplinary collaboration between psychiatrists, psychotherapists and somatic medicine can be helpful in order to tap the full treatment potential. A multimodal approach including, in addition to trauma-focused psychotherapy, social work or physiotherapy may address patients' most proximal needs and therefore potentially enhance trust, compliance and stress tolerance. Instead of imposing our (western) conceptions on our (non-western) patients, it might be most constructive (and informative) to use our patients as transcultural experts, particularly as patients often feel appreciated and more readily share their experiences.

Conclusion

Therapeutic work with (traumatized) refugees is often characterized by numerous challenges and limitations, and the ongoing confrontation with the human abyss and unalterable external hindrance can be emotionally exhausting. At the same time, it allows us to gain insight in a rich abundance of sociocultural contexts and to meet exceptional people with (for us) exceptional lives. The continuous reflection of one's own and different values and experiences puts into perspective what we consider to be indispensable or take for granted, and leaves a deep gratitude for our many conveniences and the incidental fortune of a privileged birth.

Case Report 1

Sivan, a 32-year-old married woman from Iraq was referred to our outpatient clinic by her GP. She lived with her husband and two daughters (2 and 6 years old) in a rural Swiss village, where the family was accommodated by the immigration authorities. She and the family were still waiting for their claim for asylum to be decided. Her husband had emigrated 2 years earlier, leaving his wife and two daughters with her parents in their remote home, a small village near the Turkish border.

At the time of referral, Sivan could speak only a few words in German. Only minimal communication was possible with her, so we involved a female Kurdish interpreter. The husband reported that his wife had started to show changes in her mood and behavior several months after her immigration. As time passed her behavior became increasingly peculiar; she neglected her housework, was erratic with her children and was irritable, ill-humoured, sad and weepy. She could (or would) not explain the reasons for her mood to her husband, but obviously it caused her distress and she wanted help. In initial sessions, Sivan answered the therapist's questions without elaboration and rarely spoke spontaneously. After a few weeks of therapy she gradually opened up, and it seemed that she started to find the conversation with her therapist to be beneficial. During the first year of therapy, Sivan mostly spoke about her feelings of inadequacy as a mother. She had a great deal of difficulty with her elder daughter who was now 7 years old because the girl did not obey her and had severe learning problems at school. Sivan felt responsible for her daughter's problems and asked her therapist for advice. Some 6 months after the beginning of the therapy, the family's claim for asylum was initially rejected, which caused a major relapse in Sivan's condition. The family appealed the decision and after 1 year, the family was assigned a temporary visa. The court decision was primarily based on the description of Sivan's health condition that was reported to the authorities by her therapist.

Even after 2 years of treatment, Sivan still felt unable to travel the 50 km from her home to her therapist's office alone. She would have to take a bus, then change to a train, and finally walk five blocks. She felt uneasy travelling on her own for several reasons; however, one particular reason eventually became clear: Sivan was illiterate. Only when her daughters went to school in Switzerland did she learn the Roman alphabet and slowly learn to read and write in German. When her husband found a job and could no longer accompany her, she simply had to travel on her own. Initially, this necessity troubled her a lot, but then she visibly took some pride in her new daring. She also had learned to ride a bicycle (something she never had the chance to practice in her home country) and joined the local women's gymnastics club. Around this time, she came to her therapist 1 day and proposed that they continue the sessions without the interpreter. Indeed, she had learned to speak German fairly well now and communication was possible. Not surprisingly, the therapeutic conversation changed in many ways after that. The subjects became much more personal, and Sivan addressed different topics that were never discussed before. Finally, after more than 3 years of continuous therapy, she started to tell her therapist about traumatic and haunting experiences she had been exposed to in her home country before she left. One day, when her parents were away working in the fields, three unknown men – civil officials of the police – arrived suddenly at her door. They immediately entered the house and rudely asked for her husband. She said that he was abroad and that she hadn't seen him for some time. The policemen laughed at her and started beating and groping her. While both of her children were in the room, they forced her to undress, and they raped her brutally. They left her humiliated and injured, and threatened her and her family with further harm if the family did not comply with the police. Sivan was deeply frightened, not only by the horror she had just experienced but also by the imminent danger she was in now. If her father or husband were to find out what had happened to her, she would probably be expelled by her own family. Sivan confided in her mother and told her everything. Together, they managed to conceal the crime from the rest of the family. Fortunately, she recovered passably and was able to escape with her two children to Switzerland. When Sivan started to talk about these traumatic experiences, she seemed determined to tell the entire story. The therapist did not have to persuade or urge her to do so. When she was recalling her trauma over the next three sessions, she experienced deep pain, shame, and disgust and suffered from flashbacks and intensified nightmares between the sessions. The psychological interventions were applied in accordance with the Narrative Exposure Therapy manual (Schauer, Schauer, Neuner, & Elbert, 2011). Sivan found the exposure to traumatic memories to be manageable, and she regained self-control and felt relief after a further five or six sessions conducted on a weekly basis. She still did not want to tell her husband about her trauma.

Based on an amendment to the immigration law, the family could apply for a permanent visa after they had lived in the country for 5 years and were independent from welfare for more than 1 year. Her husband had gained a good reputation as a hard-working man, and Sivan was well known among the women in the village because she had joined the local gymnastic club. After almost 5 years of treatment, Sivan's family was given a permanent resident status. Her mental health condition was almost completely normalized. The therapy could be stopped, and she continued to be seen for follow ups once or twice a year.

Case Report 2

Amir, a 26-year-old Iranian asylum seeker, was referred to our psychiatric outpatient service due to sleep disturbances and distress after obtaining a negative asylum decision. Amir was invited to a first appointment. The goal and process of the initial assessment were carefully introduced, as well as the assisting Iranian interpreter, including reference to medical confidentiality. Amir appeared suspicious, even grim, and was obviously very distressed. He insisted that he was only seeking support regarding his asylum procedure as well as his poor accommodation, but seemed unmotivated for treatment. The sessions that followed were quite challenging: Amir was easily irritated and responded to apparently innocuous questions with loud and intimidating outbursts of anger. Neither a therapeutic alliance nor an agreement regarding treatment goals could be achieved, and after three sessions, Amir terminated treatment, being provided with the address of a free legal advisory service and an information sheet on the suspected PTSD diagnosis in his mother tongue.

Four months later, Amir spontaneously appeared at the reception desk and requested an appointment. Asked about his former interruption of therapy, he mentioned mistrust and fear that sensitive information would be passed on to the Iranian government by the interpreter. The latter was therefore replaced by an interpreter with a Swiss background. In the following weeks, the situation became a bit clearer: After participating in a demonstration, Amir had apparently been arrested, interrogated and tortured, before being able to flee from his country. His asylum request in Switzerland including several subsequent appeals had been rejected (because he didn't dare to disclose his reasons for seeking asylum), and Amir was anticipating his repatriation, followed in his eyes by further persecution and, eventually, execution. In addition, his accommodation in an overcrowded asylum center with daily police roundups was amplifying intrusions and hyperarousal symptoms. Amir felt purposely mistreated by the authorities, and the social advisors in charge of his case in turn were not willing to support him due to his threatening and aggressive behavior. Not surprisingly, Amir was extremely socially isolated.

Though Amir accepted the suggested diagnoses of PTSD and major depressive disorder, he refused to talk about the experiences that had led him to Switzerland. The psychiatry resident treating Amir told his supervisor that he would not dare to do trauma-focused psychotherapy due to the impending repatriation and Amir's impaired affect regulation, particularly after having learned that several charges for aggression were reported against Amir. From time to time, however, deep desperation and suffering were shining through Amir's fierce facade which could be addressed by the therapist and allowed him to persuade Amir of a pharmacological treatment with an antidepressive medication and a neuroleptic agent for (off-label) sedation. Unfortunately, the resident had to be replaced with another clinician as treating therapist soon after due to the end of his training interval.

The following year showed few changes. Our attempts for mediation between Amir and the authorities remained fruitless, though Amir slowly developed a minimal trust in our institution. The enduring insecurity concerning his stay in Switzerland and the unaltered living conditions in the asylum center increasingly undermined Amir's last reserves. Only 1 week after his case was taken over by a staff psychiatrist for complexity and risk reasons, Amir went to his case manager's office with two bottles of fire accelerant in his hands threatening (in fragmentary German) to self-immolate if he was not transferred to another, quieter center. The police were called, and Amir was arrested for attempted malicious arson. After 3 days in prison, he was completely exhausted by his intrusions and had to be referred to a psychiatric in-patient ward due to severe self-harming behavior.

Owing to a remarkably sensitive prosecutor considering the therapist's arguments, Amir could, to his relief, be discharged from the hospital without having to return to prison. The episode, though very stressful for everyone involved, considerably strengthened the therapeutic alliance and Amir's trust in our institution. On his request, the interpreter was once more replaced, and the therapist embarked on a systematic exploration of the long history of persecution of Amir and his family beginning with the fall of the Shah regime in 1979 and including a long succession of severe traumatic experiences. With Amir's consent, this information was transmitted to a lawyer who initiated a new asylum procedure. In view of the substantial posttraumatic stress symptoms and related functional impairment, Amir was – despite his still insecure visa status – offered trauma-focused psychotherapy in which he now agreed to participate. During the next 6 months, the core traumatic experience was exposed and processed, with therapy being carefully adapted to Amir's limited distress tolerance, which led to a significant reduction of PTSD symptoms.

Despite his progress, Amir remained in a labile state with significant suicidal ideation and desperation. It took another year for Amir to be finally granted a temporary protection visa, which allowed him to take German lessons, and look for a job and an accommodation outside the asylum center. The end of 6 years of insecurity and precarious living conditions produced great joy and relief in the therapist. Amir, however, suffered a massive depressive decompensation. The fact that he was not recognized as a refugee and theoretically still could be expelled from Switzerland elicited not only anger and indignation, but bottomless resignation.

Despite an augmentation of the antidepressive treatment, he became highly suicidal and expected the therapist to support his intention to undergo assisted suicide (ironically an option that is not legally available for persons with temporary visa status). The therapist's refusal led to a critical strain on the therapeutic alliance. Amir felt abandoned and temporarily went to see other doctors hoping to have his wish fulfilled. In view of the strong suicidal ideations, a compulsory inpatient treatment was discussed, but finally refrained from, as this would have led to an irreversible withdrawal from treatment. Instead, Amir was offered continuous low-threshold attendance with the only goal being to reestablish his trust in the therapist. Amir accepted, and over the following months, depression and anger sufficiently improved to gradually allow further future-directed considerations. With the help of our social worker, a small apartment was found, and Amir was finally able to leave the asylum center. He started German lessons at our in-house language course, where he quickly made progress, and started resuming social contacts.

Today, after 4 years of therapy, Amir is working as an apprentice in a bakery. He is still suffering from minor PTSD and moderate depressive symptoms. He is still taking medication and is attending monthly therapy sessions where he mainly focuses on his many experienced losses (family, home, social status, fiancée, years of his life). He has regained his original friendliness and politeness, has made a few friends, and the contact with his social advisors is relaxed and valued on both sides.

References

Aroche, J., & Coello, M. J. (2004). Ethnocultural considerations in the treatment of refugees and asylum seekers. In J. P. Wilson & B. Droždek (Eds.), *Broken spirits. The treatment of traumatized asylum seekers, refugees, war and torture victims*. New York, NY/Hove, UK: Brunner-Routledge.

Betancourt, T. S., & Williams, T. (2008). Building an evidence base on mental health interventions for children affected by armed conflict. *Intervention (Amstelveen), 6*(1), 39–56. https://doi.org/10.1097/WTF.0b013e3282f761ff

Bettelheim, B. (1943). Individual and mass behavior in extreme situations. *The Journal of Abnormal and Social Psychology, 38*(4), 417–452. https://doi.org/10.1037/h0061208

Bisson, J. I., Roberts, N. P., Andrew, M., Cooper, R., & Lewis, C. (2013). Psychological therapies for chronic post-traumatic stress disorder (PTSD) in adults. *Cochrane Database Systematic Review, 2013*. https://doi.org/10.1002/14651858.CD003388.pub4

Brabant, Z., & Raynault, M.-F. (2012). Health situation of migrants with precarious status: Review of the literature and implications for the Canadian context—Part A. *Social Work in Public Health, 27*(4), 330–344. https://doi.org/10.1080/19371918.2011.592076

Bradley, R., Greene, J., Russ, E., Dutra, L., & Westen, D. (2005). A multidimensional meta-analysis of psychotherapy for PTSD. *American Journal of Psychiatry, 162*(2), 214–227. https://doi.org/10.1176/appi.ajp.162.2.214

Charuvastra, A., & Cloitre, M. (2008). Social bonds and posttraumatic stress disorder. *Annual Review of Psychology, 59*(1), 301–328. https://doi.org/10.1146/annurev.psych.58.110405.085650

Cloitre, M., Cohen, L. R., & Koenen, K. C. (2006). *Treating survivors of childhood abuse: Psychotherapy for the interrupted life*. New York, NY: Guilford Press.

Cloitre, M., & Schmidt, J. A. (2015). STAIR narrative therapy. In U. Schnyder & M. Cloitre (Eds.), *Evidence based treatments for trauma-related psychological disorders: A practical guide for clinicians* (pp. 277–297). Cham, Switzerland: Springer.

Crosby, S. S. (2013). Primary care management of non-English-speaking refugees who have experienced trauma: A clinical review. *JAMA, 310*(5), 519–528. https://doi.org/10.1001/jama.2013.8788

d'Ardenne, P., Ruaro, L., Cestari, L., Fakhoury, W., & Priebe, S. (2007). Does interpreter-mediated CBT with traumatized refugee people work? A comparison of patient outcomes in East London. *Behavioural and Cognitive Psychotherapy, 35*(3), 293–301. https://doi.org/10.1017/S1352465807003645

Ebden, P., Carey, O. J., Bhatt, A., & Harrison, B. (1988). The bilingual consultation. *Lancet, 331*(8581), 347. https://doi.org/10.1016/s0140-6736(88)91133-6

Eisenbruch, M., de Jong, J. T., & van de Put, W. (2004). Bringing order out of chaos: A culturally competent approach to managing the problems of refugees and victims of organized violence. *Journal of Traumatic Stress, 17*(2), 123–131. https://doi.org/10.1023/b:jots.0000022618.65406.e8

Ellis, B. H., MacDonald, H. Z., Lincoln, A. K., & Cabral, H. J. (2008). Mental health of Somali adolescent refugees: The role of trauma, stress, and perceived discrimination. *Journal of Consulting and Clinical Psychology, 76*(2), 184–193. https://doi.org/10.1037/0022-006x.76.2.184

Gorst-Unsworth, C., & Goldenberg, E. (1998). Psychological sequelae of torture and organised violence suffered by refugees from Iraq. Trauma-related factors compared with social factors in exile. *The British Journal of Psychiatry, 172*(1), 90–94. https://doi.org/10.1192/bjp.172.1.90

Gutermann, J., Schreiber, F., Matulis, S., Schwartzkopff, L., Deppe, J., & Steil, R. (2016). Psychological treatments for symptoms of posttraumatic stress disorder in children, adolescents, and young adults: A meta-analysis. *Clinical Child and Family Psychology Review, 19*(2), 77–93. https://doi.org/10.1007/s10567-016-0202-5

Jacobs, E. A., Lauderdale, D. S., Meltzer, D., Shorey, J. M., Levinson, W., & Thisted, R. A. (2001). Impact of interpreter services on delivery of health care to limited-English-proficient patients. *Journal of General Internal Medicine, 16*(7), 468–474. https://doi.org/10.1046/j.1525-1497.2001.016007468.x

Janoff-Bulman, R. (1992). *Shattered assumptions: Towards a new psychology of trauma*. New York, NY: Free Press.

Karliner, L. S., Jacobs, E. A., Chen, A. H., & Mutha, S. (2007). Do professional interpreters improve clinical care for patients with limited English proficiency? A systematic review of the literature. *Health Services Research, 42*(2), 727–754. https://doi.org/10.1111/j.1475-6773.2006.00629.x

Klasen, F., Reissmann, S., Voss, C., & Okello, J. (2015). The guiltless guilty: Trauma-related guilt and psychopathology in former Ugandan child soldiers. *Child Psychiatry & Human Development, 46*(2), 180–193. https://doi.org/10.1007/s10578-014-0470-6

Kohrt, B. (2013). Social ecology interventions for post-traumatic stress disorder: What can we learn from child soldiers? *The British Journal of Psychiatry, 203*(3), 165–167. https://doi.org/10.1192/bjp.bp.112.124958

Laban, C. J., Gernaat, H. B., Komproe, I. H., Schreuders, B. A., & De Jong, J. T. (2004). Impact of a long asylum procedure on the prevalence of psychiatric disorders in Iraqi asylum seekers in The Netherlands. *Journal of Nervous and Mental Disease, 192*(12), 843–851. https://doi.org/10.1097/01.nmd.0000146739.26187.15

Laban, C. J., Gernaat, H. B., Komproe, I. H., van der Tweel, I., & De Jong, J. T. (2005). Postmigration living problems and common psychiatric disorders in Iraqi asylum seekers in the Netherlands. *Journal of Nervous and Mental Disease, 193*(12), 825–832. https://doi.org/10.1097/01.nmd.0000188977.44657.1d

Litz, B. T., Stein, N., Delaney, E., Lebowitz, L., Nash, W. P., Silva, C., & Maguen, S. (2009). Moral injury and moral repair in war veterans: A preliminary model and intervention strategy. *Clinical Psychology Review, 29*(8), 695–706. https://doi.org/10.1016/j.cpr.2009.07.003

Maier, T. (2015). Treatment of traumatized refugees and immigrants. In U. Schnyder & M. Cloitre (Eds.), *Evidence based treatments for trauma-related psychological disorders: A practical guide for clinicians* (pp. 399–412). Cham, Switzerland: Springer.

Marcos, L. R. (1979). Effects of interpreters on the evaluation of psychopathology in non-English-speaking patients. *American Journal of Psychiatry, 136*(2), 171–174. https://doi.org/10.1176/ajp.136.2.171

Marshall, G., Schell, T., Elliott, M., Berthold, S., & Chun, C. (2005). Mental health of Cambodian refugees 2 decades after resettlement in the United States. *JAMA, 294*(5), 571–579. https://doi.org/10.1001/jama.294.5.571

Miletic, T. P., Piu, M., Minas, H., Stankovska, M., Stolk, Y., & Klimidis, S. (2006). *Guidelines for working effectively with interpreters in mental health settings*: Victorian Transcultural Psychiatry Unit Melbourne.

Miller, K. E., Martell, Z. L., Pazdirek, L., Caruth, M., & Lopez, D. (2005). The role of interpreters in psychotherapy with refugees: An exploratory study. *American Journal of Orthopsychiatry, 75*(1), 27–39. https://doi.org/10.1037/0002-9432.75.1.27

Miller, K. E., & Rasmussen, A. (2010a). Mental health and armed conflict: The importance of distinguishing between war exposure and other sources of adversity: A response to Neuner. *Social Science & Medicine, 71*(8), 1385–1389. https://doi.org/10.1016/j.socscimed.2010.07.020

Miller, K. E., & Rasmussen, A. (2010b). War exposure, daily stressors, and mental health in conflict and post-conflict settings: Bridging the divide between trauma-focused and psychosocial frameworks. *Social Science & Medicine, 70*(1), 7–16. https://doi.org/10.1016/j.socscimed.2009.09.029

Miller, K. E., Weine, S. M., Ramic, A., Brkic, N., Bjedic, Z. D., Smajkic, A., … Worthington, G. (2002). The relative contribution of war experiences and exile-related stressors to levels of psychological distress among Bosnian refugees. *Journal of Traumatic Stress, 15*(5), 377–387. https://doi.org/10.1023/A:1020181124118

Modvig, J., & Jaranson, J. M. (2004). A global perspective of torture, political violence and health. In J. P. Wilson & B. Drožđek (Eds.), *Broken spirits. The treatment of traumatized asylum seekers, refugees, war and torture victims*. New York, NY/Hove, UK: Brunner-Routledge.

Mollica, R. F., McInnes, K., Pham, T., Smith Fawzi, M. C., Murphy, E., & Lin, L. (1998). The dose-effect relationships between torture and psychiatric symptoms in Vietnamese ex-political detainees and a comparison group. *Journal of Nervous and Mental Disease, 186*(9), 543–553. https://doi.org/10.1097/00005053-199809000-00005

Mollica, R. F., Sarajlic, N., Chernoff, M., Lavelle, J., Vukovic, I. S., & Massagli, M. P. (2001). Longitudinal study of psychiatric symptoms, disability, mortality, and emigration among Bosnian refugees. *JAMA, 286*(5), 546–554. https://doi.org/10.1001/jama.286.5.546

Morina, N., Koerssen, R., & Pollet, T. V. (2016). Interventions for children and adolescents with posttraumatic stress disorder: A meta-analysis of comparative outcome studies. *Clinical Psychology Review, 47*, 41–54. https://doi.org/10.1016/j.cpr.2016.05.006

Neuner, F., Onyut, P. L., Ertly, V., Odenwald, M., Schauer, M., & Elbert, T. (2008). Treatment of posttraumatic stress disorder by trained lay counselors in an African refugee settlement: A randomized controlled trial. *Journal of Consulting and Clinical Psychology, 76*(4), 686–694. https://doi.org/10.1037/0022-006x.76.4.686

Neuner, F., Schauer, M., Klaschik, C., Karunakara, U., & Elbert, T. (2004). A comparison of narrative exposure therapy, supportive counseling, and psychoeducation for treating posttraumatic stress disorder in an african refugee settlement. *Journal of Consulting and Clinical Psychology, 72*(4), 579–587. https://doi.org/10.1037/0022-006x.72.4.579

Nickerson, A., Bryant, R. A., Brooks, R., Steel, Z., Silove, D., & Chen, J. (2011). The familial influence of loss and trauma on refugee mental health: A multilevel path analysis. *Journal of Traumatic Stress, 24*(1), 25–33. https://doi.org/10.1002/jts.20608

Nickerson, A., Bryant, R. A., Rosebrock, L., & Litz, B. T. (2014). The mechanisms of psychosocial injury following human rights violations, mass trauma, and torture. *Clinical Psychology: Science and Practice, 21*(2), 172–191. https://doi.org/10.1111/cpsp.12064

Nickerson, A., Bryant, R. A., Silove, D., & Steel, Z. (2011). A critical review of psychological treatments of posttraumatic stress disorder in refugees. *Clinical Psychology Review, 31*(3), 399–417. https://doi.org/10.1016/j.cpr.2010.10.004

Nickerson, A., Bryant, R. A., Steel, Z., Silove, D., & Brooks, R. (2010). The impact of fear for family on mental health in a resettled Iraqi refugee community. *Journal of Psychiatric Research, 44*(4), 229–235. https://doi.org/10.1016/j.jpsychires.2009.08.006

Nickerson, A., Schnyder, U., Bryant, R. A., Schick, M., Mueller, J., & Morina, N. (2015). Moral injury in traumatized refugees. *Psychotherapy and Psychosomatics, 84*(2), 122–123. https://doi.org/10.1159/000369353

Nickerson, A., Steel, Z., Bryant, R., Brooks, R., & Silove, D. (2011). Change in visa status amongst Mandaean refugees: Relationship to psychological symptoms and living difficulties. *Psychiatry Research, 187*(1–2), 267–274. https://doi.org/10.1016/j.psychres.2010.12.015

Nygaard, M., Sonne, C., & Carlsson, J. (2017). Secondary psychotic features in refugees diagnosed with post-traumatic stress disorder: A retrospective cohort study. *BMC Psychiatry, 17*(1), 5. https://doi.org/10.1186/s12888-016-1166-1

Ozbay, F., Johnson, D. C., Dimoulas, E., Morgan, C. A., Charney, D., & Southwick, S. (2007). Social support and resilience to stress: From neurobiology to clinical practice. *Psychiatry, 4*(5), 35–40.

Porter, M., & Haslam, N. (2005). Predisplacement and postdisplacement factors associated with mental health of refugees and internally displaced persons: A meta-analysis. *JAMA, 294*(5), 602–612. https://doi.org/10.1001/jama.294.5.602

Rohlof, H. G., Knipscheer, J. W., & Kleber, R. J. (2014). Somatization in refugees: A review. *Social Psychiatry and Psychiatric Epidemiology, 49*(11), 1793–1804. https://doi.org/10.1007/s00127-014-0877-1

Ryan, D. A., Benson, C. A., & Dooley, B. A. (2008). Psychological distress and the asylum process: A longitudinal study of forced migrants in Ireland. *Journal of Nervous and Mental Disease, 196*(1), 37–45. https://doi.org/10.1097/nmd.0b013e31815fa51c

Schaal, S., Weierstall, R., Dusingizemungu, J. P., & Elbert, T. (2012). Mental health 15 years after the killings in Rwanda: Imprisoned perpetrators of the genocide against the Tutsi versus a community sample of survivors. *Journal of Traumatic Stress, 25*(4), 446–453. https://doi.org/10.1002/jts.21728

Schauer, M., Schauer, M., Neuner, F., & Elbert, T. (2011). *Narrative exposure therapy: A short-term treatment for traumatic stress disorders*. Cambridge, MA: Hogrefe Publishing.

Schick, M., Zumwald, A., Knöpfli, B., Nickerson, A., Bryant, R. A., Schnyder, U., … Morina, N. (2016). Challenging future, challenging past: The relationship of social integration and psychological impairment in traumatized refugees. *European Journal of Psychotraumatology, 7*(1), 28057. https://doi.org/10.3402/ejpt.v7.28057

Schnyder, U., Bryant, R. A., Ehlers, A., Foa, E. B., Hasan, A., Mwiti, G., … Yule, W. (2016). Culture-sensitive psychotraumatology. *European Journal of Psychotraumatology, 7*(1), 31179. https://doi.org/10.3402/ejpt.v7.31179

Schnyder, U., & Cloitre, M. (2015). *Evidence based treatments for trauma-related psychological disorders: A practical guide for clinicians*. Cham, Switzerland: Springer.

Schock, K., Böttche, M., Rosner, R., Wenk-Ansohn, M., & Knaevelsrud, C. (2016). Impact of new traumatic or stressful life events on pre-existing PTSD in traumatized refugees: Results of a longitudinal study. *European Journal of Psychotraumatology, 7*(1), 32106. https://doi.org/10.3402/ejpt.v7.32106

Schulz, P. M., Resick, P. A., Huber, L. C., & Griffin, M. G. (2006). The effectiveness of cognitive processing therapy for PTSD with refugees in a community setting. *Cognitive and Behavioral Practice, 13*(4), 322–331. https://doi.org/10.1016/j.cbpra.2006.04.011

Silove, D., Sinnerbrink, I., Field, A., Manicavasagar, V., & Steel, Z. (1997). Anxiety, depression and PTSD in asylum-seekers: Assocations with pre-migration trauma and post-migration stressors. *The British Journal of Psychiatry, 170*(4), 351–357. https://doi.org/10.1192/bjp.170.4.351

Smith, P., Perrin, S., Yule, W., Hacam, B., & Stuvland, R. (2002). War exposure among children from Bosnia-Hercegovina: Psychological adjustment in a community sample. *Journal of Traumatic Stress, 15*(2), 147–156. https://doi.org/10.1023/a:1014812209051

Steel, Z., Silove, D., Bird, K., McGorry, P., & Mohan, P. (1999). Pathways from war trauma to posttraumatic stress symptoms among Tamil asylum seekers, refugees, and immigrants. *Journal of Traumatic Stress, 12*(3), 421–435. https://doi.org/10.1023/a:1024710902534

Teodorescu, D.-S., Heir, T., Siqveland, J., Hauff, E., Wentzel-Larsen, T., & Lien, L. (2015). Chronic pain in multi-traumatized outpatients with a refugee background resettled in Norway: A cross-sectional study. *BMC Psychology, 3*(1), 7. https://doi.org/10.1186/s40359-015-0064-5

van Minnen, A., Harned, M. S., Zoellner, L., & Mills, K. (2012). Examining potential contraindications for prolonged exposure therapy for PTSD. *European Journal of Psychotraumatology, 3*(1), 18805. https://doi.org/10.3402/ejpt.v3i0.18805

Van Ommeren, M., Sharma, B., Sharma, G. K., Komproe, I., Cardena, E., & de Jong, J. T. (2002). The relationship between somatic and PTSD symptoms among Bhutanese refugee torture survivors: Examination of comorbidity with anxiety and depression. *Journal of Traumatic Stress, 15*(5), 415–421. https://doi.org/10.1023/a:1020141510005

Watts, B. V., Schnurr, P. P., Mayo, L., Young-Xu, Y., Weeks, W. B., & Friedman, M. J. (2013). Meta-analysis of the efficacy of treatments for posttraumatic stress disorder. *Journal of Clinical Psychiatry, 74*(6), e541–e550. https://doi.org/10.4088/JCP.12r08225

Westermeyer, J. (1990). Working with an interpreter in psychiatric assessment and treatment. *Journal of Nervous and Mental Disease, 178*(12), 745–749. https://doi.org/10.1097/00005053-199012000-00003

Wilson, J. P. (2004). The broken spirit: Posttraumatic damage to the self. In J. P. Wilson & B. Drožđek (Eds.), *Broken spirits. The treatment of traumatized asylum seekers, refugees, war and torture victims*. New York, NY/Hove, UK: Brunner-Routledge.

Matthis Schick, M.D., is a licensed psychiatrist and psychotherapist. He is head of the outpatient service for victims of torture and war at the University Hospital Zurich, Switzerland. His research interests focus on refugee mental health, particularly on trauma and post-migration related disorders.

Naser Morina, Ph.D., is a clinical psychologist and psychotherapist at the University Hospital Zurich, specialising in traumatic stress. His specific research expertise focuses on aspects of traumatic stress research in migrants, refugees and civilian war survivors. His research theme on trauma-related disorders in refugees and post-war affected people is wide-ranging. He is senior research assistant and psychotherapist at the Outpatient Unit for Victims of Torture and War.

Ulrich Schnyder, M.D., psychiatrist and licensed psychotherapist. Professor emeritus of psychiatry and psychotherapy, University of Zurich, Switzerland. Past President, European Society for Traumatic Stress Studies (ESTSS). Past President, International Federation for Psychotherapy (IFP). Past President, International Society for Traumatic Stress Studies (ISTSS). Recipient of the 2013 Wolter de Loos Award for Distinguished Contribution to Psychotraumatology in Europe (ESTSS), and the 2016 Lifetime Achievement Award (ISTSS).

Thomas Maier, M.D., born 1967, is head of the Psychiatric Services of St. Gallen North/ Switzerland. From 2003 - 2010 he headed the Outpatient Sollten wir vereinheitlichen. Thomas Maier's research interests span from psychotraumatology to psychiatric epidemiology, transcultural psychiatry, and child sexual abuse.

Legal and Ethical Considerations Related to the Asylum Process

Jane Herlihy and Stuart Turner

Abstract This chapter sets out to cover some of the pitfalls in applying "common sense" to legal decision making relating to the asylum process and the need to engage with the wider body of general psychological knowledge. We set out a brief summary of the law, and comment on the central issue of credibility. Because the asylum seeker rarely has objective documentation of their persecution, the decision-maker usually has to consider two primary issues – first if the claim meets the threshold for acceptance and second if the claim is to be believed (credibility). Memory is taken as an example of a process that may influence the asylum claim and/or decision; for example, discrepant reporting is often taken as proof of deceit. The scientific evidence in fact suggests that this is an erroneous assumption, that memory is not fixed. It is common for memory, even memory for traumatic events, to change. It is argued that there is a need to apply expert psychological knowledge, not just in the preparation of medico-legal reports on individuals but also in making the whole system of legal decision-making more psychologically informed and more consistent with the scientific literature. After a brief consideration of interviewing issues, there is also reference to both the potential impact of vicarious traumatisation on decision-makers and the difficulties in law of tolerating uncertainty.

Keywords Asylum law · Credibility · Discrepancy · Memory · Interview Technique

---

J. Herlihy
Centre for the Study of Emotion and Law, London, UK
e-mail: j.herlihy@csel.org.uk

S. Turner (✉)
Trauma Clinic, London, UK
e-mail: s.turner@traumaclinic.org.uk

N. Morina, A. Nickerson (eds.), *Mental Health of Refugee and Conflict-Affected Populations*, https://doi.org/10.1007/978-3-319-97046-2_15

Introduction

Previous chapters have considered clinical issues. In offering treatment, as clinicians, it is always important that we respect our ethical duties and responsibilities. Although the ethics of treatment is not the focus of this chapter, it is worth reflecting on the special considerations arising from the unusual degree of dependency of asylum seekers. Often separated from family, in temporary living arrangements, having limited (or no) access to benefits, and with an uncertain future, it is hard to imagine a more precariously-placed group of people. Anyone providing clinical treatment should be aware of the possibility of intense feelings they may develop in themselves when working with a refugee or asylum-seeking client (sometimes called counter-transference). Indeed, the identification of this sort of reaction is one of the purposes of professional training. It is relatively easy for the therapist to feel that they should also be rescuer, and this may lead to distortions in the clinical relationship. Sometimes the therapist may have quite different reactions in an individual case (e.g., horror, disgust, fear, anger). It is equally obvious that these feelings must also occur within those tasked with deciding asylum claims, surely one of the most difficult of legal roles to pursue even-handedly, and that these emotions may sometimes lead to mistaken assumptions and decisions.

In this chapter, the focus will be on the legal and ethical issues involved in the process of seeking protection. It will be argued that there are important reasons for mental health practitioners to engage with this process, not only in relation to preparing medico-legal reports in individual cases but, more importantly, in helping the whole system of asylum determination to become more psychologically informed. By definition, people seeking asylum are asking to be recognised as in need of international protection. It is often impossible for health professionals to separate the demands of this legal and administrative process from therapeutic work. At the very least, key interviews with immigration officials or decision-makers or stages in the (legal) application process will easily come to dominate the (clinical) work at times. There are also stages in this process in which clinicians and mental health specialists are likely to be asked to become directly involved. In comparison with other legal activities, asylum seekers are likely to have a far smaller network of engaged professionals. This often leads to greater than usual pressures to blur boundaries, e.g. for legal advisers to engage with their clients differently based on the feelings they engender, and for health professionals providing treatment to take on the role of expert witness. Again, it is important to identify such reactions and not be led by them. The interface between asylum seeker and state often extends beyond the asylum process itself and might involve dealing with benefit applications, housing needs, family separation and so on.

The Law

When making claims for state protection, or asylum, individuals usually have to convince a state and/or judicial decision maker that they are a person with "a well-founded fear of being persecuted for reasons of race, religion, nationality, membership of a particular social group, or political opinion" (United Nations, 1951). This is a most unusual legal definition, carrying at its heart an emotional concept, in this case one of fear. Whilst this definition is the basis of international treaty, states are allowed to construct their own procedures for recognising refugees. To guide them, the United Nations High Commissioner for Refugees (UNHCR, 2011) produces a (non-binding) handbook. This states that, "The relevant facts of the individual case will have to be furnished in the first place by the applicant himself." It will then be up to the person charged with determining the applicant's status to assess the validity of any evidence and the credibility of his or her statements. In some parts of the world, states also consider other legal protection instruments, such as the European Convention on Human Rights (European Court of Human Rights, 1950) or the Convention Against Torture (United Nations, 1987), both of which can protect individuals from return (refouler) to countries where they would face serious harm.

In some parts of the world UNHCR conducts this decision-making process and these countries undertake to accept a number of these pre-decided cases. In many refugee-receiving countries where the state decides asylum claims, for example the UK, there is a two-stage process whereby the state makes an initial decision, which, if negative, can be appealed by the claimant in court. This is often the point at which clinicians and medico-legal experts get involved at the legal interface.

The Importance of the Notion of Credibility

The task of deciding if a claimant meets the criteria for international protection is often extremely difficult. Various factors stand to make the decision-making process less reliable than in other legal settings. Asylum seekers typically present without objective factual evidence (e.g., medical or detention records) from their country of origin. Judges do not usually get feedback on the outcome of their decisions to help improve their learning. It is an emotionally onerous job, due to the need to balance the responsibilities for effective state border control with the possibility that an unwise decision to return someone may result in their detention, torture and possible death.

In most branches of law one would expect the account of a claimant, defendant, or appellant to be supported (or not) by witnesses, documentation and other corroborating evidence. This is rarely the case in asylum applications or appeals. The decision maker can draw on known reports concerning the alleged country of origin, for example those produced by human rights organisations, government agencies or the United Nations. Some of these will include reference to the scale of organised violence, torture or other persecution of certain groups in the country in question. Other than this, the decision maker usually has to reach a decision based on their assessment of what is effectively the asylum seeker's apparent recollection of events (often traumatic events), with all of the potentials for distortion implicit in this statement. The decision-maker has to determine if the account that they are being given is credible.

All of this has to be performed within a highly politicised and media-dominated context of debate concerning immigration, human rights and – rightly or wrongly – terrorism and crime. This inevitable reliance on the credibility of the applicant means that there should be an important role for psychological study to help illuminate the process and to facilitate just decision-making. A report in the UK noted that Immigration Judges were required to use their "common sense and experience" to assess whether or not they believed elements of a claim (Independent Asylum Commission, 2008). We argue that this is not adequate and that there should be active engagement of research psychologists and others to ensure that higher standards of validity than this are achieved.

We are not alone in criticising the inherent subjectivity implicit in relying on judicial "common sense and experience". Indeed, the United Nations High Commissioner for Refugees (2013) report, Beyond Proof, suggests a 'structured approach' to credibility assessment in order to address the subjectivity inherent in the application of 'common sense and experience'. The report further suggests a methodology that requires decision makers to consider systematically which elements of the account are material to the claim, and to consider the claim as a whole, rather than picking out particular errant details. In addition, the authors clarify the importance of a "multidisciplinary approach". By this, they mean that decision makers should be required to draw on knowledge from disciplines such as psychology, anthropology, gender and sexuality studies, amongst others, where necessary to make a properly informed decision. Directive 2013/32/EU of the European Parliament and of the Council (2013) states that, "It is essential that decisions on all applications for international protection be taken on the basis of the facts and, in the first instance, by authorities whose personnel has *the appropriate knowledge or has received the necessary training* in the field of International protection" (our emphasis). We believe that to make decisions about people's lives that are at odds with established science is no longer acceptable.

The Importance of Psychological Input

Mental health practitioners can make helpful inroads into the process of determining asylum applications in various ways. Here liaison with immigration lawyers, medico-legal reporting and research will be considered, but this is not meant to be an exhaustive list and different approaches may be appropriate in different settings across the world.

(a) **Liaison**

Immigration lawyers often have no specialist training in mental health and yet they must interview people with high levels of distress and psychological difficulties. In many judicial systems, they have a crucial role to play in helping asylum appellants prepare a statement regarding past experiences that are claimed to give rise to a fear of future persecution or serious harm. If there is marked avoidance or dissociative behaviour (not always evident to the untrained eye), they may struggle to provide this help. Liaison between the lawyer and an experienced mental health practitioner can help to overcome some of these barriers. Simply explaining the effects of dissociation, for example, and suggesting the use of basic grounding techniques, may enable lawyer and claimant to have more productive meetings. In turn the lawyer may (with consent) be able to share information with a mental health practitioner about a judgment likely to have an important impact on health.

(b) **Reports**

Mental health practitioners are also often asked to prepare reports to assist in the decision-making process. Directive 2013/32/EU (2013) also notes that, "Certain applicants may be in need of special procedural guarantees due, inter alia, to their age, gender, sexual orientation, gender identity, disability, serious illness, mental disorders or as a consequence of torture, rape or other serious forms of psychological, physical or sexual violence". Health professionals may be engaged to address these issues.

We believe that it is very important to be clear about the exact role that is being requested of the health professional, and the basis on which the practitioner might agree to prepare a report. The simplest in some ways is the role of professional witness. Here the practitioner is expected to report the factual evidence that they collected in the clinical setting and to describe their conclusions concerning issues such as diagnosis, treatment plan and risk. This is essentially a summary of the treatment record. It must not be undertaken in a way that will mislead the decision maker or court but equally it should not stray into areas that are not part of the normal clinical assessment. The more difficult role is that of independent expert witness. The way in which these independent medico-legal reports are commissioned differs from country to country, but even when they are requested by the claimant/appellant, the writer must state and remain aware of their primary duty to the court. A very informative guide can be found in the Istanbul Protocol (United Nations, 2004).

In the UK, the claimant's lawyer usually commissions independent medico-legal reports at the stage when a refusal of protection is being appealed in court. The commissioning of such a report is often dependent on obtaining state funding – and this is not always forthcoming. Thus, for example, claims concerning prohibition of torture (article 3 of the European Convention on Human Rights) usually attract funding whereas claims concerning a right to respect for private and family life (article 8) are often not supported. In other areas of legal practice involving adversarial processes in Court, it would be common that if one "side" commissions a report, the other "side" will do so as well and then the experts then have the opportunity to argue their respective cases in court. It is extremely rare for the UK Government authorities to request a report of their own; therefore the absence of a balancing report means that the onus is on the judge alone to assess the weight to be given to technical detail in the health professional's evidence, even though this may be beyond their training and knowledge.

Those commissioning expert testimony with regard to the mental health of the claimant are rarely clinically trained themselves. In the case of lawyers and NGO advocacy groups we might expect some level of training, or at least experience of working with settled refugees. Wilson-Shaw, Pistrang, and Herlihy (2012) studied immigration lawyers' decisions to commission a report and showed that, probably due to training, there was a good awareness of common presentations of fear-based PTSD. However, even these motivated, trained lawyers relied on their own feelings of comfort and on categories of refugee experience (e.g., lawyers more frequently commissioned a report if the claimant reported rape or if there were overt PTSD symptoms of nightmares or flashbacks). They did not seem to be as good at identifying less overt presentations – such as people with more avoidant forms of PTSD, despite these being highly relevant, if the avoidance, sometimes coupled with shame, had a bearing on the ease of presenting an account of their experiences. They also tended to focus on PTSD rather than depression, although in fact, as will be described later, depressed mood can also have a strong negative impact on the capacity to present a credible account.

Practitioners setting themselves forward as expert witnesses must be clinically experienced (specifically in current work with refugees and asylum seekers) and up to date with research findings. Perhaps of equal importance, they need to be able to recognise when a question is outside their competence. They need to be able to communicate their findings clearly and, for this, additional training will be helpful.

On the other hand, even expert evidence has its limitations. In the individual, symptoms characteristic of PTSD may be observed but even if this is the case, they can never be said to prove that a specific traumatic event occurred. A conflict therefore sometimes emerges with a mental health professional finding clinical evidence of anxiety, in the form of classic PTSD symptomatology, but a decision-maker rejecting the factual basis for the initiating trauma. This is often frustrating for all concerned but it has to be acknowledged that a mental health professional cannot determine the factual basis of the claim of persecution. Finding symptoms of PTSD may sometimes be very helpful in bolstering a claim (i.e., PTSD symptoms are consistent with prior trauma) but are insufficient to bear more directly on the factual judgment. There are also many cases in which there is no evidence of PTSD and yet there is a good factual claim of persecution. It is worth recalling that most people do not develop persistent symptoms of PTSD even after the most severe trauma and therefore an excessive reliance on this single condition can lead to otherwise genuine claims being downgraded. If the diagnosis is depression, the problems of identifying cause and effect can be even more difficult.

(c) **Breadth of Evidence**

The final aspect worthy of psychological input is probably the most important. This concerns the generation and application of general research findings to the benefit of the decision-making system as a whole and as a guide to the issues likely to be relevant in any individual case.

This means moving away from the traditional medico-legal report – dealing with individual experiences, emotional responses and diagnostic conclusion. Indeed, it is often assumed that this (the medico-legal report) is the only role for the application of psychological understanding in the legal process. It has been contrasted with the evidence put forward by country experts – where there is routine presentation of general contextual and political information. This assumption was clearly articulated by a UK Senior Immigration Judge (Barnes, 2004) who considered that country evidence could be assessed in the context of other material whereas medical evidence could not.

> In the case of country evidence, the expert is not the sole source of that evidence before the court. There will almost always be other evidence going to similar issues even if not as focused on the claimant's account as the expert report is likely to be. The expert evidence can therefore be evaluated against other material much of which although of more general application will have been produced by other experts in the field. ... In contrast, there will be no similar breadth of evidence to assist in the evaluation of expert medical evidence

We argue that this is a serious misunderstanding and that, just as there is a breadth of evidence about current practice and conditions in different countries, so too there is a broad scientific literature addressing key psychological processes, for example relating to memory, general effects of anxiety and depression, disclosure and the scientific underpinning of decision-making. Current understanding and research findings in each of these areas of knowledge will be outlined below.

Memory in Everyday Situations

The asylum procedure naturally relies very heavily on memory. In order to claim asylum individuals have to relate an account which includes and explains sufficient details about their alleged persecution, flight from their country and often the journey to the host country. Interviewers and decision-makers base their decisions largely on this account and their appraisal of its credibility. It seems appropriate, then, for decision-makers to be sufficiently informed regarding how memory works, in order to understand what can and cannot be expected of people's memories.

(a) **Why and how memories normally change**

There are different categories of memory but here the main concerns are usually with the accuracy of autobiographical memory – the explicit 'memory of an event that occurred in a specific time and place in one's personal past' (Nelson & Fivush, 2004, p. 486) and, to a lesser extent, semantic memory (memory for facts and meanings).

Autobiographical memory has three main functions. It is the key to the development and maintenance of social bonds – by recalling shared experiences with others we maintain our relationships with them. It has a directive role – we can draw on past experiences to decide how to act in a current situation: in order for this to work well, we need to be able to update and reinterpret our actions in past situations, taking into account new appraisals of cause and effect. Finally, it forms a key part of our identity, giving us a sense of continuity and an awareness of how we change, and even protecting us from threats to identity. For example, in the context of persecution some torture survivors describe how they 'held onto' their sense of self, supported by autobiographical memories, perhaps of political work or of their family. It follows from these functions that crucial facets of normal autobiographical memory include the ability to adapt to different social demands, to be updated and to integrate new information.

Problems arise therefore if, within a legal framework, there is a naïve assumption that memory is fixed and unchanging; that is, that if events or facts are remembered, the content of memory will always be the same – rather like accessing a recorded video of an event. In fact, one of the features of narrative memory is that every time a specific memory is retrieved, it becomes unstable and may change. It is this new "memory" that is then "reconsolidated" into storage. In other words, every time we retrieve a memory, there is the potential for it to change (Schwabe, Nader, & Pruessner, 2014). One of the common indicators of credibility in asylum decision-making remains consistency of recall (e.g., UNHCR, 2013). For example, it may (wrongly) be argued, "This was such a bad experience that if it happened, you must remember it clearly and consistently; the fact that you have given different accounts proves that you have lied". Inconsistency may be found both within the narrative itself (internal inconsistency) and between the narrative and external facts (a large literature of studies examining memory for dates, objects, distances and other semantic memories has been ably reviewed and applied to the asylum system by Cameron, 2010). The bottom line is that inconsistency is part of normal remembering and should be applied as a criterion of credibility with great caution.

Furthermore, experimental work over many years has shown the important effect of questioning on the answers given. A prime example of the questioner effect is someone being asked what they had for dinner by their doctor ("low-fat chicken steak"), their mother ("fried chicken – just like you make it") and the chef they are trying to impress ("chicken supreme sauté") (Gyulai et al., 2013 p82). A robust literature has also shown that it is possible to suggest answers – and even memories – by changing the question. An early example can be seen in the study by Loftus and Palmer (1974) where 150 students were asked to watch a video-recording of a car accident. Afterwards one third were asked to estimate the speed of the cars "when they hit each other" (the *hit* group) and another third were asked to estimate the speed "when they smashed into each other" (the *smash* group); the remaining third were not asked this question. There was a significant effect of the question used (the *hit* group suggested an average estimate of 8.00 miles per hour; the *smash* group 10.46 miles per hour; $t(98) = 2.00$, $p < .05$). The researchers followed-up with the participants 1 week later to ask a list of 10 questions about the accident, including one enquiring if they had seen any broken glass; this question was significantly more likely to be answered positively by those in the *smash* group. This study was crucial in developing evidence that memories are reconstructed after the event – and indeed that the reconstruction can be influenced by outside factors. In the asylum system claimants may be interviewed more than once and, if the precise wording of the question differs, the answer may differ as a mere artefact of the process. It is also worth noting that very often questions are passed to the asylum-seeker through an interpreter, who may attach their own feelings to the way that questions are phrased and so there may be additional and unmeasured variance introduced into this process.

There are also interviewee effects to consider. Studies here mostly rely on the Gudjonsson Suggestibility Scale (Gudjonsson, 1997), in which a short account is read to the research participant, and then questions are asked about the text. It is possible to measure the individual participant's susceptibility to 'yielding' to suggestive questions and, after being told that they have made some errors, each person's tendency to 'shifting' or changing their answers as a result of 'interrogative pressure'. There is a large body of research into this measure and its relevance in the forensic setting but there has been very little attention to the asylum process. Negative emotional states (e. g., McGroarty & Thomson, 2013) and the perceived difference between subject and interrogator (Gudjonsson & Lister, 1984) have been found to correlate positively with suggestibility, implying that there are good grounds for further research to better understand the impact of these factors in the asylum-seeking process. The power difference between interviewer and interviewee in the asylum context probably cannot be overestimated.

Memory for repeated events may introduce further difficulties. Memories which are "vague or lack detail" can be seen as untruthful by asylum decision-makers. A UNHCR survey of practice in Europe cites the example of a female applicant who claimed to have been sexually abused repeatedly from a young age. The decision maker wrote:

> You were also vague about the details. At your substantive interview, you admitted that you do not know the dates or days of the week when he abused you. You said that he tried to abuse you in Syria but were unable to say when or provide any details. It is therefore not accepted that you were sexually abused. (UNHCR, 2013, p.141)

However, when people experience a similar event repeatedly, they normally form a 'schema' or generalized memory that covers the gist or common features of all these events. This means that they have poorer recall for specific details of each individual event. One example of this in the trauma field relates to children's reports of abuse (Bidrose & Goodman, 2000). Where there is a series of events, most of which are similar, but some are different, people can develop a generalised schema, coupled with memories for specific instances that were schema-incongruent or otherwise memorable (Brewer & Treyens, 1981; Brown & Kulik, 1977; Reed & McDaniel, 1993; Rubin & Kozin, 1984; Schrauf & Rubin, 1998). An everyday example is of eating in a restaurant – we are likely to have a 'script' for what generally happens (get seated, choose from a menu, eat, pay the bill, leave) but a better memory for the one occasion when a person at the next table collapsed, having had a cardiac arrest.

This effect can cause problems in the asylum process. Interviewers may ask about, for example, the events surrounding an individual's detention, without following up to make sure that there was only one instance of detention or of violence within detention. If there were many, and these have become conflated in the asylum seeker's memory, then a specific, detailed description of each one is unlikely to be straightforward (Herlihy, Jobson, & Turner, 2012).

(b) **Individualist/collectivist culture and memory**

People seeking asylum will often come from cultural backgrounds that differ from the predominant culture of the host country. This cultural diversity may act as a barrier to good communication. For example, there has been substantial research looking at differences between "individualist/collectivist" cultures – as an indicator of the "degree to which individuals are integrated into groups" (Hofstede, 2011). In summary, in individualistic cultures (generally Western) the self is perceived to be an independent, autonomous and self-determining unit, while in collectivistic cultures (generally non-Western and where most refugees come from) the self is perceived as interdependent and related (Herlihy et al., 2012; Markus & Kitayama, 1991).

Cultural emphasis on independence or interdependence influences parental reminiscing (Jungsook, Leichtman, & Wang, 1998) and in turn affects a child's learning. Several studies have demonstrated that mothers from individualistic cultures encourage their children to contribute their ideas to the discussion, engage more often in memory talk, use more elaborative conversations, focus on the child's role and predilections, and take a partnership role rather than a leadership role in the conversation. In contrast, mothers from collectivistic cultures tend to prompt their children to confirm the information they have already presented to them, discourage children from introducing their own ideas into the discussion, take a more directive role, and focus on social interactions, moral rules and behavioural standards (Fivush & Wang, 2005; Mullen & Yi, 1995; Wang, 2001; Wang, Hutt, Kulkofsky, McDermott, & Wei, 2006; Wang, Leichtman, & Davies, 2000). These findings suggest that, in individualistic cultures, autobiographical memory is viewed as a critical source for validating the self and a unique individual identity (Wang et al., 2006). In contrast, in collectivistic cultures identity is more strongly related to relationships and social hierarchy and thus, identity is less dependent on a unique autobiographical history (Fivush & Wang, 2005) – a requirement for the substantiation of a claim for asylum.

(c) **Memory and Emotion**

Deffenbacher, Bornstein, Penrod, and Kiernan (2004) conducted a meta-analysis of the effects of heightened stress on memory, distinguishing between the 'orienting' response of increased interest or attention to material and the 'defensive' reactions of anxiety, which lead to a 'catastrophic' impairment of memory. In one study, Valentine and Mesout (2009) recruited visitors to the London Dungeon 'Horror Labyrinth', where participants are willingly startled and frightened by a series of gruesome figures jumping out at them in the dark. One of these was an actor, co-opted to the study, who was asked to ensure that they interacted with each participant for a total of 7 min during the visit. After the visit, participants (who had not been warned that their memory would be tested) tried to identify the actor from a series of photographs. Those whose anxiety had clearly been aroused by the experience were significantly less able to identify the actor (only 17% correct) compared to those who had experienced low anxiety levels in the dungeon (75% correct identifications). Similarly, those with high state anxiety found it more difficult to recall details such as the actor's age, height, hair colour or design of his makeup. In the asylum context, this suggests that those who are most frightened by their traumatic experiences might be least able to describe them in detail. Brewin (2011) reviews this literature in detail, and suggests that PTSD appears to bring with it both enhanced and impaired memory for aspects of the traumatic experience, although he comments that additional difficulties might arise in situations where there has been prolonged or repeated exposure to trauma.

Memory and Trauma

Although the diagnosis of Posttraumatic Stress Disorder has probably attracted too much attention in asylum decision-making as specific evidence of corroboration for an account of serious harm or torture, it can still be very helpful to consider how posttraumatic symptoms (whether or not they amount to the full syndrome of PTSD) can affect the asylum-seeker's ability to present their claim.

(a) **Voluntary and Involuntary memories**

There is an increasing body of evidence suggesting that after a traumatic event, in addition to normal autobiographical memory (the sort of memories of events already considered – voluntary, verbal, structured), there are also involuntary (triggered rather than being consciously accessible) emotional memories. The latter are sensory (an emphasis on sight, sound, smell etc.), 'snapshots' rather than a structured story, and without a sense of being in the past, they are felt as a 're-experiencing' of the original event, as if in the present (for more information, see Brewin's dual representation theory (Brewin, Dalgleish, & Joseph, 1996; Brewin, Gregory, Lipton, & Burgess, 2010)). In an asylum interview, both types of memory will probably occur but they will have different characteristics and effects.

(b) **Central and peripheral memories**

There is a difference in recall between the central gist (of the chronological or emotional narrative) of an event and the peripheral details about the same event (Kensinger, 2007). For example, watching distressing videos, in analogue studies, is associated with a narrowing of attention resulting in preferential recall of the central gist at the expense of peripheral details (Loftus & Burns, 1982). In a study of memory consistency in refugees, peripheral details of traumatic events were shown to be the least stable in repeated interviews (Herlihy, Scragg, & Turner, 2002). For example, what clothes they were wearing at the time of arrest might be a central memory for someone who was then raped, and a peripheral memory for someone who was badly beaten in falaka. This lack of stability of peripheral memory is important precisely because the ability to recall consistent peripheral details may be seen as carrying weight in a legal assessment of credibility. Thus, it might appear reasonable to a lay judge to comment, "I assume that even if you are lying, you will remember that you spoke about the big event that you claim happened – the torture/beating/rape (as appropriate) – in a previous interview, and will be able to repeat this now, but if this never actually happened, you will not be able to remember the detail; that is how I will know that you are not telling the truth". Such a statement is manifestly incorrect on the basis of current scientific knowledge.

(c) **Overgeneral memory**

This body of work has been largely overlooked in relation to asylum claims because the phenomenon described is associated most robustly with depression. This is curious given the prevalence of depression in this group and highlights the importance of clinicians bringing to lawyers' and decision-makers' attention the different aspects of memory to be taken into account in valid decision-making. When people are asked to look at a cue word (e.g., 'park') and to recall a specific memory from the past that the word makes them think about, they may recall a specific event (e.g., last Tuesday I went to the park to walk my dog in the morning) or they may report an overgeneral memory referring to a category of events (e.g., I go to parks to walk my dog) or a prolonged event (e.g., last year I used to walk my dog in the park). An excessive tendency for overgeneral memory production has been robustly associated with diagnoses of major depressive disorder (see Vreeswijk & Wilde, 2004; Williams et al., 2007 for reviews) and PTSD (see Brewin, 2011, for review), and has been observed in asylum seekers and refugees with PTSD (Graham, Herlihy, & Brewin, 2014). These overgeneral memories are reasonably described by decision-makers as vague or lacking in detail, but this should be interpreted in the context of the asylum-seeker's mental state rather than as evidence suggesting lack of credibility.

Interviewing

(a) **The effects of PTSD on presentation at interview**

Little systematic work has been done on the way in which asylum claimants with psychological difficulties are perceived by decision makers, but Rogers, Fox and Herlihy (2015) report an analogue study in which trained undergraduates each watched 1 of 4 recorded versions of an actor giving an account of persecution, as if in an asylum claim. In condition 1 the actor was instructed to present rehearsed behavioural cues of PTSD (e.g., startle response, increased motor behaviour, dissociative behaviour and avoidance). In condition 2, the actor presented rehearsed behavioural cues to deception taken from the literature. Condition 3 was a combination of both these conditions and condition 4 was a neutral account with none of these behavioural cues. Instructed in making 'credibility assessment' judgments, as if an asylum decision maker, participants rated the 'trauma' presentation (condition 1) as most credible, and the mixed trauma and deception presentation as least credible (condition 3). They also answered questions designed to explore the reasons behind their decisions, which suggested that the high credibility ratings were due to what has been termed 'emotional congruence' (Kaufmann Drevland, Wessel, Overskeid, & Magnussen, 2003), which can be summed up in the comment 'he seemed understandably traumatised by events'. Emotional congruence is a worrying construct as it does not take into account other presentations of PTSD (e.g., with numbing or flattened affect). Interestingly, in the 'neutral' condition of this study (condition 4), many comments suggested that the "asylum seeker" was not believed because they were not "distressed enough."

(b) **Late disclosure**

One problem that often arises in asylum applications is the late disclosure of relevant history. Decision-makers often expect that full disclosure will take place at the earliest opportunity and when this does not happen, they may interpret the late disclosure as evidence that the asylum seeker has been rehearsed in their narrative and advised to include more traumatic events. Although this probably does happen in some cases, there are also other valid psychological explanations for this phenomenon. Bögner, Herlihy, & Brewin, (2007) conducted a study of disclosure of sexual and non-sexual violence in immigration interviews in the U.K. Ramsay, Gorst-Unsworth, & Turner, (1993) & van Velsen, Gorst-Unsworth, and Turner (1996) had previously identified avoidance as a particular feature of PTSD in survivors of sexual violence (compared to higher re-experiencing symptoms in survivors of other forms of torture); Bögner's study built on this earlier work to examine the role of shame. The sexual violence group scored higher than the non-sexual violence group on measures of PTSD, PTSD-avoidance, shame, depression, dissociation, and a study-specific 5-point measure of 'difficulty disclosing' (although difficulty disclosing was not restricted to the sexual violence group). This study (including qualitative findings, Bögner, Brewin, & Herlihy, 2010) is a good example of the application of research and scientific literature in the asylum field to investigate the sort of real-life problems identified by decision-makers, NGOs and others. Baillot, Cowan, and Munro (2009) commented on parallels and dissonances in the treatment of rape narratives between the asylum and criminal justice contexts. Anecdotal evidence suggests that even where there is growing awareness of the inappropriateness of expectation of early disclosure of sexual violence by women, this understanding is not yet being applied to men's claims. Of course, this phenomenon is not restricted to sexual assault. In the asylum context, it is likely that betrayal experiences, for example, lead to similar behaviours. Indeed any experience that preferentially increases feelings of shame is likely to be associated with late disclosure.

(c) **Interviewer effects**

'Culture of disbelief' is a phrase commonly used (Souter, 2011 extends this to culture of denial) to describe the impression that an asylum system is led primarily by the need to control borders, and thus leans towards finding ways of refusing entry, as opposed to providing state protection. Such political pressures per se are beyond the scope of this chapter, but if they are present they are likely to have an effect on the quality of information collected. For example, in a film made by a leading asylum NGO[1] in the U.K., it is argued that the more disbelieved the already traumatised asylum seeker feels, the more distressed and panicky she becomes, and therefore the more confused her account. By contrast, if she feels that her story is believed, the situation changes, "then empathy automatically comes out... she gives her all". In a meta-analysis conducted by Deffenbacher et al. (2004), the authors concluded that "it is clear that high stress levels impact interrogative recall (i.e., directed questioning) much more negatively than they do narrative or free recall," suggesting that interviewing that allows the claimant to explain the story themselves might help to mitigate the effects of the anxiety inherent in asylum interviews. It is likely that a non-judgmental stance is a better way to get fuller disclosure in asylum and related interviews.

In carefully designed analogue research, subjects were divided into two groups: "truth tellers" and "liars". The liars planned a mock crime and additionally prepared a cover story. Truth tellers planned a neutral task. Both groups were interviewed. Truth tellers provided longer and more detailed answers. When interviewed several times, no differences were found between groups in consistency over time (Giolla & Granhag, 2015). It follows that an interviewer interested in the facts of a claim should provide the opportunity for longer explanations. Furthermore, a pilot project of asylum procedures in the U.K. (Lane, Murray, D., GVA, Devine, & Zurawan, 2013) found that, even if refused legal status that would afford them protection, claimants were more likely to be satisfied and accept the decision if they felt that they had been heard and considered fully and fairly. The process of interviewing people claiming a need for international protection from persecution could – and should – also benefit from findings from well-designed, peer-reviewed research of the type increasingly undertaken in criminal law. This leaves mental health professionals with a double responsibility – firstly to continue to explain that what appear to be signs of deception may in fact be artefacts of flawed interviewing techniques, and secondly to continue to contribute to the development and dissemination of the science on which more effective interviewing could be based.

[1] http://www.asylumaid.org.uk/new-video-on-credibility-assessments-in-womens-asylum-claims/

Impact on Decision Makers

Asylum claims often entail accounts of some of the most atrocious acts that humans perpetrate upon each other, usually in the name of state or political ideology. The effects of working regularly with such material are not well known in the field of refugee law. However, by the very nature of the issues – both the emotional reaction to experiences like torture and the importance of the decision (potentially a matter of life and death) – it is likely that there is some impact. In theory, this might lead some decision makers to be more sympathetic and others to become hardened and cynical. This might go some way to explaining the wide diversity of decisions reported in a classic study of the system in the U.S.A. (Ramji-Nogales, Schoenholtz, & Schrag, 2007). Although not necessarily typical, a study of claims heard by the Refugee Review Board of Canada (Rousseau, Crépeau, Foxen, & Houle, 2002) described highly emotionally charged hearings, with board members being sarcastic with claimants, expressing anger, dismissing or trivialising horrific events and laughing amongst themselves. In psychological practice, good supervision is emphasised, not least as a way of identifying situations in which the therapist's own emotions might cloud the picture and interfere with a therapeutic effect. It is likely that similar emotions affect decision-makers but without the benefit of this sort of psychologically informed supervision.

(a) **Vicarious Traumatisation**

Vicarious traumatisation (VT) and compassion fatigue are umbrella terms often used to describe the psychological effects – well documented in therapists working with psychological trauma (Figley, 2002; Pearlman & Mac Ian, 1995) – of exposure to other people's traumatic experiences. They can involve symptoms which mirror the symptoms of PTSD, such as having nightmares about a client's trauma, or forgetting particularly stressful parts of the account, or it can mean a more pervasive change of beliefs and attitudes, e.g., seeing the world as more dangerous or untrustworthy. Unfortunately, where crucial decisions have to be made, these emotional reactions can have a major effect, for example, the unconscious attempts to reduce decision-makers' own difficulties by trivialisation of horror, cynicism and lack of empathy (Rousseau et al., 2002). In a different setting, Dembour and Haslam (2004) highlighted that, although one of the common perceptions of War Crimes Trials is that they should allow the victims space to tell their stories, close reading of the transcript at one trial before the International Criminal Tribunal for the former Yugoslavia suggested that these trials can effectively silence, rather than hear victims. Victim-witnesses are unable to dictate what they talk about or the pace of their answers; these are matters dictated by those with the power to ask questions. Moreover, "incongruously optimistic judicial remarks unnecessarily denied their suffering." A recent legal study of the U.K. Asylum and Immigration Tribunal reported 'strategies of detachment' and 'denial of responsibility' as ways of coping with the 'emotional impact of asylum work' (Baillot, Cowan, & Munroe, 2013). Although a number of qualitative studies have shown VT in family court judges (Jaffe, Crooks, Dunford-Jackson, & Town, 2003), criminal lawyers (Vrklevski & Franklin, 2008) and immigration lawyers (Westaby, 2010), no quantitative assessment of VT in immigration lawyers has been attempted, nor have potential links between VT and quality of decision-making been examined under controlled conditions in this crucial area.

(b) **Tolerating Uncertainty**

Legal and judicial professionals are forced to make binary decisions (e.g. guilt or innocence) albeit with uncertain and incomplete evidence. In the asylum context, in the absence of any independent evidence or feedback on the outcome for those denied and returned, these decisions are especially difficult. They are certainly not clear-cut decisions and yet there can be no middle ground. The outcome of any decision must be a decision to deny asylum (with the possibility of wrongful return to torture or death) or a decision to allow entry to the host country (often against a tide of social, governmental and media pressure (e.g., Free Movement, 2012)).

In a thorough audit of practice in the U.S.A., Ramji-Nogales et al. (2007) concluded that these decisions amount to a sort of "refugee roulette". Because there is no feedback from those returned to their country of origin, judges cannot learn truth from prior experience. They can only learn how they managed the decision-making process before. Inevitably, we believe, this includes learning how they had previously managed the emotional aspect of such uncertainty - and this repetition, in itself, may simply lead to a false sense of certainty.

The other frequent factor in asylum decision-making is the knowledge that some of the people before the decision maker are likely to be using systems of humanitarian protection deceitfully. Without going into the structural and political reasons why this might be so, the fact remains that some people do exaggerate accounts that would not qualify for state protection, in order to gain entry to countries. Continually having to consider whether or not one is being told lies is likely to test the most liberal of assessors and can also lead some judges to become 'hardened' by their experience.

Maroney (2011) sets out an alternative approach, a model of 'emotional regulation', drawing on psychological research and parallels from the training of doctors (who also have to make important decisions in the face of gruesome realities). It is argued that rather than asking judges to "put emotion aside" and adopt a state of judicial dispassion, they should be prepared to acknowledge and manage the emotions that they cannot help but feel. Such a model could be integrated into training programmes, without making any judgment about those participating. Mental health professionals need to be prepared to encourage and support any initiatives in this direction.

Conclusions

In this chapter, we have set out to present some of the existing evidence concerning the handling of claims for protection made by asylum seekers. As demonstrated in the U.S. by Ramji-Nogales et al. (2007), this process can amount to no more than "refugee roulette". These uncertainties can place tremendous pressure on asylum seekers, their representatives, health professionals and on those responsible for making what might be life or death decisions. We argue that as health professionals, we have an essential duty to inform decision-makers about more than the health or otherwise of an individual in a typical medico-legal report. We must also be able and prepared to describe the breadth of relevant psychological literature that pertains to the generality of reasons for acceptance or refusal of asylum-seekers. If possible, we should seek to add to this body of scientific evidence. Only in this way will there be growth of better-informed standards for justice for all those seeking asylum and safety in a new country.

References

Baillot, H., Cowan, S., & Munro, V. E. (2009). Seen but not heard? Parallels and dissonances in the treatment of rape narratives across the asylum and criminal justice contexts. *Journal of Law and Society, 36*(2), 195–219. https://doi.org/10.1111/j.1467-6478.2009.00463.x

Baillot, H., Cowan, S., & Munro, V. E. (2013). Second-hand emotion? Exploring the contagion and impact of trauma and distress in the asylum law context. *Journal of Law and Society, 40*(4), 509–540. https://doi.org/10.1111/j.1467-6478.2013.00639.x

Barnes, J. (2004). Expert evidence: The judicial perception in asylum and human rights appeals. *International Journal of Refugee Law, 16*(3), 349–357. https://doi.org/10.1093/ijrl/16.3.349

Bidrose, S., & Goodman, G. S. (2000). Testimony and evidence: A scientific case study of memory for child sexual abuse. *Applied Cognitive Psychology, 14*(3), 197–213. https://doi.org/10.1002/(sici)1099-0720(200005/06)14:3<197::aid-acp647>3.0.co;2-6

Bögner, D., Brewin, C., & Herlihy, J. (2010). Refugees' experiences of Home Office interviews: A qualitative study on the disclosure of sensitive personal information. *Journal of Ethnic and Migration Studies, 36*(3), 519–535. https://doi.org/10.1080/13691830903368329

Bögner, D., Herlihy, J., & Brewin, C. (2007). Impact of sexual violence on disclosure during Home Office interviews. *The British Journal of Psychiatry, 191*(1), 75–81. https://doi.org/10.1192/bjp.bp.106.030262

Brewer, W. B., & Treyens, J. C. (1981). Role of schemata in memory for places. *Cognitive Psychology, 13*(2), 207–230. https://doi.org/10.1016/0010-0285(81)90008-6

Brewin, C., Dalgleish, T., & Joseph, S. (1996). A dual representation theory of posttraumatic stress disorder. *Psychological Review, 103*(4), 670–686. https://doi.org/10.1037/0033-295X.103.4.670

Brewin, C. R. (2011). The nature and significance of memory disturbance in posttraumatic stress disorder. *Annual Review of Clinical Psychology, 7*(1), 203–227. https://doi.org/10.1146/annurev-clinpsy-032210-104544

Brewin, C. R., Gregory, J. D., Lipton, M., & Burgess, N. (2010). Intrusive images in psychological disorders: Characteristics, neural mechanisms, and treatment implications. *Psychological Review, 117*(1), 210–232. https://doi.org/10.1037/a0018113

Brown, R., & Kulik, J. (1977). Flashbulb memories. *Cognition, 5*(1), 73–99. https://doi.org/10.1016/0010-0277(77)90018-x

Cameron, H. E. (2010). Refugee status determinations and the limits of memory. *International Journal of Refugee Law, 22*(4), 469–511. https://doi.org/10.1093/ijrl/eeq041

Deffenbacher, K. A., Bornstein, B. H., Penrod, S. D., & Kiernan M. E. (2004). *A meta-analytic review of the effects of high stress on eyewitness memory*. Psychology Faculty Publications. Paper 1. Retrieved from http://digitalcommons.unomaha.edu/psychfacpub/1

Dembour, M. B., & Haslam, E. (2004). Silencing hearings? Victim-witnesses at war crimes trials. *European Journal of International Law, 15*(1), 151–177. https://doi.org/10.1093/ejil/15.1.151

Directive 2013/32/EU. (2013). *A Directive of the European Parliament and of the Council on common procedures for granting and withdrawing international protection (recast)*. Retrieved from http://eur-lex.europa.eu/legal-content/en/ALL/?uri=celex%3A32013L0032

European Court of Human Rights. (1950, as amended in 2010). *Convention for the protection of human rights and fundamental freedoms*. Strasbourg, 2010. Retrieved from http://www.echr.coe.int/Documents/Convention_ENG.pdf

Figley, C. R. (Ed.). (2002). *Treating compassion fatigue*. New York, NY: Routledge.

Fivush, R., & Wang, Q. I. (2005). Emotion talk in mother-child conversations of the shared past: The effects of culture, gender, and event valence. *Journal of Cognition and Development, 6*(4), 489–506. https://doi.org/10.1207/s15327647jcd0604_3

Free Movement. (2012, July 19). *Judge hung out to dry*. Retrieved from https://www.freemovement.org.uk/judge-hung-out-to-dry/

Giolla, E. M., & Pär Anders Granhag, P. A. (2015). Detecting false intent amongst small cells of suspects: Single versus repeated interviews. *Journal of Investigative Psychology and Offender Profiling, 12*(2), 142–157. https://doi.org/10.1002/jip.1419

Graham, B., Herlihy, J., & Brewin, C. (2014). Overgeneral memory in asylum seekers and refugees. *Journal of Behavior Therapy and Experimental Psychiatry, 45*(3), 375–380. https://doi.org/10.1016/j.jbtep.2014.03.001

Gudjonsson, G., & Lister, S. (1984). Interrogative suggestibility and its relationship with self-esteem and control. *Journal of the Forensic Science Society, 24*(2), 99–110. https://doi.org/10.1016/s0015-7368(84)72302-4

Gudjonsson, G. H. (1997). *The Gudjonsson suggestibility scales manual*. East Sussex, UK: Psychology Press.

Gyulai, G., Kagan, M., Herlihy, J., Turner, S., Hardi, L., & Udvarhelyi, E. T. (2013). *Credibility assessment in asylum procedures: A multidisciplinary training manual* (Vol. 1). Budapest, Hungary: Hungarian Helsinki Committee Retrieved from http://helsinki.hu/wp-content/uploads/Credibility-Assessment-in-Asylum-Procedures-CREDO-manual.pdf

Herlihy, J., Jobson, L., & Turner, S. (2012). Just tell us what happened to you: Autobiographical memory and seeking asylum. *Applied Cognitive Psychology, 26*(5), 661–676. https://doi.org/10.1002/acp.2852

Herlihy, J., Scragg, P., & Turner, S. (2002). Discrepancies in autobiographical memories—Implications for the assessment of asylum seekers: Repeated interviews study. *BMJ, 324*(7333), 324–327. https://doi.org/10.1136/bmj.324.7333.324

Hofstede, G. (2011). Dimensionalizing cultures: The Hofstede model in context. *Online Readings in Psychology and Culture, 2*(1). https://doi.org/10.9707/2307-0919.1014

Independent Asylum Commission. (2008). *Fit for purpose yet?* The Independent Asylum Commission's Interim Findings.

Jaffe, P. G., Crooks, C. V., Dunford-Jackson, B. L., & Town, J. M. (2003). Vicarious trauma in judges: The personal challenge of dispensing justice. *Juvenile and Family Court Journal, 54*(4), 1–9. https://doi.org/10.1111/j.1755-6988.2003.tb00083

Jungsook, H. J., Leichtman, M. D., & Wang, Q. (1998). Autobiographical memory in Korean, Chinese, and American children. *Developmental Psychology, 34*(4), 701–713. https://doi.org/10.1037/0012-1649.34.4.701

Kaufmann, G., Drevland, G. C. B., Wessel, E., Overskeid, G., & Magnussen, S. (2003). The importance of being earnest: Displayed emotions and witness credibility. *Applied Cognitive Psychology, 17*(1), 21–34. https://doi.org/10.1002/acp.842

Kensinger, E. A. (2007). Negative emotion enhances memory accuracy: Behavioral and neuroimaging evidence. *Current Directions in Psychological Science, 16*(4), 213–218. https://doi.org/10.1111/j.1467-8721.2007.00506.x

Lane, M., Murray, D., GVA, R. L., Devine, C., & Zurawan, A. (2013). *Evaluation of the early legal advice project*. UK Home Office Publication. Retrieved from http://socialwelfare.bl.uk/subject-areas/services-client-groups/asylum-seekers-refugees/homeoffice/1475071horr70.pdf

Loftus, E., & Burns, T. (1982). Mental shock can produce retrograde amnesia. *Memory and Cognition, 10*(4), 241–263. https://doi.org/10.3758/bf03202423

Loftus, E. F., & Palmer, J. C. (1974). Reconstruction of automobile destruction: An example of the interaction between language and memory. *Journal of Verbal Learning and Verbal Behavior, 13*(5), 585–589. https://doi.org/10.1016/s0022-5371(74)80011-3

Markus, H. R., & Kitayama, S. (1991). Culture and the self: Implications for cognition, emotion, and motivation. *Psychological Review, 98*(2), 224–253. https://doi.org/10.1037/0033-295x.98.2.224

Maroney, T. (2011). Emotional regulation and judicial behavior. *California Law Review, 99*(6), 1485–1555. Retrieved from http://www.jstor.org/stable/41345439

McGroarty, A., & Thomson, H. (2013). Negative emotional states, life adversity, and interrogative suggestibility. *Legal and Criminological Psychology, 18*(2), 287–299. https://doi.org/10.1111/j.2044-8333.2012.02046.x

Mullen, M. K., & Yi, S. (1995). The cultural context of talk about the past: Implications for the development of autobiographical memory. *Cognitive Development, 10*(3), 407–419. https://doi.org/10.1016/0885-2014(95)90004-7

Nelson, K., & Fivush, R. (2004). The emergence of autobiographical memory: A social cultural developmental theory. *Psychological Review, 111*(2), 486–511. https://doi.org/10.1037/0033-295X.111.2.486

Pearlman, L. A., & Mac Ian, P. S. (1995). Vicarious traumatization: An empirical study of the effects of trauma work on trauma therapists. *Professional Psychology: Research and Practice, 26*(6), 558–565. https://doi.org/10.1037//0735-7028.26.6.558

Ramji-Nogales, J., Schoenholtz, A., & Schrag, P. (2007). Refugee roulette: Disparities in asylum adjudication. *Stanford Law Review, 60*(2), 295–411. Retrieved from http://www.jstor.org/stable/40040412

Ramsay, R., Gorst-Unsworth, C., & Turner, S. (1993). Psychiatric morbidity in survivors of organised state violence including torture. A retrospective series. *The British Journal of Psychiatry, 162*(1), 55–59. https://doi.org/10.1192/bjp.162.1.55

Reed, H. R., & McDaniel, M. A. (1993). The enigma of organization and distinctiveness. *Journal of Memory and Language, 32*(4), 421–445. https://doi.org/10.1006/jmla.1993.1023

Rogers, H., Fox, S., & Herlihy, J. (2015). The importance of looking credible: The impact of the behavioural sequelae of post-traumatic stress disorder on the credibility of asylum seekers. *Psychology, Crime & Law, 21*(2), 139–155. https://doi.org/10.1080/1068316x.2014.951643

Rousseau, C., Crépeau, F., Foxen, P., & Houle, F. (2002). The complexity of determining refugeehood: A multidisciplinary analysis of the decision-making process of the Canadian immigration and refugee board. *Journal of Refugee Studies, 15*(1), 43–70. https://doi.org/10.1093/jrs/15.1.43

Rubin, D. C., & Kozin, M. (1984). Vivid memories. *Cognition, 16*(1), 81–95. https://doi.org/10.1016/0010-0277(84)90037-4

Schrauf, R. W., & Rubin, D. C. (1998). Bilingual autobiographical memory in older adult immigrants: A test of cognitive explanations of the reminiscence bump and the linguistic encoding of memories. *Journal of Memory and Language, 39*(3), 437–457. https://doi.org/10.1006/jmla.1998.2585

Schwabe, L., Nader, K., & Pruessner, J. C. (2014). Reconsolidation of human memory: Brain mechanisms and clinical relevance. *Biological Psychiatry, 76*(4), 274–280. https://doi.org/10.1016/j.biopsych.2014.03.008

Souter, J. (2011). A culture of disbelief or denial? Critiquing refugee status determination in the United Kingdom. *Oxford Monitor of Forced Migration, 1*(1), 48–59.

United Nations. (1951). *Convention relating to the status of refugees*, adopted 28 July 1951, entered into force 22 April 1954. Retrieved from http://www.unhcr.org/uk/3b66c2aa10

United Nations. (1987). *Convention against torture and other cruel, inhuman or degrading treatment or punishment*, entered into force 26 June 1987. Retrieved from http://www.ohchr.org/Documents/ProfessionalInterest/cat.pdf

United Nations. (2004). *Istanbul protocol, office of the United Nations High Commissioner for Human Rights, manual on the effective investigation and documentation of torture and other cruel, inhuman or degrading treatment or punishment*. Retrieved from http://www.ohchr.org/Documents/Publications/training8Rev1en.pdf

United Nations High Commissioner for Refugees. (2011). *Handbook on procedures and criteria for determining refugee status under the 1951 convention and the 1967 protocol relating to the status of refugees*. Retreived from http://www.unhcr.org/uk/publications/legal/3d58e13b4/handbook-procedures-criteria-determining-refugee-status-under-1951-convention.html

United Nations High Commissioner for Refugees. (2013). *Beyond Proof.* Retrieved from http://www.unhcr.org/uk/protection/operations/51a8a08a9/full-report-beyond-proof-credibility-assessment-eu-asylum-systems.html

Valentine, T., & Mesout, J. (2009). Eyewitness identification under stress in the London Dungeon. *Applied Cognitive Psychology, 23*(2), 151–161. https://doi.org/10.1002/acp.1463

Van Velsen, C., Gorst-Unsworth, C., & Turner, S. (1996). Survivors of torture and organized violence: Demography and diagnosis. *Journal of Traumatic Stress, 9*(2), 181–193. https://doi.org/10.1002/jts.2490090203

van Vreeswijk, M. F., & de Wilde, E. J. (2004). Autobiographical memory specificity, psychopathology, depressed mood and the use of the autobiographical memory test: A meta-analysis. *Behaviour Research and Therapy, 42*(6), 731–743. https://doi.org/10.1016/s0005-7967(03)00194-3

Vrklevski, L. P., & Franklin, J. (2008). Vicarious trauma: The impact on solicitors of exposure to traumatic material. *Traumatology, 14*(1), 106–118. https://doi.org/10.1177/1534765607309961

Wang, Q. (2001). Culture effects on adults' earliest childhood recollection and self-description: Implications for the relation between memory and the self. *Journal of Personality and Social Psychology, 81*(2), 220–233. https://doi.org/10.1037//0022-3514.81.2.220

Wang, Q., Hutt, R., Kulkofsky, S., McDermott, M., & Wei, R. (2006). Emotion situation knowledge and autobiographical memory in Chinese, immigrant Chinese, and European American 3-year-olds. *Journal of Cognition and Development, 7*(1), 95–118. https://doi.org/10.1207/s15327647jcd0701_5

Wang, Q., Leichtman, M. D., & Davies, K. I. (2000). Sharing memories and telling stories: American and Chinese mothers and their 3-year-olds. *Memory, 8*(3), 159–177. https://doi.org/10.1080/096582100387588

Westaby, C. (2010). "Feeling like a sponge": The emotional labour produced by solicitors in their interactions with clients seeking asylum. *International Journal of the Legal Profession, 17*(2), 153–174. https://doi.org/10.1080/09695958.2010.530882

Williams, J. M. G., Barnhofer, T., Crane, C., Hermans, D., Raes, F., Watkins, E., & Dalgleish, T. (2007). Autobiographical memory specificity and emotional disorder. *Psychological Bulletin, 133*(1), 122–148. https://doi.org/10.1037/0033-2909.133.1.122

Wilson-Shaw, L., Pistrang, N., & Herlihy, J. (2012). Non-clinicians' judgments about asylum seekers' mental health: How do legal representatives of asylum seekers decide when to request medico-legal reports? *European Journal of Psychotraumatology, 3*(1), 18406. https://doi.org/10.3402/ejpt.v3i0.18406

Jane Herlihy, Ph.D., is a Clinical Psychologist and Emeritus Director of the Centre for the Study of Emotion and Law in London, UK. She is an Honorary Lecturer at the University College, London, and an Associate Member of the International Association for Refugee Law Judges (IARLJ). Her particular research and dissemination focus is on the contribution that empirical psychological research can make to fair and humane legal decision making.

Stuart Turner, FRCPsych, is a Consultant Psychiatrist and the Co-founder of the Centre for the Study of Emotion and Law. He is past-President of the European (ESTSS) and International (ISTSS) Societies for Traumatic Stress Studies. He has served as trustee of the Medical Foundation for the Care of Victims of Torture, Redress, Refugee Therapy Centre and the Centre for the Study of Emotion and Law.

Part IV
Research and Clinical Advances in Refugee and Conflict-Affected Mental Health

Conceptualization and Measurement of Traumatic Events among Refugees and Other War-Affected Populations

Andrew Rasmussen, Kenneth E. Miller, and Jay Verkuilen

Abstract The literature on mental health in refugee and post-conflict populations has become quite sophisticated in modeling and measuring psychological distress. However, this has not been matched by development in approaches to measuring exposure to trauma. In this chapter we present three critiques of common practices that limit our understanding of refugee and other war-affected populations' mental health: (1) using trauma exposure checklists that are limited to measuring trauma types and not events *per se*, (2) examining trauma exposure data using factor analysis (and reflective-indicator models in general), and (3) ignoring how trauma interacts with pre-conflict conditions in models of psychological distress. We argue that addressing these critiques will bring models of mental health closer to refugees' experiences. Although not an exhaustive list, solutions should include measuring frequency and schedule of trauma exposure, conceptualizing trauma exposure as a composite variable (as opposed to a latent factor), and identifying how trauma moderates the effects of pre-existing stressors on mental health.

Keywords Trauma exposure · Measurement · Reflective-indicator models · Trauma event checklists · War-affected populations

For mental health professionals, traumatic events are often the starting point in conceptualizing refugee mental health, and are considered to be the primary class of stressors predicting emotional distress. Although in the past decade the field of mental health and psychosocial support (MHPSS) has become more sophisticated in modeling

A. Rasmussen (✉)
Department of Psychology, Fordham University, Bronx, NY, USA
e-mail: arasmussen@fordham.edu

K. E. Miller
Research and Development, War Child, Amsterdam, North Holland, The Netherlands
e-mail: Kenneth.Miller@warchild.nl

J. Verkuilen
Educational Psychology, City University of New York, New York, NY, USA
e-mail: jverkuilen@gc.cuny.edu

N. Morina, A. Nickerson (eds.), *Mental Health of Refugee and Conflict-Affected Populations*, https://doi.org/10.1007/978-3-319-97046-2_16

non-traumatic sources of distress (e.g., the inclusion of daily stressors; Miller & Rasmussen, 2010; Silove, 2013), identifying forms of distress other than posttraumatic stress disorder (PTSD) (see Rasmussen, Keatley, & Joscelyne, 2014), and developing multimodal interventions (for a review, see Nickerson, Bryant, Silove, & Steel, 2011), to date practices surrounding the conceptualization and measurement of traumatic events themselves have remained surprisingly static. This leaves the field in an awkward position regarding what is one of its central constructs: trauma exposure.

This chapter presents critiques of three common practices related to the conceptualization and measurement of exposure to trauma events. Underlying these practices—one concerning data collection, one data analysis, and one theoretical modeling—is a measurement model implicitly based on psychological symptom measurement models that we believe has become reified in the MHPSS field. This situation is problematic for two reasons: (1) events and psychological symptoms are qualitatively different and (2) reification of any model leads to stagnant research and clinical practice. Although with each critique we suggest modest solutions, our purpose in presenting these critiques is not to solve problems, but to encourage researchers and clinicians to develop measurement models that capture the breadth of meaning that reflects the impact of traumatic events in the lives of refugees.

Using Variety Scores to Represent Cumulative Trauma

We begin by questioning the most common mode of collecting trauma exposure data. Most trauma exposure measurement tools in our field are event checklists that ask respondents to indicate whether or not they have experienced particular types of potentially traumatic events (PTEs). Respondents' endorsements are then typically summed to produce composite scores that are interpreted as their cumulative trauma exposure (e.g., the Harvard Trauma Questionnaire trauma exposure portion, Mollica et al., 1992). This measurement model is drawn directly from approaches that are standard in the larger trauma research literature (e.g., the Trauma Life Events Questionnaire; Kubany et al., 2000), and reflect methods used to construct psychological symptom checklists. The most problematic assumption made when interpreting additive scores from these measures as cumulative trauma is that this interpretation lacks face validity. When respondents endorse items on these checklists, they are reacting to prompts to endorse the *types* of events to which they have been exposed, not the *number* of events to which they have been exposed. The resulting sum of these endorsements is therefore indicative of the variety of PTEs they have experienced, not their frequency. These scores are *variety scores*. Variety scores give us information about the diversity of respondents' experiences, not their cumulative experience. Using variety scores to represent frequency implies that all respondents are exposed exactly once to the types of trauma they endorse—an unlikely situation that is never tested. Moreover, researchers often refer to specific numbers of trauma events without making clear that they are not actually measuring numbers of trauma events (e.g., Lopes Cardozo et al., 2004; Powell, Rosner, Butollo, Tedeschi, & Calhoun, 2003).

One might make the counter argument that variety scores are sufficient proxies for cumulative exposure despite their lack of face validity. Indeed, it is hard to imagine that variety would not be associated with frequency to some degree. Correlations between variety and frequency are likely positive and probably moderate-to-large in effect size. Two researchers who have measured both type and frequency of war-related PTEs reported to the first author that correlations (unpublished) were .60 in a Sri Lankan sample (Nuwan Jayawickreme, personal communication, May 23, 2016) and over .85 among multiple samples in East Africa (Frank Neuner, personal communication, May 25, 2016). A correlation of .60 means that 36% of the variance in one variable is accounted for by the other and correlations over .85 increases this variance accounted for to 72%. These results suggest that the proxy argument is not without empirical support (and, thankfully, that we need not wholly discard all findings that have used variety scores to this point). Conceptually it makes sense that variety and frequency are strongly associated among samples from war-affected populations. Essential to the concept of disaster settings is the existence of numerous potential types of PTEs. This implies that using variety as a proxy for frequency is less likely to be a problem in MHPSS research than it may be for trauma research in settings with fewer PTEs.

However, there are two reasons why high associations between variety and frequency do not justify using variety as a proxy for frequency. The first relates to the face validity point already mentioned: If we wish to accurately represent the cumulative severity of PTEs, we should measure the number of times they occur. Second, and, we think, more importantly, the practice of using variety scores and not frequency limits interpretations of findings in our field. For example, the robust epidemiological finding that large majorities (across trauma-affected populations) report exposure to PTEs while only small minorities go on to develop significant psychological distress (Norris & Slone, 2014; Sachs, Rosenfeld, Lhewa, Rasmussen, & Keller, 2008) may mask meaningful differences between individuals in frequency of exposure. Similarly, the oft-cited dose-response effect—the finding that across the literature more cumulative trauma results in more posttraumatic distress (for a review in the MHPSS literature, see Johnson & Thompson, 2008)—may be underestimated by not measuring the frequency of exposure to PTEs.

Disentangling frequency and type would allow us to examine a host of clinically relevant research questions related to the "etiological role of magnitude" (Netland, 2005, p. 513) of trauma events. For example, repeated exposure to a single type of PTE might be clinically meaningful to individuals as well as statistically relevant. A few years ago a Syrian humanitarian aid worker told the first author that he and his family had been forced out of ten different homes by bombings. Although he was likely exposed to several other types of PTEs as well, simply endorsing the item "bombed" or "fled your home" on an event checklist would have substantially underrepresented his experience of war trauma. A related, clinically proximal issue is weighting. At present, summative event checklists weight all PTE types equally; this implies that something as severe as "rape or sexual assault" represents the same risk for developing posttraumatic distress as more innocuous conditions like "lack of shelter" (Mollica et al., 1992), but also that two equal cumulative scores imply the same risk even if one includes sexual assault and the other does not. It is clear from the larger trauma research literature that different PTE types have different likelihoods of resulting in psychological distress (Norris & Slone, 2014). Measures that weight PTEs in order to estimate risk without using symptom measures would aid clinical screening in the field, where lack of time and the desire to avoid unnecessarily probing of psychological distress are common complaints among MHPSS aid workers. However, weighting events *a priori* on such tools risks affirming the consequent (Netland, 2005)—i.e., weighting events based on severity sets relationships between antecedents, here events, and consequents, here symptoms, thereby predetermining the effects of those antecendents. This formal fallacy is unacceptable on logical grounds alone. But research that disentangles variety and frequency of exposure to PTEs might be used to estimate the differential impacts of types of PTEs, which in turn might be used to create weighted PTE checklists that estimate risk more accurately than using the literature based on type alone or more efficiently than using event checklists and symptom severity tools.

Other questions may be less proximal to clinical practice, though they remain important to contemporary theories of trauma and resilience in our field. For instance, how many PTEs are needed before subsequent PTEs are likely to result in symptoms of psychological trauma? Are there curvilinear relationships between frequency and distress that indicate different "tipping points" for specific types of trauma? These are empirical questions, but they cannot be answered using variety scores; they require measurement models that account for frequency as well.

Measuring the impact of trauma exposure should not be limited to measuring PTEs type and frequency alone; the schedule of their occurrence is also very likely to be important. As we have observed elsewhere (Miller & Rasmussen, 2014), people affected by organized violence experience "chronically elevated stress punctuated by intermittent PTEs" (p. 38) in which the anticipation of subsequent PTEs contributes to the development of higher levels of distress. As Ignacio Martín Baró observed in El Salvador in the 1980s, acts of violence need not occur frequently to generate widespread and enduring fear (Martín Baró, 1994). Martín Baró's observation mirrors one of the most robust findings in psychology: Of the four combinations of fixed-variable interval-ratio axes of operant reinforcement schedules, the variable ratio schedule results in behavior that is most quickly acquired and most difficult to extinguish (Reynolds, 1975). For war-affected populations, the behavior that is "acquired" from exposure to PTEs is anxiety. Events that appear both unpredictable and uncontrollable—i.e., occur on a variable ratio schedule—generally result in more distress. A variable ratio schedule of PTEs during wartime would be likely to reinforce anxiety and other forms of distress much more than predictable schedules of PTEs would. Their intermittent recurrence results in an environment of perpetual threat, which in turn increases stress and lowers stress tolerance. But these hypotheses need measurement models that account for frequency and schedule in order to be tested.

If standard trauma measurement models fail in properly estimating the frequency of PTEs, they certainly fail to capture the recurring and unpredictable nature of such events. In other words, items on war exposure checklists should not be treated as discrete event types that have or have not been experienced without regard for their number, recurrent nature, or schedule. To capture the phenomenology of trauma exposure, our measurement models must account for all three. We might begin by focusing on the composition of items so that they represent mutually exclusive event types. We might write sets of linked items, such as "Did _______________ happen to you in a particular time frame?" and, given a positive endorsement, "How many times did it happen?" or "Did it ever happen to you again?" and so forth. We might even ask respondents to rank events (e.g., as we do in clinical fear hierarchies) to aid weighting studies. Unfortunately the psychometrics of such compound items is relatively underdeveloped, with only a few articles directly addressing the issue (e.g., Liu & Verkuilen, 2013). Nevertheless, such practices would improve the reliability and validity of the data we collect on exposure to trauma.

"Factor Analyzing" Trauma Exposure

The second critique we offer concerns the use of reflective-indicator psychometric models (MacDonald, 1999; these are also known as effect-indicator models) like factor analysis to analyze trauma exposure data once they have been collected. Researchers often wish to reduce PTE checklist data using factor analysis (e.g., Hooberman, Rosenfeld, Lhewa, Rasmussen, & Keller, 2007) or principal component analysis (PCA) (e.g., Dyregov, Gupta, Gjestad, & Mukanoheli, 1999) in order to divide a list of PTEs into a smaller number of trauma exposure categories. This may be done to test whether certain categories of PTEs have different predictive power with regard to one or more outcomes (e.g., PTSD) or to facilitate comparing types across datasets with different checklists by relying on conceptual categories underlying trauma exposure. However, there are problems with the practice of using such models to create categories of PTEs.

One of the primary objections to using factor analysis with checklist data concerns the misfit between binary PTE exposure data and the statistical calculations underlying factor analysis. Trauma exposure checklist data are almost always binary—either respondents endorse or do not endorse exposure (this is also the case with checklists that differentiate direct and witnessed exposure, as each of these are also binary). Reflective-indicator measurement approaches—which include exploratory and confirmatory factor analysis, PCA, and internal consistency as measured by Cronbach's alpha—rely on association between item responses represented by covariance or correlation matrices. This is appropriate for continuous or ordinal data, both common in symptom measurement. Associations between binary data are not measured in the same manner. In particular, correlations between binary items are attenuated towards zero and related to the probability of endorsing particular items. In the case of PTEs, more common PTEs are likely to have higher correlations with each other, and rarer PTEs are likely to have higher correlations with each other, all other things being equal. In other words, item responses are likely to be associated due to rarity above and beyond any conceptual commonalities. In the factor analysis literature this is known as the problem of "difficulty" factors and leads to unclear interpretation and an overall inflation of the number of extracted factors (MacDonald, 1999). Statistical methods such as tetrachoric correlation or item response theory (IRT) deal with this problem by removing the effect of the probability of endorsing particular items. However, these methods are rarely used in the MHPSS literature (and are never default settings in statistical software packages), leading us to conclude that the majority of PTE categories derived from factor analyses are calculated incorrectly.

Although incorrect calculations are troubling to say the least, there is a fundamental conceptual error behind these calculations that is even more troubling. Reflective-indicator models purport that item responses are effects of larger, hypothetical constructs represented by the intercorrelations of responses to a set of related items, i.e., factors. In other words, item responses "reflect" latent variables that cannot be measured directly. Using these models thus implies that responses to items are (1) caused by the level of intensity of the associated latent variables and (2) somewhat interchangeable with responses to other items (i.e., no item responses are essential to defining the latent variable). Thus, psychometric findings that, in refugee samples, responses to items concerning recurrent thoughts of traumatic events, nightmares, and flashbacks load together on a single factor (Palmieri, Marshall, & Schell, 2007; Vinson & Chang, 2012), suggests that responses to these items reflect a singular psychological phenomenon, intrusive symptomatology, even though responses to each item may not uniformly contribute to the factor across studies (i.e., unequal factor loadings). Factor scores are linear combinations of estimators of hypothetical constructs that cannot be measured directly and for which there are no essential concrete indicators.

Conceptualizing trauma exposure as a hypothetical construct is problematic. When a refugee reports she was bombed, this is not an indicator that she experienced some latent bombing construct; there is a clear concrete experience of being bombed that no other experience can represent. Reports that refugees were bombed and shot and saw others being shot may all load on a single factor. However, although factor analytic software will produce output without apparent computational errors and we may be able to observe conceptual commonalities between PTEs (e.g., being bombed and shot and saw others being shot are all forms of attack with weapons) they are qualitatively quite different from each other and cannot be substituted for one another in order to represent some underlying phenomenon. Because of this, the practical interpretation of that factor is not that there exists some hypothetical "attack with weapons" construct, but rather that these events tended to occur to the same people within the particular sample of respondents in a study. This interpretation is not consistent with the conceptualization of latent factors.

This issue has been the topic of some limited discussion in the MHPSS literature. Netland's (2001, 2005) critiques of approaches to event lists in our field include the theoretical objection to using factor analysis, and suggests that PTEs should be conceptualized as *causal* indicators rather than reflective indicators. This reverses the direction between items and factors—i.e., the level of trauma exposure is caused by the level of exposure to PTEs, not the other way around. Reversing this direction means that all PTEs in a checklist are relevant to trauma exposure, and the construct of trauma exposure should thus be thought of as a composite of PTEs. PTEs do not *reflect* trauma exposure, they *comprise* trauma exposure.

Netland (2001, 2005) and Layne and colleagues (Layne et al., 2010) note that a practical consequence of modeling trauma exposure using reflective-indicator models is that important predictors of distress are often dropped from analyses. In reflective-indicator approaches, items are routinely excluded from analyses because of low covariance with other item scores. This would be acceptable if item responses represented hypothetical constructs because low covariance suggests that item content is irrelevant to latent factors. However, for sets of items that represent composite phenomena (here trauma exposure) this may well result in dropping important items (here PTEs) simply because they do not co-occur with others. In other words, single traumatic event types that do not fit into a pattern of associated events but nevertheless have large effects on mental health will likely be excluded. Using a sample of war-exposed Bosnian youths, Layne et al. (2010) compared factor-analytically derived models and composite causal models of trauma exposure and found factor analytic models did just that. Factor analytic models "reflected idiosyncratic features of how the Bosnian conflict was waged" (Layne et al., 2010, p. 1070) rather than common, latent experiences of war. Composite causal models provided more robust and theoretically relevant findings.

Underlying critiques of applying reflective-indicator models to trauma exposure is an implication that covariance may not be the operant association measure for event list data. Covariance is an appropriate measure for psychometrically bipolar traits such as attitude or liking vs. disliking, but it is unclear that PTEs are bipolar. PTE checklists are generally "pick any event" formats for which covariance is problematic at best. A relationship that might be more appropriate is proximity. Respondents who have similar profiles of PTE exposure would be judged to be similar to each other, and different PTEs that commonly co-occur could be identified. Proximity statistics such as the Jaccard coefficient (Anderberg, 1973) might be more useful in this circumstance. To date we know of no literature in the MHPSS field that uses such measures. However, proximity statistics have shown some promise in the clinical literature (Olbert, Gala, & Tupler, 2014), and we encourage researchers to explore this option.

An alternative to employing covariance-based methods that *is* frequently used is the categorical conceptualization of PTEs. Researchers might categorize PTEs based on some theoretical or phenomenological similarities (e.g., attacks with weapons) or use pre-existing documentation tools that do so (e.g., the system provided by Human Rights Information and Documentation Systems International, HURIDOCS; Dueck & Aida, 1993). This relatively simple approach allows each PTE to contribute to numerical representations of individuals' experience but groups similar types of PTEs using a composite approach in order to examine differential effects across broad categories (e.g., Priebe et al., 2010; Rasmussen, Verkuilen, Ho, & Fan, 2015). Netland (2005) recommends such conceptually based categories for PTEs, and in the absence of more sophisticated approaches such as proximity measures we second this recommendation. In as much as such conceptual categories can reflect human rights documentation efforts (e.g., HURIDOCS), this may represent an advantageous point of synergy between MHPSS and human rights fields.

Traumatic Events as Moderators in a Daily Stressors Framework

Our third critique concerns the role of traumatic exposure in most models of refugee mental health. We begin with the premise that the field is convinced that PTEs in war-affected populations are not the only sources of variance in what is captured by measures of PTSD and other forms of emotional distress. A wealth of research in the past decade has shown that non-traumatic conditions that war and political conflict create also have significant adverse effects on mental health (Betancourt, McBain, Newnham, & Brennan, 2013; Brooks, Silove, Steel, Steel, & Rees, 2011; Jordans, Semrau, Thornicroft & van Ommeren, 2012). The so-called "daily stressors model" (Miller & Rasmussen, 2010) is part and parcel of a set of models in MHPSS that account for the radiating effects of war and disaster. Earlier notable models appear in the work of Boothby (1996, 2008) and Silove (2000, 2005, 2013), among others.

The daily stressors model posits that commonly occurring stressors in individuals' immediate environment may mediate (Miller & Rasmussen, 2010) or moderate (Miller, Omidian, Rasmussen, Yaqubi, & Daudzi, 2008) the effects of trauma exposure, and that some may simply be direct effects in and of themselves (Miller & Rasmussen, 2010). That such stressors mediate the effect of trauma exposure implies that the effect of trauma exposure impacts individuals through the presence of other environmental stressors; a less strict interpretation is that trauma exposure during war is never *not* accompanied by non-traumatic stressors, and that these stressors are more proximally related (in terms of time, frequency, and relevance to daily life) to ill mental health. This mediation model has been empirically supported across disaster settings (e.g., Jordans et al., 2012). That daily stressors moderate the effects of trauma exposure implies that they make the effect of trauma exposure worse than it would be had they not existed. This is consistent with models of reduced distress tolerance (e.g., Fetzer, Peluso, & Asmundson, 2014; Vujanovic et al., 2013) and stress generation (e.g., Hammen, 2006).

Less attention has been paid to the idea that daily stressors during wartime can exert direct effects independent of the impact of trauma exposure. Those readers who have worked in the field will surely be familiar with stressors in Low and Middle Income Countries (LMIC) conflict-affected contexts that have little to do with the conflict *per se* and yet are sources of considerable distress among war-affected populations. This situation was the impetus for the "lower branch" of the 2010 daily stressors model (see Miller & Rasmussen, 2010, p. 9), which modeled the direct effects of daily stressors that do not mediate the effects of trauma exposure. Examining this lower branch leads us to consider that several such stressors may pre-date conflict. If this were the case, it may be that trauma exposure moderates the effects of such pre-conflict daily stressors on war-affected populations' mental health in addition to having direct effects of its own.

That trauma exposure might moderate the effect of daily stressors on mental health will not seem unreasonable to those familiar with the statistical models that are usually used to examine moderation. Interaction effects used to model moderation (e.g., in an ANOVA or regression model) show that the level of each variable is dependent on the level of the other—i.e., that the first moderates the second as much the second moderates the first. Theoretical pathways of moderation are modeled only somewhat more precisely in more sophisticated statistical approaches (e.g., structural equation modeling), leaving open the likelihood that cross-sectional data support trauma exposure moderating the effects of daily stressors as much as they support daily stressors moderating the effects of trauma exposure. Models to date have always started with war-related trauma exposure (an artifact of the trauma-focused roots of researchers' interest in trauma), but of course there is no reason to think that before war-related trauma there were no daily stressors in the lives of those who later were exposed to war. Indeed, what limited literature there is in our field suggests that these stressors are not uncommon and have considerable impact. Among a multinational sample of refugees, Opaas and Varvin (2015) found that adverse childhood experiences predicted postwar mental health better than war experiences. Trani and Bakhshi (2013) found that mental health in Afghanistan was linked to increased social exclusion present before war.

What might moderation look like in the field? Trauma exposure moderating the effects of daily stressors would be consistent with situations in which stressful environments are perceived as being more stressful because of exposure to PTEs. Whereas most examples in the literature to date posit that war creates daily stressors, it is likely the case that many daily stressors in LMIC conflict zones exist prior to conflicts, and that war worsens them. As an example, one might think of any of the conflicts throughout the nations of the African Sahel in the past two or three decades. Prior to these conflicts, water scarcity was a daily stressor, and the effects of war (e.g., poisoning wells in Darfur) worsened water scarcity, and likely its impact on the affected populations' mental health. Of course, the vast majority of conflict zones are in LMICs, and so we might go as far to propose that war trauma moderating the effects of pre-conflict stressors is the rule rather than the exception.

Here we formally add another component to the 2010 daily stressors model in which war-related trauma exposure may moderate the effect of pre-existing current stressors. To summarize: variance within conflict-affected populations' mental health can be partitioned into direct effects of (1) war-related trauma exposure, (2) pre-existing daily stressors, (3) daily stressors arising from the conflict situation, and (4) other stressors not directly related to war; in addition, (5) the effects of pre-existing daily stressors may be moderated by war-related trauma exposure, and (6) the effects of war-related trauma exposure may be mediated or moderated by daily stressors arising from the conflict situation. A conceptual diagram of this model is presented in Fig. 1.

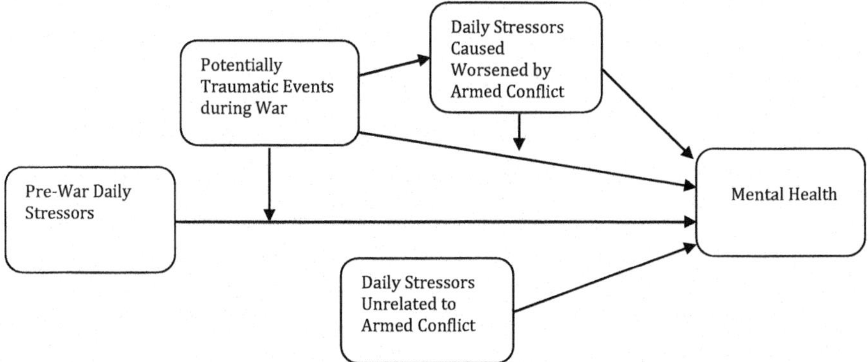

Fig. 1 Daily Stressors model with potentially traumatic events moderating the effect of pre-existing daily stressors

If war-related trauma exposure can be both mediated and moderated by daily stressors, why is there no proposed mediation of the effect of pre-existing daily stressors by war-related trauma exposure? The case for trauma exposure mediating the effects of pre-trauma daily stressors is somewhat difficult conceptually. Mediation implies that the effect of one variable is only observed in the presence of another. That the distress associated with pre-existing stressors would only be observed after trauma negates the pre-existing stressors' status as stressors. A stressor that is not stressful is no stressor at all.

We recognize that with most data that is collected in our field there is a measurement chicken-and-egg problem here: How do we convincingly show the effects of pre-existing daily stressors, war-related trauma exposure, and stressors arising from conflict when we are measuring all of them well after conflict has begun? Providing empirical support for the multiple dynamics between PTEs and daily stressors is clearly limited by our field's reliance on cross-sectional data. The few longitudinal studies that we know of do not include pre-conflict data. However, in the spirit of research that informs practice, we suggest that partitioning sources of variance into the proposed components might be meaningful in clinical fieldwork. For instance, interventions aimed at reducing the effect of pre-existing stressors should probably promote understanding of how war exposure complicates their effects. We leave it to our readers to find other meaningful implications.

In this chapter we have presented critiques of the MHPSS field's usual conceptualization and measurement of exposure to trauma: one concerning data collection, one data analysis, and a third design. Measurement models of trauma exposure have by and large relied on measuring the variety of PTEs to do the work of measuring the frequency of PTEs and have ignored the schedules of PTEs altogether. It should not be too difficult to ask participants to estimate the number of instances of particular types of trauma; although perhaps more difficult, participants might also estimate the schedule of such events and perhaps even the subjective weight of impact by ranking them. In terms of analytic approaches, most literature that has applied factor analysis (and other reflective-indicator models) to PTE checklist data has violated basic conceptual assumptions concerning the non-latent nature of trauma exposure. PTEs are concrete historical events, and not hypothetical in any way. Each PTE in individuals' experiences should be accounted for in composite models of trauma exposure. Finally, we must free our designs from the assumption that all distress in war-affected populations begins with war trauma. Exposure to war trauma is part of a larger ecosystem of stressors impacting war-affected populations. Our measurement models as well as clinical practice should reflect this reality as accurately as possible.

References

Anderberg, M. R. (1973). *Cluster analysis for applications*. New York, NY: Academic.

Betancourt, T. S., McBain, R., Newnham, E. A., & Brennan, R. T. (2013). Trajectories of internalizing problems in war-affected Sierra Leonean youth: Examining conflict and postconflict factors. *Child Development, 84*(2), 455–470. https://doi.org/10.1111/j.1467-8624.2012.01861.x

Boothby, N. (1996). Mobilizing communities to meet the psychosocial needs of children in war and refugee crises. In R. J. Apfel & B. Simon (Eds.), *Minefields in their hearts: The mental health of children in war and communal violence* (pp. 149–164). New Haven, CT: Yale University Press.

Boothby, N. (2008). Political violence and development: An ecologic approach to children in war zones. *Child and Adolescent Psychiatric Clinics of North America, 17*(3), 497–514. https://doi.org/10.1016/j.chc.2008.02.004

Brooks, R., Silove, D., Steel, Z., Steel, C. B., & Rees, S. (2011). Explosive anger in post-conflict Timor Leste: Interaction of socio-economic disadvantage and past human rights-related trauma. *Journal of Affective Disorders, 131*(1–3), 268–276. https://doi.org/10.1016/j.jad.2010.12.020

Dueck, J., & Aida, M. (1993). *HURIDOCS standard formats: A tool for documenting human rights violations*. Oslo, Norway: Human Rights Information and Documentation Systems International (HURIDOCS).

Dyregov, A., Gupta, L., Gjestad, R., & Mukanoheli, E. (1999). Trauma exposure and psychological reactions to genocide among Rwandan children. *Journal of Traumatic Stress, 13*(1), 3–21. https://doi.org/10.1023/A:1007759112499

Fetzer, M. G., Peluso, D. L., & Asmundson, G. J. G. (2014). Tolerating distress after trauma: Differential associations between distress tolerance and posttraumatic stress symptoms. *Journal of Psychopathology and Behavioral Assessment, 36*(3), 475–484. https://doi.org/10.1007/s10862-014-9413-6

Hammen, C. (2006). Stress generation in depression: Reflections on origins, research, and future directions. *Journal of Clinical Psychology, 62*(9), 1065–1082. https://doi.org/10.1002/jclp.20293

Hooberman, J., Rosenfeld, B., Lhewa, D., Rasmussen, A., & Keller, A. S. (2007). Classifying the torture experiences of refugees living in the U.S. *Journal of Interpersonal Violence, 22*(1), 108–123. https://doi.org/10.1177/0886260506294999

Johnson, H., & Thompson, A. (2008). The development and maintenance of post-traumatic stress disorder (PTSD) in civilian adult survivors of war trauma and torture: A review. *Clinical Psychology Review, 28*(1), 36–47. https://doi.org/10.1016/j.cpr.2007.01.017

Jordans, M. J. D., Semrau, M., Thornicroft, G., & van Ommeren, M. (2012). Role of current and perceived needs in explaining the association between past trauma exposure and distress in humanitarian settings in Jordan and Nepal. *The British Journal of Psychiatry, 201*(4), 276–281. https://doi.org/10.1192/bjp.bp.111.102137

Kubany, E. S., Leisen, M. B., Kaplan, A. S., Watson, S. B., Haynes, S. N., Owens, J. A., & Burns, K. (2000). Development and preliminary validation of a brief broad-spectrum measure of trauma exposure: The traumatic life events questionnaire. *Psychological Assessment, 12*(2), 210–224. https://doi.org/10.1037//1040-3590.12.2.210

Layne, C. M., Olsen, J. A., Baker, A., Legershi, J. P., Isakson, B., Pasalić, A., … Pynoos, R. S. (2010). Unpacking trauma exposure risk factors and differential pathways of influence: Predicting postwar mental distress in Bosnian adolescents. *Child Development, 81*(4), 1053–1076. https://doi.org/10.1111/j.1467-8624.2010.01454.x

Liu, Y., & Verkuilen, J. (2013). Item response modeling of presence-severity items: Application to measurement of patient-reported outcomes. *Applied Psychological Measurement, 37*(1), 58–75. https://doi.org/10.1177/0146621612455091

Lopes Cardozo, B., Bilukha, O. O., Gotway Crawford, C., Shaikh, I., Workfe, M. I., Gerber, M. L., & Anderson, M. (2004). Mental health, social functioning, and disability in postwar Afghanistan. *JAMA, 292*(5), 575–584. https://doi.org/10.1001/jama.292.5.575

MacDonald, R. P. (1999). *Test theory: A unified treatment*. Mahwah, NJ: Erlbaum.

Martín Baró, I. (1994). In A. Aron & S. Corne (Eds.), *Writings for a liberation psychology*. Cambridge, MA: Harvard University Press.

Miller, K., Omidian, P., Rasmussen, A., Yaqubi, A., & Daudzi, H. (2008). Daily stressors, war experiences, and mental health in Afghanistan. *Transcultural Psychiatry, 45*, 611–639. https://doi.org/10.1177/1363461508100785

Miller, K., & Rasmussen, A. (2010). War exposure, daily stressors, and mental health in conflict and post-conflict settings: Bridging the divide between trauma-focused and psychosocial frameworks. *Social Science & Medicine, 70*(1), 7–16. https://doi.org/10.1016/j.socscimed.2009.09.029

Miller, K. E., & Rasmussen, A. (2014). War experiences, daily stressors, and mental health five years on: Elaborations and future directions. *Intervention: The International Journal for Mental Health, Psychosocial Work and Counselling in Areas of Armed Conflict, 12*, 33–42. https://doi.org/10.1097/WTF.0000000000000066

Mollica, R. F., Caspi-Yavin, Y., Bollini, P., Truong, T., Tor, S., & Lavelle, J. (1992). The Harvard trauma questionnaire: Validating a cross-cultural instrument for measuring torture, trauma, and post traumatic stress disorder in refugees. *Journal of Nervous and Mental Disorders, 180*(2), 111–116. https://doi.org/10.1097/00005053-199202000-00008

Netland, M. (2001). Assessment of exposure to political violence and other potentially traumatizing events. A critical review. *Journal of Traumatic Stress, 14*(2), 311–326. https://doi.org/10.1023/a:1011164901867

Netland, M. (2005). Event-list construction and treatment of exposure data in research on political violence. *Journal of Traumatic Stress, 18*(5), 507–517. https://doi.org/10.1002/jts.20059

Nickerson, A., Bryant, R. A., Silove, D., & Steel, Z. (2011). A critical review of psychological treatments of posttraumatic stress disorder in refugees. *Clinical Psychology Review, 31*(3), 399–417. https://doi.org/10.1016/j.cpr.2010.10.004

Norris, F. H., & Slone, L. B. (2014). Epidemiology of trauma and PTSD. In M. J. Friedman, T. M. Keane, & P. A. Resick (Eds.), *Handbook of PTSD* (2nd ed., pp. 100–120). New York, NY: Guilford Press.

Olbert, C. M., Gala, G. J., & Tupler, L. A. (2014). Quantifying heterogeneity attributable to polythetic diagnostic criteria: Theoretical framework and empirical application. *Journal of Abnormal Psychology, 123*(2), 452–462. https://doi.org/10.1037/a0036068

Opaas, M., & Varvin, S. (2015). Relationships of childhood adverse experiences with mental health and quality of life at treatment start for adult refugees traumatized by pre-flight experiences of war and human rights violations. *The Journal of Nervous and Mental Disease, 203*(9), 684–695. https://doi.org/10.1097/NMD.0000000000000330

Palmieri, P. A., Marshall, G. N., & Schell, T. L. (2007). Confirmatory factor analysis of posttraumatic stress symptoms in Cambodian refugees. *Journal of Traumatic Stress, 20*(2), 207–216. https://doi.org/10.1002/jts.20196

Powell, S., Rosner, R., Butollo, W., Tedeschi, R. G., & Calhoun, L. G. (2003). Posttraumatic growth after war: A study with former refugees and displaced people in Sarajevo. *Journal of Clinical Psychology, 59*(1), 71–83. https://doi.org/10.1002/jclp.10117

Priebe, S., Bogic, M., Ashcroft, R., Franciskovic, T., Galeazzi, G. M., Kucukalic, A., … Ajdukovic, D. (2010). Experience of human rights violations and subsequent mental disorders – A study following the war in the Balkans. *Social Science & Medicine, 71*(12), 2170–2177. https://doi.org/10.1016/j.socscimed.2010.09.029

Rasmussen, A., Keatley, E., & Joscelyne, A. (2014). Posttraumatic stress in humanitarian disaster settings outside North America and Europe: A review of the emic trauma literature. *Social Science & Medicine, 109*, 44–54. https://doi.org/10.1016/j.socscimed.2014.03.015

Rasmussen, A., Verkuilen, J., Ho, E., & Fan, Y. (2015). Posttraumatic stress among refugees: Measurement invariance across culture in Harvard trauma questionnaire scores. *Psychological Assessment, 27*(4), 1160–1170. https://doi.org/10.1037/pas0000115

Reynolds, G. S. (1975). *A primer of operant conditioning*. Oxford, UK: Scott, Foresman and Company.

Sachs, E., Rosenfeld, B., Lhewa, D., Rasmussen, A., & Keller, A. S. (2008). Entering exile: Trauma, mental health, and coping among Tibetan refugees arriving in Dharamsala, India. *Journal of Traumatic Stress, 21*(2), 199–208. https://doi.org/10.1002/jts.20324

Silove, D. (2000). A conceptual framework for mass trauma: Implications for adaptation, intervention and debriefing. In B. Raphael & J. P. Wilson (Eds.), *Psychological debriefing: Theory, practice and evidence* (pp. 337–350). Cambridge, UK: Cambridge University Press.

Silove, D. (2005). From trauma to survival and adaptation. In D. Ingleby (Ed.), *Forced migration and mental health* (pp. 29–51). New York, NY: Springer.

Silove, D. (2013). The ADAPT model: A conceptual framework for mental health and psychosocial programming in psychosocial settings. *Intervention: The International Journal for Mental Health, Psychosocial Work and Counselling in Areas of Armed Conflict, 11*(3), 237–248. https://doi.org/10.1097/wtf.0000000000000005

Trani, J. F., & Bakhshi, P. (2013). Vulnerability and mental health in Afghanistan: Looking beyond war exposure. *Transcultural Psychiatry, 50*(1), 108–139. https://doi.org/10.1177/1363461512475025

Vinson, G. A., & Chang, Z. (2012). PTSD symptom structure among west African war trauma survivors living in African refugee camps: A factor-analytic investigation. *Journal of Traumatic Stress, 25*(2), 226–231. https://doi.org/10.1002/jts.21681

Vujanovic, A. A., Hart, A. S., Potter, C. M., Berenz, E. C., Niles, B., & Bernstein, A. (2013). Main and interactive effects of distress tolerance and negative affect intensity in relation to PTSD symptoms among trauma-exposed adults. *Journal of Psychopathology and Behavioral Assessment, 35*(2), 235–243. https://doi.org/10.1007/s10862-012-9325-2

Andrew Rasmussen, Ph.D., is an Associate Professor of Psychology at Fordham University in the Bronx, NY, USA. His work focuses on psychosocial assessment and care for displaced families across multiple stages of forced as well as voluntary migration, with particular focus on culture, trauma, and other stressors.

Kenneth E. Miller, Ph.D., is a psychologist and researcher at War Child Holland, where he develops and evaluates mental health and psychosocial interventions for war-affected children and families. His research has also focused on identifying the diverse pathways by which armed conflict and forced migration impact the mental health of civilians.

Jay Verkuilen, Ph.D., is Associate Professor of Educational Psychology at the City University of New York Graduate Center. His work focuses on psychometrics and statistics, with applications to education and mental health.

Low Intensity Interventions for Psychological Symptoms Following Mass Trauma

Katie S. Dawson and Atif Rahman

Abstract With the increased recognition of mental health as part of global health agendas, the substantial gap between mental health needs and access to evidence-based treatment services in low- and middle-income countries (LMICs) has been exposed. More than 80% of the world's population reside in these lower resource settings where exposure to adverse living conditions and mass trauma is widespread. However, less than 20% of mental health resources are managed by LMICs. Evidence-informed psychological and psychosocial interventions that have been adapted for trauma-affected LMICs and can be delivered by non-specialist providers offer one solution to filling this treatment gap. While the evidence for these low-intensity interventions is mounting, many challenges remain that impinge on the effective implementation of such interventions in these settings. These include the selection of delivery agents, the duration and methods of training and supervision, and challenges related to implementation and local government ownership. This chapter examines the current literature on low-intensity interventions in LMICs and provides a brief commentary on the existing challenges to implementation.

Keywords Low intensity psychological interventions · Global mental health · Low- and middle-income countries · Humanitarian settings · Task-shifting · Non-specialist providers · Common mental disorders

> "There is no health without mental health." Ban Ki-moon, Secretary-General, United Nations

K. S. Dawson (✉)
Psychology, University of New South Wales, Sydney, NSW, Australia
e-mail: katie.dawson@unsw.edu.au

A. Rahman
Institute of Psychology, Health and Society, University of Liverpool, Liverpool, Merseyside, UK
e-mail: atif.rahman@liverpool.ac.uk

N. Morina, A. Nickerson (eds.), *Mental Health of Refugee and Conflict-Affected Populations*, https://doi.org/10.1007/978-3-319-97046-2_17

The last two decades have seen burgeoning efforts to bring mental health to the forefront of the global health agenda. Initiatives such as the Grand Challenges in Global Mental Health (Collins et al., 2011), the Movement for Global Mental Health and the World Health Organization's (WHO) mental health Gap Action Programme (mhGAP) have sought to advance the understanding of mental health and improve diagnosis and treatment services for a wide range of mental health, neurological and developmental disorders in children and adults in low resource settings (Patel & Prince, 2010). Initiatives such as the Special series in The Lancet (2007 and 2011) and PLoS Medicine (2012) have facilitated the dissemination of key findings and developments from experts in the field, and networks such as the Mental Health Innovation Network have promoted greater collaboration within the field. More recently and for the first time, the United Nations Sustainable Development Goals, adopted in September 2015, recognised the importance of promoting mental health and wellbeing. Specifically, Target 3.4 requests that countries: "By 2030, reduce by one third premature mortality from non-communicable diseases through prevention and treatment and promote mental health and wellbeing."

In spite of these momentous developments, there is a long way to go to respond to the global mental health need adequately. Mental health constitutes a significant disease burden globally. The Global Burden of Disease (GBD) Study 2010 (Whiteford et al., 2013) estimated that mental, neurological and substance use disorders accounted for just over 10% of global disability-adjusted life years (DALYs), 2.3% of global years lost to premature mortality (YLLs), and 28.5% of global years lived with disability (YLDs). While many common mental disorders are not detected until adulthood, onset typically occurs in adolescence and DALYs have been found to peak in early adulthood (Whiteford et al., 2013). Mental ill health comes at a social and economic cost as well. In youth, mental disorders are associated with poor education achievement and health problems, such as suicide and sexual and reproductive health problems (Patel, Flisher, Hetrick, & McGorry, 2007). When these disorders persist into adulthood they can lead to considerable economic costs by means of productivity loss resulting from disability and diminished work performance, as well as the cost of providing treatment and care (Chisholm, 2006; Rehm et al., 2009).

Treatment Gap in LMICs

While the need for effective treatment for a range of mental health conditions is evident, accessibility to evidence-based psychological treatments is limited in LMICs. The vast majority of studies examining the effectiveness of psychological interventions, such as cognitive-behaviour therapy (CBT), have been conducted in high-income countries (Patel, Araya, et al., 2007). This research gap parallels the substantial treatment gap that is most pronounced in lower resource settings, where the majority of the world's population (adults and youth) reside. In fact, LMICs only manage less than 20% of the total resources worldwide to treat mental illnesses (Patel & Prince, 2010). According to World Mental Health surveys, more than 75%

of individuals who identified with disabling anxiety, mood, or substance use disorders in LMICs were not receiving care at all (Demyttenaere et al., 2004). This is due to a number of barriers, of which the low priority given to mental health in many LMICs is arguably the most notable. Government expenditure on mental health equates to less than US$2 per capita in most low resource countries, with the majority of this being directed to inpatient care (WHO, 2015). In addition, prevalence data that is gathered in these settings is often of poor quality, resulting in an inability to provide accurate GBD estimates, and thus limiting policy planning (Baxter, Patton, Scott, Degenhardt, & Whiteford, 2013). These factors are likely to contribute to the other treatment barriers that exist including limited mental health funding and infrastructure, chronic shortage of human resources, stigma associated with engaging with psychological support, and inadequate cultural adaption of treatments inhibiting local acceptability (Patel, Chowdhary, Rahman, & Verdeli, 2011; Saraceno et al., 2007).

Not only do many of these barriers impede the capacity to conduct research into the effectiveness and implementation of psychological interventions in LMIC settings, but unique challenges exist for conducting rigorous scientific evaluation of such interventions as well. These include generally poor training in research methodology, frequent attrition of staff who are looking for better opportunities and financial security, population migration (e.g., seasonal migration, seeking improved living conditions and employment) which affords particular difficulties for larger trials and cohort studies, and challenges associated with raising community awareness and appreciation of the need for mental health research.

In response to these challenges, a number of prominent experts in the field are examining different ways to improve access to evidence-based psychological treatment in LMICs. The adaptation of existing interventions, such as CBT-based interventions, into a low-intensity format has received substantial attention in the literature. Currently, there is no consensus on a definition for low-intensity psychological intervention (Bennet-Levy et al., 2010). However, the core features of these interventions include the use of fewer resources than many traditional treatments (e.g., utilising group format, having fewer sessions), use of non-therapist or remote delivery methods (e.g., bibliotherapy, e-mental health interventions) and the application of transdiagnostic approaches. Transdiagnostic treatments allow for a constellation of mental health symptoms to be addressed simultaneously by applying strategies with the same underlying principles across disorders (McEnvoy, Nathan, & Norton, 2009). In low resource settings, this may be preferable to targeted interventions that only address one condition, such as depression, and therefore require a delivery agent to be trained in multiple interventions in order to meet the diverse needs of the population.

In addition, many of these interventions have also focused on shifting the counselling role from the few mental health specialists available in LMIC settings to lay people who receive training specifically in the intervention. This process, called 'task-shifting' (or 'task-sharing'), reduces the economic cost of delivering psychological treatments, hence promoting scale-up and sustainability of such programs. Non-specialists can include community health volunteers, primary care workers, a range of auxiliary health workers, teachers and peer helpers. A review of 38 studies employing a task-shifting approach to treat depression and/or anxiety and posttraumatic stress disorder (PTSD) in developing countries found promising results (van Ginneken et al., 2013). Specifically, employment of non-specialist delivery agents (compared with usual care which typically does not involve mental healthcare) was associated with increased recovery in the adults with depression and/or anxiety 2–6 months post-treatment; and slight reductions in perinatal depression, PTSD and the quantity of alcohol consumed by adults with alcohol-use disorders. While the task-shifting approach is laudable and moves this field of low-intensity interventions in the right direction, this review highlighted the need for more rigorous scientific evaluation of its effectiveness, especially in the treatment of child and adolescent mental health problems.

Low-intensity interventions accord with levels two and three of the Inter-Agency Standing Committee (IASC) Guidelines for Mental Health and Psychosocial Support in Emergency Settings (IASC), 2007) pyramid (see Fig. 1). The pyramid is recommended to support the organisation of mental health and psychosocial services to adequately meet the needs of individuals and communities affected by emergencies. Level one describes services that seek to establish security and deliver basic care to address physical needs, such as access to food, water, shelter and basic health care. Level two includes community and family level supports for groups of people who do not require intensive mental health and psychosocial support or treatment. While some low-intensity interventions may fall under level two, the majority of such interventions comprise level three services. Level three represents those services provided for a smaller group of people who require more focused

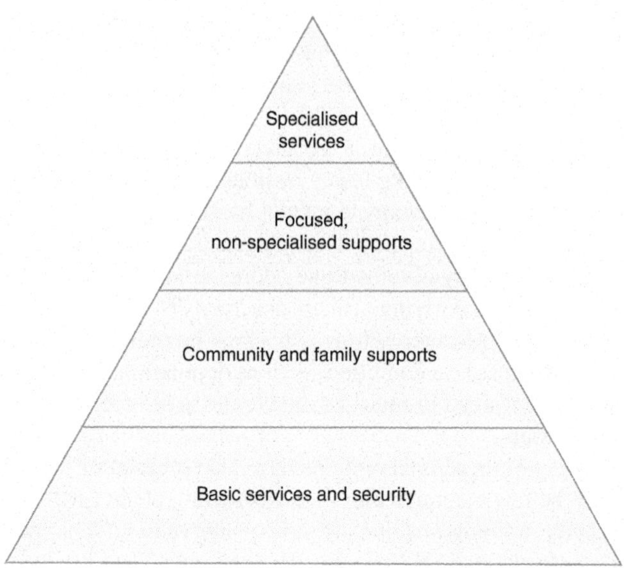

Fig. 1 Intervention pyramid for mental health and psychosocial support in emergencies. IASC guidelines on mental health and psychosocial support in emergency settings

mental health and psychosocial intervention. Finally, level four represents the more specialised services that would be required for a small percentage of people who have not benefited from supports and interventions at previous levels. These people are likely to experience significant interference to their daily functioning and have serious mental health concerns. With the potential for low-intensity interventions delivered by non-specialists to meet needs at levels two and three, qualified psychologists and psychiatrists could concentrate on providing treatment at level four.

Low-Intensity Interventions for Adults

Importantly, a number of psychological interventions for adults have proven effective when delivered by local non-specialists (i.e., adopting a task-shifting approach). For instance, a 16-session group interpersonal psychotherapy (IPT) facilitated by local non-specialist providers was shown to be effective in rural Uganda among depressed adults compared to usual care at 6 month follow-up (Bass et al., 2006). Individuals who received IPT demonstrated significant reductions in their depression symptoms and improvements in functioning. At 6 month follow-up, only 12% of individuals in the IPT condition met the diagnostic criteria for major depressive disorder, compared with 55% of those receiving usual care. Not only does this demonstrate the acceptability and effectiveness of IPT as a psychotherapeutic modality in Uganda, but it also provides support for the task-shifting model. In this study, facilitators had at least high school education but did not have any previous mental health or counselling experience. They received 2 weeks training in IPT by the researchers who had extensive expertise in implementing the intervention and providing training. However, the amount of supervision received by facilitators throughout the course of the project and the degree of fidelity to the intervention were not specified.

Similar findings were demonstrated in rural Pakistan, where a locally adapted CBT intervention for perinatal depression was delivered by volunteer community health workers (CHWs) (Rahman, Malik, Sikander, Roberts, & Creed, 2008). The CHWs were women, most of whom had completed high school but had not had any formal mental health training or experience. They received 2 days of training with 1 day refresher training after 4 months. They received monthly group supervision by a mental health specialist that lasted half a day. Mothers receiving the treatment (n = 463) demonstrated significant clinical improvement in depression symptoms, showed less disability and better overall and social functioning, compared to mothers who received usual care (same number of visits from untrained CHWs; n = 440). At 6 months, 97 (23%) and 211 (53%) of mothers in the intervention and control groups, respectively, met criteria for major depression (adjusted odds ratio 0.22, 95% CI 0.14–0.36, $p < 0.0001$). For women in the intervention group, these benefits of the treatment were sustained at 12 months– 111 (27%) and 226 (59%) of mothers in the intervention and control groups, respectively, met criteria for major depression (adjusted odds ratio 0.23, 95% CI 0.15–0.36, $p < 0.0001$).

A pilot study that employed behavioural and problem-solving techniques to treat symptoms of common mental health disorders in adults affected by mass trauma has also demonstrated promising results (Rahman et al., 2016). The study tested the effectiveness of Problem Management Plus (PM+), a brief, transdiagnostic psychological intervention developed by WHO (for a description see (Dawson et al., 2015), when compared with enhanced treatment as usual (ETAU). In ETAU, participants were seen by a primary care physician who received training in recognition and basic management of common mental disorders. The study was conducted in Peshawar, a district located in the Khyber Pakhtunkhwa province in Pakistan that has been exposed to an escalation in militant attacks in the last 5 years as well as several natural disasters. Treatment was delivered to men and women in a primary care setting by university graduates with no prior mental health training. They received 6 days of training and 2 weeks of in-field practice with less severe clients and under close supervision. Compared with ETAU ($n = 30$), PM+ ($n = 30$) resulted in improved functioning as measured by WHO Disability Assessment Scale (mean scores reduced 17.7 +/−9.2 to 6.6 +/− 6.1 in PM+ group versus 17.0 +/− 10.5 to 11.3 +/− 10.4 in ETAU group) and reduced PTSD symptoms, as indexed by the Posttraumatic Checklist-5 (mean scores reduced from 34.2 +/− 20.1 to 9.8 +/−9.1 in PM+ group versus 32.3 +/− 17.1 to 19.5 +/− 18.5 in ETAU group).

Lastly, the Common Elements Treatment Approach (CETA) (Murray et al., 2013) is exemplary of the transdiagnostic approach and has shown benefits for individuals experiencing symptoms of depression, anxiety and posttraumatic stress when delivered by non-specialists in several populations exposed to trauma and adversity. The intervention teaches counsellors eight CBT-based components that can be applied to treat a number of presenting complaints, including relaxation, behavioural activation, cognitive restructuring and exposure techniques. Counsellors are taught how to make decisions about selection, sequencing and dosing of these components to effectively tailor the intervention to the individual client. Sessions are delivered weekly for eight to 12 weeks and last a minimum of 50 minutes.

When trialled with displaced Burmese people residing on the Thai-Myanmar border, CETA significantly reduced depression, posttraumatic stress, functional impairment (e.g., self-care activities), anxiety symptoms and aggression (Bolton et al., 2014). Similar findings were demonstrated with Iraqi survivors of systematic violence (e.g., torture, unlawful imprisonment, persecution etc.) Those receiving CETA had significant reductions in posttraumatic stress, anxiety and depression scores. Overall, compared to waitlist control, the intervention showed a large effect size (Cohen's $d = 1.54$) (Weiss et al., 2015).

The above studies indicate that, in order for task-shifting approaches to be successful and scalable, existing evidence-based psychological treatments require adaptation. Specifically, treatments need to be of a lower intensity so that lay people can be trained effectively but also in the briefest amount of time. All interventions in the above studies also underwent some form of cultural adaptation. This is imperative in order to enhance the applicability and meaningfulness of interventions across different settings. An additional benefit is that low-intensity psychological treatments are more cost-effective for local providers and feasible for clients, as they tend to be brief and transdiagnostic. Specifically, several mental health problems can be effectively treated with one intervention, thus preventing delivery agents from having to be trained in multiple interventions to treat different psychological disorders.

Low-Intensity Interventions for Youth

While there are a considerable number of studies investigating the effectiveness of psychological interventions for youth, the majority of these studies have been conducted in high income settings (Gillies, Taylor, Gray, O'Brien, & D'Abrew, 2012; James, James, Cowdrey, Soler, & Choke, 2013). This is despite the WHO's recommendations for the promotion and prevention of mental health conditions in children and adolescents in their recent Mental Health Action Plan (WHO, 2013). The report, which proposes a comprehensive and coordinated response for health and social sectors to tackle mental health, stipulates,

> The early stages of life present a particularly important opportunity to promote mental health and prevent mental disorders, as up to 50% of mental disorders in adults begin before the age of 14 years. Children and adolescents with mental disorders should be provided with early intervention through evidence-based psychosocial and other non-pharmacological interventions based in the community, avoiding institutionalization and medicalization. Furthermore, interventions should respect the rights of children in line with the United Nations Convention on the Rights of the Child and other international and regional human rights instruments. (p. 16).

Several studies have demonstrated benefits for children receiving psychological treatment by non-specialist providers. For instance, a child-adaptation of narrative exposure therapy (KidNET; $n = 16$) was found to be just as effective as a meditation-relaxation program ($n = 15$) in reducing trauma symptoms and improving functioning for Tamil youth exposed to war and disaster, one and 6 months post-intervention (Catani et al., 2009). At post-assessment and 6 month follow-up, KidNET yielded effect sizes of 1.76 (CI 0.9–2.5) and 1.96 (CI 1.1–2.8), respectively. By comparison, the effect sizes for the control group were 1.83 (CI 0.9–2.6) at post-assessment and 2.20 (CI 1.2–3.0) at 6 months. Caution must be exercised when interpreting these results, as treatment was delivered in the immediate aftermath of the disaster and there was not a wait-list control condition, therefore the impact of spontaneous remission cannot be accounted for. NET demonstrated stronger results with former child soldiers in Northern Uganda, with significant reductions in PTSD symptoms compared with an academic program (mean change differences, −14.06; 95% CI, −27.19 to −0.92 and, −13.04; 95% CI, −26.79 to 0.72, respectively) (Ertl, Pfeiffer, Schauer, Elbert, & Neuner, 2011). Five to 18 year-olds exposed to trauma in Zambia benefited from ten to 16 sessions of trauma-focused CBT (TF-CBT; $n = 131$), compared to treatment as usual (TAU; $n = 126$), which comprised weekly telephone calls and monthly visits by a study assessor to monitor safety and provide necessary referrals. By comparison with children in the TAU group, those receiving TF-CBT showed a marked decrease in symptoms of PTSD resulting in an effect size of 2.39 (Murray et al., 2015).

Others have implemented classroom-based or group-based frameworks to reduce distress. For 5–6 year-old children displaced by war, a combination of group psychosocial intervention and home visits for mothers improved maternal and child mental health (Dybdahl, 2001). A brief eclectic classroom-based intervention (CBI) that integrates concepts from creative-expressive and experiential therapy, cooperative play and CBT, inclusive of trauma-processing through drawings, has showed moderate effects in reducing PTSD symptoms (mean change differences, −2.78; 95% CI, 1.02 to 4.53) and maintaining hope (mean change differences, −2.21; 95% CI, −3.52 to −0.91) in 182 Indonesian primary-school aged children when compared to a wait-list control ($n = 221$) (Tol et al., 2008). However, these differences were only upheld for girls and no significant differences were achieved on measures of depression, anxiety or parent-rated aggression. In contrast, the same intervention did not have an impact on psychological symptoms in Nepalese children, although significant changes were identified in girls' pro-social behaviour and boys' aggression and psychological difficulties (Jordans et al., 2010). Results from a randomized controlled trial of the Youth Readiness Intervention, a group-based CBT program without trauma-processing elements, showed significant post-treatment effects on emotional regulation ($\beta = 0.108$, 95% CI, 0.026 to 0.190), pro-social attitudes ($\beta = 0.151$, CI, 0.060 to 0.241), social support ($\beta = 0.134$, 95% CI, 0.025 to 0.242) and general functioning ($\beta = -0.021$, 95% CI, −0.196 to 0.154) in Sierra Leone war-affected youth (Betancourt et al., 2014). However, the intervention did not significantly ameliorate symptoms of psychological distress (internalizing and externalizing symptoms) or PTSD.

Overall, there is insufficient evidence that young people benefit from low-intensity interventions delivered by non-specialist workers (van Ginneken et al., 2013). In a systematic review of interventions for children exposed to armed conflict, Jordans, Pigott and Tol (2016) emphasised the need for improved conceptual development and cultural adaptation of child interventions. Although all interventions included in this review led to some benefit for subgroups of children (e.g., male/female gender), less than half demonstrated significant improvements on primary outcomes and five studies reported negative effects. There is an exigency for further rigorous evaluation of child-specific low-intensity interventions and task-shifting approaches.

Case Study of Problem Management Plus (PM+) for Adults: Training Community Health Workers (CHWs)

While the support for low-intensity psychological interventions delivered by trained lay-providers is mounting in the adult literature, further examination is required to determine who is best suited to deliver these interventions and what training models are both effective and sustainable. A randomised controlled trial (RCT) of a brief adapted problem-solving and behavioural intervention, PM+, was conducted in three peri-urban communities in Nairobi, Kenya (Bryant et al., 2017). Community-based interventions provide effective platforms for extending health care delivery and enhancing scalability. In this study, the research team collaborated with local primary health care facilities to employ 23 CHWs to deliver the intervention.

The CHW role was created as a means of achieving universal access to healthcare and enhancing the link between communities and the primary health system. In Nairobi, each district has a primary healthcare facility, which includes a number of CHWs that service approximately 100 households. The role of a CHW is typically voluntary and occupied by women residing in the community. Their duties can be quite varied depending on the training they have received. Many CHWs in this project provided basic health education (e.g., maternal and child healthcare, nutrition and hygiene) and referrals to specialist care. CHWs typically receive training in maternal and neonatal healthcare but do not receive training in mental health assessment or management. A key advantage of using CHWs is their familiarity with the community and the issues that are impacting women. Anecdotally, the engagement of CHWs in this research project was enhanced by their commitment to supporting those in their community.

To reach competence in the delivery of PM+, CHWs completed 8 days of classroom training followed by 2–3 weeks of in-field training where they delivered PM+ to two practice cases under close supervision. A clinical psychologist who was involved in the development of PM+ conducted the training. Active and participatory training methods were emphasised, as many women were not acquainted with classroom-based teaching. Finally, CHWs were required to pass a competency assessment before delivering PM+ as part of the RCT. This assessment required them to role-play a session while being assessed on their use of basic counselling skills, fidelity to the treatment and competency in delivering the strategies. Only three (out of 23) CHWs failed to pass this assessment and were not retained for the trial. Throughout the trial CHWs received weekly group supervision (2–3 h) from a trained local supervisor. This supervisor received 1–2 h of weekly supervision by the master trainer, who was a clinical psychologist who had been heavily involved in the development of PM+.

Women participating in the trial were all experiencing symptoms of psychological distress (e.g., symptoms of anxiety and/or depression) and impaired functioning, and approximately three quarters had been exposed to gender-based violence. Women were randomised to either PM+ or ETAU, the latter involving attendance at the PHC to see a community nurse who provided education, supportive counselling and referrals to specialised care if necessary. At the post-treatment and 3 month follow-up assessments, women in the PM+ condition reported significant reductions in psychological distress (General Health Questionnaire-12) and PTSD symptoms (Posttraumatic Checklist-5), and significant improvements in general functioning (WHO Disability Assessment Schedule-2), compared to the ETAU group. Beyond demonstrating effectiveness of PM+, the successful implementation of PM+ in a peri-urban community with CHWs also suggests that it is a simple intervention that non-specialist health workers can competently deliver.

Despite these promising findings, a number of challenges were encountered when working with CHWs. First, given their demanding roles, most CHWs reported concerns about an overwhelming increase in workload without reimbursement.

Throughout the project, monetary incentives were negotiated to motivate CWHs to remain involved and engaged in all aspects of the project. Their availability to attend training, supervision and client appointments was often obstructed by competing demands within their existing roles. These challenges raise questions regarding whether non-specialists can (a) be engaged on a voluntary basis given the demands of their role and, (b) manage a counseling role in addition to their existing roles within the health system. Using the words of McLean and colleagues (McLean et al., 2015), the latter may risk task-shifting becoming "task dumping".

A less common issue that arose was related to the client's trust in their CHW. Some clients in this trial requested that they see a CHW with whom they had not established a previous relationship. Being very well known in the community may sometimes come at a cost for CHWs when trying to build trust with clients and ensure confidentiality. Finally, some CHWs reported increased stress associated to listening to their client's stories, especially when these resonated with their own problems. While these experiences were discussed in supervision, a staff counselor was also available. McLean et al. (2015) reported similar challenges when employing CHWs while implementing a task-shifting training approach in Haiti and emphasized the need for ongoing support and supervision of staff. Further research is warranted to compare the feasibility and effectiveness of various delivery agents, while upholding sustainable training and supervision models.

Implementation and Scale–Up

With the growing body of evidence supporting the effectiveness and acceptability of psychological interventions in LMICs, it may be expected that the treatment gap is diminishing. However, while initiatives such as mhGAP recommend the use of these interventions as frontline treatment for common mental disorders, few are adopted by local ministries of health in LMICs (Thornicroft et al., 2010). One of the major barriers to accessing mental healthcare is the often limited capacity for interventions to be scaled-up by local government ministries or non-government organisations who often have small budgets for mental health and psychosocial support. Developing research agendas in collaboration with local governments with the goal of integrating psychological interventions within existing health or other service delivery facilities offers a potentially important step to enhancing scalability of such interventions. This view accords with that of Jordans and Tol (2013), who assert that merely demonstrating the efficacy of a treatment is insufficient to bridge the treatment gap. They go further to argue that treatment implementation is an imperative objective in settings where health infrastructure is deficient or in insecure and unstable settings, such as refugee camps or conflict settings.

An integral component of many of the psychological interventions trialed in LMICs is a robust training and supervision model. While quality training and supervision is fundamental to the effectiveness of any psychological intervention, current models may serve to hinder the scale-up of these otherwise helpful interventions.

Specifically, many intervention studies utilize external master trainers who are experts in delivering the intervention. These trainers are also heavily involved in the provision of supervision and ensuring fidelity to the treatment over the course of the trial. While training is often brief (i.e., less than 1 month in duration), supervision is intensive, often occurring on a weekly to fortnightly basis. This is indeed considered integral to consolidating knowledge learned in the training phase and providing support to new counselors. However, the extensive reliance on outside experts for both training and supervision is unsustainable and may restrict local partners and staff from taking ownership of and fully accepting these interventions. As the support for evidence-based treatments delivered by non-specialist providers in LMICs grows, future research needs to give attention to training and supervision models that promote sustainability. Apprenticeship models (Murray et al., 2011) and the use of technology to support distance supervision (Rahman et al., 2016) offer promise for this endeavor.

In recognition of the need to address barriers to scale-up and move beyond effectiveness studies, impact evaluation and implementation studies are becoming the focus of global mental health research. These studies examine the delivery of care within pre-existing community and health systems. For instance, Jordans et al. (2013) developed a mental health care package for children in areas of armed conflict (The Child Thematic Program) that is based on a public health model comprising prevention, treatment and rehabilitation interventions. This model allows for multiple needs to be addressed through a stepped-care approach, which accords well with the levels of the IASC guidelines pyramid (see Fig. 1). The first tier of the Child Thematic Program comprises mental health promotion activities, such as peer groups and community mental health awareness sessions. The second tier is akin to level three of the IASC guidelines pyramid, and includes the delivery of a structure psychosocial group intervention, CBI, described previously. This intervention aims to reduce symptoms of emotional distress while promoting protective factors and has undergone rigorous testing in a number of settings with mixed findings (Jordans et al., 2010; Tol et al., 2012; Tol et al., 2008). Finally, the third tier of their model comprises specialised psychological treatment for children presenting with more severe disorders that have not responded to services from the previous tiers.

The package has been implemented and tested within the community and existing health systems in a number of LMICs and overall found to be feasible and acceptable. Across several settings, the multi-tiered care package allowed for a wide reach, being available to 96, 718 children and parents, with high levels of satisfaction reported by recipients. Basic psychoeducation delivered to parents was found to reduce emotional and behavioural problems in school-aged children and although CBI demonstrated mixed findings dependent on gender and context, it provided further evidence for the feasibility and efficacy of the task-shifting approach. This study provides preliminary support for mental health care packages integrated into existing community and education services. The advantages of such an approach is the provision of mental health awareness and promotion of resiliency to a large number of people, while only providing more specialised care to those who require it. Consequently, this supports greater sustainability and cost-effectiveness over time.

It is recommended that future research adopt a broader focus, going beyond just testing the effectiveness of psychological interventions in LMICs. Rather, research should begin to meet the needs of local health systems by examining the effectiveness of implementing psychological and psychosocial interventions within existing health systems and community services. Secondly, to promote scalability of evidence-based psychological interventions, researchers should collaborate with policy makers in the planning and conducting of the research (Sharan, Levav, Olifson, de Francisco, & Saxena, 2007). Several initiatives are seeking to do just this, including PRIME (Programme for Improving Mental Health Care), a consortium of research institutions and ministries of health in five countries that seek to evaluate implementation and scale-up of mental health treatment programs. More recently, The Lancet and The Lancet Psychiatry have gathered leaders to prepare a Commission on Global Mental Health to be published on World Mental Health Day in 2017, that aims to synthesise knowledge pertaining to successful implementation and scale-up of effective interventions from diverse research participants, such as service users within the community and donors.

Conclusion

The global mental health movement is evidently making strides in establishing an evidence-base for psychological and psychosocial interventions in LMICs. However, merely demonstrating the effectiveness of treatments is not enough to bridge the treatment gap in these settings. Further, research teams need to collaborate with ministries of health and local policy makers specifically, in order to facilitate the scale-up of such interventions and make them widely available to those in the community after the research study has finished. Collaboration with policy makers requires research aims that include measurement of the financial and human resource cost of implementing mental health treatments within existing systems of care. Unfortunately, not a single country worldwide, regardless of their economic standing, invests in mental health to the degree that is proportionate to the burden of mental health disorders. Therefore, establishing feasibility of mental health treatments from a policy point of view requires focus on the cost-effectiveness of such programs.

Task-shifting is a central element of a cost-effective and sustainable model of mental health care. At least in adult populations, the literature attests to the growing evidence in support of task-shifting approaches in the delivery of low-intensity psychological interventions in LMICs. However, it remains unclear who are the best people to deliver such interventions. Previous studies have utilised different delivery agents, including volunteer community workers, paid health providers, and individuals outside of any health or community service (e.g., university students). While there are advantages and disadvantages to each of these groups of individuals, this knowledge needs to be synthesised in order to inform future research designs.

Secondly, a remarkable feature of many of the studies reviewed in this chapter is the reliance on robust training and supervision procedures delivered by outside experts. Future research should examine varied models of training and supervision that promote the up-skilling of local staff. This might include local mental health professionals or lay-providers that demonstrate exceptional skills in counselling and leadership.

Finally, a review of the literature highlights the need for greater focus on low-intensity interventions for children and adolescents. The evidence for low-intensity interventions and use of task-shifting remains mixed. This is largely due to a lack of rigorous evaluation being conducted on the numerous psychological and psychosocial interventions that do exist for young people in low income settings.

There is a long way to go to fill the treatment gap for adults and youth experiencing mental health problems, following exposure to mass trauma. However, low-intensity interventions and task-shifting approaches offer promise as affordable and scaleable solutions to this global problem.

References

Bass, J., Neugebauer, R., Clougherty, K. F., Verdeli, H., Wickramaratne, P., Ndogoni, L., … Bolton, P. (2006). Group interpersonal psychotherapy for depression in rural Uganda: 6-month outcomes. *British Journal of Psychiatry, 188*(6), 567–573. https://doi.org/10.1192/bjp.188.6.567

Baxter, A. J., Patton, G., Scott, K. M., Degenhardt, L., & Whiteford, H. A. (2013). Global epidemiology of mental disorders: What are we missing? *PLoS One, 8*(6), e65514. https://doi.org/10.1371/journal.pone.0065514

Bennet-Levy, J., Richards, D., Farrand, P., Christensen, H., Griffiths, K., Kavanagh, D., … Williams, C. (2010). *The Oxford guide to low intensity CBT interventions*. Oxford, UK: Oxford University Press.

Betancourt, T. S., McBain, R., Newnham, E. A., Akinsulure-Smith, A. M., Brennan, R. T., Weisz, J. R., & Hansen, N. B. (2014). A behavioral intervention for war-affected youth in Sierra Leone: A randomized controlled trial. *Journal of the American Academy of Child & Adolescent Psychiatry, 53*(12), 1288–1297. https://doi.org/10.1016/j.jaac.2014.09.011

Bolton, P., Lee, C., Haroz, E. E., Murray, L., Dorsey, S., Robinson, C., … Bass, J. (2014). A transdiagnostic community-based mental health treatment for comorbid disorders: Development and outcomes of a randomized controlled trial among Burmese refugees in Thailand. *PLoS One, 11*(11), e1001757. https://doi.org/10.1371/journal.pmed.1001757

Bryant, R. A., Schafer, A., Dawson, K. S., Anjuri, D., Mulili, C., Ndogoni, L., … van Ommeren, M. (2017). Effectiveness of a brief behavioural intervention on psychological distress among women with a history of gender-based violence in urban Kenya: A randomised clinical trial. *PLoS Medicine, 14*(8), e1002371.

Catani, C., Kohiladevy, M., Ruf, M., Schauer, E., Elbert, T., & Neuner, F. (2009). Treating children traumatized by war and tsunami: A comparison between exposure therapy and meditation-relaxation in North-East Sri Lanka. *BMC Psychiatry, 9*(1), 22. https://doi.org/10.1186/1471-244X-9-22

Chisholm, D. (2006). *Dollars, DALYs and decisions: Economic aspects of the mental health system*. Geneva, Switzerland: World Health Organization.

Collins, P. Y., Patel, V., Joestl, S. S., March, D., Insel, T. R., & Daar, A. S. (2011). Grand challenges in global mental health: A consortium of researchers, advocates and clinicians announces here research priorities for improving the lives of people with mental illness around the world, and calls for urgent action and investment. *Nature, 475*(7354), 27–30. https://doi.org/10.1038/475027a

Dawson, K. S., Bryant, R. A., Harper, M., Tay, A. K., Rahman, A., Schafer, A., & van Ommeren, M. (2015). Problem Management Plus (PM+): A WHO transdiagnostic psychological intervention for common mental health problems. *World Psychiatry, 14*(3), 354–357. https://doi.org/10.1002/wps.20255

Demyttenaere, K., Bruffaerts, R., Posada-Villa, J., Gasquet, I., Kovess, V., Lepine, J. P., ... Consortium, W. W. M. H. S. (2004). Prevalence, severity and unmet need for treatment of mental disorders in the World Health Organization World Mental Health Surverys. *JAMA, 29*(21), 2581–2590. https://doi.org/10.1001/jama.291.21.2581

Dybdahl, R. (2001). Children and mothers in war: An outcome study of a psychological intervention program. *Child Development, 72*(4), 1214–1230. https://doi.org/10.1111/1467-8624.00343

Ertl, V., Pfeiffer, A., Schauer, E., Elbert, T., & Neuner, F. (2011). Community-implemented trauma therapy for former child soldiers in Northern Uganda: A randomized controlled trial. *JAMA, 306*(5), 503–512. https://doi.org/10.1001/jama.2011.1060

Gillies, D., Taylor, F., Gray, C., O'Brien, L., & D'Abrew, N. (2012). Psychological therapies for the treatment of post-traumatic stress disorder in children and adolescents (review). *Cochrane Database of Systematic Reviews, 2014*(12), 1–64. https://doi.org/10.1002/14651858.CD006726.pub2

Inter-Agency Standing Committee (IASC). (2007). *IASC guidelines on mental health and psychosocial support in emergency settings*. Geneva, Switzerland: IASC.

James, A. C., James, G., Cowdrey, F. A., Soler, A., & Choke, A. (2013). Cognitive behavioural therapy for anxiety disorders in children and adolescents. *Cochrane Database of Systematic Reviews, 6*, CD004690. https://doi.org/10.1002/14651858.cd004690

Jordans, M. J., & Tol, W. A. (2013). Mental health in humanitarian settings: Shifting focus to care systems. *International Health, 5*(1), 9–10. https://doi.org/10.1093/inthealth/ihs005

Jordans, M. J. D., Komproe, I. H., Tol, W. A., Kohrt, B. A., Luitel, N. P., Macy, R. D., & de Jong, J. T. V. M. (2010). Evaluation of a classroom-based psychosocial intervention in conflict-affected Nepal: A cluster randomized controlled trial. *Journal of Child Psychology and Psychiatry, 51*(7), 818–826. https://doi.org/10.1111/j.1469-7610.2010.02209.x

Jordans, M. J. D., Pigott, H., & Tol, W. A. (2016). Interventions for children affected by armed conflict: A systematic review of mental health and psychosocial support in low- and middle-income countries. *Current Psychiatry Reports, 18*(1), 9–24. https://doi.org/10.1007/s11920-015-0648-z

Jordans, M. J. D., Tol, W. A., Susanty, D., Ntamatumba, P., Luitel, N. P., Komproe, I. H., & de Jong, J. T. V. M. (2013). Implementation of a mental health care package for children in areas of armed conflict: A case study from Burundi, Indonesia, Nepal, Sri Lanka, and Sudan. *PLoS Medicine, 10*(1), e1001371. https://doi.org/10.1371/journal.pmed.1001371

McEnvoy, P. M., Nathan, P., & Norton, P. J. (2009). Efficacy of transdiagnostic treatments: A review of published outcome studies and future research directions. *Journal of Cognitive Psychotherapy, 23*(1), 20–33. https://doi.org/10.1891/0889-8391.23.1.20

McLean, K. E., Kaiser, B. N., Hagaman, A. K., Wagenaar, B. H., Therosme, T. P., & Kohrt, B. A. (2015). Task sharing in Haiti: Qualitative assessment of a brief, structured training with and without apprenticeship supervision for community health workers. *Intervention, 13*(2), 135–155. https://doi.org/10.1097/wtf.0000000000000074

Murray, L. K., Dorsey, S., Bolton, P., Jordans, M. J. D., Rahman, A., Bass, J., & Verdeli, H. (2011). Building capacity in mental health interventions in low resource countries: An apprenticeship model for training local providers. *International Journal of Mental Health Systems, 5*(1), 30–42. https://doi.org/10.1186/1752-4458-5-30

Murray, L. K., Dorsey, S., Haroz, E., Lee, C., Alsiary, M. M., Haydary, … Bolton, P. (2013). A common elements treatment approach for adult mental health problems in low- and middle-income countries. *Cognitive and Bheavioral Practice, 21*(2), 111–123. https://doi.org/10.1016/j.cbpra.2013.06.005

Murray, L. K., Skavenski, S., Kane, J. C., Mayeya, J., Dorsey, S., Cohen, J. A., … Bolton, P. A. (2015). Effectiveness of trauma-focused cognitive behavioral therapy among trauma-affected children in Lusaka, Zambia: A randomized clinical trial. *JAMA Pediatrics, 169*(8), 761–769. https://doi.org/10.1001/jamapediatrics.2015.0580

Patel, V., Araya, R., Chatterjee, S., Chisholm, D., Cohen, A., De Silva, M., … van Ommeren, M. (2007). Treatment and prevention of mental disorders in low-income and middle-income countries. *Lancet, 370*(9591), 991–1005. https://doi.org/10.1016/s0140-6736(07)61240-9

Patel, V., Chowdhary, N., Rahman, A., & Verdeli, H. (2011). Improving access to psychological treatments: Lessons from developing countries. *Behaviour Research and Therapy, 49*(9), 523–528. https://doi.org/10.1016/j.brat.2011.06.012

Patel, V., Flisher, A. J., Hetrick, S., & McGorry, P. (2007). Mental health of young people: A global public-health challenge. *Lancet, 369*(9569), 1302–1313. https://doi.org/10.1016/s0140-6736(07)60368-7

Patel, V., & Prince, M. J. (2010). Global mental health: A new global health field comes of age. *JAMA, 303*(19), 1976–1977. https://doi.org/10.1001/jama.2010.616

Rahman, A., Malik, A., Sikander, S., Roberts, C., & Creed, F. (2008). Cognitive behaviour therapy-based intervention by community health workers for mothers with depression and infants in rural Pakistan: A cluster-randomised controlled trial. *Lancet, 372*(9642), 902–909. https://doi.org/10.1016/s0140-6736(08)61400-2

Rahman, A., Riaz, N., Dawson, K. S., Hamdani, S. U., Chiumento, A., Sijbrandij, M., … Farooq, S. (2016). Problem Management Plus (PM+): Pilot trial of a WHO transdiagnostic psychological intervention in conflict-affected Pakistan. *World Psychiatry, 15*(2), 182–183. https://doi.org/10.1002/wps.20312

Rehm, J., Mathers, C., Popova, S., Thavorncharoensap, M., Teerawattananon, Y., & Patra, J. (2009). Global burden of disease and injury and economic cost attributable to alcohol use and alcohol-use disorders. *Lancet, 373*(9682), 2223–2233. https://doi.org/10.1016/s0140-6736(09)60746-7

Saraceno, B., van Ommeren, M., Batniji, R., Cohen, A., Gureje, O., Mahoney, J., … Underhill, C. (2007). Barriers to improvement of mental health services in low-income and middle-income countries. *Lancet, 370*(9593), 1164–1174. https://doi.org/10.1016/s0140-6736(07)61263-x

Sharan, P., Levav, I., Olifson, S., de Francisco, A., & Saxena, S. (2007). *Research capacity for mental health in low- and middle-income countries: Results of a mapping project*. Geneva, Switzerland: World Health Organization and Global Forum for Health Research.

Thornicroft, G., Alem, A., Anturies Dos Santos, R., Barley, E., Drake, R. E., Gregorio, G., … Wondimagegn, D. (2010). WPA guidance on steps, obstacles and mistakes to avoid in the implementation of community mental health care. *World Psychiatry, 9*(2), 67–77. https://doi.org/10.1002/j.2051-5545.2010.tb00276.x

Tol, W. A., Komproe, I. H., Jordans, M. J. D., Vallipuram, A., Sipsma, H., Sivayokan, S., … de Jong, J. T. V. M. (2012). Outcomes and moderators of a preventive school-based mental health intervention for children affected by war in Sri Lanka: A cluster randomized trial. *World Psychiatry, 11*(2), 114–122. https://doi.org/10.1016/j.wpsyc.2012.05.008

Tol, W. A., Komproe, I. H., Susanty, D., Jordans, M. J. D., Macy, R. D., & de Jong, J. T. V. M. (2008). School-based mental health intervention for children affected by political violence in Indonesia: A cluster randomized trial. *JAMA, 300*(6), 655–662. https://doi.org/10.1001/jama.300.6.655

van Ginneken, N., Tharyan, P., Lewin, S., Rao, G. N., Meera, S. M., Pian, J., … Patel, V. (2013). Non-specialist health worker interventions for the care of mental, neurological and substance-abuse disorders in low- and middle-income countries. *Cochrane Database of Systematic Reviews, 11*, CD009149. https://doi.org/10.1002/14651858.cd009149.pub2

Weiss, W. M., Murray, L. K., Zangana, G. A. S., Mahmooth, Z., Kaysen, D., Dorsey, S., … Bolton, P. (2015). Community-based mental health treatments for survivors of torture and militant attacks in Southern Iraq: A randomized control trial. *BMC Psychiatry, 15*(1), 249–265. https://doi.org/10.1186/s12888-015-0622-7

Whiteford, H. A., Degenhardt, L., Rehm, J., Baxter, A. J., Ferrari, A. J., Erskine, H. E., … Vos, T. (2013). Global burden of disease attributable to mental and substance use disorders: Findings from the global burden of disease study 2010. *Lancet, 382*(9904), 1575–1586. https://doi.org/10.1016/s0140-6736(13)61611-6

WHO. (2013). *Mental health action plan 2013–2020*. Geneva, Switzerland: World Health Organization.

WHO. (2015). *Mental health atlas 2014*. Geneva, Switzerland: Department of Mental Health and Substance Abuse, WHO.

Katie S. Dawson, Ph.D., is a postdoctoral fellow at the University of New South Wales, Sydney, Australia. She is a clinical psychologist and consultant with the World Health Organization, Department of Mental Health and Substance Abuse, supporting the development of low-intensity psychological interventions for adults and youth affected by adversity. Her research interests include evaluating effectiveness and feasibility of mental health interventions in low-income settings with the aim of developing sustainable models of implementation.

Atif Rahman, Ph.D., MD, is professor at the University of Liverpool, UK, adjunct professor at Rawalpindi Medical University, Rawalpindi, and an Honorary Director of the Human Development Research Foundation, Pakistan. He specialises in child and adolescent psychiatry, and his research focuses on mental health of women and children in developing countries.

Development and Evaluation of Mental Health Interventions for Common Mental Disorders in Post-conflict Settings

Paul Bolton

Abstract This chapter explores the development and evaluation of mental health interventions for common mental disorders (CMDs) during the prolonged post-conflict phase. The chapter considers the selection of interventions to deal with the important combination of mental disorders typically common during this time and serious enough to affect functioning. These disorders are depression, anxiety, PTSD and/or substance abuse which are often co-morbid. Adaptation of interventions developed in one culture to another is also discussed as a prolonged and ongoing process during the pretraining, training, and implementation phases. The chapter concludes with discussion of program evaluation. Evaluation of effectiveness of mental health interventions refers primarily to impact on symptoms and functioning but also includes effects on stigma and discrimination, costs of receiving the intervention, and mortality. Other areas of program evaluation are also described – fidelity, access, uptake, and compliance.

Keywords Design · Adaptation · Intervention · Monitoring · Evaluation · Effectiveness · Fidelity · Access · Uptake · Compliance

Introduction

The term ‘post-conflict’ is used to refer to a variety of different periods. It can refer to the period immediately after cessation of fighting, when conditions are usually poor and unstable, and/or to the prolonged and relatively stable period that usually follows. Conditions during the latter period may vary: There may be recovery or partial recovery of the situation prior to conflict or a static situation without real improvement as experienced by many refugees living in camps for years at a time. The mental health needs and appropriate services during the immediate unstable phase and the prolonged stable phases are very different. Briefly, the immediate

P. Bolton (✉)
Department of International Health and Department of Mental Health, Johns Hopkins University Bloomberg School of Public Health, Baltimore, MD, USA
e-mail: pbolton1@jhu.edu

N. Morina, A. Nickerson (eds.), *Mental Health of Refugee and Conflict-Affected Populations*, https://doi.org/10.1007/978-3-319-97046-2_18

post-conflict phase will see many people exhibiting mental health symptoms which may be normal reactions to threat and difficult circumstances rather than evidence of mental illness. For example, refugees displaced by conflict and separated from family with little income and uncertainty about their future may experience sadness, loss of interest and ability to experience pleasure, weight loss, nervousness, and many of the other symptoms of depression and anxiety. In such cases the best first 'mental health treatments' would be the normal humanitarian and development aid that aims to correct as many of the situational concerns as possible, with the expectation that many symptoms will then resolve. Once the situation improves or at least stabilizes, mental health treatments can be implemented for those who continue to exhibit symptoms. Therefore, this chapter primarily deals with the development and evaluation of such mental health treatments during the chronic and stable post-conflict phase.

Which Problems to Address

In the past the conventional wisdom was that the primary mental health problem of populations experiencing conflict is PTSD resulting from traumatic experiences. However, conflicts tend to occur in settings where the population is also poor and under stress. Even in cases where this is not so before the conflict, the conflict itself tends to produce these conditions, which usually outlast the fighting. The result is that populations in post-conflict settings have not only had experiences of violence but are typically also under current financial and social stress and often ongoing danger. These multiple stressors result in various mental health problems. Studies to date suggest that, while PTSD does occur in these populations, the priority mental health issues in these contexts are depression, anxiety, and substance abuse related to the *current* situation and sundry other stresses which may vary by population (e.g., Miller, Omidian, Rasmussen, Yaqubi, & Daudzai, 2008). Multiple problems in the same person (i.e., comorbidity) is very common (e.g., De Jong, Komproe, & Van Ommeren, 2003). Among studies by the author in many post-conflict settings, presentation with a single condition is rare (e.g., Bass et al., 2013; Bolton, Bass et al., 2014; Bolton, Lee et al., 2014). Therefore, mental health programs for post-conflict populations must be prepared to focus on combinations of problems among both the population and individuals.

The choice of problems to address should be informed by their public health importance, which is a function of prevalence and severity. This approach suggests that both common and severe problems should be addressed. Severe cases are important because of their impact not only on the individual but also families. This impact on family is felt mainly as stigma and reduced function. The stigma associated with a severe mental disorder appears to be universal and substantial: Those with the disorders are often avoided, mistrusted, and not seen as priorities for assistance (Gureje, Lasebikan, Ephraim-Oluwanuga, Olley, & Kola, 2005; Link, Phelan, Bresnahan, Stueve, & Pescosolido, 1999; Thornicroft, Rose, & Kassam, 2007). In some populations the stigma of mental disorders extends to the rest of the family; for example, it may even affect marriage prospects of other family members. The reduced function associated with severe illness is equally important. Severe mental illness affects not only mental but also physical functioning (lack of energy) and social functioning (withdrawal and isolation). Its occurrence among people in the prime of life changes them from being a net contributor to family welfare and income to being a drain on the family's resources, while stigma makes it less likely that they will receive assistance to deal with their burden.

Milder cases causing reduced functioning should also be addressed as they tend to be substantially more common than severe cases (e.g., Kohler, Payne, Bandawe, & Kohler, 2015; Molla et al., 2016) and therefore also have public health importance. While still a problem, stigma is less of an issue for milder cases, which makes treatment and treatment seeking both more feasible and more acceptable.

Selection of Interventions

The Introduction described how the symptoms of common mental disorders can be the result of current environmental stressors as well as of mental disorders. For this reason, the mental health interventions that cause the greatest reduction in symptoms may be those that reduce stress by improving the environment or (if it was better before) restoring it as much as possible to what it was before the conflict. The group of activities that primarily deal with improving the environment to enhance mental wellbeing fall under the broader heading of psychosocial programs. This includes diverse activities such as providing security, getting children into school, reconnecting families, counseling people on changes they can make to reduce stress, restoring livelihoods, providing social opportunities, and providing child safe and child play areas. All are included in psychosocial programing as practiced by organizations responding to conflict, particularly nongovernmental organizations (NGOs). While the data to support the impact of these programs is limited, they are relatively inexpensive, can be implemented with minimal expertise, can reach many people, and are desirable for reasons other than reducing CMD symptoms. Providing security, employment, education, and social opportunities, for example, are worthwhile regardless of their psychosocial benefit. For these reasons it is difficult to study their psychological impact since withholding them as part of a controlled study may not be justifiable ethically. However, for the same reasons, these types of programs that have value apart from possible mental health benefits should be implemented where people are facing difficult circumstances.

Regardless of the impact of psychosocial programs, there will be persons with moderate or severe common mental disorders who will also need specific mental health treatments. While drug therapy is known to be effective for depression and useful for other CMDs, their use for these disorders in most post-conflict situations is often not feasible due to lack of resources for prescription and monitoring. For the CMDs the non-drug interventions that have shown the best evidence of effectiveness across cultures and situations (including post-conflict) are based on cognitive behavioral therapy and exposure therapy. Studies of psychotherapeutic interventions among conflict-affected populations in South America, Africa, South-East Asia, and the Middle East have repeatedly found them to be effective and acceptable for both adults (e.g., Bass et al., 2013; Weiss et al., 2015) and children (e.g., Bolton et al., 2007; Jordans et al., 2010).

The implications of these findings is that evidence-based treatments (EBTs) found to be effective in the West can be effective among post-conflict populations in other parts of the world, and that such interventions need to be appropriate for multiple and co-morbid conditions. Post-conflict interventions are therefore adaptations of one or more existing EBTs chosen on the basis of their effectiveness for depression, anxiety, PTSD and/or substance abuse.

Selection of Interventions is dependent on appropriateness and acceptability of the intervention for the local population and situation. Appropriateness refers to whether the intervention is considered likely to be effective by stakeholders. For example, if the mental health problems being addressed are thought to be medical problems then a non-medical counseling intervention may not make sense to local people. The same may be true if the cause is thought to be witchcraft. Acceptability refers to whether the intervention is something that people feel comfortable receiving. For example, males providing services to females behind closed doors is not acceptable in many cultures. Interventions that cannot be provided anonymously are less likely to be acceptable among populations where stigma surrounding mental disorders is high.

What is considered appropriate and acceptable varies by population and situation. Therefore, selecting and adapting acceptable and appropriate interventions requires an a priori understanding of the local culture and situation. This may be derived from an existing qualitative or ethnographic literature although such a literature rarely has sufficient information on mental health to inform decisions. We have found it useful to conduct brief qualitative research focused on exploring the priority mental health problems of the population, including perceived causes, what people currently do about the problem and what they feel should be done given resources not currently available. The last three topics are specifically chosen to provide information on which interventions are likely to be appropriate and acceptable. The process and rationale are described elsewhere (See 'The DIME Program Research Model: Design, Implementation, Monitoring, and Evaluation', http://www.hopkinshumanitarianhealth.org/empower/resources/tools-guidelines/the-dime-process).

An additional consideration is the selection of interventions that can be provided by local workers and not by outsiders with little or no knowledge of the local language, culture, or situation. This is partly because the demand for services will exceed the supply of outside workers who are usually expensive and only available short term, but also because implementation by local workers is critical to the adaptation and provision of the intervention in an acceptable way. While prior qualitative studies and consultations are important for identifying red flags for achieving appropriateness and acceptability, they cannot guarantee them. As local workers learn the intervention they provide key input on undetected issues, so that training workers becomes less of a one-way knowledge transfer and more of a negotiation between the external trainers and the trainees on how the intervention should be implemented. This usually results in the intervention changing over the course of the training, so much so that the author and colleagues usually provide training materials as 'drafts' at the beginning of the training, with a revised version being provided after training completion. The same process occurs when workers begin to implement the intervention under supervision of the trainers. Real life problems are identified which require adjustments based on input from the clients, the local workers and the trainers. The result is further revisions in the intervention and of the resource materials.

The reliance on local workers requires that they have the capacity to learn the intervention and that effective training can be provided. As with learning any set of skills this requires not only didactic workshops but ongoing 'on the job' training and supervision until competence is achieved. This supervisory phase also facilitates the real-life learning and adaptation described above. Previous research has demonstrated that local persons without a mental health background but with aptitude can learn to provide specific non-drug mental health treatments (e.g., Bass et al., 2013; Bolton et al., 2007; Bolton, Bass et al., 2014; van Ginneken et al., 2013). With support they can continue to provide these services after expatriate workers have gone home. Therefore, much of the intervention development described in this chapter refers to refining the treatment during local training.

Adaptation of Interventions

Appropriateness and Acceptability are issues not only in the selection of interventions but also in their adaptation for local use. Even when evidence based interventions have been selected on the basis of Appropriateness and Acceptability they still require local adjustments. This is because initial selection seeks a broad match between the local culture and the underlying concepts of the intervention including addressing the perceived causes of the problem in ways that make sense to local people. Selection using this approach should therefore result in a broadly appropriate and acceptable intervention. However, acceptability will also require more detailed changes to address problems of implementation that may not be apparent from the qualitative study or discussions with local people. Examples from programs implemented by the author and colleagues of issues that did not become apparent until implementation include: whether people are able to travel for repeated treatment sessions in terms of cost, time, and absence from other responsibilities; family opposition to treatment based on stigma; difficulty explaining the treatment using western terminology and examples; and the selection of acceptable providers in terms of social status and ethnicity. These and similar issues will need to be identified, explored, and addressed by changes in how the intervention is provided.

Adaptation also refers to training materials and manuals. Most existing materials and manuals were written for Western mental health professionals. The more that the providers of the intervention differ from this audience the more adaptation is required. There are various types of issues to consider. The first type relates to content: Most interventions have manuals and training materials that include an extensive focus on how the intervention builds on existing theories and knowledge which would be known to Western-trained mental health professionals. For those without this training these explanations may be irrelevant because they do not have this knowledge or may not even care about this aspect of the training. For them this content should be removed. Content may also have to be changed where concepts do not translate well into the local context. When adapting Cognitive Behavioral Therapy for use in Kurdistan, two of the five themes of CPT treatment – intimacy and esteem – had no local equivalent, necessitating the identification of alternative themes (Kaysen et al., 2013). In Uganda, one of the four problem areas to be addressed by Interpersonal Psychotherapy – isolation/loneliness – was not considered a relevant issue locally and so was not included in the training (Verdeli et al., 2003).

The second issue relates to translation. Mental health manuals and training materials are normally written using jargon making them difficult to translate. Much of this jargon is not necessary and its replacement by standard English (or whatever the language of the original) improves translation, particularly where translation is being done by non-technical people for non-professional trainees. For example, 'cognition' can be replaced by 'thought', 'cognitive restructuring' by 'thinking differently', 'verbal communication' by 'talking' and 'interpersonal deficits' by 'loneliness' and 'shyness' (Verdeli et al., 2003). Replacing as much jargon as possible is therefore important before sending the materials for translation.

The third consideration refers to how concepts are explained to the trainees and how the trainees will explain them to clients. This particularly refers to the use of examples which are usually rooted in the types of persons and experiences the intervention will be used for. For example, manuals of trauma interventions may exist as military (using examples of soldier's experience of war) and civilian versions (referring to criminal acts or natural disasters). The same type of adaptation is required when using these interventions in other cultures: replacing examples rooted in Western culture and experience with those more locally relevant such as that of refugees, guerilla fighters, or civilians living in war zones.

While adaptation begins with the removal of jargon and changes in content and examples based on existing knowledge and consultation with local workers, adaptation continues during the training process. As trainers explain the intervention, going through training materials and manuals, trainees are invited to raise concerns and make suggestions for changes to enhance appropriateness and acceptability. Training is designed to include this process in terms of significant additional time (2 or more days of a 10 day training) for discussion and within-training editing of the training materials and manuals. Therefore, both trainees and trainers will leave the training with revised versions of these materials.

The final stage of adaptation begins when trainees start to treat local people. Since even local trainees cannot anticipate all the issues that they and their clients will face, this is an important phase in adaptation. Examples of problems encountered by providers include opposition to working with the mentally ill by providers' families and by co-workers, low status of mental health care within the health care system, and a lack of resources for professional development due to low prioritization of mental health. Previously unanticipated client problems have included opposition to treatment as an invasion of privacy and perceived threat to family standing if the client's treatment becomes known. It is critical that the link between the trainees and trainers is maintained at this time, to make necessary changes to the intervention that address these concerns while not reducing effectiveness. This can be incorporated in the training and supervision process since training of local providers already requires prolonged detailed supervision in the form of an 'apprenticeship' (Murray et al., 2011).

In summary, intervention development is a prolonged and multi-phase process beginning with the selection of priority problems and interventions likely to address them, followed by several phases during implementation of increasing refinement to acceptability. These latter phases consist of a cascade of local inputs beginning with local partners, trainee providers, and finally ongoing and iterative inputs from actual providers and their clients. The format and provision of the intervention is therefore often quite different from the original version.

Evaluation of Interventions

There are five main elements of interventions that should can be evaluated whenever possible. While there are others that can also be explored, these five refer most directly to the capacity of interventions to have a meaningful impact on the communities in which they are provided. They are briefly described in Table 1.

Table 1 Program evaluation objectives

Construct	Working description	Indicators
Effectiveness	Impact on client symptoms and function	Change in client level indicators for symptoms and function
Fidelity	How accurately the intervention is provided, based on the training and manual	Checklist of critical provider activities
Access	Ability of those in need to make use of the intervention	Proportion of those in need of the intervention who are able to use it.
Uptake	Extent to which those with access use the intervention	Proportion of those offered treatment (or who have access to it) who begin treatment.
Compliance	Extent to which those beginning services complete them as directed by providers	Proportion of those beginning treatment who complete it as directed

It is rare for post-conflict mental health programs to measure all these elements, however measurement of multiple indicators is becoming more common. This section describes elements separately.

Effectiveness

Content

Since addressing mental disorders is the main reason for the intervention, determining how well this is achieved should be the major focus of evaluation. Mental disorders (or mental health problems generally) have five possible types of impacts, including on symptoms, functioning, stigma and discrimination, cost and mortality.

Symptoms refer to how the person experiences the problem, particularly negative effects. At this time symptoms are the only outcomes routinely measured in program evaluations. A variety of standard instruments for assessment of the symptoms of the CMDs have been adapted for use and found to be valid in multiple cultures and languages. Commonly used examples for children, adolescents, and their caretakers include the short Strengths and Difficulties Questionnaire (Goodman, Meltzer, & Bailey, 1998)) and the much longer Achenbach group of instruments for children and adolescents and their caretakers (Achenbach System of Empirically Based Assessment). Examples of adult instruments found valid across cultures are the Patient Health Questionnaire or PHQ-9, a 9 item depression instrument, (Spitzer, Kroenke, Williams, & Patient Health Questionnaire Primary Care Study Group, 1999), the 20 item Center for Epidemiological Studies Depression Scale for depression (Radloff, 1977) and 20 item PTSD Checklist (Blevins, Weathers, Davis, Witte, & Domino, 2015; Bovin et al., 2015; Wortmann et al., 2016). The author and colleagues have favored the Hopkins Symptom Checklist (Derogatis, Lipman, Rickels, Uhlenhuth, & Covi, 1974) for depression and anxiety and the Harvard Trauma Questionnaire (Mollica et al., 1992) for trauma symptoms and function, including PTSD. We have found both to reliably perform well across cultures (e.g., Bass et al., 2013; Bolton, Bass et al., 2014; Bolton, Lee et al., 2014). Their greater length than other instruments reflects a broader representation of relevant symptoms.

Reduced function is largely a subcategory of symptoms although some reduced function may be more obvious to family and observers than to the affected person (e.g., the impact of alcohol or drug use). Of particular importance is the reduced ability to do tasks and activities for others (e.g., earning income) or self-care tasks that must then be done by others (e.g., hygiene). However, reduced quality of relationships with family and friends are typically also important to the individual and family. As with symptoms there exist standard measures found to be valid and reliable across cultures. The most commonly used are the WHO Disability Assessment Schedule (Üstün, Kostanjsek, Chatterji, & Rehm, 2010) and the Short Form Survey (Ware & Sherbourne, 1992). The author usually combines these universal instruments with assessment of locally generated items referring to activities that are most important to care of self, family and community. The intent is to combine universal measurement with measurement of activities important to local people. The adaptation of symptom instruments and generation of local function items is described in the DIME manual (http://www.hopkinshumanitarianhealth.org/empower/resources/tools-guidelines/the-dime-process).

Stigma and discrimination refer to real or perceived exclusion by the community. These constructs are often included in program assessments where stigma is known to be a particular problem. Because there are many instruments available (Yang & Link, 2015) none have been widely validated across cultures. Like symptoms and function, stigma and discrimination are considered to be concepts that are readily understood across cultures and able to be accurately assessed by those experiencing them.

Costs refer to the financial costs of caring for the person and the loss of any financial contribution to family income arising from engaging with treatment. Cost measurement is rare, partly due to difficulties in defining relevant costs and measuring them accurately. At this time it is mainly undertaken as part of research, including large scale research projects by WHO and others to evaluate interventions for country-wide and global use.

Mortality refers to both directly caused death (of self or others) as well as indirect, such as by neglect. It is the least often measured outcome. This is partly because it is relatively rare and the difficulties in defining indirectly-caused mortality, and partly a reluctance by mental health program implementers to include assessment of suicidal and homicidal actions and risk. In the case of risk the author and colleagues frequently encounter reluctance because of concerns that the program may have to expend additional resources and training to address an outcome considered to be relatively rare.

Approach

The most common method of assessing effectiveness of interventions is to measure the baseline levels of CMDs, provide the intervention, and then repeat the measure. The change between pre and post intervention assessments is assumed to be the effect of the intervention.

Comparing pre and post intervention measures in this way remains the most feasible method for quantitatively assessing effectiveness. This approach has been used extensively in assessments of physical health programs as well as non-health programs. It is justified for interventions which have already shown a demonstrated impact in multiple scientific studies either in contexts like the program site or have been studied in multiple sites and found to be resistant to environmental factors. For example, most vaccines have been scientifically proven to be effective across populations and situations as long as the vaccine itself is maintained correctly prior to administration. Also, the impact of most vaccines is much greater than other factors that affect disease transmission. Under these circumstances (compelling scientific evidence and lack of other factors that affect the measured outcome) the use of the pre/post comparison method is sufficient to demonstrate effectiveness.

This is not true for mental health interventions in post-conflict populations. Severity of mental health symptoms varies over time and persons who screen into interventions are more likely to be experiencing a period of greater severity which is naturally followed by apparent improvement. This 'regression to the mean', along with a natural tendency for trauma-related mental health problems to improve with time during the post-conflict period, can cause programs to appear to be more effective than they are. Many mental health and wellbeing outcomes are sensitive to contextual factors. Improvements in personal or economic security or other aspects of the living situation can decrease anxiety and improve mood and wellbeing. Similarly, worsening of the situation can enhance symptoms. Either or both are likely since the situation in post-conflict settings is often inconstant. This makes it difficult to measure the impact of a program based on pre/post assessment comparisons alone, or even to decide whether the program was helpful, not helpful, or harmful.

Under these conditions the only accurate means of assessing impact is by comparison to an equivalent control group who did not receive the intervention. This has met with resistance from service organizations who regard withholding treatment from a comparison group for any period as ethically suspect. While ethically sound methods for conducting 'trials as program evaluation' exist (Allden et al., 2009, 'The DIME Program Research Model: Design, Implementation, Monitoring, and Evaluation', http://www.hopkinshumanitarianhealth.org/empower/resources/tools-guidelines/the-dime-process) they require some research expertise and additional resources to track and measure the control group, something that service organizations and their funders are usually unwilling to provide. At the time of writing, the group of interventions with the most scientific (i.e., controlled trial) evidence across different post-conflict cultures are the Cognitive Behavioral Therapy (CBT) based interventions (Morina, Malek, Nickerson, & Bryant, 2017; Priebe, Giacco, & El-Nagib, 2016). Therefore, evaluation of these interventions by means of measurement of fidelity combined with pre-post assessments is the most justified, although still insufficient to measure effect size. For interventions that have little widespread evidence of effectiveness, pre-post assessments are still worthwhile but lack of counterfactual evidence (in the form of a control or comparison group), which will render the results suggestive at best.

A large number of instruments exist for measuring the common mental disorders. Like evidence-based interventions, most were developed in the West. Many have been translated and adapted for use in multiple contexts and been found to perform adequately. While the existing literature suggests that depression, anxiety, PTSD, and substance abuse manifest similarly across cultures and situations, there are often variations that can reduce the local accuracy of instruments. Most questions when translated accurately perform well but some will reflect unfamiliar concepts that cannot be answered accurately. For example, with depression we have found that the concepts of 'sadness' and 'loss of interest' translate well in most places while 'hopelessness' and 'self-esteem' are difficult concepts in some languages and cultures. Translations of existing instruments therefore need to be tested among the target populations to determine how (and how well) questions are understood, through pilot testing with or without cognitive interviewing, and quantitative assessment of instrument validity and reliability (the DIME manual describes one field approach to doing so; http://www.hopkinshumanitarianhealth.org/assets/documents/VOT_DIME_MODULE2_FINAL). Programs need to use versions of instruments that they or others have tested and found valid and reliable among the population they are working with or a similar population.

Fidelity

This refers to the extent to which the intervention is provided as intended. Interventions developed in one culture or situation routinely require adaptation to others if they are to be accepted and understood. The first challenge is to identify those elements that are considered key to the success of the intervention and those that can vary as needed. Experts in the intervention must draw up lists of the critical factors which are then used to create indicators of fidelity. These indicators are compiled into checklists of intervention elements that are completed by providers and/or their supervisors on a sample of sessions with clients (or all sessions with all clients if feasible). The main use of fidelity data is not to judge fidelity at the end of the program but to correct mistakes during treatment in order to build counselor expertise while ensuring that clients receive correct treatment. Poor performance with lack of improvement results in removal of the counselor from the program. The purpose of fidelity monitoring is therefore not a measure of fidelity to the intervention/treatment manual but rather fidelity assurance through correction of mistakes as they occur and removal of providers who cannot provide the intervention correctly.

Access

While the concept of access is simple – the ability to obtain needed services – the nature of the factors that affect the ability to obtain mental health services vary greatly, such that measuring all those that are significant is rarely possible. These include the same logistic factors that affect physical health and other services, such as distance from the supply point, costs in terms of time and money, and when services are available. Measuring these factors is particularly important with respect to mental health since time, money, and distance considerations are greater for services where the client must attend frequently for repeated sessions (Gulliford et al., 2002). Other factors that are particularly relevant to mental health services include privacy in seeking services due to fear of stigma and the effects of the resulting stigma if privacy is breached. These effects include an unwillingness of the affected person to return and unwillingness of others to seek treatment and risk the same fate. Lack of faith in the intervention (appropriateness) or in the providers (acceptability) also reduces access. Measuring these factors would require a community survey, while estimating logistic issues of time, distance, and cost can often be estimated from available data based on geography and service costs. Therefore, access assessment is usually limited to one or more of these logistic factors, most commonly distance from services. Programs report the proportion of the population (based on census or other existing data) that live within a certain distance of services with the cut-off distance chosen as locally feasible in terms of time and cost of travel.

While focusing on assessing and reducing logistic barriers is important, the results are clearly inadequate in mental health programming. The author and colleagues have frequently encountered programming where 'access' defined logistically is good while the actual use of services is poor, demonstrating the importance of identifying and measuring other types of barriers. Of these, the most important in mental health are appropriateness and acceptability. These are instead more typically indirectly addressed in the measurement of Uptake and Compliance.

Uptake

Uptake is most simply what proportion of all persons who need and have access to services actually use them. However, given the difficulties in defining and measuring access, uptake is more frequently defined and measured as the proportion of persons directly offered services who then use them. This includes all persons who begin services even if they do not continue (see Compliance below). Motivation for accepting services is partly a function of their acceptability and appropriateness. When offered at a clinic it is assumed that these factors are important determinants of uptake because logistic factors are less important (since the person has come to the provider already). Therefore, uptake can be a key indicator of both and is important when these factors are not being measured by other means. Uptake is the inverse of a combination of the refusal rate for services and the 'no show' rate – those who accept services but never use them. It can mostly easily be measured and monitored based on provider and clinic records. Since low rates suggest problems with access and particularly acceptability and appropriateness, persons who refuse services should be asked why they are doing so since this may provide the best available indicator of problems in these areas short of a community-based study.

Compliance

Compliance is the proportion of those beginning treatment who complete it according to provider instructions. Like uptake, it is a function of appropriateness and acceptability but based on experience with the intervention rather than expectations. The most commonly used indicator is the number of persons who complete treatment, however the number of sessions that clients attend is helpful as a quantitative measure of compliance. Experience with psychotherapy programs suggests that number of sessions attended is also a good indicator of overall compliance since attendance is the most important issue: If clients attend sessions they usually also comply with provider instructions. Asking clients who drop out why they did so can provide useful information to redesign programs but this requires additional resources to contact clients if they end treatment without warning.

Other Perspectives

Most program evaluation refers almost exclusively to the client perspective. In recent years the importance of incorporating the perspective of other stakeholders has become apparent. The new field of Dissemination and Implementation Research focuses on the provider perspective as being key to program feasibility and sustainability. Addressing provider perspectives is considered to be important to the expansion and long term maintenance of services. While often less relevant in the post-conflict situation this can be important where the post-conflict period lasts for years. The author and colleagues have also identified two other stakeholder categories relevant to long-term sustainability and feasibility: local administration (clinic staff), and policy personnel (government or service organization leaders). For these stakeholders and for providers, instruments and assessment approaches are increasingly being developed to assess acceptability, appropriateness, feasibility, and integration with existing services. In the future this information will be collected and combined with the client-level data described in the rest of this chapter in situations where long term programming needs to be sustained by integration with existing services.

Summary

This chapter describes some of the major considerations in the development and evaluation of mental health interventions for common mental disorders in post-conflict settings. The author notes that what is appropriate varies with the type of post-conflict setting and that the highest priority interventions are often those that reduce stress by improving a difficult environment. Apart from environmental change, the interventions with the most widespread evidence of effectiveness and feasibility are currently psychotherapies based on cognitive behavioral therapy. Even these interventions require a prolonged process beginning with cultural adaptation to priority problems and conditions, followed by ongoing monitoring and iterative adjustment. The Chapter concludes with a discussion of the need to assess program performance beyond effectiveness, and to assess the needs and perspectives of other stakeholders, especially providers. This is necessary to reach the goal of instituting programs that, once outside support is removed, will be maintained and valued for as long as they are needed.

References

Achenbach System of Empirically Based Assessment. www.aseba.org. Accessed on 25 Aug 2017

Allden, K., Jones, L., Weissbecker, I., Wessells, M., Bolton, P., Betancourt, T. S., … Sumathipala, A. (2009). Mental health and psychosocial support in crisis and conflict: Report of the Mental Health Working Group. *Prehospital and Disaster Medicine, 24*(S2), s217–s227. https://doi.org/10.1017/s1049023x00021622

Bass, J. K., Annan, J., McIvor Murray, S., Kaysen, D., Griffiths, S., Cetinoglu, T., … Bolton, P. A. (2013). Controlled trial of psychotherapy for Congolese survivors of sexual violence. *New England Journal of Medicine, 368*(23), 2182–2191. https://doi.org/10.1056/NEJMoa1211853

Blevins, C. A., Weathers, F. W., Davis, M. T., Witte, T. K., & Domino, J. L. (2015). The posttraumatic stress disorder checklist for DSM-5 (PCL-5): Development and initial psychometric evaluation. *Journal of Traumatic Stress, 28*(6), 489–498. https://doi.org/10.1002/jts.22059

Bolton, P., Bass, J., Betancourt, T., Speelman, L., Onyango, G., Clougherty, K. F., … Verdeli, H. (2007). Interventions for depression symptoms among adolescent survivors of war and displacement in northern Uganda: A randomized controlled trial. *JAMA, 298*(5), 519–527. https://doi.org/10.1001/jama.298.5.519

Bolton, P., Bass, J. K., Zangana, G. A. S., Kamal, T., Murray, S. M., Kaysen, D., … Van Wyk, S. S. (2014). A randomized controlled trial of mental health interventions for survivors of systematic violence in Kurdistan, Northern Iraq. *BMC Psychiatry, 14*(1), 360. https://doi.org/10.1186/s12888-014-0360-2

Bolton, P., Lee, C., Haroz, E. E., Murray, L., Dorsey, S., Robinson, C., … Bass, J. (2014). A transdiagnostic community-based mental health treatment for comorbid disorders: Development and outcomes of a randomized controlled trial among Burmese refugees in Thailand. *PLoS Medicine, 11*(11), e1001757. https://doi.org/10.1371/journal.pmed.1001757

Bovin, M. J., Marx, B. P., Weathers, F. W., Gallagher, M. W., Rodriguez, P., Schnurr, P. P., & Keane, T. M. (2015). Psychometric properties of the PTSD checklist for diagnostic and statistical manual of mental disorders-fifth edition (PCL-5) in teterans. *Psychological Assessment, 28*(11), 1379–1391. https://doi.org/10.1037/pas0000254

De Jong, J. T., Komproe, I. H., & Van Ommeren, M. (2003). Common mental disorders in postconflict settings. *The Lancet, 361*(9375), 2128–2130. https://doi.org/10.1016/s0140-6736(03)13692-6

Derogatis, L. R., Lipman, R. S., Rickels, K., Uhlenhuth, E. H., & Covi, L. (1974). The hopkins symptom checklist (HSCL): A self-report symptom inventory. *Systems Research and Behavioral Science, 19*(1), 1–15. https://doi.org/10.1002/bs.3830190102

Goodman, R., Meltzer, H., & Bailey, V. (1998). The strengths and difficulties questionnaire: A pilot study on the validity of the self-report version. *European Child & Adolescent Psychiatry, 7*(3), 125–130. https://doi.org/10.1007/s007870050057

Gulliford, M., Figueroa-Munoz, J., Morgan, M., Hughes, D., Gibson, B., Beech, R., & Hudson, M. (2002). What does' access to health care'mean? *Journal of Health Services Research & Policy, 7*(3), 186–188. https://doi.org/10.1258/135581902760082517

Gureje, O., Lasebikan, V. O., Ephraim-Oluwanuga, O., Olley, B. O., & Kola, L. (2005). Community study of knowledge of and attitude to mental illness in Nigeria. *The British Journal of Psychiatry, 186*(5), 436–441. https://doi.org/10.1192/bjp.186.5.436

Jordans, M. J., Komproe, I. H., Tol, W. A., Kohrt, B. A., Luitel, N. P., Macy, R. D., & De Jong, J. T. (2010). Evaluation of a classroom-based psychosocial intervention in conflict-affected Nepal: A cluster randomized controlled trial. *Journal of Child Psychology and Psychiatry, 51*(7), 818–826. https://doi.org/10.1111/j.1469-7610.2010.02209.x

Kaysen, D., Lindgren, K., Zangana, G. A. S., Murray, L., Bass, J., & Bolton, P. (2013). Adaptation of cognitive processing therapy for treatment of torture victims: Experience in Kurdistan, Iraq. *Psychological Trauma: Theory, Research, Practice, and Policy, 5*(2), 184–192. https://doi.org/10.1037/a0026053

Kohler, I. V., Payne, C. F., Bandawe, C., & Kohler, H. -P. (2015). *The demography of mental health among mature adults in a low-income high HIV-prevalence context* (PSC Working Paper Series. 59). Retrieved from http://repository.upenn.edu/psc_working_papers/59

Link, B. G., Phelan, J. C., Bresnahan, M., Stueve, A., & Pescosolido, B. A. (1999). Public conceptions of mental illness: Labels, causes, dangerousness, and social distance. *American Journal of Public Health, 89*(9), 1328–1333. https://doi.org/10.2105/ajph.89.9.1328

Miller, K. E., Omidian, P., Rasmussen, A., Yaqubi, A., & Daudzai, H. (2008). Daily stressors, war experiences, and mental health in Afghanistan. *Transcultural Psychiatry, 45*(4), 611–638. https://doi.org/10.1177/1363461508100785

Molla, G. L., Sebhat, H. M., Hussen, Z. N., Mekonen, A. B., Mersha, W. F., & Yimer, T. M. (2016). Depression among Ethiopian adults: Cross-sectional study. *Psychiatry Journal, 2016*, 1–5. https://doi.org/10.1155/2016/1468120

Mollica, R. F., Caspi-Yavin, Y., Bollini, P., Truong, T., Tor, S., & Lavelle, J. (1992). The Harvard trauma questionnaire. *Journal of Nervous and Mental Disease, 180*(2), 111–116. https://doi.org/10.1097/00005053-199202000-00008

Morina, N., Malek, M., Nickerson, A., & Bryant, R. A. (2017). Meta-analysis of interventions for posttraumatic stress disorder and depression in adult survivors of mass violence in low- and middle-income countries. *Depression and Anxiety, 34*(8), 679–691. https://doi.org/10.1002/da.22618

Murray, L. K., Dorsey, S., Bolton, P., Jordans, M. J., Rahman, A., Bass, J., & Verdeli, H. (2011). Building capacity in mental health interventions in low resource countries: An apprenticeship model for training local providers. *International Journal of Mental Health Systems, 5*(1), 30. https://doi.org/10.1186/1752-4458-5-30

Priebe, S., Giacco, D., & El-Nagib, R. (2016). *Public health aspects of mental health among migrants and refugees: A review of the evidence on mental health care for refugees, asylum seekers and irregular migrants in the WHO European region* (WHO Health Evidence Network Synthesis Report 47). Copenhagen, Denmark: WHO Regional Office for Europe.

Radloff, L. S. (1977). The CES-D scale: A self-report depression scale for research in the general population. *Applied Psychological Measurement, 1*(3), 385–401. https://doi.org/10.1177/014662167700100306

Spitzer, R. L., Kroenke, K., Williams, J. B., & Patient Health Questionnaire Primary Care Study Group. (1999). Validation and utility of a self-report version of PRIME-MD: The PHQ primary care study. *JAMA, 282*(18), 1737–1744. https://doi.org/10.1001/jama.282.18.1737

The DIME Program Research Model: Design, Implementation, Monitoring, and Evaluation. http://www.hopkinshumanitarianhealth.org/empower/resources/tools-guidelines/the-dime-process. Accessed 12 Sept 2017.

Thornicroft, G., Rose, D., & Kassam, A. (2007). Discrimination in health care against people with mental illness. *International Review of Psychiatry, 19*(2), 113–122. https://doi.org/10.1080/09540260701278937

Üstün, T. B., Kostanjsek, N., Chatterji, S., & Rehm, J. (2010). *Measuring health and disability. Manual for WHO disability assessment schedule: WHODAS 2.0*. Geneva, Switzerland: World Health Organisation.

Van Ginneken, N., Tharyan, P., Lewin, S., Rao, G. N., Meera, S. M., Pian, J., … Patel, V. (2013). Non-specialist health worker interventions for the care of mental, neurological and substance-abuse disorders in low-and middle-income countries. *The Cochrane Database of Systematic Reviews*. https://doi.org/10.1002/14651858.cd009149.pub2

Verdeli, H., Clougherty, K., Bolton, P., Speelman, L., Lincoln, N., Bass, J., … Weissman, M. M. (2003). Adapting group interpersonal psychotherapy for a developing country: Experience in rural Uganda. *World Psychiatry, 2*(2), 114–120.

Ware, J. E., Jr., & Sherbourne, C. D. (1992). The MOS 36-item short-form health survey (SF-36): I. Conceptual framework and item selection. *Medical Care, 30*(6), 473–483. https://doi.org/10.1097/00005650-199206000-00002

Weiss, W. M., Murray, L. K., Zangana, G. A. S., Mahmooth, Z., Kaysen, D., Dorsey, S., … Bolton, P. (2015). Community-based mental health treatments for survivors of torture and militant attacks in Southern Iraq: A randomized control trial. *BMC Psychiatry, 15*(1), 249. https://doi.org/10.1186/s12888-015-0622-7

Wortmann, J. H., Jordan, A. H., Weathers, F. W., Resick, P. A., Dondanville, K. A., Hall-Clark, B., … Litz, B. T. (2016). Psychometric analysis of the PTSD Cchecklist-5 (PCL-5) among treatment-seeking military service members. *Psychological Assessment, 28*(11), 1392–1403. https://doi.org/10.1037/pas0000260

Yang L., & Link, B. (2015). *Measurement of attitudes, beliefs and behaviors of mental health and mental illness.*' Retrieved from http://sites.nationalacademies.org/cs/groups/dbassesite/documents/webpage/dbasse_170048.pdf

Paul Bolton is a Senior Scientist in the Center for Humanitarian Health and in the Departments of International Health and Mental Health at the Johns Hopkins University Bloomberg School of Public Health. His main interest is in the development of effective and accessible mental health services in low and middle income countries, particularly those affected by war and disasters.

New Technologies in the Treatment of Psychological Disorders – Overview, Potentials and Barriers for Conflict-Affected Populations

Jana Stein and Christine Knaevelsrud

Abstract The high number of violent conflicts around the world affects the psychological and physical well-being of thousands of civilians. Access to medical or psychological help is often limited. The growing access to digital communication-information technologies offers unique opportunities to bridge the mental health service gap by offering psychological help to a significant segment of a mentally burdened population who has experienced violent conflicts or displacement. In this chapter, different types of e-mental health approaches for trauma-related disorders including online support groups, self-help and therapist-supported online interventions, clinical video-teleconferencing and mobile mental health services will be introduced. Summary descriptions and scientific evidence will be provided for different e-mental health approaches already implemented in Western communities. Benefits and limitations of these approaches, as well as opportunities to further broaden accessibility to culturally diverse conflict-affected populations and forcibly displaced people will be discussed.

Keywords Trauma · Human rights violation · Posttraumatic stress disorder · Internet · E-mental health · Online support groups · Online counseling and psychotherapy · Clinical video-teleconferencing · Mobile mental health

Conflict and Mental Health

Violent conflict is one of the most significant characteristics of the contemporary world. Between the end of the Second World War and 2014, 259 armed conflicts were registered, with 40 armed conflicts still being active in 27 locations (Pettersson & Wallensteen, 2015). Ongoing widespread armed conflicts often involve exposure to human rights abuses like torture, arbitrary detention and forced migration. In 2015, more than 65 million people lived in forced displacement (United Nations

J. Stein (✉) · C. Knaevelsrud
Division of Clinical Psychological Intervention, Freie Universität Berlin, Berlin, Germany
e-mail: jana.stein@fu-berlin.de; christine.knaevelsrud@fu-berlin.de

N. Morina, A. Nickerson (eds.), *Mental Health of Refugee and Conflict-Affected Populations*, https://doi.org/10.1007/978-3-319-97046-2_19

High Commissioner for Refugees, 2016). Exposure to violent conflicts and the experience of forced migration have been associated with a wide range of negative consequences for social, psychological and physical well-being (Haar & Rubenstein, 2012; Hassan, Ventevogel, Jefee-Bahloul, Barkil-Oteo, & Kirmayer, 2016). Psychological symptoms like posttraumatic stress disorder (PTSD), depression and anxiety have been shown to be central subjective reactions to distress resulting from conflict and displacement (e.g., Alpak et al., 2015; Steel et al., 2009). Unfortunately, access to mental health services is limited for conflict-affected traumatized populations (Abbara et al., 2015). Mental health structures in conflict regions where people are in need of treatment are often entirely destroyed (e.g., Abbara et al., 2015). Hospitals and emergency departments have been closed and medical knowledge and equipment is lacking in many conflict areas (Haar & Rubenstein, 2012). Even in (host) countries with an established functioning health care system, psychological and medical support services are not regularly used by refugees (e.g., Morris, Popper, Rodwell, Brodine, & Brouwer, 2009). Research indicates that internal (e.g., mistrust and perceived discrimination), language and communication (e.g., no resources in the native tongue are available), cultural (e.g., unfamiliarity with mental health services) and structural (e.g., lack of accessibility, transportation, and inadequate insurance) issues may represent barriers to the utilization of face to face health services (e.g., Colucci, Minas, Szwarc, Guerra, & Paxton, 2015; Morris et al., 2009).

New Technologies in Times of Conflict

Information-communication technologies (mobile and internet sources) and social media networks have become increasingly important over the last decade. Between 2005 and 2015 the rate of internet usage increased with a compound growth rate of more than 10 per cent per year worldwide (International Telecommunication Union, 2015). Especially in developing regions internet penetration has grown, even though internet usage is considerably lower than in prosperous regions like wealthy nations in the Middle East or Western Europe (International Telecommunication Union, 2015). Similarly, the penetration of mobile cellular subscriptions has increased substantially in developing countries (International Telecommunication Union, 2015). These data clearly show that the ways in which people communicate and how information is produced, transformed and exchanged have changed enormously in recent years (Aday et al., 2013). Particularly in times of conflict, digital and online communication technologies enable and facilitate participation in the process of sharing (mental health) information with a worldwide audience (e.g., to document human rights violations and censorship) (Aday et al., 2013). When people are forced to flee from conflict, information-communication technologies have the potential to (re-) connect friends and relatives who have been separated during displacement and help to maintain contact with those who reside in the home country (Mikal & Woodfield, 2015). Additionally, internet and social media facilitate establishment of new socially supportive networks in the host country (Khvorostianov, Elias, &

Nimrod, 2012). For people who have experienced trauma in the course of conflict, the internet can be used to seek information about the impact of trauma on mental health (e.g., on web sites) or to communicate with people who have had similar experiences. However, apart from informational web sites and unstructured peer-support groups that often lack universal quality criteria and professional mental health provider involvement (Bremner, Quinn, Quinn, & Veledar, 2006), evidence-based interventions via the internet are mainly available for people living in Western societies who speak the national language (mostly English). Until now, relatively little has been done to transfer existing knowledge to conflict-affected non-Western populations and provide access to mental health interventions for individuals who are currently experiencing human rights violations or have been displaced. Therefore, the following sections aim to describe some evidence-based online applications for trauma-related care in general and to outline the transformational potential of as well as barriers to the use of these interventions in non-Western conflict-affected populations.

E-Mental Health Interventions – Integrating New Technologies in Mental Health Services

E-mental health services can be broadly defined as "the use of information and communication technology [...] to support and improve mental health conditions and mental health care [...]" (Riper et al., 2010).[1] Evidence-based e-mental health services may focus on different areas of mental health service delivery. These can include information provision and social support (e.g., educational web sites, social support groups), interventions (self-guided or therapist-supported interventions via the internet, interventions using mobile applications, virtual reality), screening, assessment and monitoring (e.g., Knaevelsrud, Karl, Wagner, & Mueller, 2007). E-mental health services can be applied as stand-alone interventions or in combination with face to face treatments (e.g., in the form of stepped or blended care) to address various psychological concerns at different stages (promotion, prevention, early intervention, active treatment, maintenance, and relapse prevention). Meanwhile, in addition to services targeting single disorders, there exist comprehensive virtual clinics that offer a wide spectrum of e-mental health services for people from Western countries. For example, the 'eCentreClinic' (www.ecentreclinic.org), the Australian 'National eTherapy Centre' (www.mentalhealthonline.org.au) and the 'This Way Up Clinic' (www.thiswayup.org.au) offer online courses for anxiety disorders, PTSD, stress, depression, obsessive compulsive disorder, and

[1] The term e-mental health (services) has already entered the scientific literature. Nevertheless, there is still no consensus statement on the definition of e-mental health. Some definitions include only interventions that are entirely delivered online. Others define e-mental health more broadly and include, among other things, online assessment, mental health promotion and prevention, treatment delivery and training of professionals (Riper et al., 2010). Terms such as telepsychiatry, online interventions and e-mental health services are often used synonymously.

other health conditions. As noted, even though different e-mental health services are applicable for a variety of disorders, in this chapter, we will emphasize low-threshold interventions, which seem to be feasible and applicable for patients with trauma-associated disorders. These include online support groups, self-guided and therapist-supported online interventions, clinical video-conferencing and mobile mental health services.

Online Support Groups

Online support groups are widely available and offer a peer-led opportunity to transfer information, resources (e.g., materials) and support by interacting with others who are, or have been, experiencing specific physical or psychological health problems (Barak & Grohol, 2011). Interaction in online support groups takes place through various internet applications (e.g., social media, forums, bulletin boards). Online support groups that are delivered and moderated by mental health professionals are often comprised of a psycho-educational and a group communication element and include a closed membership and a fixed length of time (e.g., Comprehensive Health Enhancement Support System) (Gottlieb, 2000; Helgeson & Gottlieb, 2000). The group communication component is crucial for sharing coping strategies, expressing thoughts and feelings, as well as accessing socio-emotional support (Shaw, McTavish, Hawkins, Gustafson, & Pingree, 2000; Wright, 2002). Supportive exchange with individuals who have had similar experiences may help to buffer individuals' negative reaction to stressful events and enhance well-being, life satisfaction, self-confidence and personal empowerment (e.g., Freeman, Barker, & Pistrang, 2008; Van Uden-Kraan, Drossaert, Taal, Seydel, & van de Laar, 2009). Research findings show that professionally moderated online support groups might have beneficial effects for depression and cancer-related trauma symptoms, for example, for women with breast cancer (Winzelberg et al., 2003). However, online support groups without any professional supervision have failed to show beneficial effects in Western communities (Mohr, Burns, Schueller, Clarke, & Klinkman, 2013), with some studies reporting worsening of symptoms (e.g., Kaplan, Salzer, Solomon, Brusilovskiy, & Cousounis, 2011). Unmoderated online support groups may be damaging when users misinform each other or motivate others to engage in dysfunctional behaviour (Brotsky & Giles, 2007).

Online Interventions

Online interventions are commonly understood as psychological treatments or preventive measures delivered via the internet to actively support patients in managing psychological or psychosomatic symptoms (Ebert & Erbe, 2012). Besides the provision of psycho-educational information, online interventions implement therapeutic techniques that have been proven to be efficacious in face to face settings. Online interventions are mainly based on cognitive behavioral principles and translate evidence-based components (e.g., cognitive restructuring, exposure) into an online interface. Only a few online interventions have been developed based on other psychotherapeutic concepts such as interpersonal (e.g., see Donker et al., 2013) or psychodynamic approaches (e.g., Johansson, Frederick, & Andersson, 2013). Online interventions vary with regard to the amount of mental health providers' involvement, which is on a continuum from entirely self-help programs to primarily therapist-guided online treatment or even as a supplement to face to face treatment (Ebert & Erbe, 2012).

Online Interventions – Self-Help Programs

In the context of entirely self-help programs, people interact with an online, often highly structured, self-guided program. In contrast to static psycho-educational web sites, self-help programs elicit high levels of patient involvement (Barak & Grohol, 2011). Patients are automatically guided through different modules that incorporate standardized treatment tools like demonstrations and skill exercises. In some programs, administration of treatment modules is adapted to the patients' needs and experiences; for example, based on clinical symptoms, relevant modules can be automatically identified and provided (Ruggiero et al., 2006). Feedback on the patient's performance can also be generated and administered automatically. Research indicates that self-guided interventions are efficacious for PTSD (e.g., Hirai & Clum, 2005; Steinmetz, Benight, Bishop, & James, 2012), depression (e.g., Richards & Richardson, 2012) and anxiety (e.g., van't Hof, Cuijpers, & Stein, 2009) in Western countries. Self-guided interventions for PTSD, depression and anxiety originally designed for Western communities can be effectively applied in non-Western populations (see Harper Shehadeh, Heim, Chowdhary, Maercker, & Albanese, 2016). For example, Wang, Wang, and Maercker (2013) undertook a randomized controlled trial in two parallel samples of Chinese trauma survivors (an urban sample with a variety of trauma experiences and a rural sample of earthquake survivors) to investigate the efficacy of a one-month self-help trauma intervention ('My Trauma Recovery'). The intervention was based on a social cognitive theory approach and comprised six components (social support, self-talk, relaxation, trauma triggers, unhelpful coping and professional help). Due to lack of internet access, the rural group received the intervention in a counseling center's computer room and additional technical support by volunteers. In both samples, PTSD symptoms significantly decreased over treatment. Another (pilot) study was conducted by Kayrouz, Dear, Karin, Fogliati et al. (2016) to examine the efficacy of a self-help cognitive-behavioural treatment (CBT) ('Arabic Wellbeing Course') for people with Arabic ancestry who suffered from depression and anxiety. The intervention included five online CBT modules delivered within eight weeks and was presented in English. Email contact was provided if a crisis occurred. Patients experienced significant improvements in depression, anxiety, disability and psychological distress over the course of the intervention. Treatment effects were maintained at a three-month follow-up.

Online Interventions – Therapist-Supported Programs

In contrast to entirely self-help approaches, therapist-supported interventions involve at least a minimal level of therapeutic contact between the patient and the therapist during the intervention. Therapists can provide assistance in primarily self-help programs (guided self-help) or guide the patient through the whole intervention. The form of interaction is mostly text-based and can be synchronous with real-time exchange such as via chat room conversations, be asynchronous with a delayed interaction (e.g., via email), or a combination of both (Andersson & Titov, 2014). Additional therapist support via phone calls can be provided when necessary (e.g., in case of suicidality). Therapist-supported interventions have shown substantial promise for a wide range of trauma-related psychological disorders including depression (e.g., Wagner, Horn, & Maercker, 2014), anxiety (e.g., Griffith, Farrer, & Christensen, 2010), prolonged grief (e.g., Kersting et al., 2013) and PTSD (e.g., Kuester, Niemeyer, & Knaevelsrud, 2016) in Western communities. Interventions involving therapeutic guidance tend to result in larger effect sizes than unguided interventions (Richards & Richardson, 2012). Across all studies, effects range from medium to large in size and are comparable to face to face psychotherapeutic treatment (e.g., Andersson, Cuijpers, Carlbring, Riper, & Hedman, 2014; Andersson & Hedman, 2013). Depending on the specific approach, treatment components contain psycho-education, exposure, cognitive restructuring, stress management, self-monitoring, skills training and relapse prevention (e.g., Litz, Engel, Bryant, & Papa, 2007; Spence et al., 2011). Even though interventions are typically text-based, multimedia elements, such as interactive trainings and audio/video sequences (e.g., for applied relaxation training) are sometimes included (Kuester et al., 2016). For treating PTSD in the aftermath of trauma, different online interventions exist (e.g., Spence et al., 2011). One well-established online writing treatment is 'Interapy' (Lange, van de Ven, & Schrieken, 2003), which combines CBT elements with the written disclosure approach (Pennebaker, 1997). Interapy consists of three components: self-confrontation (exposure), cognitive restructuring, and social sharing (patients are asked to write two letters to themselves or a significant other). In these letters the patients should summarize their memories of the trauma in 10 structured written accounts over five weeks, with the aim being that the client takes symbolic leave of the traumatic experience (Lange et al., 2003). Interapy involves a high level of therapeutic assistance with weekly asynchronous personalized feedback related to the patients' letters. Therapists use standardized text blocks for psychoeducation and instructions but feedback is tailored. This intervention has already been successfully administered to different trauma-affected populations (e.g., Wagner, Knaevelsrud, & Maercker, 2006) and applied in a number of Western countries. Recently, this approach has been proven to be efficacious in a non-Western conflict-affected population (Knaevelsrud, Brand, Lange, Ruwaard, & Wagner, 2015). In this study, Arabic-speaking patients with PTSD received a culturally adapted version of the Interapy treatment ('Ilajnafsy') provided by eight trained native speaking therapists. Therapists received weekly supervision from an experienced clinician. The authors noted a significantly greater improvement in symptoms of PTSD, depression, anxiety, somatization and quality of life among the treatment group relative to a waitlist control group. The completion rate was 59%. Apart from the study by Knaevelsrud et al. (2015), only few therapist-guided online interventions for depression and PTSD have been culturally adapted and studied with ethnic minority groups. For instance, Choi et al. (2012) delivered an 8-week culturally adapted online CBT ('Brighten Your Mood Program') for depressed Chinese Australians. The program included six modules with a focus on cognitive restructuring, behavioural activation, problem solving and skills training. Homework assignments, automatic reminders and weekly emails or telephone calls were implemented in the program. Depressive symptoms were reduced in the intervention group compared to a waitlist control group and the completion rate was 68%. Ünlü Ince et al. (2013) culturally and linguistically adapted a 5-week therapist-supported self-help program ('Alles Onder Controle – TR') with a focus on problem solving skills for Turkish migrants in the Netherlands. Patients received weekly emails incorporating feedback on their homework. Results did not reveal a meaningful difference between the waitlist control group and the intervention group with regard to reductions in depressive symptoms at posttreatment on the intention-to-treat analysis. Using per-protocol analysis, however, large effect sizes for reductions in depression in the intervention group were found. Kayrouz, Dear, Karin, Gandy et al. (2016) were the first to study the feasibility and efficacy of a structured therapist-supported online CBT intervention ('Arabic Wellbeing Course') in a pilot study with Arabic-speaking Australians with anxiety or depression. The 8-week intervention included five modules with a focus on teaching practical psychological skills to assist in managing symptoms. Participants engaged in brief weekly interactions with a mental health professional via email and telephone. A significant reduction in depressive symptoms, anxiety, psychological distress and impairment was observed in participants, with large pre- to post-treatment effect sizes.

Clinical Video-Teleconferencing (CVT)

In CVT, the patient and therapist communicate simultaneously via encrypted, remote video technology for diagnostic assessment, case management, medication counselling or psychotherapy (Richardson, Frueh, Grubaugh, Egede, & Elhai, 2009). When conducted as a stand-alone intervention, slight modifications of treatments that are conventionally delivered face to face need to be made (e.g., exchange of materials via mail) (e.g., Gros, Yoder, Tuerk, Lozano, & Acierno, 2011). In contrast to online interventions as described above, visual as well as auditory information can be displayed in CVT, making it more comparable to conventional treatment (Hassija & Gray, 2011). Particularly for patients who lack reading abilities or do not feel comfortable expressing feelings in writing, CVT may be more appropriate than other online interventions. CVT can either be used to conduct individual or group treatment (see Gros et al., 2013) and either from clinic to clinic (e.g., Gros et al., 2011) or from clinic to patient's home (see Morland, Poizner, Williams, Masino, & Thorp, 2015). There is a growing body of research evaluating interventions that incorporate video-based telepsychology into the delivery of mental health services in Western countries (e.g., Chan, Parish, & Yellowlees, 2015). Evidence generally suggests that video-teleconferencing is a feasible medium through which trauma-focused treatment for PTSD and related symptoms can be delivered (Gros et al., 2013). In most studies, meaningful reductions in psychopathological symptoms were observed (e.g., Germain, Marchand, Bouchard, Drouin, & Guay, 2009). Across studies, CVT administered treatment led to comparable improvements in PTSD, depression and anxiety, as well as good outcomes in treatment-related variables (e.g., retention, adherence, expectancy) relative to conventional treatment (see Gros et al., 2013). Patients reported being satisfied with video-teleconferencing even though discomfort with technical issues occurred at times (e.g., Morland, Hynes, Mackintosh, Resick, & Chard, 2011). Although findings have generally supported this modality, some trials involving exposure-based PTSD treatment found larger symptom improvements (e.g., Gros et al., 2011) and higher treatment satisfaction ratings (Yuen et al., 2015) in face to face treatment conditions. Gros et al. (2013) suggest that imaginal exposure for PTSD may be more difficult to administer via CVT than other treatment approaches (e.g., cognitive processing treatment). To date, CVT services have mainly targeted military veterans and children (Lauckner & Whitten, 2015). Research addressing the applicability of intercultural CVT for PTSD or depression is limited and primarily focused on Native Americans, Hispanic and Asian populations (Chan et al., 2015). Even though access to culturally appropriate mental health workers (e.g., with bilingual competences) is made easier by video-teleconferencing (Mucic, 2010), the use of CVT has not yet been studied systematically for traumatized populations affected by war and forcibly displaced people. Whereas some research on telemedicine in low-resource settings exists (Wootton & Bonnardot, 2015), only one study, conducted in Denmark, examined the clinical utility of CVT for psychiatric complaints with culturally diverse asylum seekers, refugees and migrants (Mucic, 2010). Video-teleconferencing was used for diagnostic assessment and the provision of culturally and linguistic appropriate treatment by clinicians educated in Sweden and Denmark. A high level of acceptance, satisfaction and willingness to use CVT was noted. However, the therapeutic modality remained unclear and no measures of psychopathological symptoms were reported. Thus, even though potentially feasible, the efficacy of CVT for conflict-affected populations still needs to be determined.

Mobile Mental Health Services

The widespread use of smartphones enables mental health professionals to incorporate smartphone applications ("apps") or mobile services (e.g., text messaging) into mental health services (e.g., Luxton, McCann, Bush, Mishkind, & Reger, 2011). In contrast to computers, mobile phones are more personal as they are commonly not shared with other people. Smartphones are available all day and frequently within arms' reach which enables patients to engage in treatment by accomplishing tasks on a just-in-time basis (e.g., coping with acute distress) (Olff, 2015). Patients might be encouraged to engage with treatment tasks through reminder messages, short motivational messages and highly personalized tools. In addition, support can be provided within a short time-frame and coping strategies or particular skills can be practiced in real-life situations (Olff, 2015). Specific tools for self-monitoring and self-management of symptoms as well as psycho-educational material can be incorporated. When the smartphone is used as a supplement to face to face therapy, communication between sessions (to sustain engagement) and after treatment (to prevent relapse) can be increased (Kuhn, Hoffman, & Ruzek, 2015). However, without professional aid, individuals seeking psychological support might have difficulties in identifying the types of tools that are needed and distinguishing between appropriate and scientifically valuable apps and other inappropriate options from the public market. Numerous mobile mental health interventions currently exist for a variety of mental health disorders and are available for download (Shen et al., 2015). Nevertheless, only few interventions are scientifically evaluated (e.g., Lewis, Pearce, & Bisson, 2012) and publicly accessible. As this field of research is very young, more time is needed to implement and evaluate these approaches. Even though not explicitly designed for conflict-affected populations and displaced people, two promising smartphone applications for trauma survivors with PTSD – 'PTSD Coach' and 'PE Coach' – should be mentioned here. The PTSD Coach was originally designed for military veterans (Kuhn et al., 2014). Using the PTSD Coach, individuals suffering from posttraumatic symptoms are encouraged to self-manage their difficulties. It can also be used to augment face to face professional care. Implementing CBT principles, the PTSD Coach provides psycho-educational material, information on finding support, self-assessment (to track symptoms over time) and self-management coping tools to reduce PTSD-related symptoms and strengthen social support. The app can be personalized by integrating one's own music, photos and contacts. The PTSD Coach is now available in different languages and thus can be used in several regions worldwide. Acceptability of and satisfaction with the PTSD Coach have been demonstrated in a study with American veterans with PTSD (Kuhn et al., 2014). Nearly 90% reported overall satisfaction with the PTSD Coach and 68% to 91% perceived the app as a helpful tool. In a community sample with PTSD the use of PTSD Coach was associated with modest reductions in PTSD symptoms (Miner et al., 2016). The 'PE Coach' is a smartphone-application for PTSD treatment developed to support the implementation and dissemination of and treatment adherence of patients and therapists to prolonged exposure (Reger et al., 2013). The efficacy of the PE Coach still needs to be investigated in clinical trials (Reger, Skopp, Edwards-Stewart, & Lemus, 2015).

Benefits of E-Mental Health Services

One of the core benefits of interventions delivered via the internet or smartphone is that culturally appropriate evidence-based support can be provided (at low costs) to patients who would otherwise not be able to obtain psychological help due to geographical, financial or temporal reasons (Lal & Adair, 2014). In particular, people who live in conflict-affected regions or have been displaced are a very vulnerable group that often remain untreated for many months or even years. The geographical independence of the patients' and providers' location makes it possible for those people to receive gold-standard psychological help via e-mental health services (Knaevelsrud et al., 2015). Moreover, interventions delivered via the internet provide the unique opportunity for patients to receive treatment while upholding their visual anonymity (e.g., in online interventions) (Andrews & Titov, 2010). Thereby, the readiness to seek help and the receptivity to psychological support may be improved (Wagner, Schulz, & Knaevelsrud, 2012). Anonymous interventions may help people who have experienced violence to confront and disclose difficult and painful memories and associated feelings. E-mental health interventions may help to overcome feelings of shame, which is particularly important for people who have experienced sexual violence and are part of a culture in which sexual assault may be regarded as the fault of the victim, leading to dishonor and worthlessness (Wagner et al., 2012). Beside the advantages of anonymity, lower fear of stigmatization, cost-effectiveness and independence of location, further benefits arise due to special technical features of e-mental health interventions. Interactive multimedia components or additional automated motivation and reminder messages can be easily incorporated in the intervention to facilitate patient engagement if required (Rochlen, Zack, & Speyer, 2004). Activities that take place during the intervention (e.g., chatting, symptom assessment) can be automatically recorded and stored properly. This feature enhances the transparency of the therapeutic process for both the patient and the provider. Stored records (e.g., educational information) can be easily accessed during or after treatment. By incorporating automatic technical features (e.g., automatic assessment of symptom change), providers are able to monitor how the patient progresses during treatment and actively give support when symptoms worsen or tailor the intervention to patients' needs if necessary (Andersson & Titov, 2014). Furthermore, supervision of less experienced providers is made easier as supervisors are able to monitor the therapeutic progress in detail and ensure that the therapeutic elements are administered properly. As online interventions are often highly structured and based on standardized texts, it is quite simple to linguistically and culturally adapt them to other cultures (Harper Shehadeh et al., 2016). Local mental health workers can be trained to provide these interventions under the supervision of experienced clinicians at a distance. Thereby, dissemination of e-mental health interventions may be further enhanced.

Barriers to E-Mental Health Services

Several challenges of implementing e-mental health interventions in low-resource settings (especially in conflict-affected countries) that warrant consideration will be discussed in this section.

Clinical Issues

One of the most significant clinical challenges associated with e-mental health services is the physical absence of the therapist. When symptoms or behaviors such as suicidal thoughts or aggression occur, the therapist is not physically present to address these urgent crises (e.g., Mitchell & Murphy, 1998). Local emergency resources such as an on-site clinician that can be contacted in the eventuality of emergencies are often limited in conflict settings (e.g., Abbara et al., 2015) or rural areas. Thus, it is essential for providers to have knowledge of patient's social support structures (e.g., family, friends, religious figures) on-site and contact information (e.g., patients' telephone number). When delivering e-mental health services (like online counselling), providers need to be properly trained to be able to deal with both clinical and technical difficulties (e.g., malfunctions) that may occur (e.g., Kuhn et al., 2015). In text-based interventions, some therapists may find it challenging to treat patients without any visual cues (e.g., nonverbal behavior cannot be observed during treatment) (Rochlen et al., 2004). Some therapists may have difficulty integrating or applying new media in their treatment due to inadequate knowledge regarding how to use these modalities (e.g., Kuhn et al., 2015).

Cultural and Regional Issues

Working with individuals from non-Western cultures requires a culturally sensitive treatment approach (Bernal, Jiménez-Chafey, & Domenech Rodríguez, 2009). Treatment receptivity and acceptance may be increased by tailoring the intervention to local customs, cultural beliefs and language (Castro, Barrera, & Steiker, 2010). Several researchers have shown that cultural values and belief systems play an essential role in how people express distress and what they believe is appropriate therapy (e.g., Hassan et al., 2015). For instance, depressive symptoms are often experienced and explained somatically in non-Western cultures (Al-Krenawi & Graham, 2000). As a result, patients might expect psychological interventions to be similar to medical treatments in terms of temporality and lack of responsibility of the patient. Patients may think that they can be "cured" rapidly and without disclosing much of their personal lives. E-mental health interventions that are time-limited and focus on practical skills may therefore be highly appropriate for patients from non-Western societies (e.g., Al-Krenawi & Graham, 2000). A directive authoritative approach incorporating high levels of therapeutic guidance during the treatment process and the use of advice giving may be required to enhance engagement (Gearing et al., 2013). Before developing and/or implementing an e-mental health intervention with people from a particular cultural group, it is essential to be familiar with the patients' psycho-cultural heritage to avoid misunderstandings (Dwairy, 2006). Thereby, if possible, close partnerships with local health care providers (in some cases also with reputed village leaders and elders) and institutions on-site with knowledge of cultural values can promote and improve acceptance of these services (Gearing et al., 2013). An additional intercultural challenge includes potential skill deficiency (Rochlen et al., 2004). Illiteracy (with regard to reading, writing and computers) is wide-spread in conflict regions leading to limited applicability of e-mental health services among people with lower levels of education. In addition, mistrust in e-mental health interventions is observed at times (e.g., Shore, Savin, Novins, & Manson, 2006). It is sometimes noted that people who have experienced trauma worry about technology itself as well as associated security and privacy issues. For example, partial hesitance towards e-mental health treatments was observed in Syrian refugees living in Turkey (Jefee-Bahloul, Moustafa, Shebl, & Barkil-Oteo, 2014). Only 45% of those who expressed a subjective need for psychiatric help, reported openness towards telepsychiatry. They were concerned about privacy issues, distortions to the therapeutic relationship and lack of familiarity with the technology. Thus, it is important to enhance recognition and knowledge of the use and effectiveness of e-mental health services in local communities. Education can further improve attitudes towards these services and thereby increase utilization of and engagement in psychological treatment (Gearing et al., 2013).

Technical Issues

Implementation of e-mental health interventions requires an existing and functioning technical infrastructure. For example, reliable electricity supply and unrestricted access to the internet are necessary conditions for providing e-mental health interventions (Jefee-Bahloul, 2014a). Even though some conflict-affected countries possess an infrastructure that allows for implementation of these interventions, some other countries may only have limited power supply (e.g., Jefee-Bahloul, 2014a) or access to the internet due to underdevelopment or attempts of dictatorial governments to restrict internet usage. Lack of information technology knowledge or internet/computer illiteracy on the behalf of the patient and the therapist might also be a major obstacle. For interventions delivered via videoconferencing, a high bandwidth capacity is additionally required. In insecure regions with a high risk of repeated and continuing violence, effectiveness and dissemination of e-mental health interventions may be reduced (e.g., difficulties with the internet connection may lead to high attrition rates) (Wagner et al., 2012). In any case, a high level of temporal flexibility is essential as unexpected (technical) events may hinder the patient's capacity to continue with and complete treatment within a specific time frame in stable as well as unstable regions.

Privacy Issues

Personal security, protection of privacy and personal data protection are important issues that should be considered. Mass surveillance, censorship, and monitoring is facilitated by new media usage (Howard, 2002). Thereby, protection of personal data that are transmitted electronically should be given priority, particularly in countries with repressive regimes. Providers should guarantee the highest level of privacy and data protection (e.g., by using encryption methods). Furthermore, patients should be educated about data and privacy protection measures (e.g., use of secure passwords) (see American Psychology Association Council on Psychiatry and Law, 2014).

Conclusion and Outlook

E-mental health interventions represent a promising alternative to providing face-to-face psychological help for people who have experienced severe stressful events in the course of conflicts or displacement. These treatments may be especially beneficial for individuals who do not have the opportunity to see a psychologist face to face (e.g., individuals living in conflict-affected settings or traumatized refugees who have been settled in rural areas in the host country that are geographically distant from treatment centers) or avoid seeking help out of shame, fear or other culturally-specific habits and conventions. Still, evidence-based e-mental health interventions for these specific populations are rare. Few studies have investigated the efficacy of these interventions for non-Western populations with PTSD and depression. Only one study (Wang et al., 2013) examined the efficacy of a self-guided intervention for traumatized patients in China and only one study by Knaevelsrud et al. (2015) investigated the efficacy of a therapist-guided online intervention for traumatized Arab patients living in North Africa or the Middle East. Results are promising with regard to symptom reduction but high attrition is frequently observed. Recently, some new projects have been initiated to adapt existing psychological interventions to the specific situation of refugees and other conflict-affected populations. New technologies (e.g., smartphones) have been used to deliver these culturally adapted interventions. One that should be mentioned here is the World Health Organization (WHO) led project 'Step-by-Step'. 'Step-by-Step' is an online self-help program for depression with minimal guidance that has been developed based on the Problem Management Plus manual (*PM+*) (Dawson et al., 2015) and adapted to the needs of people living in Lebanon. The intervention includes psycho-educational information delivered via an illustrated story, deep breathing techniques, as well as modules on behavioural activation, positive self-talk and strengthening of social contacts. The intervention is currently being pilot-tested in Lebanon for Lebanese, Syrian and Palestinian communities. In parallel, a transdiagnostic smartphone application has simultaneously been developed (based on the 'PM+' approach and initiated by the WHO) to be applied to Syrian refugees in future. Additionally, the therapy project 'Ilajnafsy' will be expanded to serve people with mental disorders other than PTSD and depression and will be optimized to apply the treatment even more efficiently (e.g., by the specific use of treatment components for specific subgroups of patients).

Besides the opportunity to provide psychological help online, advanced technologies (e.g., video-based applications via smartphone) can be a tool for supervision (e.g., case consultation) (Jefee-Bahloul, 2014a, 2014b), education, and training of local providers (e.g., Khanna & Kendall, 2015). Particularly, local native speaking mental health professionals could be qualified at a distance to treat conflict-affected populations on-site. In addition, they could learn how to conduct e-mental health interventions to serve patients from all over the world. To raise the quality of e-mental health services, it is important to develop and uphold quality standards and guidelines that cover ethical, legal and privacy issues (e.g., security of data, informed consent). Since the introduction of e-mental health services, these criteria relevant to providing high quality e-mental health services have been emphasized for the successful implementation of such services in Western communities (e.g., Manhal-Baugus, 2004). Strict training and supervision of therapists who provide e-mental health interventions, enhanced ethical codes (Rummell & Joyce, 2010), a high level of personal security, as well as scientific evaluation of the treatment are essential for comprehensive implementation and merging of existing evidence-based e-mental health interventions for conflict-affected non-Western populations.

References

Abbara, A., Blanchet, K., Sahloul, Z., Fouad, F., Coutts, A., & Maziak, W. (2015). The effect of the conflict on Syria's health system and human resources for health. *World Health & Population, 16*(1), 87–95.

Aday, S., Farrell, H., Freelon, D., Lynch, M., Sides, J., & Dewar, M. (2013). Watching from afar: Media consumption patterns around the Arab Spring. *American Behavioral Scientist, 57*(7), 899–919.

Al-Krenawi, A., & Graham, J. R. (2000). Culturally sensitive social work practice with Arab clients in mental health settings. *Health & Social Work, 25*(1), 9–22.

Alpak, G., Unal, A., Bulbul, F., Sagaltici, E., Bez, Y., Altindag, A., … Savas, H. A. (2015). Post-traumatic stress disorder among Syrian refugees in Turkey: A cross-sectional study. *International Journal of Psychiatry in Clinical Practice, 19*(1), 45–50.

American Psychiatric Association Council on Psychiatry and Law. (2014). *Resource document on telepsychiatry and related technologies in clinical psychiatry*. Retrieved from https://www.psychiatry.org/File%20Library/Psychiatrists/Directories/Library-and-Archive/resource_documents/Resource-2014-Telepsychiatry-Clinical-Psychiatry.pdf

Andersson, G., Cuijpers, P., Carlbring, P., Riper, H., & Hedman, E. (2014). Guided internet-based vs. face-to-face cognitive behavior therapy for psychiatric and somatic disorders: A systematic review and meta-analysis. *World Psychiatry, 13*(3), 288–295.

Andersson, G., & Hedman, E. (2013). Effectiveness of guided internet-delivered cognitive behaviour therapy in regular clinical settings. *Verhaltenstherapie, 23*(3), 140–148.

Andersson, G., & Titov, N. (2014). Advantages and limitations of internet-based interventions for common mental disorders. *World Psychiatry, 13*(1), 4–11.

Andrews, G., & Titov, N. (2010). Treating people you never see: Internet-based treatment of the internalising mental disorders. *Australian Health Review, 34*(2), 144–147.

Barak, A., & Grohol, J. M. (2011). Current and future trends in internet-supported mental health interventions. *Journal of Technology in Human Services, 29*(3), 155–196.

Bernal, G., Jiménez-Chafey, M. I., & Domenech Rodríguez, M. M. (2009). Cultural adaptation of treatments: A resource for considering culture in evidence-based practice. *Professional Psychology: Research and Practice, 40*(4), 361–368.

Bremner, J. D., Quinn, J., Quinn, W., & Veledar, E. (2006). Surfing the Net for medical information about psychological trauma: An empirical study of the quality and accuracy of trauma-related websites. *Medical Informatics and the Internet in Medicine, 31*(3), 227–236.

Brotsky, S., & Giles, D. (2007). Inside the "Pro-ana" community: A covert online participant observation. *Eating Disorders, 15*(2), 93–109.

Castro, F. G., Barrera, M. J., & Steiker, L. K. H. (2010). Issues and challenges in the design of culturally adapted evidence-based interventions. *Annual Review of Clinical Psychology, 6*(1), 213–239.

Chan, S., Parish, M., & Yellowlees, P. (2015). Telepsychiatry today. *Current Psychiatry Reports, 17*(11), 1–9.

Choi, I., Zou, J., Titov, N., Dear, B. F., Li, S., Johnston, L., … Hunt, C. (2012). Culturally attuned internet treatment for depression amongst Chinese Australians: A randomised controlled trial. *Journal of Affective Disorders, 136*(3), 459–468.

Colucci, E., Minas, H., Szwarc, J., Guerra, C., & Paxton, G. (2015). In or out? Barriers and facilitators to refugee-background young people accessing mental health services. *Transcultural Psychiatry, 52*(6), 766–790.

Dawson, K. S., Bryant, R. A., Harper Shehadeh, M., Kuowei Tay, A., Rahman, A., Schafer, A., & van Ommeren, M. (2015). Problem Management Plus (PM+): A WHO transdiagnostic psychological intervention for common mental health problems. *World Psychiatry, 14*(3), 354–357.

Donker, T., Bennett, K., Bennett, A., Mackinnon, A., van Straten, A., Cuijpers, P., … Griffiths, K. M. (2013). Internet-delivered interpersonal psychotherapy versus internet-delivered cognitive behavioral therapy for adults with depressive symptoms: Randomized controlled noninferiority trial. *Journal of Medical Internet Research, 15*(5), e82.

Dwairy, M. A. (2006). *Counseling and psychotherapy with Arabs and Muslims: A culturally sensitive approach*. New York and London: Teachers College Press.

Ebert, D. D., & Erbe, D. (2012). Internetbasierte psychologische Interventionen. In M. Berking & W. Rief (Eds.), *Klinische Psychologie und Psychotherapie für Bachelor* (Vol. 2, pp. 131–140). Berlin and Heidelberg: Springer.

Freeman, E., Barker, C., & Pistrang, N. (2008). Outcome of an online mutual support group for college students with psychological problems. *Cyber Psychology & Behavior, 11*(5), 591–593.

Gearing, R. E., Schwalbe, C. S., MacKenzie, M. J., Brewer, K. B., Ibrahim, R. W., Olimat, H. S., … Al-Krenawi, A. (2013). Adaptation and translation of mental health interventions in Middle Eastern Arab countries: A systematic review of barriers to and strategies for effective treatment implementation. *International Journal of Social Psychiatry, 59*(7), 671–681.

Germain, V., Marchand, A., Bouchard, S., Drouin, M. S., & Guay, S. (2009). Effectiveness of cognitive behavioural therapy administered by videoconference for posttraumatic stress disorder. *Cognitive Behaviour Therapy, 38*(1), 42–53.

Gottlieb, B. H. (2000). Selecting and planning support interventions. In S. Cohen, L. G. Underwood, & B. H. Gottlieb (Eds.), *Social support measurement and intervention: A guide for health and social scientists* (pp. 195–220). New York, NY: Oxford University Press.

Griffiths, K. M., Farrer, L., & Christensen, H. (2010). The efficacy of internet interventions for depression and anxiety disorders: A review of randomised controlled trials. *Medical Journal of Australia, 192*(11), S4.

Gros, D. F., Morland, L. A., Greene, C. J., Acierno, R., Strachan, M., Egede, L. E., … Frueh, B. C. (2013). Delivery of evidence-based psychotherapy via video telehealth. *Journal of Psychopathology and Behavioral Assessment, 35*(4), 506–521.

Gros, D. F., Yoder, M., Tuerk, P. W., Lozano, B. E., & Acierno, R. (2011). Exposure therapy for PTSD delivered to veterans via telehealth: Predictors of treatment completion and outcome and comparison to treatment delivered in person. *Behavior Therapy, 42*(2), 276–283.

Haar, R. J., & Rubenstein, L. S. (2012). *Health in postconflict and fragile states*. Washington, DC: United States Institute of Peace.

Harper Shehadeh, M., Heim, E., Chowdhary, N., Maercker, A., & Albanese, E. (2016). Cultural adaptation of minimally guided interventions for common mental disorders: A systematic review and meta-analysis. *Journal of Medical Internet Research – Mental Health, 3*(3), e44.

Hassan, G., Kirmayer, L. J., Mekki-Berrada, A., Quosh, C., el Chammay, R., Deville-Stoetzel, J. B., … Ventevogel, P. (2015). *Culture, context and the mental health and psychosocial well-being of Syrians: A review for mental health and psychosocial support staff working with Syrians affected by armed conflict*. Geneva, Switzerland: United Nations High Commissioner for Refugees.

Hassan, G., Ventevogel, P., Jefee-Bahloul, H., Barkil-Oteo, A., & Kirmayer, L. J. (2016). Mental health and psychosocial wellbeing of Syrians affected by armed conflict. *Epidemiology and Psychiatric Sciences, 25*(2), 129–141.

Hassija, C., & Gray, M. J. (2011). The effectiveness and feasibility of videoconferencing technology to provide evidence-based treatment to rural domestic violence and sexual assault populations. *Telemedicine and E-Health, 17*(4), 309–315.

Helgeson, V. S., & Gottlieb, B. H. (2000). Support groups. In S. Cohen, L. G. Underwood, & B. H. Gottlieb (Eds.), *Social support measurement and intervention: A guide for health and social scientists* (pp. 221–245). New York, NY: Oxford University Press.

Hirai, M., & Clum, G. A. (2005). An internet-based self-change program for traumatic event related fear, distress, and maladaptive coping. *Journal of Traumatic Stress, 18*(6), 631–636.

Howard, R. (2002). *An operational framework for media and peacebuilding*. Vancouver, BC: Institute for Media, Policy and Civil Society.

International Telecommunication Union. (2015). *Measuring the information society report 2015*. Geneva, Switzerland: Author.

Jefee-Bahloul, H. (2014a). Telemental health in the middle East: Overcoming the barriers. *Frontiers in Public Health, 2*(86), 53–56.

Jefee-Bahloul, H. (2014b). Use of telepsychiatry in areas of conflict: The Syrian refugee crisis as an example. *Journal of Telemedicine and Telecare, 20*(3), 167–168.

Jefee-Bahloul, H., Moustafa, M. K., Shebl, F. M., & Barkil-Oteo, A. (2014). Pilot assessment and survey of Syrian refugees' psychological stress and openness to referral for telepsychiatry (PASSPORT Study). *Telemedicine and E-Health, 20*(10), 977–979.

Johansson, R., Frederick, R. J., & Andersson, G. (2013). Using the internet to provide psychodynamic psychotherapy. *Psychodynamic Psychiatry, 41*(4), 385–412.

Kaplan, K., Salzer, M. S., Solomon, P., Brusilovskiy, E., & Cousounis, P. (2011). Internet peer support for individuals with psychiatric disabilities: A randomized controlled trial. *Social Science & Medicine, 72*(1), 54–62.

Kayrouz, R., Dear, B. F., Karin, E., Fogliati, V. J., & Titov, N. (2016). A pilot study of a clinician-guided internet-delivered cognitive behavioural therapy for anxiety and depression among Arabs in Australia, presented in both English and Arabic languages. *Internet Interventions, 5*, 5–11.

Kayrouz, R., Dear, B. F., Karin, E., Gandy, M., Fogliati, V. J., Terides, M. D., & Titov, N. (2016). A pilot study of self-guided internet-delivered cognitive behavioural therapy for anxiety and depression among Arabs. *Internet Interventions, 3*, 18–24.

Kersting, A., Dölemeyer, R., Steinig, J., Walter, F., Kroker, K., Baust, K., & Wagner, B. (2013). Brief internet-based intervention reduces posttraumatic stress and prolonged grief in parents after the loss of a child during pregnancy: A randomized controlled trial. *Psychotherapy and Psychosomatics, 82*(6), 372–381.

Khanna, M. S., & Kendall, P. C. (2015). Bringing technology to training: Web-based therapist training to promote the development of competent cognitive-behavioral therapists. *Cognitive and Behavioral Practice, 22*(3), 291–301.

Khvorostianov, N., Elias, N., & Nimrod, G. (2012). 'Without it I am nothing': The internet in the lives of older immigrants. *New Media & Society, 14*(4), 583–599.

Knaevelsrud, C., Brand, J., Lange, A., Ruwaard, J., & Wagner, B. (2015). Web-based psychotherapy for posttraumatic stress disorder in war-traumatized Arab patients: Randomized controlled trial. *Journal of Medical Internet Research, 17*(3), e71.

Knaevelsrud, C., Karl, A., Wagner, B., & Mueller, J. (2007). New treatment approaches: Integrating new media in the treatment of war and torture victims. *Torture, 17*(2), 67–78.

Kuester, A., Niemeyer, H., & Knaevelsrud, C. (2016). Internet-based interventions for posttraumatic stress: A meta-analysis of randomized controlled trials. *Clinical Psychology Review, 43*, 1–16.

Kuhn, E., Greene, C., Hoffman, J., Nguyen, T., Wald, L., Schmidt, J., ... Ruzek, J. (2014). Preliminary evaluation of PTSD Coach, a smartphone app for post-traumatic stress symptoms. *Military Medicine, 179*(1), 12–18.

Kuhn, E., Hoffman, J. E., & Ruzek, J. I. (2015). Telemental health approaches for trauma survivors. In U. Schnyder & M. Cloitre (Eds.), *Evidence based treatments for trauma-related psychological disorders: A practical guide for clinicians* (pp. 461–476). Cham, Switzerland: Springer International Publishing.

Lal, S., & Adair, C. E. (2014). E-mental health: A rapid review of the literature. *Psychiatric Services, 65*(1), 24–32.

Lange, A., van de Ven, J.-P., & Schrieken, B. (2003). Interapy: Treatment of post-traumatic stress via the internet. *Cognitive Behaviour Therapy, 32*(3), 110–124.

Lauckner, C., & Whitten, P. (2015). The state and sustainability of telepsychiatry programs. *The Journal of Behavioral Health Services & Research, 43*(2), 305–318.

Lewis, C., Pearce, J., & Bisson, J. I. (2012). Efficacy, cost-effectiveness and acceptability of self-help interventions for anxiety disorders: Systematic review. *The British Journal of Psychiatry, 200*(1), 15–21.

Litz, B. T., Engel, C. C., Bryant, R. A., & Papa, A. (2007). A randomized, controlled proof-of-concept trial of an internet-based, therapist-assisted self-management treatment for posttraumatic stress disorder. *The American Journal of Psychiatry, 164*(11), 1676–1684.

Luxton, D. D., McCann, R. A., Bush, N. E., Mishkind, M. C., & Reger, G. M. (2011). mHealth for mental health: Integrating smartphone technology in behavioral healthcare. *Professional Psychology: Research and Practice, 42*(6), 505–512.

Manhal-Baugus, M. (2004). E-therapy: Practical, ethical, and legal issues. *Cyber Psychology & Behavior, 4*(5), 551–563.

Mikal, J. P., & Woodfield, B. (2015). Refugees, post-migration stress, and internet use: A qualitative analysis of intercultural adjustment and internet use among Iraqi and Sudanese refugees to the United States. *Qualitative Health Research, 25*(10), 1319–1333.

Miner, A., Kuhn, E., Hoffman, J. E., Owen, J. E., Ruzek, J. I., & Taylor, C. B. (2016). Feasibility, acceptability, and potential efficacy of the PTSD Coach app: A pilot randomized controlled trial with community trauma survivors. *Psychological Trauma: Theory, Research, Practice, and Policy, 8*(3), 384–392.

Mitchell, D. L., & Murphy, L. M. (1998). Confronting the challenges of therapy online: A pilot project. *Proceedings of the Seventh National and Fifth International Conference on Information Technology and Community Health, Victoria, British Columbia, Canada.*

Mohr, D. C., Burns, M. N., Schueller, S. M., Clarke, G., & Klinkman, M. (2013). Behavioral intervention technologies: Evidence review and recommendations for future research in mental health. *General Hospital Psychiatry, 35*(4), 332–338.

Morland, L. A., Hynes, A. K., Mackintosh, M. A., Resick, P. A., & Chard, K. M. (2011). Group cognitive processing therapy delivered to veterans via telehealth: A pilot cohort. *Journal of Traumatic Stress, 24*(4), 465–469.

Morland, L. A., Poizner, J. M., Williams, K. E., Masino, T. T., & Thorp, S. R. (2015). Home-based clinical video teleconferencing care: Clinical considerations and future directions. *International Review of Psychiatry, 27*(6), 504–512.

Morris, M. D., Popper, S. T., Rodwell, T. C., Brodine, S. K., & Brouwer, K. C. (2009). Healthcare barriers of refugees' post-resettlement. *Journal of Community Health, 34*(6), 529–538.

Mucic, D. (2010). Transcultural telepsychiatry and its impact on patient satisfaction. *Journal of Telemedicine and Telecare, 16*(5), 237–242.

Olff, M. (2015). Mobile mental health: A challenging research agenda. *European Journal of Psychotraumatology, 6*(S4), 27882.

Pennebaker, J. W. (1997). Writing about emotional experiences as a therapeutic process. *Psychological Science, 8*(3), 162–166.

Pettersson, T., & Wallensteen, P. (2015). Armed conflicts, 1946–2014. *Journal of Peace Research, 52*(4), 536–550.

Reger, G. M., Hoffman, J., Riggs, D., Rothbaum, B. O., Ruzek, J., Holloway, K. M., & Kuhn, E. (2013). The "PE coach" smartphone application: An innovative approach to improving implementation, fidelity, and homework adherence during prolonged exposure. *Psychological Services, 10*(3), 342–349.

Reger, G. M., Skopp, N. A., Edwards-Stewart, A., & Lemus, E. L. (2015). Comparison of prolonged exposure (PE) coach to treatment as usual: A case series with two active duty soldiers. *Military Psychology, 27*(5), 287–296.

Richards, D., & Richardson, T. (2012). Computer-based psychological treatments for depression: A systematic review and meta-analysis. *Clinical Psychology Review, 32*(4), 329–342.

Richardson, L. K., Frueh, B. C., Grubaugh, A. L., Egede, L., & Elhai, J. D. (2009). Current directions in videoconferencing tele-mental health research. *Clinical Psychology: Science and Practice, 16*(3), 323–338.

Riper, H., Andersson, G., Christensen, H., Cuijpers, P., Lange, A., & Eysenbach, G. (2010). Theme issue on e-mental health: A growing field in internet research. *Journal of Medical Internet Research, 12*(5), e74.

Rochlen, A. B., Zack, J. S., & Speyer, C. (2004). Online therapy: Review of relevant definitions, debates, and current empirical support. *Journal of Clinical Psychology, 60*(3), 269–283.

Ruggiero, K. J., Resnick, H. S., Acierno, R., Coffey, S. F., Carpenter, M. J., Ruscio, A. M., … Bucuvalas, M. (2006). Internet-based intervention for mental health and substance use problems in disaster-affected populations: A pilot feasibility study. *Behavior Therapy, 37*(2), 190–205.

Rummell, C. M., & Joyce, N. R. (2010). "So wat do u want to wrk on 2day?": The ethical implications of online counseling. *Ethics & Behavior, 20*(6), 482–496.

Shaw, B. R., McTavish, F., Hawkins, R., Gustafson, D. H., & Pingree, S. (2000). Experiences of women with breast cancer: Exchanging social support over the CHESS computer network. *Journal of Health Communication, 5*(2), 135–159.

Shen, N., Levitan, M.-J., Johnson, A., Bender, J. L., Hamilton-Page, M., Jadad, A. A. R., & Wiljer, D. (2015). Finding a depression app: A review and content analysis of the depression app marketplace. *Journal of Medical Internet Research mHealth and uHealth, 3*(1), e16.

Shore, J. H., Savin, D. M., Novins, D., & Manson, S. M. (2006). Cultural aspects of telepsychiatry. *Journal of Telemedicine and Telecare, 12*(3), 116–121.

Spence, J., Titov, N., Dear, B. F., Johnston, L., Solley, K., Lorian, C., … Schwenke, G. (2011). Randomized controlled trial of internet-delivered cognitive behavioral therapy for posttraumatic stress disorder. *Depression and Anxiety, 28*(7), 541–550.

Steel, Z., Chey, T., Silove, D., Marnane, C., Bryant, R. A., & Van Ommeren, M. (2009). Association of torture and other potentially traumatic events with mental health outcomes among populations exposed to mass conflict and displacement: A systematic review and meta-analysis. *Journal of the American Medical Association, 302*(5), 537–549.

Steinmetz, S. E., Benight, C. C., Bishop, S. L., & James, L. E. (2012). My Disaster Recovery: A pilot randomized controlled trial of an internet intervention. *Anxiety, Stress & Coping, 25*(5), 593–600.

United Nations High Commissioner for Refugees. (2016). *Global trends: Forced displacement in 2015*. Retrieved from http://www.unhcr.org/global-trends-2015.html

Ünlü Ince, B., Cuijpers, P., van't Hof, E., van Ballegooijen, W., Christensen, H., & Riper, H. (2013). Internet-based, culturally sensitive, problem-solving therapy for Turkish migrants with depression: Randomized controlled trial. *Journal of Medical Internet Research, 15*(10), e227.

Van Uden-Kraan, C. F., Drossaert, C. H., Taal, E., Seydel, E. R., & van de Laar, M. A. (2009). Participation in online patient support groups endorses patients' empowerment. *Patient Education and Counseling, 74*(1), 61–69.

van't Hof, E., Cuijpers, P., & Stein, D. J. (2009). Self-help and internet-guided interventions in depression and anxiety disorders: A systematic review of meta-analyses. *CNS Spectrums, 14*(S3), 34–40.

Wagner, B., Horn, A. B., & Maercker, A. (2014). Internet-based versus face-to-face cognitive-behavioral intervention for depression: A randomized controlled non-inferiority trial. *Journal of Affective Disorders, 152–154*, 113–121.

Wagner, B., Knaevelsrud, C., & Maercker, A. (2006). Internet-based cognitive-behavioral therapy for complicated grief: A randomized controlled trial. *Death Studies, 30*(5), 429–453.

Wagner, B., Schulz, W., & Knaevelsrud, C. (2012). Efficacy of an internet-based intervention for posttraumatic stress disorder in Iraq: A pilot study. *Psychiatry Research, 195*(1-2), 85–88.

Wang, Z., Wang, J., & Maercker, A. (2013). Chinese my trauma recovery. A web-based intervention for traumatized persons in two parallel samples: Randomized controlled trial. *Journal of Medical Internet Research, 15*(9), e213.

Winzelberg, A. J., Classen, C., Alpers, G. W., Roberts, H., Koopman, C., Adams, R. E., ... Taylor, C. B. (2003). Evaluation of an internet support group for women with primary breast cancer. *Cancer, 97*(5), 1164–1173.

Wootton, R., & Bonnardot, L. (2015). Telemedicine in low-resource settings. *Frontiers in Public Health, 3*(3), 261.

Wright, K. (2002). Social support within an online cancer community: An assessment of emotional support, perceptions of advantages and disadvantages and motives for using the community from a communication perspective. *Journal of Applied Communication Research, 30*(3), 195–209.

Yuen, E. K., Gros, D. F., Price, M., Zeigler, S., Tuerk, P. W., Foa, E. B., & Acierno, R. (2015). Randomized controlled trial of home-based telehealth versus in-person prolonged exposure for combat-related PTSD in veterans: Preliminary results. *Journal of Clinical Psychology, 71*(6), 500–512.

Jana Stein, M.Sc. in psychology, is a Ph.D. candidate in clinical psychology and psychotherapy at the Freie Universität Berlin and the Centre Überleben, Germany. Her research interests include the development and evaluation of mental health services delivered via new media for trauma survivors in countries affected by mass conflict.

Christine Knaevelsrud, Ph.D., is professor of Clinical-Psychological Intervention at the Freie Universität Berlin, Germany. Her research interests include investigating mental health in refugees focusing on psychological interventions and specifically examining the potential of digitally supported interventions.

Conclusion

Angela Nickerson and Nexhmedin Morina

Large numbers of individuals across the globe have been affected by mass violence, with the number of people forcibly displaced as a result of persecution and conflict being unprecedented in recent history (UNHCR, 2017). While many people affected by war and persecution demonstrate remarkable resilience in the face of adversity, refugee, asylum-seeker and post-conflict populations also present with high rates of psychological disorders (see chapters "Mental Health Among Survivors of War in Low- and Middle-Income Countries: Epidemiology and Treatment Outcome", "Mental Health, Pre-migratory Trauma and Post-migratory Stressors Among Adult Refugees", and "Child Mental Health in the Context of War: An Overview of Risk Factors and Interventions for Refugee and War-Affected Youth"). Governments and non-government agencies across the globe are charged with supporting those individuals who cannot rely on their own governments for protection and support. These agencies have a substantial responsibility to identify and meet the needs of survivors of mass violence, often in situations of limited resources and contextual challenges. Mental health research has a critical role to play in informing the priorities and activities of those providing support in the aftermath of persecution, mass violence and displacement.

The chapters in this book provided a snapshot of the state of the research evidence regarding the mental health of conflict-affected and forcibly-displaced populations (chapters "Mental Health Among Survivors of War in Low- and Middle-Income Countries: Epidemiology and Treatment Outcome", "Mental Health, Pre-migratory Trauma and Post-migratory Stressors Among Adult

A. Nickerson (✉)
School of Psychology, University of New South Wales, Sydney, NSW, Australia
e-mail: a.nickerson@unsw.edu.au

N. Morina
Department of Clinical Psychology and Psychotherapy, University of Münster, Münster, Germany
e-mail: morina@uni-muenster.de

N. Morina, A. Nickerson (eds.), *Mental Health of Refugee and Conflict-Affected Populations*, https://doi.org/10.1007/978-3-319-97046-2

Refugees", and "Child Mental Health in the Context of War: An Overview of Risk Factors and Interventions for Refugee and War-Affected Youth"). Key theoretical perspectives that inform understanding of mental health following war and persecution were outlined (chapters "Variations of Military Violence: Structures, Interests, and Experiences of War from the 19th to the 21st Century", "Pathways to Recovery: Psychological Mechanisms underlying Refugee Mental Health", "Drive to Thrive: A Theory of Resilience Following Loss", and "A Neurobiological Perspective of Mental Health following Torture Trauma"), and prominent psychological and psychosocial interventions for supporting refugees and conflict-affected groups were presented (chapters "Narrative Exposure Therapy (NET) as a Treatment for Traumatized Refugees and Post-conflict Populations", "Culturally Sensitive CBT for Refugees: Key Dimensions", "Alcohol and Drug Misuse interventions in Conflict-Affected Populations", "Trauma Systems Therapy for Refugee Children and Families", and "Supporting Children Affected by War: Towards an Evidence Based Care System"). The final sections of this book proposed important considerations when working with traumatized refugees and conflict-affected individuals in clinical and research contexts (chapters "Clinical Considerations in the Psychological Treatment of Refugees" and "Legal and Ethical Considerations Related to the Asylum Process"), and presented recent advances in research and practice with refugee and conflict-affected populations (chapters "Conceptualization and Measurement of Traumatic Events Among Refugee and Other War-Affected Populations", "Low Intensity Interventions for Psychological Symptoms Following Mass Trauma", and "Development and Evaluation of Mental Health Interventions for Common Mental Disorders in Post-conflict Settings").

While, in recent decades, a large body of work has been amassed to guide the understanding of the psychological impact of exposure to mass violence, there remain a number of unanswered questions. In each of the chapters in this volume, authors identified areas of enquiry that need to be broached to advance knowledge regarding the mental health of refugee and conflict-affected populations, and inform the development of evidence-based interventions for these groups. Several important themes emerged from these chapters.

A number of authors proposed future directions related to research methodologies, including increasing standardization in research (chapter "Mental Health Among Survivors of War in Low- and Middle-Income Countries: Epidemiology and Treatment Outcome"), improving approaches to conceptualizing and measuring trauma exposure (chapter "Conceptualization and Measurement of Traumatic Events Among Refugee and Other War-Affected Populations"), overcoming methodological constraints in low- and middle-income countries (LMIC) (chapter "Child Mental Health in the Context of War: An Overview of Risk Factors and Interventions for Refugee and War-affected Youth"), and the implementation of innovative neurobiological and experimental methodologies to increase understanding of mechanisms underlying refugee mental health (chapters "Pathways to Recovery: Psychological Mechanisms Underlying Refugee Mental Health" and "A Neurobiological Perspective of Mental Health Following Torture Trauma"). Numerous areas were demonstrated as being in urgent need of further research, including the prevalence, prevention and treatment of substance misuse (chapter "Alcohol and Drug Misuse interventions in Conflict-Affected Populations"), the efficacy of e-health interventions (chapter "New Technologies in the Treatment of Psychological Disorders – Overview, Potentials and Barriers for Conflict-Affected Populations"), the impact of cultural adaptation of CBT interventions (chapter "Culturally Sensitive CBT for Refugees: Key Dimensions"), stress adaptation and resilience relating to sustaining the fabrics and structure of everyday life (chapter "Drive to Thrive: A Theory of Resilience Following Loss"), and how psychological factors may impact on asylum decisions to enhance justice in the asylum process (chapter "Legal and Ethical Considerations Related to the Asylum Process").

Several chapters highlighted the potential for novel approaches to facilitate research and enhance the dissemination and reach of evidence-based strategies, including the development and evaluation of low-intensity interventions to improve the scope of access to mental health services (chapter "Low Intensity Interventions for Psychological Symptoms following Mass Trauma"), e-health interventions, mobile phone applications and social media (chapters "Drive to Thrive: A Theory of Resilience Following Loss" and "New Technologies in the Treatment of Psychological Disorders – Overview, Potentials and Barriers for Conflict-Affected Populations"), as well as task-shifting approaches (chapters "Narrative Exposure Therapy (NET) as a Treatment for Traumatized Refugees and Post-conflict Populations" and "Low Intensity Interventions for Psychological Symptoms Following Mass Trauma"). A number of chapters outlined the importance of moving beyond investigations of efficacy of psychosocial interventions, to evaluating their cost-effectiveness and amenability to dissemination, especially in LMICs (chapters "Interventions for Mental Health and Psychosocial Support in Complex Humanitarian Emergencies: Moving Towards Consensus in Policy and Action?", "Narrative Exposure Therapy (NET) as a Treatment for Traumatized Refugees and Post-Conflict Populations", "Trauma Systems Therapy for Refugee Children and Families", and "Supporting Children Affected by War: Towards an Evidence Based Care System"). Several chapters discussed the importance of collaboration between academic researchers and organizations involved in mental health and psychosocial support in LMICs, to ensure that research focuses on meaningful questions with substantial implications for refugees and conflict-affected populations (chapters "Interventions for Mental Health and Psychosocial Support in Complex Humanitarian Emergencies: Moving Towards Consensus in Policy and Action?", "Alcohol and Drug Misuse interventions in Conflict-Affected Populations", "Supporting Children Affected by War: Towards an Evidence Based Care System", and "Low Intensity Interventions for Psychological Symptoms following Mass Trauma").

Governments, agencies and clinicians have a responsibility to provide the best possible support for individuals who have been exposed to war, persecution and displacement, to assist them in overcoming the psychological effects of these experiences, and support them in enhancing their capacity to adapt and thrive in the post-trauma environment. High-quality research is needed to bridge the gap between the experiences of refugees and conflict-affected groups and knowledge regarding how best to provide this support. The chapters within this book outlined a range of theoretically-driven evidence-based approaches to fostering psychological well-being amongst refugees and conflict-affected populations. In addition, a number of innovative methodologies with emerging evidence were proposed to enhance understanding, feasibility and dissemination of initiatives to provide these populations with much needed support. Collaborative partnerships between academic researchers, humanitarian actors and refugee communities to develop and implement high-quality, innovative research represent a critical pathway to ultimately providing the best possible support to individuals affected by war, persecution and displacement.

Reference

UNHCR. (2017). *Global trends: Forced displacement in 2017*. Geneva, Switzerland: UNHCR.

Angela Nickerson, Ph.D. is Associate Professor and Director of the Refugee Trauma and Recovery Program at the University of New South Wales (UNSW), Sydney, Australia. She is a clinical psychologist and conducts research into psychological and social mechanisms underlying the mental health of refugees and asylum-seekers, with the aim of informing policy and treatment development.

Nexhmedin Morina, Ph.D., is professor of Clinical Psychology and Psychotherapy at the University of Münster, Germany, and director of the Centre for the Treatment of Traumatic Stress Disorders. His research interests include investigating mental health in survivors of mass conflict as well as the evaluation of mental health services.

Printed by Printforce, the Netherlands